Comparative Criminal Justice Systems

A Topical Approach

Comparative Criminal Justice Systems

A Topical Approach

Third Edition

Philip L. Reichel
University of Northern Colorado

Upper Saddle River, New Jersey 07458

Library of Congress Cataloging-in-Publication Data

Reichel, Philip L.
Comparative criminal justice systems : a topical approach / Philip L. Reichel.--3rd ed.
p. cm.
Includes bibliographical references and index.
ISBN 0-13-091287-5
1. Criminal justice, Administration of--Cross-cultural studies. 2. Criminal justice, Administration of--Japan. I. Title.

HV7419.R45 2002
364--dc21 2001019904

Publisher: Jeff Johnson
Executive Assistant: Brenda Rock
Director of Manufacturing and Production: Bruce Johnson
Executive Acquisitions Editor: Kim Davies
Editorial Assistant: Sarah Holle
Managing Editor: Mary Carnis
Production Management: Clarinda Publication Services
Production Editor: Rosie Jones
Interior Design: Clarinda Publication Services/ Cindy Miller
Production Liaison: Adele M. Kupchik
Manufacturing Buyer: Cathleen Petersen
Manufacturing Manager: Ilene Sanford
Cover Design Coordinator: Miguel Ortiz
Formatting: The Clarinda Company
Marketing Manager: Ramona Sherman
Printer/Binder: R.R. Donnelley and Sons, Inc.
Copy Editor: Clarinda Publication Services/ Margaret Jarpey
Proofreader: Clarinda Publication Services/ Carol Singer
Cover Design: Joe Sengotta
Cover Printer: Phoenix Color Corporation

Pearson Education LTD.
Pearson Education Australia PTY, Limited
Pearson Education Singapore, Pte. Ltd.
Pearson Education North Asia Ltd.
Pearson Education Canada, Ltd.
Pearson Educación de Mexico, S. A. de C. V.
Pearson Education -- Japan
Pearson Education Malaysia, Pte. Ltd.

10 9 8 7 6 5 4 3 2 1
ISBN 0-13-091287-5

To my wife Eva,
and our sons Scott and Matt

Contents

PREFACE

Since the first edition of this book, the topic of comparative and international criminal justice has enjoyed increased attention by authors, journals, and professional organizations in criminology and criminal justice. Consistent with those changes, more undergraduate and graduate courses are being taught with comparative justice issues as the primary subject matter.

These changes are, of course, to everyone's benefit. Students of criminology and criminal justice have a much better understanding of comparative and international issues than have students of earlier generations. That knowledge is useful when those students become practitioners and increasingly must interact with justice system agents in other countries. In addition, the increased knowledge of different ways that justice is conceived and achieved, gives practitioners and policy makers ideas for improving their own system.

Hopefully the interest in, and perceived importance of, an international perspective is irreversible. This book is designed to encourage continuation of that interest and to provide a knowledge base about justice in countries around the world.

ORGANIZATION OF THE BOOK

The text is organized in ten chapters that reflect the material and order of presentation typically found in introductory books on the American system of criminal justice. That is, arrangement proceeds from concern with criminal law through examination of police, courts, and corrections. This organization distinguishes the text from other comparative criminal justice books that present detailed information on five or six specific countries. The result means this text contains less detail on the criminal justice system of particular countries, but it provides greater appreciation and understanding of the diversity in legal systems around the world.

A benefit of using the same countries for each chapter would be a sense of consistency and depth in the text. However, not every country offers the same level of contrast in all aspects of its criminal justice system. For example, describing German and French policing results in interesting and specific contrasts. But if the same countries are used to contrast the trial procedure, their similarity makes us less aware of the variation occurring in that process when other countries are considered.

Luckily, there is an alternate means for presenting information on law, police, courts, corrections, and juvenile justice. The organization used in this text follows the belief that comparison relies on categorization. That is, to best understand and explain similarities and differences among things, one must start by categorizing them. The first chapter provides the rationale for studying other systems of justice and sets down the specific approach used in this text. The second chapter reviews crime as a world problem and sets the stage for consideration of the different ways justice systems are organized in attempts to respond to the crime problem. Chapter three presents traditional material on American criminal law so the reader has a familiar and common base to use in the following chapters. Chapter four presents the four contemporary legal traditions and outlines the basic features of each. Chapter five continues material in chapters three and four by looking at substantive and procedural criminal law in each of the four legal traditions.

The next four chapters cover the topics of policing (Chapter 6), the judiciary (Chapter 7), corrections (Chapter 8), and juvenile justice (Chapter 9). Countries representing Europe, Asia, North and South America, Latin America, Australia, and Pacific islands are included in the coverage. Some make frequent appearances (e.g., Australia, France, Nigeria, Saudi Arabia) while others are less recurrent (e.g., Canada, Denmark, Mexico, Fiji). The text concludes with a concentrated look at the criminal justice system of Japan. This country was chosen for special consideration since it has a history of borrowing from other countries (a point encouraged by comparative studies) and has what many consider to be a very effective criminal justice system. Also, ending the text with an in-depth look at a particular country provides an opportunity to tie together some of the topics and items presented in earlier chapters.

PEDAGOGICAL FEATURES

- *Impact Sections:* Each chapter of the text includes an Impact section where topics mentioned in that chapter will receive greater attention and where questions raised by chapter material can be addressed. These sections should encourage mental gymnastics, suggesting things like links between countries, ideas for improving systems, and ways to encourage more global understanding. Examples include the impact guns may have on a country's crime rate (Chapter 1), how soccer and American football can explain differences between common law and civil law (Chapter 5), and the global aspects of restorative justice (Chapter 8).
- *In The News:* New to this edition are "In The News" boxes that highlight current topics relevant to chapter material. Examples include the crime of trafficking in humans (Chapter 1), the use of the death penalty around the world (Chapter 8), and England's new "parenting orders" that allows parents of misbehaving youths to be punished (Chapter 9).
- *You Should Know:* Also new in this edition are features that direct the students' attention to items providing helpful background to chapter topics. At least one "You Should Know" box appears in every chapter. Examples

include explanations of the European Union (Chapter 1), the European Court of Human Rights (Chapter 5), and a summary of similarities in delinquency around the world (Chapter 9).

- *Web Sites to Visit:* An increasing number of governments are providing Internet information about their criminal justice agencies and, in some cases, are making crime and justice statistics available. At the end of each chapter are suggested web sites where students can gather information for class discussion or for preparing term papers.
- *Key Topics and Key Terms:* Beginning each chapter is a listing of key topics and terms that students will encounter in that chapter. These have been popular aids in the two previous editions and are retained here to help direct student attention to important concepts as they read the chapter material.
- *Countries Covered:* Also continuing from earlier editions is a listing, at the chapter's start, of countries that receive particular attention in that chapter. Because different countries are discussed in each chapter this aid helps orient students about the regions and nations they will encounter during their reading.

KEY CHANGES IN THE THIRD EDITION

Subsequent editions of criminal justice text books are often necessary to update statistics, changes in law, modifications in procedures; and to include, increase, or decrease information about particular topics. All those reasons are relevant to the third edition of this book. There have actually been quite significant changes on the world scene since the second edition of this book. Important new laws and legislation are having significant impact on the way justice is administered in countries like Australia, China, England and Wales. Appropriate sections of the chapters have been modified in this edition to account for those changes.

Pedagogical improvements to the text, as outlined above, are among the more important changes in this edition, but there are also content changes in every chapter. Chapter 1 has a new, more contemporary, introduction. Chapter 2 includes new information on terrorism and cultural heritage crimes and updates both crime and victimization statistics. Chapter 3 explains the importance of the 2000 U.S. Supreme Court decision reaffirming the Miranda warning. The Chapter 4 material on China has been updated to reflect the 1997 revisions of Chinese law. New information on Hong Kong as a Special Administrative Region of the People's Republic of China is incorporated into Chapter 5. The police structures covered in Chapter 6 have all been verified and updated as necessary and new information about Europol and the Schengen Agreement has been added. Chapter 7 information on aspects of courtroom actors and court organization for each country covered in the chapter has been revised where needed. New legislation and procedures in Great Britain have especially required revised presentation. Chapter 8 now includes material on the increasingly popular topic of restorative justice. Juvenile justice procedures have undergone important changes in just about every country mentioned in Chapter 9, and that required new descriptions in Australia and England especially. Chapter 10 now includes information on the growing crime rate in Japan as an appropriate contrast to other material in the chapter that portrays Japan's system in a more glowing light.

Although comparative criminal justice enjoys increased attention, it is still in its infancy as a subject matter. As more and more text books begin to appear, more scholars attempt cross-cultural research, and more practitioners share ideas, comparative criminal justice will grow to levels we cannot yet appreciate. I hope you will find this book to be a positive contribution toward the advancement of this important field of study.

SUPPLEMENTS

- An Instructor's Manual and Test Bank, both prepared by the author, are available for adopters of this book.
- The author maintains a web site that provides information on comparative criminal justice studies in general and material related to this book more specifically. Sections at the web site provide students with hints on how to prepare research papers on comparative justice issues and has links to key web sites with additional information about law, police, courts, and corrections in countries around the world. Instructors and students are welcome to visit the site at **www.cjed.com/ccjs/ccjhome.htm**

ACKNOWLEDGMENTS

I would like to acknowledge the support I have received from many people in my attempt to provide current and accurate descriptions of the justice agencies and procedures in a variety of countries. This edition has especially benefited from the assistance of several people who were kind enough to review chapter material on their respective country. My heartfelt thanks goes out to: Ursula Smartt of Thames Valley University (England); Bankole Cole of the University of Lincolnshire & Humberside (England); Terry Bishop of the West Sussex Youth Offending Team (England); David Biles, Consultant Criminologist and Professorial Associate, Charles Sturt University (Australia); Johannes Feest of the University of Bremen (Germany); Friedrich Schwindt of the Nordrhein-Westfalen Police (Germany); Andrzej Adamski of the Nicholas Copernicus University (Poland); Paolo Iorio, lecturer in criminal procedure at the National Police School and Advisor in Prison Matters to the Ministry of Justice (Italy); and Takeshi Koyanagi of the Correction Bureau, Ministry of Justice (Japan). Despite the efforts of these colleagues there may still be inaccuracies in my descriptions of justice procedures in each of their countries. I am, of course, responsible for any such misrepresentations.

Opportunities to expand my knowledge and experience in comparative and international criminal justice have been provided by Adam Bouloukos, Frank Hoepfel, Matti Joutsen, and Graeme Newman. I thank them all and can only hope that upon reflection they believe their trust was well placed.

The staff at Prentice Hall have been wonderfully easy to work with. Kim Davies, my new editor, has provided exceptional support and encouragement and I thank her very much for making work on this edition an enjoyable experience. Developmental Editor, Cheryl Adam, provided insightful suggestions that have made this edition a much more attractive package and one that is more pedagogically sound. Her assistance was invaluable.

Finally, acknowledgment also goes to the reviewers who kindly assisted in the evaluation of the manuscript for both the first and second editions. The following people gave their valuable time and assistance in helping the various editions of this book come to publication in a better form than was first submitted. Thank you to:

Dorothy Bracey, Ph.D., City University of New York

Wilson Palacios, Ph.D., University of South Florida

David Neubauer, Ph.D., University of New Orleans

Robert J. Homant, Ph.D., University of Detroit

Joan Luxenburg, Ed.D., University of Central Oklahoma

Joseph W. Lipchitz, Ph.D., University of Massachusetts at Lowell

Jan K. Dargel, M.A., J.D., University of Tampa

William D. Hyatt, J.D., LL.M., Western Carolina University

C. Ray Jeffery, Ph.D., Florida State University

Comparative Criminal Justice Systems

A Topical Approach

Chapter 1

Taking an International Perspective

KEY TOPICS

- Reasons for studying foreign legal systems
- How an international perspective can benefit our own legal system and the world at large
- International efforts in law enforcement and adjudication
- Three ways to study foreign criminal justice systems
- Two ways to explain how criminal justice systems work in different countries
- Classification strategies
- How this book is structured

KEY TERMS

authentic strategy
cash deposit bail
classification
commercial bail
criminalization
descriptive approach
ethnocentrism
functions/procedures strategy
historical approach
institutions/actors strategy
nonfinancial bail
political approach
recognizance
synthetic strategy
three pillars

COUNTRIES REFERENCED

Australia
Canada
China
England
European Union
France
India
Japan
Mexico
Russia
South Africa
United States

Do you have confidence in the criminal justice system? Over the last several decades the American public has been disgusted and befuddled at the actions of some justice employees and the workings of parts of the system. On occasion, some police officers have behaved with bias and brutality toward suspects. Some prosecutors seem to have filed criminal charges in a selective manner. Defense attorneys have fallen asleep while their clients are on trial for their lives. Juries in civil trials have held people responsible for actions that those same people were deemed not guilty of by juries in criminal trials. Correctional officers in prisons have abused inmates, and prison programs have been denounced as having failed to rehabilitate criminals. Is it possible to have confidence in such a system? Apparently it is!

Results of an American Bar Association (1999) national survey of American citizens show 80 percent of all respondents agreeing that "in spite of its problems, the American justice system is still the best in the world." The U.S. Supreme Court fared especially well, with half the respondents expressing strong confidence in the Court versus only 18 percent expressing strong confidence in Congress and 8 percent expressing the same in the media. Importantly, considering some of the recent examples of problems cited in the previous paragraph, this confidence rating has actually increased since 1978, when a similar poll was conducted. Indeed, the levels of confidence in federal, state, and local courts have all increased. Even confidence in the local police has increased significantly. And we cannot explain these increases by arguing that the American public has become more cynical or less discerning in general, because confidence in doctors, organized religion, public schools, and the media have all decreased since 1978 (American Bar Association, 1999).

Pleased as the American public seems to be with its criminal justice system, there are complaints and concerns:

- The majority of both black and white adult Americans believe that racial profiling is an undesirable police tactic and that it is a widespread practice in the United States (Gallup Poll, 1999).
- White and Hispanic Americans tend to agree that African Americans are treated worse than other groups by the American legal system (National Center for State Courts, 1999).
- Most Americans do not believe that juries represent the makeup of their community (National Center for State Courts, 1999).

How can so many people find fault with key parts of the justice system yet still believe the American system is the best in the world? Do Americans have too idealistic a notion of their own system, or are they simply skeptical about any other country's ability to do better? Such a perspective is reflected in the term *ethnocentrism*, or the belief that one's own way of doing something is the best.

Ethnocentrism has some positive aspects. It encourages pride, confidence, and group identification. When ethnocentrism is attached to one's country, it is a key ingredient in what we call patriotism. Since feelings of patriotism and cultural identity are generally positive attributes that help make a nation strong, it is desirable for citizens to be somewhat ethnocentric about their own social institutions. And, indeed, public opinion polls in various countries show that most citizens have confidence in their own country's public institutions—even while recognizing problems with some aspects of those institutions. For example, Britons continue to view British justice as fundamentally fair despite high-profile cases over the last several years in which people were released from prison after a reexamination of evidence showed they were actually innocent (NOP Research Group, 1997).

As with many other cultural traits, ethnocentrism has negative aspects that oppose its positive ones. When ethnocentrism makes people in one group unwilling to understand and appreciate differences with people from other groups, prejudice and discrimination can result. When ethnocentrism makes it difficult, or even impossible, to be critical about the status quo, society may not experience positive change. If people believe that no other way of doing something can be useful, desirable, or even better than the current way, opportunities for improvement are missed. Preferably, citizens should balance their cultural pride and confidence with a willingness to appreciate and learn from others—even when the "others" are culturally different and geographically separate.

One goal of comparative studies is to extend a person's knowledge of people and cultures beyond his or her own group. After seeing the similarities and differences among countries and their citizens, comparative scholars have a better understanding of their own society and of ways that society might be improved. Importantly, that can be accomplished without loss of pride in one's own country or social institutions. Or, as George Santayana phrased it, "A man's feet must be planted in his country, but his eyes should survey the world" (Santayana, 1905, pp. 175–176).

WHY STUDY THE LEGAL SYSTEM OF OTHER COUNTRIES?

Because an international perspective is still new in American criminal justice curricula, it is important to spend time here showing its value. We begin with the premise that contemporary technology has provided a global communications network serving to shrink the world in the perspective of its people. It is a "small world" in terms of common problems! There is every reason to believe that the citizens of the world, through their respective governments and businesses, will become increasingly interdependent. As a result, an international perspective has both provincial and universal benefits. We will discuss these as they relate to criminal justice and from the viewpoint of Americans.

Before continuing, a few words regarding the use of the terms *America* and *American* are in order. Some authors are troubled by the use of those terms in sole reference to the United States and its citizens. Such concerns are well founded, because the North American continent is comprised of Canada, Mexico, and Central America, as well as the United States. Furthermore, because the term *America* does not distinguish either the northern or southern continent, the citizens of South American countries could also be the subjects of conversation. However, despite the insensitivity its usage may encourage, this text will use *America* as specifically referring to the United States, simply because it is so commonly used that way, and also because citizens of other North and South American countries are more correctly identified with reference to their specific country. Moreover, although the names *Canadians, Peruvians, Mexicans,* and *Panamanians* allow us to place a citizen with a particular country, a term like *United Statesian* does not roll off the tongue as easily. With apologies to our North and South American neighbors, this book uses *America* and *Americans* to refer to the United States of America and its citizens.

Provincial Benefits of an International Perspective

To understand better one's own circumstance it is often beneficial to have a point of contrast and comparison. LePaulle noted that there is a tendency to view the law of one's own country "as natural, as necessary, as given by God." This ethnocentric view actually makes the system seem uninteresting and not worthy of scrutiny. After all, why should we need to examine and appreciate what amounts to the only game in town? But, as LePaulle continues, the law of any country is more accurately the result of "historical accident or temporary social situations"(quoted in Cole, Frankowski, and Gertz, 1987, p. 19).

When we realize that the American legal system is not the only one possible, it becomes more interesting and more important to scrutinize that system. For example, the rather passive role of a judge in the American trial process takes on new meaning when contrasted with the very active judge under a civil legal system. When we read of socialist and civil legal systems making use of private citizens as lay judges, it puts the use of citizens on American juries in a new perspective. In this manner, a knowledge of alternative systems of justice provides a point of contrast. That contrast, in turn, allows the student a means and reason to gain new insight into a procedure or structure previously viewed as uninteresting and ordinary. A comparative view of legal systems allows us to understand better the dimensions of our own system. "Without such a comparison, we could

In the News

CHINESE OFFICIALS ARE BAFFLED

Americans are often accused of being oblivious to the workings, and even the geographic location, of other countries. Such criticism is not always unwarranted, but it is inappropriate to imply that citizens of other countries are fully informed about life in the United States.

During a visit to Washington, DC, a Chinese general was baffled by the 50 state flags hanging in an atrium at the National Defense University. "I thought this was one country," he told his American host, "So why so many flags?" (Pomfret, 1998, p. 1). Other official Chinese visitors have expressed surprise that cars in America stop at stoplights in what they had presumed was a wild and dangerous country.

Such misconceptions by citizens in one country about life in another country are not simply humorous misunderstandings. Pentagon officials see some of the misperceptions as rather ominous, since they could result in one military power drawing incorrect conclusions about the other. Even without military implications, the ability of countries to work together on common problems is hindered when the countries do not have a reasonably accurate understanding of each other.

be led to a false belief in the necessity and permanency of the status quo" (Terrill, 1982, p. 23).

Besides providing new insight and understanding of our system of justice, an international perspective can furnish ideas to improve that system. A technique used in one country to combat crime might be successfully adapted for use in another country. For example, a key ingredient of Japan's police system is the *koban,* or police box. Because policing in Japan is considered to be very effective and efficient, it has been studied and written about in many countries. Some researchers and practitioners argue that the koban system's community-wide deployment of police would be effective in the United States. In addition, the koban system may have important implications for the trend toward community policing in America and other countries.

No society can incorporate another culture's legal system in its entirety and expect it to work. Yet certain aspects of another system—modified to account for cultural differences—may operate successfully in a new setting. It is important to note that potentially transferable ideas come not only from countries at similar levels of development, but also from less developed countries. For example, Americans are becoming increasingly interested in mediation to settle a variety of legal disputes. As anthropologists remind us, mediation and dispute resolution have a long and distinguished tradition at the tribal and village levels in African and other countries. To ignore the experiences of those systems is imprudent and elitist.

Universal Benefits of an International Perspective

As we begin the twenty-first century, rapid travel and communication are making us painfully aware that crime no longer is confined by the geographic boundaries of individual countries. It appears that garden-variety thefts, robberies, and assaults may become less troublesome to society than offenses like the internationalization of organized crime, nuclear trafficking, international terrorism, money laundering, and the transnational trafficking of humans and human organs (see, for example, Collin, 1997; Lee, 1996; McDonald, 1997; Williams, 1999). Criminality in this new century seems to have expanded its target beyond private citizens to include communities, governments, and even nations.

Transnational crimes such as terrorism, air and sea hijacking, and drug smuggling are serious concerns that beg for a cooperative international response. Multinational collaboration is occurring, but the needed action requires a level of teamwork that countries of the world are only beginning to consider. Understandably, cooperation often starts with neighboring countries. Their common border not only presents the problem of intercountry crime but also provides both reason and opportunity to do something about it. In addition to such *neighbor cooperation, multinational cooperation* is occurring as well, as groupings of countries realize the need to develop formal agreements in their quest to control and combat crime. We will consider a few examples of both neighbor and multinational cooperation.

Neighbor Cooperation. The shared borders between the United States and Canada and between the United States and Mexico have encouraged bilateral agreements among the neighboring countries as each responds to internal and cross-border crime. Oftentimes the political "spin doctors" present the resulting cooperation between national law enforcement agencies as being more cooperative than is actually true; but each country recognizes the need for collective efforts.

The United States and Canada have longstanding agreements on law enforcement cooperation, including treaties on extradition and mutual legal assistance as well as an asset-sharing agreement. The two countries participate in the Cross-Border Crime Forum to coordinate policy matters and operation procedures so that problems can be more easily resolved. In 1998 the Royal Canadian Mounted Police became the first foreign law enforcement agency to be given access to the U.S. government's tactical drug intelligence center in El Paso, Texas (Bureau of International Narcotics and Law Enforcement Affairs—hereinafter BINLEA, 2000). Canada and the United States seem to have found a comfortable version of bilateral cooperation that U.S. officials describe as broad, deep, and highly productive. But the collegiality reflected in the U.S.–Canada arrangements has not been so easily duplicated in U.S.–Mexico arrangements.

Official policy statements between the Mexican and U.S. governments proclaim the need for collaborative efforts at stemming cross-border crime—with particular attention to drug trafficking. Specific arrangements include bilateral cooperation between law enforcement agencies, between members of the judiciary, and even between each country's military (BINLEA, 2000). The problem is not so much in getting each country to agree on what should be accomplished but rather on how the agreements are actually implemented. Specific concerns are expressed about the way U.S. agencies and personnel seem to take a rather cavalier attitude toward their Mexican counterparts. The result, critics argue, is a situation wherein the United States has the upper hand in a bilateral arrangement between presumably equal parties.

When one country takes a dominant position in its dealings with another country, the subordinate country has understandable concerns about protecting of its sovereignty. Maria Celia Toro (1999) claims that the United States has used transnational crime concerns (especially drug crimes) as a way to extend its own jurisdiction beyond U.S. borders. She cites as examples the laws providing for grand jury indictments of foreign nationals, the U.S. Supreme Court decisions that refuse to apply the Fourth Amendment to searches by U.S. law enforcement agents in foreign countries (see *United States v. Verdugo-Urquidez;* 494 U.S. 259; 1990), and the judicial processing in U.S. courts of defendants who were kidnapped from other countries by U.S. federal agents operating in that country (see *United States v. Alvarez-Machain;* 504 U.S. 655; 1992). These acts of extraterritorial enforcement of U.S. anti-drug laws pose a threat to Mexican sovereignty, according to many observers.

Deflem (1999) counters that the dominant position taken by the United States in its "cooperative" law enforcement arrangements with Mexico simply reflects the nature of international police work wherein national interests are always at stake. He notes that the Binational Drug Control Strategy between Mexico and the U.S. explicitly states that the programs are meant to uphold principles of sovereignty and mutual respect. Nevertheless, the reality is that U.S. law enforcement agencies are the dominant players in every bilateral initiative with Mexico.

U.S. government responses to claims that its actions do not reflect the principles of equality described in the bilateral agreements tend to be explanations rather than denials. The relative strength of U.S. personnel, equipment, technology, and technical know-how are presented as features that require the U.S. agencies to take the lead in law enforcement efforts. Added to those reasons is

In the News

USING MEXICAN JUSTICE

Arguments for transnational policing are often centered on the need for countries to be able to respond to crimes like drug trafficking and money laundering. Those crimes clearly deserve the most attention since they often involve criminal activities in several countries. But there is also a need for law enforcement efforts directed toward more mundane crimes where the offender has fled to a second country after having committed a crime in the first country.

In stark contrast to the problems of cross-border policing that are examined in this chapter, the actions of individual police officers and departments show how cooperative efforts between two countries can be rather easily achieved. Consider, for example, the effort of a homicide investigator in a Colorado county.

In 1992 seasonal field supervisors Juan and Aurelia Lara were robbed and killed in a rural area of Colorado's Weld County by a gang of six men—all Mexican citizens. One of the men was arrested and prosecuted in Weld County, but the other five escaped to Mexico. Sheriff's Department Investigator Al Price learned that Article 4 of Mexico's penal code provides for other nations to punish criminals using Mexico's judicial system. Using evidence provided by Investigator Price, four of the killers were apprehended in Mexico, convicted by a Mexican court, and sentenced to 35 years of hard labor at a prison near Mexico City.

The process did require some techniques not used in traditional U.S. police work. For example, Mexican authorities prefer face-to-face workings with the U.S. police officers rather than relying on phone or fax communication. Written (translated-to-Spanish) and photographic evidence is required in the Mexican courts and, as in the United States, particular rules must be followed in a particular order. But, as Investigator Price explained, when you abide by their rules, you get positive results (Mitchell, 1999).

Police departments in some Texas and California cities have also made use of Article 4, but many police departments remain unaware of the article's potential for accomplishing justice. And even when police are familiar with Article 4, preconceived notions about corruption in Mexico or presumptions about minimal cooperation by Mexican officials have kept attempts at teamwork from even beginning. Maybe an increased interest in comparative criminal justice will result in more individual police departments working together in different countries, regardless of the reluctance of politicians at the national level in each country toward cooperation.

the recognition in both Mexico and in the United States that corruption is pervasive in Mexican law enforcement.

Even though the Mexican government understands that it has a regretful level of corruption, it does not appreciate the U.S. government using that corruption as an excuse for questionable tactics. For example, in 1998 Mexican officials were made aware of U.S. Customs operatives engaging in a drug money laundering sting operation in Mexico City without having notified, or received permission from, Mexican authorities. Since sting operations are legal in Mexico only if authorized by the attorney general, the U.S. Customs operatives were considered to have violated Mexican law and sovereignty. Responses from U.S. officials ranged from understanding Mexico's concerns and looking into the situation to an argument that U.S. actions were defensible based on the need to do everything possible to bring drug traffickers to justice (Sheridan, 1998). An equally compelling argument in defense of U.S. actions in this case seems to have been a concern that corruption in Mexican law enforcement could have placed the lives of the U.S. agents in danger if Mexican officials had been notified. The U.S. Department of State has acknowledged the aggressive efforts being made by Mexico to remove corrupt officers, but it notes that corruption of public officials remains a serious problem in Mexico. As a result, the potential impact of corruption must be taken into consideration as both countries try to provide security for their personnel (BINLEA, 2000).

Mutual cooperation between neighboring nations in fighting cross-border crime seems to be of obvious benefit to both countries. But cooperative efforts are not easily achieved—especially if one country has recognized advantages over the other. A risk associated with transnational policing is the compromising of national sovereignty as more dominant countries extend their jurisdiction into subordinate countries. But a risk of not engaging in transnational policing is to give a distinct advantage to criminals who might avoid apprehension and prosecution by changing their national identification or location. Can such difficulties be overcome by arrangements between two countries? Is it, in fact, conceivable that many nations could join together in an effective cooperative effort against transnational crime and criminals?

Multinational Cooperation. An excellent example of cooperation among countries in the area of criminal justice is the *International Criminal Police Organization (Interpol).* As Chapter 6 explains in detail, Interpol coordinates interactions among police in the various Interpol member nations. While Interpol does not actually investigate cases, it does collect and disseminate information on international criminals as a way to assist member nations in solving crimes and securing the arrest, detention, and extradition of suspects. Interpol remains an excellent example of multinational cooperation involving most countries of the world, but the example we consider in this section shows multinational cooperation on a smaller scale.

The *European Union (EU)* is a treaty-based framework that defines and manages economic and political cooperation among its 15 member countries (Austria, Belgium, Denmark, Finland, France, Germany, Greece, Ireland, Italy, Luxembourg, Netherlands, Portugal, Spain, Sweden, and the United Kingdom). The EU was created in 1993 with the implementation of the Maastricht Treaty, but it is also considered a continuation of earlier treaties dating from the 1950s. The immediate precursor to the EU was the *European Community.*

The EU is described as resting on *three pillars:* European Community, Common Foreign and Security Policy, and Justice and Home Affairs. Important as the first two pillars are, our attention is focused on pillar three. The *Justice and Home Affairs (JHA)* policy deals with issues of asylum, immigration, customs, police cooperation, and judicial cooperation (Burros, Davidson & O'Beirne, 1999).

The areas of police and judicial cooperation provide especially good examples of multinational cooperation for justice purposes. Unlike the neighbor cooperation exemplified by the United States and Mexico, the EU tries to achieve cooperation among the institutions and agencies of 15 nations. A realistic goal, from the EU's perspective, is to create a European judicial space that allows Europeans to combat crime and seek justice across borders and throughout the continent.

Movement toward a common currency, the *Euro,* has taken a rocky but steady course. Some believe the EU governments will follow a similar path leading to agreement on common judicial procedures for investigating, prosecuting, and punishing some criminal acts. After all, the reasoning goes, Europeans increasingly cross their national borders to marry, work, study, buy and sell goods and services, and invest or borrow money. Shouldn't they also be able to seek and receive justice as simply and efficiently from any other EU country? The current concern about combating transnational organized crime highlights the benefits of a common judicial space. If German police want to seize the assets held by suspected criminals in Belgium, they must currently wait to get approval from a Belgian court. The very nature of organized crime activity means there will be rapid movement of people, money, and property across borders. Valuable time is

You Should Know!

THE "UNITED STATES OF EUROPE"

To help Americans understand the relationship among its member countries, the European Union has been compared with the United States. The 15 European Union countries have agreed to pool some of their sovereign powers (trade and agriculture, for example) in exchange for unity in much the same manner that the American states did to create the federal republic. Three particular endeavors for the EU at the beginning of the twenty-first century are (1) the consolidation of economic integration through establishment of the single European currency called the *Euro,* (2) the implementation of a *Common European Foreign and Security* policy, and (3) the real and democratic unification of the European continent (Prodi, 1999).

Two aspects of the EU are especially relevant to our interest in justice systems. The first is *Europol,* which makes cooperation among the EU national police forces operational. The other is the *Court of Justice,* which acts as the EU's "Supreme Court" by ensuring that treaties are interpreted and applied correctly by the EU institutions and member states. Both Europol and the Court of Justice receive closer attention in this and other chapters.

wasted when police must hold back from action until separate courts make rulings ("A single market in crime", 1999).

The tricky part, as you can well imagine, is to provide a specialized supranational judicial structure that combats transnational crime but does not violate the spirit of each country's criminal code or criminal procedure. There are precedents for such a structure. The United States has a federal judicial system that works in harmony with 50 separate state systems. Countries like Canada and Australia have found suitable ways to have federal laws and enforcement in conjunction with separate provincial and state laws. Of course, it is probably easier to get states and provinces that are part of a single nation to agree to a national judicial space than it is to get separate nations to agree to a supranational judicial space. But there are signs that the EU countries are working hard to achieve such cooperation. For example:

- *Europol* (see Chapter 6) has been in full operation since 1999 and, much like Interpol does on a larger scale, it serves to facilitate the sharing of information among EU countries about crimes and criminals. Europol also provides expertise and technical support for operations and investigations engaged in by the member nations.
- EU countries already rely on each other for protection and security under the *Schengen Agreement* (see Chapter 6), which has the goal of passport-free travel among the member nations. That means each country must provide strict identity controls at airports, seaports, and land borders for travelers arriving from countries outside the EU. Border checks of travelers moving from one EU country to another are no longer conducted, so the initial identity check becomes crucial for the governments and citizens of other EU countries to which the traveler may go.
- The police of one EU country are allowed to pursue criminals across borders into another EU country.
- There is recognition, in only a few areas so far, by one EU country of sanctions imposed by another EU country. For example, a driving-license ban in any EU country must be enforced in any other.
- *Euro-warrants* for arrest are being considered as a way to fight cross-border crime. These would be issued by a court in one EU country but could be acted upon by police in another without having to wait for an order from the first county. Some are suggesting that a *Euro-just* be established wherein a pool of magistrates from the EU countries are available to issue a Euro-warrant ("A single market in crime", 1999).

Both bilateral and multinational cooperation in law enforcement present many problems for the countries involved. However, increasing transnational crime suggests that the potential benefits of cooperative efforts might outweigh the problems. A necessary step in achieving that cooperation is an increased understanding of criminal justice systems in the various nations. Thus, more people taking an international perspective toward criminal justice will have definite universal benefits.

APPROACHES TO AN INTERNATIONAL PERSPECTIVE

An author's goal typically instructs the approach used to convey information. A police officer writing her report of a recent arrest tells the story by referring to what she heard, saw, smelled, and touched. That approach is more likely to achieve a prosecution goal than would a report providing biographical information about the suspect without reference to the suspect's behavior at the time of the incident. On the other hand, after a conviction, a presentence investigation written by a probation officer would be of little use if it fully described the event resulting in conviction but provided no biographical information about the offender.

The police officer's descriptive style and the probation officer's historical one are both necessary. The two approaches differ in their appropriateness rather than their importance. Similarly, the approach used to present information about criminal justice systems throughout the world will depend on the goal sought. There are at least three ways to study different criminal justice systems (Table 1.1). The historical, political, and descriptive approaches afford a structure that we can use to narrow and specify the goal of this text.

Historical Approach

The author of a report on the state of his country's prison system complains about the heavy cost to the treasury of maintaining prisons. Adding to the problem, prison discipline is minimal, and the convicts leave prison more corrupt than they entered. The high recidivism rate may be explained by the prison's failure to instill in its inmates any principles of morality or sense of responsibility. The author goes on to tell of another country's prison system that not only shows a financial profit but does so under more humane conditions. Prisoners in the second country are placed under severe but uniform discipline, requiring rigorous work during the day and complete isolation at night. The benefits of this inflexibly uniform system include few recommittals to the prison.

We could argue that the author's first country is the United States and the second either has a good public relations official or is a place we should send

Table 1.1 Approaches to an International Perspective

Historical Approach	Political Approach	Descriptive Approach
What mistakes and successes have already occurred?	How does politics affect a nation's justice system?	How is a country's justice system supposed to operate?
What do earlier experiences tell us about the present?	How does politics affect interaction among nations?	What are the main components of a justice system?
How can knowledge of the past prepare us for the future?	How is a country's legal tradition affected by politics?	Who are the main actors in a justice system?

observers in order to get ideas on how to improve the American prison system. Actually, the authors were Gustave de Beaumont and Alexis de Tocqueville. The country criticized was their own nineteenth-century France, and the envied system was the American penitentiary structure in 1831 and 1832 (Beaumont & Tocqueville, 1964). An early nineteenth-century American prison system being coveted as superior to others seems ironic in light of twenty-first century problems. Yet it is just that type of helpful comparison that the historical approach presents.

Beaumont and Tocqueville toured America when the Pennsylvania and Auburn systems were being touted as solutions to the new idea of imprisonment as punishment. The Frenchmen seemed to initially favor the Auburn system (quite likely for its economic benefits), but by the mid 1840s, Tocqueville spoke before the Chamber of Deputies in favor of the Pennsylvania system (see Sellin's introduction in Beaumont & Tocqueville, 1964). Despite such wavering, there is no doubt that the two travelers to the United States considered either American penitentiary system as superior to others known at the time. Their report to French citizens (Beaumont & Tocqueville, 1964) provides a classic example of the historical comparative approach. After describing its evolution and objectives, they compare the American system with Switzerland's and France's, explaining why they consider the American system superior and suggesting ways to implement it.

Beaumont and Tocqueville used an international approach for what we earlier called "provincial benefits." They wanted to improve their system and looked to other countries for suggestions. Their appreciation of the American penitentiary system's historical evolution made it easier for them to see how that system might apply to the French situation. Today their report provides a sense of history for American and French prison systems. Researchers wishing to learn from earlier mistakes and successes in each country will benefit from an international perspective incorporating a historical approach.

An understanding and appreciation of history provide the criminal justice student with information about the present and the future. Like all other social institutions, criminal justice changes over time. Ignoring the past will make it impossible to prepare for inevitable changes of the future in procedures and institutions. As Terrill puts it, "The historical approach prepares students to understand and be a part of a world of change" (1982, p. 25). Despite the changes always taking place in any society, the problems faced remain remarkably stable (McCullagh, 1984). The need for security, justice, and freedom are neither the only nor the least of those problems.

Political Approach

To understand a country's criminal justice system, we must understand its political one. Political and legal philosophies explain how and why a country treats and processes those citizens characterized as deviant (Terrill, 1982). Consider, for example, how politics might affect a country's police system.

As intense proponents of dispersed power, founders of the American republic avoided creating a single law enforcement agency with significant power at either the federal or the state level. Police responsibilities were instead decentralized throughout the country and within each state. A reason for decentralization was the fear that a large, well-organized police force could be used for misguided political purposes in the same way that the military has been used throughout history.

In 1989 events occurred to remind Americans that caution toward centralized forces is not simply a paranoid response. In December President Bush sent military troops into the Republic of Panama. Stories of looting and general disorder following the American invasion became more understandable when we learned that there was no independent police force in Panama. Instead, Panama's policing was the responsibility of the same Panama Defense Forces (PDF) that the American military was fighting. Needless to say, the PDF was unavailable for its civilian police role.

The PDF was constructed in 1983 by combining Panama's national guard, air force, navy, Canal Defense Force, Traffic Direction, Investigations Department, Immigration Department, and police force (Abad, 1989). In this antithesis of American decentralization, Panama consolidated the power of military, paramilitary, and civilian police units and placed the finished product under the authority of the republic's president. In addition, the law creating the PDF gave important functions to the commander in chief of the defense forces. Because that commander in chief, General Manuel Noriega, was the target of the American invasion, Panama had neither a military commander nor a police commissioner after American troops arrived.

A first effort of the new Panamanian government was the creation of an independent security organization called the Panama Public Force (in Spanish, *Fuerza Publica de Panama*). The PPF got off to a rocky start with problems in distancing itself from the old PDF, but it was striving toward autonomy from the military and paramilitary organizations.

Several political changes began an attempt to move Panama from the corrupt PDF to a corruption-free police force. In attempts to calm the Panamanian people's fears, the PPF was not to have a secret police like the old PDF's G-2 unit. Instead, investigations under the PPF, the citizens were assured, would be conducted by a new investigative police unit *(Policia Tecnica Judicial)* that would report to judicial authorities rather than to enforcement authorities (Sutton, 1990). This technique of linking the investigation of crimes to the judiciary rather than to enforcement personnel is common in several countries we review in later chapters.

A country's political system will influence, if not determine, its policing, court, and corrections system. The political approach recognizes the importance of politics in understanding criminal justice at a national and international level. Like the historical approach, the political approach is not the primary one we will follow in this text, but it is important nonetheless.

Descriptive Approach

A description of how something should operate provides the necessary basis for analysis and repair. Just as it would be difficult to repair a motor without knowing how that motor is supposed to function, we must understand a justice system's stated organization and structure before we can determine how closely its operation conforms to the model. Description is the essential first step in comparing criminal justice systems. The historical and political approaches are also necessary and will receive occasional attention in this book, but the descriptive approach allows us to gain an overview of a country's justice system so that we can begin to identify similarities and differences among the nations. To that end, this book emphasizes a descriptive approach when presenting information about criminal justice in other countries.

Two tactics are possible when a descriptive approach is selected for a cross-cultural textbook. One technique focuses on specific countries and describes the legal system's operation in each country. The result is a text in which the same topics (for example, law, police, courts, and corrections) are described in a separate chapter for each country (for example, England, Germany, Australia, and Japan). This strategy provides depth of coverage and gives the reader a strong background in the systems of several countries.

An alternative technique focuses on specific components of the criminal justice system and describes how different countries implement those segments. The result is a text wherein a wide variety of countries (again, England, Germany, Australia, and Japan, plus others) are referred to in separate chapters on such topics as law, police, courts, and corrections. This tactic does not provide the reader with detailed information about any two or three specific countries. Instead, the detail centers on the primary components of all systems of justice and uses various countries to highlight the variations.

Because the goals of this text include developing a better understanding of the American system of justice and gaining ideas for improving that system, the second technique seems most appropriate. In that manner, we can concentrate on already familiar concepts (that is, law, police, courts, and corrections) but do so by looking at the diversity that exists in executing those concepts. As noted, the tradeoff for showing variance is a less comprehensive review of each country. However, several countries make appearances in at least two chapters, so readers will have a nearly complete portrait of the justice system in some places, such as Germany and France.

STRATEGIES UNDER THE DESCRIPTIVE APPROACH

When differences among standard components of criminal justice systems are explored, the descriptive approach can follow two paths. One emphasizes the institutions and actors whereas the other highlights specific functions and procedures. This text follows the *institutions/actors strategy* but occasionally makes use of the *functions/procedures strategy* as well.

The Functions/Procedures Strategy

Lynch (1988) believes cross-national research would benefit from a functional rather than organizational or positional description of national criminal justice systems. He argues that there is more similarity of jobs across systems than there is among persons performing those duties. This point becomes apparent in other chapters as we look at examples like private citizens serving as prosecutors or lay judges, judges actively involved in police investigations, and probation officers who are volunteers rather than paid employees.

The argument Lynch makes is that all countries require that similar jobs be done—they just assign the duties differently. Ingraham (1987) provides an excellent example of this approach in his descriptive account of the underlying structure common to the procedural systems of the United States, France, the former Soviet Union, and the People's Republic of China. As he puts it, "Nations may differ from one another in the manner of collecting evidence, the way they sift it, refine it, and evaluate it prior to trial, and the way they present it at trial, but they all have procedures to do these things" (Ingraham, 1987, p. 17). The comparison model he develops describes procedures under the headings of intake, screening, charging and protecting, adjudication, sanctioning, and appeal. The result is a concise account comparing the four countries in each of the six categories.

As an example, we will consider the way each of Ingraham's four countries responds (at least when Ingraham was describing them) to the task of charging a defendant and protecting that defendant against abuse by the accusers. The first concern in this process is the need to protect the defendant against prolonged and unnecessary pretrial detention. Ingraham is not interested in the particular office or type of agent responsible for insuring this protection, but rather the procedures each country uses.

Police in the United States may detain a suspect for a limited time if there are reasonable grounds to believe the person is, was, or may soon be engaged in criminal activity. Short-term detention at the police station for purposes of investigation is not, however, allowed. After a formal arrest and booking, the suspect must be taken to a magistrate, who advises the defendant of her rights regarding bail and legal counsel. At that point the defendant will be released on money or property bond (or simply on her promise to return at the appointed time for a court hearing) or placed in jail until trial.

The powers of the French police to detain accused persons before trial differ somewhat from those in the United States. In cases of "flagrant" felonies and misdemeanors, the police may detain a suspect without a warrant for 24 hours so that an investigation can be conducted (Ingraham, 1987; Terrill, 1999). The prosecutor can extend the detention period for another 24 hours upon being shown additional and weighty evidence supporting guilt. The defendant cannot be detained beyond the 24 (or the total of 48) hours unless the prosecutor turns the investigation over to an investigation judge, who can then authorize temporary detention. In order to use temporary detention, the authorized punishment for the alleged offense must exceed two years, there must be reason to believe that the accused would respond negatively in the community (for example, flee, exert pressure on witnesses, or commit new offenses), or that *judicial supervision* is determined inadequate. Rather than relying on the bail system, France allows the defendant to obtain liberty before trial either with or without "judicial supervision." That procedure is a pretrial release with conditions (for example, do not leave the area, or report at specific times to particular officials) imposed by the magistrate.

Procedures in the former USSR were similar to those in France with two important exceptions. First, the Soviet periods of authorized detention were longer. In certain cases (similar to the French "flagrant offenses"), Soviet police could confine a suspect for 24 hours before notifying the procurator (essentially, the prosecutor). The initial restriction could be extended an additional 48 hours while the procurator decided whether to order release or continued "confinement under guard." The second major difference from the French system was the absence of judicial control or supervision of pretrial confinement (Ingraham, 1987). Rather than requiring a magistrate's approval for confinement under guard (similar to the French temporary detention), the Soviets authorized the person conducting the inquiry (the investigator, the procurator, or the court) to restrain the suspect.

China's Criminal Procedure Law allows public security bureaus to detain a suspect for up to three days. "Special circumstances" allow the initial period to be extended from one to four days (Ingraham, 1987; Terrill, 1999). After that extension the prosecutor has three days to approve the arrest or release the suspect. If the arrest is approved, the suspect may be held an additional two months. If the case is particularly complex, pretrial detention may be extended additional months but only as authorized by increasingly higher levels of administrators. Ingraham (1987) identified such alternatives to pretrial detention as securing a guarantor for the suspect's court appearance and confinement at the suspect's home under house arrest. It is not clear which cases allow alternatives to pretrial release or which actor or agency is authorized to grant the alternatives.

That brief review of how four countries protect citizens against prolonged and unnecessary pretrial detention provides a quick look at the functions/procedures perspective. This approach allows easy viewing of similarities among countries while drawing attention to the basic functions and procedures found in a variety of criminal justice systems. When differences become apparent, they suggest topics of conversation and debate.

For example, Ingraham suggests that by failing to allow limited periods for investigative detention prior to arrest, we in the United States may not be providing suspects the level of protection we think we are. His position is that the absence of investigative detention provisions forces American police to initiate the arrest process very early. Once the suspect is arrested and confined, pretrial release procedures come into play. American pretrial release relies heavily on bail, and arrested persons are frequently too poor to raise the necessary security. As a result, in providing safeguards against arbitrary and prolonged pretrial detention, the U.S. system actually deprives poor defendants of a measure of protection against being unfairly arrested (Ingraham, 1987).

The Institutions/Actors Strategy

A functions/procedure strategy like that championed by Lynch and by Ingraham clarifies duties and highlights the similarities among countries, but may mask important differences. Also, although that approach makes it easy to organize information for comparing a few countries, it becomes cumbersome when working with large a number of countries.

The other approach is to compare countries on the basis of specific institutions and positions charged with accomplishing particular duties. For example, Ingraham examines protection against prolonged and unnecessary pretrial detention by describing the functions and procedures used in four countries to accomplish that task. He is not concerned with the specific agency or type of officer responsible for those efforts. The alternative way to approach the topic is to emphasize such institutions as police, courts, and corrections while discussing the assigned duties of people such as police officers, attorneys, judges, and wardens.

Each approach is reasonable and useful. However, for our purposes, the institutions/actors technique is featured because it better enables the viewing of differences and can handle a larger number of countries. The chapters of this book rely on descriptions of institutions and actors, so it is an approach that will soon become very familiar to you. To illustrate the strategy, we can look briefly at how the same topic covered by Ingraham would be addressed by the institutions/actors strategy. In this case we will deal with the institution of bail as it operates in one type of justice system.

Arresting a person for a criminal offense sets into motion two conflicting goals. On the one hand, the government agency making the arrest wants to be sure that the suspect will appear at the necessary time and place for a trial regarding the charges. Opposing that goal is society's interest in being fair to the suspect, who has not yet been found guilty of anything and therefore should be allowed to move freely about and assist in preparing a defense to the charges. The extreme ways of responding to this dilemma would involve forcibly detaining the suspect until trial (the seesaw tilts toward the government's goal) or allowing the suspect to roam free until the required court appearance (a tilt in favor of fairness to the suspect). For centuries, systems of justice have sought to balance the seesaw and ensure that both goals are met. The justice system with an English heritage (that is, the common law system) developed a procedure called *bail* to equalize the conflicting goals.

As it developed in eighteenth-century England, bail in criminal cases was by *recognizance.* That is, a person pledges to meet some condition set by the court in order to obtain freedom of movement until trial. In more technical terms, a person recognizes his obligation to a judge to perform a specific act or pay a specified sum for failure to perform the act. Performing the act voids the obligation to pay. In criminal matters, English courts used the idea of recognizance as a means to guarantee a suspect's appearance in court by finding third parties, called *sureties,* who made financial pledges on the suspect's behalf (Devine, 1989). If the suspect did not show up, the sureties forfeited the agreed upon sum.

Devine (1989) points out that common law bail systems share a heritage of placing primary responsibility for an accused's court appearance upon the sureties guaranteeing the person's attendance. Five basic types of bail are identified on the basis of the primary surety or security used to ensure the accused's presence at trial (see Figure 1.1).

Commercial Bail. As conducted in the United States, commercial bail is the type of bail that many people already know about. Between the 1800s and the 1960s, American jurisdictions predominantly required criminal suspects to post commercial bail to secure their release (Samaha, 1988). Currently other programs supplement the use of commercial bail, but it still exists in most criminal courts across the country. The term *commercial* is used because the criterion for pretrial release is a financial obligation with the court. If the person shows up at the appropriate time, the obligation is voided and the money is returned to the defendant. If the person does not appear, the bond is forfeited and remains with the court.

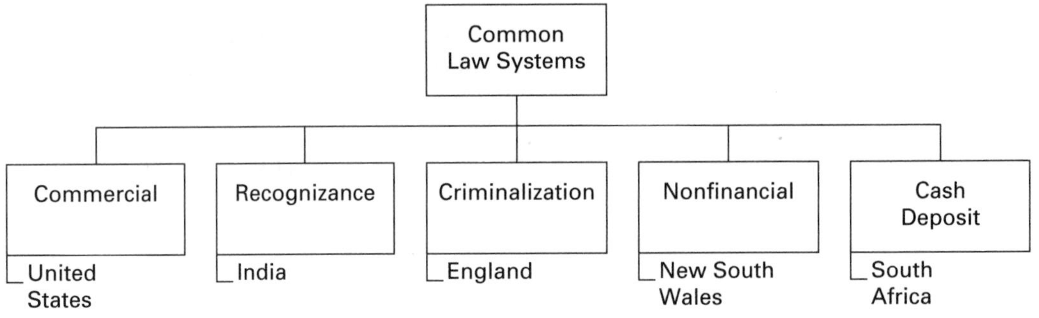

Figure 1.1 Types of Bail

This type of bail is controversial because of its possible discrimination against economically disadvantaged defendants and its spawning of the criminal justice system actor called a *bondsman.* As bail developed in America, the historical sureties came to be played by third parties willing to take a chance on a defendant in return for an opportunity to make some money. In this manner, a bondsman will advance his or her money to get a defendant released from jail to await trial. In return, the defendant will pay the bondsman a nonreturnable fee of about 10 percent of the bail amount set by the court.

Recognizance. The historical recognizance system exists today in only a few countries. Bail based on recognizance was abandoned in England in the 1970s, so today the country providing the best example of this approach is India (Devine, 1989). Pretrial release is allowed, and appearance for trial is secured, by the defendant's acknowledging an indebtedness to the court. If the defendant does not appear or fails to meet other conditions of bail, the stipulated amount "comes due." Because no cash or property is deposited with the court (neither by the defendant nor by a third party), the system is not open to criticism of economic discrimination like that directed at commercial bail. No cash is involved unless forfeiture occurs, making the Indian system similar to the historical concept of recognizance in English common law.

Criminalization. With the Bail Act of 1976, England replaced the recognizance system with a system of criminal punishment for fleeing. With this *criminalization,* failure to appear at the appointed time means that the defendant is automatically guilty of absconding and may be punished with up to three months' imprisonment, a 2000-pound fine, or both (Devine, 1989). In this manner England also avoids the opportunity for commercial bail bonding, but differently than India does.

Nonfinancial Bail. In a specific attempt to allow release on bail without the possibility of economic discrimination, the Australian state of New South Wales implemented a nonfinancial system. As a result of the Bail Act of 1978, New South Wales courts grant bail to defendants on either an unconditional or conditional basis. Unconditional release is just that—the defendants are told where and when to show up for court, and off they go. If the court believes the defendant might not appear for trial, might commit another crime, or might interfere with evidence, witnesses, or jury, conditions for pretrial release may be imposed (Devine, 1989). A conditional release might require the defendant to make periodic appearances at a specified police station, or to provide one or more persons to testify as to his likelihood of appearing in court, or to adhere to certain stipulations regarding his movements..

Cash Deposit Bail. It is possible to have a bail system that uses cash deposits but does not amount to commercial bail. The Republic of South Africa exemplifies such an approach in the way it deals with persons accused of ordinary, nonpolitical, common law crimes. Typically a cash deposit is required to secure pretrial release, and although a third party may provide the money, it cannot profit financially from doing so. If it seems reasonable to assume that the third party will be indemnified against loss of the money or will gain financial benefit as a result of making the payment, the deposit must be rejected (Devine, 1989). This system discourages the development of professional bail bondsmen despite its reliance on cash deposits.

The preceding description of five forms of bail not only exemplifies the institutions/actors (more institutions than actors in this case) strategy but also introduces an important concept used throughout this book. In identifying the five basic types of bail, we made use of *classification* to compare those types. Each of the five jurisdictions used to show a type of bail also employs other procedures. Financial conditions for bail may be imposed in New South Wales, England, and India. Both the United States and the Republic of South Africa make use of nonfinancial criteria for pretrial release. For purposes of discussion, however, we have categorized the jurisdictions according to their main method of allowing pretrial release and securing appearance for trial.

This technique of classification serves the primary purpose of providing some order to a seemingly jumbled array of institutions involved in various bail systems. Because of the classification, we have a better grasp of the different ways in which bail can be carried out in common law systems. Furthermore, the classification is an aid to memory.

It is possible, though, that we have left out an important bail type, one that does not fit into any of the five categories. Or maybe additional research will show that we have made distinctions in our classifications where none should be made. That is, maybe there should be only two types of bail instead of five. However, that is another benefit of a classification system! It is open to debate, revision, modification, and even complete dismissal. For those reasons, and others noted in the following discussion, the use of classification seems an appropriate way to approach the discussion of diverse criminal justice systems. Its importance to the remaining chapters requires an elaboration of the classification technique.

COMPARISON THROUGH CLASSIFICATION

In a popular parlor game, one person thinks of a person, place, or thing while others try to guess the object using no more than 20 yes-or-no questions. When you consider the infinite number of possibilities, it seems quite presumptuous to believe that we could guess, with no more than 20 questions, what someone else is thinking of. The fact that questioners are successful enough to perpetuate the game is a sobering thought.

A standard approach for players is to ask questions by setting up categories. For example, after determining that the object is a person, questioners may ask if it is male or female. Additional questioning may identify living or dead, famous or infamous, and eventually narrow down the person's occupation, basis for fame, and so forth. This process used to identify the object is dependent upon the players' knowledge and use of *classification.*

The Need for Classification

Classification refers to the grouping of individual objects into categories based on the objects' relationships. Through this process of naming and then grouping items into recognizable categories, we order and summarize the diversity that exists in the world. Its importance for operating in society (rather than simply winning a parlor game) becomes apparent upon realizing that survival of early humans must have been aided by an ability to recognize that individual objects shared certain properties. For example, some items were edible, whereas others made people sick. Some animals were helpful; others were lethal. The ability to distinguish the category into which a particular item fell certainly made life more pleasant.

The process of classification and the resulting classification systems have been studied most completely by scientists interested in living organisms (see Dunn and Everitt, 1982; Mayr, 1982; Stace, 1989). Terms like *taxonomy* and *systematics* are familiar from biology classes. The concept of classification, however, is helpful and applicable whenever one has to deal with diversity. From the rather frivolous example of playing "20 Questions" we can move to the more practical one of finding a book in the library. Simply mentioning the prospect of searching for a particular book from a grouping of thousands, in no order whatsoever, is enough to remind us to be grateful for the Library of Congress's classification system.

Basically, then, there is no argument on the need for classification. Instead, disagreement rests on how to classify, what criteria should be used in the process, and what the ultimate purpose of classification is. We will spend some time responding to these questions, because classification plays an important role in the structure of this text. Our guiding principle will be Ehrmann's statement: "All comparison proceeds from categorization" (1976, p. 12). The diversity of the world's criminal justice systems requires an understanding of, and appreciation for, the classification process and the resulting schemes.

Classification Strategies

Rather than tackle the difficult issue of how the classification process should take place (interested readers are referred to texts on *macrotaxonomy, mathematical taxonomy, plant taxonomy,* and *biosystematics*), let us consider the idea that each classification strategy has good and bad points. What is "best" in a particular instance depends on the goal sought. It seems more important for our purposes to be aware of what schemes are possible than to try to determine which one is superior.

Two ways of classifying are possible (see Table 1.2). The first is a *synthetic strategy* resulting in categorization of *artificial groups.* Classification of this type typically has a *special purpose* and attempts to bring order to a confusing array of objects. The terms *synthetic* and *artificial* are used with this approach because the ensuing classification is the result of scientists manufacturing a group that categorizes objects on the basis of some criteria of interest to the scientist.

Usually artificial groups are built around only one or two aspects of the object being classified. For example, a telephone book groups people alphabetically within the 26 groups of letters. A book for hikers may group flowers by color, thereby making identification easier and quicker. The classification of library books uses more criteria (for example, subject matter and author's last name) but still is essentially a "pigeonholing" exercise for the purpose of bringing order to diversity.

Although synthetic classification strategies have practical applications, such as making it easy to find a phone number, identify a flower, or track down a book, their artificial nature does not allow us to imply or deduce other information about the object. For example, we would not assume that all people listed under "S" in the phone book are females of German heritage just because our friend Helene Schneider is an Austrian woman. Because nothing else about an object is suggested, beyond the one or two characteristics used in the classification process, synthetic strategies have low predictivity.

Authentic strategies for classification provide categorization of *natural groups.* Because this scheme uses a great number of characteristics to categorize objects into groups, it is much more predictive than are synthetic systems. The terms *authentic* and *natural* are appropriate here, because scientists group objects based on factual characteristics shared by members of a group. Unlike synthetic strategies, this approach relies on verified inherent attributes rather than traits assigned or manufactured to meet some purpose that a scientist has. Humans categorized according to last names in a phone book constitute artificial groups. In contrast, humans classified according to some measure of human biology, constitute natural groups. Since this classification is based on inherent rather than assigned characteristics, it possesses the quality of predictivity. To illustrate, when scientists

Table 1.2 Classification Strategies

Synthetic Strategies	Authentic Strategies
Results in artificial groups Is based on only one or two aspects of the object Resulting classification has a practical or special purpose that brings order to diversity	Results in natural groups Is based on extensive study of the object Resulting classification allows some predictivity regarding the group's members

determine that everyone in a group of 100 humans drives erratically after imbibing a certain amount of alcohol, it seems safe to hypothesize that all (or most) other humans (that is, all other members of the same category of living organisms) would be similarly affected. Additional study may require us to revise that initial assumption to allow for variation in size, weight, and so on. Even so, a predictivity exists that is impossible with an artificial grouping. We cannot assume that a poison oak leaf is edible just because, like a lettuce leaf, it is green.

It may seem that its predictivity makes an authentic classification strategy superior to a synthetic one, but both schemes have their good and bad points. Predictivity is desirable, but it is not the sole criterion for judging classification schemes. It may be just as important and interesting to know the evolutionary history and relationships among items as it is to make predictions about the attributes of a particular object in a group. Similarly, the currently observable structure of objects in a specific category requires description and understanding regardless of any need to make predictions. These concerns with *historical relationships* and *contemporary relationships* are examples of special-purpose classifications easily handled by synthetic strategies. In these cases, predictivity is not a goal of the categorization, so natural groups are not necessary. Therefore, the classification may be adequately conducted with knowledge of only one or two characteristics of the objects involved.

Recall, for example, the classification of common law bail types presented earlier in this chapter. That categorization was determined only on the basis of what form of surety or security was used as the primary means of securing the accused's presence at trial. Such categorization resulting from a single characteristic is not helpful in predicting anything about bail in common law countries. Yet, it does suggest interesting historical questions: for example, why did countries sharing a common heritage with England develop sometimes very different techniques? Similarly, questions about contemporary relationships are generated. For example, because the United States and New South Wales share a common legal tradition, should America follow the Australian example and be more forceful in initiating nonfinancial bail systems? Questions of this type are addressed in the "Impact" section of this and future chapters.

The Role of Classification in This Book

The classification of living organisms traces its origin at least as far back as Aristotle (B.C. 384–322). It is not surprising, therefore, that some authentic systems of classification resulting in natural groups and having significant predictivity are found in biology and botany. The cross-cultural study of criminal justice systems does not share such a distinguished history. As a relatively new area of study, comparative criminal justice has not investigated its various "objects" to the extent necessary to provide authentic systems and natural groups. Today, classification in comparative criminal justice is essentially of the synthetic scheme. Synthetic strategies are important, however, because they successfully serve purposes other than predictivity.

Chapters 2 through 9 of this text are organized around particular classification schemes. Some of those approximate authentic systems with a general

IMPACT

Bail or Jail?

Ingraham (1987) suggests that American police are forced to use arrest too early. Because many American jurisdictions use commercial bail as the main way an accused can secure release from pretrial detention, early use of arrest means some poor people simply remain in jail. While awaiting trial the defendant is concerned with such things as supporting herself and/or her family; locating witnesses and aiding the lawyer in preparing a defense; and putting her affairs in order should she be convicted and sent to prison. Local citizens are not anxious to jail (i.e., punish) a person who is not yet convicted of anything, but those citizens also want to make sure the defendant appears at trial and refrains from endangering others in the meantime. These concerns are often in conflict, and American jurisdictions seem to fluctuate between which of the two is emphasized.

In the 1960s attention was directed to the problems of the defendant. Concerned that some poor people were kept in jail because they lacked cash rather than because they presented a threat to the community, some reformers sought alternatives to commercial bail. One of those alternatives, *Release on Recognizance (ROR),* is similar to the system described for India. The American version of ROR was the result of activity by the Vera Institute of Justice, which initiated the Manhattan bail project in the early 1960s. Using a point-weighing system, staff members interviewed prisoners brought in for booking. Based on the accused's responses to questions about his or her "community ties" (length of time in the community, location of relatives, employment, etc.), the staff member would determine if the person was a good risk for release simply on their promise to appear in court. The procedure was successful and popular. As a result, it supplements, but does not replace, commercial bail in many American jurisdictions today.

A more recent dissatisfaction with traditional bail procedures sides with the worries of the public and is seen in the 1984 Bail Reform Act, wherein Congress allowed federal court judges to hold defendants without bail if they believe those defendants pose a threat to the public safety. This use of preventive detention has expanded to the state level, and most states now follow the federal lead and allow bail decisions to be influenced by a concern for the threat the defendant poses to the community. In *U.S. v. Salerno* (1987), the Supreme Court upheld the Bail Reform Act's pretrial detention procedure by ruling it does not violate the Fifth or the Eighth Amendment. The reasoning behind the ruling included the justices' belief that the act was designed as a regulatory act for purposes of ensuring public safety. It was not meant to be a form of punishment.

Can an international perspective help us identify other ways to respond to the conflicting interests of the accused and the community? The four

(continued)

IMPACT

Bail or Jail? *(continued)*

alternatives to commercial bail covered in this chapter suggest there may be other choices. Some alternatives to commercial bail are already being used in American jurisdictions. In addition to the release on recognizance (as in India's system), some American courts provide for a conditional release similar to that used in New South Wales. Many alternatives, however, are consistent with the preference for a financial obligation and are (like the South African system) simply variants of the traditional American approach.

U.S. policy makers and the American public seem hesitant to support widespread movement from a financially based pretrial release system. Even if the pendulum moves from emphasis on pretrial worries of the public back to pretrial concerns of the accused, our legal history does not provide many nonfinancial examples from which to reap alternatives. This is why it is important to be familiar with and willing to borrow from the experiences of other countries. The dilemma presented by conflicting interests of the accused against those of the community will not go away. However, other countries experience the same dilemma. If our goal lies more with protecting the community, maybe we should allow the police to detain suspects for purposes of investigation. The experience of countries like France and Russia in that area may prove quite helpful. If the goal rests with concern for the rights of the accused, nonfinancial systems like those of India and New South Wales may be worthy of closer attention. In either event, an international perspective will be useful.

purpose, but most are the synthetic type having a special purpose (either historical or contemporary). In both cases, the reader should remember that classification (of either type) is being used to summarize and make sense of diversity. In addition, any classification system should serve as an aid to memory. Presenting information about a topic via a classification scheme should enable you to visualize and conceptualize the material more easily.

A final note of caution is necessary. Some people tend to view a particular classification as equivalent to a scientific theory. As such, the classification could be proved wrong. Viewing a classification in that manner is inappropriate and incorrect (see Dunn & Everitt, 1982, p. 5). Because it is a creation of reason based on accumulation of experienced data, a classification can be neither right nor wrong. It is merely an intelligible summary of information. Its value is determined by its usefulness to others. Importantly, saying that a classification is neither right nor wrong is not the same as saying that it cannot or should not be changed. If it ceases to be useful, it should be modified or discarded. "As the needs and knowledge of scientists change so must the system of classification" (Dunn & Everitt, 1982, p. 9).

THE STRUCTURE OF THIS BOOK

As explained earlier, this book uses a descriptive rather than a historical or political approach to studying comparative criminal justice. The focus is on the primary components of a large number of nations rather than providing an in-depth examination of just a few countries. This topical rather than country-by-country approach loses detail of specific countries but compensates by allowing coverage of a greater number of countries and by more clearly identifying system differences. The particular path followed with this descriptive approach emphasizes institutions and actors rather than functions and procedures. Historical and political approaches are not be ignored; neither are descriptive accounts of functions and procedures. Yet those devices provide only secondary themes here.

To aid in presenting the descriptive information, classification schemes are built around both synthetic and authentic strategies. The infancy of comparative criminal justice as a field of study requires greater use of synthetic strategies, because these can be built on only one or two criteria. The resulting artificial groups provide a sense of order to the diversity of institutions and procedures in the criminal justice systems we will encounter. The reader should remember to approach the classification in each chapter as a summary of information rather than a scientific theory. Continuing political and cultural changes occurring throughout the world present opportunities to modify the classification scheme as our knowledge of different systems expands.

With the descriptive approach used here, there is a distinct danger of providing incomplete information about some countries. Sociologists are well aware that social groups and organizations have an informal structure as well as the formal one presented to the public. A police department's organizational chart may clearly show a chain of command flowing from the police chief through bureau chiefs to division chiefs and down to section and unit commanders. What may not be shown is the department's informal policy that allows administrators to bypass a level or two when working on certain tasks or with "old friends." For example, earlier in this chapter the procedures used to ensure a suspect's right against prolonged and unreasonable detention were described for four countries. It would be naive of us to believe that those procedures, in any of the four countries, are followed to the letter by each actor every day.

The best way to identify and eventually describe the informal structure and relations of a group or organization is through participant observation over a prolonged period of time. Unfortunately, comparative criminal justice is a foundling among scientific fields of study. As a result, it has few participant observation-type research efforts. Yet, the absence of knowledge about informal workings should not preclude the use of a descriptive approach. It should only serve to remind us that there is much to learn about criminal justice organizations in our own country as well as those in other parts of the world. Although the descriptive approach provides information about only the stated workings of criminal justice institutions and actors, when you think about it, we would not want to start anywhere else. After all, it is necessary to understand how something is supposed to work before we can even begin to discern how it varies from the model.

There is a final point to make concerning the structure of this book—and the structure of the world. The last decade of the twentieth century started with dramatic and traumatic world events beginning in the late 1980s. The social, political, and economic changes brought down the Berlin Wall, saw the rise of democracy in former communist countries, encouraged the reunification of Germany and the breakup of the Soviet Union, and essentially ensured that the world would end the century in a very different place than either experts or laypeople had imagined.

The changes brought opportunities to many people in a variety of occupations, but mapmakers comprised one occupational group for whom the events were as frustrating as they were exciting. Throughout the late 1900s, media reported the futility felt by artists responsible for portraying geographic boundaries, encyclopedists attempting to prepare factual entries by publication deadlines, and college professors trying give accurate lectures on the politics of Eastern European countries. Persons interested in comparative criminal justice were placed in a similar predicament. What if a country's justice system is faithfully and accurately described in February only to find that country operating under a different political system in March? If we wait until April to describe the system, who can say that other changes will not occur in May? During times of rapid geographic change, cartographers continue to make and distribute maps. During times of rapid economic change, economists continue to debate and predict financial issues. Similarly, despite changes affecting government structures and organization, criminal justice scholars continue to describe and analyze justice systems.

Actually, the field of comparative criminal justice has an advantage over some other fields, because even rapid political and economic change cannot easily force similarly paced structural and bureaucratic change. For example, changing the former Union of Soviet Socialist Republics' name to Russia and devaluing the ruble happened more quickly than has a structural change in the way policing is provided. It is one thing to replace a country's governing body with the first democratically elected representatives in over 40 years and quite another to release all its prisoners and start over with a whole new penal system. In other words, change does not necessarily occur at the same pace in all parts of a country.

In 1991 newspaper columnist Cathy Collison enlisted University of Michigan professor Ted Hopf to answer a question posed by a 10-year-old Michigan girl. The girl wondered how long it would take the Russian government to form a democracy. She was told the change would take some time. Two of the reasons offered for the slow transition to democracy also explain why drastic changes in the Russian criminal justice system cannot suddenly occur: (1) tradition is hard to overcome, and (2) change is scary (Collison, 1991).

The comfort of tradition and the threat of change are not conditions unique to the Russian people. As a result, there is a stability in the social institutions of nations that provides a continuity in areas like the police, courts, and corrections. This is not to say that those organizations avoid change. Even when the Union of Soviet Socialist Republics existed, there were changes occurring in such areas as the role of Soviet defense counsel and the way prisons were used. The point is not that criminal justice agencies escape modification, but rather that what appears to be rapid social change affecting all aspects of a country and its people may be the start of a marathon race rather than a sprint. As you read this book's description of criminal justice in various countries, you will undoubtedly find information that is no longer accurate for that country; you may even read about a country that no longer exists in the form described. Such problems are inevitable in today's dynamic world. However, because people and their social institutions tend to find comfort in tradition and anxiety in change, the discrepancies are likely to be ones of detail rather than of the whole.

SUMMARY

This chapter introduces a book describing the different ways criminal justice can operate. That variability is shown by reference to justice systems operating in countries around the world. The study of criminal justice systems in other countries has specific benefits for our own justice system as well as for international relations. The provincial benefits include better understanding and greater appreciation for the American system based on understanding points of contrast between the different systems. In addition, an international perspective can suggest ideas to improve our system. On a broader scale, knowledge of how other countries conceive and implement the idea of "justice" is increasingly necessary. The presence and persistence of cross-national crimes like terrorism, hijacking, drug smuggling, and organized crime networks demand a cooperative international effort. Such an effort is aided when citizens of different countries are familiar with, and try to understand and respect, the institutions and procedures of other countries.

The process of studying assorted criminal justice systems can take at least three approaches: historical, political, and descriptive. This book uses the descriptive approach primarily, with attention focused on the formal workings of organizations and people driving a country's criminal justice system.

The descriptive approach allows for comparison of a number of countries. A problem with such comparison is the overwhelming diversity confronting us as we attempt to find similarities and identify differences among various systems. To aid in the process, each chapter uses a classification scheme that provides order and aids the memory process. The process of classification is achieved through two strategies: synthetic and authentic. Each strategy results in a grouping of objects (artificial or natural groups of objects) having special (the artificial groups) or predictive (the natural groups) purposes.

WEB SITES TO VISIT

- The European Union's web page at **www.eurunion.org** provides an interesting overview of the EU and has links to documents for those wishing more in-depth coverage.
- Europol's web site at **www.europol.eu.int/home.htm** has helpful information about Europol's structure and duties.
- Read Mathieu Deflem's article, "The Boundaries of International Cooperation: Human Rights and Neo-Imperialism in U.S.–Mexican Police Relationships" at **www.sla.purdue.edu/people/soc/mdeflem/zintcor.htm**

- Read Maria Toro's article, "The internationalization of police: The DEA in Mexico" at **www.historycooperative.org/journals/jah/86.2/toro.html**

SUGGESTED READINGS

Ehrmann, Henry W. (1976). *Comparative legal cultures.* Englewood Cliffs, NJ: Prentice Hall.

Ingraham, Barton L. (1987). *The structure of criminal procedure: Laws and practices of France, the Soviet Union, China, and the United States.* New York: Greenwood, an imprint of Greenwood Publishing Group, Westport, CT.

Terrill, Richard J. (1982). Approaches for teaching comparative criminal justice to undergraduates. *Criminal Justice Review,* 7(1), 23–27.

Chapter 2

Crime on the World Scene

KEY TOPICS

- How crime statistics are compiled
- Problems in reporting and recording crime
- Using crime data sets and a victimization data set to compare crime rates
- Trends in five clusters of transnational crime
- Examples of developing and testing crime theories with cross-national data
- Existing and suggested efforts to improve international adjudication efforts

KEY TERMS

cultural heritage crime
economic crime
environmental crime
international terrorism
internationally organized crime
National Crime Survey
transnational crime
Uniform Crime Reports

COUNTRIES REFERENCED

China
Saudi Arabia
Venezuela

There is an understandable tendency for a country's citizens to take a narrow view of the crime problem. In other words, their main concern is how safe they feel in their own neighborhoods. The idea that residents of some neighborhoods in other countries may be similarly concerned is only minimally interesting to the average citizen. Even if criminal activities in one country are shown to have a direct effect on crime in another, residents are unlikely to view that information as significant. After all, the government cannot do anything about "homegrown" crime; why should it be able to do anything about crime originating in some other country?

The United Nations has a less cynical outlook on the possibility of controlling national and international crime. From its universal, rather than parochial, perspective, the United Nations endeavors to measure crime, identify common crime problems, and work toward common solutions. This chapter uses those three themes to lay the groundwork for the rest of the book.

In the future envisioned by the popular *Star Trek* television shows, a unified justice system rules the universe, but for the foreseeable future, the planet Earth will likely contain as many justice systems as we have nations. Consequently, as noted in Chapter 1, it is desirable for the citizens of the world to be at least slightly familiar with one another's justice system, for as a result of changes occurring throughout the world, we now face a situation in which crime and criminals increasingly ignore national boundaries. However, before looking at the variety of ways criminal justice systems operate, let us consider the larger picture—the magnitude of the crime problem worldwide. Then we will examine how the United States' response compares with responses in other parts of the world.

THE CRIME PROBLEM

This chapter's primary goal is to introduce you to the crime problem in its world context. Because we more typically read, hear, and watch reports on crime in America, we probably know less than we should about the problems of other countries. Learning about crime in other countries will help us understand the remaining chapters, which focus on how different countries respond to crime. We begin with a discussion of how crime statistics are compiled.

During a barroom fight, John breaks chairs, tables, and glassware; hits George in the face and breaks George's nose; and then tries to get away by stealing a car parked in front of the bar. What crime or crimes do we list as having been committed by John? Although it may be tempting to argue for counting one assault, one destruction of property, and one auto theft, the Federal Bureau of Investigation's *Uniform Crime Report (UCR)* network tells the police to choose only one crime—the most serious offense (assault in this case). Of course, the police and prosecutor are not affected by this UCR directive, and John could well be charged with all three offenses. Yet, for crime-recording purposes only the assault will make it into the statistics. When the new *National Incident-Based Reporting System (NIBRS)* becomes fully functional it will be possible to record information about all crimes occurring during one incident. Even with NIBRS, however, decisions must be made about how a particular act is defined.

Try another example. Yamaguchi Yukio became angry with his wife Noriko and beat her during a domestic quarrel. Noriko died as a result of the beating. What crime—assault or homicide—is tabulated? Given your recently acquired knowledge of UCR recording practices, an answer that ignores the assault and records the homicide is understandable. In addition, if this quarrel had taken place in the United States, it would be the correct answer. However, the Yamaguchis live in Kyoto, Japan. In Japan, assault resulting in death is classified as assault rather than homicide (Kalish, 1988).

How about one more? Ladislav Urbanek forces his date for the evening, Irena Svoboda, to have sexual intercourse. Ms. Svoboda dies as a result of the rape. Both rape and homicide are, of course, serious crimes. The UCR requires that homicide be the recorded offense. However, this crime took place in the former Czechoslovakia, and they were not interested in what the UCR requires. For Czechoslovak statistics, the crime was classified as rape, not as homicide (Kalish, 1988).

These examples of differences in recording acts as one type of crime or another should make us wary of comparing crime statistics among countries. However, despite the difficulties, some information of value can be obtained if comparisons are done with due recognition of cross-cultural differences and with care in interpreting the terms used.

There are two main types of statistical data on crime in the United States. The first of these, *offender/offense statistics*, are typically kept by government agencies and range from very specific data, such as that contained in *Violent Crime in the United States* (Bureau of Justice Statistics) to data on broader subjects, such as that contained in *Uniform Crime Reports* (Federal Bureau of Investigation). Those examples happen to be at the federal level, but each state and many city governments have similar data sources and resultant publications. The second type of statistical data, *victim statistics*, is best exemplified by the *National Crime Survey* (Bureau of Justice Statistics).

The *Uniform Crime Reports (UCR)* and *National Crime Victimization Survey (NCVS)* are the most complete and frequently cited data sources on crime and victimization in the United States. As good as they are, however, they have problems. We will take a few moments to review the goals and difficulties with the UCR and NCVS, because the pros and cons here are transferable to data sources in other countries.

Uniform Crime Reports

The UCR is an incomplete nationwide system of voluntary reporting of offenses that come to the attention of police agencies and departments. Statistics are kept on 29 categories of crime broken into Part I and Part II offenses. The Part I offenses, called *index crimes*, are comprised of the four violent (homicide, rape, robbery, and assault) and the four property (burglary, larceny, motor vehicle theft, and arson) crimes believed most important for keeping detailed information on. These crimes, and, when an arrest is made, the persons believed to have committed them, are reported by police departments throughout the country.

Although providing the data is voluntary, most police agencies willingly participate by sending monthly and/or annual reports to the FBI. As a result, the

UCR provides the United States with systematic, nationwide information on serious crime across the country. Not surprisingly, however, the UCR has some reporting and recording problems. It is important to remember that our discussion of these problems should serve to indicate the difficulty of compiling data on crime in any country. Although the UCR can be criticized, few other countries have any organization that can match its efforts. The following criticisms should therefore be interpreted as highlighting universal problems.

Reporting Problems. Reporting problems with the UCR are very well documented. For the police to know about a crime, and thereby to include it in the police department's tally, the police themselves must see the offense occur or a victim/witness must report the crime to the police. Because only about one third of all crimes are reported to the police, the UCR is known to underestimate the amount of crime occurring each year. The extent to which crime is underestimated varies by type of crime (violent is reported more than is personal theft), sex (female victims are more likely to report than are male victims), and age (older victims report more than do younger victims). The dependence of the police on other citizens to report crime makes an accurate count difficult to obtain. And even when the police have been told about a crime, the potential for data problems does not end.

Recording Problems. In countries like the United States that have a decentralized system of laws and policing, identifying which category of offense has occurred is often very difficult. With its 51 systems of law, the United States presents numerous obstacles to compiling national data on crime. For example, one state may define forced illegal entry into another's home with the intent to steal something as "burglary." Another state may call the illegal entrance "breaking and entering" and reserve the term "burglary" for the taking of another's property after illegal entrance. The UCR provides police agencies with an instruction manual that helps them determine how to categorize each offense according to UCR terminology. The need for such a manual exemplifies the problems of coordinating crime statistics from numerous jurisdictions with similar yet somewhat differing laws.

Political control of crime recording is a reality that must be recognized when one is trying to interpret crime statistics. The old Union of Soviet Socialist Republics provided an extreme example of politics affecting the tracking of crime. The Communist Party of the Soviet Union set itself the task of preventing all violations of law and order, eliminating all crime, and removing all causes of deviance (Shargorodskii, 1964). Complete and accurate criminal statistics would have been a good way to judge the party's success in that endeavor, but such statistics were unavailable to Soviet criminologists. When statistics were provided, they tended to be so general that no implications or relevant variables could be identified, or so specific that generalities could not be made.

Yu and Zhang (1999) found similar recording problems in the People's Republic of China. Results from China's five-year National Crime Study (conducted between 1987 and 1991) suggest that underrecording of crime by police was a serious problem, with the police actually recording only about one third of the crimes that had been reported to them in the early years of the study. Specific efforts to improve the gathering of statistics resulted in an increase to about 60 percent by the 1990 survey. Some underrecording seems to have been built into the Chinese system, since Article 10 of China's *Criminal Law* gave police the discretion to ignore as crimes any events the officer considered to be of insignificant harm. Also, police officers themselves suggested that the use of clearance rates as a measure of police effectiveness probably encouraged underrecording in order to reach a desired clearance level. This concept of crime occurrence as an indication of police effectiveness is reflected on a broader level in the political ideology that crime rates are one of several measures of how well the Communist system is moving toward the goal of a crime-free society.

A role for politics in recording crime is not restricted to totalitarian governments. Imagine how tempted an incumbent sheriff might be during an election year to show that crime had dropped during her years in office. Similarly, the police chief may want to use statistics to convince the city council that his administration has reduced the number of drug offenses after receiving a budget supplement to fight the war on drugs. Pressure seemed especially intense during the late 1990s as a result of American media reports about the generally declining crime rates across the country. If you were a sheriff or police chief in an area where crime had not been declining, would you feel pressured to show a reduction anyway? Apparently some police officials did! During 1998 there were charges of falsely reporting crime statistics in Philadelphia, New York, Atlanta, and Boca Raton, Florida (Butterfield, 1998; Cox, 1998). Some crime went unrecorded, and some felonies were recorded as misdemeanors (e.g., burglaries became vandalism, trespassing, or missing property). In Philadelphia the statistics were so suspect that a newly hired police commissioner asked the FBI to withdraw the city's reported crime data for the years 1996 and 1997.

National Crime Victimization Survey

The first problem associated with the UCR was the underreporting of crime. People had long suspected that the UCR's estimates of crime were below what actually occurred (because it was obvious that not all crime was reported). However, not until 1973 was it possible to say specifically that less than half of all crimes are reported to the police. The turning point came with the first annual survey of American households, which questioned people about their own victimization during the preceding year. Since 1973 the U.S. Bureau of Census and the Bureau of Justice Statistics have cooperated in conducting a random national survey of crimes occurring against individuals and businesses—the National Crime Victimization Survey (NCVS). Because the resulting data are based on the report of a person actually involved in the crime, the reliance on police department records is eliminated. Not only are crimes the police know about recorded, but also those never reported to the police. As a result, we know how crime reporting varies by crime type and the sex and age of the victim, as well as the reasons given by victims for not reporting crime in the first place (e.g., "Police couldn't do anything," "It wasn't important enough").

Like the UCR, the NCVS has reporting and recording problems. Extended discussion like that given UCR problems is not necessary here because the goal is simply to provide you with reason for skepticism in considering the crime statistics of any country. The accuracy of the NCVS statistics depends on the sometimes faulty memory of the humans reporting crimes. The victim may not remember if a crime occurred within the last six months (the time period asked about) or nine months ago. Problems of overreporting occur when people misinterpret events as being criminal (for example, my bike was stolen) when they are not (the bike was forgotten about in the tool shed). Underreporting occurs when crimes involve family members or friends, and victims may therefore choose not to divulge the incidents.

The NCVS nevertheless provides important information about the actual amount of crime occurring in the country and about the characteristics of crime victims. As a result, it serves as a nice supplement to the UCR. Each organization has its own purpose, and together they provide a more accurate picture of the country's crime than either does alone.

COMPARING CRIME RATES

Because every country has similar difficulties in recording and reporting its own crime figures, crime rate comparison among countries is problematic. Industrialized countries like Japan, Australia, Canada, Germany, and Great Britain have their respective versions of the general data like that given in the UCR. As a result, there is an understandable tendency to compare, contrast, and even rank the various countries in terms of general and specific crime rates (see Figure 2.1). If the data in Figure 2.1 were used by authors of the increasingly popular "Best Places to Live" type of books, the industrialized countries would not fare very well. Yet this is exactly why such cross-cultural comparisons are frowned upon by many researchers—and even more so by government officials. The United Nations expressed that concern in this manner: "Member States are increasingly recognizing the importance of comparative work for cross-national purposes, but require reassurance that the data reported will not be used for any international numerical 'ranking' " (1990g, p. 7).

There are very good reasons why numerical rankings based on crime data should be undertaken only with caution. Consider, for example, differences in the legal definitions of crime, in the ways countries report and record crime, and even in the way the data set itself is prepared. van Dijk and Kangaspunta (2000) highlight differing recording practices by noting that police in some countries are very careful about recording every theft of a bicycle while in other countries the tracking of bicycle thefts may have low—or even no—priority. Savage (1997) found errors like miscalculation of rates and percentages greater than 100 in cross-national crime data reported by the Interpol. Also, the efficiency of criminal justice agencies is likely to make a difference. Higher rates of recorded crime in some countries may simply reflect more efficient and thorough systems for reporting and recording crime in those countries. Similarly, low rates of recorded crime rates may simply reflect system inefficiency. Crime statistics probably tell us as much about a country's justice organization as about its crime rate (United Nations, 1990g).

The danger in emphasizing the problems involved in comparing crime data is that an inference could be made that nothing can be gained from gathering and analyzing such information. Such an inference would be wrong; researchers have

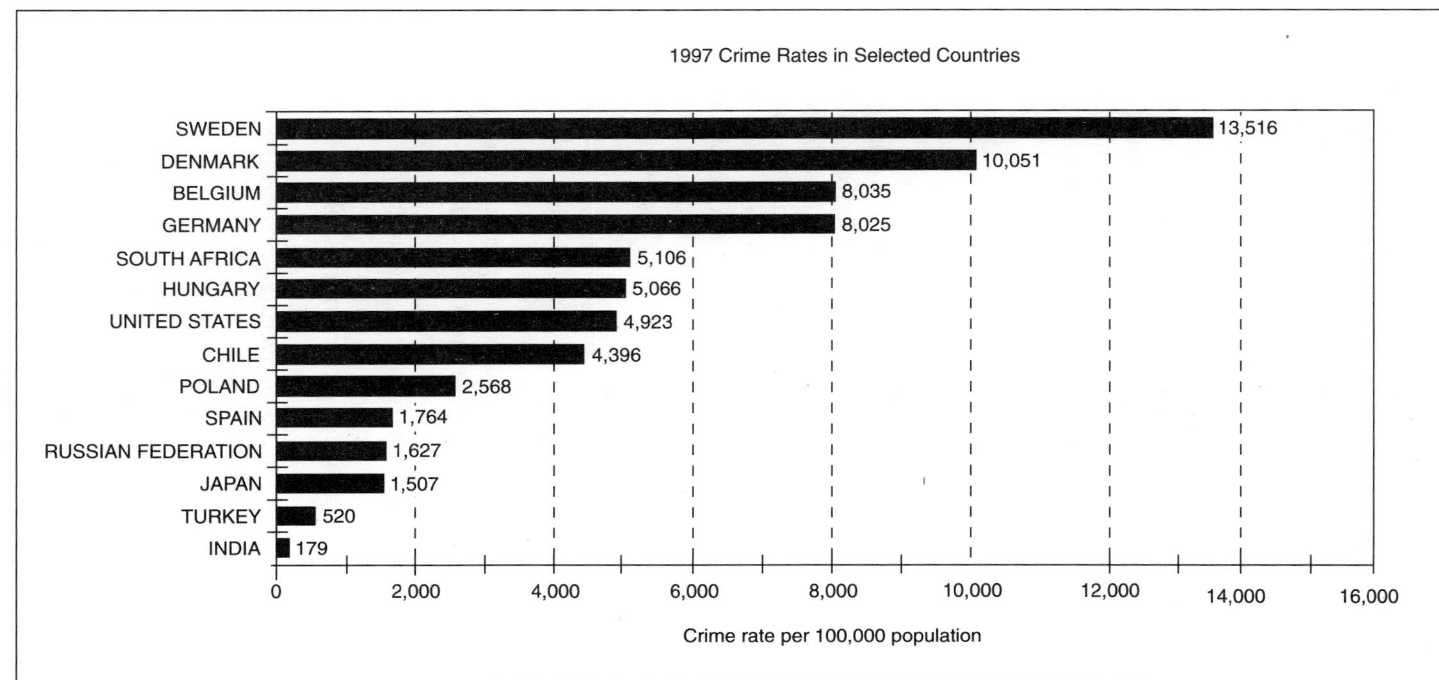

Figure 2.1 Total Crime Rate per 100,000 Population in Selected Countries, *Source:* Table developed from United Nations (2000), *Third to Sixth Survey Combined.* (Data available at www.uncjin.org/Statistics/WCTS/wcts.html). United States data from Federal Bureau of Investigation (1998). *Uniform Crime Reports 1997.* (Data available at www.fbi.gov/ucr/97cius.htm)

found several types of questions that cross-national crime data can appropriately address. For example, Bennett and Lynch (1990) and the United Nations (1990g) agree that although crime survey results cannot reliably be used to rank countries, they are appropriate for assessing the direction of change in crime over time and across nations. Other researchers have used comparative crime data to look at violence cross-nationally (Archer & Gartner, 1984; Messner, 1980); to explain the evolution of criminality over the last 200 years (Shelley, 1981); and to identify common features among countries with low crime rates (Adler, 1983). Like all provocative research, these studies have been criticized (see Beirne & Messerschmidt, 1991; Groves & Newman, 1989), but they are also recognized as important contributions to the study of comparative criminology.

Figure 2.2 shows an example of using cross-national crime data to show the relative consistency of crime rates in major cities around the world. Over a five-year period, with only a few exceptions, the same cities are found at either the higher or lower range.

Crime Data Sets

A difficulty for anyone interested in comparing crime data is to find a source containing crime information for nations around the world. Currently, the principal source is the *United Nations Survey on Crime Trends and Operations of Criminal Justice Systems.* Beginning in the 1970s and continuing today, the United Nations surveys, or *sweeps,* as they are called, are becoming increasingly sophisticated and complete in their coverage. In addition to providing data on reported crimes, responding countries are also asked to provide information about the operation of their criminal justice system through data on arrests, convictions, and prison population.

Recognizing the problems inherent in comparing crime rates among countries with different legal definitions of crime, the United Nations surveys provide a standard classification of crime definitions and justice categories. Over the years, more and more countries have adapted their own statistical definitions and procedures to coincide with the standard United Nations categories. As a result, more countries are providing data with each survey sweep. A remaining problem is the often fragmented way the questionnaire may be completed—with different officials from different bureaucracies introducing sometimes inconsistent and contradictory statistics as a country's questionnaire is filled out (Newman & Howard, 1999).

The sixth wave of the survey (covering 1995–1997) was made available to researchers in 2000. Because the data are updated as member states continue to provide information, analysis of the most recent survey typically lags a few years behind the availability of those data. For that reason, current comments about global crime rely on data from the fifth survey, covering 1990–1994.

From 1990 to 1994, many countries reported falling crime rates, but on average crime continued to rise in the 1990s as it had in the 1980s. As Figure 2.3 shows, the most common crimes reported around the world are theft and burglary. When countries are grouped by region, the Arab states report a lower crime rate than other regions for all crimes except drug-related offenses (for which Eastern Europe is lowest). Property crimes rates, like burglary and theft, are highest in Western

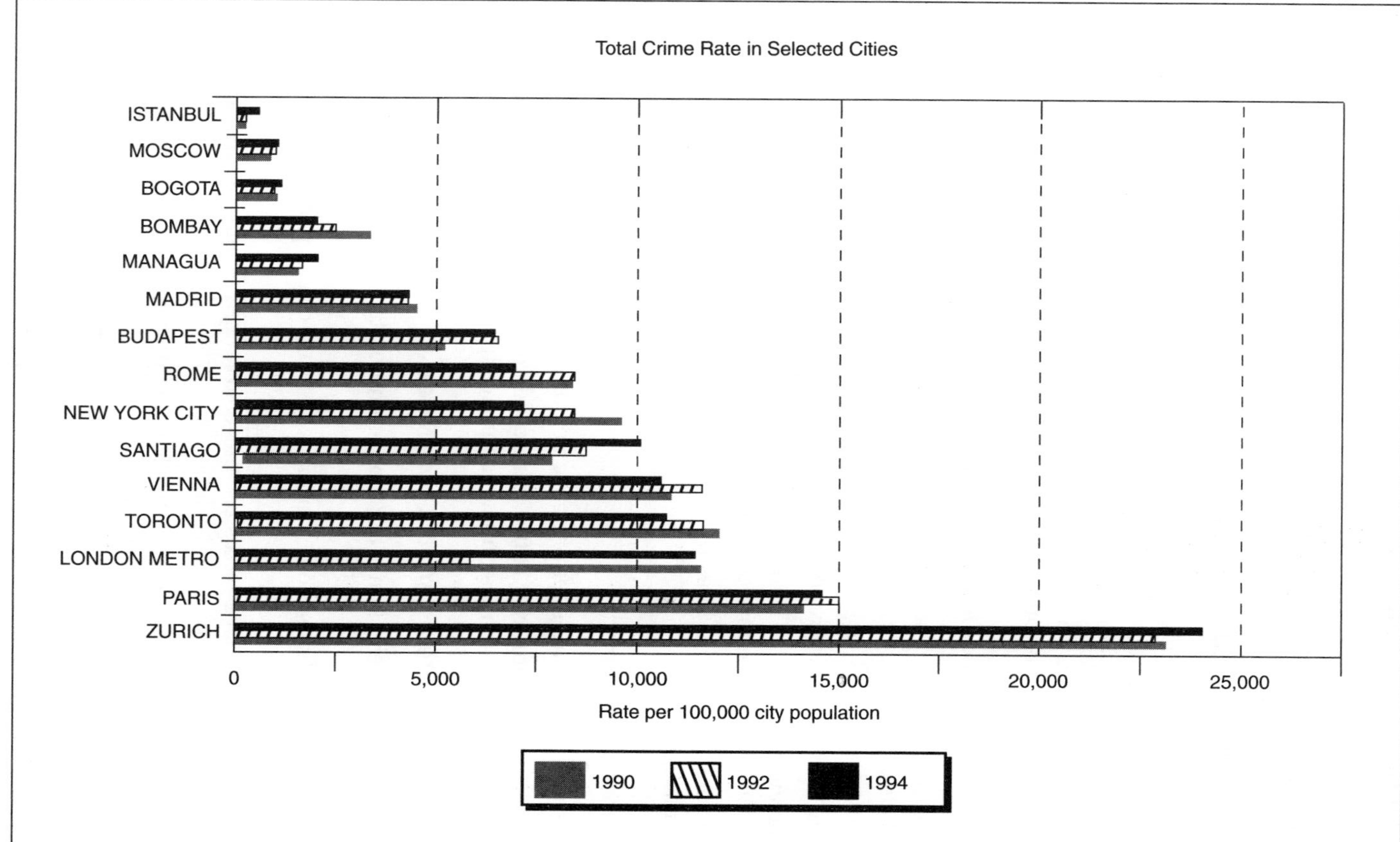

Figure 2.2 Total Crime Rate per 100,000 City Population in Selected Cities (ordered by 1994 rate). *Source:* Table Developed from United Nations. (1997), *Fifth United Nations Survey of Crime Trends and Operations of Criminal Justice Systems.* Data set available from Crime Prevention and Criminal Justice Branch, United Nations Office at Vienna, P.O. Box 500, A-1400 Vienna, Austria. Data for this table are from the data set available in October 2000.

You Should Know!

COMPARING WITH CAUTION

The temptation to compare countries on the basis of reported crime requires significant restraint. Newman and Howard (1999) and Lewis (1999) provide many reasons for caution that can be grouped under four broad categories:

Statistics Are Political Statements

- The open announcement of a country's crime statistics is often made only after the information has been rigorously checked for both its "validity" and for the impression it creates.
- At times, countries have made crime data available to the United Nations survey but have not provided that information to their own citizens.

Problems in Defining, Reporting, and Recording

- Types of crime that seem comparable are often not (e.g., comparisons of homicide are confounded by how deaths from drunken driving are recorded).
- Many crimes are not reported to the police.
- Some events reported and recorded as crimes may not actually be crimes, and some crimes reported are never officially recorded.
- Decisions to record crimes may be affected by concerns about job evaluation measures.

Comparison Problems

- The structure and number of police personnel varies among the countries.
- Whereas some countries count crimes when the police become aware of them, others count crimes only when police forward them for prosecution.

Varying Social Features Affect Crime Rates

- Countries where telephones are more common tend to report a higher proportion of crime.
- Countries where household insurance is more developed report a higher proportion of crime.
- Countries where police forces use more advanced technology tend to find a higher proportion of actual crime.
- Countries with more available medical facilities may have lower homicide rates than countries with less accessible medical facilities.

Europe and North America. Violent crime, like homicide and robbery, is highest in North America, Latin America, and Africa (Lewis, 1999).

Homicide presents an especially interesting crime for comparison purposes (see this chapter's "Impact" section). In addition to being universally considered the most serious of offenses, homicide rates appear to be especially reliable indi-

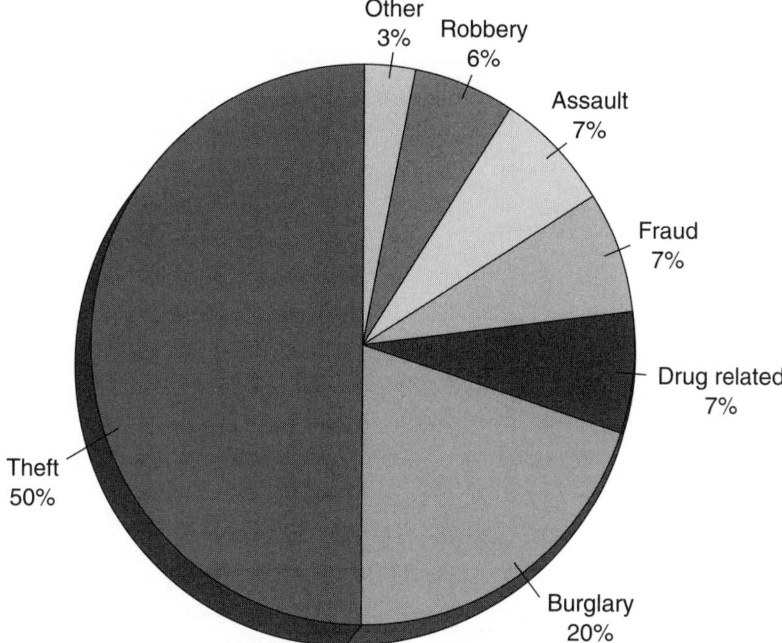

Figure 2.3 Crime types reported in the Fifth United Nations Survey, 1994. *Source:* Data are from the *Fifth United Nations Survey on Crime Trends and Operations of Criminal Justice Systems.* Data set available at www.uncjin.org/Statistics

cators of the actual occurrence of that crime (see Newman & Howard, 1999, pp. 12–13). The lowest median reported homicide rates are in Arab states and Western Europe. The highest reported rates are in Latin America and sub-Saharan Africa. North American rates, including those for the United States, fall in the mid-range. However, the North American standing is likely a result of Canada's low homicide rate providing a contrast with the rather high U.S. homicide rate.

Victimization Data Set

For reasons similar to those giving rise to the NCVS in the United States, several other countries are making use of victimization studies to supplement their own police-based statistics. Because official crime statistics from police sources require victims to report an offense, there is concern that cross-national comparison of crime statistics may compare reporting habits as much as crime incidents. We know, for example, that in many countries the likelihood that a crime will be reported to police is affected by such things as the seriousness of the offense, but we do not know how cultural differences may affect crime reporting from one country to another. Do cultural differences make Italians more or less likely to report theft than Saudi Arabians? Are Colombians more or less likely to report assaults than Canadians? At this point we cannot answer such questions. However, attempts at data gathering that is similar to the NCVS process have begun, and

Guns in America

A goal of comparative studies is to provide a point of contrast so we can better understand our own country. As more countries participate in projects like the *United Nations Survey on Crime Trends and Operations of Criminal Justice Systems (UN Survey)* and the *International Crime Victim Survey (ICVS)*, it is possible to place crime in the United States in a broader context.

Using data from both the UN Survey and the ICVS, van Dijk and Kangaspunta (2000) note that crime in the United States is rather similar to that in Canada. Both the United States and Canada have relatively high burglary rates and car-related crimes. But when compared with England, the United States may have less of a burglary problem. Langan and Farrington (1998) used victim surveys and police statistics to conclude that England's burglary rate was almost double America's, as was its motor vehicle theft rate. However, while the United States may look relatively good in regard to property crimes, the picture is not so rosy for violent crime. Despite the fact that serious violent crimes are relatively more prevalent in the countries of the former Soviet Union (e.g., Estonia, Kazakhstan, and the Russian Federation), the United States stands out with high rates, especially in contrast to other industrialized nations like Canada and the Western European countries (van Dijk & Kangaspunta, 2000).

The violent crimes of homicide and robbery are especially high in the United States, where those crimes often involve the use of guns. In fact, a frequent explanation for the greater violence in America is the country's high rate of gun ownership. Presumably, the more lethal the weapon being used in a violent confrontation, the more likely that death will be the result. In countries where lethal weapons are more readily available, therefore, we might expect homicides to be higher. And, indeed, an international study of firearm regulation found that, in general, countries with higher firearm ownership rates among their citizens also have higher firearm-related death rates, including homicide rates (Walker, 1999). To complicate an otherwise straightforward conclusion, though, we have the odd fact that Finland and the United States report the highest rates of civilian firearm ownership, but Finland has a much lower rate than America for homicide victims killed by a firearm (Walker, 1999, figures 6.4 and 6.7). Consequently, data like these are seldom considered the final answer for either side in the firearm debate.

Since 1997 each state and territory in Australia has implemented the *Nationwide Agreement on Firearms.* That agreement provides uniformity in a country where firearm laws had previously differed greatly across the states and territories. When the merits of the agreement were being debated it was not unusual to have the United States put forward as an

IMPACT

Guns in America

example, the *Australian Institute of Criminology (AIC)* issued a press release in 1996 noting that Australia's rate of firearm-related homicide was 0.4 per 100,000 population compared to 0.7 in Canada and 6.3 in the United States. In the United Kingdom, where guns are less pervasive, the firearm homicide rate was 0.1 per 100,000 (Australian Institute of Criminology, 1996). Responding to that data, the Great Australian Gun Law Con web site complained that the AIC was engaging in "cherry picking" data by choosing only those examples that supported its argument. The anti–gun control argument was that the AIC had ignored data from other countries and had not allowed for any cultural differences among countries. Offering its own country comparisons, the Gun Law Con web site noted that Switzerland and Norway are almost saturated with military firearms and have little firearms control yet a lower gun-death rate than Australia. And Mexico, with strict firearm controls, borders the United States and has a gun-death rate more than double America's (Gun law con, 2000).

The debate continues, and the increased availability of reliable crime statistics from a greater number of countries will mean more opportunity for the United States to compare its crime problem with crime in other countries. In doing so, we may be able to better determine our relative strengths and weaknesses.

comparative researchers are gaining more information about crime from the victims' perspective.

The *International Crime Victim Survey (ICVS),* sponsored by the United Nations Interregional Crime and Justice Research Institute, is currently receiving and evaluating data from its third survey sweep (covering data from 1996 and 1997). The first two surveys (in 1989 and 1992) had participation from more than 20 countries and 14 cities. By late 2000, the third sweep had resulted in receipt of data from over 55 countries.

Overall victimization rates in industrialized countries from the 1996–1997 survey showed relatively high counts (above 25 percent of the respondents in each country) in Canada, England and Wales, France, the Netherlands, Scotland, and Switzerland (the United States showed a 24.2 percentage). Countries with relatively low counts (under 20 percent) included Austria, Finland, and Northern Ireland (Mayhew & van Dijk, 1997). Trends identified where countries responded to one of the earlier surveys and the 1996/1997 survey, indicated that risk of victimization generally declined for citizens in Canada, Finland, and the United States. Risk of victimization increased between the earlier and the more recent survey for people in England and Wales, France, the Netherlands, Scotland, and Switzerland.

In their analysis of data from the first two victimization surveys, van Dijk and Mayhew (1993) found that within Europe the most consistent increases were in thefts of and from cars. Car ownership also increased during that period, but to a lesser degree than the victimization rate. van Dijk and Mayhew (1993) note that some police sources suggest the opening of the borders with eastern European countries increased the demand for stolen cars.

Reporting of crime to the police shows some consistency over countries by type of crime. Data from all three surveys (Mayhew & van Dijk, 1997; van Dijk & Mayhew, 1993), show that more than 50 percent of all thefts from a car, bicycle thefts, and burglaries were reported in most countries. Less than 50 percent of all cases of personal theft, and threats/assaults were typically reported. Least often reported—about 10 percent in all the countries providing the data—were sexual offenses. The most frequent reasons given for not reporting any of these crimes were that the incident was "not serious enough" or that the "police could do nothing" about it (van Dijk, 1999). These reasons did not vary much across countries, but nonreporters in Poland and Spain more often said that "the police wouldn't do anything about it." That lack of confidence in the police may help explain why Poland and Spain had the lowest percentage of crimes reported to the police in the 1989 and 1992 surveys. The average percentage for reporting was 48.9 percent, with Scotland (62.3 percent), France (60.8 percent), and New Zealand (59.7 percent) showing the highest reporting levels.

Obviously information from these victimization studies can be quite useful for increasing our understanding of crime within countries. They provide a nice addition to police-based statistics, but we must not conclude that the methodological problems in police statistics are missing from victim-based measures. For example, the *International Crime Victim Survey* found that victimization most often occurred, regardless of the country, near the victim's own home or elsewhere in the local area. Only 4 percent of the victimizations occurred while the respondents were outside their own country. Interestingly, the Swiss provided an exception; 16 percent of their reported incidents took place outside Switzerland. This point becomes methodologically important because victimization rates in Switzerland may overstate the actual vulnerability of the Swiss in their own country. Just as police-based statistics may overstate the crime rate in popular tourist areas having a low native population, victim-based statistics may overstate the rate in countries with well-traveled citizens. This is just one of several problems presented by victimization studies. Just as police-based statistics are useful as long as we remember their limitations, the victim-based measures are welcome additions for comparative criminology, but they are not a methodological solution.

CRIME TRENDS AND CRIME THEORIES

Crime has economic, social, and personal costs. As the incidence of crime rises, governments must use more and more of their budgets to respond to the crime problem. Such financial costs are especially burdensome for developing countries, but even developed countries feel the financial hardship brought by crimes like smuggling, financial fraud, and currency manipulation, as well as the more traditional crime types. High as the financial costs are, the social and personal costs of suffering brought by crime may be even higher. Crime can eat away at the moral order, provoke fear among citizens, and can certainly be damaging to people's well-being. An understanding of crime trends and the causes of criminality may help reduce the incidence of crime, and these are areas of study where comparative criminology may prove very beneficial.

Crime Trends

Since the mid 1980s, the United Nations has expressed concern about what was initially called *transboundary criminality* but today is more often called *transnational crime.* While recognizing the difficulty in defining transnational crime, the United Nations relies on a general definition of offenses whose inception, perpetration, or direct or indirect effects involve more than one country (United Nations, 1995, p. 4). Five clusters of these criminal acts were of initial concern: (1) internationally organized crime, (2) terrorist activities, (3) economic offenses involving more than one country, (4) crimes against cultural heritage, and (5) crimes against the environment (United Nations, 1990f). By the mid 1990s (United Nations, 1995), discussion was more likely to refer to specific crime categories (for example, theft of intellectual property, illicit arms trafficking, and computer crime) rather than crime clusters. However, the cluster approach allows for a more convenient presentation here.

Internationally Organized Crime. There is a tendency to consider organized crime as bound to specific countries. For example, the Italian Mafia, the American Cosa Nostra, and the Japanese *Bōryokudan* exemplify criminal syndicates linked to particular territories. Yet in the last few decades, organized criminality has increasingly shed its parochialism and is less confined by national boundaries. Jamieson (1995) explains the transnational dimension of Italian organized crime and suggests that there are few regions of today's world untouched by Italian Mafia presence or influence. Narcotics smuggling is the main transnational activity for Italian organized crime, but tobacco smuggling and arms trafficking have an increasingly expanded role. With the emergence of new markets in Eastern European countries during the 1990s, the continued internationalization of crime was inevitable. In the early 1990s authors were already commenting that organized crime was a part of life in many Central and Eastern European countries. The primary player in those activities was, and is, the Russian mafia, which created particular problems for fledgling democratic institutions (American Society of Criminology, 1995).

Advantages of organized crime include providing an effective distribution system for illegal goods and services. As the market for such goods and services expands beyond a criminal organization's original territory, it is simply good business for that organization to similarly expand its distribution. International expansion can mean that the organization members involve themselves in activities in another country, such as the involvement of the Japanese *Bōryokudan* (also called the *yakuza*) in Brazil and Korea (Kaplan & Dubro, 1986). More commonly, however, crime syndicates in one country develop relationships with those of one or several other countries. In that way, for example, drugs like heroin, cocaine, and marijuana reach the United States from sources as diverse as Colombia and Afghanistan.

Drug trafficking is one of the most visible activities involving organized crime on an international basis. The innumerable actors, efficiently organized division of labor, production and distribution systems that are national and international in scope, and multinational political base combine to make drug trafficking an underground empire (Martin, Romano, & Haran, 1988). The opportunities for criminal activity in the new countries of Eastern and Central Europe were apparently too good for many crime organizations to ignore. For example, Colombia's powerful Cali drug cartel did not wait to seek access into possible Czechoslovakian and Polish markets. In October 1991 Czechoslovak authorities seized 100 kilograms of cocaine that had been hidden in a truckload of Colombian coffee (Castro, 1991). The coffee was traced to a Polish ship that had stopped in Colombia, so Polish officials also got involved. Their investigation discovered another 100 kilograms of cocaine sitting in a Warsaw warehouse.

Another activity where an effective distribution system is necessary for the crime to be completed is illegal immigration. The worldwide smuggling of immigrants has mushroomed since the early 1990s. Estimates have as many as 500,000 people (for example, illegal labor migrants and asylum seekers without founded claims) from countries like China and India being smuggled into Western Europe at fees from as low as $250 to highs of $25,000 (Schmid & Savona, 1995). Most of those people are young males, but there is also illegal traffic in women for the sex market and in children for the adoption market. Schmid and Savona (1995) note that the criminals involved in smuggling people are often also engaged in arms and drug smuggling—and do not hesitate to use violence to defend all their smuggling operations.

Western European countries are experiencing increased illegal immigration from eastern, central, and southern Europe, and from northern Africa. In the United States, illegal immigrants enter from every part of the world, but in the early 1990s the top five countries of origin for illegal immigrants were Mexico, El Salvador, Guatemala, Canada, and Poland (McDonald, 1997). Although many of these immigrants had entered illegally across the U.S. border, a substantial proportion (41 percent) entered legally but overstayed their visas. In addition to being a crime itself, illegal immigration brings about the additional crimes of manufacturing and selling fraudulent documents, bribing public officials, and victimization of the illegal immigrants. The links to these collateral crimes make illegal immigration profitable for organized crime and challenging for the world's democracies to control.

Drugs and migrant trafficking provide only a few examples of organized crime's illicit goods and services. Other activities especially suitable to a network of criminal alliances include trafficking in weapons, industrial secrets, migrant labor, female and child prostitution, and works of art (United Nations, 1990b). The resulting individual, social, political, and economic damage in developed countries is widely recognized, but less attention has been given to the destruction that organized crime activities cause in developing countries. As the United Nations (1990b) points out, organized crime in developing countries often infiltrates public administration and political structures (including the armed forces). As a result, it can undermine the democratic process and distort a society's ethical norms.

International Terrorism. The United Nations defines *international terrorism* as "terrorist acts, the author or authors of which plan their actions, are directed or come from, flee to and seek refuge in, or otherwise receive any form of assistance

In the News

TRAFFICKING IN HUMANS

When Rosa was fourteen, a man came to her parents' home in Veracruz, Mexico, and asked her if she wanted to make money in the United States. At the time Rosa was working in a hotel cleaning rooms, and the man told her she could make many times her salary by doing the same work in the United States. Rosa persuaded her parents to let her go, and a week later she was smuggled into the United States through Texas to Florida. Upon her arrival in Florida she was told that her job would consist of having sex with men for money. Since she was a virgin, her new "employers" repeatedly raped her to teach her how to have sex. Rosa was confined to trailers, where she serviced customers throughout the day. Since her customers did not always wear condoms, Rosa soon became pregnant and was forced to have an abortion. She was returned to the brothel almost immediately (Statement of Rosa, 2000).

Rosa is only one of many women and children who provide stories about the transnational crime of trafficking in persons. *Human trafficking,* which typically refers to the recruitment, transport, or sale of humans for the purpose of exploiting their labor, always involves the use of deception, coercion, or debt bondage. Although trafficking occurs within countries as well as across borders, it is the cross-border version that qualifies as a transnational crime.

About 50,000 people are brought into the United States each year against their will, but the practice of trafficking occurs in virtually all countries and takes many forms. Forced prostitution is common, but so is bonded domestic servitude, sweatshop labor, forced marriage, and the pressing into service of child soldiers (Department of State, 2000; Koh, 1999). Women and girls are especially popular targets, but traffickers also seek men and boys.

Efforts by individual countries are resulting in legislation to strengthen national enforcement efforts, and international endeavors are making the trafficking of humans a priority for many organizations. For example, to better enable governments and the international community to respond to the trafficking problem, the United Nations Office for Drug Control and Crime Prevention launched the *Global Programme Against Trafficking in Human Beings.* A particular goal of the program is to bring to the forefront the involvement of organized crime groups in human smuggling and trafficking (United Nations, 1999).

from a country or countries other than the one in which the acts themselves take place" (1990f, p. 6). The U.S. Department of State also keeps track of terrorist incidents. When combined with information from the United Nations, these data show some interesting geographic changes during the 20 years from 1968 to 1988. In 1968, 32 percent of the incidents took place in North America, but in 1987 the percentage dropped to zero. Conversely, terrorist acts increased in the Asia/Pacific region from 0.8 percent in 1968 to 20.8 percent in 1987. In 1968, 68 percent of terrorist incidents took place in either Latin America or North America. In 1987, 65 percent took place in the Middle East or the Asia/Pacific area.

During the 1990s North America remained comparatively untouched by international terrorism (see Figure 2.4). The majority of 1999 incidents occurred in Latin America and Western Europe (53 percent of the 390 incidents), whereas only two were recorded in North America. Although the number of incidents in North America has been comparatively few, their impact has been dramatic. The single North American incident in 1993 (the World Trade Center bombing in New York City) resulted in 6 deaths and some 1,000 injuries. That number of casualties far exceeded the number of casualties in the next highest region (178 casualties from the 185 incidents in Europe) during that year.

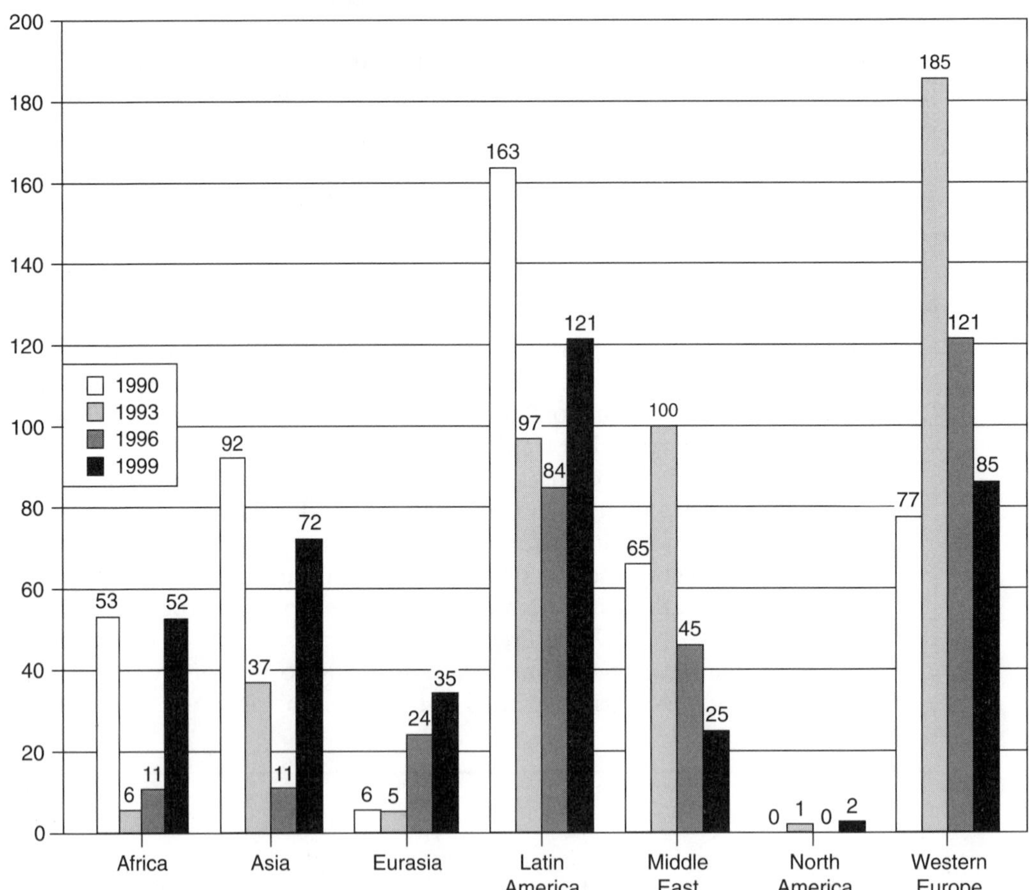

Figure 2.4 International Terrorist Attacks by Region, 1990–1999. *Sources:* (1) 1990 data from Department of State (1994), *Patterns of global terrorism, 1993*. Washington DC: Office of the Secretary of State, (2) 1993 data from Department of State (1997), *Patterns of global terrorism, 1996*. Washington, DC: Office of the Secretary of State, (3) 1996 and 1999 data from Department of State (2000), *Patterns of global terrorism, 1999*. Washington, DC: Office of the Secretary of State.

In addition to the harm to specific victims of terrorism, this form of international crime brings about increased tensions between countries, dramatically influences national and international politics, and affects the economy (for example, tourism) of even those countries not directly involved.

Economic Crimes. Economic crimes of an international type can be divided into those benefiting a corporation and those benefiting an individual (United Nations, 1990f). The first category of harmful acts or crimes includes activities that maximize, maintain, or obtain economic profit for multinational corporations. Typical of such acts is transnational corporate bribery, wherein company officials persuade government or business personnel in foreign countries to behave favorably toward the corporation (Beirne & Messerschmidt, 1991). Although the transaction may benefit specific people or companies in each country, it is also likely to harm other citizens through increased prices, decreased wages, and exploitation of an already impoverished populace.

The quest for corporate profit also results in transnational corporations "dumping" on a country certain products banned or not approved for sale in another country. Contraceptive devices, lethal drugs, toxic pesticides, and other items have been sold or distributed to a variety of countries and have harmed thousands of people (Beirne & Messerschmidt, 1991), especially in Third World countries.

The second category of economic crimes involves those benefiting an individual. For these offenses, private persons represent their international activities as perfectly legitimate when in fact the intent is to defraud individual investors, public or private institutions, or governments. Sometimes with the help of organized crime, these individuals operate to launder money, smuggle, provide prostitutes, make weapons deals, assist in the "adoption" of children, and manipulate investments. The result is harmful to the citizens and social structure of both developed and developing countries.

Crimes against Cultural Heritage. Patrimonial crimes violate a country's heritage through the unlawful procurement or acquisition of archaeological and artistic objects that are classified as part of the cultural legacy of a country. We do not often think of such thefts as particularly frequent nor in the context of international crime. However, the number of such incidents has increased in recent years so that today systematic theft and even simple plundering by occasional thieves threaten the cultural property of nations (United Nations, 1990a; United Nations, 1995).

The most destructive pillaging occurs in developing countries, with the spoils being sent to the developed countries. Since World War II, the United States has been cited as "the largest single buyers' market for stolen or illegally exported cultural property" (Greenfield, 1989, pp. 236–237). But other countries certainly take part—and some with little sign of guilt. For example, the National Gallery of Scotland included a statement in its catalog of Spanish and Italian paintings that the gallery's *El Medico* by Goya was stolen from the Royal Palace in Madrid in 1869 (Greenfield, 1989).

The problem is not a new one. In 1970 the General Conference of the United Nations Educational, Scientific and Cultural Organization *(UNESCO)* adopted a

Convention on the Means of Prohibiting and Preventing the Illicit Import, Export and Transfer of Ownership of Cultural Property. By December 1999, 91 nations had accepted or acceded to the convention, but few of those were developed countries (e.g., Australia, Canada, France, Italy, United States). Because developed countries are the most important markets for the cultural objects, their nonaccession to the convention has limited its impact on illicit traffic.

In a continuing attempt to highlight the importance of the theft of cultural property as an international issue, the International Institute for the Unification of Private Law *(UNIDROIT)* drew up a new treaty in 1995 to complement the 1970 UNESCO Convention. The resulting UNIDROIT Convention on Stolen or Illegally Exported Cultural Objects had been signed or acceded to by 34 countries in early 2000. In doing so, those countries (about 20 percent of which are considered developed countries) have agreed to minimum rules of uniform law concerning stolen or illegally exported cultural objects (UNIDROIT, 2000).

Even if a significant number of developed countries accepts the UNESCO or the UNIDROIT Conventions, it is questionable whether such regulations can have an impact. The United Kingdom, for example, has problems with the convention's position on the return of cultural items to the claiming country. Should France return the Venus de Milo to Greece? Should all the Egyptian mummies in museums throughout the United States, and elsewhere be returned to Egypt? Should the Natural History Museum in London return the skull of the Middle Stone Age, Broken Hill Man, to Zambia, where miners discovered it in 1921? Because there is no time limit on how long the protected items must be in a territory for a state to claim it for the national heritage, and given the very imprecise phraseology as to what is protected, it is unlikely that developed countries will change their position on existing international regulations.

Despite what may be reasonable concerns regarding existing regulations, we cannot lose sight of the breadth and growth of this problem. UNESCO estimates that more than 50,000 art objects were smuggled out of India during the 1980s (Greenfield, 1989). Turkey, which has been called an "open-air museum," has some 200,000 monuments, 10,000 tombs, and 3,000 ancient cities providing a supermarket for looters (Walsh, 1991). Drawing the world public's attention to the problem is a necessary first step, and one that is being slowly taken. *Time* magazine underscored the crisis by noting:

> *The art of the world is being looted. From New York to Phnom Penh, from ancient ruins in Turkey to up-to-date museums in Amsterdam, precious records of human culture are vanishing into the dark as thieves steal with near impunity. (Walsh, 1991, p. 86)*

Information from the Interpol database showed that by mid 2000, Italy, France, the Czech Republic, Poland, the Russian Federation, Germany, and Belgium were the countries reporting the most thefts of cultural objects (Interpol, 2000). Possibly, as crimes against the cultural heritage are more often committed against such developed countries as those in Europe and North America, patrimonial crimes will receive a more concerted response. Yet because museums are more abundant in prosperous countries, the poorer nations continue to serve more as suppliers than as preservers.

Environmental Crimes. The opening of Eastern Europe and continued development in other parts of the world present a challenge for environmentally sound economic and social development. Unfortunately, it is a challenge not easily met, because problems worldwide are so serious that some consider offenses against the environment to be crimes against humanity (United Nations, 1990b). Air, water, and land pollution cease to be an exclusively national problem when the result reaches beyond the initiating country's borders. The massive use of chemical herbicides, detergents, and inorganic fertilizers, and the careless and indiscriminate disposal of poisonous and radioactive industrial waste, exemplify new forms of transnational crime.

Environmental offenses, as, for example, those that result in damage to the ozone layer and acid rain, present challenges to the traditional and narrowly interpreted concepts of sovereignty and criminal responsibility. The harm caused to the environment threatens life and property around the world, not stopping at the offending country's borders. As a result, some argue that the response to such offenses should no longer fall within the jurisdiction of a single country. The alternative, though, is not at all clear. Delegates at the Eighth and Ninth United Nations Congress on the Prevention of Crime and the Treatment of Offenders considered actions ranging from new laws to reparation for damages. As with many other problems at national and international levels, there is more agreement on the goal than on how it should be achieved.

Crime Theories

Facts about national and international crime trends are appropriately followed by explanations of those facts. Such mental gymnastics, which are the domain of comparative criminology, actually fall outside this book's focus. Our interest in comparative criminal justice systems is more concerned with the structures and procedures nations use to deal with offenders than with how those countries explain the criminals' behavior and crimes' occurrences. Of course, there is necessarily some overlap in those interests. Countries with high rates of crime may require different justice systems than those with low rates. Similarly, different justice systems may partially explain why one country has a higher crime rate than another. In either event, explanations for criminal behavior and of the distribution of crime are inevitably linked to a society's method of social control.

A thorough examination of how criminological theory is applied to cross-cultural and international crime statistics is not possible in this book. The subject is important and intriguing enough, though, to warrant at least the brief discussion that folllows: Neapolitan compared six *low violent crime* (LVC) nations with *six high violent crime* (HVC) nations and found that the countries in each grouping could be distinguished according to five categories of factors (Neapolitan, 1999, pp. 269–271):

- **Social integration versus disorganization**—LVC nations achieved social cohesion and social order through strong kinship and community systems, and the countries exhibited long-term political and social stability.

- **Economic stress versus support**—HVC nations had at least moderately serious poverty problems.
- **Care versus abuse of children**—LVC nations tended to at least moderately respect the rights of children and to have procedures for helping deprived children.
- **Official/approved violence**—Violent crime in HVC nations tended to be a reflection of an overall culture of violence as indicated by long-term violent insurgencies and by excessive extrajudicial violence by police, military, and vigilante groups.
- **System corruption and efficiency**—HVC nations had criminal justice systems that were corrupt, inefficient, and had lost the respect of most citizens. The systems in LVC nations were more likely to be fair and just, if not always highly efficient.

Neapolitan summarizes his findings by noting that the factors leading to high violent crime rates are cumulative and interactive (1999, p. 271). Any suggestion that a single, or even a few, factors can effectively and correctly explain why crime rates differ among countries is presumptuous. But that doesn't mean researchers should neglect studying the impact of particular variables when developing crime theories. Just to give you an idea of how some theorists use comparative analysis, we will highlight the variables of religion, socioeconomic factors, and the role of the situation. Keep in mind that this exercise simply exemplifies the point; it is not meant to be a review essay covering the research that considers possible links between these variables and crime.

Religion. It is popularly believed that religion's promotion of a morally correct lifestyle will likely provide a negative correlation between religiosity and criminality. That is, individuals living a morally correct life should have a low crime rate. Studies over the last several decades provide contradictory evidence on the link between religiosity and crime or deviance, but a study by Stark, Kent, and Doyle (1982) set a standard to which more recent studies respond. That research was not comparative in nature, but it took a position that intrigued investigators and encouraged comparative studies.

Stated most simply, Stark et al. (1982) found that in communities where religious beliefs are strong, the resultant moral values suppress the delinquency rate. The key point is the emphasis on "community." Stark et al. take an ecological perspective and argue that "religion only serves to bind people to the moral order if religious influences permeate the culture and the social interactions of the people in question" (1982, p. 7). This concept of religion "permeating the culture" is the element that comparative criminologists find intriguing.

The Kingdom of Saudi Arabia is a country where religion permeates the culture. More specifically, Saudi Arabia operates under the guidelines of the laws of Islam as provided in the writings, statements, and deeds of the prophet Muhammad. Islamic law (the *Shari'a*) not only provides the country's legal system but also is effectively the standard governing all individual behavior and social relations. In other words, the *Shari'a* (religion) permeates Saudi culture and society. In this sense, Saudi Arabia presents a unique opportunity to test the hypothesis that criminality will be low where a culture of religiosity is strong. Though neither were designed to test that specific hypothesis, studies by Ali (1985) and Souryal (1987) provide data relevant to the general point.

Both Ali (1985) and Souryal (1987) note the difficulty in comparing crime rates in Saudi Arabia to rates in other countries. In addition to methodological problems mentioned earlier, Saudi Arabia presents two unique obstacles. First, *Shari'a* allows, and even encourages, nonlegalistic response to misbehavior. Criminal complaints are often resolved through arbitration even before a police record is made (Souryal, 1987). That practice obviously means that crime is underreported in official statistics. Even homicide statistics are probably higher than official counts, since the *Qur'an* condones punishment by the victim's family under a feuding model rather than a court system (Groves, Newman, & Corrado, 1987).

The second methodological problem when one is working with Saudi statistics comes from the kingdom's use of the Arabic lunar calendar based on an Islamic year *(Hijri)*. Instead of the 365 days in a Gregorian calendar year, a *Hijri* year has only 354 days. In addition, a *Hijri* year usually overlaps with two Gregorian years, so any seasonal effect on crime may be confused when one undertakes cross-national comparison of crime statistics. Both Ali (1985) and Souryal (1987) are well aware of these problems and try to accommodate them. We will first look at Ali's findings.

Ali compared criminal statistics in Saudi Arabia for the Islamic year 1401 (basically November 9, 1980 to October 29, 1981) with 1981 statistics for the United States generally and Ohio specifically. He found Saudi Arabia's rate (per 100,000 population) for all reported crime was 159, compared with a rate of 5625.9 in the United States and 5284 in Ohio for the seven UCR index crimes (Ali, 1985). He also compared specific crimes (taking definitional problems into consideration) and found that both violent and property offenses in Saudi Arabia were far below those in the United States. Ali attributes the lower Saudi crime rates to a "profound internalization of Islamic religious values among Saudi people . . . [and to] a firm and uncompromised implementation of the Islamic penal code" (1985, p. 54).

Souryal's (1987) comparison was more global in nature. He contrasted official Saudi statistics from 1970 to 1975 with world rates of reported offenses as found in the first United Nations survey (1970–1975) of crime rates. Saudi Arabia fared well in the comparison, with a murder rate about one fourth that of the combined world rate (that is, 1 per 100,000 compared to 3.9 per 100,000). For property crimes, the combined world rate was 908.5 compared to the Saudi rate of 1.4, while the world rate for sex offenses was about five times the Saudi rate (24.2 to 5).

In an attempt to isolate the role of *Shari'a* as distinct from Middle Eastern culture, Souryal also compared Saudi Arabia crime rates with those in neighboring Islamic countries. He noted that although the other countries are influenced by Islamic law, only Saudi Arabia uses the *Shari'a* as its sole legal system. Criminal justice in other Arabic countries is influenced by things like codification and precedent through their dealings with other nations. Saudi Arabia's leadership in the use of orthodox *Shari'a* law provided one variable to set it apart from neighboring countries. Comparison of Saudi crime rates with rates in other Islamic nations may therefore reveal any effect the *Shari'a* has on criminality.

As with the combined world data, the Kingdom of Saudi Arabia appears to have a crime rate lower than Arabic countries incorporating state law. For the categories of murder, property crimes, and sexual offenses, the Saudi rate consistently fell below that of six other Arab countries. Souryal highlights the comparison with Kuwait, which is culturally, ethnically, and religiously similar to Saudi Arabia. The primary difference between the countries, for Souryal, is that Saudi Arabia applies *Shari'a* law to crime whereas Kuwait does not. The average Saudi murder rate from 1970 through 1979 was 0.482 per 100,000 population compared with Kuwait's rate of 3.05. Similar results were found for property crimes (7.44 in Saudi Arabia and 111.90 in Kuwait) and sexual offenses (3.2 for the Saudis and 28.05 for Kuwait).

Souryal concludes that incidents of crime under *Shari'a* law in Saudi Arabia are far fewer than those in the world generally and are even below the rates of similarly situated Arab countries. Both Ali (1985) and Souryal (1987) suggest that the penetration of religion (that is, the *Shari'a*) throughout Saudi society is an important variable in explaining the low crime rates. In this manner, the researchers seem to support the Stark et al. (1982) claim that crime and delinquency are suppressed in communities where religiosity is strong.

Socioeconomic Factors. One of the exciting, and irritating, things about criminology research is the way that results can vary depending on the type of analysis conducted and the variables used. For example, Groves et al. (1987) also studied the link between religiosity and crime, with Islam exemplifying cultural permeation. Unlike Souryal (1987), these researchers assumed that Islamic cultures can be grouped together whether their legal system is solely *Shari'a* or also incorporates state law. Their resulting comparison is on combined crime rates between 14 Islamic countries and 33 non-Islamic countries. Saudi Arabia is not included among the Islamic countries in this sample, which uses the countries responding to the first United Nations crime survey (1970–1975).

Groves et al. (1987) found significant differences in the theft and fraud crime rates, with the non-Islamic rate being roughly ten times greater. Although not significant, differences in the rates of robbery and drug abuse were in a similar direction. What sets the Groves study apart from that of Ali (1985) and Souryal (1987) is its reluctance to claim that Islamic religion suppresses crime. Instead, Groves and coworkers looked for other variables that might explain the noted differences, namely, the per capita *gross domestic product (GDP)* indicator, which shows a country's level of economic development. Inclusion of that variable eliminated all significant effects of Islamic religion in explaining crime rate variation. Groves et al. concluded that "it is the high level of economic development that is strongly related to high crime rates, rather than Islamic religion being related to low crime rates" (1987, p. 500).

Shichor (1990) also looked at the relationship between crime and socioeconomic factors from a cross-national perspective. He predicted that socioeconomic change leads to a degree of *anomie,* wherein a country's people feel that there are no guidelines for their behavior. If problems of individual adjustment to the changing social situation creates opportunities and conditions for crime, Shichor reasoned, increased socioeconomic development should be accompanied by an increase in property crime. Simultaneously, socioeconomic indicators should be negatively related to violent crime, because those types of offenses are usually more prevalent in rural societies. He used Interpol's *International Crime Statistics* to test his reasoning.

Homicide (representing violent crime), larceny (representing property crime), and the total volume of crime comprised Shichor's dependent variables. The independent variables were population size and change (developing nations have a rapid population increase), public health (for example, infant mortality rate, number of hospital beds) and communication/education (for example, number of newspapers and education expenditures). Upon applying these variables to 44 nations, Shichor concluded that "homicide rates were negatively correlated with indicators of modernization, while larceny and total crime rates showed a positive relationship with them" (1990, p. 74). As one explanation, Shichor suggests that availability of material possessions increases with economic development. When that availability is accompanied by increased cultural emphasis on having those possessions, an increase in property offenses seems to naturally follow. Also, compared to developing countries, modern countries likely have more efficient law enforcement, more accurate recording methods, and citizens who more willingly report crimes. Each of those factors may help explain why an increase in property crime rates seems to accompany modernization.

The Role of the Situation. Both religion and socioeconomic factors provide a macrolevel analysis of cross-national crime data. Some researchers are also interested in more microlevel investigations as they attempt to identify patterns in the spread and distribution of crime. LaFree and Birkbeck (1991) provide just such an analysis in their look at situational characteristics of crime.

Working on the assumption that crime is more likely to occur in some situations than in others (that is, crime is "situationally clustered"), LaFree and Birkbeck (1991) considered situational variables present when specific personal contact crimes were committed. The cross-national aspect of this study results from their taking victimization samples in the United States and in Maracaibo, Venezuela. The authors freely admit to significant differences between the two samples (one being of a country, the other of only one city in a different country), but they argue that for their purposes the differences become a strength. Because their goal was to test the generalizability of hypotheses about situational characteristics of crime, diverse samples yielding similar patterns could only make their resulting arguments more potent.

Upon comparing data for the crimes of assault, robbery, and pickpocketing in the United States and assault, robbery, and property snatching in Maracaibo, the authors found some interesting similarities. In both countries, assault typically involves single victims, private locations, men, and offenders acquainted with the victim. Correspondences likewise occurred for robbery, which in both samples involved public domains, lone victims, strangers, and incidents taking place outside buildings. Finally, pickpocketing and property snatching shared the variables of involving a lone victim who was a stranger to the offender and occurring in a public place (LaFree & Birkbeck, 1991).

If other investigations continue to show cross-national similarities in crime "situations," comparative criminologists will have provided valuable information to such fields as victimization studies. More specific to our purpose, LaFree and Birkbeck remind us that microlevel analysis of cross-national crime data is as appropriate and possible as the macrolevel studies, using variables like religion and socioeconomic conditions.

Both macro- and microlevel investigations provide an opportunity to test the applicability of criminological theory to crime in places other than the theory's country of origin. That is an important activity, because the alternative results in *criminological ethnocentrism,* wherein criminological concepts and generalizations about one society are assumed to apply to all others. A preferred approach for comparative criminology might be what Beirne (1983) calls *methodological relativism,* which allows an observer to design cross-cultural generalizations while at the same time maintaining respect for cultural diversity. Whether it is ventured to achieve a general theory of crime, to test a theory's generalizability, or to modify theories for different cultures, cross-national study of crime is an important endeavor. Nevertheless, because this book's focus is on response to crime, rather than on its occurrence and distribution, the topic of comparative criminology must be set aside.

SUMMARY

This chapter sets the stage for the rest of the book by presenting crime as a worldwide problem requiring a reaction from nations individually and collectively. Problems in preparing crime statistics are noted, but as long as the user is aware of their limitations, the various crime and victimization data sets provide useful information.

Cross-national crime statistics are especially useful in identifying trends in certain crimes with international impact. The five clusters of such crimes are internationally organized crime, terrorism, economic offenses, crimes against the cultural heritage, and crimes against the environment. The statistics are also useful to test and develop crime theories. The variables of religion, socioeconomic factors, and the role of the situation are offered as examples of comparative analysis making use of cross-cultural data.

The chapter's "Impact" section looks at the impact gun ownership may have on the violent crime rate in the United States. It is possible that comparison of crime rates among countries will provide each country with a more objective view of its own crime rate.

WEB SITES TO VISIT

- Visit web sites of organizations working against the trafficking of humans. You will find many of them listed by the U.S. State Department at **www.usinfo.state.gov/topical/global/traffic/#organizations**
- Get the most recent information of international terrorism at the Office of the Coordinator for Counterterrorism at **www.state.gov/s/ct/** and at the Centre for the Study of Terrorism and Political Violence at **www.st-and.ac.uk/academic/intrel/ research/cstpv/**
- Interpol is actively involved in the recovery of stolen works of art. Visit the Interpol site at **www.interpol.int/Public/WorkOfArt/Search/RecenThefts.asp** to see some recently reported thefts.

- Read the UNIDROIT *Convention on Stolen or Illegally Exported Cultural Objects* (1995) at **www.unidroit.org/english/conventions/c-cult.htm** and compare it with the older (1970) *Convention on the Means of Prohibiting and Preventing the Illicit Import, Export and Transfer of Ownership of Cultural Property* at **www.unesco.org/ culture/laws/1970/html_eng/ page1.htm**

SUGGESTED READINGS

Adler, Freda. (1983). *Nations not obsessed with crime.* Littleton, CO: Fred B. Rothman.

Moors, Cindy, & Ward, Richard (Eds.). (1998). Terrorism and the new world disorder. Chicago: Office of International Criminal Justice Publications.

Neapolitan, J. L. (1999). A comparative analysis of nations with low and high levels of violent crime. *Journal of Criminal Justice, 27*(3), 259-274.

Newman, G. (Ed.). (1999). *Global report on crime and justice.* New York: Oxford University Press.

Shelley, Louise. (1981). *Crime and modernization.* Carbondale, IL: Southern Illinois University Press.

van Dijk, J. J. M. (1999). The experience of crime and justice. In G. Newman (Ed.), *Global report on crime and justice* (pp. 25-42). New York: Oxford University Press.

Chapter 3

An American Perspective on Criminal Law

KEY TOPICS

- Essential ingredients of justice systems
- General characteristics of criminal law
- Major principles of criminal law

KEY TERMS

actus reus	legal guilt	presumption of guilt
concurrence	*mens rea*	procedural criminal law
crime control model	penal sanction	specificity
due process model	politicality	substantive criminal law
factual guilt	presumption of innocence	uniformity

COUNTRIES REFERENCED

England
Mexico
United States

As explained in Chapter 1, this book uses categorization and classification to describe various legal systems. However, to get to the point where classification is helpful, it is desirable to identify a basic foundation for all legal systems. After this is done, subsequent classification proceeds in a more logical fashion because it flows from a single source. To that end, this chapter centers on the basic components of any justice system: delineating the laws and specifying the manner of enforcement. The former, called *substantive law,* and the latter, *procedural law,* provide the common ingredients and basic foundation of any legal system. The way in which a society achieves the two objectives yields the variety found among the world's justice systems.

Although our primary interest is studying that variety, we must remember that one benefit of an international perspective is a more accurate perception of our own legal system. Obviously, that position works only if our own system is sufficiently understood so that similarities and differences become apparent. It is assumed that readers of this text have more than a layperson's comprehension of the American system of criminal justice. Because of that assumption, detailed information about police, courts, and corrections in the United States is minimal. It is less likely, though, that readers will have a similar level of knowledge regarding criminal law. Introductory-level textbooks in criminal justice provide several chapters on American police, courts, and corrections, but seldom contain more than one chapter concerning criminal law itself. This fact is rather ironic, because it is criminal law that gives those other topics their "reason for being." Ironic or not, specifics of criminal law are seldom as well comprehended as are the terms and processes associated with American policing, adjudication, and punishment.

This chapter aims to accomplish two tasks: (1) to explain the basis for the American system of justice, and (2) to facilitate an appreciation of the essential ingredients of all justice systems: substantive and procedural criminal law. The second goal relies on the American system as its explanatory vehicle because, in cyclical fashion, appreciation of other systems requires understanding how our own operates.

ESSENTIAL INGREDIENTS OF JUSTICE SYSTEMS

Two problems need resolving before any society can implement an institutionalized pattern of criminal justice. First, the laws must be delineated. Next, the manner of enforcement must be specified. The way a society resolves these problems involves the essential ingredients of any legal system. These activities are of equal importance and provide a sound basis for diagramming the basic foundation of legal systems. However, simply stating the existence of this foundation is not sufficient. To allow comparison and contrast, it is necessary to examine these ingredients more closely. That examination is aided by identifying key features of each ingredient.

Figure 3.1 and Table 3.1 illustrate the essential ingredients and their key features in terms of a justice paradigm. As the figure and table show, an institutionalized pattern of justice rests on the definition of rules (substantive law) and the determination of their enforcement (procedural law). In turn, delineation of rules specifies the requirements to be met for something to qualify as a law and the criteria used in deciding if a particular behavior is criminal (see Figure 3.1). The first

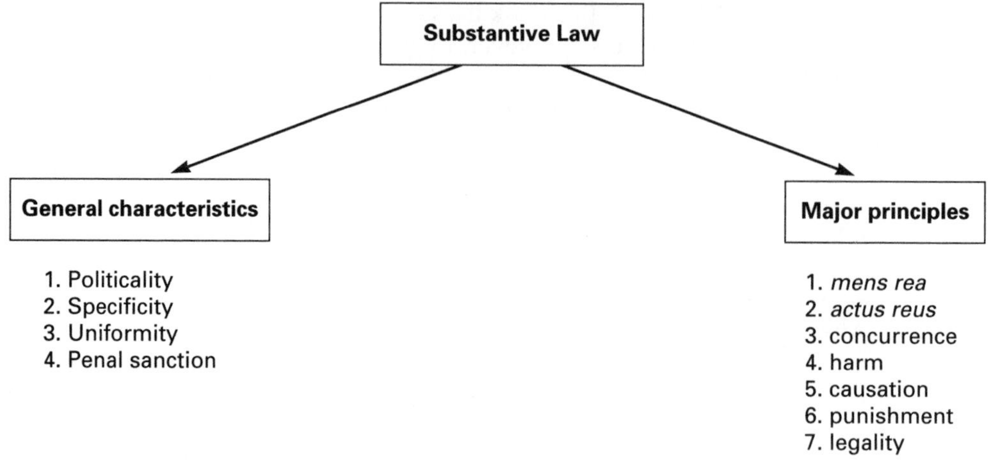

Figure 3.1 Substantive Law

condition, requirements to qualify as a law, can be called the *general characteristics of law.* The second condition, determining if a particular behavior is criminal, comprises the *major principles of law.* Importantly, both the general characteristics and the major principles are discussed here in terms of law in Western nations. Although it hints of ethnocentrism, such tunnel vision is necessary at this point to assure us of having a common base from which to view the law and legal systems in other countries.

Just as we can analyze two aspects of the definition of laws, we can also bifurcate the manner in which the rules are implemented (see Table 3.1). The rules

Table 3.1 Procedural Law

Crime Control Model	Due Process Model
Assumes freedom is so important that every effort must be made to repress crime.	Assumes freedom is so important that every effort must be made to ensure that government intrusion follows legal procedure.
Seeks to make decisions that will identify factual guilt.	Seeks to make decisions that will identify legal guilt.
Follows rules that emphasize the repression of criminal activity.	Follows rules that emphasize containing the government's level of intrusion into citizens' lives.
Emphasizes efficiency of action (i.e., speed and finality).	Emphasizes legitimacy of action.
Requires a high rate of apprehension and conviction by early exclusion of those not likely to be guilty.	Insists on a formal, adjudicative, adversarial fact-finding process, even though such restraints may keep the process from operating with maximal efficiency.

can be activated to emphasize repressing rule violation (crime control model) or to contain the system's level of intrusion into the citizen's life (due process model). As Packer (1968) presents those two models, they are less bound to specific legal systems than are the characteristics and principles of criminal law. Therefore, the comments that follow about procedural law are applicable to a wider range of legal systems than is the following analysis of substantive law.

Substantive Criminal Law

An interest in the manner in which definitions of criminal behavior evolve is a concern of substantive law. *Black's Law Dictionary* defines substantive law as "that part of law which creates, defines, and regulates rights." The penal, or criminal, code of each state provides examples of these laws.

The Criminal Code of Colorado, for example, defines robbery as follows:

> *(1) A person who knowingly takes anything of value from the person or presence of another by the use of force, threats, or intimidation commits robbery.*
> *(2) Robbery is a class 4 felony* (Colorado Revised Statutes, *2000).*

Georgia, on the other hand, has this definition:

> *(a) A person commits the offense of robbery when, with intent to commit theft, he takes property of another from the person or the immediate presence of another:*
>
> *(1) By use of force;*
> *(2) By intimidation, by the use of threat or coercion, or by placing such person in fear of immediate serious bodily injury to himself or to another; or*
> *(3) By sudden snatching.*
>
> *(b) A person convicted of the offense of robbery shall be punished by imprisonment for not less than one nor more than 20 years* (Criminal Code of Georgia, *2000).*

Notice that in addition to defining (at different lengths) what constitutes the crime of robbery, the statements also specify what punishment will be attached to that crime. A class 4 felony in Colorado requires a sentence of at least two but no more than six years followed by a three-year mandatory parole period. Although both states define the crime of robbery, the definitions and punishment vary. Despite the differences, both are examples of substantive law, because they each serve two purposes: (1) they define the behavior subject to punishment by the government and (2) they specify what the punishment will be for those committing that offense.

Such definitions are not easily arrived at. Many criteria must be met before a definition qualifies to be a criminal law. Even more standards are necessary before a specific act is considered to be criminal. Consider, for example, the development of the law of theft. As explained by Hall, the law of theft provides an example of how something comes to be defined as illegal and of how the definition can change over time.

Hall notes that prior to the fifteenth century the crime of theft essentially referred to the taking of property without the owner's consent. Today it has a broader meaning and encompasses acts wherein property was lawfully obtained but then appropriated for the taker's own use (for example, swindling, embezzlement, misappropriation). The turning point came in the English "Carrier's Case" of 1473. The defendant (the carrier) was hired to carry certain bales (probably wool, cloth, or both) to Southampton. Rather than fulfilling his obligation, he carried the goods to another place, where he broke open the bales and took the contents. He was apprehended and charged with a felony (Hall, 1952).

Today the felony charge of theft seems only reasonable. Then, however, common law recognized no criminality in a person who came legally into possession of an item and then converted the item to his own use. The reasoning behind such a position was that the owner of transported goods was responsible for protecting himself by employing trustworthy persons. If his trust turned out to be misplaced, it was unfortunate but not illegal. After all, *trespass* (unlawful interference with a person's property) was an essential part of the definition of theft. It seemed impossible for a person to commit trespass upon items he possessed.

Despite what would appear to be an ironclad defense, the court eventually found the defendant guilty of larceny. The verdict was based on reasoning by Justice Choke (one of three justices hearing the case), who argued, "I think that where a man has goods in his possession by reason of a bailment he cannot take them feloniously, being in possession; but still it seems here that it is felony, for here the things which were within the bales were not bailed to him, only the bales as an entire thing were bailed" (quoted in Hall, 1952, p. 9). In other words, the defendant had legal possession of the bales but not of the contents of those bales. The defendant could have sold the bales intact or left the bales unopened in his house, but when he opened them and took the contents, he committed a felony.

Hall suggests that this new interpretation of what constitutes larceny was a result of changing social conditions and pressing social interests. Specifically, Hall notes political and economic conditions that preceded and possibly influenced the outcome of the Carrier's Case. First, consider the political conditions. The king at the time was Edward IV, who, like his predecessor Henry VI, occasionally "consulted" with judges before they handed down a decision. Hall reviews the comments of several chroniclers of the time and concludes that Edward IV was likely to interfere with decisions made at several court levels.

With these political considerations, Hall also emphasizes important economic ones. The Carrier's Case occurred at a time when the economic structure of England was dramatically changing. Alteration of the manorial system and the destruction of serfdom resulted in a situation where more than 3000 merchants were engaged in foreign trade as the sixteenth century began. Hall suggests that it would be hard to believe that as the old feudal structure based on agriculture gave way to a new order based on industry and trade, the king would be standing by as a casual observer. Edward IV, supportive of merchants and of trade relations with other countries, was himself a merchant engaged in many private ventures. With this background, and because the merchant "stolen" from was foreign, Hall believes that Edward IV had good reason to use this case as one requiring his "consultation" with the justices. The combination of political and economic conditions brought together the monarchy and the mercantile class and their shared interest in secure transport of wool and cloth. Such new arrangements required a new rule—so the law, which had lagged behind the needs of the times, was brought into more harmonious relationship with the other institutions by the decision rendered in the Carrier's Case (Hall, 1952, p. 33).

The difficulty in defining something as criminal has led some legal theorists to explain substantive criminal law by reference to its general characteristics and its major principles. A review of those characteristics and principles allows us to appreciate the complexity of our legal system.

General Characteristics of Criminal Law. Table 3.1 shows four general characteristics of Western criminal law (Sutherland & Cressey, 1978):

- Politicality
- Specificity
- Uniformity
- Penal sanction

If any of these four is not present, the activity prohibited or required cannot be called criminal. *Politicality* refers to the fact that only violations of rules made by a government authority can be crimes. Rules can be made by many groups and individuals. A basketball coach can tell her players what time they must be in their dorm room; an employer can tell his employee what to wear to work; a teacher can require students to prepare a paper following a certain typing format. If players, employees, and students violate those rules, they may be subjected to punishment for having done so. They have not, however, committed a crime, because a government authority did not make the rules.

For people to know in advance what particular behavior they must do (for example, in some states citizens must come to the aid of a police officer upon request) or refrain from doing (for example, shoplifting), criminal law must be specific. Korn and McCorkle (1959) relate an example of a case (*McBoyle v. United States*, 283 U.S. 25, 1931) in which the defendant had his conviction of interstate transportation of a stolen airplane set aside. The trial court convicted McBoyle under a statute prohibiting the taking of a motor vehicle or "any other self-propelled vehicle." Because of the airplane's relatively recent invention, the Supreme Court believed such words as "self-propelled vehicle" still brought to many people's mind a picture of vehicles moving on land rather than through the air. Because the legislature had not specifically included airplanes in the statute, their theft was not prohibited. In a 1945 Virginia case (cited in Hall, 1960, p. 39), a court set aside a charge of disorderly conduct on a bus because the statute specified only car, train, or caboose. Although each of these examples may cause some people to wince at the "technicality" of the law, it is important to consider Justice Holmes's remarks in the McBoyle case:

> *It is reasonable that a fair warning should be given to the world in language that the common world will understand, of what the law intends to do if a certain line is passed. To make the warning fair, so far as possible the line should be clear (cited in Korn & McCorkle, 1959, p. 103).*

Criminal liability should be uniform for all persons despite social background or status. The definition of a crime should not allow one kind of person to commit the act without blame while legally sanctioning a different category of person for the same behavior.

Finally, to qualify as criminal law there must be some punishment that the government will administer. Without a *penal sanction* the rule becomes more of a guideline than a prohibition of crime. It may seem strange that a government would try to make some behavior criminal without providing a punishment for that behavior, but it has happened. For example, some states define adultery as a crime but provide no criminal punishment for its occurrence. Because it can be used in civil court as a basis for divorce, the states believe that it serves a purpose. The following definition of *criminal law* incorporates each condition:

> *A body of specific rules regarding human conduct which have been promulgated by political authority, which apply uniformly to all members of the classes to which the rules refer, and which are enforced by punishment administered by the state (Sutherland & Cressey, 1978, p. 6).*

As neat and concise as all that sounds, it is obvious when we look at our criminal laws that the preceding definition is an ideal, relating more generally to Western legal systems and to the American system particularly. There is no requirement that "law" in general needs to be specific or have a sanction before citizens of some society view it as law. Similarly, politicality becomes problematic when, for example, a revolutionary tribunal enforces its decrees. Even uniformity is breached in the United States when we direct laws to specific categories of people, such as prohibiting some citizens from disobeying authority figures, skipping school, or leaving home simply because they are under a certain age.

Despite such problems, these criteria are appropriate and provide a fair description of what constitutes criminal law in much of Western society and in several other places as well. For our purposes, they provide a context and terminology that will be helpful as we look at other legal systems.

Major Principles of Criminal Law. There are different criteria to be met in deciding if a particular behavior is criminal. Something that is often hard for the layperson (and even criminal justice employees) to understand is why or how a defendant who seems so obviously guilty can avoid prosecution. At times an explanation lies in the absence of one or more of the following conditions. Jerome Hall (1960) has suggested seven criteria as constituting the major principles of Western law (see Figure 3.1):

- *Mens rea*
- Act *(actus reus)*
- Concurrence
- Harm
- Causation
- Punishment
- Legality

Mueller summarized these by suggesting that crime refers to legally proscribed (legality) human conduct (act), causative (causation) of a given harm (harm), which conduct coincides (concurrence) with a blameworthy frame of mind *(mens rea)* and which is subject to punishment (punishment) (Hall & Mueller, 1965, p. v).

The requirement for a guilty act *(actus reus)* reminds us that having bad intentions is not enough. Behavior is criminal only (with exceptions that will shortly be noted) when the individual acts in a prohibited way or fails to act in a required way. In addition, that behavior must be linked in a causal way to some harm considered detrimental to social interests. Consider the following illustration. Suppose that John poisoned Bob with every intent to kill him. Bob is taken to the hospital, where he recovers from the poison but dies of the antidote. Although John's overt act was the necessary first link in the chain of events culminating in Bob's death, it was not John's act that caused the harm (death). Instead, another event (administration of the fatal antidote) intervened between that first link and the final result. John could, of course, still be guilty of several other crimes, such as assault or maybe attempted murder. However, as Korn and McCorkle (1959) point out, this principle has been the basis for successful appeals in homicide cases where victims died of negligent medical care instead of the bullet that caused the need for the care in the first place.

The requirement for a guilty mind *(mens rea)* can be difficult to understand because of confusion between motivation and intent. A young boy may be motivated to take food from a grocery store without paying because his family is starving. Although some see that as an acceptable motivation, the criminal law cares only about the boy's intention. His intent, clearly, was to steal. His motivation may be considered by the store owner, police, prosecutor, and judge as they decide what action to take. Yet as far as criminal law is concerned, the boy intended to take another person's property without paying and has therefore stolen.

The existence of a harmful act and the presence of mens rea are not enough to show that a crime has occurred. It also must be shown (with exceptions noted as follows) that there was fusion of intent and conduct (that is, *concurrence*). Consider a strange case that Hall (1960) relates. In 1896 an Ohio medical student tried to kill a young woman with whom he had been having an affair. He gave her a large dose of cocaine in Ohio, believing the cocaine would kill her then and there. He then took what he believed to be her dead body into Kentucky, where he decapitated it. Medical evidence established that the woman had been alive at the time of the decapitation in Kentucky. A Kentucky court found the man guilty of murder (*Jackson v. Commonwealth,* 100 Ky. 239, 1896), but Hall makes a point relevant to our discussion. An argument can be made that there was no intention to kill or injure a human being at the time of the decapitation, because the man believed that the woman was already dead. Hall suggests that because the court believed the defendant thought she was dead when he decapitated her, the court should have found that the mens rea did not concur with the actual killing. On that basis, Hall believes, the court decision was wrong, because it violated the principle of concurrence.

As we look over the seven conditions for crime, it becomes easier to appreciate the difficult job that attorneys, judges, and juries sometimes have in determining if and how these things fit together. As if the task were not difficult enough, there are some exceptions to those conditions that may come into play. For example, we modify the requirement that a harm must be caused by some behavior, so attempts and conspiracy are themselves crimes. Also, the requirement of *mens rea* is modified in strict liability cases, which consider the individual responsible despite intent. Most strict liability laws concern public welfare offenses (sale of adulterated food, violations of building regulations), but some relate to serious felonies (Hall, 1960). An example would be the felony-murder rule found in some states. If a death occurs while the offender is committing a felony, that offender may be held criminally responsible for the death even if there was no intent on his part to kill the victim.

Despite those instances of strict liability, intent is an essential part of our legal conception of criminal responsibility. In cases where intent is absent, the defendant is not criminally responsible for an act that would otherwise be a crime. For example, many of us would not define as criminal a five-year-old child who opens the mailboxes in his apartment complex and throws his neighbors' mail into his wagon to empty later in the sandbox. We also might question a legal system that brings charges of assault against a woman who caused great physical harm to a man trying to rape her. In each example our objection seems based on the belief that the child and the woman were not responsible for the acts, though they may have constituted a crime. We may even smile with a sense of self-satisfaction that we live under a system where such behavior can be excused or justified in appropriate cases. Problems arise, however, when presenting cases not so clear-cut. What would we think if that boy had been ten instead of five, or maybe fifteen? What if the man were unarmed, smaller, and physically weaker than the woman, yet she chose to protect herself by shooting him? The question of responsibility in these situations will not result in as much agreement among us. The Model Penal Code (American Law Institute, 1985) notes seven generally recognized defenses based on absence of criminal intent. Each state will phrase the defense in its own way and may not even have all seven. One, insanity, is commonly found and provides a good example of one way to approach the question of responsibility.

Under Anglo-Saxon law and well into the thirteenth century, the mentally deranged were treated much like any other criminal. Eventually "insanity" was accepted as a condition negating blameworthiness. Yet deciding what constituted insanity remained a problem. The "wild beast test" developed in the thirteenth century was among the first methods used. It said that a madman was one "'who does not know what he is doing, who is lacking in mind and reason, and who is not far removed from the brutes"' (Hall, 1960, p. 475). The first long-lasting criteria for determining insanity came in 1843. In that year a court found Daniel M'Naghten not guilty of murdering Edward Drummond because M'Naghten was suffering from delusions. Specifically, M'Naghten felt pursued by several enemies, including Sir Robert Peel, who was England's prime minister at the time. M'Naghten killed Drummond while believing that Drummond was actually Peel. The public outcry in response to the acquittal resulted in a request by the House of Lords for the judges of the Queen's Bench to present their views of the insanity defense. Their response, considered by the judges to be a restatement of existing law rather than an innovation (Hall, 1960), was called the *M'Naghten rule*. They established a "right from wrong" test with the following necessary to show insanity: (1) At the time of the crime the defendant was operating under a defect of reason so as to be unable to know the nature or quality of the act; or (2) if the defendant was aware of the act's nature, he did not know the act was wrong (see Moran, 1985).

From the 1850s to the 1970s, the M'Naghten rule was the primary means for determining insanity in the federal and most state courts in the United States. Some states supplemented M'Naghten with an "irresistible impulse" test that assumed that people may have known their act was wrong but they could not control the impulse to commit it. Sometimes called the "policeman-at-the-elbow" test, the irresistible-impulse modification accepts the right-versus-wrong concept but presumes that persons may have such a compulsion to commit a crime that they would do so even if they knew the act was wrong and a police officer was present and watching.

Today fewer than half the states still use the M'Naghten rule (with or without the irresistible-impulse modification). Increasingly popular among state legislators is the Model Penal Code definition from the American Law Institute (ALI), which reads:

> *A person is not responsible for criminal conduct if at the time of such conduct as a result of mental disease or defect he lacks substantial capacity either to appreciate the criminality [wrongfulness] of his conduct or to conform his conduct to the requirements of law. (American Law Institute, 1985, Section 4.01)*

Under this standard (also called the *Brawner rule* from *U.S. v. Brawner*, 1972), criminal responsibility is linked to "substantial capacity to appreciate" rather than "being unable to know" the wrongfulness of the act.

The difficulty of deciding whether a lack of criminal responsibility is best linked to not knowing right from wrong, to mental disease or defect, or to irresistible impulses, is a continuing problem. Since the much criticized verdict finding John Hinckley, Jr., not guilty by reason of insanity in the attempted assassination of President Ronald Reagan, the federal government and many states have sought modification and even abolition of insanity defenses. At the federal level, the Insanity Defense Reform Act of 1984 set a new criterion for determining insanity in federal criminal trials. In many ways it is a return to the M'Naghten rules, because the defendant must be shown to have been unable to appreciate the wrongfulness of his acts. However, it also borrows from the ALI test in linking the inability to appreciate wrongfulness to a severe mental disease or defect. In another important modification of previous standards, the Insanity Defense Reform Act requires that the defense prove insanity. Previously, the burden of proof fell on the state to show that the defendant was sane. Now, in the federal courts, defendants can be required to prove their insanity, thus making such a plea more difficult.

Some states have adopted the new federal guidelines, but others have chosen to make the insanity defense more difficult, or even impossible. In 1982 Idaho provided an example of the latter position when it abolished the insanity defense (Geis & Meier, 1985). By 1988 two other states (Montana and Utah) had followed Idaho's lead (Zawitz, 1988). Under the Idaho statute, defendants can be examined before trial to determine if they are fit to proceed to trial. If not, they are placed in a mental facility until such time that they can adequately participate in their defense. Defendants found fit to go to trial are subject to only two kinds of verdicts: guilty or not guilty. If the defendant is found guilty, his or her mental condition can be considered for sentencing purposes (Geis & Meier, 1985).

You Should Know!

GUILTY BUT INSANE

Since *mens rea* is an essential element of criminal responsibility, the concept of "guilty but insane" sounds like an oxymoron to some people. After all, if a person is insane at the time of the crime, how could she have had the mental state necessary to form criminal intent?

The finding of "guilty but insane" or, in some states, "guilty but mentally ill," is usually considered to be a legislative response to public frustration with insanity defenses. Actually, the insanity defense is infrequently used (less than 2 percent of cases going to trial) and is seldom successful even when it is used (Albanese, 2000). But since the public perceives the insanity defense as mostly a way for defendants to "get away" with something, about 12 states now have laws allowing a person to be held criminally responsible for an act even though he may not have had the mental capacity to form *mens rea*. As the Alaska law reads: "A defendant found guilty but mentally ill is not relieved of criminal responsibility for criminal conduct. . . ." (*Alaska Statutes* 12.47.030).

When one country interprets the importance of intent and criminal responsibility in such a variety of ways, we must expect similar variations among nations. Although the substantive law in each country invariably addresses such issues as responsibility, there are differences in how that concept is interpreted and incorporated. If we remember the example of the insanity plea and its variations in the United States, we will be better able to understand differences in issues of substantive law under other legal systems.

Procedural Criminal Law

In Figure 3.1 substantive criminal law was conveniently divided into its general characteristics and major principles. Similarly, as Table 3.1 describes, procedural criminal law also has two components. Although general characteristics and major principles theoretically carry equal weight in substantive law, the bifurcation of procedural law results in two components that are unlikely to be found in equal proportion. Instead, procedural criminal law is likely to emphasize one philosophy over the other at any given time.

The *due process model* and *crime control model* were described by Packer (1968) as separate value systems competing for priority in the operation of the criminal process. Although neither is said to correspond to reality or represent a best approach, they are effectively used to understand the operation of the process. In that manner, the models provide a technique for discussing a variety of criminal justice systems. Because neither model is deemed better than the other, procedural law in different justice systems can be described without making value judgments. Chapter 5 takes exactly that approach. However, as noted earlier, gaining an international perspective is benefited by establishing a parochial base. Therefore, we will see how Packer's models help us understand American procedural law so that we can more fully appreciate the workings of procedural law in other countries. We begin by reviewing aspects of the American Constitution that relate to the criminal process.

Constitutional Provisions for the Criminal Process. After creation of the new Constitution of the United States, some framers expressed concern that the document contained the seeds of a tyranny by government. Discussion focused on adding a bill of rights to restrict the powers of the new federal government. Thomas Jefferson favored such a declaration of rights when he wrote to James Madison:

> *Let me add that a bill of rights is what the people are entitled to against every government on earth, general or particular, and what no just government should refuse . . . (Boyd, 1955, p. 440). The inconveniences of the Declaration [of Rights] are that it may cramp government in it's [sic] useful exertions. But the evil of this is short-lived, moderate, and reparable. [The absence, however, of a Declaration is] permanent, afflicting, and irreparable (Boyd, 1958, p. 660).*

The proponents' voices were so strong that the first Congress to meet following the adoption of the new Constitution submitted 12 amendments for consideration by the states. Ten of those were ratified by 1791, and they have become known as the Bill of Rights. For purposes of criminal law, the Fourth, Fifth, Sixth, and Eighth Amendments have particular relevance. The others are not unconnected to criminal law, but typically have a more tangential link. For example, the First Amendment references to restrictions on religion, speech, press, assembly, and petition have been the source of controversy in trial proceedings (conflicts between a free press and a fair trial) and confinement of prisoners (may a Satanist practice his religion while in prison?).

In the interest of focus, we will highlight only the Fourth and Fifth Amendments. The Sixth (providing for such things as the right to a speedy and public trial before an impartial jury, and for the assistance of counsel) and the Eighth (prohibiting excessive bail, excessive fines, and cruel and unusual punishment) are relevant to procedural law but involve topics more appropriate for other sections of this book. However, before addressing the Fourth and Fifth Amendments, there is one other to note. When drafted, the U.S. Constitution was not intended to protect individual citizens from the unfair enforcement of state laws. In the spirit of states' rights, and with greater fear of the federal government than of the state government, citizens expressed interest in controlling the closest thing they had to a monarch and Parliament. That the Bill of Rights limited only the federal government was made most clear by Chief Justice Marshall in the *Barron v. Baltimore* (1833) decision:

> *Had the framers of these amendments intended them to be limitations on the powers of the State governments, they would have imitated the framers of the original Constitution, and have expressed that intention. . . . These amendments demanded security against the apprehended encroachments of the General Government—not against those of the local governments (32 U.S. 243, at 250).*

That view held until after the Civil War, when protection of citizen rights gained new concern and attention. The Thirteenth Amendment abolished slavery, but in response to continued violation of rights, Congress adopted the Fourteenth Amendment in 1868. The portion of the amendment affecting criminal justice reads, "No State shall . . . deprive any person of life, liberty, or property, without due process of law. . . ." Since the amendment's adoption, the meaning of the phrase due process has been a point of controversy. One resolution rests on the theory that the provisions of the Bill of Rights are incorporated into the due process clause of the Fourteenth Amendment and therefore applicable to the states as well as the federal government. This legal theory has served as the basis for many U.S. Supreme Court decisions. The Court selectively has made certain Bill of Rights stipulations binding on state governments. In this manner, the U.S. Supreme Court can tell any state how to proceed (due process) when that state seeks to deprive a citizen of life, liberty, or property. Because of the Fourteenth Amendment, the procedural conditions of the Fourth and Fifth Amendments must be followed by state governments in criminal proceedings.

The Fourth Amendment says, "The right of the people to be secure in their persons, houses, papers, and effects, against unreasonable searches and seizures, shall not be violated, and no warrants shall issue, but upon probable cause, supported by oath or affirmation, and particularly describing the place to be searched and the persons or things to be seized."

Importantly, this amendment does not prohibit all searches. Only those that are unreasonable are not allowed. The problem becomes one of defining "unreasonable" and, by implication, "reasonable." Since the 1960s, the U.S. Supreme Court has dealt with the question in the context of "searches and seizures" by the police. One type of police procedure governed by the Fourth Amendment would be the stopping and frisking of a citizen. In *Terry v. Ohio* (1968), for example, the U.S. Supreme Court held that police could stop and search three men whom the officer had observed prowling in front of some store windows. The search produced guns on two of the men, and the justices said the search was a reasonable precaution for the officer's safety. Further, after lawfully arresting a person, the police may conduct a "search incident to the arrest" to include the surrounding space in which a suspect could reasonably be expected to obtain a weapon or destroy evidence (see *Chimel v. California,* 1969).

Independent of, yet associated with, the Fourth Amendment is the judicially developed regulation known as the *exclusionary rule*. In the 1961 case of *Mapp v. Ohio,* the U.S. Supreme Court held that state courts must, just as the federal courts had been doing since 1914, exclude from trial any evidence obtained in violation of the privileges guaranteed by the U.S. Constitution. Such violations have come to include such things as an absence of a warrant, lack of probable cause to arrest, or the use of a defective warrant. In addition, under the "fruits of the poisonous tree" doctrine, evidence generated by or directly obtained from an illegal search also must be excluded. The primary purpose of the exclusionary rule was to deter police misconduct or, when misconduct has occurred, to return the "case" against a suspect to its position prior to the violation.

It is not comforting to hear about the release of an "obviously guilty" person because the evidence gathered against him could not be used at trial. This is particularly troublesome when the violation is something trivial, such as an incorrect warrant form. One result of efforts to modify the exclusionary rule has been a *good-faith exception,* which the U.S. Supreme Court put forth in *United States v.*

Leon (1984). The Court ruled that evidence obtained through an illegal warrant need not be excluded at trial if the police could show that they got the evidence while reasonably believing they were acting according to the law. The extension of the good-faith exception to include warrantless cases has not been decided by the Court, but in 1988 the House of Representatives added such an exception to the Omnibus Drug Initiative by a 259 to 134 vote. Its impact has yet to be tested, but it does reflect a public desire to continue movement away from a strict application of the exclusionary rule.

According to the Fifth Amendment, "No person shall be held to answer for a capital or otherwise infamous crime, unless on a presentment or indictment of a Grand Jury . . . nor shall any person be subject for the same offense to be twice put in jeopardy of life or limb; nor shall be compelled in any criminal case to be a witness against himself, nor be deprived of life, liberty, or property, without due process of law. . . ."

Obviously, several aspects of the Fifth Amendment relate to procedural criminal law, but we will consider only that section regarding compelled self-incrimination. Consistent with the adversarial process and its requirement that the state must prove the defendant's guilt, the protection against compelled self-incrimination links to the Fourth Amendment's prohibition against unreasonable search and seizure and the Sixth Amendment's right to counsel. In the context of the Fifth Amendment, self-incrimination is interpreted more specifically in reference to whether a confession was voluntary and not coerced, and whether due process was followed while a confession was obtained. This second point, the process followed in obtaining a confession, was addressed in a 1966 U.S. Supreme Court decision.

On the evening of March 3, 1963, an 18-year-old girl was abducted and forcibly raped in Phoenix, Arizona. Ten days later, police arrested Ernesto Miranda at his home, took him to the police station, and placed him in a lineup. The victim immediately identified Miranda, who was then placed in a room and interrogated by the police. After two hours of interrogation, Miranda signed a confession, admitting that he had seized the girl and raped her. At the trial, defense counsel pointed out that the police did not tell Miranda about his right to counsel and to have counsel present during the interrogation (a point that had been decided earlier in *Escobedo v. Illinois*, 1964). Miranda was convicted, but on appeal the U.S. Supreme Court overturned the conviction (*Miranda v. Arizona*, 1966) and ruled that the confession (self-incrimination) could not be used, because the police did not tell Miranda of his right to remain silent. The Court specified the procedural safeguards to be followed before statements made during a custodial interrogation could be used against the defendant. Those safeguards have become known as the *Miranda warnings*. In general, individuals who are in police custody, and are being interrogated, must be advised of their rights before any statement they make can be used against them. "Police custody" refers to the restraint of a person's freedom in any significant way. "Interrogation" refers to questioning initiated by law enforcement authorities to elicit an incriminating statement.

As concerns were expressed in recent decades over the exclusionary rule, displeasure was also voiced with the Miranda decision. Advocates of a "get tough on crime" policy favored modifications to the Miranda warnings that would allow police more flexibility to accept statements by suspects. For example, a

In the News

MIRANDA UPHELD

Since the 1960s, critics have complained about the hands of police and prosecutors being tied by the proliferation of "rights for the criminal." Although the "criminal's rights" are also the Bill of Rights, it is important that the public should feel justice is being done; therefore, after the *Miranda v. Arizona* ruling in 1966, the U.S. Congress passed Section 3501 of the Omnibus Crime Control Act of 1968. Section 3501 was an attempt to overrule Miranda by declaring that failure to read the rights is just one of several factors to be used in deciding if the statement was made voluntarily. As it turned out, the federal government never tried to enforce Section 3501, and its constitutionality had never been challenged—until a U.S. Court of Appeals ruled in 1999 that a statement by defendant Charles Dickerson could be used against him at his trial. Citing Section 3501, the Court of Appeals said the police failure to read Dickerson his rights prior to his statement was not sufficient in itself to suppress the statement.

The case went to the U.S. Supreme Court, and in *Dickerson v. United States* (2000, No. 99-5525) the Court issued what was called by many people one of its most important criminal law rulings in several decades. In a 7-2 vote, the Court refused to discard the Miranda decision and reaffirmed that police must warn criminal suspects of their Miranda rights ("Supreme Court reaffirms," 2000).

The Court's decision to uphold Miranda was based in part on how the Miranda rights have become such a basic part of the justice process. Generally speaking, both liberals and conservatives live comfortably with Miranda. Neither police nor prosecutors believe the restrictions imposed by the Miranda decision are troublesome. Reading a suspect his or her rights does not prevent police from obtaining statements from those suspects, and prosecutors have not found that Miranda hampers the prosecution of cases. The police still obtain confessions (since 80 to 90 percent of all suspects waive their Miranda rights), and prosecutors dismiss only a few cases because of Miranda problems (American Bar Association, 1988; Rosen, 2000).

statement volunteered by the individual—that is, one in which there is no questioning by officers and which the individual freely makes—does not require Miranda warnings. Generally, on-the-scene questioning is also exempt, because at this stage the investigation has not reached an accusatory phase. In *New York v. Quarles* (1984), the Court included a "public safety" exception to Miranda. In situations where there is an immediate need to protect the public safety, the Court decided that this need takes precedence over the suspect's Fifth Amendment privilege against self-incrimination.

In *Colorado v. Spring* (1987), the Court reinstated the murder conviction of John Spring, who was arrested on firearms charges during a hunting trip. Not knowing that the police also suspected him of murder, Spring waived his right to remain silent. The Colorado Supreme Court ruled that his statements to police could not be used against him, because he should have been told, before waiving his rights, that they would ask about the murder. The U.S. Supreme Court disagreed, saying, "the Constitution does not require that a criminal suspect know every possible consequence of a waiver." The Court will continue to explain, modify, and refine the Miranda ruling as more situations present themselves. And as it does so, we will continue to see the pendulum swing between competing philosophies that stress control of crime and those that want to regulate the actions of justice officials. The resulting controversy between those philosophies is the basis for Packer's distinction between crime control and due process.

Decisions like those in Escobedo, Miranda, and Mapp seem to support a due process model to the extent that they restrict police behavior in favor of protecting citizen rights. The trend toward a more conservative public and U.S. Supreme Court in the 1980s and 1990s brought increased complaints that rights of "criminals" were more protected than were rights of "law-abiding citizens." That opinion reflects a position of the crime control model.

Crime Control Model. Under the authority of the Fourteenth Amendment, the U.S. Supreme Court has tried to stipulate the requirements of due process when government action is taken against a citizen. The result is American procedural law. Analysis of the form that law takes is aided by Packer's earlier mentioned models. The procedural law can emphasize efficiency of action (crime control model) or legitimacy of action (due process model).

The value system underlying the crime control model assumes that repression of criminal behavior is the most important function performed by the criminal justice process (Packer, 1968). The primacy of this function is necessary to ensure human freedom and allow citizens to be secure in person and property. The criminal justice process guarantees this goal of social freedom by efficiently operating to screen suspects, determine guilt, and appropriately sanction convicted persons.

To operate successfully, the crime control model requires a high rate of apprehension and conviction following a process that emphasizes speed and finality. Packer (1968) compares the model to an assembly-line conveyor belt moving an endless stream of cases to workers standing at fixed stations as they perform their respective operations and thus move the case to a successful resolution. Speed of the conveyor belt is kept high as long as there are no ceremonious rituals cluttering the process and slowing advancement of the case. Speed is also achieved when the cases are handled in a uniform and routine manner. In this sense, the crime control model is appropriately identified as an administrative, almost managerial, model (Packer, 1968).

An emphasis on finality means reducing chances to challenge the process or the outcome. Borrowing Packer's metaphor, we can point to the problems created when assembly-line workers are constantly subjected to review and second-guessing by supervisors. These interruptions while doing your job are bad enough, but imagine the damage to "finality" when workers are constantly having returned to them products presumably finished several weeks or months earlier. The metaphor is, of course, transparent. An efficient criminal justice process means that as a case proceeds from victim/witness to police, then to prosecutor, each "worker" performs his or her job in a speedy manner without fear of later veto.

A successful conclusion under the crime control model is one that excludes, at an early stage, persons apprehended but not likely to be guilty, while securing prompt and lasting conviction of the rest. Packer uses the concept of "presumption of guilt" to describe the orienting attitude toward those not excluded because of probable innocence. The presumption of guilt is important in the crime control model, because it allows the system to deal efficiently with large numbers of cases. This model expresses confidence in the screening process used by police and prosecutors when they release the "probably innocent" suspects and sustain action against the "probably guilty" ones. That is, after determining sufficient evidence of guilt to permit further action, all subsequent activity directed toward suspects is based on the view that they are presumed guilty (Packer, 1968).

Packer warns us not to think of presumption of guilt as the opposite of the presumption of innocence. These concepts are different, rather than being opposite ideas. Specifically, the presumption of innocence is a concept directing authorities about how they are to proceed—not what they are to believe. That direction includes a warning to ignore their belief (that is, presumption of guilt) while processing (where they presume innocence) the suspect/defendant. Because the presumption of guilt is simply a prediction of outcome, authorities can believe suspects are "probably guilty" while treating them as if guilt remains an open question.

It is apparent in this review of the crime control model that the early administrative fact-finding stages are of utmost importance. Subsequent stages of adjudication should be as abbreviated as possible to ensure speed and finality.

Due Process Model. If the due process model were put in charge of the assembly-line conveyor belt formerly run by the crime control model, one of the first changes would be an increase in the number and frequency of quality control inspection points. The speed and finality used by the crime control model to achieve its goal is seen by the due process model as inviting abuse of government power. Built upon concepts like the primacy of the individual and the limitation of official power, the due process model insists on a formal, adjudicative, adversarial fact-finding process. If this means that the process is slowed down and lacks finality, then so be it. As Packer says, "Precisely because of its potency in subjecting the individual to the coercive power of the state, the criminal process must, in this model, be subjected to controls that prevent it from operating with maximal efficiency" (1968, p. 166).

One way to implement its antiauthoritarian values is with the doctrine of legal guilt. *Legal guilt* can be distinguished from *factual guilt* in the following manner. Police Officer Williams observes Peter Jones run up to Virginia Spry and grab Virginia's purse and then run down the sidewalk. Officer Williams, the fastest runner in the department, catches Jones from behind, places him under arrest, and begins questioning him about the robbery. Jones immediately admits to the criminal act and, with the corroborating observation by Officer Williams, we can safely say that Jones is in fact guilty of the crime. Under the crime control model, this "presumption of guilt" would result in a rapid and final determination of guilt. However, under the due process model, emphasis is on the manner in which a government official (initially, Officer Williams) used her authority to intrude in the life of Peter Jones. The officer's actions are appropriately reviewed to determine their legality. If it is determined, for example, that Jones's confession was extracted without him being informed of his right to remain silent, the

IMPACT

Due Process, Corruption, and Fighting Crime

Is it possible to have so little due process that corruption of government officials is standard procedure? Is it possible to have so much due process that crime is allowed to flourish? Countries are constantly looking for the best balance between the due process and the crime control models. This "Impact "section looks at this issue with assistance of examples from the criminal justice systems of Mexico and England. We then look at attitudes of the American public regarding appropriate powers for the government.

Because of an assumed link between the civil liberties held by the public and corruption of the government, the topic of corruption is receiving increased attention (see McCormack, 1996). Transparency International is a not-for-profit, nongovernment organization that seeks to counter corruption at international and national levels. Each year Transparency International releases a *Corruption Perception Index (CPI)* that reflects the perception of businesspeople, political analysts, and the general public regarding corruption in countries around the world. The 2000 CPI found Nigeria, Yugoslavia, and the Ukraine to be perceived as the most corrupt of 90 nations, while Finland, Denmark, and New Zealand were perceived as the least corrupt (Transparency International, 2000). Obviously there is also corruption in other countries—for example, the United States was perceived as the fourteenth least corrupt country; but see Glazer (1995) on police corruption. Yet for present purposes, consider the case of Mexico.

Mexico, which has ranked among the lower one third of countries on the CPI since the mid 1990s, has had problems with police corruption for many years. Quiñones (1994) reports a vast ladder of corruption, with the street officer being the most visible level in a pyramid scheme that actually enriches police commanders more than street officers. Some of the Mexico City police officers compare themselves to the old Southern sharecroppers in the United States who were poorly paid, charged for their equipment, and worked long hours. If, at the end of their shift, the street officers do not have enough money to pay off the police commanders, the officers risk harassment or transfer to a job where they must survive on their legal, and meager, salary. This situation does not encourage appropriate attention to the civil liberties of Mexico's citizens. Police, citizens, and government officials have recognized the problem and are attempting to resolve it (see Quiñones, 1994), but it is not an easy task.

Most would agree, with Mexican citizens at the forefront, that loss of civil liberties because of corrupt officials can have no redeeming aspects. However, what if the loss, or reduction, in civil liberties is accomplished without corruption? In 1994 (effective in 1995) England responded to increasing crime by modifying both the methods used to identify crime occurrences and to adjudicate defendants (American Broadcasting Company,

(continued)

Due Process, Corruption, and Fighting Crime *(continued)*

1994). Identifying crime was made easier through increased use of surveillance cameras on London streets—without much protest from civil libertarians. At least one commentator suggested the attitude in England might indicate that the British do not fear their government as much as Americans do. Another change in British procedure, which did bring opposition from civil libertarians—but support from police—related to the defendant's right to remain silent. The right to silence was not challenged; however, it became allowable to consider a defendant's silence as an indication of guilt (Shaw, 1995).

Contemporary patriot groups, and others, criticize the U.S. government as being secretive, deceitful, and even corrupt. Such attitudes would seemingly make it difficult to reduce the due process rights that exist in the United States. Yet the complexity of the issue becomes apparent when we ask ourselves what powers the government should have as it attempts to protect us. In other words, are contemporary Americans satisfied with the balance we have struck between crime control and due process? Although no one would argue for giving up so much civil liberty that corruption is widespread, would some be willing to relinquish a few liberties in exchange for promise of safer neighborhoods?

In 1995 the Associated Press commissioned a nationwide telephone poll of adults regarding their opinion about new powers the government could be given to try to prevent terrorism ("Poll finds Americans," May 4, 1995). Thirty-eight percent would give the government the power to ban people from speaking on radio or television if they advocate antigovernment violence. Sixty-five percent would support the power to search for and seize weapons from groups that might be planning terrorism, even if the groups had not committed any crime. Fifty-four percent of the random sample put public security ahead of people's civil liberties. If the American public prefers a crime control model over a due process model, should the courts follow that lead?

confession cannot be used against him. A result of losing the confession as evidence may mean that the case against Jones is dropped or lost in court. According to the due process model, Jones was not "legally guilty" of the purse snatching, because rules designed to protect him and to safeguard the integrity of the process were not in effect. Factual guilt may be apparent or even legitimately known, but legal guilt must be validly decided via the previously determined process.

There is a tendency to suppose that the values of the due process model are opposite those underlying the crime control model. That position would be incorrect, because it implies that the due process model is uninterested in repressing crime. Instead, the differences are best seen with reference to procedure rather than outcome. Cole (1986) distinguishes the values of each model in the following manner: The crime control model assumes that freedom is so important that every effort must be made to repress crime, whereas the due process model assumes that freedom is so important that every effort must be made to ensure that criminal justice decisions are based on reliable information. Each model seeks to guarantee social freedom. One does so by emphasizing efficient processing of wrongdoers, whereas the other emphasizes effective restrictions on government invasion in the citizen's life. Who is the greater threat to our freedom? The criminal trying to harm us or our property, says the crime control model. The government agents like police officers and prosecutors, says the due process model. Yet both criminals and government agents can invade our interests, take our property, and restrict our freedom of movement. Social freedom requires that the law-abiding citizen be free from unjustifiable intrusion by either criminals or by government agents. Unfortunately, it does not appear possible to achieve both goals simultaneously. One is emphasized at the expense of the other, but neither can be identified as qualitatively better. Although we may have an individual preference for one over the other, it would be incorrect to attribute intrinsic superiority to our choice.

SUMMARY

An understanding of basic criminal law concepts is important for appreciating any country's legal system. This chapter used terms well-known to many of you, so we can begin the journey to other countries with familiar baggage. The two essential ingredients to any justice system are substantive law and procedural law. The former concerns the definition of rules, whereas the latter specifies their enforcement. Substantive criminal law is made up of general characteristics that allow identification of some act as criminal, and major principles that determine if a particular behavior is criminal. Procedural criminal law is implemented through either a crime control model or a due process model. Although each of these models seeks to ensure the social freedom of citizens, they emphasize different, and often conflicting, ways to achieve that goal.

This chapter emphasized American perspectives, mechanisms, and terminology to provide a common base on which future chapters can build. However, do not confuse the need for a common base with a suggestion that the American way of doing justice is necessarily the best in all instances. As noted in Chapter 1, one of the benefits of taking an international perspective is to identify ways that other countries might handle certain functions more efficiently, effectively, and fairly than we do. As we analyze criminal justice in other countries, it is important to set aside our understandable biases that America's way of doing things is the only reasonable or correct way. Such ethnocentrism hinders our ability to understand and appreciate alternative systems.

WEB SITES TO VISIT

- Check out "A Brief Summary of the Insanity Defense" at **ua1vm.ua.edu/ ~jhooper/ insanity.html** which presents a history going back to the Garden of Eden.

- Visit The Oyez Project (Northwestern University) at **oyez.nwu.edu/** and do a title search on some of the cases discussed in this chapter. Several of them provide multimedia activities associated with the case.
- The criminal law encyclopedia provided at **www.nolo.com/encyclopedia/crim_ency.html** provides a very good overview of many terms and concepts discussed in this chapter.

SUGGESTED READINGS

Ferdico, John, N. (1999). *Criminal procedure for the criminal justice professional* (7th ed.). Belmont, CA: West/Wadsworth.

Hall, Jerome. (1960). *General principles of criminal law* (2nd ed.). Indianapolis: Bobbs-Merrill.

Packer, Herbert. (1968). *The limits of criminal sanction.* Stanford, CA: Stanford University Press.

Chapter 4

Legal Traditions

KEY TOPICS

- Basic features making up the common legal tradition
- Basic features making up the civil legal tradition
- Basic features making up the socialist legal tradition
- Basic features making up the Islamic legal tradition
- Cultural components of legal systems
- Private law and public law
- Balance of powers and separation of powers
- Substantive components of legal systems
- Procedural components of legal systems

KEY TERMS

canon law
codification
Corpus Juris Civilis
custom
equity
feudalism
ijtihad
indigenous law
issues of fact
legal tradition
legal system
Marxism-Leninism
mazalim
particularization
points of law
precedent
principle of analogy
qadi's
Qur'an
Roman law
Russian law
Shari'a
stare decisis
Sunna
written code

COUNTRIES REFERENCED

China
England
France
Mexico
Roman Empire
Russia
United States

LEGAL SYSTEMS AND LEGAL TRADITIONS

The legal systems in today's world can be divided among four families, or traditions. Each legal tradition has unique elements that influenced its development and form. This chapter identifies some of those foundations for each tradition, then compares them in terms of cultural, substantive, and procedural components.

Since it is obviously impossible to discuss the legal system of every country of the world separately, they must be grouped according to similarities. The existence of sovereignty and nationalism means that the legal system (that is, legal institutions, procedures, and rules) in one country is not exactly duplicated in any other, yet certain countries do share "legal traditions" with one another (Merryman, 1985, pp. 1–3). These traditions are the basis for their groupings.

A legal tradition puts the legal system into a cultural perspective. It refers to deeply rooted and historically conditioned attitudes about things like the nature of law, the role of law in society, how a legal system should be organized and operated, and the way law is or should be made, applied, or perfected (Merryman, 1985). From this perspective, it is possible to analyze the legal systems of a considerable number of countries at one time. In doing so, however, we must not forget the variability of systems within the traditions. England, New Zealand, and New Jersey share a common legal tradition but do not have identical legal systems. Similarly, France, Germany, and Italy have their own legal systems but can be grouped in the same legal tradition along with the separate legal systems of Argentina and Brazil. See Figure 4.1 for one representation of how countries might be categorized according to their legal traditions.

Today legal scholars identify three or four legal traditions (some call them legal families). This number has not been consistent throughout history, and some formerly prominent legal traditions no longer even exist. We will concentrate on four contemporary traditions but must first mention some historically significant ones.

In 1928 law professor John Henry Wigmore published a three-volume work on the evolution of the various legal systems. A 1936 version not only revised and expanded the information but also incorporated the three previous volumes into one library edition. This prototype of comparative legal studies still sets the standard for comprehensive coverage. Wigmore (1928) believed there had been 16 legal systems in the world: Egyptian, Mesopotamian, Chinese, Hindu, Hebrew, Greek, Roman, Maritime, Japanese, Mohammedan, Celtic, Germanic, Slavic, Ecclesiastical, Romanesque, and Anglican. By 1936 Wigmore saw six systems as having completely disappeared as legal structures (Egyptian, Mesopotamian, Hebrew, Greek, Celtic, and Ecclesiastical). Five survived as hybrids (Roman, Germanic, Slavic, Maritime, and Japanese). The Chinese, Hindu, and Mohammedan remained essentially unmixed, and the two newest (Romanesque and Anglican) were hybrids.

A momentary retreat to before the time of Christ will instill an appreciation for the maturity of the idea that law is an instrument for social organization. If, in the process of gaining that appreciation, we gain a sense of humility as well, that is all to the good. After all, in some ways our contemporary legal systems have existed for less time than others have been extinct.

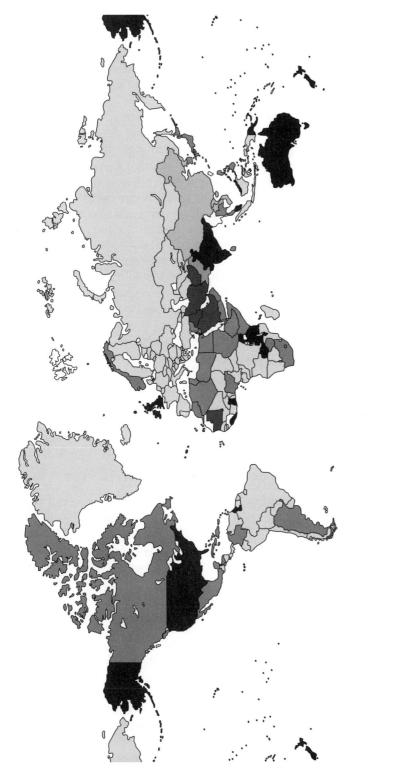

Figure 4.1 Countries with Similar Legal Traditions. *Note:* Type of legal tradition was determined from review of information in *The World Factbook* (http://www.odci.gov) and from the Library of Congress Country Studies (http://1cweb2.loc.gov/frd/cs/cshome.html).

The Egyptian legal system extends back as far as 4000 B.C., but it was especially well organized by the Fourth Dynasty (2900–2750 B.C.). By that time, the Egyptian king, or pharaoh, ruled as a theocrat with divine authority coming from the sun god Osiris through his son Horus. In this manner, the source of law and justice was presumed to be divine but was received by way of the pharaoh, who appointed chief judges.

As sole legislator, the pharaoh provided codes that set down the proper behavior of his people. The particular procedures for implementing the codes were more likely handled by the chief judges. Disputing parties brought their case before a judge, who listened to their oral arguments. The trial judge was expected to "be quiet while [listening] to the words of the petitioner. Do not treat him impatiently. Wait until he has emptied his heart and told his grief" (Wigmore, 1936, p. 30).

In its more than 4000-year existence, the Egyptian legal system obviously passed through many stages and in the process formulated some principles that western society could have profited from observing. The discovery of a 250 B.C. bail bond for a jail prisoner's release, and a recognition of women's independence and equality with men in some legal relations, remind us that we more "modern" citizens may be in many respects mere revisors instead of innovators.

In the region between the Euphrates and Tigris rivers (basically, Iraq today), the Mesopotamian civilization emerged and fought off successive waves of conquest until the arrival of Persians and Greeks in the centuries before Christ. The legal system developed by these traders emphasized commercial law and has provided reasonable examples of today's deeds, partnerships, and other contract forms.

The most notable achievement of the Mesopotamian legal system was the Babylonian law called the *Code of Hammurabi.* King Hammurabi's (circa 1792–1750 B.C.) code is one of the first known bodies of law. The laws, engraved on stone tablets, emphasized property rights and spoke to such issues as theft, ownership, and interpersonal violence.

The Hebrew legal system started with Moses receiving the two tablets of stone and the recording of the first five books of the Bible (known as the Torah, or Ancient Law). That first period (about 1200–400 B.C.) was followed by the Classic period (300 B.C.–A.D. 100) in which rabbis developed the law. The Talmudic period (200–500) saw the consolidation of records and was followed by the Medieval period (700–1500) of private codes and commentaries. Finally, the Modern period (1600–1900) saw the Hebrew language and legal system relegated to secondary standing as Jews became more linked to national (territorial) norms. Actually, Wigmore (1936) suggests that the Hebrew system ended as a strictly legal system with the end of the Classical period. After A.D. 100, Hebrew law was replaced in Palestine by Roman rule, and since then Jewish law has operated mainly as local custom and as ceremonial and moral rules.

Writing before the 1949 establishment of a communist People's Republic of China, Wigmore (1936) identified the Chinese legal system as the oldest continuing legal system. It has now followed the way of other pre–Christian era systems and lives only in a borrowed format. Possibly more so than in other systems, the Chinese legal system relies heavily on a philosophy of life. Specifically, the belief in a law of nature wherein all parts harmoniously adjust to each other was basic to Chinese law and justice.

The implications of such a philosophy were provided great clarity through the words of Confucius (551?–479? B.C.) The Confucian philosophy emphasized a government of men rather than of laws: the government will flourish with the right men but will decay without them. A result of that perspective was a situation where a single official directly ruled each province or locality. That magistrate, or governor, would collect taxes, serve as chief priest, provide moral guidance, and dispense justice. The emperor in Peking kept the governor in office as long as law and order prevailed and the people remained content and prosperous.

Law and order among content and prosperous people was best achieved, according to Confucius, through moral force and the rule of reason. Strict technical rights and insistence on principle were deemed inappropriate and unnecessary under the Chinese system. Instead, compromise was the goal to achieve, and mediation or arbitration (in today's terminology) was the means to that end. Operating without lawyers, the accused, accuser, and witnesses were questioned by the magistrate. In his efforts at dispensing justice, the judge was expected to operate from the position that nothing is so important that it cannot be compromised for human welfare, comfort, or dignity. With convictions like that, the Chinese joined the Egyptians, Mesopotamians, and Hebrews in providing the world a foundation for continually evolving legal systems.

TODAY'S FOUR LEGAL TRADITIONS

As the preceding review suggests, the decision to place the various legal systems into categories is easier than deciding how many categories to use and what to name them. Some scholars suggest that there are just two legal traditions while others use three or four groupings. Rene David (David & Brierley, 1968) has provided one of the more frequently cited groupings: common, civil, socialist, and religious/philosophical. Missing from most categorizations of legal traditions is a reference to customary, or *indigenous,* legal systems. An obvious reason for this is that indigenous systems do not share a common legal tradition—they are, by definition, confined to a particular locale and are essentially independent of outside influences.

The classification strategy most useful for this text is one using the four legal traditions established by David. His last category, religious/ philosophical, has included such important legal systems as Hindu and Judaic; but the most important contemporary example is the Islamic legal tradition. For purposes of simplicity and clarity of discussion, this Islamic legal tradition will serve as the fourth category. It is important to remember, however, that it is really only one of several legal traditions falling into the religious/philosophical category. Of the other three (common, civil, and socialist), the American reader is most familiar with the *common* legal tradition, because the United States falls into that general category. The *civil* tradition, oldest of the four, is today's primary competitor with the common legal tradition and can be found in some format throughout the world. The *socialist* legal tradition is both the youngest of the four and may be the first of the four to die out. However, even in a weakened state, the socialist tradition has influenced the countries where it appeared in a manner not easily tossed aside. As such, the socialist legal tradition deserves our attention and consideration as we review the major legal traditions in today's world.

You Should Know!

INDIGENOUS LAW

Indigenous law refers to the traditional obligations and prohibitions that a group of people requires its members to follow. Similar terms for these kinds of norms and sanctions include *customary law, unwritten law,* and *folk law.* Because indigenous law is a culture's original law, it has influenced the development of the four contemporary legal traditions. That point is apparent in this chapter's review of the subtraditions shaping each of the four legal traditions.

Although this book restricts coverage of indigenous law to its role in developing the civil, common, socialist, and Islamic traditions, the topic has broader importance. Not only are some countries best identified even today as following indigenous law (for example, the Federated States of Micronesia, the Marshall Islands, and Palau), but some populations within nations are best understood with reference to their customary procedures. For example, Pommersheim (1995) helps us understand tribal law in Native American culture, and Zatz (1994) provides insight into popular justice issues. Possibly the most intriguing work on indigenous law is the two-volume compilation of essays by Renteln and Dundes (1994). A review of those books will give you a broader understanding of both the existence and importance of indigenous law.

Lund (1996) reminds us that contemporary society can benefit from experiences of more traditional legal forms as he notes examples of prison alternative sentences with roots in customary law. For example, a magistrate in Alaska sentenced Henry, an Alaska Native, to keep the wife of the man Henry assaulted supplied with food and firewood while the husband recovered in the hospital. The sentence meant Henry would be working double-duty during the coldest months of the winter as he provided for both his own family and that of his victim. Lund explains that similar sentences of this "bush justice" are regular occurrences in Alaska's smaller cities and villages.

Before embarking on a review of each tradition, it is necessary to note that no legal system is a pure example of a particular legal tradition. As shown by the category of "Combination" in Figures 4.1 and 4.2, some countries are more accurately described as combining aspects of several traditions. This is especially true in countries colonized by nations that imposed their particular brand of law on an existing indigenous legal system. Further complicating matters are those countries subjected to multiple colonization periods by nations with different legal systems. As a result, we find countries like some in Africa that use combinations of common and Islamic law, and some in South America where both civil and common influences shaped the legal system. It is appropriate to keep these combined systems in mind as we discuss the four legal traditions—not because they challenge the use of four categories, but because they remind us that the categories are artificial groupings that try to bring order to a confusing array of legal systems.

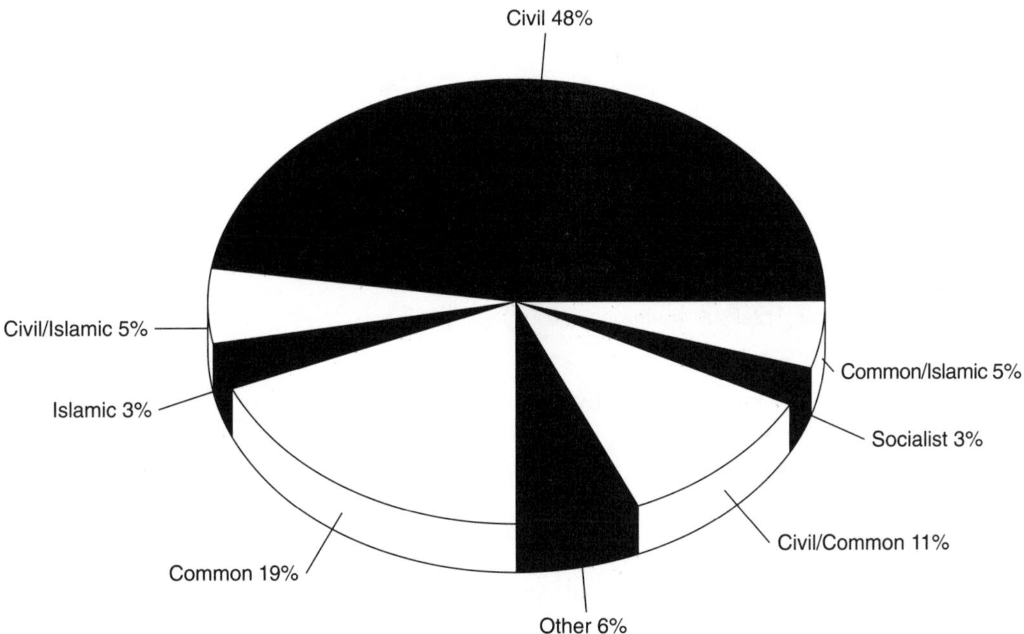

Figure 4.2 Countries by type of legal system *Note:* Type of legal system was determined from review of information in *The World Factbook* <http://www.cia.gov/cia/publications/factbook/index.html> and the Library of Congress Country Studies <http://lcweb2.loc.gov/frg/cs/cshome.html>

Common Legal Tradition

Although not the oldest, the common legal tradition provides a familiar base for discussing the history and essential features of a legal tradition. After covering that more native material, we can move to less familiar traditions.

The Romans occupied Britain from about A.D. 50 to the start of the fifth century. At that point, only the groundwork for the Roman law (civil legal tradition) had been laid. By the time the *Corpus Juris Civilis* was published (A.D. 533), the Romans in Britain had been pushed out by Germanic tribes like the Saxons and the Angles. St. Augustine's efforts at converting Britain to Christianity (A.D. 597) provided some Roman influence in terms of church law, but this early period served mainly to provide a base for a separate legal tradition called *common law.*

The common legal tradition developed from several sub-traditions. Those include feudal practices, custom, and equity (see Figure 4.3). An overview of each provides information helpful in understanding the basics of common law.

Feudal Practices. The primary political and military system of the Middle Ages (about A.D. 500 to 1450) was *feudalism.* Under this system, a lord provided vassals with land in exchange for military and other services. By the 1200s, when feudalism was in decline, several layers of feudal relations existed. For example, the vassals of an important baron (the vassals' lord) were in turn the lord of their

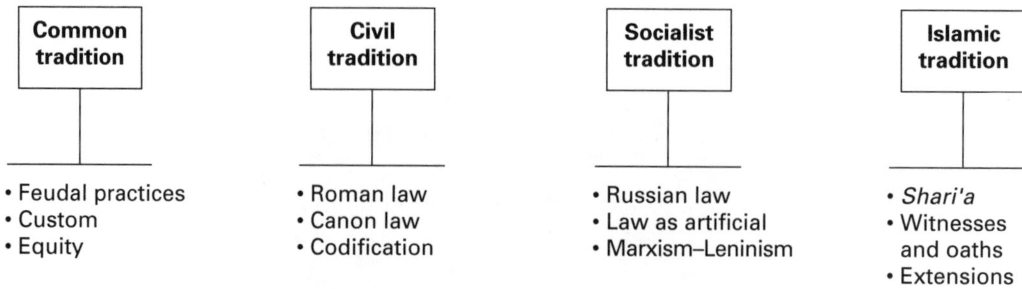

Figure 4.3 Developmental sub-traditions in four legal traditions

own vassals. Obviously, not everyone could be a landholder. Someone had to do the work necessary for keeping the lord (at whatever level) viable. A variety of peasant villagers provided this service in their role as agricultural workers in the lord's estate or manor.

Inevitably, differences arose among vassals at various levels, between vassals and their lords, and among villagers in a manor. Before the Norman Conquest (1066) of England, a nonfeudal Anglo-Saxon political system provided dispute settlement through assemblies of freemen sitting in shire and hundred courts. Upon his arrival in England, William the Conqueror (1066–1087) chose not to abolish the existing Anglo-Saxon process. Instead, he set up an orderly government with stern enforcement of royal rights. A new system of royal courts was developed with the primary interest of settling disputes of landholders. For example, a baron (beholding to his lord the king), presided over disputes between the baron's vassals. In doing so, the baron drew upon the advice of his other vassals (the disputants' peers) in arriving at a judgment. Failure by a vassal to answer an order to appear (summons) in court could result in the lord's reclaiming the vassal's land.

Disputes among the villagers were deemed more appropriately handled by the lord of the manor than by a royal court. If the manor court was unavailable or inappropriate, villagers could turn to traditional *shire* or *hundred courts.* In this manner, England retained Anglo-Saxon influences on its legal system into the early twelfth century. Law under Henry I (1100–1135) continued to be mostly Anglo-Saxon and administered at a local level according to widely varying regional custom (Plucknett, 1956). Even so, the administrative machinery, such as *royal courts,* placed by William I and Henry I provided the base for a common law dominating the realm. The realization of a common law occurred with Henry II (1154–1189) and allows us to turn to custom as the next sub-tradition of common law.

Custom. Henry II saw the reign of his predecessor, Stephen (1135–1154), as a period without law and troubled by civil war. Henry's grandfather, Henry I, on the other hand, ruled over a more orderly kingdom. In addition, in the 100 years since the Norman Conquest, both royal courts and the separate system of church courts had grown and become involved in many jurisdictional disputes. Henry II sought to return order to the kingdom and to solve disputes between state and church courts. One of his efforts resulted in the Constitutions of Clarendon

(1164), which listed customs said to be the practice during the reign of Henry I. The 16 articles forming the Constitutions provided custom as a basis for building order and served to declare the proper relation between church and state. The significance of custom must be elaborated.

The principal element in most premodern legal systems was custom. Not surprisingly, custom was an essential aspect of court decisions under Anglo-Saxon law and the English feudal process. Importantly, however, custom was not always consistent by geography or by social standing. Local village customs settled disputes among peasants and other villagers. Occasionally, those customs contradicted the habits of vassals, lords, and other freemen. Plucknett (1956) notes that village customs in England frequently kept a woman's property free from her husband's control and allowed her to enter into contracts on her own. Bourgeois custom did not allow such behavior by women. This point becomes important because the common legal tradition was built upon only one of these custom types. Specifically, common law was the custom of landholders as accepted and interpreted by the royal courts. It is appropriate to keep this point in mind as we discuss custom's role in the origin of common law.

According to Blackstone (I *Comm* 53–54), legal custom is ancient (no one can remember its beginning); continuous (it has never been abandoned or interrupted); peaceable (it has the common consent of those using it); reasonable (in terms of "legal" reason); certain (ascertainable); compulsory (it is not obeyed at option); and consistent (one custom cannot contradict another). As complete as that definition might sound, we must still consider the question of how custom is determined. One way to decide if a custom met the criteria for being a good legal custom was the jury system. Presumably, if a freeman's peers settle a dispute by using principles that reflect common and immemorial custom, the decision exemplifies common law. Or, as Blackstone put it, "The only method of proving, that this or that maxim is a rule of the common law, is by showing that it hath been always the custom to observe it" (I *Comm* 68).

The origin of common law in custom makes *precedent* a basic concept in the common legal tradition. When stated as a policy, precedent is called *stare decisis,* which means courts are expected to abide by decided cases. However, we must be careful here not to imply that courts before the sixteenth century had anything even resembling the modern principle of precedent or policy of *stare decisis.* The distinction is best handled by referring to the work of medieval judge Henry de Bracton. Bracton saw the courts of his time (mid-thirteenth century) as foolish and ignorant corruptors of doctrine, deciding cases by whim instead of by rule (Plucknett, 1956). In an attempt to return to the rule of law, Bracton reviewed the original plea rolls (immense in number and weight, and without index) from the courts. He used those documents to research legal principles and then to identify cases as historical evidence for the accuracy of his statements.

Note that this process of Bracton's was different from studying cases and deducing rule of law from them. For Bracton, a case could illustrate a legal principle and provide proof that the principle was once applied; but the case was not in itself a source of law (Plucknett, 1956). In other words, Bracton was searching for evidence of custom, and that custom could be identified through reference to several cases. As a result, court decisions were governed by custom, not by the case or cases cited as proof of that custom.

The movement to citing prior cases as binding (that is, the movement to precedent in its modern sense) instead of simply showing custom, began in the sixteenth century. Still, it was the seventeenth century before the practice became established. Specifically, decisions of the Exchequer Chamber (where the judges were the state chancellor and the treasurer) were held to be binding on other courts. Even so, the process was not really entrenched until the nineteenth century brought a strengthening of the House of Lords and the organizing of a single court of appeals. Therefore, custom is not only a basic component of common law, but it also is what has allowed precedent and *stare decisis* to become essential features.

Equity. The early history of equity (from the Latin *aequus,* meaning "fair" or "just") links it to the sub-traditions of feudal practices and custom. Yet it differs from those because of its eventual standing as a separate legal system both conflicting and cooperating with common law.

In the early stages of development, the king was in constant contact (usually through his council) with the various judges and courts across the country. In an informal manner, cases moved from court to court with little difficulty and without excessive regard to jurisdictional boundaries. Judges, in close cooperation with the king's council, had considerable discretion, especially in procedural matters. With the fourteenth century came significant elaboration of the judicial system responsible for implementing the common law. As a result, the contact between monarch and judge became infrequent, and the court's discretion in handling matters was correspondingly reduced. By the mid 1350s we find courts refusing to bend procedural rules, even in a sense of "fairness," and instead declaring that judges were bound to custom and to taking a strict definition of statute (Plucknett, 1956).

Not surprisingly, this inflexibility in the royal courts led to unhappy people who were unable to obtain justice. These people turned to the king and asked him to add fairness to the law. The king's agent in such matters was the chancellor, who had responsibility for guiding the king's conscience. Traditionally, the chancellor was also a church official, but with the growth of the office and expansion of responsibilities, laymen came to be appointed chancellor in the fourteenth century. Simultaneously, then, judges were isolated from the king while another royal office, with direct access to the monarch, was strengthened. The outcome of these events was the institutionalization of equity as an important aspect of law in England.

The chancellors decided conflicts between law and morals based on morality rather than technical law. Therefore, in Chancery court, decisions were based on the equity of the case without concern for the procedural necessities (David & Brierley, 1968). By the fifteenth century, the chancellor was essentially an autonomous judge deciding cases in the name of the king. This situation did not always sit well with common law judges. To appease them, the fifteenth- and sixteenth-century chancellors often called upon the judges to explain a point of law.

The cross-pollination of ideas between common law courts and Chancery courts benefited both. Common judges learned that technicalities were not an excuse for reaching obviously wrong decisions, and the chancellors came to understand better the law and its application. In addition, Chancery courts aided common law courts by providing relief to procedural and substantive defects in the common law system. Plucknett (1956) identifies such faults as slowness, expense, inefficiency, technicality, antiquated methods of proof, and suspicions of volunteer witnesses as particular areas where Chancery courts helped common law courts.

Having one court system existing primarily to correct the defects of another court system is not desirable in perpetuity. Something had to give. Over the centuries, the rules of equity became as strict, consistent, and "legal" as those of the common law. The growth and formalization of equity finally provided an opportunity to unite the two legal systems, and in 1875 a Judicature Act removed the formal distinction between the two courts. Common law was now complete. From a historical base (feudal practices), the common legal tradition had basic principles (custom) and a sense of fairness (equity).

Civil Legal Tradition

Because the phrase *civil law* is familiar to American readers, it is necessary to distinguish the term's general use from its use in reference to a legal tradition. In its more typical usage in the United States, civil law is set against criminal law because it deals with private wrongs instead of the social wrongs handled by criminal law. In that manner, civil law deals with such matters as contracts, ownership of property, and payment for personal injury. However, in its original meaning, civil law referred to the code of laws collected by the Roman emperor Justinian. The *Corpus Juris Civilis* set the stage for subsequent law not only with Justinian's successors but eventually with Napoleon and his *Code Civil* (Code Napoleon) as proclaimed in 1804. The use of civil codes as a legal tradition spread across Europe and to such places as Quebec, Canada, and South America. As a result, in much of the world, the term *civil law* brings to mind a legal tradition based on *written codes,* not a specific type of law dealing with private wrongs. Because our concern throughout this book is with criminal justice systems, we will have no need to use civil law in reference to those laws regulating individual disputes. So when you read about civil law systems and civil legal traditions, place it in the context of a code of laws as first developed for the Roman Empire.

Just as the common legal tradition developed from several basic subtraditions, the civil tradition has its own underpinning (see Figure 4.3). Specifically, we look at the role played by Roman law, canon law, and codification.

Roman Law. Civil law's claim of being the oldest contemporary legal tradition rests on its link to Roman law. In turn, Roman law was the result of statutes, edicts of magistrates, and the interpretations of jurists (Kolbert, 1979; Watson, 1970).

Three legislative bodies created Roman law statutes. The *comitia centuriata* and *comitia tributa* enacted statutes known as *lex* (a collection of laws). The *concilium plebis* enacted *plebiscitum,* a law passed by the common people. These laws were binding only on the average citizen unless the Senate made it binding on the nobility and senators. The earliest form of written Roman law dates to 451 and 450 B.C., when a council of 10 men inscribed 12 bronze tablets with specifics

You Should Know!

HOW ABOUT SCANDINAVIA?

Scandinavian countries (i.e., Norway, Sweden, Denmark, Finland, Iceland, and the Faroe Islands) present an interesting problem in categorizing countries as falling into one of four legal traditions. Some have argued for a separate Scandinavian legal tradition, since these countries do not fit neatly into any of the four traditional families. Others have simply placed Scandinavian law as a subgroup of the civil legal tradition, or have described it as falling between the common and civil traditions.

The problem, as Lillebakken (1996/1997) notes, is that Scandinavian law relies on codes (making it similar to civil law countries), but those codes have been developed in a rather unsystematic manner rather than as a specific codification document designed to replace all prior law (making it dissimilar to civil law countries). Also, when applying the law, Scandinavian judges are expected to base decisions on specific statutes (similar to judges in civil law countries), but the courts also cite legal precedents supporting their decision (similar to judges in common law countries). Contradictions like these simply remind us that a four-category classification of legal traditions may be convenient, but it is also rather artibrary.

concerning the rights of Roman citizens. These Twelve Tables were approved as *lex* by the *comitia centuriata* in 450 B.C. They provided the basis for private rights of Roman citizens, consisted mainly of ancient custom, and concerned procedure more than substantive law. For example, the opening passage of the Twelve Tables states, "If a man is summoned to appear in court and does not come, let witnesses be heard and then let the plaintiff seize him. If he resists or absconds, the plaintiff can use force. If he is ill or too old, let the plaintiff provide a beast to bring him: but if he declines this offer, the plaintiff need not provide a carriage . . ." (quoted in Kolbert, 1979, p. 13).

Superior magistrates, especially the praetor, of Rome issued edicts that initially identified how magistrates planned to fulfill their duties. Complaints between Roman citizens were taken to the Urban Praetor, who handled cases of Roman *jus civile* (private law). By issuing edicts at the start of his term, the praetor could identify the principles he would follow during his one year in office. Although the edict was valid only for that praetor's term, a tendency developed for praetors to borrow from their predecessor's edict. This certainly is different from *stare decisis* in common law, but it does suggest an early means of attaining consistency in procedure (Watson, 1970). A more appropriate link between the praetor and common law refers to a means for attending to fairness. In this manner, the edicts became a body of law known as the *jus honorarium,* which was to Roman law what equity was to common law (Kolbert, 1979). Advance notice of the procedural rules he would follow allowed the praetor to give the process a sense of fairness.

Finally, Roman law was the result of interpretations by jurists. These jurists were statesmen knowledgeable in the law, not lawyers or legal practitioners in the modern sense. The emperor would confer upon certain jurists the right or privilege of giving written opinions on cases. Those opinions would become binding on the parties in the dispute. Because jurists also could write on imaginary cases, there came to be an extensive, and often contradictory, collection of legal opinions on a variety of cases. At this historical point, the emperor Justinian entered and provided one of the most important legal documents in the civil legal tradition.

Justinian became emperor in 527, succeeding his uncle Justin. As one of his first acts, he charged 16 experts with examining the existing juristic writings and refining the massive bulk of material then serving as Roman law. The resulting *Corpus Juris Civilis* was meant to eliminate incorrect, obscure, and repetitive material. Further, it was to resolve conflicts and doubts while organizing the remaining material into some systematic form (Merryman, 1985). At its completion in 533, the *Corpus Juris Civilis* stood as the sole authority for the laws and juristic writings.

Interestingly, most of the material in the *Corpus Juris Civilis* was over 300 years old and, therefore predated Christianity. Emperor Constantine (275–337) was the first Roman emperor to become Christian, and Theodosius (346–395) made Christianity the sole religion of the empire. Obviously, Justinian's compilers had access to some 200 years of ecclesiastical law that they chose to ignore. Although church law did not have much impact on Roman law, it was an important factor in the development of the civil legal tradition.

Canon Law. The Roman Catholic Church developed canon law to govern the Church and the rights and obligations of her followers. Roman civil law was the universal law of the worldly empire, and canon law was the universal law of the spiritual realm (Merryman, 1985). Civil courts administered Roman civil law, whereas ecclesiastical courts managed the canon law.

The primary source providing the specifics of canon law were the various *decretal letters.* These decrees were authoritative papal statements concerning controversial points in doctrine or ecclesiastical law. Basically, any matter the papacy considered relevant to the well-being of the whole Christian body public was potential subject matter for a decretal letter. The decretal letter had official and binding force and in essence was a judicial verdict signifying appropriate behavior and thought.

With the Church claiming jurisdiction over the entire life of Christians, potential conflict with the state was inevitable. In fact, the papacy and the government in Constantinople were in serious conflict from the time of Pope Leo I (440–461) onward. By Pope Gregory's time (590–604), canon law had secured a foothold in the legal system of the empire. Ullman (1975) suggests that a main reason for this ascendancy of canon law was its flexibility. With Gregory, canon law operated as a living law, providing a written system of law for contemporaries. The Roman law, as codified in the *Corpus Juris Civilis,* stood in stark contrast with its centuries-old standards. Canon law developed from real situations in the current time period and was flexible enough to absorb features of other systems, like those of the Germanic tribes.

By the ninth century, both Roman law and canon law had experienced their heyday. Germanic and other invaders provided modifications as the empire collapsed, but by the eleventh century each had reestablished itself as superior systems. Law became a major object of study at Bologna and other Italian universities, and Italy became the legal center of the Western world (Merryman, 1985).

Scholars from many countries came to study the *Corpus Juris Civilis*, and, as a result, it provided a base for a common law of Europe *(jus commune)*. This situation prevailed until the fifteenth century, when the idea of national sovereignty gave rise to national law. The foundation had been laid, however, and Roman civil law, and canon law to a lesser extent, remained a large part of the legal systems in western Europe.

IMPACT

AMERICA'S CIVIL LAW TRADITION

The United States is among the countries identified with the common legal tradition. Yet the lack of surprise with which you read that statement distorts the role played by the civil tradition in America's history. Consider, for example, the role played by Spanish and Mexican civil law in the development of the American West.

Even after receiving statehood (1850), California was feeling the impact of centuries under a civil legal tradition. For example, upon their arrival in California, Americans found Mexican lawmen called *jueces de campo*, or judges of the plains. In 1851 the California legislature repealed all prior laws with one exception—the statute relating to judges of the plains (Ruiz, 1974). Mexican law required all cattle runs and drives passing through a city, town, or village to be inspected for brands and ownership by the judges of the plains. Those judges could arrest suspected cattle or horse thieves and take them to the nearest magistrate. In the absence of any English equivalent, the California legislature gave this Mexican law enforcer the same powers as a sheriff, constable, or police officer.

California's use of the judges of the plains exemplifies the necessity of making adjustments in applying English common law to a dramatically different culture. Settlers in the American frontier had to stretch their imagination when applying the ancient customs and traditions of eleventh-century England to the legal problems that arose with the cattle drives and gold rushes of the nineteenth-century West.

The civil law tradition also predisposed some areas to recognize the usefulness of law codes. Miners' codes served as bodies of law in western mining camps from Colorado to California. These rough but workable rules and processes provided a means to record claims, to decide whose claim was first, to settle disputes among claimants, and to enforce decisions of miners' "courts" (Friedman, 1973). Answers to such questions were not easily identified in English common law.

IMPACT

AMERICA'S CIVIL LAW TRADITION

Despite flirtations with codification and the civil tradition, the legacy followed by American legal systems has been that of the common law. Admittedly, Louisiana did more than flirt with civil law. Louisiana Codes of 1808, 1825, and 1870 borrowed heavily from the French Code Napoleon. As a result, Louisiana judges decide cases (private more than public law) chiefly on the basis of codes rather than prior decisions. The complicated history of the civil law in Louisiana (nicely reviewed by Tucker, 1956) reminds us that aspects of the civil tradition have helped shape a specifically American legal system.

Undoubtedly, one area in which law in America (and indeed in all common law countries) has become more civil-like is with the increased reliance on statute as an important source for law. Yet, even when the legislature plays a primary lawmaking role, we view the resulting statutes in a special way. As Sereni explained, "The content of statutory provisions is not authoritatively established unless and until they have been construed by the courts" (1956, p. 66). For example, the U.S. Congress can pass a law prohibiting the burning of the American flag. In a country where codification prevails, the courts would be obliged to find all flag burners guilty and apply the appropriate punishment. Because of the common legal tradition in the United States, a law prohibiting flag burning is not "authoritatively established" until the courts accept it as such. As this flag burning example shows, then, despite the obvious increase in statutes as a source of law, countries following the common legal tradition are still distinguished from their civil tradition cousins in terms of the power courts have to evaluate the legislature's work.

Codification. The components of the civil legal tradition have relied primarily on written (codified) laws. Though not fully realized until the *Corpus Juris Civilis,* Roman civil law had a tradition, dating back to the Twelve Tables, of laws being binding because they were authorized and recorded. Canon law supported the codification principle through papal decrees. Codification became so entrenched that in 319 Emperor Constantine could declare, "The authority of custom and long usage is not slight but not to the extent that it will prevail against reason or against statute" (quoted in Kolbert, 1979). Roman law and canon law provided a tradition of codification that, in turn, emphasized a revolutionary nature of law and stressed its written form.

When Justinian announced the *Corpus Juris Civilis,* his goal was to abolish all prior law. When the French codified their law in the Code Napoleon, all prior law in those areas was repealed. Of course, both *Corpus Juris Civilis* and the Code Napoleon had principles of prior law incorporated in the new codes. However, in each case, and by implication in all cases of codification (Merryman, 1985;

Sereni, 1956), the codes received their validity not from a previous incarnation, but from their incorporation and reenactment in the new code.

The relevance of codification's revolutionary nature becomes clearer when contrasted with common law. For example, Merryman (1985) notes that codes exist in common law jurisdictions (for example, the codes of Louisiana and California); but those codes are not based on the ideology or cultural reality that support French or German codes. Specifically, codes under common law do not abolish all prior law in their field (that is, they are not revolutionary). Instead, they claim to perfect and supplement it. The view of civil law codes as replacing, instead of extending, prior law more appropriately distinguishes the civil and common traditions than does the presence of codes themselves.

Besides its revolutionary nature, codification is distinguished by its written form. Some people argue that civil law is distinct from common law in that the former is written and the latter is unwritten. This distinction is misleading. Actually, the distinction between written and unwritten law has little to do with whether the law is put in writing (Postema, 1986). *Unwritten law* exists in the customs of the community and is binding by that fact, regardless of whether someone wrote it down. *Written law,* on the other hand, exists and is binding because it was enacted by a recognized authority (for example, a monarch or a legislature) following formal procedures.

Codification gives civil law a revolutionary character and written format that adds to its separate identity among legal families. Upon combining those features with the historical links to Roman and canon law, we have the basic ingredients of the civil legal tradition.

Socialist Legal Tradition

The socialist legal tradition is the newest of the four discussed here, but its roots are as deep as those of the other three. Not all comparative legalists believe that the socialist legal family constitutes a separate tradition. The historical link between civil law and law in socialist countries leads some to believe that these legal systems are simply a modification of the civil law tradition (see Quigley, 1989, for a particularly persuasive argument). However, I side with David (David & Brierley, 1985), Hazard (1969), and Merryman (1985), who are among those believing that a close look at law under socialism clearly identifies distinctions warranting a separate category for a socialist legal tradition. Admittedly, political and economic changes beginning in 1989 have modified the legal system in many former socialist countries. Other countries, such as China, Cuba, North Korea, and Vietnam, were less affected by challenges to traditional socialism. The result is a legal-tradition category with several legal systems implementing shared characteristics in a variety of ways. That is why we use the term *legal tradition* rather than *legal system* in this discussion.

To identify a separate socialist legal tradition, we must begin with the development of Soviet law. In this process, we must remember that just as the civil legal tradition owes part of its existence to a political entity no longer existing (that is, the Roman Empire), the socialist legal tradition is traced to the former Soviet Union. As such, the legal system of the Union of Soviet Socialist Republics (USSR) provided the philosophical, and sometimes technical, base for a socialist legal tradition. As socialism spread, other countries set up a new legal system borrowing from the Soviet model but placed in their own cultural situation. So the components of Soviet law (*Russian law*, a view of law as artificial, and *Marxism-Leninism*) became the basic elements of the socialist legal tradition (see Table 4.1).

Russian Law. In 395 the Roman Empire divided into eastern and western parts. The civil legal tradition was more closely tied to Rome and the Western Empire, although influence from the eastern section via Justinian was immense. Russian legal history borrows more from the Eastern, or Byzantine Empire, primarily because Russia's contact with the eastern "Romans" did not occur until the tenth century. By then, Byzantine law, as a historical extension of Roman law, was becoming more closely linked to canon law.

As with all legal systems, customary norms oriented the initial legal effort of Russians. With the public conversion to Christianity around 989, custom was reduced to writing so that, in the Byzantine tradition, it could be related to the influence of the Church. Of the various princes becoming involved in recording laws, Grand Prince Iaroslav the Wise (1015–1054) is credited with compiling the first Russian Code of Laws. Iaroslav's *Pravda* is a brief document based on customary law with emphasis on penal law (see the English translation by Vernadsky, 1947). A crowd of independent states made up Russia until Mongol invaders destroyed Kiev in 1240 and made Russia part of the Mongol Empire. The Mongols were primarily interested in maintaining power and collecting taxes, and produced little change in Russian life, but they did prevent Russian contact with the new ideas dramatically changing western Europe during the Renaissance in the 1300s and 1400s.

The Russian princes surviving under Mongol domination still played the roles of judges and rule makers in their principalities. Russian law near the close

Table 4.1 Some Cultural Components of Legal Traditions

	Common Tradition	**Civil Tradition**	**Socialist Tradition**	**Islamic Tradition**
Do legal rights and obligations lie with the individual (private law) or the state (public law)?	Public law, with both the individual and the state having a legal personality.	Public law when concern is with the state's legal personality; private law when concern is with the individual's legal personality.	Public law, because the state has an interest in all transactions.	Private law, because the concern always centers on the individual's legal personality.
What is the position of the judiciary in relation to other government branches?	Courts share in balancing power.	Courts have equal but separate power.	Courts are subordinate to the legislature.	Courts and other government branches are subordinate to the *Shari'a*.

of the fifteenth century was essentially a series of private collections consisting of princely enactments and, secondarily, of customary and Byzantine law (Zigel, 1974). Control by Mongols essentially ended by 1490, and in 1497 the Grand Prince of Moscow issued a new Code of Laws for all territories subject to Moscow. This code was a digest of the earlier laws and the first formulation of the basic principles of a new monarchical regime. One of those principles gave the grand prince, soon to be called the *czar,* authority to decide how his various lords must judge in their courts (Vernadsky, 1947; Zigel, 1974).

With the reign of the czars came the firmly established idea of law as reflecting the will of a monarch. Customary law was still relevant, because princes and czars felt no need to establish rules for everyone and for all situations. That is not to say that customary law limited their power. Instead, princes and czars simply felt no challenge to their authority if customary law was used to handle disputes in which they had minimal interest. The indifferent attitude of rulers toward firmly establishing a countrywide code lasted until 1832. Before that date, attempts to modernize Russian law are more accurately described as efforts to consolidate and explain than to reform and redesign. In 1832 a codification of Russian law was finally established, and in 1855 a penal code was created. Though late by western European standards, Russia finally had a written law.

Law as Artificial. The English came to appreciate the rule of law as binding because it recognized immemorial custom. The Romans and western Continentals came to appreciate the rule of law as binding because it was appropriately authorized and recorded. The Russians never came to appreciate the rule of law at all. This is not meant to be a disparaging statement. It is simply recognition of a difference in the Russian attitude toward law compared to the attitude toward law held by other Europeans. As an old Russian proverb expresses it, "Law is like a wagon tongue, it goes wherever you turn it" (Reshetar, 1978, p. 250).

On the Continent and in England, people considered law a natural complement to morality and a fundamental base for society. This idea did not take root in Russia. David and Brierley (1985) suggest that this is partly due to the absence of Russian jurists and the late appearance of a Russian university (1755) and a Russian legal literature (mid- to late nineteenth century). Perhaps more important is the point that written law was foreign to Russian mentality. Law was deemed the arbitrary work of an autocratic sovereign, a privilege of the bourgeoisie and, therefore, of no import to the common person. Russians took for granted that the sovereign was above the law. The impact that this view of "law as artificial" had on the Russian people becomes clearer as we move to the role played by Marxist philosophy. A basic tenet of Marxism-Leninism is that under communism the need for law will wither away. That concept would likely have been difficult for twentieth-century British, French, or Germans to accept. Yet in Russia, where law had been essentially ineffective and artificial for hundreds of years, people found the concept neither surprising nor unreasonable (cf. David & Brierley, 1985).

Interestingly, Chinese history reflects some traditions similar to those in Russia. Clark (1989) points out that the Chinese people have never been treated very well by their governments, and as a result, the citizens are not inclined to wholeheartedly trust and respect government of any type. Because law was provided by those very governments, the Chinese also came to view it as rather artificial. As a result, Chinese reaction to misbehavior has a long tradition of being handled in an informal (that is, nongovernmental) manner by the people most directly involved in the violation.

In several of the remaining chapters we will see examples of this Chinese preference for grassroots handling of crime. It will be good to remember that China (arguably the best contemporary example of the socialist legal tradition) shares some historical and cultural features with Russia. That common heritage may partly explain why a socialist legal tradition, with its concepts like "law as artificial," was more acceptable to China's people.

Marxism-Leninism. The Bolshevik revolution (November 7, 1917) provided the primary ingredient for a separate socialist legal tradition. To this point, the history of Russian law, and even the idea of law as artificial, could have provided the background for yet another country joining the civil legal tradition. The communist revolution in Russia forced its legal development to take a different path.

Marx and Engles had proposed a scientific socialism based on their understanding of laws ruling the development of society and humanity. Vladimir Lenin, who was appointed head of the new Soviet state after the Bolshevik victory, had been absorbed in the study of Marxism. Unfortunately, neither Marx nor Lenin provided real specifics about establishing a legal system once a communist revolution occurred. Instead, general principles had to suffice for about five years until codification began. Meanwhile, courts loyal to the working class were instructed to apply the old imperial codes as interpreted by the revolutionary consciousness of the judges.

The primary principle directing the new Soviet law was the idea that law is subordinate to policy. Law was a means to be used by the leaders to achieve some desirable end. It was not an absolute value dictating the leader's conduct. The history of law in Russia meant that the people did not see this idea as necessarily original. Because law is artificial, the reasoning went, it might just as well be subordinate to policy as it was in the past to the will of princes and czars.

The policy to which law is subordinate places the rights of the collectivized economy and the socialist state above the idea of law or the rights of an individual. Socialists view this subordination to policy as an improvement. Although agreeing with bourgeois-democratic revolutions that claim all people are equal before the law, the Marxist adds that law is sacred to the bourgeois because it is his design, enacted with his consent, and exists for his benefit and protection (Terebilov, 1973). With all that going for him, the socialist asks, why wouldn't the capitalist believe that the rule of law is supreme?

In 1992 one of the first examples of the potential for damaging consequences when following a "law is subordinate to policy" course was made public ("Russia's system on trial," 1992). Andrei Chikatilo, a 56-year-old former schoolteacher, was tried in a Russian court for raping, slaying, and partially cannibalizing 52 victims. The case attracted attention not only because of its gruesome nature but also because it highlighted some of the defects of the former Soviet legal system. For example, following a policy of placing ideology above public safety, residents of the town where the murders (which started in 1978) occurred were not warned for more than five years that a maniac was killing young women and children. Furthermore, Soviet authorities eventually admitted that, in an attempt to solve the crimes and stop the killings, they executed the wrong man before Chikatilo was arrested near a murder scene in late 1990 ("Russia's system on trial," 1992).

The Chikatilo case is an extreme example (and not one that could happen only in a socialist legal system), but it does accentuate types of problems that might develop when law is used by leaders to achieve some desirable end rather than as an absolute value dictating the leader's conduct. By seeing law as a tool, rather than an absolute value, Lenin argued that law could well serve the purposes of socialism. Also, despite examples like the Chikatilo case, those purposes are presumed to benefit society. More specifically, socialist law—and this is clearly a distinguishing feature—exists to serve both economic and educational goals.

Socialism demands greater effort by leaders in respect to economics than capitalism requires of its leaders. As a result, the economic task of socialist law is significant. Of course, law can come to the aid of capitalist economies also, but it presumably does so with its moral grounding intact (see David & Brierley, 1985). For example, law in a capitalist economy tells its citizens to observe the rules of justice and morality and, as a result, the society will enjoy economic order. Socialist law says it will help provide the desirable economic order and the result will be justice and morality for the citizens. Thus, the socialist attitude toward law is the complete reverse of the capitalist attitude.

More than once, Lenin identified the educational nature of socialist law (see Terebilov, 1973). That is, Lenin believed that law must be used in a socialist state to educate citizens in a spirit of new, socialist relations and in the new rules of the community. Judges were charged with the duty of ensuring the success of gov-

In the News

EDUCATION THROUGH EXECUTION

A Chinese expression proclaims that one must "kill the chicken to frighten the monkey." The expression takes application in China's frequent use of the death penalty for offenses ranging from property and public order crimes to violent offenses. A belief in killing the chicken to frighten the monkey is a good example of the view that law must be used to educate (deter, in this case) potential offenders. To this end, Chinese officials have made sure that executions are well publicized and accompanied with appropriate propaganda. Lepp (1990) explains that news of executions is spread throughout the country with the aid of television, radio, and the press. Occasionally, an execution is conducted in public or a corpse might remain exposed after the punishment is applied.

Amnesty International (1998) suggests that despite the appearance of broad publicity of executions in China, there are probably even more executions than are publicized. In their 1998 report, Amnesty International cites "incomplete" figures of 1067 people known to have been executed in China during 1998. China, along with the Democratic Republic of Congo, Iran, and the United States, account for 80 percent of executions worldwide.

ernment policy by actively participating in educating the people. As David and Brierley (1985) put it, Lenin's philosophy was that socialist law, and the decision of judges, should be so reasonable that every honest citizen, including the person losing the case, would support and agree with the law that served as the basis for the decision.

Because law is an aspect of policy in a socialist system, the courts do not exist just to interpret and apply the law. They also must help ensure the success of government policies by educating the people. Socialist law does not establish a rule of order by providing a principle for use in solving disputes. Instead, it is a means of guiding society toward the communist ideal. This position is clearly held today in the People's Republic of China as will become apparent in later discussions in this text of public legal education in China. In fact, the use of law to "educate" misguided Chinese citizens does not even have to wait until the court stage. Chinese police can impose the administrative penalty of "re-education through labor" on persons whose offenses are not serious enough to justify criminal punishment handed out by the courts (Turack, 1999).

With the economic and educational assistance of law and the legal system, the socialist state can progress to communism. Under this philosophy, once the goal of communism is achieved, crime ceases and there is no need for law or the legal machinery. Until that time, laws, police, courts, and prisons are necessary to ensure that everyone faithfully observes and obeys government instructions (Terebilov, 1973). The government policy and instructions (that is, socialist law) to be obeyed have their main source in legislation, because that is the simplest and most straightforward way to express the will of the people. Generally, this was accomplished via the deputies of the various Soviets. More specifically, it was secured by legislative actions of the Supreme Soviet.

Socialist Legal Tradition After the USSR's Demise. As noted earlier, we are discussing a socialist legal tradition, not a Soviet legal tradition. Other countries falling within the socialist legal family share aspects of the Soviet tradition. Specifically, the Marxism-Leninism perspective of law being subordinate to policy and the economic/educational functions of law, are common throughout the socialist tradition. In 1990, for example, two Chinese public security officials wrote of ways to "prevent and punish law-breaking criminal offences [sic] by comprehensively employing political, economic, administrative, educational, cultural and legal means" (Bo & Yisheng, 1990, p. 1). The placement of "legal means" at the end of that list was probably not accidental—not because the preference is for extralegal or even illegal means, but rather because legal means under the socialist tradition is merely one of several social forces to be used for keeping order.

The role Russian law played in creating a socialist legal tradition is relevant to other socialist countries only to the extent that it helped form Soviet law. The view of law as artificial was not as entrenched in many post–World War II socialist countries as it had been in pre-1917 Russia. As a result, the legal systems of some of those new socialist countries were anything but duplicates of the Soviet legal system. Even so, the philosophical base in Marxism provides sufficient similarity to assign membership in a socialist legal tradition.

The term *legal tradition* refers to cultural aspects of law as well as to the technical attributes. For example, Louisiana's historical link to civil law and its reliance on codification is not enough to place it in the civil legal tradition. Similarly, even dramatic political and economic changes in a country will not automatically move the country from one legal tradition to another. For example, Warsaw Pact nations did not undertake an unrestricted adoption of the Soviet legal system after World War II. Poland, Hungary, and the German Democratic Republic retained technical aspects from their civil law heritage. Just as Soviet law considered the civil law history of those countries while getting them to accept socialist legality, any subsequent political and economic changes in those nations cannot dismiss the 50-year heritage of socialism.

Movement away from Communist Party monopoly does not require, nor could it achieve, complete disregard for the role socialism played in each country's legal history. Thus, Danilenko and Burnham (1999) explain that political and legal reforms have largely reunited the Russian legal system with the civil law family, but the remnants of the socialist past continue to set Russia apart from other members of the contemporary civil legal tradition. Therefore, identification of a separate socialist legal tradition remains necessary for the future not only so that we can understand existing socialist nations, but also so that we can appreciate both the changes occurring and those that are necessary as other countries try to leave the socialist legal tradition.

Islamic (Religious/Philosophical) Legal Tradition

As noted at this chapter's start, the last legal tradition covered here is the religious/philosophical. Although it has included such important legal systems as the Hindu and Judaic ones, its primary contemporary example is Islamic law.

With over 1 billion followers, Muslims represent about 20 percent of the world's population. As a base of comparison, Roman Catholics are about 17 percent *(2000 World Almanac and Book of Facts)*. Muslims live all around the world but have their highest concentrations in the Middle East, Africa, and Asia.

Along with Christians and Jews, Muslims believe in one God, whom Muslims call Allah. Allah's messenger was the prophet Muhammad (570?–632), who had been preceded by Jesus and the Old Testament prophets. The religion preached by Muhammad is Islam (Arabic for "submission"), and its followers are "those who submit to Allah" (Muslims).

Compared with the other three legal traditions, Islamic law is uncommon in its singularity of purpose. Islam recognizes no distinction between a legal system and other controls on a person's behavior. In fact, Islam is said to provide all the answers to questions about appropriate behavior in any sphere of life.

As a legal tradition, Islam is unique among the four discussed here. Although each of the other three took some principles and techniques from religion, the traditions themselves remained distinct and separate from religion. Islamic law, however, is intrinsic to Islamic faith and life in Islamic countries. Importantly, not all Muslim societies are correctly identified as solely bound by Islamic law. Countries like Jordan and Kuwait have both civil and Islamic aspects in their legal system, whereas other nations combine Islamic and common traditions (for example, Kenya and Nigeria) or even have a socialist aspect (Algeria). Muslim countries providing the clearest examples of widespread use of Islamic law include Afghanistan, Iran, Iraq, and Saudi Arabia.

Like all religions, Islam has sects, the *Shi'ite* and *Sunni* branches being the primary ones. Even within the sects, different schools of thought developed regarding legal questions. As a result, Islamic law is not uniformly applied throughout Islamic countries any more than civil, common, or socialist law is consistent across nations following those traditions. Yet despite variation in the way Islamic law is interpreted and applied, media reports often portray it as a harsh and inflexible system that is inappropriate in today's world. Certainly there are criminals who have been amputated, beheaded, and stoned under Islamic law. However, there have also been criminals whose punishment has been set aside because of their victim's forgiveness. In fact, the *Qur'an* encourages forgiveness with the same vigor that it advocates retaliation. That point, which becomes more clear in the following discussion, is good to keep in mind so that our media-inspired notions of Islamic law do not prevent a more dispassionate understanding of its operation.

Islamic law is best discussed by referring to some of its primary components. Specifically, we review the role played by the *Shari'a,* the use of witnesses and oaths, and the *mazalim* and civil extensions (see Figure 4.3).

The Shari'a. Before Muhammad, Arabic tribes operated under customary law, of which blood revenge was a major tenet. After the angel Gabriel called Muhammad to be a prophet, Muhammad preached about the need to replace old tribal loyalty with equality and brotherhood among all Muslims. In 622 he fled from harassment in Mecca to greater appreciation in the city of Medina. As his prophet status spread, Muhammad was asked to judge disputes between Muslims. Generally, he followed the customary law of the town (to the extent it was consistent with Islamic principles) but in cases where that law was lacking, he turned to Allah for direction. Muhammad provided no tables, commandments, codes, or digests. Instead, Allah's revelations and Muhammad's own behavior provided answers to the quarrels and questions of the townsfolk. In time, these events comprised the primary ingredients of Islamic law: the *Qur'an* and the *Sunna.*

Islamic law is called the *Shari'a,* "the path to follow." In its purest form, it consists of the writings in the *Qur'an* (the holy book of Islam) and the *Sunna* (the statements and deeds of the Prophet). However, even taken together these two elements do not make up a comprehensive code of law. In fact, they hardly constitute the bare skeleton of a legal system (Coulson, 1969). Therefore, added to the primary sources were two secondary sources of law: analogical reasoning *(qiyas)* and consensus by jurists *(ijma).*

The *Qur'an,* as the "word of God," was recorded by scribes and edited by scholars. It has little legislative material, with only about 10 percent of its 6237 verses containing rules. Only some 200 of those actually deal with legal issues in the strict sense of the term (Lippman, McConville & Yerushalmi, 1988, p. 26). In any event, the *Qur'an* provides the laws as given by Allah. Islamic law, then, is considered by Muslims to be the divinely ordained system of God's commands; to deny that point would be to renounce the Islam religion.

The second basic source of the *Shari'a* contains the collected actions and sayings of Muhammad. This *Sunna* includes reports *(hadith)* that explain, clarify, and amplify (but do not add to) the *Qur'an*. For example, in the area of substantive criminal law, the *Sunna* advises:

> *Three classes of offenders are not to be punished: the child before coming to age, the sleeper until he wakes up, and the insane until he becomes sensible (quoted in Lippman et al., 1988, p. 30).*

In applying the *Qur'an* and *Sunna,* two camps formed. One side took a strict interpretation and believed that every rule of law must be derived from the *Qur'an* or the *Sunna.* The other camp believed that human reason and personal opinion should be used to elaborate the law. In the eighth century, the disagreement resulted in the first fundamental conflict of principle in Islamic jurisprudence (Coulson, 1969) and provided the foundation for one of two secondary sources of Islamic law.

In the early ninth century, the jurist Shafi'a proposed a compromise that some authors claim earned him the title "father of Muslim jurisprudence" (Coulson, 1969). Basically, Shafi'a sided with the strict interpreters while acknowledging that there were gaps that human reason was helpful in filling. Human reasoning, he believed, had to be subordinate to principles established by divine revelation in order to make sure it did not result in human legislative authority. Cases not seemingly answered by the *Qur'an* or *Sunna* were handled by a process known as *reasoning by analogy,* or *qiyas.* These decisions were to make use of human reasoning as long as that reasoning had divine law as its starting point. For example, Lippman et al. (1988) note that some judges have sentenced committers of sodomy (not mentioned in the *Qur'an* or *Sunn*a) to the same penalty the *Qur'an* provides for adultery by reasoning that sodomy and adultery are similar offenses.

The next secondary source of the *Shari'a* draws upon the knowledge of legal scholars. Following Muhammad's death, the caliphs (leaders of the Muslim community) made use of consultants to help in the proper interpretation of the *Qur'an* and *Sunna.* Not surprisingly, some scholars became more prominent than others, and each had supporters for his interpretations. Schools of legal thought developed around four particular jurists (Malik, Hanifa, Shafi'i, and Hanbal). By the end of the ninth century, the four schools had developed documents telling how their school interpreted questions or solved unique cases. This process was known as the *doctrine of consensus,* or *ijma.* When qualified jurists had unanimous agreement on a given point, their opinion was considered binding and having absolute authority. Recall the use of English juries to identify custom and common usage. Similarly, Muslims used a "jury" of scholars to identify the appropriate meaning of a *Qur'anic* text. Because there was consensus among jurists about how to resolve a unique problem, an opinion by an individual judge was transformed to a statement of divine law.

With the *Qur'an* and *Sunna* serving as primary sources, and *qiyas* and *ijma* as secondary, the *Shari'a* was complete. Yet, although the law was God-given, its application fell to humans. A feature Muslims developed to apply the law was a reliance on witnesses and oath taking. Their importance under Islamic law and uniqueness among the world's legal traditions allow them to be highlighted as a basic, distinguishing component of Islamic law.

Witnesses and Oaths. The mechanism for administration of *Shari'a* is the *qadi's* court. Originally, there were no provisions for courts with many judges, for counsel by laypeople, nor for any system of appeals. Instead, the single *qadi* sat in judgment over the facts of the case and how the law should apply. The facts were created primarily through oral testimony as substantiated and validated by reliable witnesses. In fact, a *qadi's* primary task was to certify a person as having the necessary qualities to assure the truthfulness of his statements.

The importance of witnesses and oaths has been a hallmark of Islamic law since its earliest development. The *hadith* in the *Sunna* was validated by naming the line of respected men through whom the stories about the Prophet had passed. In other words, a recollection about Muhammad's statements or actions was considered true because trusted and reliable men passed the recollection from generation to generation. The tradition of Islamic law, then, is to seek truth through statements made by reliable people.

The *Shari'a* does not distinguish between private and public law. Therefore, for purposes of *Shari'a,* there are no public wrongs to which the "state" must respond. Actions common law would see as "crimes" (public wrongs) are handled in the same manner as actions called "torts" (private wrongs) in common law. If accusation of a *Qur'anic* or *Sunna* violation is made under *Shari'a,* the accuser is responsible for initiating the action. Consequently, upon being assaulted or

In the News

OATHS AND EVIDENCE IN ISLAMIC LAW

A very controversial trial in Pakistan in 1995 provides some insight into the use of oaths and evidence under Islamic law (Dahlburg, 1995; Rashid, 1995). Two Christians were convicted of blasphemy against Islam (a crime that carries mandatory death) after being accused of scrawling anti-Islamic slogans on a mosque wall. The conviction was interesting because it was based on oaths rather than evidence.

The offending words had been immediately washed off the walls, so there was no evidence supporting the accusations. There was not even testimony as to the nature of the writing because witnesses who had seen them refused to repeat the words in court. They were too offensive for devout Muslims to say aloud, the witnesses said. The defense attorneys argued that there was no evidence against their clients, but the trial judge disagreed and found the two men guilty. The judge reasoned that the allegations were so serious that no faithful Muslim would falsely make them.

The idea that an accusation must be true or the accuser would not make it seems unusual to may observers. In fact, a Pakistani appeals court agreed there was no evidence on which to base guilt, and the convictions were overturned. Regardless of the appellate ruling, the lower court's decision is instructive because it highlights the role some judges play in oral statements given by devout Muslims. In the absence of evidence, oral testimony and oaths are considered effective ways to determine truth under Islamic law.

stolen from, for example, it becomes your responsibility to bring a complaint against the offender. You show the truthfulness of your complaint (that is, prove your case) by presenting witnesses on your behalf and/or taking appropriate oaths. The *Qur'an* and *Sunna* set down the number of witnesses and type of oath required. For example, proof of adultery requires four witnesses, whereas theft can be proved with just two (see Lippman et al., 1988, pp. 42–45).

Accusers must always shoulder the burden of proof. They do this by calling witnesses who give oral testimony to the truth of the accuser's claim. The witnesses must be male adult Muslims (some *qadi* allow two women to count as one man) of high moral character. The witnesses must testify directly about their personal knowledge of the truth. Upon presenting the required number of qualified witnesses, the *qadi* rules in favor of the accuser. This is done without cross-examination of the witnesses or even presentation of evidence for the defendant. The problem, as you can well imagine, is that few offenses occur in the presence of two or more witnesses. Unless four devout male Muslims were watching while the defendant committed adultery, or two such witnesses observed the defendant burglarize a home, it would be difficult to win a case via witnesses alone.

Without any real evidence, judgment is for the defendant. More often, however, some evidence exists but is simply incomplete. At this point, the tradition of oath taking enters the court procedures. As Rosen (1989) describes it, the oath under *Shari'a* is very different from its quaint ritual status in western jurisprudence. Under Islamic law, witnesses are not sworn before testifying, nor is there any punishment for perjury. In fact, given the nature of the proceeding, the law assumes that a person may well make statements that do not bear on the truth. Rosen (1989) compares the process to bartering in the marketplace. Statements are tossed out in court to get a reaction in the same manner that one tosses out a price at the bazaar just to see how the merchant responds. In the courtroom, witnesses speak freely, and judges inquire cleverly, but no one is held to the implications of truth until truth is attached via an oath.

Oaths are taken either toward the character of the parties or the actual occurrences in the case. However, the key oath in *qadi* court is the decisory oath. If neither side can present adequate support for its claim, one party may challenge the other to take an oath in support of the latter's assertions. If the opponent does so, he automatically wins. Or he can refer the oath back to the challenger, who may achieve victory by then swearing as to his own truthfulness.

At this point, the power of the *qadi* comes into play and makes this oath-taking process different from similar procedures in other systems. In Islamic law the *qadi* decides which party will first challenge the other to take an oath. This is important, because the first to swear wins the case without the other having opportunity to rebut or in any way continue. In other systems the priority is determined by who is the plaintiff or defendant in the case. Here the *qadi* designates. He does so by looking for the person presumed most likely to know what is true about the matter at hand, or the one presumed to have been carrying out his or her tasks correctly. That person is then designated as the one first to be challenged to take the oath (Rosen, 1989).

The oath works under *Shari'a* because it is believed that false swearers will suffer the consequences on judgment day. The seriousness with which Muslims approach oath taking is shown by many cases in which persons have maintained their testimony right up to the moment of oath taking only to stop, refuse the oath, and surrender the case (Lippman et al., 1988).

Extensions of Islamic Law. The core of Islamic law is relatively inflexible. Conservative Islamic jurists claim that God, through the texts of Islamic law, offers the solution to every contemporary problem. Others have not always found Allah's guidance to be clear, consistent, and current. In fact, the idealistic scheme of procedure and evidence under *Shari'a* has required, since medieval times, alternative jurisdictions.

The non-*Shari'a* jurisdictions have taken many forms over the centuries. Petty commercial affairs were handled by the old inspector of the marketplace. Petty criminal cases went before the chief police officer. A "master of complaints" heard cases that the *qadi* failed to resolve (Coulson, 1969). Starting in the eleventh century, the collective description for these jurisdictions has been *mazalim,* or complaints court. The common feature of these courts was the significant discretion allowed in matters of procedure and evidence. Their charge was to resolve cases in the most effective way by using the best available evidence (Coulson, 1969; Lippman et al., 1988).

Mazalim jurisdictions provided a way for the ruler to have criminal and civil cases settled without submitting to the rigid requirements of *Shari'a.* These new "secular" courts were acceptable under Islamic law because the *Shari'a* gives the ruler power to enforce the law, to direct public security, and to maintain social order. The *mazalim* courts expanded to the point that their *qadi* were seen as representing the law of the ruler whereas *qadi* in *Shari'a* courts were regarded as representatives of Allah's law (Lippman et al., 1988).

As contact with western nations increased in the nineteenth and twentieth centuries, Islamic countries saw a need to make increased use of non-*Shari'a* courts and procedures. In areas like commerce, the ancient *Shari'a* simply could not respond to modern developments. In criminal law, the severe punishments demanded by *Shari'a* were regarded as antiquated and more appropriate for a tribal society. Modernization took the form of adopting European-style codes in many Islamic countries. By the end of the nineteenth century, *Shari'a* law had been generally abandoned in areas of commercial law, general civil law, and criminal law (Coulson, 1969). With the creation of new court systems (like the earlier *mazalim* jurisdictions) law became openly secular. The *Shari'a* remained responsible primarily for family law.

The westernization of Islamic countries and their law continued with minimal complaint until the 1970s. In the last quarter of the twentieth century, Muslim traditionalists clamored for a return to the purity of Islamic heritage. The wealth and influence of some Muslims allowed them to realign their business practices with their religious beliefs and laws. The changing pattern of world wealth meant that western business people could no longer dictate all the specifics of trade relations. Moreover, the Iranian revolution and the growing strength of more fundamental strains of Islam in Egypt, Syria, and elsewhere meant considerable pressure for tighter adherence to Islamic orthodoxy (Tomkins & Karim, 1987).

Despite movement toward affiliation with other legal traditions, Islamic law enters the twenty-first century as a separate tradition. Like the other three, the Islamic legal tradition will encompass diverse legal systems and undoubtedly be influenced by civil, common, and socialist countries. Nevertheless, it gives all appearances of maintaining its footing in the traditions of *Shari'a*, oaths and witnesses, and some modern version of *mazalim*.

COMPARING THE LEGAL TRADITIONS

Because a goal of this text is to use classification strategies to provide a sense of order to diverse institutions and procedures, it is appropriate to identify more carefully the similarities and differences among the four legal traditions (common, civil, socialist, and Islamic). Our classification strategy choices, you will recall, are either *synthetic* or *authentic* in nature. The former, resulting in artificial groups, requires knowledge of only one or two aspects of the groups being classified. The latter, which provides natural groups, depends on extensive investigation of the objects.

Many legal scholars and comparative criminal justicians have written about legal traditions (see Cole et al., 1987; David & Brierley, 1968; Terrill, 1982), but not as many have attempted a comprehensive analysis comparing the traditions based on some common criteria (see Ehrmann, 1976; Ingraham, 1987). The shortage of detailed information means that any current classification of legal traditions is most accurately described as synthetic rather than authentic. This means that the categories of common, civil, socialist, and Islamic should be seen as artificial groups arrived at based on some one or two criteria of interest to the scientist.

Predictivity is the main quality lacking in synthetic versus authentic classification. With the natural groups resulting from authentic classification, we could be told that a country's legal system falls in the civil legal tradition and immediately predict characteristics of that system. With synthetic groups, though, the best we can do is assume that the country has cultural similarities or links to western Europe, and speculate that the country's system might therefore share ideas with western Europe about such things as the appropriate source of law and the correct role of judges. The great variability of systems within each tradition means that we cannot yet (and maybe never will) achieve an authentic classification of legal families. A much more extensive investigation of the various systems and a clearer understanding of their characteristics must precede any progress toward identifying natural groups of law systems. Until then, we must rely on artificial groups like the four presented here.

Because artificial groups depend on the criteria chosen by the person doing the classification, the resulting categories reflect his or her interests. My interests are threefold: the values and attitudes supporting legal systems (cultural component), the characteristics of law in each system (substantive law), and procedures by which each system enforces the law (procedural law).

Chapter 3 explained that two essential ingredients of any justice system are substantive law and procedural law. With these components, law is delineated (substantive law) and the manner of enforcement is specified (procedural law). The cultural component is also important, because it often provides the key ingredient distinguishing legal systems between, and even within, legal traditions. For example, the state of Louisiana has specific substantive and procedural elements linking it to the civil legal tradition. However, the cultural elements of law in Louisiana are undoubtedly closer to those of Arkansas and Texas than to France.

In this chapter, certain aspects of each legal tradition have already been identified. Several of these speak of cultural elements relevant to the historical development of that legal tradition. Yet so far, discussion has not addressed specific areas of substantive and procedural law. To place comments about the four traditions in a broader context, we will now compare and contrast each in terms of cultural, substantive, and procedural aspects. Because remaining chapters provide country-specific information, this chapter continues its general discussion of the four traditions and saves individual treatment for later chapters.

Cultural Component

Although the role of culture is often noted as indispensable to understanding a country's legal system (see Friedman & Macaulay, 1969; Merryman, 1985; Rosen, 1989), it remains one of the least researched areas. Custom in common law, codification in civil law, the Russian view of law as artificial, and the importance Muslims place on oath taking are examples of cultural elements that help us appreciate each legal tradition. Sometimes the cultural differences hide similarities among the traditions. For example, Lippman et al. (1988) suggest that the Islamic restrictions on what evidence is allowable shows a shared belief with the common law principle that it is better to release a guilty person than to punish one who is innocent.

Similarly, some traditions are culturally alike in certain ways but have very different operations as a result. For example, the civil law tradition and the Islamic tradition share a religious heritage but with greatly disparate impact. Canon law under the civil tradition operated in a highly civilized world where law enjoyed great prestige. Christianity lacked interest in the actual organization of society, so there was no need to have church law replace, for example, Roman law. Thus, Roman law spread throughout the West without conflicting with the Christian religion (David & Brierley, 1968). The same was not true for Islamic law. By its very nature, Islam is all encompassing. Its relevance to all aspects of the individual's life includes the organization of society, the role of social institutions, and the norms appropriate for human behavior. Islamic law had to replace any existing legal system as it spread from Medina.

By drawing attention to points such as these, the comparative justician seeks to identify similarities and differences among legal traditions. As examples, we will briefly consider the cultural components concerning "public and private law," and the "balance/separation of powers" (see Table 4.1).

Private and Public Law. The idea of private law and public law is a useful distinction in comparing legal systems. In the sense used here, the terms refer to a "legal personality." That is, where do legal rights and obligations lie? Under civil law the question requires two answers. Some matters are the sole concern of the individuals involved. Those individuals come as equals before the judge, who serves as referee in the matter. The legal rights and interests lie with the private individuals and, in its truest form, the right to sanction rests with the individual as well. Public law, in the civil tradition, refers to rules governing activities of the state or of persons acting in the public interest. A separate system of laws, of courts to hear such cases, and of procedures regulating the whole process is a feature of the civil tradition.

Under common law, the distinction between public and private law is not so clear. Common law does not provide separate systems for handling private and public disputes. Both types of questions go before the same courts of law, are heard by the same judges, and are governed by similar rules. Cases involving state action are placed in the same position as those involving the action of ordinary citizens (Schwartz, 1956).

The absence of a distinction between public and private law in the common tradition is historically based. Essentially, English common law is predominantly public law, because the courts were justified in settling disputes only because of the lord's (finally, the Crown's) interest in the case. In this manner, the public or state was given a legal personality. In the capacity of a "personality," the state could bring claims against an individual. Civil law also recognized a legal personality of the state, but claims initiated by that "personality" progressed through the separate legal system set up for that purpose.

The idea of the state having a legal personality is not present under the Islamic tradition. The *Shari'a* took no steps to define the interests of the community or public. Consistent with the Arabic emphasis on the individual, the Islamic legal tradition gives primacy to private law (Lippman et al., 1988). As noted earlier, the *Shari'a* exists to orient the private lives of Muslims and their relations with each other. Like the common tradition, a single legal system appropriately hears all types of disputes. However, instead of justifying this as resulting from a widespread interest by the state, Muslims justify it as a general concern with the individual.

The socialist tradition is more like common law in that law is regarded as primarily public rather than private. In fact, Lenin proclaimed that all law is public law. By that he meant that there is a state interest in every transaction, even those traditionally private in nature (Hazard, 1969). Because the interests of a private person are of secondary importance under socialism, there is no role for private law in the socialist tradition. At this point the socialist and common traditions part ways. Although the common tradition may emphasize public law, it still recognizes private law as relevant and appropriate—just not requiring a separate system of justice as required by the civil tradition. In the socialist tradition, public law is more than emphasized—it stands alone, with no other category of law being recognized.

Balance/Separation of Powers. One of the more important cultural changes in modern times was the eighteenth-century political and intellectual revolutions in most western nations. Especially significant were documents like the American Declaration of Independence and the French Declaration of the Rights of Man and of the Citizen. These manuscripts offered ideas about human equality and the relationship between state and citizen. We quickly notice political, economic, and intellectual aspects of the revolutions, but there were important legal ramifications as well. Consider first the impact these events had in the civil and common law countries.

Members of the French judicial aristocracy were targets of the French Revolution because of their tendency to identify with the landholders. Repeated efforts toward reform had been obstructed by courts refusing to apply new laws, interpreting them contrary to their intent, or hindering attempts of officials to administer them (Merryman, 1985). The situation differed from the one found in England (and America), where judges had more often been on the side of the individual against a power-wielding ruler. English citizens did not have the French fear of judicial lawmaking and of judicial interference in administration.

Another reason for targeting French judges was their failure to distinguish clearly between applying law and making law. Montesquieu and Rousseau had argued for the importance of establishing and maintaining a separation of governmental powers. Especially important was a clear distinction between legislative and executive duties on the one hand, and the duties of the judiciary on the other. In the French Revolution, this emphasis on separation of powers led to a system designed to keep the judiciary from intruding into areas reserved for the other two powers: lawmaking and execution of the laws. Again, this situation differed from that found in the American colonies. The system of checks and balances developed in the United States does not try to isolate the judiciary, nor does it try to approximate the sharp division of powers typically encountered in civil law countries. Essentially, the judiciary was not a target of the American Revolution the way it was in France (Merryman, 1985).

Following the French lead, European countries moved to separate the three governmental powers so that the judiciary could be isolated. In America and England, a system of checks and balances was used without any particular interest in isolating the judiciary.

Although the common law tradition operated with a judiciary that balanced the power of the legislature and the executive, the civil tradition functioned with a judiciary separated from the other two branches of government. This separation of powers is one explanation for the development of a separate legal system for public law. It also, of course, reflects a greater suspicion of the judiciary under the civil tradition than was present in the common legal tradition (Merryman, 1985).

Despite the different paths taken, both civil and common law traditions rely on each government part as a source of law. As will be explained later, there are important differences with regard to which government area is emphasized as the primary source of law, but for now we need only point to the expectation that each part has a role to play. The socialist legal tradition rejects the separation-of-powers principle and instead invests all power in the hands of the legislature (for example, the National People's Congress in China). As a result, socialist courts are not the equal of the legislature, either by isolation from that branch or by serving as a check and balance to that branch (see Seay, 1998 for a concise review). The implications of this situation for the duties of a judge and the function of the court are that, like socialist courts, Islamic courts do not operate as a counterbalance to the legislature and executive. Instead, consistent with its emphasis on private law, the Islamic court serves as a stabilizing device among contending persons (Rosen, 1989). Actually, under classic Islamic theory, neither the state nor the courts were instruments for the application of law. Instead, each was to focus on the individual and perform its respective duties in a way that allowed individuals to carry on with their own affairs.

There are other intriguing and important questions about the cultural component of legal traditions. It would be good to know such things as the attitude of people toward their courts, what type of people and cases go to court, the extent to which courts are used or avoided, and so on. Yet such questions still await an interested scientist. Preliminary information on cultural views, like the role of the state in human affairs and the positioning of various parts of government, is sufficient at least to propose a rudimentary design for the structure of each legal tradition. The cultural suspicion of the judiciary in many pre–French Revolution civil law countries has already helped explain the civil tradition's preference for separate public and private law systems. Similarly, the lack of distrust of common law judges explains that tradition's satisfaction with a single system hearing both public and private disputes. The trust/distrust distinction also suggests that the common law may be more willing to provide judges with lawmaking powers.

The Islamic emphasis on private law emanating from a divine source means that we should not be surprised to find the Muslim judge playing a restricted role in lawmaking (he cannot take Allah's place) or law applying (he is there to assist individual rather than state interests). At the other extreme, cultural aspects of socialist law suggest that those judges will actively represent state interests, because all law is public law. Still, like the Islamic *qadi,* we would not expect the socialist judge to be involved in lawmaking, in this case not because law is viewed as coming from God but because lawmaking falls to the socialist legislature, which operates at a governmentally superior level. Keeping points like those in mind, we turn to the substantive and procedural components of the legal traditions.

Substantive Component

In its broadest sense, substantive law concerns where laws come from (see Table 4.2) and how they are defined. More specifically, as explained in Chapter 3, substantive law is composed of internal and external characteristics. Chapter 5 provides detailed information about the internal and external characteristics of criminal law in several countries, so here we can concentrate on a broader question of substantive law: Where do the laws come from?

Any legal tradition must consider the role local custom plays as a source of law. The *Qur'anic* part of Islamic law is supposed to be of divine origin, but, besides its divine inspiration, the *Sunna* certainly reflects Muhammad's understanding of local custom. Socialist law began in the Soviet Union by taking ad-

Table 4.2 A Substantive Component of Legal Traditions

	Common Tradition	Civil Tradition	Socialist Tradition	Islamic Tradition
The primary source of law is	Custom	Written code (provided by rulers or legislators)	Principles of the socialist revolution	Divine revelation

vantage of the customary view of law as artificial and using existing courts to initiate implementation of the new tradition. In the civil legal tradition, codes substituted for prior custom. Under common law, decisions by judges reflected custom and provided it with legitimacy. Unfortunately, a summary like this is misleading. Custom played a role in all four traditions, but the actual source of law in each does not equally reflect custom.

Primary Source of Common Law. For the common legal tradition, the primary source of law is custom. Law is a public expression of society's entrenched vision of right and wrong, good and bad (Postema, 1986). Like the civil law, common law rests on certain principles. The difference between the two is that for common law the principles exist as generally accepted tradition instead of through writing. Writing them down reveals, not creates, the principles. Because the traditional way of identifying custom was through the court rather than legislative process, judges came to play a pivotal role in common law. A decision by a judge was accepted as legal recognition of a custom. In this sense, the judge "made law" by accepting the custom as binding in a particular case. The absence of a cultural suspicion about judicial actions, and the tradition of accepting principles other than those specifically written by rulers and legislators, gave the common law judge lawmaking and law-applying authority.

Primary Source of Civil Law. The primary source of law in the civil tradition is the written code. The code, which is complete and self-sufficient, is provided by the ruler or the legislature. Of course, completeness is a problem since the codes would become unreasonably extensive if they anticipated all possible acts and the specifics of every case. Instead of offering direct and specific solutions to particular problems, codes supply general principles from which logical deduction provides a resolution in each case (Sereni, 1956). In this manner, civil judges need only identify the applicable code principle to decide a particular case. The solution is expected to be reached through an independent process of legal reasoning that the judge can identify and explain. This process allows the judge to apply the law, but not to make it—exactly what the cultural tradition of separation of powers had in mind. Therefore, under the civil legal tradition, the solution to each case is to be found in the provisions of the written law, and the judge must show that the decision is based on those provisions.

Primary Source of Socialist Law. The socialist legal tradition shares with the civil tradition a view of law as stemming from written codes. The difference is that civil codes are the work of special-interest groups (rulers and the bourgeoisie), whereas socialist laws represent the ideals of the socialist revolution. In that sense, the principles of the revolution are the primary source of socialist law. Further, because socialism does not regard law as an absolute value (whether divine, state-imposed, or traditional in nature), it is merely a means to achieve socialist and communist ideals. Because law is just an instrument, it stands to reason that judges have a similar role and therefore cannot be a source of law. So, like the judges under civil and Islamic traditions, socialist law judges are expected to apply—not make—the law.

Primary Source of Islamic Law. Islamic law is presumed to be of divine origin. Its primary sources, the *Qur'an* and the *Sunna,* specify the legal principles linked to right and wrong behavior. Its authority is based on God's commands instead of long-held traditions or directives by state power. In fact, its divine nature means that no worldly authority can change it, let alone supplement it. So, like civil law judges, Islamic *qadi* must turn to written documents for solutions to disputes. Also like their civil counterparts, *qadi* cannot do more than identify the correct principle for use in a particular case. The difference lies in the source of that principle.

Procedural Component

If law under each tradition really came only from the source identified in the preceding paragraphs, few legal systems of any type could remain effective. The belief that state authorities anticipate every nuance of each potential dispute is just as unreasonable as trusting that ancient custom provides useful guidelines for contemporary behavior. Similarly, believing that God's pronouncements for appropriate behavior today are the same as those provided in the sixth century requires as much faith as accepting utopian theories of a nineteenth-century philosopher and a twentieth-century revolutionary. Obviously, each system had to provide ways to update, modify, fill in the gaps, and supplement the various sources of law in their respective legal traditions. The ways in which that was done brings us to the final topic for this chapter: the procedures for solving problems of flexibility (see Table 4.3).

Flexibility in Common Law. The concept of *stare decisis* has the potential to tie common law to the vestiges of the past. When judges are expected to decide the present case similarly to the way like cases were decided in the past, it seems unlikely that much change can occur. Maybe even more important, what happens when the court is presented with a case that seems very dissimilar to preceding ones? Luckily for the judge and, therefore, for nations under this tradition, common law provides for flexibility by empowering judges to develop solutions to unique cases by "making law" (Postema, 1986). The only restraint requires the solution to be built from a base of existing law. The result is law established by

Table 4.3 A Procedural Component of Legal Traditions

	Common Tradition	Civil Tradition	Socialist Tradition	Islamic Tradition
How is flexibility provided?	Judge-made law and particularization	Variation in reasoning and definition, and identification of issues as either questions of law or of fact	Principles of analogy and directions from higher-level courts	*Mazalim* courts and the process of *ijtihad*

judicial decision and precedent rather than issuing from statutes, codes, or divine proclamation.

Another technique to achieve flexibility under common law is the practice of *particularization.* A review of U.S. Supreme Court holdings in any subject area quickly exemplifies this point. The common legal tradition limits court decisions to very particular facts. Two cases may involve stopping a suspect and searching the suspect's person and surrounding area. However, in case A, the suspect was walking away from the reported scene of the crime, while in case B the suspect was running away. The particular behavior of the suspect may well make the cases different in the court's eyes. As a result, the judge in case B may decide that the decision in case A did not set a precedent for the situation now before her. So the case B judge has the flexibility to make law for this "unique" case.

Flexibility in Civil Law. The civil legal tradition faces a similar problem but for different reasons. The idea of a state authority (for example, legislature, parliament, and the like) reducing to writing all the necessary components of substantive and procedural law cannot be seriously proposed. Yet that is the objective under civil law. Ideally, the civil law judge simply extracts the facts in the case, finds the appropriate provision from the legislature, and applies it to the problem. As Merryman (1985) explains, if a relevant provision is not found, the fault is assumed to lie with either the judge (who obviously cannot follow clear instructions) or the legislator (who failed to draft clearly stated and clearly applicable legislation). Unfortunately, the ideal is, like most ideals, unrealistic. Relevant provisions often cannot be found, so where is the flexibility needed to handle those situations?

One way to provide flexibility in civil law is to recognize that deducing a solution from a necessarily general legislative provision may lead judges to different conclusions. That is, different judges will often employ different reasoning, which will lead to different results (Sereni, 1956). As long as the judge shows how the decision proceeds logically from the rule stated by the legislature, the solution should be regarded as acceptable. Similarly, the civil tradition allows for changes in meaning over time. Earlier civil courts may have correctly ruled in their time, but subsequent modification in the meanings attached to words in the written law allows and requires contemporary courts to arrive at different findings with reasoning as sound as that of their predecessors.

The civil legal tradition gains flexibility by giving judges authority to characterize issues as either problems of law or problems of fact. Particularization in common law and the characterization of judicial precedents as law have resulted in more law in common law countries than in civil law countries (Sereni, 1956). The result is the designation of many issues as *points of "law"* instead of simply *issues of "fact."* This is an important distinction, because a legal issue, once recognized as such, must be followed. A factual issue is presented at face value and without authoritative connotation.

While common law requires many issues to be considered questions of law, civil law provides courts with the discretion to view those same issues as questions of fact. Consider, for example, issues about evidence and testimony. A civil court judge may find it strange to keep an important piece of evidence or relevant testimony out of court. Yet for that judge these are issues of fact—did this person commit this offense? For the common law judge, the same issues may be legal ones—was this evidence or testimony gathered in the appropriate (legal) manner? Obviously, providing the civil court judge discretion to decide whether an issue is a factual or legal question gives that tradition a degree of flexibility not found under common law.

Flexibility in Socialist Law. An early technique for flexibility used in the socialist tradition was the *principle of analogy.* Article 10 of the Soviet Union's 1922 Criminal Code instructed judges (and prosecutors) to punish, by analogy, any acts deemed socially dangerous even if they were not defined as criminal by the code (Hazard, 1969; Reshetar, 1978). This open-ended provision of substantive law provided the court with great flexibility to define something as criminal and determine the necessary punishment. As long as the act being prosecuted was analogous to one prohibited in the code, socialist law could prosecute and sanction the offender.

The usefulness of punishment by analogy is highlighted upon discovering how loosely drafted were some code definitions of crime. For example, the crime of hooliganism referred to intentional acts that seriously disturbed public order and showed clear disrespect for society (Chaldize, 1977). With a definition like that, it was easy to argue that a particular offense was analogous to something prohibited in the code. Use of the principle became excessive, and in 1932 the courts were chastised for applying the law to acts not at all analogous to those prohibited by the code. In 1936 Stalin (of all people) brought a temporary lull in use of the principle when he demanded stability of laws (Hazard, 1969). After regaining vigor in 1941, the use of analogy was finally dismantled with revision of the Soviet criminal code in 1958.

Through the mid 1990s, the Chinese code also incorporated the principle of analogy. Under Article 79 of the code, a person committing a socially dangerous act not specifically prohibited by law could still be punished if the act was analogous to something that was specifically prohibited. McCabe (1989) reports an example of analogy's application when a Chinese citizen sold his passport to another person. Selling a passport was not explicitly prohibited by the code, so the offender was punished under the prohibition against forgery. With the 1997 revision of Chinese law, the principle of analogy seems to have been rejected. Article 3 of the revised criminal law says that persons shall not be convicted or punished for acts that are not explicitly defined as criminal (Taiyun, n.d.). The degree to which China's courts are implementing that provision has not yet been determined.

Today flexibility in socialist law, even in China, relies on more widely accepted procedures than just the principle of analogy. Especially important is the role played by the higher-level courts. Like the civil court judge, the judge in the socialist tradition is expected to decide by reference to principles recorded in a set of codes. To aid in that process, the supreme court in socialist countries watches over the ways in which judges interpret laws and administer justice. When the supreme court deems something inappropriate, it issues directives that lower-court judges must follow. The flexibility, then, lies not so much with the ordinary court judge, but is still found in the court system.

Flexibility in Islamic Law. The rigidity of the *Shari'a* required Islamic law to develop procedures for flexibility very early. The importance of flexibility procedures for the development of Islamic law was highlighted earlier in this chapter where we discussed *mazalim* courts. The *mazalim* courts gave flexibility to Islamic law by providing opportunities for rulers to make law. Of course, it was not called lawmaking, because only Allah could do that. Instead, the rulers' "laws" were seen as administrative and enforcement requirements. These rules supplemented and enforced the *Shari'a* in a way that essentially provided secular legislation.

The closest thing the *Shari'a* itself has had to flexibility was the early process of *ijtihad*. During the first several centuries of its growth, Islamic law allowed jurists to interpret independently the *Qur'an* and *Sunna* when deliberating a case. This process provided significant flexibility, because each judge could arrive at a decision based on his understanding of the law as it related to the current case. By the tenth century, it was determined that sufficient opinions had been written regarding interpretation of the *Qur'an* and *Sunna*. The door of *ijtihad* was closed, and future generations of jurists were denied the right of independent inquiry (Coulson, 1969). Instead, jurists had to follow the doctrine of their predecessors. Why close a procedure allowing flexibility? Coulson (1969) believes that Muslim lawyers, like those the world over, were creatures of precedent who saw law as primarily a way to stabilize social order. Each legal system has periods when law remains static, with settled rules in line with the temper of society. If Islamic law remained settled and stable for an extremely long time, it was because Islamic society itself remained relatively unchanged. Importantly, since the mid-twentieth century, Muslim jurists and judges in some countries have been allowed to determine the rule of *Shari'a* by independent interpretation of the basic texts. Though not widespread, the practice of reopening the door of *ijtihad* is providing a degree of flexibility that may allow *Shari'a* law to retain important influence as part of the Islamic legal tradition.

SUMMARY

Four legal traditions are identifiable today. Although there is considerable variety of legal systems within each tradition, it is possible to distinguish a common heritage making up each legal family. The common legal tradition is familiar to American students, because it developed in England and had significant impact on the legal system of the United States. Important aspects of its development include feudal practices, the importance of custom, and the concept of equity. The civil legal tradition is the oldest of the four contemporary families; its roots extend back to Roman law and canon law as it emphasizes codification. Getting its start in the Soviet Union, the socialist legal tradition built upon Russian law and a view of law as artificial, but took its specific form from Marxist-Leninist philosophy. Finally, the Islamic legal tradition has a divine source in the ingredients making up the *Shari'a* and customary Arabic reliance on oaths and witnesses. Various extensions of Islamic law have allowed it to continue in modern circumstances, and, given the ascendancy of Islamic fundamentalists, will continue to be a force in Muslim countries.

Attempts to compare the four traditions are most appropriately handled by considering certain cultural, substantive, and procedural components. In that manner, we can identify how law is emphasized as either public or private, the relationship between the judiciary and other organs of government, the primary source of law, and how each tradition responds to the problem of flexibility. With this basic understanding of four categories of legal traditions, we are ready to tackle more specific topics concerning particular countries.

WEB SITES TO VISIT

- Visit the Native American and Aboriginal Law web site at **www.nesl.edu/ research/ native.htm** for good information and interesting links. For other aboriginal information check out the links at **www. bloorstreet.com/ 300block/ablawleg.htm**
- The Avalon Project at the Yale Law School provides access to historical legal documents (e.g., the Constitutions of Clarendon) at **www.yale.edu/ lawweb/avalon/ avalon.htm**
- Read some extracts from early English law to get an idea of the terminology used in Anglo-Saxon times at **www.yale.edu/lawweb/avalon/medieval/ saxlaw.htm**

SUGGESTED READINGS

Danilenko, G. M., & Burnham, W. (1999). *Law and legal system of the Russian Federation.* New York: Juris Publishing.

David, Rene, and Brierley, John E. C. (1985). *Major legal systems of the world today* (3rd ed.). London, England: Stevens and Sons.

Lippman, Matthew R., McConville, S., and Yerushalmi, M. (1988). *Islamic criminal law and procedure: An introduction.* New York: Praeger.

Melton, Ada P. (1995). Indigenous justice systems and tribal society. *Judicature,* 79 (3).

Merryman, John H. (1985). *The civil law tradition* (2nd ed.). Stanford, CA: Stanford University Press.

Pommersheim, F. (1995). *Braid of feathers: American Indian law and contemporary tribal life.* Berkeley, CA: University of California Press.

Chapter 5

Substantive Law and Procedural Law in the Four Legal Traditions

KEY TOPICS

- Aspects of substantive law in the four legal traditions
- Aspects of procedural law in the four legal traditions
- Three ways to implement the process of adjudication
- Contrasting the adversarial and inquisitorial adjudication process
- Supporting the rule of law through judicial review

KEY TERMS

adversarial adjudication
common law crime
concentrated model of judicial review
diffuse model of judicial review
inquisitorial adjudication
Islamic adjudication
judicial review
mixed model of judicial review
private law
public law
Rechtsstaat

COUNTRIES REFERENCED

Argentina
Austria
Brazil
China (PRC)
England
France
Germany
Greece
Italy
Mexico
New Zealand
Portugal
Russia
Scotland
United States
Venezuela

The discussion of law in this chapter continues the general theme begun in Chapter 4. The similarity in topics means that there is no reason to change classification schemes. The four legal traditions are reviewed here in terms of their substantive and procedural aspects. This chapter includes more detailed reference to particular countries as means of explanation, but its focus remains broad.

SUBSTANTIVE CRIMINAL LAW

You will recall that substantive law deals with defining criminal behavior. With its general characteristics, substantive law provides citizens with information about what behavior is required or prohibited (specificity) and explains what may happen to people who misbehave (penal sanction). Further, substantive law assures citizens that the law comes from a legitimate authority (politicality) and will be applied by that authority in an unbiased manner (uniformity).

Those four general characteristics of substantive criminal law—specificity, penal sanction, politicality, and uniformity—admittedly reflect a Western bias. Similarly, the seven major principles of criminal law—*mens rea, actus reus,* concurrence, harm, causation, punishment, and legality—are criteria linked to Western law. There is a danger in applying these general characteristics and major principles to non-Western systems if we insist that they are in any way superior to other legal standards. However, if they serve merely as a point of contrast, the characteristics and principles can provide a useful comparative technique. Therefore, as an aid to comparison, we use traditionally Western aspects of substantive criminal law to describe law in other legal traditions.

General Characteristics and Major Principles

Every known legal system relies on some version of *politicality* to create and define criminal behavior. The authority may take forms like a tribal chief, a monarch, a supernatural force, a court official, or an elected body of citizen representatives. Whatever its form, it has the authority (either granted by the citizens or taken by force) to make laws. Similarly, every legal system provides some type of punishment, or *penal sanction,* to people who misbehave. Sanctions might range from a required apology to execution of the offender, but in each instance the offenders should understand that they have misbehaved and must suffer the consequences.

Providing citizens with specific information *(specificity)* about their obligations is difficult but remains a universal ideal. American vagrancy laws and laws against hooliganism in the former Soviet Union are examples of laws lacking specificity. Although the intent of laws without specificity is obviously not to trick the citizen, sometimes that is the result. Political authorities in both countries agreed that specificity is a desirable attribute of criminal law. It is also, however, difficult to achieve.

American and Russian citizens have experienced these laws being applied with prejudice. Some citizens in each country seem above the law, whereas others have the law applied to them with obvious vigor. Such absence of *uniformity* does not mean that citizens and authorities in each country see uniformity as an undesirable characteristic of law; rather, it is an ideal we are striving for (or at least want to give the appearance of doing so) despite falling short at times.

Extensive discussion of how different legal traditions or systems view the four general characteristics of substantive law is unnecessary since they are universally accepted as appropriate ideals. What country would not describe its laws as demonstrating, or striving for, politicality, specificity, uniformity, and penal sanction? We must find more debatable and identifiable aspects of criminal law if we wish to distinguish among legal traditions or systems.

The major principles of substantive law also present ideals, but the seven internal requirements have the advantage of being more often applied than their four philosophical cousins of general characteristics. *Mens rea, actus reus,* concurrence, harm, causation, punishment, and legality are used to identify a particular behavior as criminal. As such, they can provide a mechanism to compare legal systems on points like the requirements each uses to show criminality. We will provide a brief example of how a few countries deal with the idea of criminal responsibility, because that concept incorporates several of the principles.

The *Penal Code of the Federal Republic of Germany,* which provided the base for unified Germany's penal code, assigns criminal responsibility to persons acting intentionally (*mens rea* and *actus reus*) to violate a criminal statute, but Germans do not assign criminal capacity to anyone under age 14. Further, if the act is the result of a mistake of fact or necessity, the actor is not criminally responsible. Similarly, persons acting in self-defense do not act unlawfully. Those modifications of criminal responsibility by defenses and justifications should look familiar to Americans (*Penal Code of the Federal Republic of Germany,* 1987).

In a comparable manner, the *Italian Penal Code* says that no one may be punished for an offense unless at the time it was committed the actor was responsible. For the Italians, one is "responsible if he has the capacity to understand and to will" (*Italian Penal Code,* 1978, p. 32). As do the Germans, the Italians require a person to be age 14 before criminal responsibility is attributed. The Italians further specify that offenders from ages 14 through 17 shall be responsible, but subject to reduced punishment, if the person had capacity to understand and to will. Other justifications and excuses for criminal responsibility in Italy include accidents, physical compulsion (similar to duress in American jurisdictions), self defense, and necessity (*Italian Penal Code,* 1978).

Islamic law requires the presence of both criminal conduct and criminal intent to show criminal responsibility. As part of criminal conduct, Muslim jurists say that criminal responsibility also demands causation. However, recall the example in Chapter 3 wherein Bob, having been poisoned by John—who had intended to kill Bob—dies from the poison's antidote rather than from the poison. Because Bob's death was not the direct cause of the poison administered by John, John cannot legally be charged with murder. Had the Bob and John story occurred in an Islamic law jurisdiction, the outcome could be quite different. Sanad points out that under Islamic law, "a person is held criminally responsible even if some contributing factors intervene to assist in bringing about the criminal result as long as these factors are insufficient to bring about the result by themselves and do not break the causal relationship between the result and the act or omission, which remains the principal cause" (1991, p. 86).

Criminal intent, as Islam's second requirement for criminal responsibility, is taken to mean an evil state of mind (that is, *mens rea*). Muslim scholars distinguish between general and specific criminal intent by viewing the former as inferred whenever someone voluntarily participates in criminal conduct, but general intent is not always sufficient to show criminal responsibility. There are times when specific intent must be proved. In this sense, specific intent seems to refer to the need to prove that the person intended to commit the particular act under question and did so without justification or excuse. Because Islamic law will withhold criminal responsibility in such circumstances as coercion and necessity, it is possible for a person to have committed an illegal act with general intent (for example, he knowingly hit another person) but without specific intent (for example, he did so only to protect himself from the assailant).

Some of the Islamic reasons for withholding responsibility add an interesting twist on similar ones found in other countries. For example, infancy is a defense to crime under Islamic law, but Muslims believe that criminal capacity increases with age. As a result, criminal capacity is not possible until age seven is reached, because younger children are not viewed as able to reason. Children between age seven and the onset of puberty have partial criminal capacity and therefore have some criminal responsibility—though not for *hudud* or *quesas* crimes (discussed later in this chapter). After the onset of puberty, a person can be held fully criminally responsible as long as she is of sound mind. Because puberty plays such an important role in assigning responsibility, we might expect it to be well defined by Muslim jurists. Actually, Sanad (1991) reports considerable disagreement. Some scholars say that it is determined by age (either 11 or 12, depending on the scholar), whereas others say it varies in males and females, and still others argue that some signs of puberty should be used in making the judgment.

This brief review of how some countries view criminal responsibility reminds us that the similarity among countries can be just as interesting as the differences. As a final example, before moving to a discussion of substantive law in each legal tradition, let us look at how Germany, France, and Italy handle the insanity defense. As Chapter 3 pointed out, the insanity defense has generated considerable debate in the United States as to what the most appropriate phrasing should be. Do you suppose other countries have come up with better wording?

Section 20 of the *Penal Code of the Federal Republic of Germany* excuses those suffering from a mental disorder as follows:

> *A person is not criminally responsible if at the time of the act, because of a psychotic or similar serious mental disorder, or because of a profound interruption of consciousness or because of feeblemindedness or any other type of serious mental abnormality, he is incapable of understanding the wrongfulness of his conduct or of acting in accordance with this understanding. (*Penal Code of the Federal Republic of Germany, *1987, p. 55)*

The code goes on in section 21 to also excuse persons of "diminished capacity." Here, if the perpetrator's ability either to understand the wrongfulness of his conduct or to act in accordance with that understanding is substantially diminished (rather than absent as in section 20), he is still criminally responsible but subject to a reduced penalty.

The *French Penal Code* specifies that a person is not criminally responsible "if, at the time of the conduct, that person is stricken with a psychic or neuropsychic disorder which prevents him or her from understanding or controlling his or her acts" (*French Penal Code of 1994,* 1999, p. 38). However, the code goes on to explain that a person so stricken remains punishable—but the court will take into account that circumstance when it determines the penalty.

The *Italian Penal Code* distinguishes between total and partial mental deficiency. For the former, Article 88 states,

> *Anyone who, at the time he committed the act, was, by reason of infirmity, in such a state of mind as to preclude capacity to understand and to will shall not be responsible. (* Italian Penal Code, *1978, p. 32)*

On the other hand, partial mental deficiency is

> *Anyone who, at the time he committed the act, was, by reason of infirmity, in such a state of mind as to greatly diminish, without precluding, his capacity to understand and to will, shall be liable for the offense committed; but the punishment shall be reduced. (* Italian Penal Code, *1978, pp. 32–33)*

These codes seem to leave the definition of mental deficiency as unmanageable as have the legislators in the United States. That does not, of course, give Americans a basis for gloating, but instead emphasizes the difficulty of attempts to be fair when assigning criminal responsibility. Such issues in the area of substantive criminal law present worldwide problems. Although specific examples like those just given are useful in showing both similarity and difference, it is necessary to move to a more general discussion as we consider substantive law in the four legal traditions.

Substantive Law in the Common Legal Tradition

As the historical home of the common law, England presents an excellent example of that tradition's substantive law. Because common law was unwritten law, there was no source to which one could turn and read a list of crimes and their punishments. Identifying what was criminal relied on earlier decisions by judges and through reference to community folkways. As a result, the earliest common law offenses, called *felonies,* included crimes like murder, robbery, rape, arson, and larceny. These serious transgressions were punishable by death or mutilation and by loss of property. The judiciary could also identify other offenses, called *misdemeanors,* which were deemed less serious.

It seems that crimes under common law were essentially "pulled out of a hat" held by the judge. Even if the judge was a political authority applying penal sanction in a uniform manner, where was the specificity? If the judge got to decide what was criminal, how could citizens have any advance warning? The answer relies on the concept of *immemorial custom.* The "hat" from which a judge pulled the crimes was the norms guiding people in that community. Because everyone presumably shared these norms, everyone well knew what behavior was acceptable. Custom provided specificity.

Scotland provides a good contemporary example of substantive criminal law in the common legal tradition. Along with England, Wales, and Northern Ireland, Scotland helps compose the United Kingdom. These four countries operate under a single government but have three separate legal systems. The systems of England, Wales, and Scotland have more in common with one another than they do with Northern Ireland, but even the Scottish system differs from that of England and Wales. At this point, our general discussion need only note that Scotland is considered a member of the common legal family. More particularly, Scottish courts continue to take an active role in judge-made substantive law.

Although most common law countries view legislation as the appropriate task for lawmakers (as will be discussed), Scotland continues the common law traditions of judge-made law in addition to legislation-based law. This position may be related to the absence, until 1999, of a specifically Scottish parliament. Prior to the reestablishment of a parliament separate from that of the United Kingdom, the Scots relied on their representatives in the Parliament at Westminster to provide necessary laws. But that body never showed much interest in the substantive criminal law of Scotland (Jones, 1990). As a result, the traditional flexibility that common law allows the court is embraced by the Scots as a strength of the system.

The High Court of Justiciary has a "declaratory power" that allows the Court to punish obviously criminal acts even though such behavior was not punished in the past. That power has not been explicitly used since 1838, but the High Court continues to create new crimes but without citing its declaratory power as authority. Jones (1990) cites the cases of *Khaliq v. H. M. Advocate* (1983) and *Strathern v. Seaforth* (1926) as examples where the High Court invoked the power. The latter case, though older, provides the better example of this technique.

In the *Strathern v. Seaforth* case, the accused had used another person's automobile without permission. However, he had no intention of permanently depriving the owner of his property; hence, there was no intent to "steal" under existing Scottish law. Nevertheless, the High Court decided it was wrong to secretly take and use any property belonging to another. With that phraseology, the Court created a new crime.

In addition to creating new crimes, the Scottish judiciary can also decide if an old crime has simply been perpetrated in a new way. This is done in the court's role of applying common law principles to new circumstances. Again, Jones (1990) offers an interesting example. At common law *malicious mischief* identifies acts that involve serious and willful damage to another's property. All relevant precedents before 1983 involved physical damage to the property in question. However, in *H. M. Advocate v. Wilson* (1983), Scotland's High Court extended the crime of malicious mischief to cover economic loss as well as property damage. The Court did not intend to create a new crime; it was simply applying existing law to new circumstances.

The perseverance with which Scotland holds to the tradition of judge-made substantive law is not repeated in most other common law countries—and is likely to weaken in Scotland also as the Scottish Parliament becomes comfortable with its role. With expanding populations and increased heterogeneity, common law countries found it increasingly difficult to rely on custom to inform citizens of their obligations. The problem was intensified in colonies, where the ancient ways of English villages provided little support for handling unique problems in the new surroundings. In America, for example, criminal law became essentially a matter of statute. By 1900 most states technically recognized the possibility of *common law crime,* but other states had specifically abolished the concept (Friedman, 1973). In the latter states, statutes said all crimes were listed in the penal code. If the code did not require or prohibit the behavior, it was not a crime—even if a judge believed such behavior was customarily abhorred.

Substantive Law in the Civil Legal Tradition

It may surprise you to learn that some people, mostly in civil law countries, find the common law to be crude, unorganized, and culturally inferior to civil law. In fact, Merryman (1985) suggests that the civil law lawyer's attitude of superiority over common law lawyers has become part of the civil law tradition. As he puts it, a lawyer from a relatively undeveloped Central American country may recognize the United States' advanced economic development and standard of living, but will find comfort in thinking of our legal system as undeveloped and of common law lawyers as relatively uncultured people (Merryman, 1985).

One basis for the civil lawyer's lack of appreciation for the common law concerns the substantive law. Even though common law jurisdictions have moved more toward statutory crimes and procedures, the civil law holds much more closely to the principle that every crime and every penalty must be embodied in a statute enacted by the legislature. The civil lawyer sees common law courts violating this principle every time people are convicted of common law crimes and every time judges prohibit relevant evidence and make rules regarding criminal procedure.

As we saw in Chapter 4, an early emphasis on the idea that crime existed only through statute enacted by a legitimate authority was a prime characteristic of the civil legal tradition. Add to that the belief that average citizens should be able to easily find, read, and understand the law, and you have the reasoning behind codification. The French saw this point as especially true in the areas of criminal law and procedure. In fact, a criminal code was the first object of codification in revolutionary France.

As England is home to common law, so France can argue for a similar heritage regarding civil law. France, like most civil law countries, has divided its various laws into public law and private law. The criminal laws are in the public law category, and, as expected in a civil law system, they are the result of specific legislation resulting in a written document. The two primary documents are the *Code of Criminal Procedure* and the *Penal Code.* The former specifies how to investigate a case and how to try a person charged with a criminal offense. Substantive law is prescribed in the *Penal Code,* which identifies the types of offenses and their respective punishments. There are other sources of substantive law, but a written law defines all criminal offenses.

The *French Penal Code* has five Books:

- Book I, called the General Part, includes provisions applicable to all offenses (e.g., stipulations regarding criminal liability and responsibility).

- Book II describes felonies and misdemeanors against the person (ranging from the broad "person" category of humanity to the very individual category of "personality") and specifies the applicable penalties.
- Book III describes felonies and misdemeanors against property (ranging from traditional larceny provisions to the newer category of money laundering) and specifies the applicable penalties.
- Book IV describes felonies and misdemeanors against the nation, state, and the public place (e.g., treason, terrorism, and corruption) and specifies the applicable penalties.
- Book V describes other felonies and misdemeanors (e.g., public health offenses and cruelty toward animals) and specifies the applicable penalties (*French Penal Code of 1994*, 1999).

Although the terms *misdemeanors* and *felonies* are used in translations, criminal offenses in France actually divide into the three categories of *crime* (serious felonies), *dèlit* (less serious felonies and misdemeanors), and *contravention* (violations). These distinctions not only refer to the seriousness of the offenses but also indicate which court will hear the case. Offenses classified as *crimes,* heard before the highest-level court (Assize Court), are punishable by imprisonment for life or a specific number of years (i.e., 30, 20, or 15), although the judge has discretion to reduce the authorized prison term or, for some crimes, impose a fine or a non-prison penalty as add-ons to a reduced prison sentence. A Correctional Court hears *dèlits,* which are punishable by a prison term between six months and ten years, a fine, or a noncustodial sentence like probation. *Contraventions* can result in a fine or a noninstitutional sentence (e.g., probation or community service) and are heard before a Police Tribunal (*French Penal Code of 1994*, 1999; Terrill, 1999).

Such organization of crimes and jurisdiction is exactly what proponents argue is the advantage of codification over common law. The presumption is that criminal codes under civil law are clear, have no conflicting provisions, and are without gaps (see Merryman, 1985). With those features, citizens can know their rights and obligations, and judges can simply apply the appropriate provision of the code as cases come before the court. One result of this approach is an extremely comprehensive code book that tries to anticipate all possible actions to prohibit. Another approach is to develop codes that express general principles to guide judges when they try cases.

Common law jurisdictions have increasingly relied on statutes (that is, codes) to express substantive law. As a result, there are fewer differences today between the ways common and civil law countries define crime and prescribe punishment. However, some illustrations may still prove instructive. Consider, for example, how the state of Colorado and the countries of Italy and Germany define the crime of theft.

As an example of a common law jurisdiction, the state of Colorado provides a standard definition of theft:

> **(1)** *A person commits theft when he knowingly obtains or exercises control over anything of value of another without authorization, or by threat or deception, and:*

(a) *Intends to deprive the other person permanently of the use or benefit of the thing of value; or*

(b) *Knowingly uses, conceals, or abandons the thing of value in such manner as to deprive the other person permanently of its use or benefit; or*

(c) *Uses, conceals, or abandons the thing of value intending that such use, concealment, or abandonment will deprive the other person permanently of its use and benefit; or*

(d) *Demands any consideration to which he is not legally entitled as a condition of restoring the thing of value to the other person* (Colorado Revised Statutes, *2000).*

The statute then specifies theft as either a misdemeanor or a felony (hence subject to the appropriate punishment) depending on the value of the thing involved. In additional subsections (numbered 2 through 8) the statute addresses such issues as thefts committed two or more times within six months and the increased penalty when the victim of theft is elderly or handicapped.

It seems unlikely that theft codes under a civil legal tradition could be more complete or precise than they are in Colorado. In fact, as noted earlier, codification either can be very comprehensive or can rely on general principles. Although Colorado legislators seem to prefer a code that tries to anticipate most contingencies, some countries of the civil legal tradition are more comfortable with providing guiding standards rather than specifics. As a result, their codes are comparatively short.

The German code on theft has two subsections:

(1) Whoever takes moveable property not his own from another with the intention of unlawfully appropriating it to himself shall be punished by up to five years' imprisonment or by fine.

(2) The attempt is punishable (*Penal Code of the Federal Republic of Germany*, 1987, p. 190).

Two other sections of the German code define the related crimes of aggravated theft and armed theft/gang theft, but in each instance the code explains the terms *aggravated, armed,* and *gang,* rather than modifying or elaborating the term *theft*.

The French are even more succinct:

Article 311-1: Larceny is the fraudulent taking away of any thing belonging to another.

Article 311-2: The fraudulent taking away of energy to the detriment of another also constitutes larceny (*The French Penal Code of 1994*, 1999, p. 163).

Both the German and French codes are relatively concise. In both examples, it is apparent that these countries of the civil legal tradition do not see the goal of codes to be that of providing specific solutions to particular problems. Instead, codes are meant to supply general principles from which logical deduction provides a resolution in each case. So, as described in Chapter 4, civil judges need only identify the applicable code principle to decide a particular case. The principle expressed regarding theft in Germany and France seems to be the idea that it is illegal to take something that doesn't belong to you. When a theft case is brought to court, German and French judges are expected to use logical deduction to determine whether the circumstances of the case show that the defendant did indeed take something that didn't belong to him.

Interestingly, it is the code (statute) from the common legal tradition that provides greater detail and specificity. Are Colorado legislators trying to limit judicial discretion by providing such detail that the law is not open to interpretation by the judge? Or, could it be that because Colorado, as a common law jurisdiction, follows the concept of judicial precedent, its codification process requires more elaboration to incorporate various case law relating to theft? Such questions as these are intriguing but lie outside the scope of our present discussion. Instead, the statute and codes relating to theft merely provide examples of substantive law in both the common and civil legal traditions. With that background we are ready to look at substantive law in the socialist and Islamic traditions.

Substantive Law in the Socialist Legal Tradition

The socialist tradition owes much to the language and structure of the *Criminal Code of the Russian Soviet Federated Socialist Republic.* Borrowing from its civil legal tradition roots, socialist law is codified, but the resulting code may not provide citizens with much information about what is allowed or disallowed. Article 6 of the Russian Republic Code defined a crime as "any socially dangerous act or omission which threatens the foundations of the Soviet structure . . ." (quoted in Terrill, 1984, p. 333). Specific description of criminal acts did not have to be provided, because anything "socially dangerous" was criminal. This version of civil law's codification principle set socialist law apart from its European heritage. After revisions and added specificity in the 1920s and 1950s, Soviet law remained comparatively ambiguous.

The criminal code of the People's Republic of China is based in part on the Russian Code (see Berman et al., 1982). The PRC Code, which was revised in 1997, continues the socialist tradition of imprecision over specificity. Crimes are defined in Chapter II, Section 1, Article 13 of the code as

> *All acts that endanger the sovereignty, territorial integrity, and security of the state; split the state; subvert the political power of the people's democratic dictatorship and overthrow the socialist system; undermine social and economic order; violate property owned by the state or property collectively owned by the laboring masses; violate citizens' privately owned property; infringe upon citizens' rights of the person, democratic rights, and other rights; and other acts that endanger society, are crimes if according to law they should be criminally punished. However, if the circumstances are clearly minor and the harm is not great, they are not to be deemed crimes* (Criminal Law of the People's Republic of China *1997).*

The 1958 revision of Soviet criminal law attempted to clarify the laws and eliminate their erratic enforcement. The *Fundamentals of Criminal Legislation* became the primary source of substantive law (Savitzky & Kogan, 1987). Also developed were the *Law on Criminal Responsibility for Crimes against the State, the Law on Criminal Responsibility for Military Crimes*, and the *Fundamentals of Criminal Pro-*

cedure. Each republic in the Soviet Union had to modify its criminal code to conform with the basic principles of the new legislation, and again the Russian Republic provided the model. A new definition described crime as "a socially dangerous act (an action or omission to act) provided for by the Special Part of the present Code which infringes the Soviet social or state system . . ." (quoted in Terrill, 1984, p. 335). This improved definition increases specificity by reference to the "special part" of the code, which lists the major criminal acts, specifies the elements constituting each, and indicates the punishment that can be imposed.

The PRC Code's version of the Soviet "special part" is found in the code's Part II: Special Provisions. The 10 chapters of Part II (*Criminal Law of the People's Republic of China*, 1997) cover offense categories like "crimes endangering national security" (e.g., acts with the goal of overthrowing the socialist system), "crimes undermining the order of socialist market economy" (e.g., smuggling, counterfeiting, or sabotage of collective production), and "crimes of disrupting the order of social administration" (e.g., keeping state personnel from carrying out their duties, or assembling a crowd to disturb order at public places). Part II also specifies the punishment for each crime. Penalties include execution by shooting, but more often are stipulated as life imprisonment or imprisonment for a specific number of years.

Criminal responsibility under Chinese socialist law is accorded to anyone who has reached age 18. A person who has reached age 14 and who commits murder, serious injury to another, robbery, arson, habitual theft, or other crimes seriously undermining social order is also held criminally responsible (*Criminal Law of the People's Republic of China*, 1997). Persons between the ages of 14 and 18 are given lesser punishment for any crimes they commit. Other circumstances affecting criminal responsibility include mental illness (the offender's family must provide strict surveillance and arrange for medical treatment), physical condition (e.g., a deaf-mute or blind person may be exempted from punishment or receive a lesser penalty), and actions intended to prevent danger.

Substantive Law in Islamic Legal Tradition

Substantive law in the *Shari'a* identifies three categories of crime: *hudud*, *quesas*, and *ta'azir*. *Hudud* crimes are offenses against God and require mandatory prosecution. As the most serious crimes, *hudud* offenses have fixed penalties as specified in the *Qur'an* and *Sunna*. The seven *hudud* crimes are adultery (including fornication), defamation (slander), drinking alcohol in public or private, theft, highway robbery, apostasy (rejection or abandonment of Islam by one who professes Islamic faith), and corruption of Islam (transgression of Islam). Flogging is the required punishment for adultery, defamation, and drinking alcohol (although the alcohol drinker could also be exiled). Highway robbery requires death by crucifixion or cutting off both hands and feet. The punishment for apostasy (after refusal to repent and reconvert) is beheading, as is the punishment for corruption of Islam (Souryal, Potts & Alobied, 1994, p. 258).

***Hudud* Crimes.** Because *hudud* crimes are decreed by Allah, they are absolute, universal, and cannot be subjected to interpretation by judges or government officials (Souryal et al., 1994). In addition, the punishment for a *had* (singular of *hudud*) must be harsh and swift because such an act violates the sanctity of God and threatens the integrity of society. The harshness of Islamic punishment is often noted by Westerners, who highlight punishments like beheading, stonings, whippings, and amputations. Too often ignored by those same Westerners is an equally important aspect of *Shari'a*—rigorous rules of evidence. We will use the crime of theft to understand better the *hudud* crimes and their punishments.

The *Qur'an* (Chapter 5: 38) requires that men or women who steal must have their hands cut off. This harsh penalty reflects the belief that theft not only deprives the owner of property, but it also creates fear, distrust, and apprehension in the community. For a society to be truly Islamic, all men and women have the right to protection of their spiritual, intellectual, and physical needs. This right is attached to a corresponding duty that requires each person to respect the person and property of everyone else or be punished for failing to show such respect (Lippman et al., 1988). Souryal et al. (1994) compare this attitude with the "broken windows" criminological theory (see Wilson & Kelling, 1982) that suggests punishment of minor offenses will forestall the occurrence of more major crimes.

Importantly, the *Shari'a* realizes that such a harsh penalty as amputation must be applied only when there is no doubt about the nature of the act and about the offender's guilt. The first point, the nature of the act, is important, because the act is theft for *had* purposes only when the property taken exceeds a certain value and is taken from a secure location in a clandestine manner. Souryal et al. (1994) explain that the schools of Islamic thought agree that stolen property must have a minimum value, but they disagree as to what that minimum is. Yet even monetary value is not the sole consideration when determining if the act was one of theft. Siddiqi (1985) exemplifies items not worth guarding—that is, without value—as dry wood, hay, game, fish, and other things found in great quantity in the land. Similarly, there is no amputation for stealing items like milk and fruit, which quickly spoil, or for theft of prohibited items (for example, alcohol), because the offender need only claim his intent was to destroy the harmful item.

The requirement that the item be taken from a secure location in a clandestine manner takes us to the second point, proof of the offender's guilt, that must be addressed before the *had* penalty is applied. This is where the rules of evidence serve to control the inappropriate application of the penalty. Souryal et al. (1994) explain that the victim has the responsibility to show a *had* offense has occurred. The *had* of theft cannot be established, and therefore the amputation punishment cannot be imposed, unless the victim is shown to have exercised reasonable care in safekeeping the property. The judge must determine if the stolen property had been kept in a safe place as required for a *had* theft.

Only two kinds of evidence are accepted as proof of guilt in *hudud* crimes: confession and eyewitness testimony (Souryal et al., 1994). An admissable confession is one made voluntarily, unequivocally, in detail, and during court proceedings. Also, because the consequences are so grave in *hudud* crimes, a confession can be withdrawn at any time before the punishment is applied. If the withdrawn confession was the only evidence against the accused, the judge will set aside the sentence and retry the accused in accordance with *ta'azir* rules. When the evidence is eyewitness testimony, guilt is established by providing a required number of eyewitnesses. That number varies according to the *had* offense being tried. For theft, two male witnesses are required. If there is any doubt about the nature of the offense or the guilt of the accused under *had* criteria, the accused can still be subjected to *ta'azir* law.

Quesas Crimes. *Quesas* crimes are those offenses that require retaliation by the victim or victim's family. Some *quesas* are very serious—murder, for example—but because they are acts against individuals more so than against God and his community of believers (the criteria for *hudud* offenses), they are less grave than *hudud* crimes. *Quesas* are not always given a specific and mandatory criminal definition in the *Qur'an,* so the behavior constituting these offenses has evolved through academic, judicial, and political supervision. They include voluntary homicide, involuntary homicide, intentional physical injury, and unintentional physical injury. The last two categories include crimes of assault, battery, and other acts not resulting in death.

Souryal et al. (1994) point out that the uninformed observer might think that Islamic law requires a more severe penalty for theft (a *had* crime) than for murder. That would be an inaccurate assumption because a fixed penalty (for example, amputation for theft) does not necessarily make the punishment more or less severe than a negotiated one. Murder, for example, is punished by beheading. However, because murder is a *Quesas* crime it is open to negotiation. That negotiation may take the form of restitution if both parties agree.

This idea of restitution replacing retaliation is consistent with an aspect of Islamic law that is often overlooked—the expression of forgiveness and charity. Although the *Qur'an* clearly prescribes retaliation for *quesas* offenses, it just as clearly encourages forgiveness. The expression of that forgiveness is found in the use of *diyya,* which Al-Sagheer defines as "money paid to a harmed person or his heir in compensation for a felony committed against him" (1994, p. 85).

When *diyya* can be paid, the amount paid and the recipient of payment are all covered by specific rules. For example, in cases of murder the *diyya* amount varies from the equivalent of 100 camels for a Moslem male to the equivalent of 50 camels for a Moslem female. Payment is typically made by the offender or the offender's blood relatives.

Ta'azir Crimes. *Ta'azir* offenses include acts condemned by *Shari'a* or *Sunna* but not listed among *hudud* or *quesas* crimes (for example, eating pork, giving false testimony, bribery, and espionage). In addition, *ta'azir* crimes are acts that violate proper Islamic conduct (for example, obscenity, provocative dress, traffic violations). Finally, as we saw in the earlier discussion of theft, acts that are *hudud* and *quesas* crimes but that fail to meet the rigorous rules of evidence are placed among *ta'azir* offenses (Souryal et al., 1994).

Prosecution and punishment of *ta'azir* crimes is discretionary. The court and religious elders determine these issues in light of the damage caused, the offender's circumstances, and the social and spiritual significance of the crime. Any imposed punishment for *ta'azir* offenses should be rehabilitative in nature and can range from long-term imprisonment or light corporal punishment, to counseling and payment of restitution (Wiechman, Kendall & Azarian, 1996). When deciding the appropriate punishment, judges are encouraged to be flexible and choose a punishment they believe will help the offender and deter others from commiting the same crime.

PROCEDURAL CRIMINAL LAW

As you can see, issues of substantive law do not vary much among the four legal traditions. Each considers similar acts to be criminal, and they all debate questions such as criminal intent and responsibility while struggling with defenses to crime. The real differences among the traditions fall in the area of criminal procedure.

Chapter 3 presented two models of procedural law: one of due process and another of crime control. Because neither model corresponds to reality nor represents an ideal, they are offered simply as techniques to understand how the legal process operates. Each model seeks to guarantee social freedom, but the crime control version does so by emphasizing efficient processing of wrongdoers, whereas the due process model emphasizes restrictions on government invasion into citizens' lives.

Consider, for example, the topic of *public law* versus *private law* in terms of the crime control and due process models. While the civil legal tradition distinguishes between private and public law, the other three traditions do not. The division of public and private law presents interesting problems when the civil legal tradition deals with criminal matters. Private law, which deals with disputes between individual citizens, has been the primary concern of civil law since Roman times. Public law, under the civil legal tradition, deals with relations between citizens and public officials or agencies. Its focus on public matters makes it more administrative than legal in nature. It provides a way for citizens to complain about the way social institutions and officials are acting.

Distinguishing between public and private law presents a problem when criminal law is categorized. Originally crime was considered the concern of private law, because the wronged person was expected to initiate action against the offender. When crimes came to be seen as also affecting the whole society, the public began to share an interest in what had been a solely private area. As the state (public) developed a legal personality, criminal law came to have a public component with two aspects. First, in addition to the victim, the public at large was harmed and had the right to sanction the wrongdoer. Second, the state took from the wronged citizen the obligation to investigate, prosecute, and punish the offender. That development was not a problem under common law, because the same courts handled both public and private law. However, civil law countries were presented with the dilemma of leaving crimes a matter of private law or switching them to the jurisdiction of public law courts.

The dilemma was resolved by keeping crimes in the private law domain. However, that solution meant that the officials in private law courts were asked to judge the actions of government officials (for example, police officers and prosecutors), a matter more comfortably handled by the administrative judges hearing public law complaints. This positioning of criminal law as part of public law but managed by the regular (that is, private law) courts helps explain why civil law systems seem to emphasize the crime control model.

The French, for example, do not view public law as law in the strict sense. Instead, public law is essentially administrative law, useful to help keep society operating. The "true" law, for French citizens, concerns relations between individuals, where the state simply serves as an impartial arbitrator. The public and administrative aspect of criminal law requires the state to play a more active role.

French citizens allow their government a degree of discretion, and even arbitrariness, because society's interest is directly involved in catching and punishing the criminal. The general attitude is that as long as officials like police and prosecutors act in a spirit respecting the liberty and equality of citizens, it is not so important whether the law is strictly followed. "After all, criminal law is public, and public law is different from private law" (David, 1972, p. 121). The result, to return to the metaphor in Chapter 3, is an assembly line where workers are able to complete their task with minimal interference from suspicious supervisors concerned with the ways in which workers do their job.

There are many aspects of procedural law and unlimited points to use for comparing legal systems. We will concentrate on just two general topics: the adjudicatory process and judicial review. In each instance you will find examples of legal systems following what seems to be one or the other of Packer's models. Just remember, Packer (1968) presents the two models as being different without labeling one as better than the other. We should view them the same way.

Adjudicatory Processes

The process of adjudication is typically either *adversarial* (also called *accusatorial*) or *inquisitorial* in nature (see Table 5.1). Both systems have the finding of truth as a fundamental aim, and each is guided by the principle that the guilty should be punished and the innocent left alone (Jörg, Field & Brants, 1995, p. 42). The differences between the two are in their assumptions about the best way to find the truth.

Table 5.1 The Adjudicatory Process

	Adversarial Systems	Inquisitorial Systems
Who Plays the Role of the Accuser?	Role of accuser moves from the individual to the state in an evolutionary continuation of private vengeance.	The state as accuser replaces the individual in a developmental substitution for private vengeance.
How Is Truth Determined?	Truth is said to arise from competition between opposing sides, so the emphasis is on the trial phase.	Truth is said to arise from a continuing investigation, so the emphasis is on the screening process.
Where Does Power Lie?	Power is shared by the prosecutor, defense, judge, and jury, so the judge exerts influence indirectly in the role of referee.	Power is concentrated more in the judge, so the judge exerts influence directly in the role of investigator.
What Level of Cooperation Is Expected of the Defendant?	Defendant is neither expected nor required to cooperate with the investigation or court officials.	Defendant is expected, but not required, to cooperate with investigation (including court) officials.

The adversarial system is often considered the successor to private vengeance. As societies evolve, the power to initiate action first lies with the wronged person (the accuser). That power eventually extends to relatives of the "victim," then to all members of the person's group, and finally to the government responsible for the well-being of the person. In time, then, the accuser moves from being the individual to being the state (as in *State of Texas v. Jones*). The setting for the accusation is before an impartial official serving as referee (judge). Because the disputing parties (the state and the accused) behave in a manner similar to a contest, they are considered adversaries.

The inquisitorial process also shows societal evolution, but along a different path. Here the wronged person is eliminated as private accuser and replaced with a public official. Unlike the adversarial process, the inquisitorial process does not keep the public official in the role of accuser. Instead of accusation, there is now investigation. Because the parties are not engaged in a contest, a referee is not necessary. Instead, the impartial official (judge) serves as an inquisitor actively seeking to determine what transpired.

In general terms, the common legal tradition makes use of the adversarial process, whereas the civil legal tradition follows one of inquisition. Because of its civil roots, the socialist tradition also exemplifies the inquisitorial process. The Islamic legal tradition offers a unique combination relying on private accusation in an inquisitorial-type setting. Because these distinctions provide one of the most common comparisons of legal systems, we should consider them in greater depth.

Inquisitorial Process. One of the first things necessary to an understanding of the inquisitorial process is to separate it from the term *inquisition*. The Spanish Inquisition of the late fifteenth century was notorious for its use of torture to compel cooperation in its religious investigations. The only thing it had in common with today's inquisitorial process was the prominent role given the judges. The judge is at the center of the fact-gathering process in the inquisitorial system, but torture is not.

By the mid-sixteenth century, the inquisitorial method was standardized and required for all French courts. Terrill (1984) identifies the major characteristics of that process as (1) the positioning of the king's prosecutor as a party to the suit in every criminal case, and (2) the use of two magistrates during the course of the investigation and the trial. The first point is important because it recognized the state's (that is, the king's) interest in the case and abolished the accusatory idea of trials as duels between two parties. The second point highlights the primary and active role judges, instead of attorneys, play in a civil law system.

Rather than a competition between opposing sides, a trial under the inquisitorial system is more like a continuing investigation. The parties in the case must provide all relevant evidence to the court. The judges, not the attorneys for the plaintiff or defendant, then call and actively examine witnesses (Abadinsky, 1988). In this way the inquisitorial system assumes that truth can be, in fact must be, discovered in an investigative procedure. Because parties on either side may have an interest in hiding the truth, the state must be involved early and continually in the investigation.

Trials play an important role in civil proceedings, because the inquisitorial procedure does not include a guilty plea as Americans know it. A defendant's confession of guilt is not the same as a guilty plea, and instead serves as additional evidence to be evaluated (Ingraham, 1987). Yet the resulting civil law trials are not similar to those under common law in either their form (see Chapter 7) or their length. Matti Joutsen (personal communication, August 1, 1997), suggests that civil trials are shorter, especially compared to American trials, because continental Europeans may be more willing than Americans to admit their guilt and take the punishment. Reasons for that cooperation might include a more efficient adjudication process and the "light" sentences Europeans face compared with sentences in the United States.

There is no civil law equivalent to the American model of *plea bargaining*, whereby a defendant enters a guilty plea in court in exchange for a stipulated bargain. Joutsen (personal communication, October 23, 1997) explains that a plea bargain in the sense of an overt agreement between the defendant and the prosecutor as to the charges is neither theoretically possible nor practicably advisable. In theory, a plea bargain would violate the principle of legality that requires civil law prosecutors to bring charges for what the suspect is alleged to have committed, not for what he or she is willing to admit to. As a practical matter, the reality of day-to-day prosecutorial work does not include opportunities for negotiation between prosecutor and the defendant or defense counsel.

Pizzi (1999) agrees that there is no exact parallel to plea bargaining in most European trial systems; but he believes the fiscal realities of all Western countries dictate the use of "incentive mechanisms" that allow a case resolution without requiring a full-blown trial. For example, Weigend (1993) explains that Section 153a of the *German Code of Criminal Procedure* assumes public interest in prosecution can be satisfied by having the offender make a payment or perform some action that will benefit the public. Under that section, misdemeanor offenders can avoid a criminal trial and a conviction by paying a sum of money to the victim, a charitable organization, or the state, or by performing some act of public service. Since the payment or action precedes conviction, the offender must consent to the "conditional dismissal," which seems to give this sanction a "bargained" aspect.

Although civil and socialist legal traditions both use the inquisitorial process, they implement it in slightly different ways. For example, an independent judiciary typically performs the inquisitorial function in civil law systems. Under socialist law, an agent of the police or prosecution often takes the role. Despite such variation, the inquisitorial process involves a procedurally active judge and rather passive lawyers. This situation is nearly the opposite of that in the adversarial process, which has a procedurally passive judge and rather active advocates.

Adversarial Process. The adversarial process assumes that truth will arise from a free and open competition over who has the correct facts (Samaha, 1988). The struggle is between the state on one side and the defendant on the other. This "sporting" or "fighting" system of justice developed from the *trial by ordeal* in the tenth to thirteenth centuries, wherein a battle settled disputes between parties. The victor was assumed to have "truth" on his side, so a triumphant accused was cleared of the charges whereas a defeated one was deemed guilty.

As trial by combat grew in popularity, procedures for conducting the ordeal received increased attention. The language setting forth the rules of the proceeding and the language used in that proceeding became very exacting. Procedure became so important that, some authors believe, the adversarial process became a system emphasizing procedure over substance. As a result, each side plays a game in which the players use the law (especially procedural rules and rights) to gain an advantage or act as a bargaining chip (Ingraham, 1987).

Waldron (1989) identifies two safeguards of the adversary system. First, it uses cross-examination (in place of swords) to challenge or destroy a witness's testimony. Each side has a chance to question the honesty of witnesses, search for biases, and figure out what witnesses actually know instead of what they think they know. Second, instead of power being granted to a single position, the prosecution, defense, judge, and jury, share it. The prosecutor represents the state in trying to prove the defendant's guilt. The defense attorney argues the client's innocence and ensures that the accused has all the legal protection possible. The judge serves as the referee in this contest and guarantees that the players abide by the rules. This system of checks and balances differs from the inquisitorial process, which concentrates more power in the judge's position.

Importantly, just as variation exists among countries using the inquisitorial system, the adversarial process is not the same in all common legal traditions. One of the clearest examples of such differences are the ways in which American and British defense counsels approach a jury trial. Americans who are used to hearing emotional and dramatic orations by a lawyer on behalf of the client would be quite surprised at the apparent detachment, lack of interest, and absence of aggressiveness displayed by an English solicitor or barrister.

When representing the client, English barristers do not see their function as obtaining an acquittal by using procedural rules in the hope the prosecution will stumble. Of course, it is not fair to say that American defense attorneys see their duty as constantly erecting procedural barriers. However, one does not have to be especially cynical to believe that such action occurs in the American courtroom. Some authors (see Graham, 1983) are convinced that it occurs much more frequently than in the British courtroom.

The English barrister tends to approach a trial as something to be decided on the basis of contested facts. The jury should inflict punishment on the defendant only if the jury is sure that the prosecution's story is true. But since the barrister has an attitude of acceptance toward punishment applied to a defendant who is proved guilty, some (especially Americans) may see the barrister as detached and uncommitted to the defense of the client.

Graham (1983) speculated on the reason why English barristers do not become more aggressive during the trial. He decided that the barrister's working conditions are the main reason. Unlike the American defense counsel (especially a privately hired one working in a large law firm), barristers usually work alone. They prepare much of their own cases and appear in court with the frequency of an American public defender in a large city. Such factors make it difficult to maintain an aggressive posture with each new case. As a result, the appearance of the adversarial process looks rather different in these two common law countries. Nevertheless, the contrast between the adversarial and inquisitorial methods are still more pronounced than any differences within the two systems.

Contrasting Adversarial and Inquisitorial Processes. Barton Ingraham developed an intriguing and helpful model of criminal procedure that allows us to compare and contrast procedures in a variety of nations. The application of his model to procedural criminal law resulted in the identification of four areas where inquisitorial and adversarial procedures differ:

1. The inquisitorial systems emphasize the screening phase of the criminal process with the idea that a careful investigation will determine factual guilt. The adversarial systems emphasize the trial phase, where the idea that complex rules of evidence to produce substantive results will ensure the defendant a fair trial.
2. The adversarial systems are much more likely to restrict the involvement of the judiciary in both the investigatory and adjudicatory process. The direct involvement of the judge in inquisitorial systems contrasts with his or her more indirect involvement in adversarial systems.
3. Because the inquisitorial system assumes that all involved persons are seeking the truth, the defendant is expected (though not required) to be cooperative. That cooperation includes supplying information to investigators and answering questions at trial. The adversarial systems, on the other hand, neither expect nor require the defendant to assist investigators. The burden of proof is on the prosecutor, who assumes that the defendant will maintain silence.
4. The role of the judge in adversarial proceedings is primarily one of referee. The attorneys develop and present their respective cases, and then a jury decides between the two versions of the facts. The court in an inquisitorial system is another investigator with the added power of being able to decide the case. The judges ask most of the questions and develop the facts, while the attorneys exist more to argue the interpretation that the court should give those facts (see Ingraham, 1987, p. 121).

Ingraham believes that the main objectives of the inquisitorial system are a search for truth and the achievement of procedural justice. Are these objectives different from those of the adversarial system? The adversarial approach differs in the sense that the quest for truth and justice officially begins at the trial stage, because information from the investigation is not considered until presented in court. Then each side presents its own private version of the truth, and the judge or jurors must decide who is the most convincing. As a result, the importance of how a person is adjudicated seems a more important objective in the adversarial process than determining whether the accused actually commited the crime. This point is similar to the distinction made in Chapter 3 in terms of legal guilt versus factual guilt. One might argue that although each system seeks to determine both types of guilt, the inquisitorial emphasizes the latter (factual guilt) while the adversarial highlights the former (legal guilt).

Just as common law and civil law systems borrowed aspects of codification and precedent from each other, so too have the inquisitorial and adversarial systems exchanged procedures. For example, the common law systems adopted a public prosecutor to file criminal charges without relying on a grand jury. Rules of discovery compel some sharing of evidence between the opposing

Soccer Versus Football!

Pizzi (1999) has an especially interesting way to contrast the adversarial and inquisitorial systems. He uses a sports analogy of American football versus European soccer. A notable difference between these two sports—and between the adversarial and inquisitorial justice systems—is in the way rules are applied. In the European trial system and the popular European sport of soccer, rules are relatively few in number and rather easy to express. In the American trial system and the more popular (among Americans) sport of football, rules are numerous and complex.

- The rules of soccer are expressed rather easily with statements like a player cannot intentionally trip someone or push someone off the ball or engage in dangerous play.
- In football the rules are often made complicated by the exceptions: (1) certain players on the offense may move (but only in certain directions) before the ball is snapped, but other players may not even flinch; (2) the defense can block offensive players, but only certain ones and—for some—only within a specified distance from the scrimmage line.

In addition to a different emphasis on rules, the sports also differ on how those rules are enforced:

- In soccer, one referee, on a large playing field, has sole responsibility for controlling play among the players as they move quickly about the entire field. Two assistant referees follow the play from the sidelines to help with decisions in locations where the referee may not be well positioned. But only the referee has a whistle, and only the referee can stop play.
- A football game, which is played on a smaller field, requires six to eight officials and many whistles. Any of those officials can stop play whenever they believe a rule infraction has occurred—which, given the extensive and complex rules, can be quite often.

One effect of the different rules and their enforcement is that soccer is played with minimal interruption and a tendency to let the players play. Minor infractions may be ignored and the referee stays in the background as much as possible. In football, on the other hand, nonenforcement of the rules simply to avoid interrupting the flow of the game would be shocking to players and fans alike.

Throughout his intriguing book, Pizzi uses this soccer/football analogy to distinguish the inquisitorial and adversarial trial systems. The Europeans seem to have reflected a similar spirit in both their trials and their sport. Like a soccer game, the inquisitorial system has rather clearly expressed rules of procedure that are relatively few in number. And, as we see more clearly in Chapter 7, overseeing the process is a primary official

IMPACT

Soccer Versus Football!

who tends to stay in the background and let the court-room players play. A few assistants (two or three citizens serving as lay judges, help the professional official (the judge) make decisions.

The trial system preferred by rule-obsessed Americans, the argument goes, reflects a football game with many complex rules that provide most any courtroom official (e.g., judge, prosecutor, defense counsel) with an opportunity to stop play and get a ruling on whether an infraction has occurred. Both soccer and football games eventually end, and each provides a clear outcome. Trials following either an inquisitorial or adversarial process also end—but the outcome may not always be clear. Was the accused really guilty? Does a heavy reliance on procedural rules prevent the players from playing? Are outcomes of either sporting events or trials influenced by the degree to which play is controlled and how often it is interrupted? Would sport fans resent game outcomes that proclaimed winners on the basis of who best followed the rules (a "legal win") regardless of who scored the most points (a "factual win")?

sides, resulting in a "search for the truth" more similar to an inquisitorial than adversarial process. Also, the role of the common law judge has increased in areas like plea negotiation and what evidence the jury will be allowed to hear. The results of this cross-pollination are systems where each contains elements of the other (Ingraham, 1987; Merryman, 1985). The resulting mixture is not, however, as complete as that found in Islamic law.

A Mixed System. Islamic procedural law is a mixed system combining adversarial and inquisitorial aspects. Because the *Shari'a* is a religious law based on divine command and revelation, it did not develop through judicial precedent or legislative codification. Furthermore, it does not require the administration of justice to be a combined office (for example, the inquisitorial judge) or divided into many (for example, the adversarial attorneys, judge, and jury). Identifying Islamic procedural law is not so easy. Though the sacred law prescribes penalties for criminal acts, it does not specify the means used to apprehend the offender and bring him to justice. The matter is left to the discretion of the state (Awad, 1982).

Because of this discretion, Islamic law has features of both procedural types. The inquisitorial process seems to predominate, because historically there has been little division between the judge and the investigator. In addition, the defense attorney's role is not so much adversarial as it is one of presenting favorable evidence, safeguarding against improper incrimination, and overseeing the criminal judgments. Simultaneously, such adversarial provisions as the right to confront accusers, maintain silence, and a modified presumption of innocence reflect adversarial interests.

A peculiar twist given procedural law by Islamic justice is the differing provisions for separate categories of offenders and its impact on the presumption of innocence. *Shari'a* judges place suspects into one of three categories: "(1) the accused is from the pious and righteous group; (2) he is among the disobedient and immoral; or (3) his character is unknown though neither righteous nor immoral" (Awad, 1982, p. 100). These categories help judges decide the appropriate procedures to follow when a person is accused of a crime. When presented with a person of the first category, jurists usually give no credibility to the accusations. After all, the person is pious and righteous and therefore deserves the benefit of doubt. Because accusations against the sinful and immoral person are more likely to be true, given his or her lifestyle, limiting the accused's rights and freedoms in the quest for truth is permissible. Persons in the third category are generally placed with the immoral and subjected to the same restrictions.

As these examples from several countries show, there is greater diversity among nations in terms of procedural criminal law than we found on issues of substantive criminal law. However, this focus on the adjudicatory process might lead us to believe that procedural law issues are essentially differentiated on the basis of which legal tradition a country follows. That assumption would be incorrect, because there are differences in procedural law both among and between the legal traditions. One area of variation is linked to the concept of judicial review. As we consider that topic, we will see that procedural criminal law shows variation beyond that which is explained by legal tradition affiliation.

Judicial Review

The phrase "laws change but the Law must remain" is commonly used to express the concept of *Rechtsstaat,* or *the rule of law.* That point reduces to the question of whether a country views its law or its government as supreme. A Soviet journalist expressed it this way: "Putting people to death, the English king broke the law; by putting people to death, the Russian Tsar created the law. . . . It is one thing when lawlessness tramples right, living in the consciousness of society, and quite another thing when lawlessness becomes right" (Feofanov, 1990–1991, p. 21).

As Figure 5.1 shows, reaching a position of *Rechtsstaat* requires a nation to first recognize the supremacy of certain fundamental values. Those values may have either secular or divine origin as long as they are understood to reflect basic and ultimate principles. After being recognized, the fundamental values must be reduced to written form. A country's constitution often accomplishes this task. Finally, the trip to *Rechtsstaat* requires a nation to provide procedures that hold its government to the tenets of this higher law. If citizens cannot challenge laws made by the country's legislature or ruler, the concept of a higher law is lost. For example, say that the legislature in a country whose constitution assures freedom of religion passes a law prohibiting Muslims from operating a place of worship. If citizens cannot challenge the substance of such a law as violating fundamental values (recorded in the constitution), the concept of *Rechtsstaat* is emasculated.

The procedures supporting the rule of law need to be of two types: those related to questions of substance, and those related to questions of administration. Questions of substance are similar to the example of the Muslims prohibited from worshiping in a country guaranteeing freedom of religion. Questions of

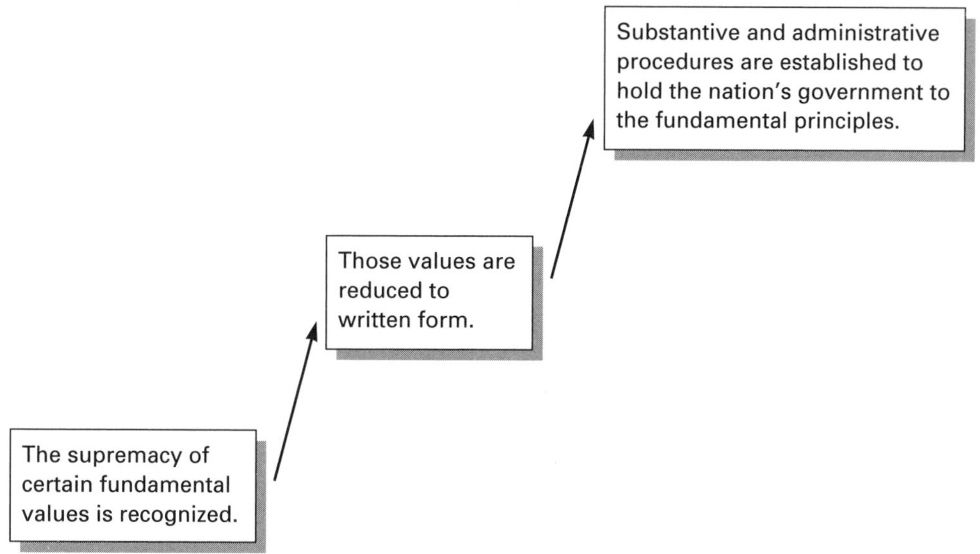

Figure 5.1 Flowchart for Achieving *Rechtsstaat*

administration, on the other hand, deal with how the government enforces its statutes and is itself subject to the law. Consider, for example, a case of Soviet pretrial detention.

A Soviet journalist (Feofanov, 1990–1991) became aware of a defendant who had been kept in prison for five years and 11 months while awaiting his trial. The journalist asked the USSR Procuracy if such action was consistent with the principles of law and justice. The response was basically one of surprise that someone believed that a thief should be set free just because the term of pretrial confinement was violated. The government official explained that the defendant was accused of a crime that warrants a 15-year sentence. From the official's point of view, if the person is eventually convicted and six years are subtracted from that sentence, nothing so terrible has happened. The situation is worsened, in Western eyes, by the fact that the Procuracy was the very agency that the Soviets used to monitor such behavior. When the law is deemed inapplicable to certain citizens or agencies, it cannot have an independent value, and there is no *Rechtsstaat.*

Of the three steps to a rule of law (that is, recognizing supremacy of certain values, reducing them to writing, and providing a way to hold the government to those laws), the third is particularly interesting. The first two steps are rather well accomplished today and show little differentiation—at least in the common and civil legal traditions. A rule of law, if it exists, in the socialist and Islamic traditions must be approached differently. Consequently, we will review ways to hold the government accountable in common and civil legal families and then turn to the question of *Rechtsstaat* under socialist and Islamic law.

The process by which governments are held accountable to the law is called *judicial review.* The term refers to the power of a court to hold unconstitutional and, hence, unenforceable any law, any official action based on a law, or any other action by a public official that the courts deem in conflict with the country's

In the News

HONG KONG AND THE RULE OF LAW

In mid 1997 Great Britain relinquished its control over Hong Kong, and that small but prosperous territory became a Special Administrative Region of the People's Republic of China. Hong Kong, which had been under governance of the British parliament since 1842, had followed the common legal tradition established under the English rule. With its transfer to China, the Hong Kong legal system became affiliated with a socialist legal tradition.

A topic of particular concern for many Hong Kong citizens was the impact that the transfer to China would have on the rule of law that had been firmly established under British rule. Some argued that Hong Kong's prosperity was due in part to the confidence businesses had that legal disputes would be handled with reference to the written law and with impartial justice. Not everyone was convinced that Beijing would respond with a similar concern for the rule of law. For example, in 1996, despite a long-term contract, a McDonald's restaurant was summarily ousted from its location in Beijing ("Hong Kong's legal system," 1997). In Hong Kong the sanctity of contract would not have allowed such immediate eviction without deliberate court action. Similar concerns were expressed for criminal law issues, since Hong Kong's Basic Law (a mini-constitution for Hong Kong providing some autonomy after the hand-over to China) could present difficulties for the Chinese authorities.

By 1998 Beijing had pretty much maintained a hands-off approach to Hong Kong, and the rule of law seemed undisturbed. But in 1999 Chinese officials denounced a ruling by the Hong Kong Court of Final Appeal on the right of children to seek abode in Hong Kong (Stephen, 1999). Although not a criminal justice issue, the ruling is important for our purposes because it concerns the power of Hong Kong's Court of Final Appeal. Specifically, does that court have the authority to rule on whether an act of the Chinese Peoples' National Congress is consistent with the Basic Law? Mainland China says the court does not have such authority. It has been apparent to many observers that Hong Kong's "honeymoon" period is drawing to a close, and judicial autonomy in Hong Kong will likely be compromised as the former British colony moves from affiliation with a common legal tradition to a socialist legal tradition.

basic law (see Abraham, 1986). One of two models can be used to accomplish judicial review (see Brewer-Carias, 1989; Cappelletti, 1989). The *diffuse model* is decentralized and allows a wide variety and large number of courts in the country to rule on issues of constitutionality of laws. The *concentrated model* is centralized by restricting issues of the constitutionality of laws to a specific state agency (see Figure 5.2).

The diffuse model had its origin in the United States and is now found primarily in Britain's former colonies (for example, Canada, Australia, India). It is not, however, confined to countries following the common legal tradition. European countries such as Norway, Denmark, and Sweden have procedures that are

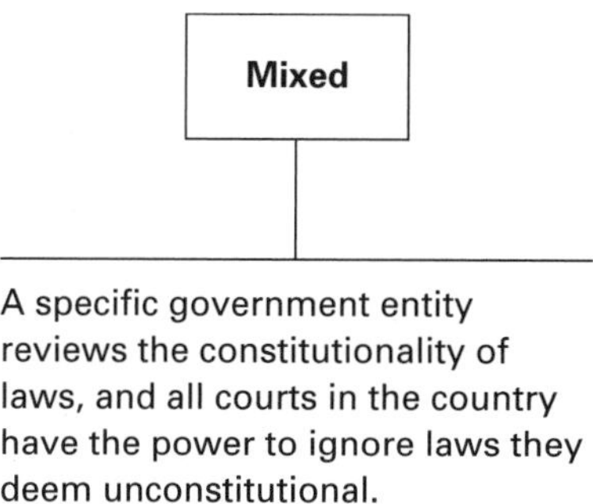

Figure 5.2 Models for Accomplishing Judicial Review in Common and Civil Traditions

very similar to the American prototype, as do the Latin American countries of Argentina and Mexico. The concentrated model was first established in Austria in 1920, then spread to such European countries as Germany, Italy, and Spain. Not surprisingly, some countries fail to fit neatly into one of these two models. These *mixed-model* countries (for example, Venezuela, Colombia, Brazil, and Switzerland) offer interesting variations of judicial review, and as a result they also warrant our attention (see Figure 5.2).

Diffuse Model for Judicial Review. The diffuse model gives a country's entire judiciary the duty of constitutional control. This approach follows the assumption that the judiciary functions to interpret the laws in order to apply them in concrete cases. When two laws conflict, the judge must determine which of the two prevails and then apply it. In countries with a rigid constitution, the judge is expected to decide by deferring to the higher law, because a constitutional norm prevails over an ordinary legislative norm. Therefore, in countries following a diffuse model of judicial review, any judge having to decide a case where an applicable legislative norm conflicts with the constitution must disregard the former and apply the latter. As a result, even low-level courts can rule a statute unconstitutional or declare police action as violating a suspect's fundamental rights.

Providing all judges and courts the general power to act as constitutional judges is a consequence of the principle of the supremacy of the constitution (Brewer-Carias, 1989). For example, the Constitution of the United States includes a Supremacy Clause that makes clear the link between the principle and the diffuse model. A clause in Article 6, section 2 states:

> *This Constitution, and the Laws of the United States which shall be made in Pursuance thereof; and all Treaties made, or which shall be made, under the Authority of the United States, shall be the supreme Law of the Land; and the Judges in every State shall be bound thereby, any Thing in the Constitution or Laws of any State to the Contrary notwithstanding.*

After establishing the constitution as supreme, and empowering judges at all levels to act as a constitutional court, the diffuse-model countries are left with a potential problem. Because judges at all court levels and regions can rule on constitutionality, the potential for conflicting opinions and rulings is great. How does a system of diffuse judicial review respond to the danger of different judges reaching inconsistent results on close questions? Countries in the common legal tradition respond to that problem with the aid of *stare decisis.*

An emphasis on *stare decisis* reduces the danger of inconsistent rulings by requiring judges to follow their own prior decisions and the precedents of higher courts. In the United States, the presence of a single national supreme court and the requirement that lower courts follow its superior precedents, ensures the uniformity of constitutional adjudication. The civil legal tradition countries using a diffuse system of judicial review cannot, customarily, rely on *stare decisis.* Instead, as we will see, they use related concepts (for example, in Mexico), set up special procedures (for example, in Argentina), or establish special courts (for example, in Greece). In such ways, countries with a civil legal tradition and a diffuse system of judicial review are able to resolve problems of uncertainty and conflict arising when numerous judges make decisions on constitutionality of laws (Brewer-Carias, 1989). An overview of judicial review in three countries will highlight these modifications while elaborating on the system of diffuse judicial review.

Like many other Latin American countries, Argentina and Mexico were influenced by the constitutional system of the United States. This presented some problems in the area of the judiciary, because those same countries had modeled their legal system after the civil legal tradition of European countries. In the area of judicial review, many Latin American countries eventually moved from the American diffuse system to a mixed system combining this common law feature with their civil law system. Argentina and Mexico, however, remained faithful to the American system (Brewer-Carias, 1989). Understandably, each country also added its own modifications, but they clearly follow a diffuse model of judicial review.

Article 31 of the Constitution of the Republic of Argentina says, in part, the Constitution and the laws passed by Congress are "the supreme law of the Nation" (quoted in Brewer-Carias, 1989, p. 156). Further, Article 100 makes the Supreme Court and the various inferior courts competent to hear cases related to the Constitution and congressional laws. As in the United States, therefore, all Argentinian courts can declare legislative acts, as well as executive and administrative acts and judicial decisions, to be unconstitutional.

In its appellate jurisdiction, the Argentinian Supreme Court of Justice hears two kinds of appeal. For *ordinary appeals,* the Supreme Court reviews particular

You Should Know!

JUDICIAL REVIEW AT A SUPRANATIONAL LEVEL

Judicial review is most correctly viewed as the way a specific country provides for oversight of government actions in relation to legal principles established by that country. The affiliation of European countries via treaties and conventions presents an interesting modification of the traditional concept of judicial review. For example, the member states of the Council of Europe have agreed to abide by the principles established in the *European Convention on Human Rights (ECHR).* Enforcing the ECHR are the European Commission of Human Rights and the European Court of Human Rights. It is the Court to which our attention is directed.

The European Court of Human Rights, sitting in Strasbourg, France, hears cases regarding compliance by individual countries with the ECHR. The United Kingdom offers a good example of this judicial review at a supranational level since the UK only recently incorporated the ECHR into domestic law via the Human Rights Act of 1998.

Although the UK was an original signer (in 1950) of the ECHR, the convention was not incorporated into domestic law until October 2000 when the Human Rights Act became effective. As a result of that incorporation, British courts are able to issue a declaration of incompatibility when the court determines that legislation conflicts with the ECHR. Further, British citizens (like the citizens of all countries that have incorporated the ECHR into their domestic law) who believe that their domestic court has failed to protect an ECHR right can petition the European Court of Human Rights to ask that court to rule on the legislation's compatibility with the ECHR. British penologist Ursula Smartt (personal communication July, 2000) believes the incorporation of the Human Rights Act will result in challenges to several existing UK laws on topics related to the housing, treatment, and discipline of prisoners. Judicial review, at least for the countries signing the ECHR, exists at a supranational as well as national level.

decisions made by the National Chamber of Appeals and serves as a court of last resort for such matters. It is the second type of appellate jurisdiction, *extraordinary appeals,* which provides Argentina's special procedure for judicial review.

Any party having direct interest in a case decided at the provincial superior court or at the National Chambers of Appeals level can bring the case before the Supreme Court of Justice. The primary restriction for such access is that the case must involve a constitutional issue. In this manner, the Supreme Court provides final interpretation of the Constitution. For that reason, extraordinary appeal is the most important means for judicial review of state acts.

Judicial review in Mexico is directly linked to the *judicio de amparo* (trial for protection), which in turn comes from the Mexican Constitution. The trial for *amparo* (constitutional protection) comprises five different aspects: protection of fundamental constitutional rights, procedures against judicial decisions that incorrectly apply legal provisions, judicial review of administrative action, protection of the agrarian rights of peasants, and reviews on the constitutionality of legislation.

In addition to covering similar topics, Mexican and American judicial review share an appreciation for the concept of judicial precedent. As noted earlier, the absence of *stare decisis* in civil law countries makes it difficult for them to use a diffuse system of judicial review. Mexico integrated diffuse judicial review into its civil legal tradition by developing *jurisprudencia* as a procedure similar to *stare decisis.*

In cases when the law of *amparo* is at issue, precedents from previous federal court decisions are considered binding for lower courts. This process is similar to *stare decisis* in common law but differs in an important respect. Whereas *stare decisis* relies on a single decision, Mexican *jurisprudencia* (precedents from previous decisions) require five consecutive decisions to the same effect (Brewer-Carias, 1989).

These similarities with judicial review in the United States are balanced by other aspects that set the Mexican system apart. Possibly most important is the restriction of *amparo* jurisdiction to federal level courts. Therefore, judicial review is not a power of all courts in Mexico as it is in America.

In addition to the Latin American countries that followed the American lead on diffuse judicial review, the model also caught on in a few European countries. Greece is especially noted for having a judicial review process that is very similar to that of the United States.

The 1927 Greek constitution expressly established judicial review powers of all courts, and the idea has remained through the present 1975 constitution (Brewer-Carias, 1989). There are three primary areas of difference between Greek and American judicial review. First, in common law countries, the constitutional issue must be raised by one of the parties in the case. In Greece, the courts have power to review the constitutionality of legislation even when there is no case before them that challenges that legislation. Second, neither the *stare decisis* doctrine nor the Mexican version of *jurisprudencia* exists in Greece. Therefore, decisions of the higher-level courts are not made obligatory for those at the lower level.

The third distinction between Greek and American versions of diffuse judicial review is the Greek addition of a special court to rule on constitutional matters. Greek courts are organized in three separate branches, which hear, respectively, civil and criminal cases, administrative cases, and public audit and financial matters. Because all courts in each branch have the power of judicial review, it is possible that the court of last resort for each branch will render contradictory and conflicting judgments on constitutional issues. To resolve such problems, the 1968 constitution established a Constitutional Court. The 1975 constitution reconstructed that court into a Special Highest Court, which provides a corrective measure to a judicial review process operating in three different court branches.

Concentrated Model for Judicial Review. The alternative to diffuse judicial review is a concentrated approach. The distinguishing feature of the concentrated system of judicial review is the use of a single state organ to act as a country's constitutional judge. That entity can be the Supreme Court of Justice, acting as the highest court in the judicial hierarchy, or a specialized court organized outside the ordinary court hierarchy. In either situation, the country's constitution expressly creates and regulates the agency responsible for upholding the supremacy of that constitution.

The idea that a constitution should create and specify the process of judicial review is a distinguishing feature between the diffuse and concentrated models. For example, neither the U.S. Constitution nor the Argentinian Constitution (as examples of the diffuse models) conferred judicial review power on the courts. Instead, both constitutions simply note their supremacy and the duty of all courts to make decisions consistent with their contents. By default, not by decree, all courts in the United States and Argentina are constitutional courts. In the concentrated model of judicial review, there is no doubt concerning which agency decides constitutional questions. That duty falls to a very specific state organ, identified in the country's constitution itself.

Most adherents of this position are civil law countries, but some socialist countries either adopted the model (for example, Yugoslavia) or are flirting with the procedure. The archetype is Austria, but the concentrated model was also adopted by Italy (1948) and West Germany (1949). More recent followers include Cyprus (1960), Turkey (1961), and the Russian Federation (1993). The countries following this model tend to believe more strongly in the separation of powers (rather than simply checks and balances) and the supremacy of statutory law. The concentrated model refuses to grant judicial review power to the judiciary generally. The ordinary judge must accept and apply the law as he finds it; judicial review is undertaken by a specialized court or tribunal.

Austria provided the model for concentrated judicial review when its 1920 constitution created a constitutional tribunal *(Verfassungsgerichtshof).* This 14-person court was reinstituted in 1945. Members are appointed by the president of the republic after recommendations from the Parliament. They have life tenure to age 70 and possess the power to review the constitutionality of legislation and decide jurisdictional disputes (Abraham, 1986). Since 1920, Austrian citizens have been able to file complaints when they feel their constitutional rights have been violated by an act of administration. Since 1975 complaints have also been allowed regarding a violation of rights by an act of legislation.

Germany's federal constitutional court, the *Bundesverfassungsgericht,* was created in 1951 (for West Germany). It consists of 16 judges, all of whom have considerable past judicial, legal, professional, or other high public experience. Half are elected by the lower house (Bundestag) and half by the upper house (Bundesrat) of Parliament. The judges serve a nonrenewable 12-year term. They hear cases brought by agencies, institutions, and certain individuals. The court decides the constitutional validity of any federal or state statute and protects the fundamental rights and privileges of citizens on both substantive and procedural issues.

Italy's constitutional court *(Corte Costituzionale)* was established in 1948 and began functioning in 1956. This 15-member body is staffed with distinguished persons having at least 20 years' experience as practicing lawyers, experienced judges, or professors of law. The judges are appointed for staggered nine-year terms with five selected by the president of the republic, five by three-fifths vote of Parliament, and five by the ordinary and administrative judiciary. The *Corte Costituzionale* is the final interpreter of the constitution and has the power to declare both national and regional laws unconstitutional.

In the News

THE DEMOCRATIZATION OF RUSSIA

Russia's Constitutional Court—established in 1991, but more clearly defined under the 1993 Constitution of the Russian Federation—is the first court in Russia to be given the authority to decide constitutional issues. As such, it was offered by many observers as the first credible evidence that Russia was poised to become a genuinely law-based state.

In the traditional Soviet system there were many organizational and procedural features, related to Communist rule, that undermined the independence of courts and served to make the judiciary subordinate to the legislature. For example, the Ministry of Justice provided "oversight" over the courts of general jurisdiction, and as a result the courts were subject to pressure by that ministry (Danilenko & Burnham, 1999). Further, the idea that the judiciary could rule on the legitimacy of legislative action was in conflict with socialist ideology that saw Communist social policy as dominant over any state organs.

The 1993 Constitution changed the balance of power so that the legislative, executive, and judicial branches are defined as separate and equal. Judges are independent and subject only to the Constitution and federal law (Article 120).

The Supreme Court of the Russian Federation is the highest judicial authority on civil, criminal, and administrative cases, but the Constitutional Court, which has 19 judges, decides cases regarding the compliance of various legislation with the Constitution. Where the Court determines the legislation to be in conflict with the Constitution, the legislation is made invalid (Article 125). This procedure of judicial review places Russia with those countries following a concentrated model. The Constitutional Court must wait until a designated body (e.g., the President of the Federation, the State Duma, the Supreme Court of the Federation) asks the Court to make a ruling regarding specific legislation.

With constitutional courts like those in Austria, Germany, and Italy, the concentrated model of judicial review achieves the same goal as the diffuse model: to provide procedures for holding the government to certain fundamental values. France offers another way to achieve the same end. In France, the belief that courts should not engage in any lawmaking at all prevented placement of "judicial review" within the judiciary. Instead, in 1958 the French created the Constitutional Council *(Conseil Constitutionnel)*. Unlike the constitutional courts of other European countries, this entity lies outside the judicial system (Abraham, 1986). Neither individuals, groups, nor courts of law can appeal to it. The council is composed of all the ex-presidents of France plus nine other persons selected (three each) by the president of the republic, the president of the senate, and the president of the National Assembly. The nine appointed members serve one nonrenewable nine-year term of office, and the ex-presidents serve for life.

The council has wide-ranging duties (see Brewer-Carias, 1989), only one of which is judicial review. It accomplishes the judicial-review duty by striking down laws or declaring them unconstitutional after they are drafted by the parliament but before the president signs them into law. A single opinion is delivered, without concurring or dissenting opinions, and that judgment is final and binding. However, because the council is not a court of law, its decisions can be enforced only by the council's ability to persuade the courts. Two things especially keep the council from representing an example of judicial review (Abraham, 1986). First, private individuals cannot challenge the constitutionality of a law; so, for example, there can be no French equivalent to America's Clarence Earl Gideon and his challenge to the absence of defense counsel for indigents. In addition, when challenges are authorized, they can be only on the law's substance, not on its procedural application. As a result, challenges like those in the United States on search and seizure procedures are not considered by the French Constitutional Council.

Mixed Model for Judicial Review. Because the concentrated and diffuse systems of judicial review can exist in countries with either a common or civil legal tradition, it is not surprising that mixed systems of judicial review sometimes occur. Brewer-Carias (1989) believes that countries like Portugal and Venezuela exemplify mixed systems.

The Portuguese constitution of 1976 and its 1982 revision established a complete system of judicial review, which has elements of concentrated (including the French version) and diffuse models. The Constitutional Court, created by the constitution as part of the judicial hierarchy, represents the concentrated aspect. Along with the establishment of the Constitutional Court, the Portuguese constitution authorizes all courts in the country to avoid implementing any law deemed by the court to be unconstitutional. This rule, of course, agrees with the diffuse model. Similarly, building on a 100-year tradition, Venezuela's 1961 constitution established the Supreme Court of Justice as competent to review the constitutionality of laws. Simultaneously, the Civil Proceedings Code allows all courts in Venezuela to declare inapplicable laws the court deems unconstitutional. These combinations of diffuse and concentrated systems of judicial review provide Venezuela and Portugal with two of the most extensive systems of judicial review in the world (Brewer-Carias, 1989).

Brazil's new constitution (1988) places it among countries with mixed systems of judicial review (Dolinger, 1990). Although Brazil originally followed the United States and used a diffuse model, constitutional reforms over the years kept adding aspects of a concentrated model. As a result, any Brazilian judge at any court level today can ignore law that he or she considers unconstitutional for the current case (Dolinger, 1990). Additionally, the Brazilian Supremo Tribunal Federal not only rules on the constitutionality of laws related to the case immediately before it but also can declare unconstitutional any action initiated by the office of the attorney general of the republic.

Judicial Review in the Islamic and Socialist Traditions. As noted earlier, discussion of a *Rechtsstaat* in Islamic and socialist law must differ slightly from its discussion under common and civil legal traditions. Countries in the common and civil families usually (France being an exception) follow one of two judicial-review models to hold their governments accountable to fundamental values. In all cases, those values have been reduced to written form through a constitution. Under Islamic law, the fundamental values are presented in the *Qur'an* and *Sunna*. Under socialism, law is subordinate to policy.

Islam very clearly accepts the supremacy of fundamental values or laws. Those laws preceded the state, and the state exists solely to maintain and enforce them. The *Shari'a* records the fundamental values, so Islamic law meets the first two criteria for achieving a *Rechtsstaat:* recognition of the supremacy of fundamental values and reducing those values to written form. For those viewing the rule of law as desirable, the problem with the Islamic tradition is that it goes no further than the first two steps.

The *Shari'a* does not visualize any conflict between the interests of the ruler and of the citizen. As a result, there are no procedures (judicial or otherwise) to review the actions of government. Substantive questions cannot be brought by citizens, because the law is considered to be of divine origin and valid for all time. To question the legitimacy of a law would mean that a Muslim is questioning Allah. Similarly, questions regarding the procedures used to enforce the law are inappropriate because Muslims are told to give allegiance to the existing authority, regardless of the nature of that authority (Coulson, 1957). Unjust rulers and their inappropriate procedures will be punished by Allah in the next world.

The absence of any system to provide a remedy against the abuse of individual rights by government agents means that Islamic law does not completely operate under a rule of law. The recognition and written account of fundamental values is not backed up with formal procedures by which citizens can hold their government accountable to those values. Instead, the Islamic tradition simply counsels against abuse and relies on faith that rulers will hold themselves answerable. "To the power of the ruler who is supported by adequate physical force the *Shari'a* sets no other limits than those which he finds in his own conscience" (Coulson, 1957).

In terms of achieving a *Rechtsstaat*, Islamic law is similar to the common and civil legal traditions in recognizing and reducing to writing certain fundamental values. It differs from the other two by having incomplete mechanisms for judicial review to force the government to abide by the same values it requires of the citizens. Socialist law differs from the other three by failing even to recognize fundamental values, let alone reducing them to writing or providing procedures to hold the government accountable. The phrase "failing to recognize" is actually inappropriate because socialism rejects the notion of law as an absolute value. Instead, socialist policy is the absolute, and law is the subordinate. In other words, a *Rechtsstaat* is absent in the socialist tradition by design, not mistake.

Because socialist legality exists to advance the interests of the state, there has been only indirect interest in protecting the welfare of individual citizens. The possibility of inappropriate government behavior is recognized, but the judiciary is certainly not viewed as the appropriate monitor. In China, for example, the Supreme People's Court (the country's highest court) cannot invalidate a law passed by the National People's Congress. Interestingly, however, the Court has assisted the Congress in drafting legislation (Terrill, 1999). Instead of having the judiciary oversee government activities, socialist systems rely on the procuracy as the agency responsible for supervising the activities of administrative agencies. Because this is not part of the judiciary, examinations of violations of law by state officials is initiated by this investigative body rather than by individual citizens. The absence of judicial authority to rule on the legitimacy of legislation means that law is subordinate to policy and as a result, judicial review is not an aspect of the socialist tradition.

SUMMARY

Every legal system must address issues of substantive and procedural law, but each system may approach the terms differently. This chapter takes the admittedly Western-linked perspective on substantive and procedural law as first presented in Chapter 3 and uses these concepts as a comparative aid in discussing legal systems.

Looking at substantive law in each of the four legal traditions, we found that defining what was criminal and specifying the punishment included reliance on judges (common legal tradition), legislators (civil legal tradition), a variety of government agencies (socialist legal tradition), and on God (Islamic legal tradition). Regardless of who or what is doing the defining, it is apparent that each legal tradition has some difficulty with several or all of the general characteristics and major principles associated with substantive law.

Procedural law was addressed with specific attention to the issues of the adjudicatory process and judicial review. Adjudication typically follows an adversarial or inquisitorial model. Both models seek the truth in claims made by the state against an individual. The inquisitorial process (civil law systems and socialist law systems) seems like a continuing investigation with all parties cooperating to determine what happened. The adversarial process (common law systems), on the other hand, is more obviously a contest between competing sides, where truth is said to lie with the victor. This is especially true in the United States' version of the adversarial process. Adjudication under Islamic procedural law seems a combination of the inquisitorial and adversarial models.

The procedure of judicial review was introduced as an important way to ensure that a government abides by the fundamental values of a nation. In this way a *Rechtsstaat*, or rule of law, can be achieved, because the government, like its citizens, is made accountable. One model of judicial review is the diffuse design, wherein all courts in a country have authority to find laws unconstitutional. This decentralized model is used in the United States and in some civil law countries, so it is not attached to particular legal traditions. The concentrated model for judicial review follows a centralized design and invests all constitutional review power in a single state organ. Some countries have successfully adopted aspects of both diffuse and concentrated models and as a result are said to have a mixed model for judicial review. Still other countries (for example, some under the Islamic and socialist legal traditions) do not seem to operate under a rule of law and as such have incomplete or nonexistent procedures for judicial review.

WEB SITES TO VISIT

- The International Constitutional Law web site at **www.uni-wuerzburg.de/law/info.html** is an ambitious project that allows comparison of constitutional documents from many (planning for all) countries.

- There are many translations of the Qur'an available on the Internet. Visit **www.quran.org.uk/** to identify some of those sites and to see other types of information available on the Qur'an.
- Read about the criminal procedure law of China at **www.enstar.co.uk/china/ law/blw/crimproc.htm** and about the criminal law of China at either (1) **l-a-law-firm.com/library/law/criminal/criminal.htm** or (2) **www.qis.net/chinalaw/prclaw60.htm**

SUGGESTED READINGS

Guarnieri, C. (1997). Prosecution in two civil law countries: France and Italy. In D. Nelken (Ed.), *Comparing legal cultures* (pp. 183–193). Aldershot, England: Dartmouth.

Ingraham, Barton L. (1987). The structure of criminal procedure: Laws and practice of France, the Soviet Union, China, and the United States. New York: Greenwood, an imprint of Greenwood Publishing Group, Westport, CT.

Pizzi, W. T. (1999). *Trials without truth.* New York: New York University Press.

Sanad, Nagaty. (1991). The theory of crime and criminal responsibility in Islamic law: Shari'a. Chicago: Office of International Criminal Justice.

Souryal, Sam S., Potts, Dennis W., and Alobied, Abdullah I. (1994). The penalty of hand amputation for theft in Islamic justice. Journal of Criminal Justice, 22, 249–265.

Chapter 6

An International Perspective on Policing

KEY TOPICS

- Centralized and decentralized supervision of police forces
- Singular and multiple number of police forces to be supervised
- Example of centralized single systems of policing
- Example of decentralized single systems of policing
- Example of centralized multiple coordinated systems of policing
- Example of decentralized multiple coordinated systems of policing
- Canada's contracting system for providing police services
- Example of centralized multiple uncoordinated systems of policing
- Example of decentralized multiple uncoordinated systems of policing
- Issues of corruption in policing
- Issues of international cooperation in policing

KEY TERMS

Bereitschaftspolizei
Carabinieri
centralized policing
contract policing
Cuerpo Nacional de Policia
decentralized policing
Europol
Gendarmerie Nationale
Guardia Civil
Interpol
koban/chuzaisho
Kriminalpolizei
Policia Judicial Estatal
Policia Judicial Federal
Policia Municipal
Policia Preventiva
Policia Rural Estatal
Polizia di Stato
Royal Canadian Mounted Police
Schengen Group
Schutzpolizei

COUNTRIES REFERENCED

Canada	Italy	Nigeria
France	Japan	Spain
Germany	Mexico	United States

In Japan, Seicho Matsumoto's fictional Inspector Imanishi travels throughout the nation to investigate a case. No one seems to mind the fact that Imanishi-san is with the Tokyo Metropolitan Police Force yet is interviewing witnesses, asking questions of local police officers, and apparently having the run of the country with no regard for jurisdictional boundaries.

A continent away, Georges Simenon has his French Inspector Maigret investigate crime scenes under the watchful eye of deputy public prosecutors and upstart examining magistrates. Meanwhile, farther north in the Netherlands, police Commissaris Van der Valk (courtesy of Nicholas Freeling) must deal with an Officer of Justice who operates as an amalgam of a French public prosecutor and examining magistrate. Also in the Netherlands, but operating at lower ranks, Detective Adjutant Grijpstra and Sergeant de Gier (from the pen of Janwillem van de Wetering) work the Amsterdam streets, making decisions on such matters as the distance between a prostitute and the bar down the street. Because prostitution is illegal within 200 feet of a public place selling alcohol, police (who may actually be looking for drugs) may want to stop and question the streetwalker.

Police-procedure novels showing officers with nationwide jurisdiction, having to work under the direction of an examining magistrate, reporting to a combination prosecutor-judge, or dealing with laws that allow prostitution only on certain parts of the street, may raise questions of credibility from American readers. However, upon realizing that the U.S. police structure and organization, as well as procedures followed, are just one of several models available, American readers may find such novels to be doubly intriguing.

In fact, the American model of policing is more unusual than common. A basic principle of the American republic was the notion that the states and federal government would share power. In terms of maintaining law and order, the power was to be primarily at the state level. As if to emphasize the point, the U.S. Constitution mentions only two crimes (counterfeiting and treason) and avoids any mention of a national police force to protect federal property and enforce federal laws (Johnson, 1981). Taking their cue from the federal government, the states avoided direct involvement in law enforcement and delegated such duties to the local communities. This seemed appropriate, because crime was a local phenomenon and thus local authorities were presumed to know best how to respond to violators.

A result of this assignment of responsibilities was an absence of federal and state law enforcement agencies in accordance with a general decentralization of policing throughout the country and within each state. Even when the federal government increased its involvement in law enforcement, Congress, instead of investing all authority in one agency, divided enforcement responsibilities so that each federal department has investigative units responsible for enforcing laws relevant to that department's jurisdiction. The result ranges from U.S. Department of Agriculture agents enforcing specific legislation like food stamp regulations to the Federal Bureau of Investigation (Department of Justice) investigating over 200 different types of cases, (e.g., robbery of federally insured banks, interstate racketeering, transporting stolen property across state lines).

This chapter focuses on the various ways policing is structured around the world. You should bear in mind that this is only one of many ways policing might be presented in a comparative book. Comparison of police duties, training of officers, how police handle human rights issues, procedural law and the police, and the presence and nature of specialized units are also appropriate topics. Because one chapter does not provide an opportunity for too great a variety of issues, only two other points are presented here: police misconduct and the growth of international cooperation in law enforcement. However, we begin with the structure of police departments.

CLASSIFYING POLICE STRUCTURES

"The organization of the police is a curious subject. To begin with, it is boring" (Bayley, 1992, p. 509). That statement is not a very good way to encourage people to keep reading, but it is the way David Bayley chose to begin one of his articles on the topic of police structure in different countries. He resumes his discouraging start by adding that the subject is also "basic, inconsequential, fateful, and diversionary" (p. 510). Despite such inglorious traits, the organization of policing is regarded as so important that it is often considered a key issue for such central values as human rights and political freedom. Before dismissing such claims as grandiose, consider your reaction to a proposal that U.S. jurisdictions replace all local police departments with a single federal police agency having authority to enforce national and state laws across the country. As suggested earlier, tampering with the structure of decentralized American policing would be viewed by some as tantamount to tampering with the Constitution itself.

Arguing that the topic of police organization is important, even if boring, is easier than deciding how it should be presented. Rhoades and Moore (1992) reviewed attempts to categorize police organization, some of which contrasted only two types of structures and others of which compared as many as six. The use of just two categories has resulted in distinctions between the *kinship model* of policing versus the *ruler-appointed model* (see Reith, 1975) and the *common law model* versus the *continental model* (Rhoades & Moore, 1992). Authors recognizing three or four categories have considered whether a country's policing is *fragmented, centralized,* or *integrated* (see Hunter, 1990) and have evaluated the interplay of *structure, function,* and *source of power* (see Mawby, 1990). Jiao (1997) finds theoretical support for four models that distinguish among *police professionalism, community policing, problem-oriented policing,* and a *security orientation.*

David Bayley (1985; 1992) suggests a categorization on the basis of *dispersal of command* and *number of forces.* It is Bayley's scheme that directs our review. Here the concepts of centralization/decentralization and single/multiple forces serve as a base for a typology of worldwide police structures. Because multiple forces, either centralized or decentralized, can work together (coordinated) or at cross purposes (uncoordinated) the result is the six-cell matrix found in Table 6.1.The following analysis and discussion borrow heavily from Bayley's work.

Table 6.1 Types of Police Structures

	Dispersal of Command	
	Centralized	**Decentralized**
Single	Ireland Israel Nigeria Poland Saudi Arabia	Japan
Multiple Coordinated	Austria France England and Wales	Australia Canada Germany India
Multiple Uncoordinated	Belgium Italy Spain Switzerland	Mexico United States

Source: Adapted from *Patterns of Policing* by David H. Bayley. Copyright (c) 1985 by Rutgers, the State University of New Jersey. Additional information from David H. Bayley, (1992), Comparative Organization of the Police in English-speaking countries, *Crime and Justice, 21,* 509–545.

Bayley's criterion to identify a system as either centralized or decentralized is the stated locus of control. The emphasis is on "stated," because it is possible for a system to be one way in principle but another in actuality, meaning that the resulting categorization may not always reflect the actual condition. France, for example, has multiple police forces whose day-to-day operations are decided at the unit level. Structurally the command is from Paris, but it is seldom applied. Using the criterion of stated locus of control, France has a centralized police command. Bayley (1985) realizes that this criterion is deceptively simple, because it ignores the reality of informal command relationships. Yet until there are more comparative studies, Bayley's provides a sensible option.

Bayley's typology is especially helpful for understanding relationships among the countries in a particular cell and between countries in different cells. It also provides a concise way to describe policing in many different countries by emphasizing the similarities rather than being confused by the differences. In other words, like all good classification schemes, Bayley's typology of police structures summarizes and makes sense of diversity.

Upon understanding the characteristics of each category for police structures you can assign immediately a new structure to the appropriate category. For example, Kurian says, "Mexican police forces exist at the federal, state and municipal levels through many overlapping layers of authority" (1989, p. 258). We also know that Mexico's main federal police is part of the Ministry of Government; that each state and the federal district has its own police force; and that police delegations, headed by a comandante, operate in large urban areas. Applying Bayley's classification scheme to these characteristics should result in your assignment of Mexico to the cell containing "decentralized" (a different authority supervises the force at each level) "multiple" (there are at least three types of police) "uncoordinated" (there are apparently overlapping layers of authority) police structures.

With the aid of Bayley's categorization, we now move to a description of one police system falling into each major type found in Table 6.1. Because the United States uses a police system that is less often found, it seems fitting that we better understand what most countries are doing. We do that by describing the police systems in countries that fall into each of six cells in Bayley's typology. The six countries representing each cell are Nigeria (centralized, single), Japan (decentralized, single), France (centralized multiple coordinated), Germany (decentralized multiple coordinated), Spain (centralized multiple uncoordinated), and Mexico (decentralized multiple uncoordinated).

Centralized Single Systems: Nigeria

The idea of one national police force responsible for enforcing a single set of laws throughout an entire country sounds strange to Americans. However, as Table 6.1 shows, that system is perfectly acceptable to the citizens of many countries. Nations as diverse as Poland (Adamski, 1997), Saudi Arabia (Alobied, 1989), and Israel (Bensinger, 1989) find it possible to operate effective governments with a single national police force. Nigeria is another country falling into this category and, because it provides an opportunity to consider police in a Third World country, is used here to exemplify the type.

Thirty years before gaining independence from the British in 1960, Nigeria had merged its Northern Constabulary, the Southern Police Force, and the Lagos Police Force into the Nigeria Police Force (Kayode, 1976). The continued existence of independent regional police departments and community police forces alongside that national force provided a decentralized system. Given the local conditions and political climate of the time, this decentralized law enforcement provided a sense of autonomy and stability for each administrative area.

As independence took hold during the 1960s, Nigeria moved toward a very centralized police model. A turning point occurred in 1964, when the first Nigerian head of the Nigeria Police Force took office. Before that date, every inspector-general of the national police was British (Kayode, 1976). The next step to complete centralization and Nigeriazation of law enforcement was the gradual integration of remaining local police forces into the Nigeria Police Force. The first group of local officers reported for training at the federal police college in 1968. By 1980 the merging of local police into the federal force was completed for all Nigeria.

The Nigeria Police Force is headquartered in Lagos and operates under the leadership of an Inspector General of Police (see Figure 6.1). Prior to a 1999 democratic election, Nigeria was under a military leadership that might suggest that the police force would be under the supervision of the Ministry of Defenses. Actually, though, it exists as a separate body that is part of the military administration. Reflecting that link, the Inspector General of Police is a member of the Supreme Military Council, the Federal Executive Council, and the Council of States (Iwarimie-Jaja, 1988b). Five assistant inspector generals each supervise one of the five departments at central headquarters (Igbinovia, 1989). These departments, labeled A through E in Figure 6.1, have responsibility for such activities as

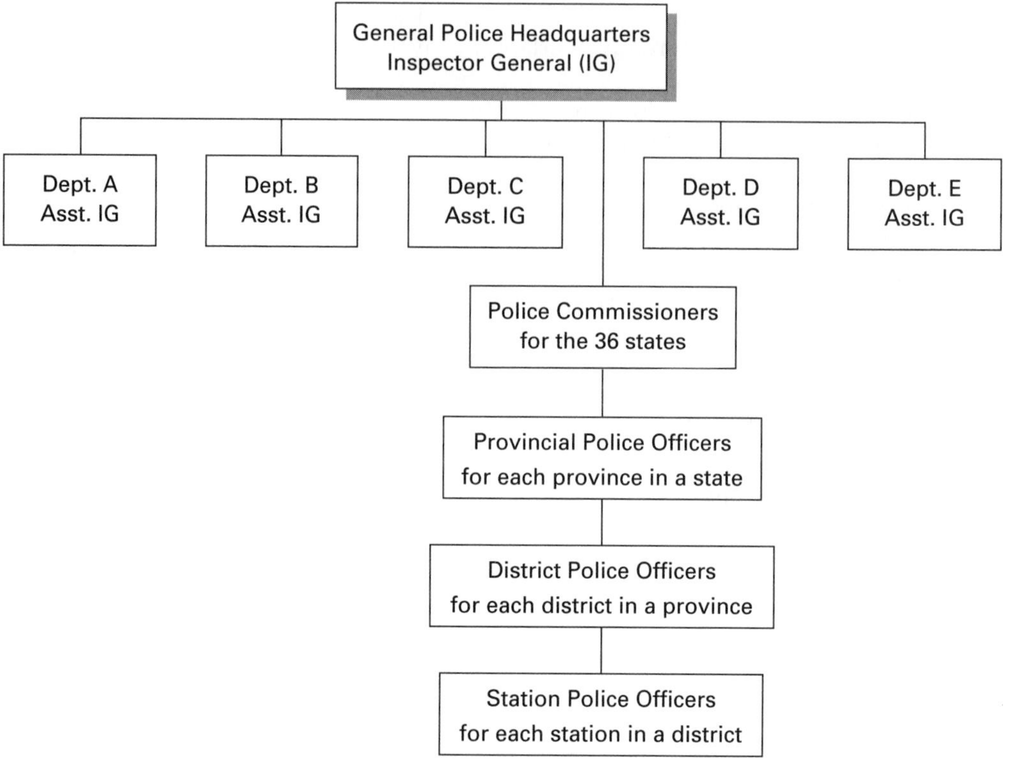

Figure 6.1 Nigeria's Police Organization

general administration (Department A), communications and transportation (Department B), general financial matters (Department C), criminal records and investigation (Department D), and a special branch (Department E) responsible for internal security and countersubversive activities.

Below central police headquarters in the organizational hierarchy are police commands in each of Nigeria's 36 states. A commissioner of police heads each of the police commands, which are located in the 36 capital cities. Below the commissioner are the provincial police officers, then the district police officers, and finally the station officers.

The tasks of policing and the manner in which they are carried out are similar to those of any other modern nation. Patrol, either foot or automobile, is handled by uniformed officers, who are usually unarmed except for a billy club or baton. Foot-patrol officers walk their beat during both day and evening hours. Two-way radios provide contact with police headquarters, the nearest police station, or patrolling police cars.

Motorized patrol is of four types: roundabout, antirobbery, highway, and police accident (Igbinovia, 1989). The roundabout patrol involves the assignment of officers to the important traffic circles (roundabouts) in the cities. This positioning allows police officers to watch all movements in the area, report suspicious behavior, and respond quickly to instructions from the police station. Antirobbery patrol teams, as their name implies, are mobile units charged with apprehending persons caught in the act of robbery or intercepting those believed ready to commit a robbery. The highway patrol units have access to ambulances, motorcycles, and sophisticated communications equipment. These officers enforce traffic laws, aid accident victims, and respond to crimes committed on highways. The police accident patrol responds to instances of hit-and-run driving and tries to prevent or reduce deaths from road accidents.

The centralized single police forces of countries like Poland, Saudi Arabia, Israel, and Nigeria show us just one way of providing law enforcement in a country. The fact that these countries vary considerably in size (Israel is slightly larger than New Jersey whereas Saudi Arabia is one third the size of the United States) and population density (Nigeria has 322 people per square mile and Saudi Arabia 15) suggests that geography alone is not a likely variable to explain the occurrence of this type of police structure. Nor does government type seem to predict a single centralized police force, because even these few examples include a democratic state (Poland), a monarchy with a council of ministers (Saudi Arabia), a parliamentary republic (Israel), and a federal republic under, until recently, a military leadership (Nigeria).

A country's preferred police structure is not easily explained as the result of one or two clearly identifiable features. A people's history, culture, traditions, and links to other people are only some of the topics to be considered in trying to understand a country's social institutions. Such disciplines as political science, history, sociology, psychology, and anthropology are among those that may provide answers. For our purposes, we must be content with appreciating the variety and foregoing the analysis. In presenting the other examples of police structures, we continue to rely on descriptive accounts rather than analyzing the reasons that various countries share a similar police structure.

Decentralized Single Systems: Japan

Japan is offered as the sole example in Table 6.1 of a single police force under decentralized command. Not only are examples scarce for this category, there is disagreement about even Japan's placement in that cell. However, to understand the disagreement it is necessary first to examine the structure of Japanese policing—so we begin at that point.

A combination of pre–World War II reliance on centralization and the remnant of a decentralized format imposed by occupation forces after the war helps explain Japanese policing as an example of a single force under decentralized command. The Tokugawa shogunate (1600–1868) provided for law enforcement through an elaborate system wherein town magistrates (or their delegates) served in roles we would today call police chief, prosecutor, and judge. Average citizens also played an important part, because they were grouped into organizations and made mutually responsible, and collectively liable, for any crimes or disorder caused by each other (Ames, 1983). The shogun provided a central authority over this policing arrangement through his links to town magistrates and the citizen organizations.

With the Meiji Restoration (1868–1912), Japan began gathering ideas about policing from the West. When Kawaji Toshiyoshi was sent to Europe in 1872, he was charged with investigating the police structures in several countries. Upon his return to Japan later that same year, Kawaji recommended police reorganization along the lines of France (Westney, 1987). The result was the 1873 establishment of the Home Ministry, which provided direct control over prefectural administration. The Police Bureau, within the Home Ministry, allowed the ministry to control police activities throughout Japan. It was centralization like this that the Allied occupation forces found potentially destructive to the newly established peace. As a result, like their counterpart in post–World War II Germany, Allied occupation forces in Japan decided to decentralize Japanese policing.

Ames (1983) and Chwialkowski (1998) describe how the American advisers made suggestions for a reorganized Japanese police that would closely follow the American model. With the new Police Law of 1947, the Home Ministry was abolished, police were relieved of administrative duties (for example, issuing permits, regulating public health, construction, and similar businesses), and autonomous police units were established. All cities and towns with populations of 5000 and over were told to establish a police force, and as a result some 1600 independent municipal police departments were organized. The smaller towns and villages were policed by a new National Rural Police, which was organized at the prefecture level with very limited national level involvement (Ames, 1983).

Like the citizens of the new West Germany, which we will discuss shortly, the Japanese had immediate problems with these structures imposed by the occupation forces. Difficulties in providing financial support for the local police and the presence of undesirable influence from politicians and gangsters were of particular concern. Finally, in June 1951 the Police Law was amended to allow smaller communities to merge their police forces with the National Rural Police. Eighty percent of the communities with autonomous police forces quickly disbanded their independent force and joined with the rural police.

In 1954 a new Police Law abolished the dual system of municipal and rural police and integrated the two types into prefectural police forces (Ames, 1983; Kurian, 1989), which provided the base for today's structure.

The Structure of Japanese Policing. Japan now has three main law enforcement organizations (see Figure 6.2). The National Public Safety Commission, under the direct authority of the prime minister, is responsible for all police operations and activities in Japan. Ames sees this remnant from decentralization times as a relatively ineffective approach to maintaining public control of the police. The typically elderly and conservative men serving on the commission "almost always defer to police decisions" (Ames, 1983, p. 199). As a result, the police are independent of effective formal external checks on their power and operation.

The National Police Agency (NPA), the second of the three main organizations, serves as a central supervisory agency for the Japanese police system. The NPA is not a separate police force, and its officers perform strictly supervisory duties. This agency compiles crime statistics, furnishes criminal identification services, procures police equipment, and supervises police education and training (Ames, 1983). The NPA is headed by a commissioner general and consists of five bureaus: Police Administration, Criminal Investigation, Traffic, Communications, and Security.

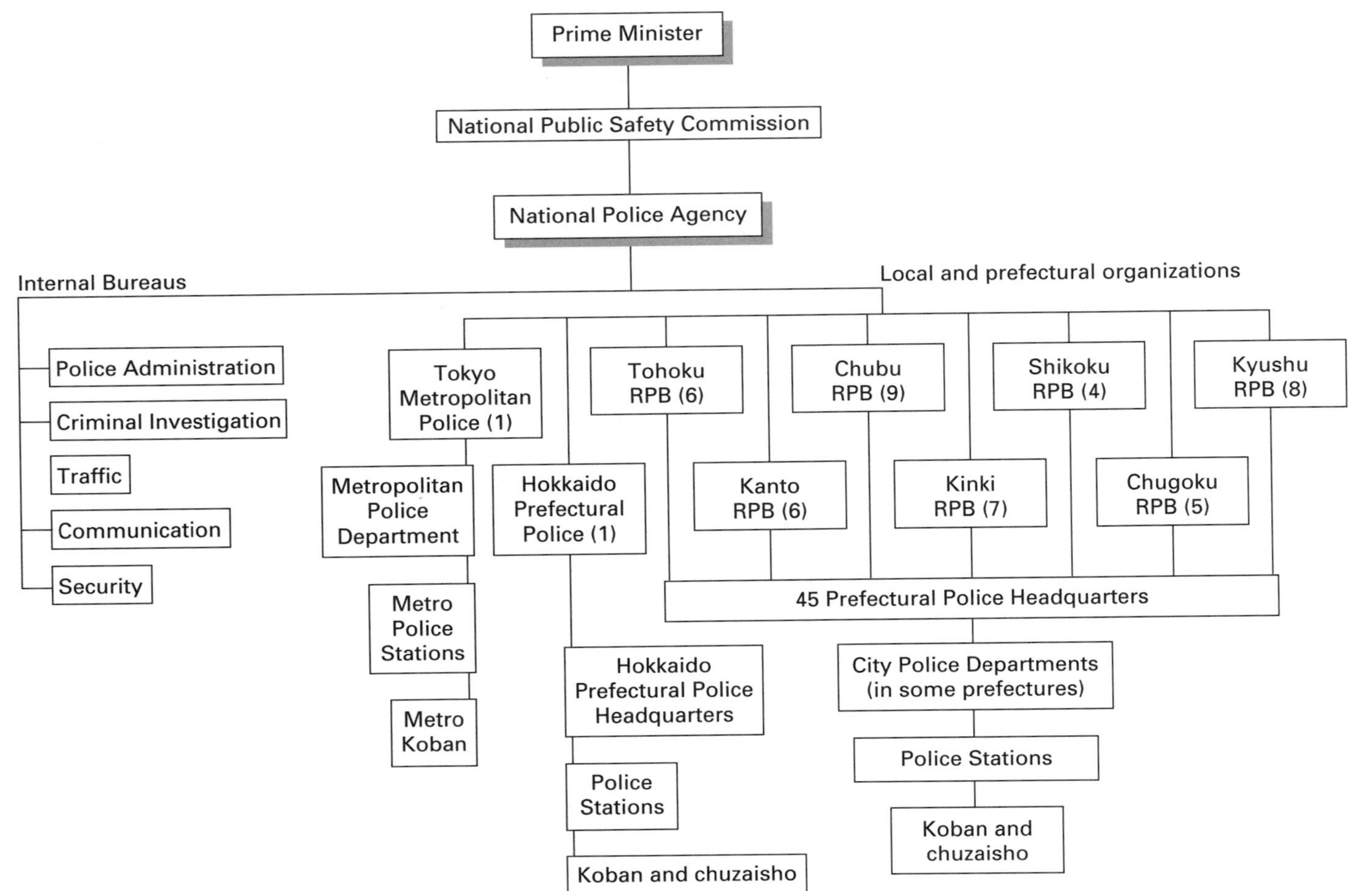

Figure 6.2 Japan's Police Organization

Providing a step toward decentralized command are seven *regional police bureaus (RPBs),* which serve as a liaison with the prefectural police. In addition to the seven RPBs, two police communications divisions also operate under the NPA (see Figure 6.2). These divisions provide structural integration of the country's largest city police force (Tokyo Metropolitan Police Communications Division) and for Japan's only region that is also a prefecture (Hokkaido Prefectural Police Communications Division).

The only agencies to perform actual police work in Japan are the local and prefectural organizations. That might seem to make Japan an example of a centralized (command is from a common national agency) multiple (there are different local forces) police structure. However, this is where Japan offers a singular example to Table 6.1. Japan is divided into 47 prefectures that are similar in concept to American states and in size to large American counties. The organizational chart in Figure 6.2 indicates (in parentheses) the number of prefectures in each of Japan's regions (for example, the Tohoku region has six). Each prefecture has one police headquarters from which chiefs and assistant chiefs control everyday police operations.

It is at the prefecture level that confusion arises about whether Japan has single or multiple forces and whether it is a centralized or decentralized structure. The highest-level officials at prefectural police headquarters (for example, chief and senior police superintendents) are employees of the NPA. That fact would suggest a single rather than multiple force. All other officers (for example, police superintendent, police inspector, police sergeant, policeman) are employed by the prefecture and at the prefecture's expense. The prefecture-employed police are primarily found at the organizational levels below Prefectural Police Headquarters—suggesting multiple rather than single forces. Based on Figure 6.2, an assumption that police in the police station and *koban/chuzaisho* levels are prefectural employees would be correct in most cases. Furthermore, each prefectural police department is supervised by the prefectural public safety commission under the prefectural governor's jurisdiction.

The 47 prefectures are themselves divided into districts. Each district has its own police station area under the direct control of prefectural police headquarters. Some of the police station boundaries correspond to city boundaries, but larger cities often have several police stations (Ames, 1983). Officers start their shift by reporting to the police station headquarters and are then deployed throughout the station boundaries. Because the NPA supervises and trains both its employees (the highest level officials at prefectural headquarters) and the prefecture employees (the regular police officers), and is the administrative unit for all police operations, Japan seems to have a single police force. Yet that single force clearly operates under a dispersal of command to the prefectural level. That means we have the unusual situation of a single force with decentralized command (see Bayley, 1992).

The area covered by a police station further divides into small jurisdictions linked to police boxes called *koban* and *chuzaisho. Koban,* which are located in urban areas, are staffed by two to twelve officers in a single shift. The specific number varies according to the area covered by the *koban.* Ames (1981), Bayley (1991), and Parker (1984) provide interesting descriptions of *koban* based on their individual experiences in Japan. Koban vary in size and shape from kiosk-like structures at busy street intersections to a quaint house on the bank of a canal. Between these extremes are *koban* operating from a thin, two-story building crammed among tall office buildings or a room sandwiched between the bar below and a restaurant above. Bayley (1991) identifies the only common features to the *koban* as a round, red light globe hung over the front door and dull gray interior walls.

Chuzaisho are the *koban* of rural areas. These police boxes are more typically built like the houses of their village. The *chuzaisho* includes a living area for the assigned police officer and his or her family. Parker (1984) highlights the close ties that develop between an officer and the community by noting that the *chuzai-san* ranks with the village headman and school principal as top town officials.

Deployment of officers to the neighborhood level will sound familiar to those with a knowledge of concepts like community-oriented policing. Chapter 10, which gives detailed coverage of Japan, continues discussion of this intriguing aspect of Japanese policing.

Centralized Multiple Coordinated Systems: France

Bayley (1985; 1992) distinguishes between multiple coordinated and multiple uncoordinated systems to demarcate situations where several forces operate within defined jurisdictions from those where several forces have overlapping authority. He reminds us, however, that all national governments create police agencies with authority for areas that transcend the concerns of subordinate government units. Examples include the FBI in the United States and Canada's Royal Canadian Mounted Police. So technically all multiple-force countries have uncoordinated systems, because there is inevitably a national-level agency with overlapping authority.

Bayley assigns a country to a coordinated or uncoordinated cell according to his judgment about the level of importance attached to the central government's responsibilities in the total view of policing. In a coordinated police system, enforcement by the central government is deemed relatively unimportant. Central authority is curtailed by such techniques as limiting its jurisdictional area and allowing it to intervene only at the request of local authorities. Alternatively, uncoordinated forces are independently active, have responsibility for many offenses, and can act without prior approval of local authorities. Although recognizing that multiple-force countries are necessarily uncoordinated, we will follow Bayley's lead and for purposes of description and education distinguish some as coordinated.

Table 6.1 places countries like Austria (see Harnischmacher, 1989) and England and Wales (see Bayley, 1992) among the centralized multiple coordinated type. The England and Wales placement would likely irritate some British observers and therefore, deserves brief justification. There are 43 police forces in England and Wales. Forty-one are provincial forces and two serve the London area: the London Metropolitan Police (with Scotland Yard being its Criminal Investigation Department) and the City of London Police. The Home Office (that is, the central government) has direct supervision over the London Metropolitan Police and indirect supervision over the provincial police and the City of London Police. The controversy about England and Wales being an example of a centralized police command is based on how "indirect" the Home Office supervision is over the other 42 police forces.

The argument for England and Wales as having decentralized policing is supported by the organizational structure that has the central government sharing administrative responsibility for provincial policing with each local chief constable and with a local police authority. Each police authority has some (49 percent) financial responsibility for its police, appoints the chief constable and assistant chief constables, and determines the size of its police force and the number of people needed for each rank. Because of these local influences, British citizens and politicians cringe at the suggestion that they have a national police force with multiple agencies.

Although the role of local police authorities seems like a good criterion for a decentralized system, persons arguing for England and Wales as a centralized system point out that the Home Office provides 51 percent of the police funding, approves the appointment of the chief and assistant constables, and supervises annual inspections of each department (Hirschel & Wakefield, 1995; Terrill, 1997). As a result, many authors believe centralization is a fact that is becoming increasingly apparent. Bayley explains that "although public opinion remains dead set against the creation of a national police force, Britain may be moving in that direction . . . [since] the central government has created the structure of policing and powerfully influenced its operating policies" (1992, p. 533). Similarly, Terrill says that despite English protestations, "in both theory and fact, however, the central government has enormous control and influence over the police, and it appears to be increasing" (1997, p. 11). Hirschel and Wakefield (1995) and Bayley (1992) see the expanded Home Office role in selecting and training chief constables, the greater willingness of chief constables to accept Home Office policy directives, and the increased movement toward coordination of police activities throughout the country as shifting the center of power from the local authorities to the Home Secretary. So, with no intent to offend British feelings, England and Wales are included here among the centralized multiple coordinated police types. A less controversial example of this type is France, to which we now turn our attention.

French policing dates back at least to 1666 and Louis XIV's creation of a Lieutenant-General of Police for Paris. The holder of that position had both administrative and judicial tasks ranging from controlling prices, weights, and measures, and inspecting markets to apprehending criminals and developing surveillance of suspected traitors. This office was abolished after the French Revolution, and Napoleon appointed a Minister of Police, who initially focused on information gathering and state security (Roach, 1985).

Nineteenth-century changes finally settled down when the Municipal Code of 1884 set the terms of commune (France's smallest division of local government) organization. The office of mayor was created, and the holder of that office was given control over police services (Kania, 1989). The result was a system of local policing operating in conjunction with the national police.

In 1941 the Vichy government established the basic structure of French policing with the *Gendarmerie* policing the rural areas and the *Police Nationale* having responsibility for urban policing. In this manner, French policing reflects the multiple coordinated type, because each force has separate jurisdictions. Actually, each is also under a different ministry, as will be described, but because the ministries make up the central government, the police system is centralized.

The French are proud of their forked version of centralization (see Figure 6.3). Since Napoleon's time, they have consistently refrained from placing control of the police under a single authority. In fact, Stead (1983) suggests the absence of a Minister of Police is a conspicuous strategy to avoid the concentration of force in the hands of a single person. The chosen alternative gives the Minister of the Interior administrative control over the civil police (the *Police Nationale*), while the Minister of Defense has similar control over the *Gendarmerie Nationale.* The Minister of Justice even gets into the act with its judicial control of the civil police and the gendarmes in the investigation of crime.

Gendarmerie Nationale. The *Gendarmerie* is the older of the two police forces. It is responsible for enforcing the law in the rural areas of France and in communities of fewer than 10,000 people. The fact that there are few densely populated

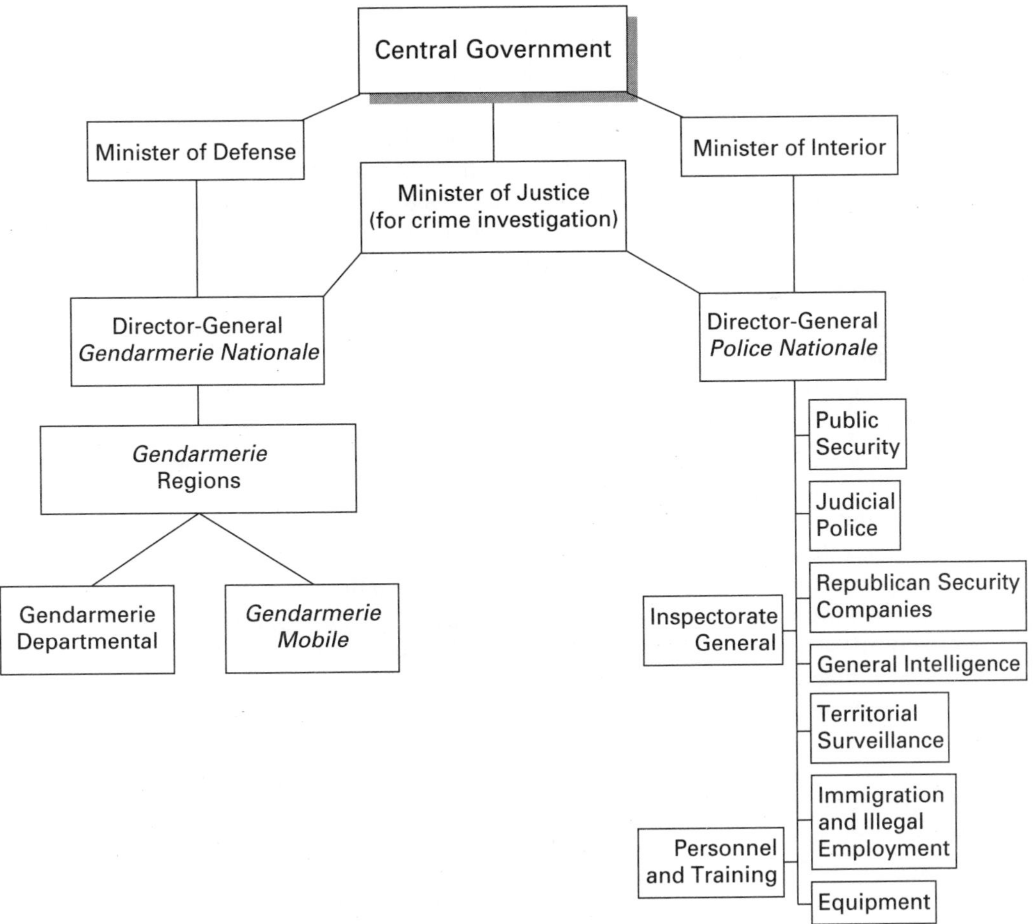

Figure 6.3 France's Police Organization

metropolitan areas means that 95 percent of French territory and nearly half its population are the *Gendarmerie's* responsibility ("The Gendarmerie Nationale," 2000; Horton, 1995).

A director general, who is responsible to the Minister of Defense, controls the *Gendarmerie.* The military linkages should not, however, detract attention from its sophisticated and highly successful style as it conducts typical civilian policing duties of patrol, surveillance, maintaining public order, and criminal investigation. The policing of France's road traffic and smaller towns is carried out by personnel meeting high recruitment and training standards using quality equipment that would be the envy of most police forces.

The *Gendarmerie* have two significant subdivisions. The first, the Departmental *Gendarmerie* are divided into brigades and include specialized units for such tasks as criminal investigation, prevention of juvenile delinquency, and the patrolling of roads, mountains, and air traffic. The other subdivision is the Mobile *Gendarmerie,* which is a public-order force with semimilitary training. Sometimes referred to as the anti-riot police, the Mobile *Gendarmerie* units are housed in barracks and are distributed throughout the country. Their principal mission is the maintenance or reestablishment of order, so the units can be deployed on short notice at the government's request. The squadrons are mobile through their armored vehicles, light tanks, and helicopters.

Police Nationale. Stead (1983) points out that most foreigners seem to assume that all French police are gendarmes. The similarity of uniforms fosters that confusion, and the high visibility of gendarmes (constantly in uniform and on patrol throughout the country) makes the assumption understandable. The *Police Nationale* is the larger of the two forces, with over 125,000 personnel (Horton, 1995). Operating primarily in urban centers of more than 10,000 in population, the *Police Nationale* is administrated by a director general under the Ministry of the Interior.

Eleven services, or directorates, control and coordinate the operational work of the police (French Ministry of Interior, 2000). Several of these are similar to departments found in Anglo-American policing. For example, the Directorate of Public Security uses uniformed patrol officers and plainclothes inspectors for policing the cities. The Directorate of Judicial Police controls and coordinates the *Police Nationale*'s detective work. Through subdirectorates, the judicial police have responsibility for such things as forensic investigation, criminal statistics, banditry (for example, gang crime, aggravated theft, kidnapping), and white-collar crime activities like counterfeiting and art forgery. Importantly, the Directorate of Judicial Police also controls the Regional Crime Services. Those services make inquiries into organized, professional, and transient crime by coordinating efforts of the urban police, over which they have authority in more serious criminal matters.

The *Police Nationale* has its own version of the Mobile *Gendarmerie.* The military style (they are based in barracks and their officers have military rank) of the Republican Security Companies (CRS) disguises their civil nature. Although not armed to the level of the Mobile *Gendarmerie,* the CRS can move equally fast, wherever needed, as they fulfill their duties of maintenance and restoration of public order.

The remaining directorates have such duties as monitoring the police forces—including investigation of complaints about police behavior (Inspectorate General); collecting and interpreting information on social, political, and economic trends—including infiltration of extremist groups (Directorate of General Intelligence); repressing activities harmful to the interests of France—for example, counterespionage and antiterrorist duties (Directorate of Territorial Surveillance); controlling the movement of people and foreign publications to and from French territory (Central Directorate for the Control of Immigration and Illegal Employment). The two remaining services are responsible for the central control of police personnel and training (Directorate of Personnel and Training) and for the central control of the materials and equipment used by the National Police (Directorate of Equipment).

A presumed benefit of a centralized police force is an increase in cooperation and efficiency. As just described, the two great French police forces seem to embody those characteristics and well illustrate what is good about centralization. A prime example would be the urban police (Public Security) turning serious cases over to the regional crime service. As Stead describes it,

> *Here one sees the value of a national police system: the urban police inform the regional crime service, which in turn transmits any important intelligence to the Central Directorate in Paris. The latter, in certain cases, circulates it throughout the country, and this can lead to cross-checks and association of data. Thus, the usefulness of centralization, coordination, and cooperation becomes clear (Stead, 1983, pp. 121–122).*

Americans are more used to seeing police agencies at odds with one another than engaging in such a spirit of cooperation. The local police complain that the FBI takes credit for breaking a case, or a city police department withholds evidence from the sheriff's department in the hopes of making its own unaided arrest. Those examples seem more typical of America's version of interagency cooperation. But we should not be too quick to assume that France avoids similar problems (see Horton, 1995; Stead, 1983). As Stead points out, police everywhere and throughout time have been reluctant to share their hard-won knowledge. "It is hardly to be avoided that when two distinct organizations, heirs to very different traditions, are pursuing the same ends, there will be competition and rivalry" (Stead, 1983, p. 127). A source of friction, for example, centers on the inevitable growth of towns and the expansion of suburbs. When a town of 9000 expands to over 10,000, the policing should pass from gendarmes to the *Police Nationale.* Yet the gendarmes have policed the area for as long as anyone can remember and see no reason that they should suddenly leave. Similarly, as city suburbs extend to the countryside, the *Police Nationale* come to regard the new area as their jurisdiction despite the presence of the *Gendarmerie Nationale.* It appears that despite the tranquility of force coordination on paper, there is less harmony in practice.

Further indication that the French system is not as synchronized as they would like is suggested by a January 1983 law authorizing locally controlled police. Horton (1995) estimates there are now over 2800 municipal police departments, with around 10,000 police personnel. The units seem to have come into existence as President François Mitterrand and his Socialist Party sought to carry out their campaign promise of decentralization and increased local control over governmental services. Some cities, Kania (1989) believes, were displeased with the policing services provided by the national government and took advantage of the opportunity to create their own force.

The existence of the local police units presents a problem for our placement of France with the police systems under a centralized command. If the *Police Municipale* is under local rather than central authority, that suggests a decentralized system. At this time, however, there are several reasons to downplay the importance of the mayors' police and to keep France among the countries with a centralized police system. These reasons include the municipal police forces' typical size, duties, and authority.

Police Municipale units are usually small and have police powers engaged primarily in general crime prevention, direct deterrence of criminal elements, and the arrest of persons caught in criminal acts (Horton, 1995; Kania, 1990; Kania, 1989). Because the mayors have considerable latitude in developing their police agencies, substantial variation exists in the duties given each force. In towns with significant tourist traffic, the *Police Municipale* are primarily order-maintenance personnel. In other cities, they are weapons-carrying, crime-fighting, traditional cops. In both instances, however, these *Municipales* are supplements to—not replacements of—the *Police Nationale* and the *Gendarmerie.* The municipal police have only limited enforcement powers and no general investigative powers. In cases of serious crime and for criminal investigations, they are expected to call the *Police Judiciaire,* the *Gendarmerie,* or the *Police Nationale.*

Despite their autonomous authorization, the municipal police are linked to the *Police Nationale.* Their selection, educational, and training requirements are similar to those of the National Police, and their uniforms are so alike that French citizens are easily confused about their distinction. Although empowered by the city, the *Police Municipale* must comply with the regulations and laws of the national government.

For these reasons, and because most French cities have not formed municipal police units, it seems appropriate to retain France among the countries operating a centralized multiple coordinated police structure.

Decentralized Multiple Coordinated Systems: Germany

Quite a variety of countries have police systems that are composed of several forces under the command of different government levels. Table 6.1 suggests Australia, Canada, and India are examples. Each of Australia's six states and two territories has its own police force (Swanton et al., 1989) with jurisdiction defined by the state and territorial boundaries. An exception is the Australian Federal Police, which enforces federal statutes throughout the country (compare it to the FBI in the United States) as well as having responsibility for the Australian Capital Territory. India has 25 state forces plus national units stationed in seven Union Territories. Canada, which receives closer attention in this chapter's "Impact" section, has police forces at the municipal, province, and federal levels. A common trait among these countries is the coordination each has been able to

You Should Know!

WAS THAT A MOUNTIE?

Canada falls among the decentralized multiple coordinated police systems. There are three levels of Canadian law enforcement (federal, provincial, and municipal), with control and supervision decentralized to the government at each level. Yet the differences are not always apparent. For example, during a visit to North Vancouver, you will find *Royal Canadian Mounted Police (RCMP)* officers providing police services to that city. Should you need a police officer as you leave North Vancouver and travel across the rural parts of British Columbia, you will be directed to the provincial police, whom you will easily recognize, because they are still the RCMP. Of course, if the federal police stop you anywhere in the province, you will again see the now familiar RCMP uniform.

Just as you think you have this system figured out, you fly from Vancouver to Toronto. After renting a car at the airport, you drive to your hotel and pass a police car with "Metro Toronto Police" painted on the door. Inside the car is a police officer wearing a non-Mountie uniform. The next day you decide to drive to Ottawa. With a concern for the provincial police, whom you correctly assume to be responsible for catching speeders on the highway, you look for officers like the ones you saw in British Columbia. Unfortunately, while concentrating on remembering the Mountie uniform, you are pulled over by a police officer wearing an Ontario Provincial Police uniform.

Canada's police structure is not as strange as your visit may lead you to believe. In fact, it is very straightforward. As noted above, there are three distinct levels operating under the supervision of federal, provincial, and municipal authorities. The different experiences in British Columbia and Ontario are simply the result of Canada's provision for contract policing. The province of British Columbia and its city of North Vancouver have each contracted with the RCMP (the federal agency) to provide the province and some cities with police services. The province of Ontario and its city of Toronto have chosen to provide their own provincial and local law enforcement. See this chapter's "Impact" section for more on the idea of contracting for police services.

achieve among its multiple and decentralized police forces. Germany, the example provided here, shows similar characteristics.

The occupation of Germany by Allied forces after World War II provides a relevant recent history for German policing. The Potsdam Agreement of 1945 provided the Allies with the task of decentralizing, democratizing, and demilitarizing areas of public life in each defeated country's zone of occupation. Although there was agreement on the need to decentralize the police, the Allies had different ideas about what decentralization was, and the goal was approached differently by the British, French, and Americans (Fairchild, 1988; Thomaneck, 1985).

To the British, decentralization meant regionally organized police under the watchful eye of civilian police authorities. The system the British established in

Germany was remarkably similar to that found in Great Britain. Also, as in Britain, the police function in this occupation zone was limited to the maintenance of law and order and the detection of crime. This meant that the traditional administrative functions of German police (for example, registration of all residents, environmental health, building permits and regulations, road supervision) were transferred to other administrative departments.

The police administrative functions were retained in the French zone. Also, the French saw nothing inherently bad in centralized control of the police, so that structure was essentially retained, with a concession to decentralization being the granting of some police functions to small-town mayors. Again, the similarity to the structure of policing at home—in this case, France—was not well hidden.

Americans retained central police control as an organizational principle, but only in communities with fewer than 5000 inhabitants. Larger communities had locally controlled communal police in much the same way that American cities have their own local police. This plan represented the greatest difference from the traditional German organization. In the American zone, mayors were made responsible for setting up police forces and providing for weapons, clothes, and supervision.

Not surprisingly, Germans found the mixture of police structures to be inconvenient, inappropriate, and ineffective. In 1949 German officials complained that communal police forces in small towns were impractical. In 1950 the Allied High Command decided that each state government (in then West Germany) could centralize its police at the state level. Gradually, cities gave up their local police force until each state passed police laws regulating the activities and organization of the newly centralized police. By 1955 all northern German states had completed the reconstruction of their police. In 1975 Munich ceased its communal police force, and the reconstruction was finally complete for all West Germany.

Today, the day-to-day operations of German policing is decentralized to the state *(Länder)* level (see Figure 6.4). Federal forces exist, but policing is essentially a state matter. The two primary federal agencies are the Federal Office of Criminal Investigation and the Federal Border Patrol. The Federal Office of Criminal Investigation has a broad range of federal and international duties and operates under the Federal Ministry of the Interior. It serves as the central headquarters for law enforcement in Germany and is the conduit for electronic data interchange between federal and state police. The Federal Border Patrol, also out of the Federal Ministry of the Interior, guards the frontiers of the republic—except in Bavaria, which has its own border police. This force may also provide reinforcement to state police forces if requested (Fairchild, 1988; Schwindt, 2000).

Each German state controls its own police force, with the federal government acting as a liaison and coordinating agent. Despite the potential for great divergence, there is considerable similarity among the various state police. The glue providing the similarity is made from tradition and from the fact that the laws enforced in each *Länd* are rather standard. As Schwindt puts it, "Anyone involved with the police would hardly notice any difference from one federal state to the other" (2000). The trend is toward even greater similarity. For example, before 1976 the police in each state wore different uniforms. In that year, a standard uniform (with different state sleeve patches, cap emblem, and rank insignia) was introduced and in 1980 made mandatory. After unification in 1990, the five states

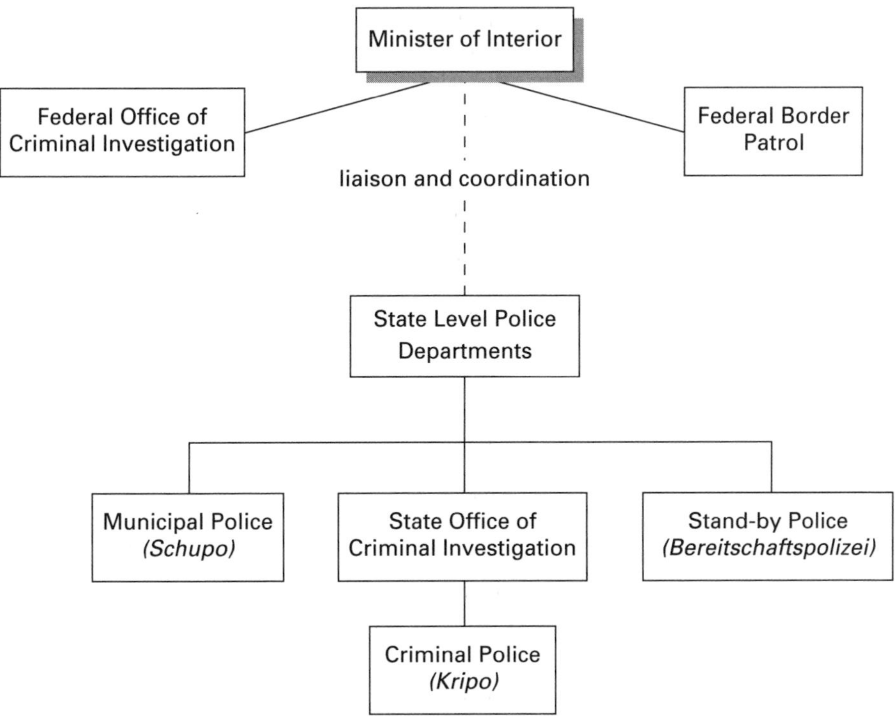

Figure 6.4 Germany's Police Organization

of the former East Germany also adopted the standard uniform (see Harlan, 1997 for a discussion of the unification of German policing).

The typical structure of policing in the *Länd* involves a three-part division (Kurian, 1989; Thomaneck, 1985; Schwindt, 1992). The *Schutzpolizei* (typically shortened to *Schupo*), are the uniform-wearing police and have the highest visibility and broadest range of duties. They are the first to arrive on the scene of all types of crimes and are initially responsible for all aspects of enforcement and investigation. Patrol is mostly by car, but the *Schupo* also have mounted police units, canine units, and armed police officers working in helicopters.

Soon after the *Schupo* have determined that a crime has occurred, or have identified a suspect, the criminal police, or *Kriminalpolizei (Kripo)*, are called in. The *Kripo* are plainclothes officers similar to detectives in the United States. They have the authority to search and seize and are responsible for developing a case and initiating charges against suspects. Linked to the *Kripo* in every *Länd* is a State Office of Criminal Investigation. This central headquarters for the *Kriminalpolizei* is responsible for gathering all significant information and documents used for the prevention and investigation of criminal offenses (Kurian, 1989; Schwindt, 1992). Personnel at this central crime-fighting headquarters analyze information, conduct crime lab activities, and notify police throughout the *Länd* about the current crime situation.

The third police organization is the *Bereitschaftspolizei*, or "stand-by police." The officers in this paramilitary force are quartered in barracks and act only in units rather than as individual police. Traditionally their function has been the training of young police officers. As the name suggests, their public function is to support the *Schupo* when large numbers of police are needed for crowd control, emergency activities, serious accidents, and the like.

Centralized Multiple Uncoordinated Systems: Spain

Upon recalling the rivalry between the *Police Nationale* and the *Gendarmerie,* you may question the claimed cooperation between those two French police forces. However, a review of uncoordinated forces quickly shows us that any problems encountered between the French police groups pale in comparison to those in uncoordinated systems like the ones in Belgium, Italy, and Switzerland (see Bayley, 1992). Italy, for example, has five national police forces: the *Polizia di Stato,* the *Carabinieri,* the Finance Police, the Prison Service, and the Forestry Police (Iorio, 1995). The first two have the most general policing duties and are the ones that best typify the lack of coordination. Like the French system, Italy sets one police force under its Ministry of Defense (the *Carabinieri*) and focuses on—but is not restricted to—rural law enforcement. The other force, the *Polizia di Stato,* operates under the Ministry of Interior and is responsible for law enforcement throughout the country. Problems arise because the *Carabinieri,* when engaged in police duties, is supposed to follow directions from the Interior Ministry. However, institutional rivalry, competition, and a somewhat high degree of animosity between the two police forces persuade the *Carabinieri* to be more responsive to orders from the Ministry of Defense. The result is a centralized system with multiple, yet uncoordinated policing (Cammett and Gibson, 1989; Collin, 1985). Similar problems confront Spain's police system.

Spanish police forces can trace their history to the twelfth century, but the first modern versions were formed in 1829 with the *Carabineros* and in 1844 with the *Guardia Civil.* Today Spain has three major law enforcement systems: the *Cuerpo Nacional de Policia (National Police Corps),* the *Guardia Civil* (Civil Guard), and the *Policia Municipal* (Municipal Police). The system is considered centralized because all forces operate under the authority of the national government. The Minister of the Interior has responsibility for policing in Spain, but within the ministry the task specifically falls to the Director of State Security. Even the Municipal Police are ultimately linked to the central government, because those local forces are governed by the same 1986 law that regulates the two national forces (see Figure 6.5).

Guardia Civil. The oldest national police force in Spain is the *Guardia Civil* (Civil Guard). This force was patterned after the French Gendarmerie and has always considered itself part of the army. The Civil Guard has defended government policy over the years and has successfully prevented challenges to have it demilitarized. Today it has responsibility for policing the rural parts of Spain, patrolling the highways between cities, controlling firearms and explosives, guarding certain installations, and protecting such areas as the coast, the frontiers, ports, and airports (Kurian, 1989; Macdonald, 1987).

The Civil Guard is headed by director general who is responsible to both the Ministry of the Interior and the Ministry of Defense. Some problems aris-

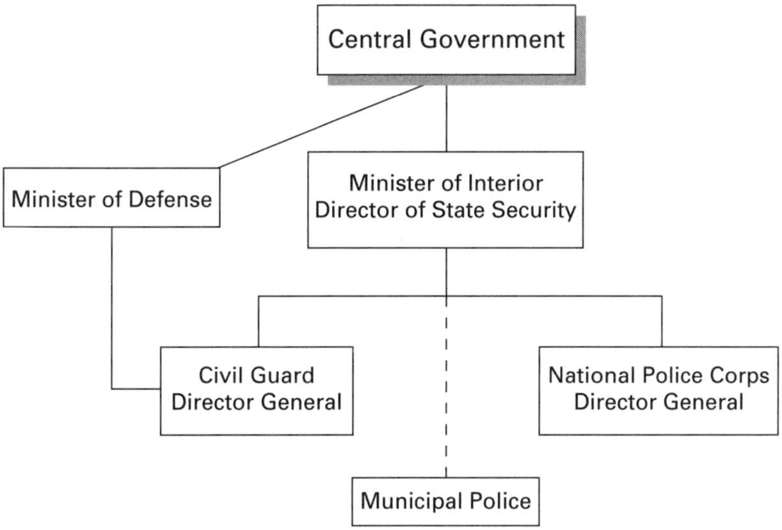

Figure 6.5 Spain's Police Organization

ing from this dual accountability are considered here, but first we can note that the 1986 law tries to respect the Civil Guard's military character while shifting power toward the Interior Ministry.

The Civil Guard's history and military links have given it an ultraconservative perspective that Morn and Toro (1989) describe as providing a remaining symbol of Franco's dictatorship (1939-1975). In fact, the guard seems to be having a hard time moving into the new era of policing. Incidents of corruption have marred its public image, and there is fear among liberals that increased crime and terrorism may inspire the rise of neo-authoritarianism in the guard (Morn and Toro, 1989).

Terrorism by Basque and Cataluna separatists is a particular problem for the guard, because the guard is considered to represent the national government against which these separatist movements are fighting. The guard's base of operation in the countryside and smaller towns also increases its vulnerability to attack. In 1997 the Civil Guard adopted a territorial distribution that established zones under the command of a high ranking officer of the guard. This partitioning may provide increased organization and efficiency for the guard (Departmento de Internet Guardia Civil, 2000)

Cuerpo Nacional de Policia. If the Civil Guard is a symbol of Spain's past, the National Police Corps represents a new order and provides a symbol of democracy (Morn and Toro, 1989). The national police are a combination of two earlier forces: the Armed and Traffic Police *(Policia armada y de trafico)* and the Superior Police Corps *(Cuerpo general de policia).* The former was a uniformed urban force under military control. The latter served as a plainclothes investigative police with a highly political purpose and was accused of repressive gestapo-like tactics (Macdonald, 1987; Morn and Toro, 1989). When the two were united in 1986, the new National Police Corps took responsibility for policing Spain's urban areas. Today the National Police Corps (with the Superior Corps as its detective component) operates in all provincial capitals and in municipalities with over 20,000 residents. Its responsibilities include issuing identity cards and passports, supervising private security forces, and enforcing gambling and drug laws.

The National Police Corps is headed by a director general of the police who reports to the Minister of the Interior through the Director of State Security. The separate and distinct nature of the two police forces before their combination has caused some turmoil as Spain tries to improve police efficiency and eliminate rivalry between the previously divided units. Attempts to reduce such problems have included the institution of common training and entrance procedures along with a clean break with any military links to the Armed and Traffic Police.

Other obstacles confronting the National Police include relatively weak relations with the public, new crimes for which the National Police seem unprepared, and problems with recruiting and deployment of personnel.

Response to the public relations problem has included attempts at more friendly contact with the people, but the citizens remain resistant. New offenses like international drug trafficking and organized crime seem to have grown with little interference from the National Police in general and the Superior Corps (as the detectives) more specifically. As if those difficulties were not sufficient to keep reformers busy, current recruitment and deployment practices receive criticism. The force draws heavily from the southern provinces and Madrid, so the northern provinces, already expressing strong feelings in favor of independence, are given tacit support for their contention that they are an occupied zone. In addition, as police officers gain experience and seniority, they typically earn transfers to less hostile areas of the country. In a manner reminiscent of deployment practices in the United States (see Cole, 1986, p. 251), the younger, less experienced officers are assigned to the most unruly areas (Morn and Toro, 1989). That inexperience may lead to a public perception (possibly an accurate perception) of ineffective policing.

Despite problems and growing pains, the National Police Corps represents an important aspect of Spain's move toward democracy and greater police accountability (Morn and Toro, 1989). Also, though it is an even more recent arrival than the National Police, the Municipal Police provides another step away from the repressive police tactics of Spain's past.

Policia Municipal. Municipal Police officers are recruited locally, are typically unarmed, and wear uniforms that vary in design from city to city. Because every municipality, from the largest cities to those under 100 people, is authorized to create its own police force, these units would seem to make Spain's system decentralized. However, as mentioned earlier, the Municipal police are regulated by the same 1986 law that governs the National Police and the Civil Guard. That law restricts the Municipal Police duties to protecting city buildings, traffic control, and assisting other police forces in such tasks as crowd control.

The Municipal Police are prominent figures on the streets of larger towns and cities. The largest of these local forces, the Security and Municipal Police Delegation of Madrid, is substantial enough to have two specialized units: the Citizens' Protection Patrol and the Ecological Patrol (Kurian, 1989).

Uncoordinated Policing. Spain's 1986 law attempted to improve police efficiency by eliminating parallel structures, dual command systems, and intercorps rivalry (Macdonald, 1987). The endeavor was successful to a great extent, but Spain's police system remains correctly classified as uncoordinated rather than coordinated. Macdonald (1987) identifies several areas of conflict among the three law enforcement units. First, both the National Police Corps and the Civil Guard have some authority to operate anywhere in the nation despite the presumed urban/rural jurisdictional division. The National Police can go anywhere their criminal investigation and intelligence operations take them, and the Civil Guard can follow any lead their inquiries may present. That national authority becomes especially troublesome when the crime areas for each police force overlap. For example, drug trafficking falls in the National Police Corps' concern with drug crime but is also linked to the Civil Guard's charge to protect ports and airports and to halt smuggling operations. When both national police forces investigate the same criminal activity and can conduct that investigation throughout the country, the potential for confusion is considerable.

The lack of coordination is not just between the two national forces. Under the Spanish system, every member of any police force is automatically a member of the "Judicial Police." In that role, the police assist the judges and prosecutors as they investigate a crime. Prior to 1986 this provision caused some problems, because the police often took a leadership role in investigations whereas the court personnel simply followed. The 1986 law reasserts judicial power and makes units of Judicial Police functionally responsible to the courts although still administratively linked to the Ministry of the Interior. Because Municipal Police officers can act as Judicial Police where necessary, criminal investigation under court direction may at times rely on police from three different forces. Again, the possibility of confusion and working at cross purposes is increased by such an arrangement.

The 1986 law takes specific interest in trying to avoid disorder and create cooperation among the police forces. The law stipulates that police units must act in accordance with the principle of reciprocal cooperation and even sets penalties of dismissal or suspension for officers not so behaving (Macdonald, 1987). If both national forces find themselves involved in the same action, the first force committed is to continue its operation until the Civil Governor or the Ministry of the Interior rules on jurisdiction. The fact that the law must include these provisions reinforces the characterization of Spain's policing system as involving a centralized command with multiple uncoordinated forces. It is now time to see how decentralized policing handles the problem of supervising its multiple forces.

Decentralized Multiple Uncoordinated Systems: Mexico

The United States, with more separate police forces than any country in the world, is easily the most extreme case of a decentralized multiple uncoordinated system. There are over 17,000 state and local law enforcement agencies in the United States (Maguire, Snipes, Uchida & Townsend, 1998). As if that multiplicity of effort were not enough, there are times when the jurisdictions of these agencies and that of the federal forces overlap. The result is an uncoordinated system that deserves brief elaboration before considering the example of Mexico.

Both city and county forces are usually considered local policing in the United States. Although city police chiefs typically owe their position to a mayor or city council, the sheriff is an elected official responsible for policing the unincorporated areas of a county. Local police officers enforce the laws of their state and the laws and ordinances passed by the city and county governments. As a county force, sheriff's deputies have authority throughout the county, including the ability to enforce state and county laws being violated in towns and cities. As a courtesy, sheriff's deputies are unlikely to operate in a municipal police jurisdiction without being invited by the police chief.

Because the primary enforcement of state laws is the responsibility of local police, the police agencies at the state level tend to have specific duties. For ex-

IMPACT

Would Canada's System Work in the United States?

As this chapter points out, police systems are either centralized or decentralized (although Japan presents a unique combination). The United States' version of extreme decentralization not only places us in the minority among nations but also attracts criticism as being too complex, inefficient, and expensive. Is it possible that other countries use a police structure that we should consider? If so, an intriguing alternative is provided by our neighbor to the north.

The Royal Canadian Mounted Police (RCMP) is a force as familiar to Canadians as the FBI is to U.S. citizens. Like its American counterpart, the RCMP is a federal agency dedicated to the enforcement of federal statutes and executive orders. In addition to federal-level policing, Canada also provides province and local policing. Although the responsibility for administration of justice actually lies with the provinces, a province can fulfill that duty by contracting with the federal government to provide policing services. Eight of Canada's 10 provinces have chosen to contract with the federal government and have the RCMP operate as the provincial police. In these cases, the RCMP is under the direction of the provincial attorney general while being under administrative control from the Ottawa headquarters (Kurian, 1989). The exceptions to federal contract policing for the province are Ontario and Quebec. In those provinces, the Ontario Provincial Police and the Quebec Police Force provide law enforcement.

Municipal police forces include those in cities, towns, villages, and townships. Like their counterparts in the United States, these local police departments, when grouped together, make up the country's largest body of police. As the "street cops," they handle most of the crime and are the primary enforcers of the law. The Canadian municipal forces differ from their American neighbors in two important ways:

IMPACT

Would Canada's System Work in the United States?

1. The local Canadian officer may actually be a member of the RCMP with whom the city has contracted for policing.
2. The local Canadian officers have the authority to enforce all laws in their jurisdiction—including certain federal statutes, the criminal code and the statutes of their province, and municipal bylaws. Local police officers in the United States enforce city codes and state laws but do not have the authority to enforce federal statutes.

Municipal contracting for police services is done with the province. Because the RCMP serves as the provincial police for eight provinces, the local police officer ends up being a Mountie if the municipality contracts with the province to provide police services. Quebec lacks a legal provision for contracting with its municipalities to provide policing, so Ontario is the only province where non-RCMP provincial police do contract policing for municipalities (Kurian, 1989).

The contracting system is very cost effective for both provinces and municipalities. The procedure began for economic reasons during the 1930s (Talbot et al., 1985) and continues today for similar reasons. The province is charged a percentage of the actual per capita cost for RCMP expenses. That charge is low enough that provinces and municipalities can maintain a highly efficient police system for a reasonable cost.

Canada's system of contracting for police services may be appealing to Americans since we already contract for things like defense counsel and correctional services, and some communities contract with their state police/patrol for law enforcement. Expansion of this option for police services would not violate the American preference for decentralization, but would require greater coordination of effort and might mean giving up some local control.

If increased contracting occurs, who will be the contractor? Would local governments contract with each other but not with the state level? Would any state be willing to contract with the federal government for very specific services? Or would local and state governments contract with private companies? Private security companies might be able to provide traditional police services for some communities. Maybe the future structure of American policing will include a variety of both private and public police forces under command structures that are centralized in one case (e.g., a national private police corporation) and decentralized in the other (e.g., traditional city, state, and federal agencies). Even if that would be too extreme, can you think of alternatives or modifications that could use private policing in the traditionally public arena?

ample, states may have police agencies responsible for patrolling the highways in the state, providing police services to state colleges and universities, enforcing state regulations on items like alcohol, and policing the state's parks and recreation areas. In many states these duties are divided among several agencies with names like Highway Patrol, University Police, Public Safety Officers, Bureau of Investigation Agents, and Park Rangers. In other states many tasks are consolidated and assigned to one agency, often called the State Police, who provide services ranging from highway patrol to criminal investigations.

Even federal level law enforcement reflects America's commitment to decentralization of policing. Command authority in federal law enforcement splits in two ways. First, policing divides between military and civilian agencies. Their authority is further apportioned within the military and civilian agencies themselves. Military law enforcement, for example, typically rests with traditional police-type agencies like the Military Police and three investigative agencies: the Naval Investigative Service, the Air Force Office of Special Investigations, and the Army Criminal Investigation Command (McGuire, 1988). These agencies are responsible for the investigation of crimes committed against U.S. military personnel or property, and crimes committed by military personnel. Command authority within federal civil law enforcement is divided among various federal departments, agencies, and bureaus, but rests primarily in the Department of the Treasury and the Department of Justice. In the spirit of decentralization, division of authority does not even stop at the department level.

A result of this proliferation of agencies is an occasional overlapping of jurisdictions. State police jurisdictions tend to be large, but confined to unincorporated areas and highways. County police (sheriffs) usually share authority with state and municipal forces. Although their jurisdiction might be geographically small in comparison, municipal forces have been known to find themselves working cases that state and even federal agencies have laid claim to. Our neighbor to the south is faced with a similar situation.

Kurian (1989) describes Mexico's police system as imitating the American system by having forces at the federal, state, and municipal levels with many "overlapping layers of authority" (p. 258). Dispersing of agencies even occurs within each of these levels (see Figure 6.6). The federal level, for example, includes the General Directorate of Police and Traffic, the Judicial Police, the Federal Highway Police, Mexican Immigration Service, Secretariat of Finance (customs officers), and other smaller agencies. The larger and the smaller agencies all report to different federal government agencies.

The primary federal force is the *Policia Judicial Federal* (Federal Judicial Police). The FJP are organized along population lines. Separate units are in each major metropolitan area, and for rural districts, one unit is responsible for a large geographic area. Each FJP unit is headed by a commander who reports directly to a state commander of the FJP. The state commander, who is located in the capital of each of Mexico's 31 states, reports to the director of the FJP. That director, in turn, reports to the federal attorney general. FJP *agentes* (officers) are often persons with the correct political connections and are likely to have had experience as military officers (Wilkinson & Malagùn, 1995).

Each Mexican state may structure its police system somewhat differently, but Wilkinson and Malagùn (1995) offer the state of Tamaulipas as exemplify-

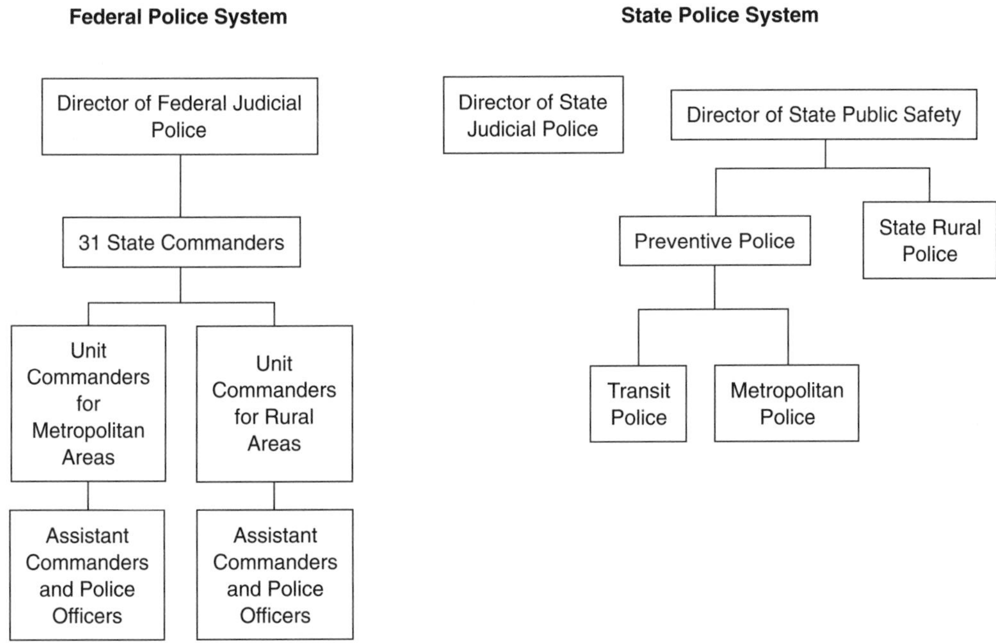

Figure 6.6 Mexico's Police Organization

ing a widely used organization. In that structure, state police are divided into two major subdivisions: the *Policia Judicial Estatal* (State Judicial Police) and the *Policia de Seguridad Publica* (Pubic Safety Police). Each force is commanded by its respective director, working from the state capital. The director of the State Judicial Police heads the agency responsible for investigating serious crimes and apprehending offenders at the state and local levels.

The Public Safety Police has its own subdivisions into the *Policia Rural Estatal* (State Rural Police) and the *Policia Preventiva* (Preventive Police). In carrying out their enforcement duties in rural areas, the State Rural Police perform functions similar to those of county sheriff's deputies in the United States. Wilkinson and Malagùn (1995) note that officers among the State Rural Police, at least in Tamaulipas, are largely undereducated compared to those of other police agencies. Because they are drawn primarily from rural areas, where education is not highly valued or widely accessible, they tend to be farm workers with appropriate political connections.

Continuing the spirit of decentralization, even the Preventive Police are subdivided at the municipal level. The *Policia de Transito* (Transit Police) are responsible for traffic control and violations of traffic law. Upon encountering a criminal violation, the Transit Police attempt to secure the suspect and crime scene and then will notify the State Judicial Police, who take the case from that point. The *Policia Preventiva Uniformada* (Metropolitan Police) may arrest persons accused of committing both major and minor crimes, but in major crime cases they must turn the suspects over to the State Judicial Police. When a major crime is reported, but no suspect is apprehended, the Metropolitan Police notify the State

Judicial Police, who take the case for further investigation (Wilkinson & Malagùn, 1995).

Compared with the information available to U.S. citizens on policing in Canada, there is remarkably little information about the police structure for our southern neighbor. When Americans do hear anything about Mexican police, the information is practically always negative. Allegations and proven instances of brutality, criminal behavior, and corruption on the part of police in Mexico make it hard for Mexico's citizens as well as outsiders to view the country's police force favorably. Upon his election to Mexico's presidency in 2000, Vicente Fox announced plans to overhaul the country's notoriously corrupt and inefficient police forces ("Fox to shake up," 2000). His planned "top-to-bottom" renovation would restructure nearly all police institutions and would break the existing political ties between police and the presidency. Mexican citizens have been anxiously awaiting the implementation of Fox's plan and the opportunity it could bring to provide the country with a more professional police system. Concerns about police corruption are not limited to Mexico. Unfortunately, corruption in law enforcement seems to be a worldwide problem that varies more by degree than existence.

POLICING ISSUES: POLICE MISCONDUCT

Police misconduct might range from accepting gifts and free meals to protecting the illegal activity of others or committing crimes directly. An even broader definition might include actions that violate citizens' and suspects' procedural rights or exhibit discriminatory behavior toward minority group members. Although there may be disagreement among police and citizens regarding the evil attributed to such low-range versions of misconduct as accepting gifts and free meals, it is safe to assume that behavior at the other extreme (for example, committing crimes, excessive use of force, unequal treatment based on race) is universally despised.

U.S. citizens are constantly reminded of police misconduct by a seemingly neverending thread of media reports about graft, corruption, beatings, and criminal activity. It is clearly an important problem and one that courts, commissions, talk show hosts, editorial writers, average citizens, and police officers themselves have addressed with great seriousness and concern. Glazer (1995) explains that for many decades the misconduct was explained by police officials as instances of a "few bad apples" misbehaving and giving the rest of the barrel a bad name. More recently, some criminologists are suggesting the "barrel" itself might be rotten. That is, police work may actually breed misconduct by perpetuating a culture that encourages or at least tolerates police misbehavior. Comparative studies may help answer such questions by finding similarities and contrasts in the occurrence of police misconduct in different countries.

Bracey (1995) notes that until the mid 1970s, studies of police corruption tended to focus on the United States. She reminds us that extensive corruption of the police had also been found in India, Saigon, Singapore, Hong Kong, and rural Italy (see Bracey, 1995 for appropriate citations), but that northern Europe seemed relatively free of similar misconduct by its various police forces. However, police scandals in London and Amsterdam between the mid 1970s and

In the News

HIRE WOMEN AND REDUCE CORRUPTION?

Can corruption among police officers be solved by simply hiring more women officers? Officials in a few countries have thought so.

In 1999 the Mexico City government briefly tried to combat police corruption by taking ticket books away from traffic policemen and leaving the issuing of tickets to policewomen ("Something for a refresco," 2000). The officials argued that women are less corrupt. But, men in the traffic police outnumber women by nine to one, so the result was mostly one of making traffic offenses ten times as hard to enforce—as well as ten times as tempting for policewomen to take bribes. But maybe the trick is to hire even more women, as Peru has tried to do.

Leaders in Peru, believing that women are more honest than men, have turned to women police officers for traffic enforcement in the streets of Lima (Koop, 1998). By 1999 Peru's president Fujimori hoped that all of Lima's 2500 traffic officers would be female. About one fourth of the traffic officers were female in 1998, and the first recruits quickly gained a reputation among drivers as incorruptible—quite unlike their male counterparts, most of whom overlooked traffic infractions for bribes as small the price of a candy bar. As a Lima taxi driver said, the women seem less interested in collecting money and more interested in doing the job—"but let's wait to see if they stay that way" (Koop, 1998).

early 1980s led many to conclude that at least the potential for corruption is present in any police force.

In 1996 allegations of corruption in Australia's largest police force—the Australian Federal Police—shook the country. According to reports, members of the AFP were involved in bribery, protection rackets, drug trafficking, and child pornography ("Corruption inquiry," 1996). A board of inquiry criticized senior force officials for failing to identify and root out entrenched corruption. In Asia, the Nepalese Police are said to torture persons under investigation by administering beatings, using rollers on the thighs, and even burning homes (SAHRDC, 1997).

On the African continent, the United Nations Commission on Human Rights reports that police in Togo have used excessive force when investigating reports of crime or attempting to arrest a suspect, and that in Zaire the police display an arrogant abuse of power that has resulted in plundering expeditions and seemingly arbitrary killings of citizens. Upon turning their attention to Latin America, the UN Commission found plausible the general view in Chile that the uniformed police use brutal treatment and torture on suspected common criminals or even witnesses (Human Rights Internet, 1996).

Reports from the Human Rights Watch concluded that Brazilian police frequently beat, torture, and commit summary executions with little fear that their behavior will receive any negative sanction from the government (Human Rights Watch, 1997c). Expressing particular concern about the plight of street children around the world, the Human Rights Watch reports that police are abusing and killing street children in India (Human Rights Watch, 1996b) and submitting street children in Bulgaria to physical abuse and other mistreatment—both on the street and in police lockups (Human Rights Watch, 1996a). Street children in Kenya are subject to frequent beating, extortion, and sexual abuse (Human Rights Watch, 1997a).

Police in Switzerland are said to be racist in their dealings with foreigners and with Swiss citizens of non-European descent, and institutional racism is said to be prevalent in such British mainstays as Scotland Yard (Reid, 1999; Wiseberg, 1997). Police in Egypt are accused of torturing suspects at police stations and detention centers to encourage confessions (Human Rights Internet, 1996). We could, unfortunately, go on. However, the point is surely made by now—police misconduct, from taking bribes to extrajudicial executions (explained away as "shootouts," if explained at all), occur without regard to the type of police structure followed.

Certainly one can argue that levels and types of police misconduct vary by time and country, but keep the big picture in mind for a moment: police misconduct is undeniably pervasive. How should we interpret this pervasiveness in terms of causes and solutions? Are certain "personality types" attracted to police work in all countries? If police misconduct flourishes only when it is tacitly supported by upper command, why do commanders worldwide seem to approach their supervisory duties so similarly? Does power corrupt? When any society gives some of its citizens the authority to control the behavior of other citizens, will that power inevitably corrupt the controllers?

This book is not an appropriate place to discuss at any length the proposed theories of corruption (interested readers should see Bracey, 1995, and almost any introductory criminal justice textbook). However, the idea that police work itself might breed misconduct is intriguing because of its comparative implications. In other words, if police misconduct results from the occupation itself, we should expect to find misconduct by police officers everywhere. Evidence thus far suggests the truth of this occupational explanation of police misconduct. Confirmation awaits the interested researcher.

POLICING ISSUES: GLOBAL COOPERATION

Both crime and criminals increasingly ignore national boundaries. Because transnational crime and the reaction to it have significant consequences for citizens of every country, the second policing issue considered here is the international response to transnational crime.

Cross-national cooperation among law enforcement agencies seems to have been a concern of European countries before other nations appreciated the need for teamwork. The close proximity of European countries and the desire to provide citizens with easy mobility around the continent encouraged procedures that allow citizens to cross borders—and, unfortunately, law-abiding citizens are not always distinguishable from law-violating ones. Consequently, it is not surprising that arrangements for police cooperation among countries have progressed further in Europe than elsewhere.

By the start of the twenty-first century, three structures had developed to enable cross-national cooperation in Europe: (1) the International Criminal Police

Organization (Interpol), (2) the European Police Organization (Europol), and (3) the Amsterdam Treaty/Schengen Agreement.

International Criminal Police Organization (ICPO)—Interpol

The idea of international cooperation in police activities was first introduced in 1914 (with the French as primary advocates) but the onset of World War I postponed action. Attempts were again made in 1923 (Austrian instigation this time), and headquarters for the International Criminal Police Commission (ICPC) were established in Vienna until World War II caused suspension of activities. Finally, in 1946 the French offered a building near Paris for the reestablishment of a headquarters. The ICPC continued to grow and in 1956 was renamed the *International Criminal Police Organization (ICPO—Interpol).* In 1966 Interpol moved to Saint

You Should Know!

INTERPOL FAQs

Is Interpol an International Police Force?

- No. Interpol is an international organization that has coordinated police international cooperation between its member nations since 1923.

Does Interpol Actually Investigate Cases?

- No. Investigations are conducted by the national police forces of member nations under their own sovereign laws. Interpol's role is to supply criminal information of a transnational nature to these national police forces.

How Does Interpol Communicate?

- Each member country establishes a National Central Bureau staffed by its own police force and communicates via an independent e-mail network that covers the globe. The system provides a secure and rapid means of communication using encryption.

Does Interpol Collect Information on International Criminals?

- Yes. The Interpol General Secretariat has established a database of information on all internationally wanted criminals or missing individuals, with their photographs and/or fingerprints.

How Is an Internationally Wanted Criminal Traced?

- At the request of a member country, the General Secretariat issues a "Red Notice" to all members. That notice contains sufficient details of the case, description, personal details, criminal history, photograph, and fingerprints of an internationally wanted criminal. Member nations use that information to locate, arrest, and detain the suspect pending an extradition application.

Cloud (outside Paris) and in 1989, having outgrown its Saint Cloud building, moved to new facilities in Lyons, France.

One of the most curious aspects of Interpol's status is the organization's very legitimacy. It is not based on an international treaty, convention, or any similar document. The multinational group of police officers who drew up its constitution never submitted it to their respective governments for approval, authorization, or ratification (Fooner, 1989). Yet Interpol is treated as a legitimate organization by most governments of the world. Nations must apply for membership, appoint delegates, pay dues, and abide by the organization's rules. With recognition now from, and working relations with, such prestigious organizations as the United Nations, the Council of Europe, the World Health Organization, and the World Customs Organization, Interpol remains a legal curiosity but stands on firm ground.

Interpol has two interrelated governing bodies, the General Assembly and the Executive Committee. These are decision-making bodies with supervisory powers. Charged with implementing the decisions and recommendations adopted by the two governing organs is the General Secretariat. The General Secretariat is composed of permanent departments (e.g., Liaison and Criminal Intelligence; Legal Matters; Technical Support) that provide the framework for the day-to-day operation of Interpol.

The key to Interpol's success in achieving international police cooperation is found in its structure of *National Central Bureaus* (NCBs). Interpol identified three primary factors that hamper international cooperation (Interpol, 2000):

- The different structures of police forces around the world makes it difficult for officials in one country to know which department in another country has authority to deal with a case or supply information.
- The use of different languages can become a barrier to communication and may discourage or even interfere with communication.
- Differences among legal systems may present problems ranging from frustration to inability to cooperate.

To overcome these potential problems, Interpol established NCBs in each of Interpol's member states (numbering 178 in 2000). Each country provides space, supplies, and personnel to serve as a liaison for Interpol communication and to handle requests from other member countries. Because each country controls its own NCB, they differ widely in size, personnel, and level of activity. However, each NCB has three responsibilities: (1) maintain open channels to all police units in its own country; (2) maintain connections with the NCBs of all other member countries; and (3) maintain liaison with the General Secretariat. In this manner, the NCBs provide a contact point in each member nation to allow the coordination of international criminal investigation.

So Interpol is not a force of international detectives with worldwide jurisdiction; it instead serves as a global conduit for communication and data sharing for member nations (Benyon, 1997). Operating through the NCB network, any police officer or agency in a member country has access to global policing services when faced with a problem involving foreign jurisdiction.

Determining the appropriate police agency to serve as a country's NCB is not difficult in countries with centralized systems. With greater decentralization, though, the difficulty increases. In the extremely decentralized United States, it would be practically and politically unsuitable to name a state or local police department as the country's representative to Interpol. Instead, the NCB of the United States is in Washington, DC, where it exists as a separate agency within the Department of Justice.

The United States' commitment to Interpol increased dramatically in the 1970s and 1980s and remains strong today. The need for such a system is the result of increasing internationalization of crime and the sheer volume of foreign nationals now living in or visiting the United States. To respond to these situations, it is increasingly apparent that even local police need an international channel of communication available at their level. As a result, even the decentralized police system in America is participating at a local level in a multinational effort in policing.

Europol

Europol, the European law enforcement organization, was established in 1992 with the Maastricht Treaty on the European Union (EU). After ratification by the member nations and the passage of some needed legal statutes, Europol was able to take up full operation in 1999. From its headquarters in The Hague, the Netherlands, Europol operates under a mandate for preventing and combating such criminal activities as illicit drug trafficking, illicit vehicle trafficking, trafficking in human beings, terrorism, and money laundering (Europol, 2000). As that list suggests, initial efforts at cooperative policing are directed toward criminal activities that require an organized crime structure and that typically involve operations in several countries. That is exactly the kind of criminal activity that calls for a multinational cooperative response since the criminals do not confine their activities to a single country's border.

Europol supports crime prevention and combating duties by facilitating the exchange of both personal and nonpersonal data among the Europol liaison officers who represent the various law enforcement agencies. In addition, Europol provides member countries with strategic reports and crime analysis based on information supplied by member nations or generated by Europol itself and other agencies. Finally, Europol provides expertise and technical support for operations and investigations engaged in by member nations.

You will note from that review of Europol activities that there is no separate Europol police agency with law enforcement authority across the EU. This is an important point since it is not often clear to laypeople that Europol is a framework to facilitate cooperative efforts among different countries, not a free-standing police agency that engages in independent investigations and makes arrests. And, of course, it is just that type of facilitative arrangement that fits in with contemporary versions of multinational police cooperation. The idea of a "Supranational Bureau of Investigation" with agents assigned throughout the EU, charged with enforcing laws applicable to all citizens in each member nation, seems a bit far-fetched today. Far more reasonable and workable in preventing and combating cross-border crimes is an agency like Europol that can coordinate the efforts of different policing systems rather than imposing yet another police agency upon each member country.

The Amsterdam Treaty/Schengen Agreement

In 1985 five countries (Belgium, France, Germany, Luxembourg, and the Netherlands) signed the *Schengen* (from the Luxembourg city) *Agreement*. The original five were joined by Portugal and Spain in 1991 and later by Austria, Greece, and Italy. The goal of the Schengen Agreement was to, eventually, provide unhindered travel among European member states—with assurance of very strict identity controls at airports, seaports, and land borders for travelers arriving from countries outside the European Union. In addition, various Schengen treaties address questions about allowing police to pursue criminals across borders and attempt to set up a data bank designed to allow sharing of information among the Schengen Group.

The database, which seems similar in concept to Interpol's system of information exchange, has been termed the *Schengen Information System (SIS)*. The system consists of a central system computer (C-SIS) in France linked to national computers in each Schengen Group country (N-SIS). Data on either persons or objects is entered into the C-SIS by each participating country and is copied to each N-SIS computer within minutes. The possibility of independent data entry into a common database gives Schengen Group members more control over the data than is allowed by Interpol, which distributes information only from the General Secretariat.

The SIS is seen as the cornerstone of the Schengen Agreement as it provides a level of protection for the now open borders. The agreement divided "Schenegenland's" borders into outer frontiers with the rest of the world and inner frontiers where people may move from one country to another without stopping at border booths and barriers. That means that the countries on the outer frontier are responsible for prohibiting wanted persons, criminals, persons under surveillance, and other "undesirables" from penetrating the outer frontier. In return for removal of frontier checks, the SIS gives police and other agencies in member countries access to identical information on persons and property (Benyon, 1997).

The problems of achieving cross-national cooperation is seen in the difficulty the Schengen Agreement had in getting established. Inner frontier border controls for the original seven Schengen countries were removed in 1995. By the late 1990s other eligible countries (that is, EU countries) had either chosen not to join or had been prevented from joining. The "chose-not-to" group included Ireland and the United Kingdom—each wishing to maintain passport control at its internal borders. The "not-sure-you're-ready" group included Austria, Greece, and Italy. Because those countries would be responsible for the outer frontiers, some of the original Schengen members needed convincing that they could effectively control the borders with non-Schengen countries. All three countries eventually allayed such fears and became Schengen partners.

Measures to which Schengen countries have agreed include (European Union, 2000) the following:

- The removal of checks at common borders, replacing them with external border checks.
- A common definition of the rules for crossing external borders.
- The introduction of rights of surveillance and hot pursuit.
- The strengthening of legal cooperation through a faster extradition system and faster distribution of information about the implementation of criminal judgments.
- The creation of the Schengen Information System (SIS).

Despite initial difficulties, the Schengen Agreement was deemed a success and it is now—with the Treaty of Amsterdam (effective May 1, 1999)—incorporated into the legal and institutional framework of the EU. The United Kingdom and Ireland are the only EU countries not fully participating in Schengen (both countries prefer to maintain their own checks on anyone entering their territory), but the agreement is applied to some non-EU countries as well. Norway and Iceland, for example, abide by Schengen, and efforts are being made to eventually provide free movement with other non-EU countries. Such effort will bring Europe closer to a free-travel continent without loss of protection from criminals. Just as important, it will demonstrate how countries can cooperate to combat transnational crime and criminals. That concept of international cooperation is a perfect way to conclude this chapter.

SUMMARY

This chapter was organized around the concept of variation in police structure. Building from Bayley's (1985) classification scheme, we categorized police structures according to their type of supervision or command (centralized or decentralized) and the number of forces being supervised (singular or multiple). When multiple forces are supervised, Bayley noted some work well together (coordinated) while others seem to operate at cross purposes (uncoordinated). Upon putting these conditions together, a typology was created yielding six possible cells, each containing a different police structure.

Countries like Ireland, Israel, Nigeria, Poland, and Saudi Arabia each have a single police force reporting to a centralized command. Japan presents a unique combination of a single police force with command decentralized to the prefecture level. The simplicity of a single police structure has not, however, made it a worldwide favorite. Other countries accept the central government as appropriate for supervision purposes but show a preference for having multiple police forces to report to that central authority. France was highlighted as a country falling into this division, because both its *Gendarmerie* and *Police Nationale* report to ministries of the central government. Although some conflict exists between the French forces, they are considered coordinated because they basically respect their assigned jurisdictions. In Spain, on the other hand, the multiple forces of *Cuerpo Nacional de Policia, Guardia Civil,* and *Policia Municipal* have overlapping responsibilities and jurisdiction. The result is an uncoordinated system.

Countries that have decentralized police services also provide examples of both coordinated and uncoordinated efforts. Germany was highlighted as a coordinated multiple police system because its different state police forces are coordinated by the federal government serving as a liaison and coordinating agent. The United States presents the most extreme form of decentralized multiple uncoordinated policing, but Mexico was highlighted to provide the international perspective.

Finally, the chapter included a brief look at two of the many important issues that can be addressed regarding policing around the world. After a review of police misconduct in a variety of countries, we were left with questions about the effect of police work on police officers and the type of person that might be attracted to police work. The chapter ended with discussion of important ways that countries have tried to work together to combat the ever increasing cross-national nature of both crime and criminals.

WEB SITES TO VISIT

- Read about the French *Gendarmerie Nationale* on the official site for the Ministry of Defense at **www.defense.gouv.fr/gendarmerie/organisation/index.html** You can translate the page with the assistance of **www.bablefish.altavista.com**
- Visit the official page the Spain's *Guardia Civil* at **www.guardiacivil.org** Some pages have English translations but for others you can use **www.bablefish.altavista.com**
- Keep track of programs for police cooperation in the European Union at sites like **europa.eu.int/scadplus/leg/en/s22004.htm**
- Visit the website for the U.S. National Central Bureau at **www.usdoj.gov/usncb/** to read about U.S. cooperation in Interpol.

SUGGESTED READINGS

A number of interesting police procedure novels are set in foreign countries, many of them written by authors of these countries. Some, like Georges Simenon's Inspector Maigret series and the Inspector Imanishi stories by Seicho Matsumoto, are popular enough to be translated into English. Others are written in English and are widely available. From Britain, the works by P. D. James and her Commander Dalgliesh are more linked to police procedures than are Agatha Christie's mysteries using private investigators. James Melville's series about Inspector Otani provides easier access to the Japanese scene than do the less available (in English) works by Seicho Matsumoto. From France, in addition to Simenon's Inspector Maigret, consider Nicholas Freeling's Henri Castang mysteries. The Netherlands provides the setting for Inspector Van der Valk (Nicholas Freeling) and for Janwillem van de Wetering's intriguing stories featuring Detective Adjunct Grijpstra and his assistant Sergeant de Gier.

More traditional suggestions include:

Bayley, David H. (1985). *Patterns of policing: A comparative international analysis.* New Brunswick, NJ: Rutgers University Press.

Das, Dilip. (1995). Can the police work with people? A view from France. *The Police Journal, 68* (4), 333–344.

Fairchild, Erika S. (1988). *German police.* Springfield, IL: Charles C. Thomas.

Harlan, J. P. (1997). The German police: Issues in the unification process. *Policing: An International Journal of Policing Strategies & Management, 20*(3), 532–554.

Horton, C. (1995). *Policing policy in France.* London: Policy Studies Institute.

Chapter 7

An International Perspective on Courts

KEY TOPICS

- The primary actors in the criminal justice process
- Differences in legal training and career tracks
- Different ways prosecution is carried out
- Different ways counsel for defense is provided
- The role of professional judges and laypeople in the adjudication process
- The need for an independent judiciary
- Laypeople serving as judges or jurors
- Examples from each continent of variation in court organization
- Questions on the presumption of innocence and the concurrent consideration of guilt and sentencing

KEY TERMS

adjudication continuum	people's assessors	private prosecutor
jurors	presumption of guilt	professional judges
lay judges	presumption of innocence	public prosecutor

COUNTRIES REFERENCED

China	France	Nigeria
England	Germany	Saudi Arabia

The criminal trial of O. J. Simpson held the attention of many Americans throughout much of 1995. Many people disputed the jury's decision, but just about everyone agreed that this version of the American trial process was a more convoluted and prolonged operation than it should have been. How do you suppose the trial would have progressed in other countries? In some, there would have been no jury. Instead, a panel of professional and lay judges would have heard the arguments—and even questioned the witnesses. Even countries with a jury system would have provided a very different performance. Consider Russia. After the collapse of the USSR, Russia reintroduced jury trials—which it had used from 1864 to 1917—to its court process. The revival began gradually in 1993 with only certain regions using a trial by jury for defendants accused of serious felonies. By the end of the 1990s, as Danilenko and Burnham (1999) explain, the right to a jury trail was still being used for only a very narrow category of extremely serious offenses. Since the O. J. Simpson criminal trial would likely qualify as one where a Russian defendant would have the right to a jury trial, let us consider some of the ways such a trial would have differed from its American version ("What if the O. J. Simpson trial," 1995):

- In a Russian trial, the victims' families not only would be permitted to question Simpson in court, they would be *obliged* to do so.
- In addition to closing arguments by the prosecution and the defense, a member of each victim's family in a Russian trial could address the jury in an emotional closing statement—with few of the restrictions that bind American trial lawyers.
- If the prosecution could not allude to any violent episodes in Nicole and O. J. Simpson's past, the victims' relatives could probably get away with it in a Russian trial.
- A hung jury would be unlikely in a Russian trial—it takes only seven of the twelve jurors to support a conviction or acquittal. Also, if the Russian jury were evenly split, a judgment of acquittal would be automatic.
- There are no mistrial motions in Russia.

The concern of this chapter is with the institutions that different countries establish to bring a defendant to justice. Of course, when looking at particular social institutions, we also must consider the people who work there. Recall that Chapter 1 distinguished between a functions/procedures strategy and an institutions/actors one. The former highlights the similarities among legal systems but in doing so masks their differences. In several ways, Chapters 3 through 5 followed a functions/procedures approach, because they presented general material about legal systems according to separate traditions. As a result, you now have general information about the function of law in four legal families and some specific information about legal procedures in countries representing each family. You do not, however, have much understanding of who carries out those functions and procedures or in what setting they work. That information is what the actors/institutions strategy provides. Of course, it is not possible to speak of the "who" and "where" without occasional reference to the "what." Therefore, as we learn about the actors and institutions in various countries, we must be intermittently reminded of the functions and procedures.

We approach these topics by looking first at the actors Americans know as the prosecutor and defense counsel. We then turn to the players responsible for deciding the outcome of a case. These adjudicators can be either professionals or laypersons. Finally, we consider the stage upon which these performers carry out their duties.

PROFESSIONAL ACTORS IN THE JUDICIARY

The primary actors in the criminal process are the advocates (prosecutor and defense counsel) and the judge. These three positions indicate possible career tracks in the legal profession. Other choices might include legal scholar, corporate attorney, notary, or other forms of public and private legal work. The ease with which a law school graduate can move among these occupational areas helps show whether a country has a unified or separated legal profession. In the former, all legal professionals are considered to have the basic knowledge and training to participate in any of the fields. In the latter, each field has distinct entrance requirements that restrict horizontal movement by the legal professionals. Part of the difference results from how a country educates its law students.

Variation in Legal Training

Americans tend to associate legal education with graduate work undertaken after the student has completed a general college or university education. This process is actually uncommon from the world perspective, because civil law countries, and even legal studies in England, provide training in law at the undergraduate level.

Like college training almost everywhere, legal studies under the civil law tradition are usually general and interdisciplinary rather than professional (Glendon, Gordon & Osakwe, 1985). As a result, civil law graduates are not trained to begin the practice of law immediately. Instead, those wishing to enter a legal profession need further practical training. The American law school graduate, on the other hand, is expected to be prepared to do any type of legal work with only a minimal apprenticeship.

The type and duration of training in the civil law vary by country and also according to the kind of legal career the new graduate wants to pursue. Shortly after receiving the university degree in law, new civil lawyers are given the option of being a private lawyer, a judge, a government lawyer (basically a public administrator), or a legal scholar. Entrance into each legal profession typically depends on the applicant successfully passing an exam and completing a period of apprenticeship. With different educational backgrounds, occupational choices, and career entrance requirements, it is not surprising that countries vary regarding the role and social position of their legal professionals.

Lawyers in America often find themselves in the peculiar position of being in a prestigious occupation while also serving as the butt of many jokes. Actually, jokes and negative comments about lawyers have been around since the late sixteenth century. Shakespeare's Dick the butcher said, "The first thing we do, let's kill all the lawyers" *(King Henry VI, Part II)*, as he was making suggestions in support of Jack Cade's promise of a better society. In colonial America outright belligerence often took the form of hostile legislation. McDonald (1983) reminds us of the pre-Revolutionary dictum that it was not deemed necessary, or even advisable, to have judges learned in law. The hostility came primarily from the landed gentry and the clergy, both of whom feared the loss of their power and status to a lawyering class. The role of lawyers in England and the United States continues to occasion feelings of contempt as well as respect among the citizens.

Lawyers in civil law countries seem to fare better in some respects. Certainly, they are not the catalyst for jokes as much as the lawyers in common law countries are, though neither are they regarded with great respect. Part of the public perception of civil law attorneys results from the variety of distinct professional careers from which they choose. Graduates not wanting to become judges can follow a path leading to positions like public prosecutor, government lawyer, defense advocate, or private attorney. The specific career decision is made early and places the young graduate on a rather precise path.

The distinctions among the various legal careers in civil law countries may seem unusual to Americans. In the United States, the legal profession is more unified and allows lateral movement by lawyers from one type of position to another. For example, recent law school graduates may initially serve in a district attorney's office or as a public defender in order to get some experience and a reasonable starting salary. After a few years in that field, they may then set up an independent practice where criminal law plays only an insignificant role.

The legal fields in civil law countries are much less unified. Civil lawyers often develop separate skills, images, and professional associations as they follow their chosen legal path. This process results in knowledgeable and rather efficient personnel, but it also causes some problems. Results of the early career decision and separation of professions include isolation, inflexibility, professional rivalries, jurisdictional problems, and communication difficulties (Merryman, 1985). In an attempt to lessen the chances that a new university graduate will make an uninformed career choice, some countries (for example, Germany) require law graduates to engage in a period of practical training. Over a period of many months or several years, the "interns" experience the work of judges, government lawyers, and private attorneys. Drawing on those experiences, the still rather recent graduate can choose a legal profession with a better idea of what the career will involve.

Advocates in the socialist tradition tend to follow the same process as those in civil law countries. The law degree, offered at the undergraduate level, is essentially under the control of the universities rather than the legal profession itself. The members of the legal profession are primarily state employees with a status similar to that of other civil servants (Glendon et al., 1985).

Differences between the socialist and civil legal professions are primarily in terms of integration. Instead of having distinct and separate legal fields, the socialist legal profession is highly integrated. As in the United States, this means that socialist lawyers have horizontal mobility to move from one branch of the profession to another without facing additional entrance requirements.

The term *jurist* designates all members of the legal profession for most socialist countries just as the term *lawyer* is applicable to the members of America's legal profession.

A notable exception to the socialist format is Poland. Both under socialism and now under a democracy, university law graduates can choose one of several legal professions. After passing relevant exams and working in the area for the required time, the person is accepted into the ranks of government attorney, private attorney, and so on. As a result, the Polish model follows the civil law tradition more closely than the socialist one. Each branch of the Polish legal profession has specific post law-school training requirements that restrict, without totally foreclosing, horizontal mobility.

Just as Poland's separated legal profession varies from the socialist tradition, and did so even under socialism, so England departs somewhat from the common law practice of a unified legal profession. The positions of *barrister* and *solicitor* provide the basis for a bifurcated system of advocates in England. Terrill (1984) compares them to physicians who are general practitioners (solicitors) and those who are specialized surgeons (barristers). For example, when members of the public need general legal advice or assistance, they usually turn to a solicitor.

Barristers, the more specialized practitioners, can make arguments before higher-level courts where solicitors have restricted access. The solicitor's right to full audience in lower courts, but only limited hearing in higher courts, means that after preparing a case for the higher level, the solicitor must employ a barrister to make the arguments. The British legal system relies on the presenting of oral arguments, so his or her verbal skills and specialized talents make the barrister a respected figure in that system.

General comments about Islamic advocates are difficult to make. The parties in legal disputes are infrequently represented by counsel (Lippman, McConville, & Yerushalmi, 1988) and legal training typically results in scholars instead of practitioners. In Saudi Arabia, for example, persons wishing positions as advocates or judges follow a religious rather than traditional legal education (Amin, 1985). After five years in a preparatory religious school (similar to a secondary-level education), potential legal actors attend a *Shari'a* law school in Mecca, Riyadh, Jeddah, or Medina. Those law schools do not have university status, but after graduation, persons wishing advocate status can request a practicing certificate from the Ministry of Justice. The necessary license to practice before the *Shari'a* Courts is issued in each locality by a committee presided over by a chief justice of that locality (Amin, 1985). Persons wishing a judicial appointment must be selected by the appropriate committee in the Ministry of Justice. After such selection, the aspirants must complete a three-year course of judicial training at the Higher Judicial Institute.

In other Islamic countries, advocates follow a path closer to that of the civil legal tradition. In Iraq and Sudan, for example, aspirants to the legal profession must be law graduates of recognized universities (one of three in Iraq and one of two in Sudan). Graduates must then be accepted to the Iraqi or Sudanese bar and serve as an apprentice for one (Sudan) or two (Iraq) years with a practicing advocate.

Variation in Prosecution

Prosecution of criminal cases is accomplished through either private or public prosecutors (see Figure 7.1). The oldest process (private prosecution) allows the victim or victim's relatives to initiate action against the offender. Where private prosecution is retained today, it is typically alongside public prosecution rather than standing as a country's sole system. However, it can still be an important and effective procedure even if it is not the only, or even primary, means of prosecution. For example, Matti Joutsen (personal communication, August 1997) explains that in some civil law jurisdictions victims can (and in some jurisdictions, *only* the victim can) prosecute for certain categories of offenses, like trespass or libel. In several jurisdictions (e.g., Austria and Germany), victims can serve as "subsidiary prosecutors" in that they have extensive rights of presenting evidence, requesting that certain witnesses be called, commenting on evidence, and otherwise addressing the court. In some jurisdictions (e.g., Austria, Germany, Sweden), the victim can prosecute if the public prosecutor refuses to do so.

Finland provides a particularly interesting continuation of private prosecution by granting the victim a full right to serve as prosecutor completely independently of the public prosecutor. Reforms proposed in the late 1990s may result in restricting the victim's independence to cases where the public prosecutor refuses to prosecute, but even then the victim is able to serve as a subsidiary prosecutor (Joutsen, personal communication, August and November 1997). In any case, victims are allowed to appear in court and present claims or charges different than those brought by the prosecutor. The victim even has the full right to appeal the case—even if the defendant is found not guilty. In practice, Joutsen notes, most victims in Finland prefer to let the public prosecutor handle the case. However, even if it is not often used, the existence of the provision certainly gives victims in Finland a prosecutorial power not frequently found today. Instead, prosecution in countries around the world tends to be initiated by the government (i.e., public prosecution) rather than the individual (that is, private

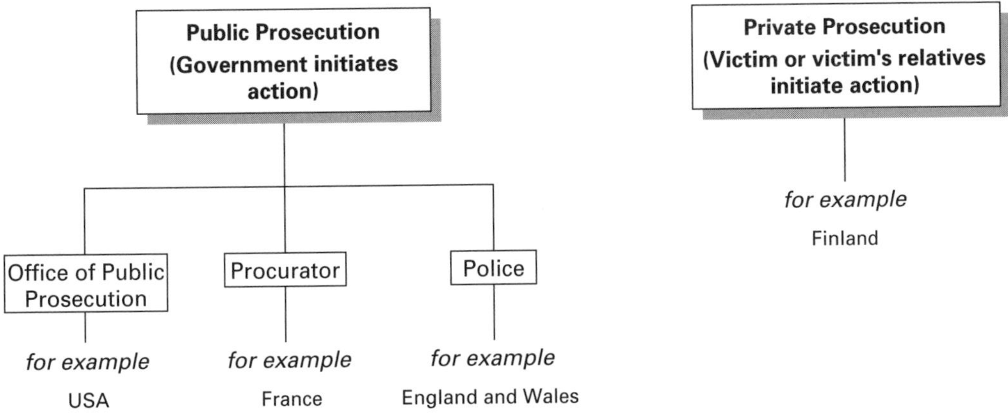

Figure 7.1 Variation in Prosecution

prosecution). For that reason, we focus on variations in the way public prosecution is managed.

Public prosecution can be conducted by an office of public prosecution, by a procurator, or by the police (again see Figure 7.1). To exemplify each type, we will look at the United States, France, and England and Wales.

United States. As noted earlier, colonial Americans were not keen on the idea of lawyers. Because of that, private prosecution, rather than public prosecution by a government attorney, dominated the colonial system of criminal justice. For example, in colonial Pennsylvania, victims with a criminal complaint against another person were responsible for initiating action against that person. The victim informed the justice of the peace (whose fees the victim would pay) about the charge. The victim then attended pretrial hearings, ensured the appearance of witnesses, and hired an attorney to plead the case if the victim did not wish to argue it himself (Steinberg, 1984). It was the private citizen who pursued the case to its conclusion.

As the authorities before whom all prosecutions were initiated in colonial Pennsylvania, the aldermen (members of the municipal legislative body) and justices of the peace (judicial magistrates with limited jurisdiction) were the most important criminal justice officials. Procedures for prosecuting criminal cases were so simple and informal that by 1802 the justices complained that all the criminal cases left no time for more important civil matters (Steinberg, 1984). A solution to this problem, at least in misdemeanor cases resulting in dismissals or acquittals, allowed juries to charge the private prosecutor all the court costs. Felonies were not included for fear that doing so would discourage private citizens from prosecuting serious crimes.

Because the early 1800s were times without an organized, modern police force, the enforcement of the law was still primarily the responsibility of a community's residents. The method used by the citizens involved the private citizen's starting criminal action against someone by initiating procedures at the office of the neighborhood alderman. A portion of the alderman's income was from a fee attached to each case. All criminal cases began in these offices. Although the alderman did not have the power to make the final disposition, it was here that decisions were made about how far a case would proceed in the criminal justice process.

Either the alderman or the grand jury screened most of the private criminal cases out of the judicial system. If an alderman accepted a case, it had to be given to the grand jury for formal indictment. Obviously, there was very little for a public prosecutor to do in this system of law enforcement. Most cases were resolved at the citizen-alderman level, and although aldermen were officers of the state, they were noticeably dependent on the private citizens who provided their fees (Steinberg, 1984). Because their role was judicial, the aldermen could not independently initiate a case. Therefore, if the private citizen did not start things rolling, the alderman (even if he knew of the wrong committed) could not prosecute the case for the private citizen.

None of this should be taken to suggest that public prosecutors did not exist during this time period. Until 1850 the official title for such persons was "deputy attorney general," and they had responsibility for prosecuting serious offenses or "great public wrongs." However, because most cases were minor offenses that were fully resolved by the aldermen, the public prosecutor was seldom called upon. The obvious question becomes, what did the public prosecutors actually do? In cases where an alderman chose not to go to a grand jury, the public prosecutor did nothing. For the rest of the cases he served as a clerk, organizing the court calendar and presenting cases to grand and petit juries. He conducted the prosecution's case in many but not all trials of serious crimes. For most cases, he could be, and perhaps was even expected to be, replaced by a private attorney. Essentially, the public prosecutor had very limited freedom to decide how a case would be handled (Steinberg, 1984).

The idea of a public prosecutor with minimal discretion strikes Americans as very strange today. Contemporary public prosecutors in the United States have significant discretion. They decide whether a case will be carried forward, what the formal charges will be, and even if the charges should later be dropped. It seems unlikely that such discretion was a twentieth-century creation. Steinberg (1984) suggests that the existence of discretion has not changed, but its location has. In these early years of American justice, discretion was in the hands of the alderman, grand jury, petit jury, and private citizens. Citizen discretion was especially overwhelming at each stage of the process, compared with the powerlessness of the public prosecutor. For example, at any point the parties could end the proceedings by simply settling their dispute and not making court appearances.

The public prosecutor's role began changing as the private citizen's role in law enforcement began to decline. According to Steinberg (1984), public disturbances could not be effectively quelled or prosecuted by private citizens. During the 1840s and 1850s, the problem of public order reached crisis proportions. Philadelphia responded to these problems by increasing its police watch in 1850 and then consolidating the police force in 1854. Also in 1854, "the prosecuting attorney's title was officially changed to district attorney, the office was made elective, and the officer was required for the first time to 'sign all bills of indictment and conduct in court all criminal or other prosecutions in the name of the commonwealth'" (Steinberg, 1984, p. 580).

The discretionary power of the district attorney increased slightly over the next 25 years, but private prosecution remained popular and served to limit that discretion. The end of this situation was in sight, however. Complaints grew about private settlements between aldermen and the parties, about the failure of private prosecutors to appear before grand or petit jurors, and about the petty content of the cases themselves. Finally, in 1874 Pennsylvania set in motion changes that effectively altered the relationship between citizens, police, and the courts. The main characters in the criminal justice system became officers of the state (police and public prosecutors) instead of private citizens. Equally important, neither police officer nor prosecutor were officers of the court. Instead, they were independent law enforcement agencies whose purpose was to channel some cases into the courts while resolving others in alternative ways. The effect of the change occurred almost immediately. The percentage of felonies heard by the courts rose, and conviction rates increased, whereas the number of dismissed cases declined dramatically. This shift from a criminal justice process relying upon citizen initiation to one dominated by state initiation provided the power and discretion now housed in the office of public prosecutor.

It is important to note that private prosecution has not been completely abandoned in the United States. In some jurisdictions (for example, Arkansas, Kentucky, North Carolina, Tennessee) victims may retain, at their own expense, private prosecutors to move a case through the criminal justice system (Robin & Anson, 1990). The private prosecutor acts under the supervision of the local public prosecutor's office but provides victims an opportunity to take criminal legal action in cases (for example, misdemeanors) for which the public prosecutor gives low priority. Despite those few jurisdictions holding to the private prosecution concept, public prosecution is well entrenched in the American system of justice. The result is a person the prosecutor, said, at the least, to have broad discretionary power (Newman, 1986) and at the extreme, to be the most influential person in America in terms of the power he or she has over the lives of citizens (Reid, 1987).

France. Discussing public prosecution in countries of the common legal tradition is fairly straightforward—you describe the office of public prosecutor. When attention turns to prosecution in countries of the civil tradition, discussion becomes a bit more complicated. The main reason for that is the civil tradition's (more accurately, the inquisitorial process's) emphasis on the investigative stage and the office of procurator. The *procurator* is a person acting in the place of someone else. In this case, a government attorney takes action for a private citizen who has been wronged. Importantly, procurators act for society and are not simply out to defend state interests. This means procurators do not so much have the duty of securing a conviction as they have the duty to assure justice is done and society's interests are served (Terrill, 1999). France provides a good example of the prosecutorial role under a civil legal tradition, so we will briefly describe prosecution in that country.

There are three key players in the French prosecution process: the judicial police, the procurator, and the examining magistrate. Recall from Chapter 5's discussion of the inquisitorial procedure that the trial is essentially a continuation of the investigatory process. Furthermore, judges play a more active role and attorneys a more passive one compared to those positions under an adversarial procedure. As we recall these circumstances, the idea of prosecution involving three players (police, prosecutor, and judge), representing three seemingly distinct (at least for Americans) stages, makes a bit more sense. Let's begin with a brief description of each player.

The role of judicial police can actually be taken by a member of the *Police Nationale*, the *Gendarmerie Nationale* (see Chapter 6), a prosecutor, or a few specific government officials (for example, mayors). The judicial police operate (regardless of the force or office they are under) at one of three levels: officers, agents, and assistant agents. Judicial police officers have the most authority and can investigate the most serious offenses, order a suspect detained for investigation, and be given even broader authority by an examining magistrate. Judicial police agents and judicial police assistant agents have more restricted authority (though agents obviously have more than their assistants) and function primarily to assist the officers in carrying out their duties.

The results of the investigation by judicial police are given to the procurator. Like their counterpart in a public prosecutor's office, the procurator has the discretion to charge a person with an offense or to dismiss the case. In the spirit of private prosecution, the French also allow victims to initiate legal proceeding either by direct presentation to the court or by adding a civil component to the criminal charges (Pease & Hukkila, 1990). The civil claim (e.g., collecting compensation for damages to person or property) can be heard concurrently with the criminal case (Terrill, 1999).

French procurators are part of a civil service hierarchy headed by the Minister of Justice. Below the Minister are the Attorney General for the Court of Cassation and the Attorneys General for each court of appeal. The Attorneys General supervise their own staff and the procurators *(Procureurs de la Republique)* for each court of General Jurisdiction in that appellate district (Frase, 1988). The procurators determine appropriate charges against the accused, prosecute less serious felonies and most misdemeanors, and direct the work of the judicial police. They also handle serious felonies that fall outside the jurisdiction of the Attorneys General.

Examining magistrates, who are chosen from among the court judges, serve three-year renewable terms. Article 81 specifies, "The examining magistrate shall undertake, in conformance with law, all acts of investigation that he deems useful to the manifestation of the truth" *(French Code of Criminal Procedure,* 1988). In this manner the judiciary has the role of an investigation director who assigns and supervises activities of the judicial police and the procurator. The examining magistrate cannot, however, open an investigation unless requested to do so by the procurator or the victim (Frase, 1988).

Four types of investigations are anticipated by the *French Code of Criminal Procedure:*

1. Investigations of flagrant offenses
2. Formal judicial investigations
3. Preliminary investigations
4. Identity checks

All investigations are conducted under two general principles. First, official investigation of the facts should be fair in the sense that they attempt to uncover both favorable and unfavorable evidence, and that brutal or deceptive methods will be avoided. Second, all investigatory steps are to be thoroughly documented in writing (Frase, 1988). Although all four types of investigation are important, the first two allow the broadest investigatory powers and the last two the narrowest. To exemplify the process we will consider just the first two, because they are more involved. In doing so, we can come to understand the role of the French procurator.

Flagrant offenses are defined as those that are in the process of being committed or have recently been committed. In such cases, the judicial police, procurators, and examining magistrates are given extensive search, seizure, and detention authority. There are procedural safeguards over that authority (for example, house searches must be witnessed by persons independent of the searching authorities), but there are no legal standards similar to probable cause under common law regarding, for example, where police may look for evidence (Frase, 1988). After considering the results of the investigation of a flagrant offense, a procurator determines whether to charge the accused with a *contravention* (least serious), a *délit*, or a *crime* (most serious). The eventual charge will determine whether the accused is simply released on a promise to appear or held in custody to await (within two working days) court arraignment. In addition, the procurator may decide that a judicial investigation is needed (if the charge is for a *contravention* or *délit*) or required (when the charge is for a *crime*).

A formal judicial investigation, which is conducted by an examining magistrate, is mandatory when the procurator charges a serious felony *(crime)* and optional when *délit* or *contravention* charges are filed (Frase, 1988). During the judicial investigation, the magistrate can issue arrest warrants and detention orders and can initiate interrogations of the accused and the victim. When the judicial investigation is deemed complete, the accused is either released or formally charged.

Later in this chapter the French court system is described and reference is again made to the French procurator. At that point you will be reminded that the procurator has a rather limited role in the actual conduct of the trial. Despite differences in the role of French procurator as compared to the U.S. prosecutor, we must remember that both exemplify public prosecution. That is a key point, because the existence of public, rather than only private, prosecutors reaffirms the idea that "crime" is a public wrong.

England and Wales.[1] The role of a public prosecutor with primary responsibility for taking action against criminal offenders is an even more recent idea in England. Before 1985, the decision to prosecute rested with the police, not a public prosecutor. To initiate action against a suspect, the police in England and Wales hired solicitors and barristers who would present the police (that is, public) complaint in court. To help fulfill their prosecutorial duties, most police forces had solicitors on staff to handle the most serious cases (Hughes, 1984; Emmins, 1988). These solicitors were simply employees of the police and lacked decision-making power about the nature of eventual charges. When an "in-house" person was not available, police hired solicitors from the community. As with the private citizen, when a police case went to a higher court, a barrister was hired.

In 1879 England created the office of the Director of Public Prosecutions (DPP). However, the office's growth was remarkably slow until the mid 1980s. Before 1985 the DPP's role was limited to only exceptionally important or difficult cases. That limited role was dramatically changed when the Prosecution of Offences Act of 1985 transformed the position by requiring the DPP to prosecute all criminal proceedings initiated by the police.

Because the increased responsibility and duties thrust upon the DPP would be too great a burden for the existing structure of the office, the Prosecution of Offences Act also created the Crown Prosecution Service (CPS). Chief Crown Prosecutors are responsible for the operation of the Crown Prosecution Service in their area. Branch offices in each area handle prosecutions for a grouping of Mag-

[1]This section has benefited greatly by input from a colleague in the United Kingdom. While the author remains responsible for any inaccuracies present in the description provided, professor Ursula Smartt at Thames Valley University (London) has done her best to help provide accurate and current material.

istrates' Courts—the CPS does not provide prosecutors in the Crown Court. A senior crown prosecutor heads the branch office and oversees the activities of the crown prosecutors and other staff (Ashworth, 1995; Sprack, 2000).

As the CPS provides England and Wales with a national prosecution service, it is important to distinguish it from both a procurator and a public prosecutor system. The difference from the procurator system is clear because the CPS is not involved in the investigation stage—as, for example, is the French procurator. In fact, because the procurator is simply one of three groups (police, procurator, judge) responsible for prosecution, the separate duties of the CPS explicitly set it apart from a procurator system.

It is not as easy to distinguish the CPS from an office of public prosecution. The office of public prosecutor, at least in American jurisdictions, is one with significant discretion at all stages of the judicial process. Court decisions have secured that discretion by identifying public prosecutors as responsible for determining the circumstances under which criminal charges are filed, initiating the prosecution process, and deciding if prosecution should be discontinued (Neubauer, 1996). This discretion stands in marked contrast to the role of the CPS, which is involved in a case *only* when it receives it from the police. "The Crown Prosecution Service has no right to be informed of cases and cannot insist that any advice they give [regarding prosecution of a case] is accepted until the police decide to prosecute" (Keenan, 1992, p. 83).

The police and the CPS are supposed to operate in concert, but that goal is apparently not being achieved to everyone's satisfaction. Since the creation of the CPS there has been increasing antagonism between the two because the CPS does not always take on every case the police bring to prosecution. Cases may be dropped by the CPS for lack of evidence, for example. Sprack notes that the number of cases discontinued by the CPS in the Magistrates' Courts was at 12 percent in 1998–1999 (2000, p. 61).

Once a person is charged by the police, the relevant papers are sent to the local CPS branch office, where the evidence is reviewed. The CPS lawyer reviewing the evidence decides if the charges are justified and can discontinue proceedings when prosecution seems unwarranted. If additional or alternative charges are needed, the CPS lawyer can have them added when the accused appears in court.

The ability of the CPS lawyer to discontinue proceedings is one of the primary changes from the pre-1985 system. When police were solely responsible for determining charges and initiating prosecution, advocates simply followed the wishes of the police. Today the CPS has a partial role in initiating prosecution and a prominent role in determining if prosecution will continue, but it still seems appropriate to have England and Wales as examples of police-initiated prosecution (see Figure 7.1). References to the CPS are careful to note that the initial decision to prosecute still rests primarily with the police in England and Wales. Ashworth and Fionda note that "the initial decision to prosecute is usually taken by the police, and that the principal function of the CPS is the review of cases passed to them by the police for prosecution" (1994, p. 895). Similarly, Keenan (1992) explains that although the CPS has provided a formal separation of prosecution from detection and investigation, "the police continue to decide whether to prosecute, caution, or take no further action in the first instance" (p. 83).

Variation in Defense

Variation in the way nations go about prosecuting cases is continued in the procedures countries develop to defend those citizens being prosecuted (see Figure 7.2). In the *Shari'a* courts of Saudi Arabia and other Islamic countries, professionally trained lawyers do not have a monopoly on legal representation. In fact, Muslims have traditionally acted for themselves or nominated others, relatives or character witnesses, to act for them. Today's restrictions on representation by nonprofessionals have reduced the layperson's use of the courts, but lawyers still are not required personnel in the Islamic justice process.

The former Soviet Union provided an active role for nonprofessionals in the prosecution and defense of criminal defendants. If a person were accused of a crime, coworkers could secure a colleague of the accused to go to court as a "social defender" to testify about the defendant's good moral character and work habits. On the other hand, if the accused's work habits and other characteristics were not appreciated, colleagues could send a "social accuser" to speak against the defendant. In this manner, the public's interests were represented in court on a level equal to those of the defendant.

Despite these examples of laypeople helping in the defense of an accused, most countries rely on legally trained professionals to help defendants present their case. Before the mid-nineteenth century, legal protection for people unable to hire an attorney was primarily the result of charitable acts. Men such as Saint Yves of Brittany—"'a lawyer and yet not a thief, to the wonder of the people'—were canonized for their work in representing the impoverished" (Cappelletti & Gordley, 1978, p. 516). Even the more organized programs faded in and out of use with changes in monarchs. When legal assistance programs were in use, it was not always clear just who benefited from the assistance, under which circumstances it would be provided, and by what process the assistance would be carried out.

Figure 7.2 Variation in Defense (Keep in mind that variation exists within as well as among countries. The countries identified as exemplifying each general type may be accurately placed under another type as well. For example, Mexico also has an Assigned Counsel government-support system, and most countries under a socialist legal tradition also provide legally trained defense counsel.)

More modern programs in the West began in 1851 with French legislation designed to remove financial barriers that the poor encountered during litigation. A 1901 act established a national system of *bureaux* to determine eligibility in that program. Italy (in 1865) and Germany (in 1877) also initiated programs that allowed judges to appoint lawyers, serving without pay, to assist in the defense of an impoverished defendant (Cappelletti & Gordley, 1978).

In the twentieth century, provisions for the defense of poor people around the world have continued to improve, but not always quickly. A 1972 French re-

In the News

DEFENSE COUNSEL IN RUSSIA TODAY

The 1993 Constitution of the Russian Federation provides that every person detained in custody and everyone accused in a criminal case has the right to defense counsel from the moment of arrest, detention, or charge, whichever comes first (see Article 48). The provision for defense counsel from the moment of arrest is an important modification to the procedures existing under Soviet law. In fact, this was such a bone of contention during Soviet times that the defense counsel issues became one of the first reforms to be discussed once Soviet power began to fade (Danilenko & Burnham, 1999).

As a result of the new constitutional provision, the criminal investigator on a case must now include defense counsel in any investigative activities unless the suspect/ defendant has waived the right to counsel. Should the investigator not abide by this provision, any evidence gathered after counsel should have been involved may be excluded at trial.

Because early representation by counsel is a relatively new requirement in Russia, many of the details are still being worked out. Some people argue that counsel merely has to be present during the preliminary investigation since counsel's presence will prevent the worst kinds of abuses. Others prefer that counsel take a more active role. The active role proponents are in a more difficult position because the procedural rules are rather restrictive regarding defense counsel activities. For example, defense counsel cannot directly call witnesses—as they could, for example, in a American preliminary hearing. Questioning of witnesses by Russian defense counsel is subject to approval by the criminal investigator.

Also, as in most civil law countries, the defense is not expected to conduct its own independent investigation of the facts of the case. Instead, defense counsel relies on the testimony gathered by the investigative team. American defense counsel would likely find the inability to interview all the defense witnesses and as many prosecution witness as will talk to them as being a major obstacle to preparing a defense. But in Russia and other civil law countries, defense counsel seems to assume that it would be unethical (e.g., witness tampering) to contact prosecution witnesses. Similarly, it is believed that neither the investigator nor the trial judge would believe any witness for the defense who had been contacted by defense counsel. Such procedures and beliefs remind us that the inquisitorial process is a much more of a collegial one than is the adversarial system (Danilenko & Burnham, 1999).

form substituted a system of aid paid by the state for the previous "charity" with unpaid lawyers providing legal assistance to the poor. However, the nineteenth-century Italian innovation of judge-appointed lawyers providing uncompensated legal assistance remains essentially unchanged some 130 years later (Cappelletti, 1989).

Latin American countries provide examples of the slow movement toward establishing adequate means of legal assistance to poor defendants. Following their historical roots, the legal systems of most Latin American countries borrowed defense provisions from Spain, France, and Portugal. As a result, the assigned counsel (typically serving without pay) system was adopted throughout Latin America by the end of the nineteenth century.

Today two basic kinds of assigned counsel operate in Latin America (Knight, 1978). In the first, a judge appoints lawyers from a list of practicing attorneys in the area. Lawyers appointed in this manner typically serve without pay as they fulfill their charitable obligation. The second type of assigned counsel involves the use of lawyers paid by the state. These "public defenders," operating in the criminal courts of such countries as Mexico, Argentina, Brazil, Peru, and Paraguay, work full time for the court or part time for both court and private clients.

Besides the assigned counsel system, some Latin American countries have national or state legal assistance programs. In Chile's national plan, the Ministry of Justice gives money directly to the Chilean Bar Association to finance the judicial assistance service *(Servicio de Asistencia Judicial)*. The other popular Latin American alternative to assigned counsel is law school legal assistance clinics (Knight, 1978). For example, besides Mexico's government-employed lawyers *(Defensores de Oficio)*, some law schools provide free legal service through neighborhood legal assistance offices. In addition to providing needed legal assistance to poor citizens, these programs give law students, and recent graduates, important practical training.

General comments about the legal assistance systems in continental and Latin American countries provide the necessary overview of worldwide options. Even in these brief remarks you should see similarities with the primary legal assistance procedures in the United States. We have government-supported programs similar to those in such countries as France, Chile, and Mexico. Like many European and Latin American countries, we also have programs that depend on judges to assign counsel from lists of available attorneys. American states also have jurisdictions where defense attorneys are full-time government employees. A review of defense systems on other continents would reveal few variations from these themes. Yet it is still instructive to highlight the defense system of a particular country.

THE ADJUDICATORS

Journalist Iurii Feofanov relates an Eastern parable as he reflects on the idea of a state governed by law:

> *A certain youth was sent to a sheik, famous for his wisdom, to study the laws. For ten years, the youth wrote down the pronouncements of the holy sheik on his scrolls. When he returned to his native land, now a mature man, he took along*

> *an ass loaded down with bales. In them were the scrolls of wisdom. This man then began to judge his countrymen. Whoever came, he would immediately unfold a scroll and read off a dictum. People marveled at the learning of their countryman. But they did not understand what to do; they would ask again, and he would give them a new dictum, even wiser than the first. And so they stopped going to the wise man. One time, he traveled into the mountains to teach people about the laws. Crossing a stream, the ass sank with all his load. The wise man was in despair: how could he now issue judgments? And when people came to him, being without his scrolls of wisdom, he would now for the first time ask again: "What did you say your problem was?" And when he looked into the matter carefully, he would begin to remember what he had been taught and he said what had to be done. He spoke so clearly and wisely that people could only marvel. From that time on, the fame of the learned man spread. And they would say about him: "Earlier, a wise ass would teach us, now it is the wise man himself" (Feofanov, 1990–1991, pp. 15–16).*

From the perspective of the common legal tradition, that parable might be interpreted as criticizing the civil tradition's reliance on codes (the scrolls carried by the ass) for dispensing justice. However, Feofanov used the parable to support the civil legal tradition's belief that law is best envisioned as general principles instead of specific rules. He interprets the parable in this way: "the ass with the 'scrolls of laws' sank in the mountain stream but the principles of law remained in their original sense within the memory of the wise man and judge" (Feofanov, 1990–1991, p. 17). In this manner, the common legal tradition is disparaged as being loaded down with so many specific rules covering every individual problem that the legal system sinks from its own weight.

A distinguishing feature between the civil and common legal traditions is the former's preference for codes that clearly set forth general principles for judges to follow as they dispense justice. The latter's preference is for judges to follow specific guidelines as set down in similar cases handled by the same or other judges. A goal of both traditions is to provide uniformity of justice. The common tradition sees that as best achieved when judges follow decisions in similar cases, whereas the civil tradition feels that the goal is reached by judges following the same general principles. In either case, achieving the goal is linked to the behavior of an adjudicator.

In a sense, the adjudication process is the *raison d'être* for a justice system. Citizens and agencies of the government make use of the justice system when they seek resolution of some dispute. Whether the dispute concerns a private or public wrong, some process for adjudication must be part of the resolution. The preceding parable highlights the role that a judge plays in the decision, but in some justice systems others are recruited to assist the judge.

Plato was among the first to champion a role for laypersons in the criminal process. As he explained it, "In the judgment of offenses against the state the people ought to participate, for when anyone wrongs the state all are wronged and may reasonably complain if they are not allowed to share in the decision" (quoted in Ehrmann, 1976, p. 95).

Today the United States is among only a few countries that take Plato's suggestion to the extreme. In the infrequent case where a jury is used, Americans are relying on laypeople to decide the defendant's guilt or innocence while a judge, separate from those laypeople, controls the proceedings. The seriousness of the task before these members of the public, acting without legal training, is highlighted daily by judges across the country. Although a fictional account, the words of Judge Larren L. Lyttle in Scott Turow's best-selling novel, *Presumed Innocent,* give a feel for the role and mission of American jurors.

Murder defendant Rusty Sabich watches as the prospective jurors for his case are brought into the courtroom. Of the 75 people, 12 will be chosen to decide his fate. As a former prosecutor, Sabich knows that most jurors are going to begin the trial with a pro-prosecution bias. After all, jurors usually tell themselves, the police and prosecutor think the guy is guilty, so who am I, a mere citizen off the street, to say he isn't guilty? The only way Sabich can maintain hope is his knowledge that Judge Lyttle has a reputation for emphatically explaining to the jury such concepts as the presumption of innocence. Sabich listens carefully as the judge begins by telling the potential jurors what the case is about.

> *[Judge Lyttle] has probably seen a thousand juries chosen during his career. His rapport is instantaneous: this big, good-looking black man, kind of funny, kind of smart. . . . He is skilled in addressing juries, canny in divining hidden motivation, and committed to the foundation of his soul to the fundamental notions. The defendant is presumed innocent. Innocent. As you sit here you have gotta be thinking Mr. Sabich didn't do it.*
>
> *"I'm sorry, sir. In the first row, what is your name?"*
>
> *"Mahalovich."*
>
> *"Mr. Mahalovich. Did Mr. Sabich commit the crime that he is charged with?"*
>
> *Mahalovich, a stout middle-aged man who has his paper folded in his lap, shrugs.*
>
> *"I wouldn't know, Judge."*
>
> *"Mr. Mahalovich, you are excused. Ladies and gentlemen, let me tell you what you are to presume. Mr. Sabich is innocent. I am the judge. I am tellin' you that. Presume he is innocent. When you sit there, I want you to look over and say to yourself, There sits an innocent man" (Turow, 1987, p. 234–235).*

The parable of the "wise ass/wise man" and the story of Judge Lyttle's speech to potential jurors suggest extremes in the assignment of people to adjudicate a dispute. At one extreme is a professionally trained judge with sole responsibility for hearing the dispute, determining guilt or innocence, and assigning appropriate sanctions. At the other extreme, carrying out the same duties, is a panel of citizens, minimally knowledgeable in the law. Using these extremes as ideal types for purposes of analysis suggests the continuum in Figure 7.3.

Notice that we are referring only to decisions of fact (that is, did the accused commit the offense?) when speaking of the adjudication process. Courts will often decide questions of law as well as ones of fact. In those instances, the court will rule on such things as the legality of police procedures in the arrest, or the constitutionality of the law that the accused supposedly violated. When dealing with questions of law, courts typically rely only on professional judges. Those judges may be at the mercy of political or religious leaders when making their decisions, but the decision is given by the judge. For questions of fact (and even

Figure 7.3 Variation in Adjudication: An Adjudication Continuum

question of law in some jurisdictions), however, several countries provide input from laypeople. It is to this process we refer when speaking of the adjudication continuum. After considering the issue of presumption of innocence, we will deal with players at the continuum's ends and middle, then look at country-specific examples along that continuum.

Presumption of Innocence

We covered the distinction between presumption of guilt and presumption of innocence in Chapter 2, but a brief review is in order because this issue relates to the mindset of adjudicators as they consider a case. To the extent that civil law systems follow a crime control model, one could argue that they presume the guilt of a defendant. Or, as Packer (1968) might put it, the investigation by civil law system officials is assumed to identify any accused person who is probably innocent. Similarly, people whom the investigation does not exclude are probably guilty. Therefore, subsequent action against those people proceeds under a presumption of guilt. Conversely, one could argue that common law systems emphasizing a due process model presume the innocence of a defendant. Proponents of that system might argue that the assumption of innocence is necessary because the investigatory stage is not as complete nor intensive as it is under civil law. As a result, common law officials cannot be so sure they have already excluded the "probably innocent."

Maybe instead of trying to view one legal system as presuming guilt, another presuming innocence, and a third as presuming nothing, it is best to try to appreciate how a country's legal system tries to avoid prosecution of probably innocent people. Some choose to weed out the innocent in the early stages with intensive investigation of suspects, whereas others believe that the procedures themselves can be used to do the weeding as the suspect/defendant moves through the system.

It is difficult not to ask which system is more just. Merryman (1985) tells of a comparative scholar who said that if he were innocent he would prefer to be tried in a civil law court, but if he were guilty he would rather be tried by a common law court. Merryman (1985) believes that comment considers criminal procedure in civil law to be more likely to distinguish accurately between guilty and innocent. But whichever system —and whatever the presumption—the adjudication process relies on people to make that distinction. It is to those people that we turn our attention.

You Should Know!

PRESUMING INNOCENCE IN CHINA

Reference to a presumption of innocence concerns the broad issue of how a defendant is viewed as he or she comes before the court to interact with the various players. More specifically, does a legal system presume that the accused is innocent or guilty upon arrival at the court stage of the justice process? For example, an important addition in the 1996 Revision of China's Criminal Procedure Law was Article 12, which states, "No person shall be presumed guilty unless the people's courts find them so in accordance with the law" (*Criminal Procedure Law of the People's Republic of China*, 1998). Prior to that addition, Chinese law seemed to reject a presumption of innocence.

The 1979 Chinese Code of Criminal Procedure did not specifically provide for a presumption of innocence, and historically the Chinese courts placed great emphasis on confession. In fact, Berman et al. (1982) said the accused in China was not told in advance what evidence would be used against him. He was not allowed to see the entire record of the preliminary investigation and even his lawyer, who could see the record, was not to give the defendant any details. The reason offered for this seemingly strange rule was that full disclosure of the evidence would tend to taint the voluntary character of a confession. That is, a confession following full realization of the evidence against a person could not be as sincere as one given before the accused knows what the prosecutor knows.

Professional Judges

During the 1980s, some 300 judges and court workers were killed in Colombia. That number includes half the 24-member Colombian Supreme Court, who were killed on a single day in 1985. Most of the murders were linked to drug traffickers and their attempts to stall government repression of their activities. Because they were an essential link in the punishing or extradition of the drug dealers, being a Colombian judge became a high-risk occupation.

In 1991 Colombia tried to provide greater safety to those persons still willing to serve as a judge. Under the "anonymous judge" program (Marcus, 1991), armed guards took accused drug smugglers, for example, into a small courtroom. Instead of facing a judge, the defendant sat with his lawyer and a court reporter while staring into a bulletproof one-way mirror. Behind the mirror, the judge, known to the defendant only by a number, watched the proceedings in the safety of anonymity. When it was necessary for the judge to speak, his voice was electronically disguised in a further attempt to lengthen his career and life.

Stories of killing judges and court officials are unusual but not lacking. Between January 1988 and June 1989, a report on harassment and persecution of judges and lawyers identified 145 such officials who had been attacked or threatened with violence, detained, or killed (United Nations, 1990c). The countries with the most cases reported were the Philippines (28), Colombia (23), and Peru (15). Colombia received particular attention because of groups like the "Extraditables" that threatened to murder 10 judges for every Colombian extradited to the United States.

Harassment and persecution of judicial officials is of greater concern than just a humanitarian interest in the well-being of these people. When the judiciary does not feel free to function, the law cannot operate. The Colombian legal system faced severe problems when judicial officials were executed, compelled to resign, or forced to leave the country. In the face of violence, those judges trying to hold court found few people willing to testify. Colombia's reliance on oral testimony meant that cases made little progress. Combine that with a shortage of technical facilities for crime investigation and the result is an ineffective court system. The problem may not be as stark in other countries, but a judiciary subject to manipulation by others is a well-recognized problem. We will take a look at procedures used in various countries to ensure their judiciary is able to act independently.

An Independent Judiciary. In 1986 the General Assembly of the United Nations passed a resolution for the Basic Principles on the Independence of the Judiciary. Those principles emphasize that the independence of the judiciary should be guaranteed by the state and enshrined in the constitution or law of each country. This position was taken in the belief that an independent judiciary is indispensable for implementing everyone's right to a fair and public hearing before a competent and impartial tribunal (United Nations, 1988).

It is hard to imagine that any country would take a stand against an independent judiciary. In fact, most governments claim that the United Nations' Basic Principles are already embodied in the constitution or laws of their countries. Yet after seeking information from nongovernment agencies, the United Nations found that the basic principles were not always fully respected, despite the public stance taken by government officials.

The judicial system of the former Soviet Union provided an example of a judiciary with questionable independence. The Soviet judiciary fell under the political leadership of the Communist Party of the Soviet Union (CPSU) and the various agencies of state power. Despite its political placement, the USSR constitution declared its Supreme Court to be independent and subject only to the law. The party and state agencies were categorically prohibited from interfering in the examination of specific cases before the court. Yet in practice the Soviets were not able to end the intervention of party and Soviet organs in judicial activity. In the early 1980s, 25 percent of people's judges polled by the USSR Academy of Sciences said that they were subjected to unlawful influence. By 1986 the chairman of the USSR Supreme Court suggested that "'the main reason for judicial error is the violation of the principle of the independence of judges'" (quoted in Petrukhin, 1988–1989).

The frustration of the USSR Supreme Court chairman correctly identifies the importance of an independent judiciary. A country's judiciary can deal with all crimes (including abuse of power by government agents) only when it exists separate and independent from the legislative and executive branches. How do countries seeking an independent judiciary go about finding people to serve as judges? Strange as it might seem, some countries rely on the legislature and executive branches. Other nations use committee recommendations, and still others hold public elections. Of course, various combinations of these approaches are also possible. Some countries seek a more clear-cut separation of government powers and have made the judicial service a bureaucratic career that can be chosen by persons formally educated in the law.

The variability by which judges arrive at their positions deserves closer attention. After all, every country's goal (or at least the publicly stated one) is to provide citizens with an independent judiciary. Only in this way can judges be free to decide in an impartial manner the disputes brought forward by citizens and government officials.

Becoming a Judge. The people who adjudicate legal disputes typically come to their position in one of two ways: selection by others or self-selection. When the selection of judges is by others, it takes the form of either appointment or election. The people chosen usually have already gained experience as attorneys and, especially when chosen for higher courts, may have attained a certain level of distinction in the legal profession.

Appointment to the magistracy can be by the executive or by a special committee. For example, the president of the United States appoints (with the consent of the Senate) federal judges, and the British prime minister selects judges for the House of Lords. Special committees sometimes appoint judges through recommendations to the executive (for example, Israel) or a member of the executive's cabinet (for example, Germany). In some Latin American countries (for example, Bolivia, Honduras, and El Salvador) judges of the highest court appoint members of the lower courts (Hitchner & Levine, 1981).

Election of judges by the people is not frequently found in countries of the world. The United States provides an exception; the majority of American states select judges through some form of popular election. Even in the United States, several states are moving toward a combination appointment/election process (see discussion of the Missouri merit selection plan in introductory criminal justice texts like Albanese, 2000; Schmalleger, 1997).

Judges also can be elected by a country's legislature. Hitchner and Levine (1981) say that this process is used to free judges from executive control (for example, some Central American states), to ensure political reliability (for example, the former USSR), or to provide appropriate distribution of desirable characteristics (for example, judges on the Swiss Federal Court must reflect the German-, French-, and Italian-speaking aspects of Swiss culture).

In the self-selection process, judicial service is chosen as a career after the completion of one's formal legal education. In countries with this process, graduates with law degrees choose among such careers as prosecutor, defense counsel, private attorney, or judge. When choosing a judicial career, the aspirant typically takes a state examination and, if successful, begins serving as an adjudicator. In some countries the new judge will attend a special school, but more often will immediately be sent to a remote part of the country to begin service at the lowest-level courts (Merryman, 1985). Promotion in the court hierarchy and transfer to more desirable locations result from some combination of seniority and proved ability.

Self-selected judges are most often found in countries following the civil legal tradition, but the process is also found in Islamic countries (for example, Saudi Arabia). Because civil law judges have the duty of applying rather than making law, their function is essentially a mechanical one. Judges in the common law tradition are more involved in lawmaking and are often expected to be knowledgeable enough in the law to render creative decisions. One result of this distinction is the perception that common law requires experienced and renowned persons to serve as judges, whereas the civil law operates well with a civil servant or expert clerk. After all, the judicial process in civil law should be a fairly routine activity (Merryman, 1985). The judge is presented with a fact situation, and his duty is merely to link that situation with the appropriate legislative provision and then to pronounce the solution that the union automatically produces. That process, one could argue, can as easily be completed by a young law school graduate as by a celebrated lawyer with many years of legal experience.

Lay Judges and Jurors

When Americans think of laypeople participating in the court process, they typically picture 12 citizens sitting off to one side of the courtroom. The right to a trial by jury has been cherished for quite some time in America's history. Thomas Jefferson provided the reasoning for such a procedure:

> *Were I called upon to decide, whether the people had best be omitted in the legislative or judicial department, I would say it is better to leave them out of the legislative. The execution of the laws is more important than the making of them (quoted in Moore, 1973, p. 159).*

Participation of laypeople as jury members is only one way that citizens take part in the adjudication process. In some countries laypeople sit at the court bench with professional judges and enter into the decision-making process from that location. These two means of participation (juror or lay judge) identify the primary ways in which citizens provide a judiciary with input from the common folk. After an overview of each strategy we will look at country-specific examples of how these techniques operate.

Juries. Although similar assemblies existed in continental Europe before the eleventh century (see Moore, 1973), England is considered the birthplace of the jury. The first type of jury, as it developed after 1066 in England, decided if an accusation against a person was well founded. Sometimes that accusatory jury determined guilt or innocence. Yet eventually two types of juries were established, with the accusatory one called the *grand jury* and the verdict one becoming the *petit* or *trial jury*.

The early trial juries either assembled and stated what they knew about a particular crime, or were told to go into the countryside and establish facts about the alleged crime. To accomplish that duty the jurors talked to neighbors, picked up hearsay information and rumors, and spoke with the accused and the accuser. After gathering their evidence they would reassemble and draw a conclusion about guilt or innocence (Stuckey, 1986). If the accused was found guilty, he was given the punishment prescribed for the crime. Soon not only the jurors expressed what they had learned about the crime, but witnesses might even appear before the jury and relate what they knew about the accusation.

The witnesses' knowledge, like that of the jurors, was often no more than rumor or hearsay, so the jury might give little weight to their testimony. This was particularly true if the witnesses portrayed the accused as innocent. The reason for discounting witness testimony and deciding contrary to what appeared to be the facts rested in the jurors' fear of the king (Stuckey, 1986). The jurors knew that the king's justices often had advance information about a crime because of reports from the sheriffs and the coroners. If the justices believed that the jurors had presented a false verdict, the jurors would be required to make atonement (a payment of property or money) or be punished.

The bias toward conviction in a trial by jury meant that many accused preferred other systems for exoneration. For example, before its abolishment in 1215, many an accused opted for *trial by ordeal.* Here the accused had to do some physical feat as a call to the Deity for help in determining guilt or innocence. It was presumed that God would enable the innocent to do the required ordeal, while the guilty would fail in his performance. Such required feats included holding a red-hot iron or removing a large rock from a boiling pot of water. After the test, the accused's hand was wrapped; then three days later he appeared before a priest who unwrapped the wound and determined if it had healed. A healed hand showed innocence, an unhealed one guilt.

Trial by compurgation was another alternative. This system used "character witnesses" for both the accused and the accuser to take oaths asserting the truthfulness of their respective statements. The technical language of the required oath (an error when repeating it meant guilt) and the general unreliability of the oath helpers (compurgators) did not make this option especially popular. The remaining choice was *trial by battle.* The accused and the accuser would go into actual combat with each other, usually using battle-axes. Like trial by ordeal, the "winner" in the battle was said to have had the assistance of God and therefore must be innocent (Stuckey, 1986).

Efforts to "encourage" the accused to submit to *trial by jury* included the placing of weights on his chest in increasing amounts until he submitted to a jury trial. Even then, the accused often preferred being crushed to death in an effort to save his possessions for his family, rather than having them confiscated by the king should the jury convict him.

As time passed the king could no longer confiscate property as payment for crimes. Equally important, jurors were no longer punished or required to make atonement for possible erroneous verdicts, and the testimony of witnesses received greater consideration. It was this newer concept of the jury trial that the colonists brought with them to America. By 1673 trial by jury had become an important procedure in Virginia, the Massachusetts Bay Colony, New York, and Pennsylvania (Moore, 1973). Jury trials continued to play a major role in the development of the American republic as the colonists prepared for the Revolution. The Declaration of Rights of the First Continental Congress (1774) included trial by peers as a "great and inestimable privilege." In the Declaration of Causes and Necessity of Taking Up Arms (1775) the colonists claimed that they had been deprived of "the accustomed and inestimable privilege of trial by jury in cases affecting both life and property." And the Declaration of Independence (1776) gave as one reason requiring separation "for depriving us, in many cases, of the benefits of Trial by Jury." The place of honor American revolutionaries gave jury trials continues today in the hearts of Americans, although very few cases ever get to the jury stage.

Lay Judges. During the late eighteenth and early nineteenth centuries, the appeal of jury trials influenced legal developments, first in France and then other European countries. It became obvious that the jury trial was not suited to criminal proceedings in civil law systems (Ehrmann, 1976). Instead, the "mixed bench" provides a functional equivalent to the jury trial. This process is common today in both civil and socialist law systems. Private citizens and professional judges combine into a single body responsible for deciding questions of fact, and occasionally law, while determining guilt and punishment. As full participants in the trial process, lay judges on mixed tribunals represent another use of the public in civil legal systems.

Germany's use of lay judges is discussed here, but before considering that country's rather effective use of the mixed bench, we need to point out that lay judges can sometimes be more show than substance. In the former Soviet Union, for example, lay participants in the adjudication process, called "people's assessors" (as they are still called in China), were observed by foreigners, and even some Soviets, to be little more than puppets of the professional judge with whom they sat.

Being a people's assessor was not a full-time responsibility, because the assessor usually spent no more than two weeks per year hearing cases. Because of their limited involvement, assessors often had no understanding of the law except to the extent that they might have read the handbook provided them or listened to lectures presented by jurists. Yet officially the lay judges were on an equal footing with the professional judge (Terebilov, 1973). If one of the three tribunal members disagreed with the other two, the dissenting member had to sign the judgment and provide a written minority opinion. Not surprisingly, judges occasionally suppressed assessor activity in the deliberation room, as the Soviets themselves complained, and frequently determined a sentence without consulting the assessors (Petrukhin, 1988–1989).

The role of people's assessor seemed a simple way to ensure civilian participation (Terrill, 1984) and to represent the voice of peers (Barry & Barner-Barry, 1982). But despite such laudable motives, the Soviet judicial system was criticized for judges putting pressure on people's assessors to come to a particular decision. Petrukhin (1988–1989) notes that contrary to the law, assessors were summoned at the judge's discretion instead of in a sequential order. This meant that judges hearing controversial cases could summon the more submissive and obedient assessors to ensure agreement with the judge's position. Even when given the opportunity to participate actively, the assessors' lack of training suggested that they were not likely to challenge the advice and counsel of the professional judge unless they happened to be especially assertive.

The more typical use of lay judges is exemplified by such countries as Germany. When used in accordance with the original intent, the lay judges provide an intriguing alternative to the jury system as a means of providing citizen input to the trial process. They stand as a contrast to the law systems that prefer to rely almost totally on professional judges and avoid any active participation by laypeople. That point brings us back to the adjudication continuum (see Figure 7.3).

Examples along the Adjudication Continuum

Before we consider country-specific examples of the continuum types, it is important to emphasize the continuum's analytic purpose. As with all ideal-type constructs, the extremes are not represented by any real-life example. Still, for purposes of analysis we can identify examples that are closer to one end or the other. Similarly, whenever you have two ends, there must be a middle; that is, there should be mid-range examples that serve as a balance between the two extremes. Below the continuum line in Figure 7.3 are names of countries that arguably exhibit characteristics running from one ideal type to the other. To provide structure for our discussion of adjudicators, we will consider these countries as they relate to either a heavy reliance on judges or on laypeople in the adjudicating process. To set the boundaries, we will look at the extremes and then move toward the middle.

Saudi Arabia. It may seem strange to have Saudi Arabia toward the "judge heavy" end of an adjudication continuum. During the discussion of judicial review (Chapter 5), this same country exemplified the absence of complete judicial review, and that might imply the absence of judicial power. However, we must remember that judicial review concerns the ability of the judiciary to rule on actions of the legislature and the executive. For purposes of an adjudication continuum, we are looking only at the more traditional role of the judge as he or she decides disputes between citizens or between the government and a citizen. In other words, does the adjudication process rely more heavily on a single judge or a group of laypeople in deciding the question of guilt?

Chapter 4 discussed the importance of witnesses and oath taking in the Islamic court. It is apparent from that review that adjudication in a *qadi* court relies on that judge's ability to direct independently the activities of the accused, the defendant, and any witnesses. Granted, the *qadi* is in turn directed by the *Qur'an,* which stipulates the number of witness and types of oaths necessary for conviction. Yet it is still the *qadi,* without the assistance of any laypeople, who decides if the witnesses and oaths are acceptable. The *qadi* may not have judicial independence and may lack the power of judicial review, but in the courtroom he, and he alone, adjudicates the cases brought before him.

The procedure in *Shari'a* courts of Saudi Arabia is very straightforward and informal (Moore, 1988; Solaim, 1971). When both plaintiff and defendant are present, the *qadi* listens first to the plaintiff and then to the defendant. Each side may refute the other's arguments and may bring witnesses to support his side. The *qadi* is responsible for determining that the witnesses are of good character and is also charged with cross-examining the witnesses. The courtroom is often a simple, small office. These close quarters allow the judge to carefully observe the parties and their reactions. Witnesses may be standing within two feet of the accused.

At the conclusion of testimony, the *qadi* renders his decision, which must include a summary of the facts and the legal reasoning supporting the decision. Moore (1988) explains that the standards on which the decision is based are not, however, clearly defined. For example, the *qadi* is not bound by precedent, nor even by his own prior decisions. He is not required to follow the decisions of a higher-ranking judge. It is, therefore, difficult to dispute the decision of a *qadi* or even to understand its basis from the record. Instead, the judge is simply told to rely on the evidence and testimony as produced by the parties and *Shari'a* principles as the *qadi* knows them.

Other Islamic law countries also reject jury trials in favor of adjudication by a single judge or panel of judges. The *qadi* are typically professional judges rather than laypeople. However, the Islamic Revolutionary Courts (established in Iran after the 1979 revolution) include an individual "trusted by the people." Entessar (1996) explains that the "trusted" person is one of a three-member panel that also includes a civil judge and a religious judge. Although each panel member presumably has similar power, in the late 1980s (the period being described by Entessar) the Revolutionary Courts were dominated by the religious judge.

The heavy reliance on a judge for adjudication purposes is consistent with how *Shari'a* sees a just and impartial trial. Under Islam, there is no need to have laypeople involved in adjudication, because judges are assumed to be unbiased. This assumption is more than just a "hope" because it has its base in Islam itself. Sanad explains that Muhammad commanded judges to be just in their judgments, and is reported to have made his point as follows:

> *The judges are of three kinds, two of them go to Hell and one to Heaven. A judge aware of the right and ruled in accordance with it, then he goes to Heaven, and a judge ruled by ignorance he is in Hell; and a judge who knew the right but deviated from it, he is in Hell too (quoted in Sanad, 1991, p. 83).*

Because, from the Muslims' perspective, judges want to go to Heaven, they will rule fairly and do not need to be monitored by laypeople. A judge-heavy adjudication process is the result.

England. Figure 7.3 places England at the "heavy reliance on laypeople" end of the adjudication continuum. Actually, English courtroom policy allows a much more active role for the judge than does American procedure (Hughes, 1984). In the English tradition, the court will often question witnesses and take a rather active role in the proceedings. At the conclusion of prosecution and defense presentations, the judge may deliver a summary and instructions to the jury. Those comments may include the judge's opinions on witness credibility and may express a particular view of the case.

Judges must be careful with this opportunity to influence the jury via the summary, because the defense could appeal on the grounds the judge went too far in trying to persuade the jury. However, Zander (1989) believes that judges can normally make the summing up "appeal-proof" while at the same time indicating (for example, through body language) their true opinion of the facts. Because the judge in criminal cases knows of any criminal record the accused may have (a fact the jurors do not know), there is likely a temptation to exert improper influence on the jury. In the United States such a temptation is avoided by having judges sum up only on the law and not on the facts. Zander (1989) does not think English judges abuse their power, but there are also many cases in English criminal law that resulted in a retrial or even a not-guilty verdict on appeal because a judge was deemed to have misdirected the jury (U. Smartt, personal communication, July 11, 2000).

Although judges have a fairly involved role, it remains for the English jury to adjudicate questions of fact. On that basis, England is correctly placed on the continuum, because laypeople have an active role as jurors. Additionally, as discussed later in this chapter, laypeople in England are used as magistrates and in that capacity have an even more active role in the justice process.

While the English jury trial would look more familiar to Americans than would the process in countries outside the common legal tradition, it still seems unusual. A first impression would likely be surprise at the placement of the key courtroom actors. In the English courtroom, the opposing barristers sit next to each other and wear identical wigs and robes. Instead of being at his barrister's side, the accused sits in the dock at the rear of the courtroom. The jury never sees the defendant talk directly with the defense counsel (Graham, 1983).

Before 1972 English jurors were selected from a group of persons occupying a dwelling with a certain taxable value. This procedure did not provide much of a cross section of the population and tended to exclude women and low-income people. Acts of Parliament in 1972 and 1974 required jury panels to be chosen at random from all those on the electoral register (i.e., voter registration list) who are between18 and 70 years old and have lived in the United Kingdom for at least five years since age 13. Hughes suggests that the process may not be as random as the legislation intended, and he cites reports of court officials purposefully selecting more men than women, few minority group members, and even avoiding persons with certain family names (Hughes, 1984).

Randomness is also believed to be achieved in selecting British juries by avoiding, as much as possible, the American practice of *voir dire.* In that procedure, the American adversaries question potential jurors to identify possible biases for or against the defendant. By using an allotted number of "challenges," both prosecutor and defense attorney can have some jurors they believe are most likely to favor the opposing side excluded from service. English jurors, on the other hand, arrive at their position without having to suffer such questioning by prosecutor and defense counsel. The result, some cynics have suggested, is a situation where English trials start once the jury selection ends, while American trials are essentially over after the jurors have been "picked." Actually, challenges to particular jurors are possible in the British system. It does not happen often, but either the prosecution or the defense may challenge a potential juror. The challenge, which would be called a *challenge for cause* in an American courtroom, must be for a particular reason. One of the lawyers knowing the potential juror would be an example of a good reason, as would an argument that the potential juror has a criminal record or is biased. The judge determines whether the challenge will be allowed.

Following closing speeches by prosecuting and defense counsels (defense always having the last word), the British judge summarizes the evidence for the jury and, as noted earlier, may even comment on the credibility of witnesses. Basically, the judge is allowed to express an opinion about the defense as long as questions of fact are left to the jurors. Such action by the judge would be distressing to American defense counsels, who are given considerably more leeway in their attempts to win over the jury with emotion and oratory when the facts of the case may not be enough.

Germany. The enthusiasm that American revolutionaries had for jury trials was repeated by revolutionaries in the French Revolution and the nineteenth-century bourgeois European revolutions. The rising middle classes saw participation in criminal proceedings as a weapon in the fight against aristocracy, the professional judiciary, and overpowering monarchs (Ehrmann, 1976). The idea caught on in France and spread to most civil law countries, but it proved a disappointing experiment.

The Europeans tried to incorporate the common legal tradition of a jury into their civil legal tradition system without otherwise modifying their system. The inquisitorial trial format, the importance of the investigatory stage, and the active role of the judge made it difficult for jurors to follow the evidence presented under civil legal procedure. In their confusion regarding their role, European jurors often asked the judge for advice. The advice was provided in forms that would be totally inadmissible in an Anglo-American jury trial (Ehrmann, 1976).

Today the classical jury system is primarily a common law tradition. Some civil law country examples exist, though. France uses nine lay jurors (initially chosen from voting rolls) to hear cases involving serious criminal trials before the Courts of Assize. However, the French version seems unusual to those familiar with the English and American juries, because the French jurors join three professional judges upon whom the jurors are dependent for explanations of both law and facts (Terrill, 1999). Austria, on the other hand, has eight jurors deciding on their own about the defendant's guilt or innocence. In addition, as noted at this chapter's start, some Russian jurisdictions have started using juries in cases where defendants are accused of serious felonies.

The French use of both professional judges and laypeople signals, but does not illustrate, the more typical direction of courts following the civil law. That is, instead of using laypeople who independently and bindingly determine guilt or innocence, countries of the civil legal tradition are more likely to use a "mixed bench," wherein two or three laypeople work with professional judges to adjudicate criminal cases. This approach seems better suited to the inquisitorial process, because the laypeople and professional judges are expected to work together toward sound verdicts and sentences. Germany provides a particularly good example of the mixed-bench approach.

The German people used the jury system in the 1840s and briefly in Bavaria after World War II. For the most part, however, recent German history has involved the use of citizens as lay judges rather than as jurors. Specifically, the community chooses fellow citizens to serve on the bench with professional judges. These lay judges have full powers of interrogation, deliberation, voting, and sentencing.

Lay judges serving in criminal courts are called *Schöffen.* They serve in courts of limited jurisdiction and in the higher-level courts with general jurisdiction. An accused criminal will be tried in a court with professional and lay judges, unless it is for a petty offense or—paradoxically—for certain very serious political offenses (e.g., treason, genocide, terrorist conspiracy, etc.). There are two types of mixed trial courts. The *Schöffengericht,* a lower-level court of limited jurisdiction (one professional and two lay judges), and the *Grosse Strafkammer* (with three professional and two lay judges). When the *Grosse Strafkammer* is hearing a very serious crime (murder, manslaughter, etc.) the

IMPACT

Concurrent Consideration of Guilt and Sentence

Under the American system of justice, sentencing hearings typically follow trials—sometimes by as much as several weeks. One reason for this procedure is to provide time to gather information about the defendant for use by the judge in determining the appropriate sentence. The probation department, for example, will need time to complete a presentence investigation. Because determination of guilt and determination of sentence are separate procedures, the rules governing trials in the United States differ greatly from those controlling sentencing hearings. Consider the law of evidence. In the United States, it limits the nature and sources of information to be considered during the guilt phase of a trial, but there are few such limits at the time of sentencing. And the restriction on evidence about the defendant's prior criminality vanishes after conviction. As a result, there are few evidentiary or other restraints placed on the court during the sentencing phase.

German and French law, on the other hand, do not separate the guilt-finding and sentencing functions (Tomlinson, 1999; Weigend, 1983). The French do not even have a word that is equivalent to our word "sentencing." Tomlinson explains that the notion of sentencing does not really exist in France. Instead, a judgment convicting a defendant also imposes the relevant penalty—there is no concept of conviction as separate from sentence. The trial court finds the facts, decides upon the verdict, and determines the sentence, all in one proceeding. Because the two aspects are not separate activities, there is no need to distinguish, as in America, between evidence admissible relevant to guilt and other types of evidence. The trial court must gather simultaneously the information necessary to reach a verdict and to arrive at an appropriate sentence.

The standards used in Germany to collect evidence about guilt and sentencing may seem rather loose to many Americans. For example, hearsay evidence may be introduced, and the closest thing to an exclusionary rule is the barring of evidence gathered in such extreme situations as deception, illegal threats, and hypnosis. Evidence about the defendant's character, including prior convictions, can be introduced even if the defendant refuses to testify! Germany's Code of Criminal Procedure recommends introducing evidence of prior offenses only "as far as necessary." Yet in practice the defendant's criminal record is usually read into the court record just before the closing arguments of the trial (Weigend, 1983).

Germans do not view the unified trial (that is, simultaneous determination of guilt and sentence) and the unstructured manner of gathering evidence as unjust. Their confidence in the fairness of the procedures is based on two facts:

IMPACT

Concurrent Consideration of Guilt and Sentence

1. The absence of an unsupervised lay fact-finder (an American jury).
2. A tradition of the inquisitorial procedure.

Together, these facts result in a different approach to truth-seeking. First, the German court system does not have to control the deliberations of lay jurors through complicated rules of evidence. The lay judges discuss and decide cases with the professional judge and are under that judge's continuous guidance and advice. The German system relies on the professional judge's ability to explain to the lay judges the relevance and weight of the evidence. Professional judges, because of their training and experience, are presumed to know how properly to assess evidence without the guidance of formal rules (Weigend, 1983).

Consideration of this different way of conducting a trial highlights distinctions between the inquisitorial and adversarial systems. In America, truth emerges in an indirect fashion from a contest between the people involved. Therefore, as in any other "competition," procedural rules to guide and regulate the contest are of foremost importance. In Germany, the truth comes directly to the court through questioning of persons most likely to know it. That does not mean that the truth can be sought at any cost, but the German system does put less emphasis on formality and rules of evidence. The difference is made clear in Weigend's (1983) comment that a German judge would think it absurd to limit testimony from a witness who is about to convey useful information on the defendant's need for rehabilitation simply because the witness was called to testify about the offense. The loss of truth Weigend explains, would be regarded as much more harmful than upsetting the sequence of taking proof.

court is referred to as a *Schwurgericht*. Decisions of the lower-level courts, with and without lay judges, can be appealed to another mixed court, the *Kleine Strafkammer* (with one professional and two lay judges). All of the more serious cases can be appealed only for points of law and only to a purely professional court.

The lay judges are assigned to sessions over a period of four years. Usually they serve an average of one day per month. If their service ever exceeds 24 days in one year, they can ask to be stricken from the list of lay judges. Because a defendant lacks choice between a bench or jury trial, it is easier than it would be in the United States to figure out the number of lay judges needed over a four-year period. In addition, the date and length of a German trial is more predictable. This is because the judge in the inquisitorial system determines the evidence to introduce, the witnesses to summon, and the general nature of the proceedings.

As a result, German trials tend not to be as long as those in America. There are other time-savers as well. Because there is no jury, the rules of evidence are uncomplicated, and there is never a need to remove a jury while attorneys make motions and arguments the jurors should not hear. Finally, "hung juries" are eliminated, because decisions on guilt can be made with less than a unanimous vote.

As in the United States, the participation of the lay public is the result of efforts to ensure representation of the average citizen. Selection of the *Schöffen* varies by region since there is no federal standard. In some parts of Germany (e.g., the rather small Bremen), the names are handpicked by the political parties. In other parts (e.g., the very big Nordrhein Westfalen), the *Schöffen*-list is drawn from the population registers. *Schöffen* may repeat their service as long as it has been at least eight years since they last served. The state courts determine via formula the number of citizens required and call the necessary principal lay judges *(Hauptschöffen)* and a number of alternates *(Hilfschöffen).*

Notably absent from this process is a procedure similar to American *voir dire,* where either prosecution or defense challenge lay judges. But even though there is no German counterpart to the *voir dire* process, it is possible to challenge the persons on the nomination list and the chosen lay judges. Moreover, lay judges chosen for a particular trial can be challenged for bias—as can the professional judges. Nevertheless, such challenges are rare. The presiding judge has responsibility for the composition of the court, but a *Schöffe* must inform the judge if he or she does not feel completely free in considering the case.

We now have a better understanding of the actors involved in the judicial process of different countries of the world. It is time to move on to the second part of the actors/ institutions strategy and consider the stage on which these actors play: the courts.

VARIATION IN COURT ORGANIZATION

A review of court organizations around the world reveals a strange combination of similarity and uniqueness. The similarity comes from the seemingly universal use of a basic organizational structure composed of lowest-level, mid-level, and highest-level courts. We find uniqueness when we look more closely and see many possible variations on that basic theme. Attempts to classify the various organizations into only a few categories would be fruitless. In some countries a dual system operates, with courts at the state or province level coexisting with courts at the federal level. In other countries the system is so centralized that one simple three-tiered structure handles criminal, civil, and administrative cases in the same courts with the same judges. Criminal, civil, and administrative disputes may be under the jurisdiction of three separate court hierarchies in other countries. Some countries include a system of religious courts with an autonomous system of secular courts.

Obviously, finding three or four common variables to use in categorizing the systems is an unwieldy assignment. The most reasonable approach for handling the profusion of organizations is simply to describe some variations to show the different ways in which a basic theme can be played. In the absence of a reasonable classification scheme, we will simply consider examples from some countries covered in other chapters and a few new nations to ensure a broad-based representation.

France

The courts of France are organized into two major systems: the ordinary, or regular, courts, and the administrative courts (Harvard Law School Library, 2000). The simplicity of the French system stops at this point, however, because each system has separate and distinct hierarchies that even the French authorities consider quite complex. Confusion regarding court jurisdiction required the creation of the eight-member *Tribunal des Conflits*. This tribunal, presided over *ex officio* by the Minister of Justice, makes unappealable decisions regarding the system to which a case will be assigned.

Because the ordinary courts handle both civil and criminal cases, our discussion will be restricted to that area. Further, as seen in Figure 7.4, there are different lower- and intermediate-level courts for civil and criminal cases. We will follow the hierarchy for criminal cases. First, because there are some common features of trials at each court level, an overview of court procedures will be helpful before we tackle the inevitable differences.

In the most general sense, French defendants do not enter pleas in their courts. In principle, all cases go to trial, and whether the accused agrees with or fights the charges is simply another piece of evidence for the court to consider. Obviously a full-fledged trial in all instances would be too burdensome for

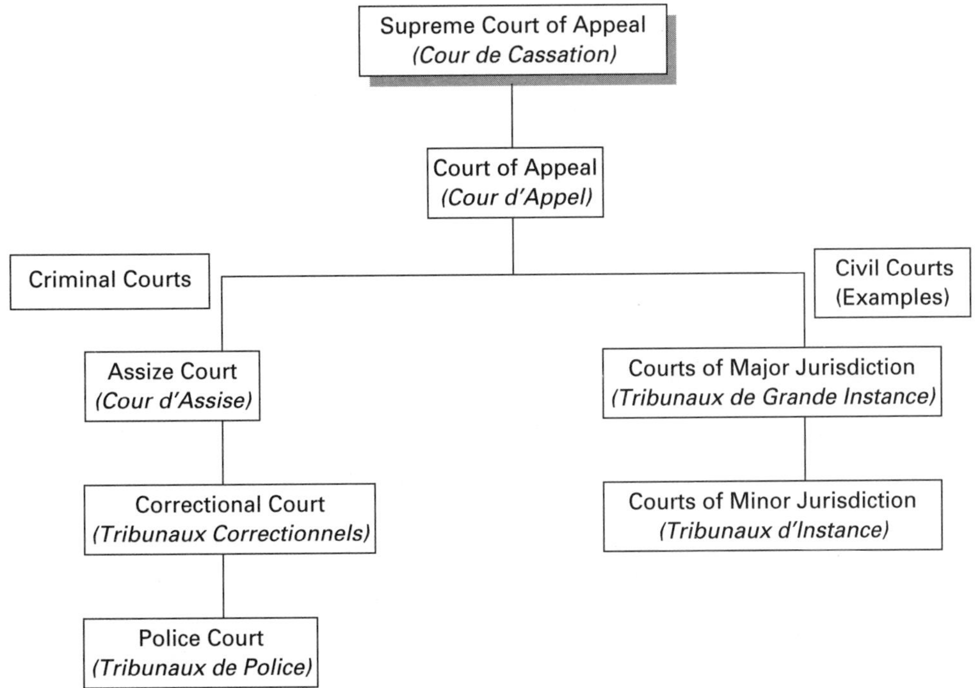

Figure 7.4 Ordinary Courts of France

almost any country, but especially an industrialized nation like France. As a result, there are several procedures and practices (especially at the lower-court levels) that are designed to save time and discourage unnecessary litigation (Frase, 1988). At the lowest tier (police court) trials can be completely avoided through trial substitutes. At the next higher tier (correctional court) there are several ways (see the following discussion) to condense the process.

During a trial, regardless of the court level, any prior convictions of the accused are admissible as relevant evidence. In fact, from an American perspective, French trial courts seem bound by few restrictions on the kind of evidence that can be introduced. This apparent permissiveness may be explained by three factors (see Frase, 1988):

1. Fact-finding in France is dominated by professional judges rather than lay jurors, so procedural safeguards need not be as stringent as in systems where laypersons have a significant role.
2. Because there are not separate guilt-finding and sentencing phases to French trials, all evidence relevant to sentencing must be admitted at the same time as that relevant to guilt.
3. For determining both guilt and sentence, the French believe it is better to judge the whole person (including past behavior and character) rather than just the current charges.

The trial itself is conducted by the presiding judge at each court level. The accused is given an opportunity to provide a statement to the court, after which the attorneys can pose questions (usually through the judge) to the defendant. The accused, who is not put under oath, is not required to answer any of the questions; but the court is not prohibited from drawing unfavorable conclusions from that silence (Frase, 1988). After interrogating the accused, the court calls in the witnesses, places them under oath, and asks them to provide information that they have regarding the offense and the accused. The presiding judge may interrupt the witnesses' narrative to clarify ambiguities and encourage relevance. The attorneys can also question the witnesses, but they do so under restricting guidelines. Following the last witness, the prosecution and the defense attorneys (always in that order) make their closing arguments. With that brief overview in mind, let us look more closely at the different types of French courts.

Trial Level: Police Court. The basic tribunal for minor offenses subject to a fine is the Police Court *(Tribunal de Police)*. These courts are spread throughout the country and are presided over by justices of the peace, who are required to live in the tribunal's jurisdictional area. Although several judges may be assigned to the court, a single judge makes the decision.

When trials occur in Police Court they are invariably brief and simple. More typically, adjudication occurs without an actual trial and even away from the actual courtroom (Frase, 1988). A substitute for the trial is used when the prosecutor sends information on the case to the court and the judge believes that the matter can be handled simply with a fine. The court notifies the prosecutor of the fine's amount, and the prosecutor (if he or she does not object to foregoing the trial) informs the accused. The accused has 30 days to either pay or object. If either prosecutor or accused objects to this procedure, the case is set for trial in police court.

Trial Level: Correctional Courts. Criminal or Correctional Courts *(Tribunal Correctionnel)* are above the Police Courts in the hierarchy. These courts have jurisdiction over lesser criminal offenses and can assign penalties of up to 10 years imprisonment. A panel of three or more (but always an uneven number) judges hears the cases and reaches a decision by majority vote.

The accused appearing before this court has the right to counsel (either retained or appointed), but counsel is not required unless the accused suffers from some disorder that could compromise the defense (Frase, 1988). Because witnesses are allowed, the trial process would be rather time-consuming if not for the fact that both defense and prosecution typically rely on pretrial statements and information from any judicial investigation instead of bothering with witnesses.

The proceedings are further consolidated by having rather permissive rules of evidence. As the Code states it, "Except when the law provides otherwise, offenses may be established by any manner of proof, and the judge shall decide according to his thorough conviction" (*French Code of Criminal Procedure,* 1988). When the Correctional Court can use any manner of proof to find the accused guilty, the proceedings are not prolonged by many questions of law.

The court can announce its verdict and sentence immediately after closing arguments, later the same day, or even at a later date. Whenever announced, the judgment must include both the disposition and the reasons for that decision.

Trial Level: Assize Court. The Assize Court *(Cour d'Assise)* has original jurisdiction in serious felony cases and can assign penalties ranging from fines to life imprisonment. An interesting aspect of the Assize Court is its use of a lot-chosen jury of nine citizens who sit with three judges to hear cases of original jurisdiction (Abraham, 1986). Jurors chosen by lot are not automatically impaneled, because the prosecution has four peremptory challenges and the defense has five (Frase, 1988). The three judges include a presiding judge who is always a member of the *Cour d'Appel* (the next higher-level court) and two other magistrates who may come from the *Cour d'Appel* or a local lower court.

During the trial, and with the presiding judge's approval, the jurors and other two judges can question the accused and the witnesses. Also, the prosecution and defense can submit questions for the presiding judge to ask.

After hearing the last witness and the closing statements, the presiding judge instructs the jurors on their duty to determine the accused's guilt or innocence. Rather than a standard of proof like "beyond a reasonable doubt," the Assize Court jurors and judges are told that for determination of guilt, "the law asks them only the single question, which encompasses the full measure of their duties: 'Are you thoroughly convinced?'" (*French Code of Criminal Procedure,* 1988; Article 353). The law does not ask them how they became convinced but instead requires them to ask themselves what impression the evidence and the defense made on their reason. If those impressions "thoroughly convinced" the juror or judge that the accused is guilty, then he or she is obligated to vote accordingly.

Voting by judges and jurors is by secret ballot, with conviction requiring at least eight of the twelve members. A vote for conviction is followed by a vote on the penalty. From the penalties proposed by the members, the one imposed will be that receiving a majority vote.

Appellate Level: Courts of Appeal. At the level of the Courts of Appeal *(Cour d'Appel),* both the previously separate civil and criminal systems come together. These courts take appeals not only from the civil and criminal courts below but also from such special courts as the Commercial Court and Juvenile Court. Each of the 27 judicial districts *(Chambres)* has a Court of Appeal. Each court has three to five judges (seven in the Parisian court) who hear the case and make decisions on both points of law and points of fact (Abraham, 1986; Rhyne, 1978). Decisions on points of fact are final, while those on points of law can be appealed to the *Cour de Cassation.*

Appellate Level: Supreme Court of Appeal. The court of last resort in the French hierarchy is the Supreme Court of Appeal *(Cour de Cassation).* This highest-level court has five civil chambers and only one chamber hearing criminal cases. The court, which lacks original jurisdiction, is headed by a president and must have seven judges (from a total of fifteen) present to hear a case.

The term *cassation* derives from the French *casser,* which means "to break" or "to smash" (Abraham, 1986). The term is appropriate for this tribunal, because the court's power is limited to voiding the legal point of a case. When the *Cour de Cassation* decides that the lower court inappropriately applied a point of law, the case is returned for retrial to a different court at the same rank and of similar category. However, if the new court disagrees with the Court of Cassation's position (and the new court has the right to do that), the case goes once again before the Court of Cassation (Council of Europe, 2000). At this second appearance, the full court hears the case. This opinion, now considered an authoritative interpretation on the point of law, must be followed by the lower tribunal.

England

The English court design includes a rigid structural segregation between the country's criminal and civil courts. In fact, a separate criminal jurisdiction has existed for over 700 years (Abraham, 1986). But the two separated judicial hierarchies typically make use of the same judges to hear the cases brought forward. For our purposes, only the criminal court hierarchy is of concern (see Figure 7.5).

Trial Level: Magistrates' Court. At the lowest level of the criminal court hierarchy are Magistrates' Courts. Unpaid lay magistrates (also called justices of the peace or JPs) preside over these highly visible tribunals that Edward II (1307-1327) established near the end of his reign. Over 30,000 JPs now work in more than 500 Magistrates' Courts throughout the country. Lay magistrates are appointed by the Lord Chancellor upon advice from a local advisory committee.

In certain jurisdictions, especially larger cities, Stipendiary Magistrates are more likely than JPs to be found at the helm of the Magistrates' Courts. More than 150 Stipendiary Magistrates are at work in London, for example, and about

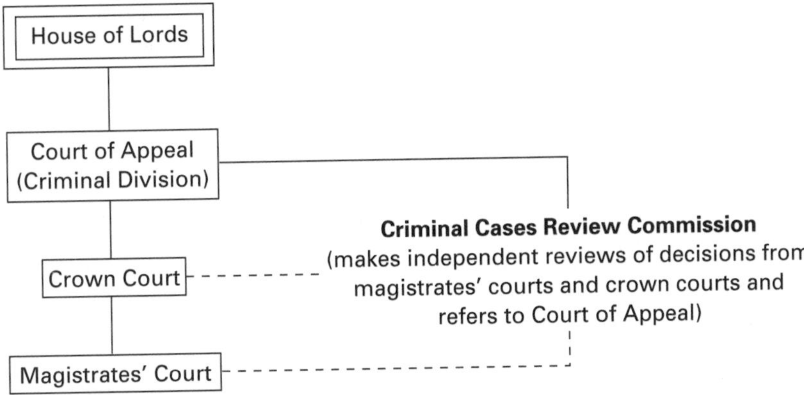

Figure 7.5 English Court Organization

25 more have appointments in the provinces. As the title suggests, the Stipendiary Magistrate receives a regular salary. Also, unlike the justice of the peace, the Stipendiary Magistrate must be a full-time professional lawyer (Magistrates Association, 2000; U. Smartt, personal communication, July 11, 2000).

The Magistrates' Courts serve as the workhorse for the English criminal jurisdictions with the vast majority of criminal cases beginning and ending here. The trials at this lowest-level court are conducted without a jury and before two or three JPs. When a Stipendiary Magistrate heads the court, he or she hears the case alone.

Defendants before the Magistrates' Court are typically unrepresented by counsel and find themselves subjected to proceedings that are conducted at a dazzling speed. The rapid action is surprising, because the JPs are lay magistrates, both in the sense of being unpaid and in terms of not needing a legal background. It might be expected that such a person would run a rather deliberate and time-consuming courtroom. Luckily, because Magistrates' Courts have such a heavy workload, that situation does not occur. The court's efficiency may come in part from the presence of lawyers volunteering as magistrates (there is no prohibition against legally trained people becoming JPs), but is more clearly the result of the management by the court's clerk.

The magistrates' clerks often are, but are not required to be, legally trained. They are assigned to the Magistrates' Courts, where their duties range from helping unrepresented defendants to advising the magistrates on points of law or procedure, though not on the decision (Emmins, 1988). The clerk provides advice when asked by the magistrates but may also offer advice even if unasked (Keenan, 1992). Although the JPs receive basic legal training, they are typically pleased to accept their clerk's advice on matters of law.

Trial Level: Crown Court. Immediately above the Magistrates' Court level is the Crown Court, which the Courts Act of 1971 established. This court, which has both appellate and original jurisdiction, is the first level at which an accused is entitled to a trial by jury. The Crown Court, authorized to sit anywhere in England and Wales, is typically presided over by a professional circuit judge. On occasion, the presiding official is a recorder who has been selected from barristers with at least 10 years' experience and has agreed to be available on a part-time basis to hear cases.

The Crown Court hears cases involving serious offenses and carries out its duties with great pageantry and fanfare. All contested trials take place before a jury. In such cases, the jury alone decides whether the defendant is guilty or not guilty. The Criminal Justice Act of 1967 allows a majority verdict (for both conviction and acquittal) when jurors vote 11 to 1 or 10 to 2, although a unanimous one is preferred. To that end, the judge will accept a majority decision only after the jury has had two hours (or longer if the judge thinks the case requires it) to reach a unanimous verdict (Emmins, 1988).

Appellate Level: Court of Appeal. The Court of Appeal hears appeals on conviction (e.g., a flaw in the proceedings had occurred at trial) and sentence (e.g., the sentence was excessive) by defendants from the Crown Court. The prosecution cannot appeal a verdict of acquittal. The appeals come to the Criminal Division of the Court of Appeal. Sitting without a jury, this court hears appeals based on the transcripts of the evidence taken at the trial. The court is presided over by the Lord Chief Justice.

Several high-profile cases involving the miscarriage of justice in the 1980s and 1990s (e.g., the Guildford Four and the Birmingham Six) caught the attention of the British media and public. In a 1993 report to Parliament, a Royal Commission on Criminal Justice recommended that an independent body be established to consider suspected miscarriages of justice and, when appropriate, to arrange for their investigation. When the investigation reveals matters that should be considered further by the courts, the case is referred to the Court of Appeal. As a result of this recommendation, the Criminal Appeal Act of 1995 was passed and the Criminal Cases Review Commission (CCRC) was established as an independent body responsible for investigating suspected miscarriages of justice in any Crown Court or Magistrates' Court in England, Wales, and Northern Ireland (Criminal Cases Review Commission, 2000).

The CCRC started handling casework in 1997, and in October 2000 it had its 100th case referral. A few cases were handled posthumously. For example, the case of Mahmood Mattan, hanged in 1952, was referred to the Court of Appeal in 1997, and Mattan's conviction was quashed in 1998 when the Court ruled that the conviction was "unsafe" because of unreliable evidence from the main prosecution witness. Decisions about whether a case should be referred to the Court of Appeal is made after a review by Case Review Managers determines that pertinent evidence or arguments were not considered at the original trial or appeal. Upon passing case review, the final decision on referring a case is made by the 15 Commission Members, either singly or in three-member groups (Criminal Cases Review Commission, 2000).

Appellate Level: House of Lords. In addition to its function as the upper House of Parliament, the House of Lords provides the accused with a court of last resort—but access is very restricted. If the appeal is on a point of law involving "general public importance," and the appeal is supported by the Court of Appeal or by the Appeal Committee of the House of Lords itself, the case may proceed to this final stage. At any one time there are nine to eleven Law Lords who have been appointed by the Queen on the Prime Minister's advice, who in turn was advised by the Lord Chancellor. Three Law Lords are required to constitute a court, but five normally sit to hear an appeal (Council of Europe, 2000; Keenan, 1992).

Nigeria

Nigeria is located on the West African coast near its namesake river the Niger. As they did in several other parts of Africa, the British began colonizing important areas of Nigeria in the late 1800s. The important port of Lagos was taken as a British colony in 1861 and then incorporated with the rest of southern Nigeria in 1906 as the Colony and Protectorate of Southern Nigeria. Independence was won in 1960, but in 1966 the fairly new Federal Republic of Nigeria was placed under a federal military government that held all executive and legislative power. In 1989 the military lifted a ban on political activity, and in 1999 a civilian government was reestablished with the election of President Olusegun Obasanjo.

Before 1861 Nigeria's courts consisted primarily of village officials hearing cases involving the community and family elders handling family disputes. The system seems to have worked fine for the Nigerians, but the British found it ineffective for their purposes. British merchants had trouble using the existing courts to enforce payment of debts by their local customers. To assist in this process, the British government established a judicial system wherein a resident agent (British consulate) regulated trade between British merchants and their local customers (Iwarimie-Jaja, 1988a). With this foothold, an English court system began to spread throughout Nigeria.

Nigeria's courts are found at both the federal and state levels (see Figure 7.6). At the federal level the highest court is the Supreme Court of Nigeria. The Supreme Court consists of the chief justice and a number of associate justices as may be prescribed by federal legislation. The justices are appointed by the president upon advice from the legislature. The Federal Court of Appeals, consisting of a president and a number of justices as prescribed by legislation (but at least three must be knowledgeable in Islamic law and three in customary law), hears appeals from the Federal High Court, the State High Courts, *Shari'a* Courts of Appeal, Customary Courts of Appeal, and other courts. The Federal High Court, with a chief justice and at least five other judges, has original jurisdiction in federal law violations and in cases involving the federal government versus individuals or states, or states versus states.

The highest level court in every state is the State High Court. Each court is headed by a chief judge, appointed by the state governor, and supported by such number of judges as is prescribed by state law—also appointed by the governor, but upon advice by a judicial commission. This court hears and decides any civil and criminal case involving state law. Below the State High Court in the judicial hierarchy are the Magistrates' Courts—the workhorses of Nigeria's court system.

The court structure at the state level is complicated by the inclusion of Customary Courts providing for traditional law and also by the declaration of at least four states (all in the North) to implement Islamic law throughout the state. States providing for traditional law have Customary Court judges who typically

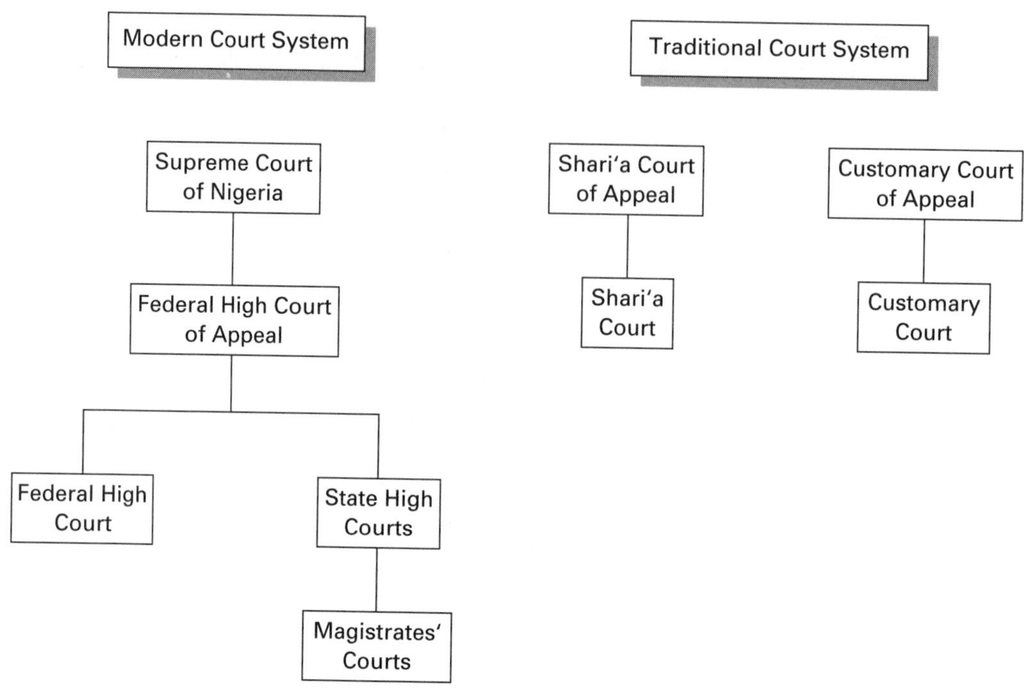

Figure 7.6 Nigeria's Modern and Traditional Courts

are lay people without formal legal training, but who have the age and experience to be knowledgeable of the customary laws of their clans. States that have declared Islamic law process both civil and criminal cases (at least those involving Muslims) through the *Shari'a* Courts. Rulings from the Customary Courts (where they exist) may be appealed to the state-level Customary Court of Appeals that stands below the Magistrates' Court level. Cases appealed from a *Shari'a* court go to a state-level *Shari'a* Court of Appeals and, as needed, to the Federal Court of Appeals.

The federal and state courts comprise Nigeria's modern court system but since that system was initially imposed on Nigeria by colonial rule, it is not a popular one with Nigerians. Iwarimie-Jaja (1988a) notes that although the modern court system has spread to all aspects of life in contemporary Nigeria, the Nigerians do their best to avoid the courts.

Efforts to bypass the formal courts may result from the delays typical in the modern system. Oloruntimehin (1992) notes that such delays keep many people, who are presumed to be innocent, in terrible, overcrowded, unhygienic prisons while they await their trial. In addition, the people hesitate to serve as prosecution witnesses because of their aversion to the court. Whether the Nigerians' efforts to shun the modern court are a result of the delays in getting a complete judgment in a case, or because the people have little confidence in modern courts, the typical Nigerian prefers more traditional ways to settle a dispute.

The preference for traditional justice systems over modern ones provides an opportunity to look at a level of court operation that is often neglected. The Customary and *Shari'a* courts, specifically, provide Nigerians the chance to use more traditional ways to resolve conflict. These traditions can involve the intervention of chiefs and elders or even consultation with oracles, juju (amulet), shrines, and the like (Iwarimie-Jaja, 1988a). Cases dealing with personal injury and those involving crimes can all be handled from a perspective of traditional customs and religious beliefs. The specific mechanisms used to deal with these situations are the Customary and *Shari'a* Courts.

Nigerian Customary Courts are especially popular in the southern states, where they dispose of cases by reference to established customs, beliefs, and values. In the northern states, with a primarily Islamic population, Islam encompasses all aspects of the people's life. *Shari'a* Courts give these Nigerians a means to decide cases on the basis of Islamic law.

Both types of courts play a very important role for the Nigerian people. Ebbe (2000) and Iwarimie-Jaja (1988a) believe that these courts continue to exist because the modern courts are considered ineffective for many issues, irrelevant for others, and lack credibility on issues where they could be relevant. For example, the Magistrates' Courts are where most felony cases are tried, so it is this court that provides the average Nigerians with most of their knowledge about how modern courts operate. Unfortunately, the present operation is not one that instills trust. Crucial facilities, from accommodations to secretarial assistance, are lacking, and magistrates may have to take notes and write judgments in longhand. Additionally, the high level of discretion given magistrates results in considerable sentence variation from judge to judge (Oloruntimehin, 1992). As a result, Nigerians are provided few reasons to find legitimacy in the formal court setting.

Upon considering Cole's (1990) description of cases before the Magistrates' Court, it becomes easy to understand why many Nigerians seem disillusioned with movement away from tradition. For example, Cole relates the following exchange between a defendant and court officials:

> *Court Clerk: Are you guilty or not?*
> *Defendant: Let me explain, I . . .*
> *Clerk: Stop wasting our time; are you guilty or not?*
> *Defendant: (silent)*
> *Clerk: The . . . accused person, not guilty, my lord.*
> *Defendant: No . . . I was just . . .*
> *Clerk: Shut up!*
> *Magistrate (to defendant): You are either guilty or not guilty.*
> *Defendant: (silent)*
> *Clerk: Defendant pleads guilty, my lord.*
> *Magistrate: I find the accused person guilty as charged.*
> *Clerk: As your lordship pleases (Cole, 1990, p. 306).*

The proceedings in this defendant's trial would not continue without a plea being duly recorded, but one wonders how freely (or accurately) that plea was entered. Cole (1990) also reports instances of defendants being ridiculed in court, called a liar, and subjected to police misbehavior. If Nigerians are told that such behavior symbolizes a modern court system, it is little wonder that many prefer the traditional justice systems over those imposed by a foreign power.

China

With the formation of a communist dictatorship in 1949, the People's Republic of China (PRC) began a path that would join it with those countries following a socialist legal tradition. The Chinese Communists sought to modernize the legal system by looking to the Soviet Union for ideas. Although a Soviet pattern was followed in the ensuing decades, the PRC was not quick to put her new legal system in writing. Comprehensive codes of substantive and procedural law were generated only in 1979 and revised in 1996, but those codes reflect the influence of the USSR as the birthplace of socialist legal systems. China's versions find a counterpart in the USSR's 1960 Code of Criminal Procedure and the Criminal Code. Even with the 1996 revisions, China's legal system remains in the socialist mold (Jie, 2000). One explanation for the delay in producing codes of criminal law and of criminal procedure rests on the viability of China's preexisting informal judicial system. That system is important enough in the PRC that it must be included in our discussion of China's courts.

Victor Li (1978) titled his book comparing law in China and the United States *Law without Lawyers*. That title nicely characterizes the informal justice structure that some consider the lowest tier of the PRC's criminal justice system (Rojek, 1985). A main benefit of the informal system is the absence of lawyers, law being an occupation that the Chinese have never awarded much prestige. Although lawyers are becoming more prominent in today's China, it remains to be seen if they will become more acceptable to the public. There is, after all, a well-entrenched dislike for attorneys dating at least to Imperial China, when one could receive a three-year sentence for helping litigants prepare documents (McCabe, 1989). An 1820 imperial edict referred to lawyers as "litigation tricksters" and "rascally fellows (who will) entrap people for the sake of profit" (Li, 1983, p. 103). Such attitudes are hard to turn around, so it should be of little surprise that in the mid 1990s there were only about 102,000 practicing lawyers in China (Jie, 2000).

In the absence of reliance on legally trained professionals to handle disputes, Chinese citizens turned to each other (see Clark, 1989; Li, 1978; Situ & Liu, 1996; and Rojek, 1985). The foundation for the resulting informal justice structure are the People's Mediation Committees (PMCs), composed of 10 to 20 people, to which everyone in China, except small children, belongs. The PMCs, which number about 1 million, are organized at places of work, neighborhoods, schools, and the like, so each person is likely to belong to several such groups (especially one at work and one in the neighborhood). The resulting peer pressure from these constant companions provides the glue holding together an informal sanctioning process.

In the tradition of socialist legality, China believes that education must play a primary role in the justice system. Because the PMCs have historical ties to Confucianism and are based on the belief that moral education through mediation is the best way for communities to resolve conflict, they fit very nicely with the socialist view of law.

The PMCs serve as a conduit for the norms and values that upper levels of government believe are appropriate. Government officials use the mass media to spread such information as legal norms, and then the PMCs furnish a setting to discuss and enforce those norms. Importantly, the norms provided by the central

In the News

ARE THE CHINESE BECOMING MORE LITIGIOUS?

Although it is not clear that the Chinese public is becoming more accepting of criminal lawyers, there does seem to be greater acceptance of using lawyers to handle civil disputes. Rosenthal (1998) describes the case of Sun Lili, who became pregnant without the required advance permission of her employer's family-planning office. Sun, a hotel banquet assistant, was given the choice of quitting or having an abortion. Instead, she protested and decided to have the child—knowing she would probably be fined by her employer and receive a few other sanctions. She and her husband were stunned when company officials heaped on penalties equivalent to nearly a third of her yearly wages and refused to pay medical expenses associated with the pregnancy and birth of her daughter. Sun and her husband, Zhang, responded in a very un-Chinese manner. They hired an attorney and sued.

A decade ago such a suit would have been unthinkable, but today ordinary people all over China are suing employers, state enterprises, and even the local police (Rosenthal, 1998). Legal reform in China appears to be encouraging Chinese citizens to take legal action against the previously unchecked powers that be. Sun and Zhang lost in two courts, but their lawyer was planning an appeal, and some of their fellow citizens have been successful in similar suits. As stories of such success spread around the country, an increasing number of administrative law cases are being initiated.

It is undetermined at this point whether criminal cases will also result in an increasing use of lawyers hired by defendants. Jie (2000) explains that China's legal service institutions and practitioners have been increasing. In addition to law courses for full-time students, various institutions offer legal education through evening courses, correspondence courses, and television courses. It may be that reference to China as a country of "law without lawyers" (as Victor Li titled his 1978 book) will be a misnomer.

government are simply general policies indicating priorities and directions (Li, 1978). Actual application of those general principles is, government officials believe, more appropriately done at the local level. One obvious result is that different local groups will interpret the general principles differently. Such variation is not considered bad. Central authorities issue a single general policy, and then local units adapt that policy to suit local needs and conditions (Li, 1978). Consistency with socialist principles is assured by having the PMCs operate under the guidance of local governments and the local people's courts. Members of the PMCs, who are elected for three-year terms by the people living or working in the PMCs' jurisdiction, serve as volunteers and must be "solid citizens" (Jie, 2000; Situ & Liu, 1996).

Through a process of discussion and persuasion, the small groups respond to everything from misbehavior and outright deviance to questions of health care and family planning. Justice is provided in this informal way without the use of lawyers or courtrooms. Since, however, the utopian ideal of pure communism has not been achieved in the PRC, or anywhere else, there is also the need for a more formal justice system.

China's formal justice system uses four layers of courts, organized along territorial lines (see Figure 7.7). The Supreme People's Court serves as the highest tribunal in the country. Below it in the hierarchy are the Higher People's Courts, Intermediate People's Courts, and the Basic People's Courts. Court officials at each level are elected and recalled by the people's congress relevant to each court level. The courts are essentially agencies of the central government and do not have judicial independence in a manner similar to courts in Western countries (McCabe, 1989). Central government supervision is not direct, but instead is routed through judicial committees appointed by the various people's congresses. The judicial committees review court activities, discuss major difficult cases, and concern themselves with other court-related issues.

The Supreme People's Court, which is made up of several subcourts or branches, handles cases impacting the entire country. It interprets statutes and provides explanations and advisory opinion to the lower courts. Because those interpretations, explanations, and advice must be consistent with socialist principles, the Supreme People's Court is supervised by the National People's Congress—that is, the Communist Party. The Supreme People's Court must also approve all death sentences imposed by Intermediate or Higher People's Courts. The Higher People's Courts are found at the province and autonomous region levels and in autonomous cities (Beijing, Tianjin, and Shanghai). The Intermediate People's Courts handle cases similar to those at the Higher People's Court

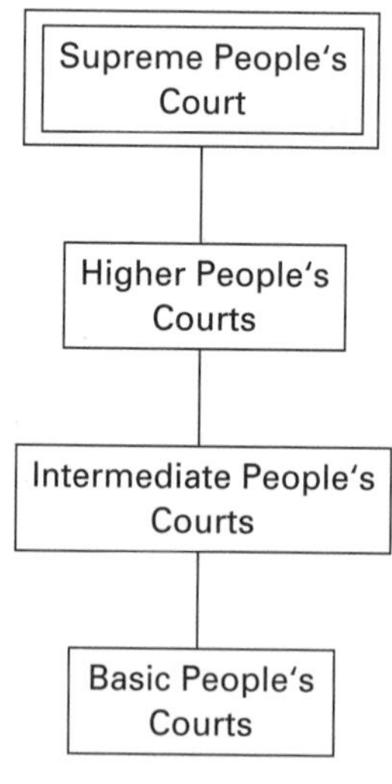

Figure 7.7 China's Court Organization

level, but they perform their duties at the municipal or prefecture level (McCabe, 1989; Situ & Liu, 1996).

The workhorses in China's formal court system are the Basic People's Courts. Operating at the rural county level and the urban district level, these courts have original trial jurisdiction over ordinary criminal and civil cases. Davidson and Wang (1996) note that in recent years district courts in larger cities like Beijing and Tianjin have also established neighborhood-based courts to help relieve the district court's caseload. Discussion of the Basic People's Court activities gives us a chance to look more closely at some of the players and procedures in Chinese courts.

Because the Chinese system is more inquisitorial than adversarial, the trial is essentially a continuation of the investigation. The investigation is begun by the procurator before the trial. Following the Soviet model of the 1950s, China developed a national procuracy responsible for investigating and prosecuting cases at each government level. When the court has decided to open the court session and adjudicate the case, it must first determine the adjudicators. In each type of court, the adjudicators are a collegial panel of judges and laypersons (called "people's assessors"). In the Basic People's Court and the Intermediate People's Court that panel will consist of three judges or a combination of a total of three judges and people's assessors. If a case in either the basic or intermediate court is considered suitable for "simplified procedures" (e.g., cases in which defendant can be sentenced to less than three years imprisonment and where the facts of the crime are clear and the evidence sufficient) adjudication can be made by a single judge (*Criminal Procedure Law of the People's Republic of China*, 1998).

For cases of first instance in the High People's Court or the Supreme People's Court, the panel has three to seven judges (but always an odd number) or a combined total of three to seven judges and people's assessors. Other key personnel in the trial are the defendant, procurator, defenders (a lawyer, relative, or lay advocate), victims, witnesses, and interpretors (all defendants have the right to use their own spoken and written language in court proceedings).

The trial proceeds through defined steps, which Davidson and Wang (1996, p. 149) have summarized as including the following:

- Court is called to order and the judge introduces all the participants.
- The charges are read and the defendant advised of his rights.
- The judge and people's assessors question the defendant.
- The procurator makes a statement, questions the defendant, and verifies evidence.
- The defender enters a statement and questions the defendant.
- The procurator and defender present their arguments.
- The defendant, if he or she so chooses, makes a statement.
- After a brief recess allowing the panel to deliberate, court is reconvened.
- Defendants found innocent are dismissed. Those found guilty are told the crime for which they have been found guilty and the criminal punishment (if any) that will be applied.

There are obvious similarities in these steps with those found in trials of common and civil legal traditions, but Table 7.1 highlights some interesting points of comparison.

Saudi Arabia

The Saudi Arabian judiciary is actually dual in nature. A hierarchy of *Shari'a* Courts exercise general and universal jurisdiction, whereas a separate system of specialized tribunals has jurisdiction over specific issues. Our concern, however, is with the *Shari'a* Courts. Chapter 5 noted that although *Shari'a* law has aspects of both inquisitorial and adversarial procedures, the former seems to predomi-

Table 7.1 Points of Comparison in Chinese and American Trial Procedures

China		United States
	Arrest	
Public Security Bureau		Police
	Defense Counsel	
Provided by state		Provided by state to indigents
	Prosecution	
Procurator also acting as an active investigator		Prosecutor who is not very active as an investigator
	Adjudicators	
Collegial Bench with professional judges and people's assessors		Jury of laypeople
	Prosecution Philosophy	
Emphasis on protecting the public and less so on the defendant		Emphasis on protecting the rights of the accused and less so toward the victim
Emphasis on confession (those confessing get a lighter sentence) with the possibility of innocent people confessing		Emphasis on plea bargaining (those bargaining are subjected to a less severe penalty) with the possiblity of innocent people pleading guilty
	Trial Philosophy	
No presumption of innocence at trial		Presumption of innocence until found guilty
Trial is primarily to review facts, consider mitigating factors, and sentencing		Trial serves to determine guilt or innocence
Those found guilty have the right to appeal		Those found guilty have the right to appeal

Source: Adapted from Robert Davidson and Zheng Wang, (1996), The court system in the People's Republic of China: With a case study of a criminal trial. In O. N. I. Ebbe (Ed.), *Comparative and international criminal justice systems: Policing, judiciary and corrections* (pp. 139–153). Boston: Butterworth-Heinemann.

nate. An example of this is the absence of any dividing line between the investigation and trial stages. But the result is not a purely inquisitorial process, because there is no investigating magistrate supervising the investigation. Instead, interrogation of suspects is conducted by designated officials whose positions fall either above or below that of the judge. Specifically, the interrogation is conducted by the *wali al-mazalim* or the *al-mohtasib* (Sanad, 1991). The former's post is traditionally higher than that of judge, and its holder can actually rule on cases outside the judge's jurisdiction. The *al-mohtasib*, on the other hand, is inferior to the judge but has the duty of assuring correct enforcement of Islamic *Shari'a.*

The interrogation phase obviously has significant influence on the eventual trial outcome, so Islamic law provides several safeguards to the accused at this stage. One of these relates to Chapter 4's discussion of the basic features making up the Islamic legal tradition. As noted in that chapter, the oath plays an important role in the judicial process—so important that its impact is felt as early as the interrogation. Sanad (1991) explains that in cases of *hudud* and *qisas* crimes, the authority in charge of interrogation is not allowed to require an oath from the accused. The concern is that an accused who actually committed the crimes might be tempted to state untruths, thereby compounding his misconduct by false swearing. The duty of proving *hudud* and *quesas* acts falls on the accuser, and Muslim jurists are told that silence of the accused is not considered evidence.

When a case moves on to actual trial, the Saudi Arabian system provides a three-tiered court structure with trial and appellate level courts (see Figure 7.8). The king, who as head of the Saudi judicial system appoints and removes all

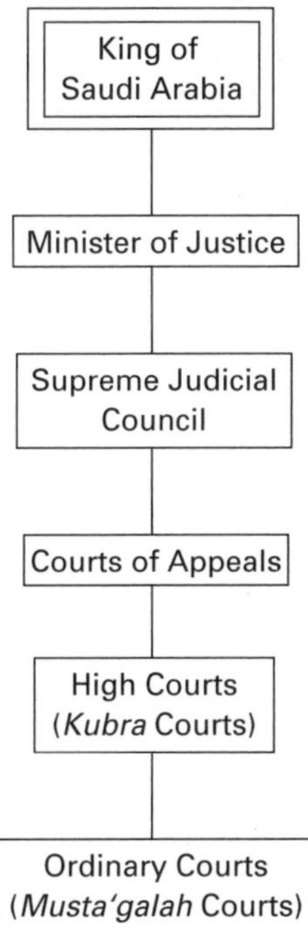

Figure 7.8 Saudi Arabia's Courts

judges, may act as a source of pardon and can serve as the final court of appeals to determine if the verdict conforms to the *Shari'a*. At a more practical level, the Ministry of Justice (appointed by the king) presides over the *Shari'a* judicial system.

The *Shari'a* Courts are ones of general jurisdiction and as such may hear civil and criminal matters. In fact, a single judge might hear a criminal case immediately after hearing a civil one. In the hierarchical structure, ordinary courts (Courts of Urgent Affairs) are at the bottom and, progressing upward, we find the high courts (*Kubra* Courts) and then the Courts of Appeal. The ordinary courts *(Musta'galah)*, presided over by a single Islamic judge *(qadi)*, are the lowest-level *Shari'a* Court, and exist in nearly every town. They deal with minor domestic matters, misdemeanors, small claims, *ta'azir* crimes allowing discretionary penalties, and with *hudud* offenses of intoxication and defamation (Human Rights Watch, 1997b).

The high courts of *Shari'a* law (*Kubra* courts) have exclusive jurisdiction over *hudud* and *quesas* crimes and general jurisdiction to hear cases on appeal from the lower courts. A single judge hears the case unless a sentence of death, stoning, or amputation is called for, which requires a three-judge panel then ratification by the king (Amin, 1985; Moore, 1996; Moore, 1987).

Before moving to the appellate level court, we should look briefly at some aspects of the trials in the ordinary and high courts. The right to defense, for example, is definite if not specific. *Shari'a* includes many admonishments favoring an opportunity for the accused to tell his or her side of the story. One caliph cautioned his judges, "If an adversary whose eye had been blinded by another comes to you, do not rule until the other party attends, for perhaps the latter had been blinded in both eyes" (quoted in Sanad, 1991, p. 81). The right to defend oneself against accusations by another does not necessarily require the services of a professional lawyer. In fact, although the accused has a right to retain an attorney, the presence of a defense attorney does not eliminate the defendant's right to defend himself or herself. The attorney is merely the defendant's agent.

Chapter 5 noted that Islamic procedural law is not easily identified, because the sacred law does not specify what means should be used to bring offenders to justice. Sanad (1991) elaborates this point in his discussion of the rules of evidence in criminal trials. He believes that the majority of Muslim scholars maintain that evidence in criminal cases must be restricted to testimony and confession. Judges cannot base a criminal conviction on other kinds of evidence (for example, prior personal knowledge). Within these two types of evidence are more specific rules for their use. Regarding testimony, for example, at least two witnesses (one legal school says a single witness) must provide consistent testimony before a conviction on *hudud* and *quesas* crimes can be rendered.

Not just any witness is acceptable when testimonial evidence is given. The witness must be an adult male (one school accepts two females as equivalent to one male) known to have good memory, sound mind, and good character (Sanad, 1991). Even with these characteristics, a witness's testimony may not count if he or she is a family member or is suspected of having feelings of either animosity or partiality toward the accused or accuser.

Confessions, the second kind of evidence, are more complicated than a simple admission of guilt by the accused. To be valid the confessor must be a mature, mentally sound person who gives, with free will, a confession that is neither doubtful or vague. A coerced confession is not only inadmissible, but requires the coercer to be punished (Sanad, 1991). Despite that seemingly straightforward statement, Moore (1987) notes that flogging and long detention of suspects refusing to confess does occur in Saudi Arabia. This point reminds us that not all cultures agree on what might constitute coercion.

Once a judgment is given, the appeals process may come into play. The Islamic systems view the appealing of decisions to higher courts somewhat differently than do other legal traditions. *Shari'a* is not case law, so the judge is not bound by decisions of other judges, whether in a higher court or not, or even by his decisions in the same court. More important than the absence of case law is the Islamic rejection of generalized legal reasoning.

When deciding a case, the *qadi* was traditionally limited to highly particularized legal rules instead of general legal concepts. His task was to decide which of the very specific and detailed rules most closely fit the particular facts before him (Shapiro, 1981). Because a major purpose of appeals courts is to provide uniform legal rules to make justice similar throughout the country, the Islamic approach has little use for the appellate process. In the absence of a need for uniformity of law, appellate courts become unnecessary.

Despite the lack of a historic need for an appeals process, many Islamic countries now provide some type of appeals court. Although this may show an interest in providing some uniformity to the law, it also reflects the influence of Western legal ideas and a need to accommodate activities in the growing secular areas of law.

Two Courts of Appeal operate in Saudi Arabia; each hears appeals from a specific part of the country. Each court divides into departments to hear cases of criminal law, personal status, or complaints not falling into either of those two categories. Three-judge panels hear appeals except, once again, sentences of death, stoning, or amputation. Panels of five judges hear those cases.

The Supreme Judicial Council is the highest judicial authority in the *Shari'a* system. The council's 11 members do not actually serve as a court. They can review decisions by the Courts of Appeal but in cases of disagreement must refer the case back to the Court of Appeals for reconsideration.

SUMMARY

This chapter looked at the judiciary from an institutions/actors perspective. Beginning with how the primary actors in a judicial system arrive at their positions, we considered various processes of legal training. Because every system has some type of prosecutor and defense attorney, we then looked at the different ways those positions are implemented. In addition to prosecution and defense, each legal system has actors responsible for adjudicating the case brought to court. An adjudication continuum illustrated the variation in adjudicator types by identifying systems that rely heavily on a professional judge (for example, Saudi Arabia), whereas others emphasize a role for laypeople (for example, England). Still other countries prefer a mixed bench, wherein professional judges and laypeople sit together to judge the facts of a case (for example, Germany).

Because these actors must have a setting for their performance, we next looked at different ways courts can be structured. Because the diversity here does not lend itself to easy classification into types, we simply looked at examples from several countries to show the variation. The formal structure was typically emphasized, although the informal justice system in some countries (for example, China and Nigeria) was pertinent to a more complete understanding of that country's judiciary.

WEB SITES TO VISIT

- Use the Harvard Law School library's web site at **www.law.harvard.edu/library/ research_guides/french_legal/french_laws.htm** to conduct research on French law.
- Read more about the Crown Prosecution Service at **www.cps.gov.uk/**
- The National Center for State Courts provides an impressive list of links to courts in more than 15 countries at **www.ncsconline.org/Information/info_court_ web_sites.html#international**

SUGGESTED READINGS

Council of Europe. (2000). *Judicial organisation in Europe.* Strasbourg, France: Council of Europe Publishing.

Emmins, Christopher J. (1988). *A practical approach to criminal procedure* (4th ed.). London, England: Blackstone Press Limited.

French Code of Criminal Procedure (G. L. Kock and R. S. Frase, Trans.). (1988). Littleton, CO: Fred B. Rothman.

Li, Victor H. (1978). *Law without lawyers: A comparative view of law in China and the United States.* Boulder, CO: Westview.

Lippman, Matthew, McConville, Sean, and Yerushalmi, Mordechai. (1988). *Islamic criminal law and procedure.* New York: Praeger.

Moore, Richter H., Jr. (1996). Islamic legal systems: Traditional (Saudi Arabia), Contemporary (Bahrain), and Evolving (Pakistan). In C. B. Fields and R. H. Moore, Jr. (Eds.), *Comparative criminal justice: Traditional and nontraditional systems of law and control* (pp. 390–410). Prospect Heights, IL: Waveland.

Chapter 8

An International Perspective on Corrections

KEY TOPICS

- Problems in determining imprisonment rates
- Corrections in Australia
- Racially disproportionate incarceration rates in Australia and United States
- Corrections in Poland
- Corrections in Japan
- Types of community corrections

KEY TERMS

assignment
deterrence
diversion
incapacitation
rehabilitation
retribution
transportation
volunteer probation officers

COUNTRIES REFERENCED

Australia
Japan
Poland
United States

It is always dangerous to make statements implying universal agreement. We do not, however, go too far out on a limb by saying that all societies want social order. It would be more dangerous to say that they all agree on what social order means. This chapter concentrates instead on those aspects of social order that most societies try to achieve.

Social order's form may vary from one country's desire to have extreme conformity and consistency among its people, to another country's view of order as allowing as much individuality and diversity as reasonable. It is neither possible nor appropriate to identify one view as correct. It is, however, necessary to see the differences if we want to understand how each country tries to achieve social order.

Some countries develop strategies to achieve social control by emphasizing conformity to a cultural standard for behavior. Japan is an example of this type of response. Other countries, like Poland, seek social control by appealing to each person's sense of civic obligation. Still others (the United States may be an example) believe that social control is best obtained by penalizing misbehavior.

With such different social control strategies, it is not surprising that countries often develop distinct techniques to control misbehaving citizens. The effect of capital punishment is always the death of the offender, but how that penalty is achieved varies considerably. Consider, for example, the French execution of Damiens.

In 1757, as punishment for assaulting King Louis XV, Robert François Damiens was condemned to make the *amende honorable* before the main door of the Church of Paris. Foucault (1977) quotes the account left by an observer of the punishment as follows:

> *The sulphur was lit, but the flame was so poor that only the top skin of the hand was burnt, and that only slightly. Then the executioner, his sleeves rolled up, took the steel pincers, . . . especially made for the occasion, . . . and pulled first at the calf of the right leg, then at the thigh, and from there at the two fleshy parts of the right arm; then at the breasts. Though a strong, sturdy fellow, this executioner found it so difficult to tear away the pieces of flesh that he set about the same spot two or three times, twisting the pincers as he did so, and what he took away formed at each part a wound about the size of a six-pound crown piece. After these tearings . . . the same executioner dipped an iron spoon in the pot containing [molten lead, boiling oil, burning resin, and sulphur melted together, and he liberally poured it] over each wound. Then the ropes that were harnessed to the horses were attached with cords to the patient's body; the horses were then harnessed and placed alongside the arms and legs, one at each limb. . . . The horses tugged hard, each pulling straight on a limb, each horse held by an executioner (Foucault, 1977, pp. 3–4).*

Today France does not even have the death penalty. In fact, just 80 years after Damiens's execution, France was looking at a very different form of punishment. In 1837, also in Paris, Leon Faucher drew up rules for a facility housing young prisoners. The rules included a nine-hour workday; two hours per day devoted to instruction in reading, writing, drawing, and arithmetic; several recreation periods; and two full meals with several rationings of bread throughout the day (Foucault,

1977, p. 6). Within an 80-year span in the same city, punishment went from gruesome torture to enlightened reformation.

Most countries experience a similar variation in preferred forms of punishment. Within 35 years of Damiens's execution in France, Americans had established Philadelphia's Walnut Street Jail as the country's first true correctional institution. For 15 years before Faucher designed his Paris facility for young offenders, Americans had debated the benefits of two correctional philosophies. Both the Pennsylvania and Auburn systems provided imprisonment as a humane alternative to corporal and capital punishment.

Ironically, whereas France abandoned the death penalty as a punishment, the United States has made increased use of it since 1977. Let's compare some accounts of recent American executions to the description of Damiens's execution:

- Upon first receiving the 1900 volts, Evans clenched his fists and arched his body into the restraining straps. Sparks and flames crackled around his head and white smoke seeped from under the hood—but he did not die. A

In the News

EXECUTIONS AROUND THE WORLD

Records are not complete for all countries, but Amnesty International estimates that at least 1625 prisoners were executed in 37 countries around the world in 1998 (Amnesty International, 1999b). Eighty percent of all known executions took place in China (over 1000), the Democratic Republic of Congo (over 100), the United States (68), and Iran (66 known). Hundreds of executions were also reported in Iraq, but Amnesty International was unable to confirm most of those reports. Adding to the grimness of China's high number of executions are reports that organs from prisoners executed in southern China are being sold to patients from Hong Kong for liver transplants. The practice would not be as controversial if the organs were donated voluntarily, but suspicions are aroused since Chinese law does not require consent from convicted criminals ("Organs from executed," 2000).

About one half of the world's countries have abolished the death penalty in law or practice (Amnesty International, 1999a). Most Western European countries are abolitionist, and as Central and Eastern European countries continue movement toward democratization they too have abolished capital punishment. In North America, Canada has abolished the death penalty for all crimes, but in both the United States and Mexico death penalty statutes vary by state jurisdiction. All the former British colonies in the Caribbean have death penalty statutes, with Jamaica and Trinidad having particularly high numbers of people on death row. Among Latin American countries, about one half have abolished capital punishment.

Countries in the Middle East generally retain the death penalty as an important sanction under *Shari'a*. In Saudi Arabia (with about 30 executions per year), beheading by sword is an official method of execution, and it is used especially against drug traffickers. Death sentences, which are usually carried out in public, are also imposed for murder and armed robbery.

second jolt was administered. His chest rose against the straps and a stream of saliva ran down the front of his prison smock—still, he was not dead. It took three tries, but the state of Alabama finally executed convicted murderer John Louis Evans III.

- Hours before his execution, convicted killer Robert Brecheen was found in his holding cell, groggy and breathing heavily from an overdose of sedatives ("Killer revived," 1995). Brecheen was rushed to the hospital where his stomach was pumped and officials declared him mentally fit to be executed by Oklahoma a mere two hours later than scheduled (Harris, 1983).
- It took Mississippi 30 minutes to execute Emmitt Foster in 1995. Lethal injection does not usually take so long, but this time the officials had tightened the leather straps that bound Foster to the gurney so tightly that the chemicals could not flow through his veins. The coroner, who entered the death chamber twenty minutes after the execution began, noticed the problem and had the straps loosened. Death was pronounced several minutes later (Radelet, 1999).

These examples of variation in capital punishment show the vast array of techniques countries use to control misbehavior and achieve social order. This chapter describes some of those differences. The problem is deciding which one or two of the various punishment forms best shows country differences. Similarly, countries vary by the justifications they emphasize for administering punishment and the goals they perceive punishment serving. Although they are not mutually exclusive, reasons for punishing offenders have included protection of society, the seeking of revenge, securing an orderly society, and changing the offender. Before identifying the primary thrust of this chapter, we must familiarize ourselves with these different perspectives.

VARIABILITY IN JUSTIFICATION FOR PUNISHMENT

The classic justifications and goals for punishment are retribution, deterrence, rehabilitation, and incapacitation. *Retribution,* possibly the oldest of these, is considered by some to reflect a basic human tendency toward vengeance. The argument for retribution is that punishment is a necessary and natural response to persons violating social norms. Its most explicit depiction is in the "eye for an eye, tooth for a tooth" dictum of biblical times. A goal of retribution is to retaliate for the wrong done in such a way that the nature of the punishment reflects the nature of the offense (Newman, 1978). For example, the Germanic tribes in northern Europe of the Middle Ages were very protective of their forests. In fact, the penalty for illegally cutting down trees was execution. In an effort to have the "punishment fit the crime," the offender was executed in a manner that would reflect the crime itself. So persons taking the life of a tree by cutting off its top were buried in the ground from the shoulders down. A plow was then taken across the offender's head and his life was lost by topping, just as the tree had been topped.

The *deterrence* fork has two prongs: specific and general deterrence. Specific deterrence means that the offender is punished for the express purpose of deterring his or her personal acts of future wickedness. General deterrence means that

IMPACT

Global Aspects of Restorative Justice

Punishment has typically been justified on the basis of retribution, deterrence, rehabilitation, or incapacitation. Today, however, we increasingly hear a restorative rationale for punishment. Restorative justice attempts to make the victim and the community "whole again" by restoring things, as much as possible, to how they were before the crime occurred. To achieve its goal of repairing the damage caused by the offender, restorative justice requires equal attention be paid to the offender, the victim, and the community. Because contemporary justice systems tend to concentrate on the offender—at the expense of a concern for either the victim or the community—persons seeking to know more about restoration find themselves turning to tribal and aboriginal systems for information.

Saudi Arabia presents an aspect of restoration that was briefly mentioned in Chapter 5 but deserves elaboration here. Since *Shari'a* does not view the state as having a legal personality, wrongs are always considered actions against an individual. Obviously, this view of crime sets the stage for a very victim-oriented legal system that allows and even encourages nonlegalistic response to misbehavior. Criminal complaints under *Shari'a* are often resolved through arbitration even before a police record is made. Even such serious crimes as homicide may never be brought to formal trial, since the *Qur'an* condones at least two types of responses that do not involve the court system: retaliation and compensation.

Retaliation by a victim's family is an accepted response to murder under Islamic law. The *Qur'an* explains that "retaliation is prescribed for you in the matter of the slain; the free for the free, and the slave for the slave, and the female for the female" (2:178). Similarly, any intentional, serious, but nonlethal harm inflicted upon a human body can also be responded to with retaliation. The *Qur'an* repeats the Torah's version of retaliation in noting that "life for life, eye for eye, nose for nose, ear for ear, tooth for tooth, and wounds equal for equal" (5:45). But an important distinction between Islam's version of retaliation and a pure *lex talionis* is that the *Qur'an* clearly tempers retaliation by encouraging forgiveness. For example, the "life for life" verse continues by noting that "if any one remits the retaliation by way of charity, it is an act of atonement for himself" (5:45). Expression of that charity or forgiveness is found in the concept of compensation in the form of *diyya*.

When retaliation is not used in response to murder, or for felonies against the person, it is typically replaced by *diyya*. Al-Sagheer believes that *diyya* is best defined as "money paid to a harmed person or his heir in compensation for a felony committed against him" (1994, p. 85). Although *diyya* may have a deterrent function, it is considered a way to rid society, including the victims and their families, of any grudges toward the offender. It

(continued)

IMPACT

Global Aspects of Restorative Justice *(continued)*

attempts, in other words, to make the victim and the community whole again.

Rules govern the cases in which *diyya* can be applied, the amount to be paid, and by whom it is paid (Al-Sagheer, 1994). For example, in cases where a human life has been taken, the *diyya* amount varies from the equivalent of 100 camels for a Moslem male to the equivalent of 50 camels for a Moslem woman. Payment is typically made by the offender or the offender's blood relatives, but the burden of payment may occasionally fall to the Saudi Arabia State Treasury (for example, when the offender has not been identified).

With appropriate modifications by the adapting culture, nations around the world are turning toward a restorative-justice paradigm for at least parts of their justice system. Some countries have indigenous examples from which to draw (e.g., aspects of Aboriginal justice provides the base for some Australian and New Zealand procedures), but even where a domestic foundation is present, countries are enthusiastically borrowing restorative-justice ideas from each other (see Ward, 2000).

Examples of a restorative justice paradigm taking hold in American communities is seen in the increased use of mediation for resolving conflicts and in a greater variety of non-prison sanctions (e.g., increased use of fines, community service). Both mediation and prison alternatives show a concern for the victim and the community as well as being a response to the offender's behavior. As American communities continue to move toward restorative-justice procedures they may benefit from studying traditional justice in non-Western countries as well as procedures being developed in countries that rely on more modern systems.

the offender is punished in the belief that the penalty will prevent other people from committing a similar crime.

Rehabilitation was recognized as a legitimate goal of punishment as early as the eighteenth century, when the Quakers encouraged the reforming of offenders into productive members of society. During its peaks and valleys of acceptance over the last several centuries, rehabilitation has taken a variety of forms. In one version, it follows a medical model wherein the offender (or patient) is classified (or diagnosed) according to his or her problems (or illness). The classification committee (or physicians and pathologists), composed of psychologists, social workers, clergy, health workers, educators, and the like discuss the offender's needs and develop a treatment plan. Successful completion of the treatment plan is expected to make the offender better able to operate as a law-abiding member of society.

Incapacitation as a punishment goal refers, in its most general sense, to restricting an offender's freedom of movement. Presumably, society is protected when the offender cannot move freely about in the community. Historically, incapacitation was achieved almost solely through incarceration in jails and prisons. Other techniques included corporal punishments (for example, the stocks in colonial America) and the pre-1991 Soviet Union's use of a passport system to control movement of Soviet citizens throughout the country (Shelley, 1990). Incapacitation of the future is likely to rely on technology to restrict the offender's movement. The increased popularity of electronic monitoring devices probably foretells gadgets that will allow constant monitoring of a person's movement and immediate analysis of blood and urine samples.

Retribution, deterrence, rehabilitation, and incapacitation are not always mutually exclusive, but it is often difficult for several of them to operate together. Although a penal system may be effectively based on a combination of retribution and deterrence, it is more difficult to merge, for example, rehabilitation with retribution. Also, the location where the punishment is administered may affect the ability to realize each goal. General deterrence is possible only in an open society where the public is kept informed of the application of punishments. Movement is more easily restricted in a prison than in an open community. Rehabilitation that might be achieved in a community setting might be impossible in the confines of a secure prison.

The punishment systems in three countries are described in this chapter. All four justifications for punishment are found in each country, but they vary in terms of the emphasis that one or two are given over the others and in terms of the location deemed appropriate for achieving punishment's goals. Our point of departure for discussing each country is the prison system. With this focus, we can find examples of countries that make minimal use of imprisonment, others that rely heavily on their prisons, and still others that seem to portray a middle point.

A discussion of legal systems and aspects of criminal law fell nicely into four legal families in Chapters 4 and 5. Describing differences among police forces was aided by reference to the number of forces and their type of command in Chapter 6. The variation in forms, justifications, and goals of punishment among countries is more difficult to categorize. Still, remembering Ehrmann's dictum that "all comparison proceeds from classification" (1976, p. 12), we will attempt a categorization of countries using one form of corrections, imprisonment as punishment.

IMPRISONMENT AS PUNISHMENT

Imprisonment as punishment, rather than as a way to detain someone for trial or to hold the person for other punishment, has become popular around the world. It is certainly not the only form social control has taken, but it is common enough to warrant close attention. Imprisonment as punishment occurs in most societies and provides one way to categorize countries.

Determining Imprisonment Rates

A popular way to compare countries on their use of imprisonment is to measure their respective incarceration rates as shown in Figure 8.1, which presents the basic formula to determine a country's rate of imprisonment *(Ir)*. Using this

$$Ir = \frac{\text{Number of Persons in Prison}}{\text{Total Population of Country}} \times 100{,}000$$

Figure 8.1 Determining Imprisonment Rates

formula, we find that the imprisonment rate for the United States in 1999 (Beck, 2000) was 476 [(1,366,721 / 287,126,261) × 100,000 = 476]. It is easy, then, to figure an imprisonment rate for any country, providing that its total population and the number of persons in its prisons on a particular date are known. Unfortunately, the simplicity is deceiving!

There are definitional and methodological problems when we figure imprisonment rates in this manner. Definition problems come from differences about what counts as a prison and who counts as a prisoner. For example, Canadian prisons include federal penitentiaries, provincial prisons, some jails, and community correctional centers. In the United States, state and federal prisons are counted, but inmates in jails and community corrections facilities are typically excluded. The 476 rate arrived at by using the formula in Figure 8.1 excludes the American jail population. When the jail population is included (as it is in Figure 8.2), the incarceration rate becomes 682. As a result, comparing Canadian and American imprisonment rates means that Canada will have a more broadly defined numerator in the equation than will America with its usually provided "prison only" figure. A similar problem is posed by the question of whether juvenile facilities are counted as prisons, and whether countries that send mentally ill criminals to hospitals include those hospitals among their prison count.

Besides the problem of deciding what constitutes a prison, there is the additional problem of deciding who is a prisoner. In some countries, pretrial detainees spend months or years awaiting trial. In other countries, the average stay in an unconvicted status is comparatively short and may not count as prisoner status. Also, some persons may be in prison for civil rather than criminal offenses. Is it appropriate to count persons serving time for nonpayment of fines with others who are truly criminal offenders? Because neither the establishment (that is, the prison) nor the unit (that is, the prisoner) of count is universally defined, any comparison of countries concerning prison population is problematic (Rahim, 1986).

There are also methodological problems with calculating incarceration rates. First, the numerator and denominator may not correspond. For example, the numerator comes from the adult population (where juveniles are not counted as prisoners) of a country, but the denominator includes persons of all ages living in that country. The result, therefore, reflects a downward bias, because a country with a high proportion of juveniles shows a low incarceration rate even with a high prison population. South Africa had a 1999 estimated general population of 40,100,000 and a 1999 prison population of 161,163 (Walmsley, 2000), yielding an incarceration rate of about 400 per 100,000 general population. However, because 35 percent of the South African population is under age 15 (*Statistical Abstracts of the United States: 1999*), the incarceration rate per 100,000 adults is 615. Countries wishing to use incarceration rates as a political or public relations tool can conveniently manipulate both numerator and denominator when presenting information on their use of imprisonment.

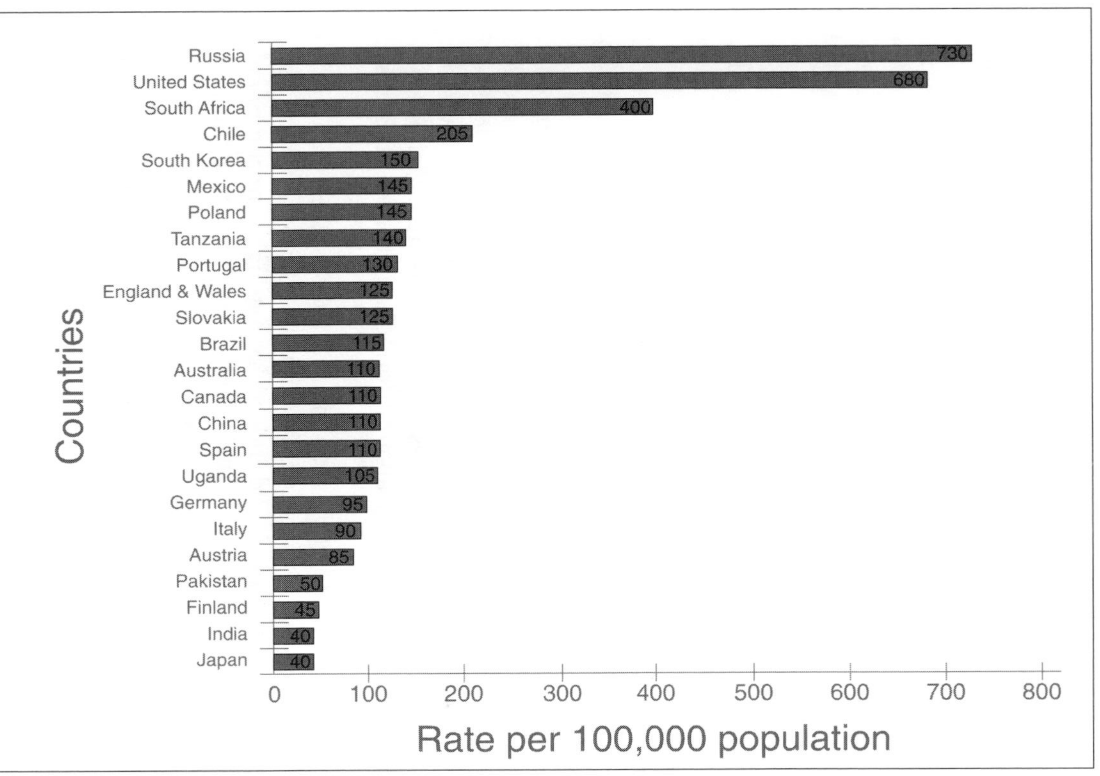

Figure 8.2 Imprisonment Rates for Selected Countries: 1999 *Source:* Adapted from Roy Walmsley (2000), *World Prison Population List,* 2nd ed [Research, Development and Statistics Directorate Report No. 116] London: Home Office. Available at **www.homeoffice.gov.uk/rds/pdfs/r116.pdf**

Another problem with the denominator in the traditional *Ir* formula is its implication that everyone in a particular country has a random chance of being imprisoned. That, of course, is not true. Instead of reflecting a random selection process, a country's imprisonment rate is more correctly given per 100,000 arrests, crimes, prosecutions, or convictions (Buck & Pease, 1993; Lynch, 1988; Rahim, 1986). Other problems come from using the number of persons in prison on a specific date rather than the number of admissions to prison over a certain time. Lynch (1988) calls the former figure "stock design" and notes that the likelihood of an offender's being in prison on a given day is a function of sentence length. Therefore, stock designs overrepresent more serious offenders with longer sentences. Lynch prefers the "flow design," because it takes the number of admissions over time and thereby separates the tendency to incarcerate from the length of sentence served. The flow design has its disadvantage too in that it risks double-counting inmates who may be released and then returned during the time period for technical reasons rather than having committed a new crime.

Rahim (1986), Lynch (1988), and Buck and Pease (1993) offer alternative formulas to find a country's use of imprisonment. Rahim thinks the rate should be the number of persons sentenced to prison divided by the number of persons convicted during the same year. Lynch prefers dividing the number of persons admitted to prison by the number of arrests made during the same year. Buck and Pease (1993), expanding on both Rahim and Lynch, applied this reasoning to their analysis of European imprisonment rates from 1985 by expressing the number of prisoners in relation to recorded crime rather than to total population. Because some countries might record quite trivial crimes compared to those recorded in other countries, Buck and Pease suggested it is even more appropriate to compare the prison population to the number of prosecutions in a country. Of course, there is then the problem of some countries prosecuting more trivial offenses than do other countries. Well, then, how about a formula that takes offense seriousness into account?

When Buck and Pease performed the calculations, they found that England and Wales (typically high in comparison with other European countries when the traditional *Ir* formula is used) did indeed have a higher prison population per conviction of the most serious offenses—but a much lower population per conviction of the least serious offenses. The point that England and Wales are harsh (that is, likely to imprison) toward the most serious offenders but lenient (that is, unlikely to imprison) to the less serious is hidden when the traditional *Ir* formula is used.

Despite the appropriate criticism offered by Buck and Pease (1993), Lynch (1988), and Rahim (1986), we will still use the traditional method to find incarceration rates, because of a lack of the necessary numbers to compute rates as suggested by critics of the traditional method. Incarceration rates are difficult to come by, and those few sources providing them typically use the old "total prisoners divided by total population" method. Therefore, despite its problems, the traditional incarceration rate is best for comparing the largest number of countries, and as such, becomes the means for our categorization of countries (see Figure 8.2). Yet, we will heed the warnings of the critics and proceed cautiously in applying the results of these calculations.

You Should Know!

ISRAEL LEADS MIDDLE EAST IN BAR MITZVAHS!

Does the title for this box seem painfully obvious to you? If so, that is the point Buck and Pease (1993) are making about the traditional way to figure a country's imprisonment rate. They suggest that expressing a prison population in relation to national population is rather like expressing the number of bar mitzvahs as a proportion of national population. A headline proclaiming Israel as leading the Middle East in bar mitzvahs might lead some readers to suspect it has something to do with there being a lot of Jewish people in Israel.

What Buck and Pease are saying is that just as bar mitzvahs are triggered by Jewishness, imprisonment is triggered by crime. So comparing bar mitzvah rates across countries without attention to the proportion of Jews in each country is much like comparing imprisonment rates across countries without attention to the amount of crime in each country.

Using Imprisonment to Maintain Social Order

Figure 8.2 orders selected countries around the world from high to low rates of imprisonment. Note that there does not appear to be any pattern based on which legal tradition the country belongs to. Statistics are mostly unavailable for countries in the socialist and Islamic families, but civil and common law countries are well dispersed throughout the list. It would be difficult to argue that use of imprisonment is a function of the legal family of a country.

Given the definitional and methodological problems just noted, it seems unwise to try to make distinctions among countries with somewhat similar rates. It probably is not safe, for example, to claim that Australia uses imprisonment less than does Spain and more than Canada. The rates in the three countries are just too close together to discuss reasons for differences that may not exist—or may exist in a different order if measured otherwise. On the other hand, it seems unlikely that definitional and methodological problems account for Poland's standing in comparison with Japan's. A difference of over 100 suggests, at the very least, that one country imprisons its citizens more than does the other country. Similarly, a country like Australia, whose rate falls midway between the two, probably really does provide a middle example.

This chapter describes the prison system of Poland, Australia, and Japan, but prison is only one side of the coin. If Japan is not incarcerating its offenders, what happens to them? Similarly, Poland cannot keep everyone locked up, so what happens to those released from prison or who are never sent there? Answering these questions requires a look at the alternatives to prison each country uses. We begin in the middle, with Australia.

CORRECTIONS IN AUSTRALIA

To paraphrase a Down Under saying, "Australia is such a different place because God made it last and he was tired of doing the same old thing." Australia's penal strategy is not the platypus of the world's corrections systems, but it does have some unusual features in addition to the more common characteristics that make it similar to its common law cousin, the United States. To emphasize both the unique and the ordinary, this discussion of Australian corrections highlights historical and contemporary issues. In the process, the stage is set for discussing Poland, a country where corrections seem almost always to imply prison, and Japan, a country where corrections apparently suggests more than just imprisonment.

Some of Australia's distinctive correctional characteristics include its

1. History as a penal colony
2. Disproportionately high incarceration rate of indigenous Australians
3. Wide variation in incarceration rates among states
4. Creativity in using alternatives to prison

Interestingly, those same distinctive characteristics show some similarity between Australia and the United States. We begin with the shared heritage of serving as a receiving port for England's banished criminals.

Australia's History of Transportation

Australia provides a unique example in studying imprisonment, because it is the only continent settled as a penal colony. For that reason, a discussion of corrections in Australia is a discussion of that nation's most fundamental historical roots (Chappell, 1988). One of the reasons that England turned to Australia to send some of its criminals was the growing resentment in the American colonies to this British practice. This shared correctional heritage between the United States and Australia warrants brief attention.

During medieval times a popular way to relieve a village of the burden of misbehaving citizens was to force them to leave the village. The problems those people might cause at the next village was of little concern to the first village. This banishment was desirable from the perspective of the sending village because (1) there was no need to worry about the future behavior of the offender; (2) the procedure was cheap compared to other means of social control; and (3) the exiling village could ignore the opinions of the receiving village. Eventually this practice of banishment led to the punishment response known as *transportation*.

In setting up a system of transportation, the British Parliament passed an act in 1598 providing that persons be sent to "such parts beyond the seas as shall at any time hereafter" be assigned (quoted in Shaw, 1966, p. 23). Like banishment, transportation allowed a society to get rid of troublemakers, but it had the added advantage of providing people to carry out dangerous and unpleasant work. It was this new advantage that provided a link between transportation and colonization. A motherland could get rid of its misfits and at the same time provide its colonization efforts with a labor pool. By the early seventeenth century, the American colonies were receiving a rather steady stream of English convicts, who would provide labor for the fledgling settlements just as later convicts would assist with the eighteenth-century development of Australia. Although recognizing the human misery associated with transportation, twentieth-century authors often make the argument that transportation was a penal practice that worked by helping the economic development of colonies (Chappell, 1988; Shaw, 1966).

In 1615 the English Privy Council ordered persons found guilty of robbery or any felony other than willful murder, rape, witchcraft, or burglary to be transported to either the East Indies or the American plantations as laborers. Despite these early beginnings, it was not until the eighteenth century that transportation became a major part of English law. The Transportation Act of 1718 declared its purpose as being to deter criminals and to supply the colonies with labor. Transportation was possible as a substitute for execution, an act of royal mercy, a reprieve or commutation of punishment, or as a form of punishment itself.

The option of transportation or execution applied to a wide range of misdeeds. In 1797 crimes punishable by death included counterfeiting gold and silver coins, murder, arson, rape, sodomy, piracy, burglary, highway robbery, picking pockets, shoplifting, stealing horses, cutting down trees in a garden, sending threatening letters, and a host of other offenses. Crimes for which transportation was itself a possible punishment included grand larceny, receiving or buying stolen goods, stealing letters, theft under one shilling, assault with intent to rob, stealing fish from a pond or river, stealing children with their apparel, bigamy, and others.

The actual process of transporting the convicts was contracted out to individuals. The contractor was given the rights to the convict's labor in the colonies, and he could sell those services to the planters. If the convict had enough of his own money, he could buy off his servitude and basically turn his punishment into mere banishment. All the American colonies except those in New England received some convicts at some time; most went to Maryland and Virginia, where agriculture was more labor-intensive. Although many settlers benefited from the extra labor, not all colonists were pleased with the policy of transportation. Maryland tried to banish it in 1676, and by 1697 several other colonies had expressed their displeasure with it. For a time, England sent most of its transportees to the West Indies, but in 1718 the Transportation Act revived mainland trade, and the convicts were sent to America in even greater numbers. In 1722 Pennsylvania prohibited the receiving of transported convicts, and a year later Virginia did the same (Shaw, 1966). In fact, Virginia even went one more step and in 1740, when England asked the colonies for troops for the Spanish war, Virginia enlisted ex-cons!

Although there are no official figures, historians estimate that some 50,000 convicts were transported to the American colonies prior to 1775. In 1775 the rising resentment of the colonies toward England led, not surprisingly, to refusing to serve any longer as the dumping ground for English convicts. Undaunted and patient, the English found a replacement colony in a new continent Captain James Cook had claimed for Great Britain a mere five years earlier.

In January 1788, after eight months at sea, 11 British ships landed in Sydney Cove. Of the more than 1000 people going ashore, nearly 750 were prisoners being transported from England as punishment for a variety of offenses. From that date and until 1840, English prisoners were continually transported to New South Wales, and until 1867, to other parts of Australia (O'Brien & Ward, 1970). They represented both men and women who had been convicted of a wide range of offenses. The typical transportee was sentenced for theft, had been a propertyless laborer, and was 26 years of age (Hughes, 1987). In all, about 160,000 prisoners were transported to Australia.

Hughes (1987) suggests that "the System" as convict transportation to Australia was called, passed through four stages. During the first stage (1787–1810), transportation was primarily used to clear out the English jails and to help declare a new English presence in the Pacific. Only about 7 percent of the total number of transportees were sent to Australia during these first 23 years.

The second stage, lasting from 1811 through 1830, saw a significant growth of social problems in England. Population increases, runaway unemployment, and the growth of slums were stirred together in a caldron brewing crime. To this stew, the British Parliament finally authorized the new police force championed by Sir Robert Peel. The success of the "peelers" provided an ever-increasing supply of felons for the British courts to handle. When these conditions in Britain were matched with Australia's post-1815 demand for convict labor, the resulting push-pull connection furnished some 31 percent of the eventual total of transportees.

From 1831 through 1840, the System peaked and then began its decline. Nearly 32 percent of the 160,000 transportees arrived during these nine years. Alternative ways of handling British criminals were still at the discussion level. The former colonists in America were experimenting with penitentiaries as an alternative to corporal and capital punishment, but similar suggestions in England developed very slowly. Reformists in England were increasingly outspoken in their complaints about the slavery aspects of transportation. In addition, opposition by Australians was taken more seriously. After all, 50 years of settlement provided the Australian colonists with a voice to be reckoned with. The Australians increasingly disliked the competition that convict labor presented for jobs and came to resent the continuous dumping of fresh convicts on their soil. As a result, in 1840 all transportation to New South Wales ceased.

With a lingering death from 1841 to 1868, the System provided convict labor primarily to Van Diemen's Land (now known as Tasmania). When that reception point dried up in 1853, a last dribble of convicts was sent to Western Australia to help colonists settle that difficult part of the continent. By 1868 transportation was all over (Hughes, 1987).

In his fascinating and detailed account of the transporting system in Australia, Hughes (1987) suggests that proponents had hoped it would do four things: sublimate, deter, reform, and colonize. *Sublimation* would remove the criminal class, or a good slice of it, from England and put it where it could do no further harm. The cause of crime was believed to be in the individual—not in society or social structure—so it made sense to amputate this sickness.

By the 1830s proponents' hopes centered more on general *deterrence.* It was assumed that banishment across the seas would terrify the innocent away from crime. But the problem became one of convincing Great Britain's lower class that Australia was a terrible place to go. Verses written as early as 1790 suggested that Botany Bay might have been viewed as a paradise compared to the drudgery of Mother England. The bravado in letters the transportees sent home, the wishful thinking of those at home, and the often true examples of ex-cons prospering in Australia all made it difficult to portray transport to Australia as something to be feared.

Reformation was a distant third among the aims of transportation. However, at least one author suggests that the System provided the "most successful form of penal rehabilitation that had ever been tried in English, American or European history" (Hughes, 1987, p. 586). Hughes takes this position because of the benefits seemingly linked to the assignment system. Despite its inherently exploitative nature, assignment may have provided transportees with a sense of value in work and a motivation to obey the law. This result, in turn, led directly to the fourth purpose of transportation: *colonization.*

Most convicts were *assigned* (lent out) by the government as laborers to private settlers. A few (maybe one in 10) were kept by the government to labor on public works projects. Wealthy British settlers were enticed to the distant colony with offers of free land and free labor. Assigned labor was not simply something to do with people who had been punished by transportation; the labor was, in fact, the punishment.

Assignment was the early form of today's open prison. Instead of herding men together in gangs, assignment dispersed them throughout the bush and kept them in working contact with the free. It fostered self-reliance, taught them jobs, and rewarded them for proper completion. The work was hard, but not really harder than what the settler had to do for himself. It was not slavery, because the assigned man worked within a watchful set of laws and rights. For example, convicts exiled to Australia served a fixed term and then became free. All had, within limits, the right to sell some portion of their labor on the free market and could bring their "master" to court for ill treatment. Although the situation should not be romanticized, there were aspects to it that contradict the horror stories reformists told in the 1830s.

Contemporary Australian Corrections

Chappell (1988) believes that the legacy produced by Australia's convict past had specific influence on the eventual structure of its criminal justice system. The responsibility of controlling a largely disobedient population led to an early reliance on centralized authority. Individual settlements, villages, and even small cities were not able to support the necessary organizations to provide police, court, and correctional services. The states, which were each separate colonies of Britain, therefore provided these services in their own geographic territories. That initial dependence on the larger government unit established a pattern that became formalized with the 1901 creation of a Commonwealth of Australia.

The new Commonwealth provided a federal government, but, following the traditional pattern, each of the member states was charged with administering its own criminal laws and criminal justice systems. In fact, the federal (Commonwealth) government gave state courts the power to adjudicate and determine cases involving federal criminal laws—with the state acting under federal authority. The Australian Federal Police enforces Commonwealth criminal laws and is responsible, under contract, for policing in the Australian Capital Territory (ACT). Prosecution of federal defendants is accomplished by the Commonwealth Director of Public Prosecution and those convicted are sentenced by state judges acting under Commonwealth authority. Unlike the United States, there are no county or local jails and no federal penitentiaries (although the ACT does have a correctional system with noncustodial options and is considering establishing a prison). As a result, the sentence imposed on federal offenders is carried out in state prisons or by other state correctional services. Basically, the Australian correctional system is the responsibility of the six states (New South Wales, Victoria, South Australia, Queensland, Tasmania, and Western Australia) and the Northern Territory.

Australia's nine major systems of criminal justice administration (six states, two territories, and the federal system) clearly fall in the common legal tradition. Yet its decentralization to the state level makes it closer to the United States model than to either Canada or England (Sallman & Willis, 1984). Instead of a single unified system applicable to all counties (see England) or one giving the national government responsibility for criminal law (see Canada), Australia entrusts her state bodies with criminal justice administration (see the United States). The primary difference from the American system is Australia's limited federal involvement in criminal justice.

Prisons in Australia

There are nearly 80 state prisons throughout Australia, with New South Wales having the most (21) and Tasmania the least (3). The pattern in most states is to place about one half of the prisoner population in one large prison and disperse the remaining half among a number of smaller prisons.

Commonwealth (Federal) Prisoners. Of the total prisoner population, about 3.5 percent are federal convicts serving their sentence in a state prison. Section 120 of the Australian Constitution requires the states to provide prisons for offenders against the laws of the Commonwealth. The states do not receive direct compensation for providing that service to the Commonwealth, but federal officials presumably take it into account when the general funding allocations to the states are being determined. The absence of any prisons operated by the Commonwealth means that people sentenced to prison for violating a federal law are subject to the discretion of judges for the state in which the federal law was breached.

One result of this practice is discrepancy in the sentences that federal offenders receive when convicted of the same offense but in different jurisdictions. For example, offenders of the federal drug and fraud laws (the most common convictions for federal criminals) may receive different sentences in New South Wales than they would in Western Australia. The argument supporting such inconsistency is that state and federal prisoners should receive similar treatment for similar offenses. Thus, if a New South Wales drug conviction brings a three-year sentence, so should a federal drug conviction when the crime occurred in New South Wales. Furthermore, because the states are required to provide places in prison for federal offenders, and because the Commonwealth does not directly pay the cost of housing its prisoners in state prisons, the states understandably believe they have much to say about how those offenders will be sentenced.

Intracountry Variation in Incarceration Rates. The decentralization to the state level makes it difficult to describe an "Australian" corrections system. We would rightfully balk at a suggestion that American corrections can be described by reference to one, or even several, of the 50 states. Likewise, a discussion of Australian corrections in general, and imprisonment more particularly, is hampered by the variation among the states and the Northern Territory. However, just as authors write textbooks on American police, courts, and corrections without having to do a different book for each state, so there are similarities that allow some general comments about Australian corrections. In the interest of fairness, occasional reference to the situation in different jurisdictions is appropriate.

An early reliance on community corrections (in the form of assignment) made Australians familiar with, if not accepting of, an alternative to imprisonment. Correspondingly, the knowledge of experiments with penitentiaries in the United States and in England provided an impetus for building similar facilities for offenders not suitable for assigned labor positions. This combination seems to have given Australian states a rather mid-road perspective on the proper place to achieve penal goals: a mixture of both prison and community. The result is Australia's middle placement in a listing of incarceration rates around the world (see Figure 8.2).

Although Australia's incarceration rate overall is at mid-range, there is actually considerable variation within the country (see Figure 8.3). Since Australia

		Ir per100,000 **adult** population	
Australia (March 1999)		142	
	Northern Territory	476	
	Western Australia	209	
	Queensland	197	
	New South Wales	144	
	South Australia	122	
	Tasmania	89	
	Victoria	79	
	Australian Capitol Territory	52	
United States (December 31, 1998)		461	
South		520	
	High = DC	1913	(combined jail and prison)
	Low = WV	192	
West		417	
	High = NV	542	
	Low = UT	205	
Midwest		360	
	High = MI	466	
	Low = MN	117	
Northeast		328	
	High = NY	397	
	Low = ME	125	

Figure 8.3 Imprisonment Rate *(Ir)* Variation in Australia and the United States. *Sources:* Australia data from Australian Bureau of Statistics (2000), *Prisoners in Australia.* Available at **www.abs.gov.au/ausstats.** United States data from A. J. Beck, & C. J. Mumola (1999), *Prisoners in 1998* [NCJ 175687] Washington, DC: Bureau of Justice Statistics.

prefers to provide imprisonment rates based on the total adult population (i.e., those people actually eligible to be imprisoned) rather than total population, the numbers discussed in this section differ from the those used for Figure 8.2. For example, in 1999 Australia's imprisonment rate was 142 per 100,000 adult population, but the rate for individual jurisdictions varied from 79 in Victoria to 476 in the Northern Territory (Australian Bureau of Statistics, 2000). Similar intracountry differences have been consistently reported since 1961, while the country's average rate has remained relatively stable.

Considerable variation is found in the incarceration rates among states in the United States as well. In 1998 the prison (that is, not including persons in jails) incarceration rate for the United States was 461. However, as in Australia, that rate masks considerable diversity, ranging from the District of Columbia's unbelievable 1913 (although this figure includes the total jail and prison population) to Minnesota's rate of 117 (see Figure 8.3).

Explaining differences in the incarceration rates among jurisdictions within a country is as difficult as explaining rate differences among a grouping of countries. As we discovered when working with comparison of crime rates in Chapter 2, it is not possible to identify one, or even a few, variables to adequately explain differences in crime among countries. Methodological, definitional, and cultural problems mean that we can only make "best guesses" in this area of comparative criminal justice. The same holds true for drawing conclusions about the differing incarceration rates among nations. The best we can do is remember Chapter 2's warning that conclusions drawn on rate comparisons are tentative and possibly misleading. That caution applies, though certainly less so, to a comparison of jurisdictions within a country as well as those among countries.

With this warning in mind, let us consider one explanation offered for the differences among Australian states: a disproportionate rate of Aboriginal imprisonments. As you will see, researchers believe that this situation has little impact on the intracountry variation, but it highlights an important aspect of Australian corrections and deserves closer attention.

Disproportionate Incarceration Rates. In discussing Australian imprisonment rates, Biles (1993; 1986) refers to claims that Australian Aboriginal people are the most imprisoned ethnic group in the world. In the United States, African Americans comprise 13 percent of the general population but are 49 percent of the prison population (Beck & Mumola, 1999). This 4 to 1 ratio indicates a serious problem in America, but consider the 11 to 1 ratio of Aboriginal prisoners (19 percent) to the total Aboriginal population (2 percent) in Australia (Broadhurst, 1996).

Broadhurst (1996) analyzed 1995 data and found the national imprisonment rate for Aboriginal people was 1756 per 100,000 Aboriginal adults. That compared with a rate of 117 per 100,000 of all adult Australians. After calculating a disparity ratio (the incarceration rate of Aboriginals to non-Aboriginals), Broadhurst found variation ranging from a disparity of about 18 to 1 in South Australia and Western Australia to 2 to 1 in Tasmania. A disparity ratio of 13 to 1 was the national average for Australia.

Attempts to explain the interstate variations in imprisonment rates have been mostly unsuccessful. Even after controlling for demographic characteristics like urbanization, the proportion of young males or Aborigines in the population, single-parent families, police force size, and crime severity, researchers have not been able to account for all the variance (Broadhurst, 1996). The size of the Aboriginal population in each jurisdiction accounts for much of the variation, but not all. Thus far, the differences in imprisonment rates among the states and territories is most frequently argued as a result in administrative traditions, community attitudes (for example, demands for punishment), and colonization practices (Broadhurst, 1996).

Although the disproportionate imprisonment rates for Aborigines cannot explain different rates among the jurisdictions, they do highlight a dilemma for Australian criminal justice by showing the problems of forcing a foreign justice system upon a native population. Aborigines were officially recognized as British subjects in 1837 and were thereby afforded the protection and rights accompanying such status. Unfortunately, British justice was not always understood, appreciated, or even wanted by the Aborigines. Midford (1992) suspects that local Aborigines had a lack of comprehension or sense of justice about the whole process. A news report from 1842 relates a conversation between a government official and an Aborigine convicted of murdering a fellow Aborigine and thereby sentenced to life in prison. The Aborigine could not understand why the governor punished him so severely: "If a White man kills a White man, we never interfere—some time back, the White men killed many of the natives and the Governor took no notice, now why should the Governor take any notice of me, if I kill a fellow native, that steals my wife, or kills my brother, when it is according to our law?" (quoted in Midford, 1992, p. 12).

The Aborigines' experiences in the Australian justice system remain problematic today. Improvements have been made since the late nineteenth century, when a newspaper noted that the rundown collection of wooden sheds where Aboriginal prisoners were kept was a place where "the nigger is both happy and comfortable" (quoted in Midford, 1992, p. 14). Certainly problems of prejudice and discrimination remain, but also troublesome are the ever-present cultural barriers that work against equal treatment for Aboriginal people. Consider, for example, difficulties arising from Aboriginal concepts of time, name, and social relations.

Tribal Aboriginals seldom use clocks or calendars and may not even know their date of birth. Prisoners have had their length of sentence explained to them by the number of dry seasons they will be locked up. Police are frustrated in their investigation of deaths when trying to interview people who cannot speak the dead person's name. In a ripple effect, living relatives with the same name as the recently deceased person must use another name for the appropriate time. Inappropriately, the police may record such a name change as using an alias (Midford, 1992; Palmer, 1992). Also there is always the danger that police will use a taboo name when speaking to a victim, witness, or suspect and thereby violate Aboriginal custom and reduce the Aborigine's community standing.

Social relations among Aboriginals also make their incorporation into this imposed justice system very difficult (Midford, 1992; Palmer, 1992). Avoidance relationships, wherein people may not normally speak or even look at each other, make it difficult for some prisoners to work or live together. Obligation relationships, wherein one shows duty and respect to a kin, present problems for Aboriginal prison officers and police aides, because their official status does not override kinship requirements. Because the term "family" has a broad meaning for Aboriginals, prison administrators encounter difficulties in trying to be fair to all prisoners while recognizing cultural differences in deciding about "family" visits and emergency leaves.

One attempt by Australia to respond to the special circumstances presented by Aboriginal prisoners is the suggestion that private Aboriginal prisons be established. In fact, an Aboriginal community corrections center has been established in Queensland. Known as Gwandalan, this facility is a minimum-security prison in a metropolitan area. Biles (1993) describes it as a prerelease and postrelease residential facility operated by Aboriginal staff and owned by the Brisbane Tribal Council. Even though specialized facilities and programs may be a genuine attempt to address the problem of Aboriginal overrepresentation, Biles and others understand that the problem has no easy or quick solution.

Cultural differences and the prejudice and discrimination they engender are not, of course, limited to relations between Aboriginals and other Australians (see Tonry, 1997a; 1997b). Tonry says "members of minority groups are overrepresented among crime victims, arrestees, pretrial detainees, convicted offenders, and prisoners in every Western nation" (Tonry, 1997a, p. vii). It is difficult to find a country anywhere in the world where charges of institutionalized racism and discrimination are not levied. Blacks in South Africa; Turks in Austria; Koreans and Burakumin in Japan; Finns in Sweden; Moroccans in the Netherlands; Latinos, African Americans, and Native Americans in the United States; and the list, unfortunately, goes on. Australia's response to the problems of its minority population is an unhappy combination of informal and formal policies.

The informal (some say, paternalistic) handling of Aboriginals is especially apparent at sentencing. In Queensland, for example, a 1965 law allowed judges to order Aboriginal offenders to reserves rather than sentencing them to prison. Because this could be done even if the accused had not been convicted, it was possible for Aborigines to be compulsively detained on settlements or reserves. Even today, an Aborigine living in Australia's more remote areas is occasionally punished according to tribal law rather than in the formal courts. The comments of one judge choosing to release a juvenile to "the traditional ways of his people" rather than a state facility, illustrates this philosophy: "It is, I think, sad but true that to many aboriginal children a term of imprisonment tends to be regarded as a sign of manhood and a much more comfortable experience than those designed over the centuries by their own people as the transition from childhood to manhood" (quoted in Gifford and Gifford, 1983, p. 121).

Despite the use of informal methods, Aboriginal offenders are still most likely handled by the formal machinery and are overrepresented at each stage of the criminal justice system. Their disproportionate number in Australia's prisons is especially problematic, because it seems to indicate discrimination in the use of community-based alternatives. Their typical poverty status means that many Aborigines lack the necessary funds to gain access to nonprison sentences like fines. Further, community service work or compliance with probation orders may be difficult to carry out because the required behavior may not be culturally acceptable (Leivesley, 1986). However, Australia's willingness to try a variety of community-based programs suggests that more opportunities for placement of Aboriginal offenders may be possible in the future.

Community-Based Corrections. Despite the considerable difference in incarceration rates, Australia and the United States make similar use of community-based corrections. When all types of correctional supervision in both countries are totaled, Australia and the United States each have about 30 percent of their convicted adults in prisons and the remaining percentage under some form of community-based supervision.

Since the mid 1980s, Australia has pursued the principle that prison should be a sentence of last resort (Zdenkowski, 1986). That perspective was influenced by the growing cost of prisons and by the disillusionment with prison either as a place for rehabilitation or as a means of deterrence. Consequently, community alternatives to prison are emphasized in Australia. But just as the use of imprisonment varies by state and territory, so too does the use of community alternatives.

Three types of community corrections are common in the Australian states and territories: probation (sometimes called "supervised recognisance"), community service/work orders, and parole (Walker & Biles, 1986). *Probation,* or supervised recognisance, is possible for any conviction where imprisonment may be imposed. A court releases adult offenders to a fixed time period under a probation order. The time period ranges from about three months to over five years, but around 60 percent of the probationers serve a two- or three-year sentence. While under a probation order, the offender receives supervision, guidance, support, and referral services from paid and volunteer staff.

For Australia as a whole, probation is the most frequently used community-based corrections procedure. Within each jurisdiction, except South Australia, probation is the most common form (Walker & Biles, 1986). Yet even in South Australia, nearly half the people under community corrections are sentenced to a supervised suspended prison sentence, which is in fact an order under the Offenders Probation Act. In South Australia, probation—or a first cousin to it—still provides the most used form of community corrections.

Community service or *work orders* are alternatives to imprisonment in which the court requires offenders to make restitution by performing a set number of hours of community service work. The required hours range from around 25 to over 500, but national statistics show about 75 percent falling between 100 and 300 total hours (Walker & Biles, 1986). Because this is an alternative to imprisonment, a wide variety of offenses have been committed by persons under this sentence. In Victoria, for example, all persons other than those convicted of treason or murder are eligible for community service/work orders.

Parole (called "release on licence" if the person is being released from a life imprisonment sentence) refers to early release from prison. At the discretion of a parole board, the prisoner can serve the difference between his minimum and maximum sentence (that is, the parole period) under supervision in the community. Nationally, about 14 percent of the persons in community-based corrections are under parole or licence. Over 60 percent of the parolees serve a parole period of over 18 months but under five years.

Although probation, community service, and parole are common to the eight Australian jurisdictions, some of the unique community-based options are worth noting. For example, New South Wales makes use of presentence supervision orders for persons convicted but awaiting sentence. The offender's performance under community-based supervision is assessed before a penalty is imposed.

After this short (usually less than 12 months) trial period, the sentencing judge presumably has more information useful in determining an appropriate sentence for the offender.

In Victoria, *attendance centre orders* provide the court with a noncustodial sentencing option where the period of imprisonment can be served in the community. This penalty combines restitution in the form of community work with a requirement of regular attendance at an attendance centre. During the one- to twelve-month time period, the offender goes to the center to participate in a variety of personal development activities.

The willingness of Australian state governments to support community-based programs has pleased many criminologists, who see government policy as supporting their recommendations based on criminological theory. Some suggest that the government support for prison alternatives has more to do with economic concerns than humanitarian ones, but even these cynics are pleased with Australia's innovations in community corrections.

From its origins as a penal colony to its contemporary standing as a modern industrialized nation, Australia has maintained an intriguing combination of the standard and the unique. Its mid-range use of imprisonment and its development of community alternatives provide an appropriate position from which to view other countries falling toward the extremes on the incarceration continuum.

CORRECTIONS IN POLAND

In 1989 Poland and Hungary took steps toward ending more than 40 years of totalitarian rule. Over the next five years all the countries in central and eastern Europe experienced extraordinary political and social changes, including independence from the Soviet Union, establishment of an independent Russian state, splitting of Czechoslovakia into the Czech Republic and Slovakia, new membership in the United Nations, and application for membership in the Council of Europe. Realizing that a country's criminal justice system is a key indicator of its level of democracy and the degree to which human rights are respected, reform of that system become a priority for these countries. That reform was, and remains, no small task because it requires revision of law, procedures, policies, practices, and attitudes in all components of the criminal justice system.

Roy Walmsley (1995) provides an excellent account of the progress and problems that 16 of the Central and Eastern European countries have had in reforming one particular aspect of their respective criminal justice systems—the prison systems. Before we look at Poland as a specific example of what has happened in this region of the world, it is appropriate to report on Walmsley's findings for the area as a whole, which will help us place the Polish situation in context.

Reforming Prison Systems in Central and Eastern Europe. One of the first problems confronting the emerging democracies was trying to reform a prison system based in old buildings in great need of repair. Comments by the Human

Rights Watch after a visit to Polish prisons in 1987 were probably applicable to many prisons in central and eastern Europe at the time:

> *The physical environment of many and perhaps most of these institutions is intolerable. They are ancient, overcrowded, damp, stuffy, cold in winter and hot in summer. Sanitary conditions often verge on the indecent (Helsinki Watch, 1988, p. 7).*

Walmsley (1995) explains that the lack of attention to prison facilities was understandable when we remember that socialist ideology posited that crime would disappear in a socialist society and there would be no need for prisons. Today, given competing demands for money to refurbish facilities throughout society, new prison philosophies must be implemented in the old institutions.

Compounding the problem of dated facilities, the move toward a market economy in these countries had the unfortunate, if not unexpected, result of increasing crime. Growth in thefts, violent crimes, money laundering, drug trafficking, protection rackets, and other crimes overloaded the criminal justice system at all levels. Long delays in processing people through the system meant long stays in pretrial detention. Because in many Central and Eastern European countries, pretrial detainees are held at the same institutions as sentenced prisoners, that increase had direct impact on prison populations.

In almost every Central and Eastern European country, the numbers held in penal facilities were greater at the decade's end than at its start (see Table 8.1). Particularly notable increases were in Belarus, Croatia, and the Czech Republic, where proportions at least doubled. Yet despite the herculean nature of the task, there are clearly identifiable positive developments throughout Central and Eastern Europe. Walmsley (1995) notes, for example, desirable changes to the organizational structure, an enthusiasm toward progressive policies, and a professionalism among prison administrators and employees. Poland provides a good example for a closer look at corrections in Central and Eastern Europe.

The Example of Poland. During nearly 45 years as the Polish People's Republic, Poland's imprisonment rate never dropped below 100 per 100,000 general population. Moving from a 1945 low of 107, it peaked at 372 in 1973. Between 1980 and 1988 it stayed in the 200 range with a low of 205 in 1984, and a high of 295 in 1985.

One reason for the fluctuating imprisonment rate was the use of general amnesties, which often released large numbers of prisoners. Thirteen amnesties since 1945 resulted in a lowered imprisonment rate 12 times. The exception, 1983, involved a partial amnesty to imprisoned Solidarity leaders and to other Solidarity leaders willing to turn themselves in before October 31. The net result was an insufficient number to affect the overall imprisonment rate. The most recent general amnesty, in 1989, gave Poland its lowest incarceration rate (Ir = 106) since 1945, but within one year it was inching back up again (Siemaszko, Gruszczyńska & Marczewski, 2000). As Table 8.1 shows, by 1999 Poland's imprisonment rate was back up to 147. A look at sentencing options will help us better understand some of the reasons Poland retains its comparatively high incarceration rate.

Table 8.1 Central and Eastern European Imprisonment Rates (*Ir*)

Country	*Ir* per 100,000 Population 1991	*Ir* per 100,000 Population 1994	*Ir* per 100,000 Population 1999[a]
Belarus	140	290	575
Bulgaria	80	95	145
Croatia	20	50	50
Czech Republic	80	160	225
Estonia	280	290	310
Hungary	120	130	150
Latvia	320	350	360
Lithuania	235	275	385
Moldova	255	280	275
Romania	110	195	222
Slovakia	85	135	125
Slovenia	25	30	50

[a]Data for Belarus is from 1997; data for Bulgaria, Croatia, and Slovakia is from 1998.
Sources: 1991 and 1994 data from Roy Walmsley (1995), *Developments in the prison systems of central and eastern Europe* (HEUNI paper no. 4). Helsinki, Finland: The European Institute for Crime Prevention and Control. 1999 data from Roy Walmsley (2000), *World Prison Population List,* 2nd ed. [Research, Development and Statistics Directorate, Report No. 116] London: Home Office.

Sentencing Options in Poland

The 1970 Penal Code, still in effect in the mid 1990s, provides for sentence types ranging from fines to incarceration. The law does not provide for a specific penalty for any given offense. Instead, the court may choose the sanction it will impose from a grouping of principal and accessory penalties. The principal penalties are (1) the immediate deprivation of liberty, (2) the conditionally suspended deprivation of liberty, and (3) fines. In addition, there are two special principal penalties: (4) 25 years of deprivation of liberty, and (5) life imprisonment. The death penalty was abolished with the new Penal Code of 1997. Accessory penalties, which are imposed in conjunction with a principal penalty, include sanctions like the deprivation of public rights, the deprivation of parental rights, the prohibition of holding specific jobs or engaging in particular activities (Adamski, 1997). The non-fine and non-special principal penalties will be considered in greater depth.

Deprivation of Liberty. Deprivation of liberty (that is, imprisonment) is the most incapacitative sentence. Table 8.2 shows that while the total number of sen-

Table 8.2 Non-Fine Sentence Types in Poland (Percent of Total Non-Fine Sentences)

Year	Total Non-Fine Sentences	Deprivation of Liberty (%)	Sentence Suspended (%)	Limitation of Liberty (%)
1990	86,380	33.7	60.2	6.1
1995	145,398	22.2	72.8	5.0
1997	152,845	16.8	76.0	7.2

Source: A. Siemaszko (Ed.) (2000), *Crime and law enforcement in Poland,* Warsaw, Poland: Oficyna Naukowa. Available at **iws@iws.org.pl**

tences has increased since 1990, the percentage of prison sentences has actually declined. Although this sentence can range from three months to 15 years, the average sentence length is two years. This sanction is looked at more closely in the following discussion of prisons.

Conditional Suspension of a Prison Sentence. The conditionally suspended deprivation of liberty, which is the most commonly imposed penalty, allows the offender to remain in the community. Conditional suspension of imprisonment includes sanctions that require certain actions of the offender but do not require reporting to a court official (as required by a suspended sentence in some countries). However, this same sentence may also place the offender under supervision of a court official (as probation does in some other countries). Conditional suspension of a prison sentence is used for cases of "intentional" offenses where the sentence would not exceed two years of deprivation of liberty. It is also applicable in cases of "unintentional" offenses where the sentence would not exceed three years of deprivation of liberty. The judge sets the term of suspension between three and five years.

With the suspension, the court can impose a fine, demand an apology to the victim, require obligations like abstaining from alcohol or submitting to medical treatment, and can have the defendant perform community service, find work, go to school, or report to a supervising authority. Should the person commit a new offense or not abide by the conditions of suspension, the judge may send him or her to prison.

Limitation of Liberty. The limitation of liberty is a noncustodial penalty allowing the offender to remain at liberty in the community under certain restrictions. As with the broader conditional suspension of sentence, limitation of liberty can include placing the offender under supervision. Limitation of liberty can be for three months to two years and requires specific behavior while the offender retains freedom of movement in the community.

The penalty typically takes one of three forms: supervised community work, wage deductions, and compulsory employment for those offenders without a job. If the conditions are not met, the court can impose a fine. Should the fine not be paid in time, the judge can impose a prison sentence.

Ostrihanska et al. (1985) cite the educative (emphasizing work) benefits of the limitation of liberty penalty, but claim that it was less popular in the 1980s than in the 1970s. Those authors do not provide data on its use in the 1970s, but in 1983 only 6 percent of those found guilty received this sentence. Some consistency is found in recent years, with limitation of liberty constituting 6 percent in 1990, 5 percent in 1995, and 7 percent in 1997 (see Table 8.2).

Since 1990 the total use of the conditional suspension of a prison sentence (that is, the sum of sentence suspended and limitation of liberty in Table 8.2) has increased from 66 percent to 83 percent of all non-fine prison sentences. Those numbers make the suspended sentence the most frequently applied penal measure in Poland. Before looking more closely at community placement of offenders, we must become familiar with the custody option.

The Use of Imprisonment in Poland

There are about 140 institutions in Poland for sentenced offenders (Adamski, 1997). That number includes closed prisons (61), open prisons (40), semi-open work centers (23), prison hospitals (15), and houses for where sentenced mothers can stay with their children (2). The prisons operate at capacity, but overcrowding is not as severe as it was in the 1980s.

The living conditions for prisoners have improved since the mid 1980s but remain austere. Prior to the reforms, prisoners were sometimes kept in the semidarkness of dirty and stifling cells. Inspectors found prisoners sleeping on wooden boxes instead of beds, living without running water, made to use sanitary buckets in the absence of toilets, and being fed at irregular times (Bulenda, Holda & Rzeplinski, 1990). With the start of noticeable reforms in 1986, problems in prisons were openly discussed. Prison staff began conscientious efforts to make real improvements in the prison environment (Płatek, 1998b). Indication of success is found in a more relaxed daily routine for prisoners, access to more recreational activities, reduction in the amount of time the prisoner must stay in a locked cell, and increased use of furloughs to visit family members. These changes are best considered in the context of Poland's current use of imprisonment.

Prisoners in Poland, as is true in most other countries, include both convicted and unconvicted people. As explained in the earlier discussion of imprisonment rates, the category of "prisoner" typically includes persons in detention while the charges against them are investigated or while they await their trial. In the United States, people in this situation who are not on some form of pretrial release are kept in jails operated by city or county governments. We do not often think of persons awaiting trial as "prisoners" (although we may use the term "inmate"), because they have not been found guilty of anything and are not serving time in a prison. However, our perspective and our usual elimination of people in detention from our imprisonment statistics are not shared by most other countries.

Although both convicted and unconvicted (that is, detained) persons share the prisoner label, they are not treated in the same manner. Our discussion of imprisonment in Poland would be incomplete if the situation of the detainees were omitted, so we begin at that point.

Preliminary Detention in Poland

Preliminary, or pretrial, detention is a procedure authorized by the court. In general, preliminary detention can be used when the collected evidence is sufficient to indicate that the accused committed the crime and at least one of the following is also present:

1. There is good reason to fear that the accused may go into hiding, especially if he has no permanent residence in the country or when his identity cannot be established.
2. There is good cause to assume the accused will try to get others to commit perjury or will otherwise try to obstruct the criminal proceeding.
3. The charge is for a felony or intentional misdemeanor punishable with the deprivation of liberty up to at least eight years, or if the accused has been sentenced by a court of the first instance for the penalty of deprivation of liberty of three years and over.
4. There is good reason to believe the accused may again commit a crime against life, health, or public safety, especially if he or she has threatened to commit such an offense.

After determining that the appropriate criteria exist, the court of first instance can set preliminary detention for up to 18 months or, in the case of a felony charge, for no more than two years (Adamski, 1997; Bulenda et al., 1990).

Since mid 1990, preliminary detention is conducted only in the houses of detention, which number about 70, under the direction of the Minister of Justice (Adamski, 1997; Bulenda et al., 1990). Unlike American jails, the detention houses are sometimes physically attached to regular prisons and under the same administration as the prisoners. In 1990, 48 of the prisons had sections for detainees.

The presence of both convicted and unconvicted persons in what appears to be the same physical structure makes it difficult to identify some facilities as prisons or detention houses. For example, in 1991 at the Bialoleka facility near Warsaw, some 1700 persons under preliminary detention were being housed in four buildings, each having four units or floors. In a physically distinct section of the compound, separated by gates and walls, another 450 prisoners were housed in a similar setting. The only way for an uninitiated observer to distinguish between the groups is the knowledge that detainees get to wear their own clothes whereas convicted prisoners must wear prison uniforms.

The difficulty of differentiating detainees and prisoners is not lost on Polish academics and officials. Some (for example, Bulenda et al., 1990) express concern that the use of the same buildings and personnel for both convicted and unconvicted persons provides an undesirable organizational symbiosis. There should be, critics argue, noticeably different conditions for persons in the two situations.

Prisons in Poland

Polish officials believe that work, education, and cultural activity provide the means by which offenders can be resocialized (Płatek, 1990a). Of the three, work was especially emphasized under socialism. The 1970 Penal Code said the purpose of a prison sentence is to: "accustom the prisoner to work and observe the legal order, thus preventing his relapse into crime" (Ostrihanska et al., 1985, p. 61). Even after the change in government, work remains a desirable goal and is considered a way to instill socially desirable attitudes in the prisoner.

Fewer jobs are available for prisoners today, because the economic changes have, among other things, meant that prison industries cannot keep pace with the outside competition. On the prison grounds are various workplaces. Inmates make gloves in converted cells, build furniture in regular buildings, and do construction work outside, making prefabricated sections for buildings. These areas are not as busy as they were before 1989, but every effort is made to provide work, and an accompanying fair wage, to all prisoners. A major problem for prison administrators in the1990s was providing prisoners with employment. Adamski (1997) notes that the number of inmates in the total prison population who worked while serving their sentence decreased from 54.8 percent in 1990 to 21 percent in 1995.

The rehabilitation of prisoners and their restoration to society are primary goals of imprisonment in Poland (Mozgawa & Szumski, 2000). The basic means by which these goals are achieved is through activities related to work, education, and cultural endeavors. The principal location for providing the activities is a prison facility rather than a community setting. The 1997 code provides for three types of prison regimen: (1) Individually Programmed, (2) Therapeutic, and (3) Normal. Voluntary participation is required for the individual program, but prisoners are simply assigned to the other two. An important aspect of the new code is a sanctions-enforcement part that allows prisoners to have contact with the outside world, considerable access to printed and broadcast media, temporary leave on furlough, and increased opportunities for outside members of the public to interact with prisoners on prison grounds (Mozgawa & Szumski, 2000). Poland is also trying to reduce the number of people imprisoned for nonpayment of fines by providing an option for community service lasting from one to twelve months. In fact, increased use of community sanctions is an obvious direction being taken as Poland responds to its still high incarceration rate.

Community Placement in Poland

Community supervision in Poland can be either obligatory or optional. As noted earlier, supervision is possible for sentences of conditional suspension of a prison sentence, but it is also used in other cases where the court believes the offender needs supervision. When supervision is required instead of a prison term, it operates like probation in other countries. The person reports to a professional supervision officer, but lay volunteers augment the professional staff. The use of lay citizens lends an informality to supervision and shows offenders that they have a friend. The Polish system assumes that the volunteers also will benefit from this process. Because of their interaction with offenders, the volunteers will presumably come to understand better the role society plays in the development of criminal behavior.

The Polish version of parole allows for release from incarceration after serving two thirds of the sentence, achieving the aims of punishment, and receiving a favorable prognosis. The minimum time to serve before parole is one half of the sentence for young adults, and three quarters of the sentence for recidivists. The time spent on parole cannot be less than one year (three years for recidivists) nor longer than five years. As noted earlier, the penitentiary court makes the parole decision at the request of the warden, prisoner, and prisoner's counsel. The release may require direction by the community supervision officer, but such supervision is mandatory only for recidivists.

Earlier in this chapter we noted that countries differ in their opinions about the appropriate location for achieving punishment goals. Poland's high imprisonment rate suggests that, at least for its years under socialism, the goals were best achieved in an institutional setting. Even since the change in government, Poland still makes greater use of prisons than do many other countries. Rapid changes were not possible since no infrastructure for community supervision existed through most of the 1990s. Although probation and parole existed under socialism, they were not fully used or formally integrated into the country's penal philosophy. Even as Poles seek to change the location for achieving penal goals from prisons to the community, the process will be long and controversial. Płatek, who says that it is hard to find Polish examples of community supervision and community-based corrections, suggests two reasons for Poland's delayed development in this area: (1) the courts are not willing to share power with the people, and (2) Poles believe it is the court's role, rather than the public's, to devote time to wrongdoers (Płatek, personal communication, January 12, 1992). Such attitudes not only will limit the involvement of citizen volunteers in working with offenders but also will hinder development of paid professionals to supervise persons receiving suspended sentences. However, the growing importance of community supervision is seen in the increased number of professional probation officers. The professional probation officers, who are attached to the courts, have increased along with the greater use of conditional suspended prison sentences. By 1998, professional officers were 14 percent of all probation officers (both professional and volunteer). In 1989 professionals were only 5 percent of the total (Siemaszko, et al., 2000). That increase suggests that Poland is building a stronger infrastructure for a more formal probation system.

The shortage of noncustodial alternatives to prison is not a problem only for Poland. In his review of Central and Eastern European countries, Walmsley (1995) noted that judges in all those countries have very few options between fines and imprisonment. Developing a viable probation system is considered too expensive, and many people consider alternatives like community service to be an unwanted reminder of the forced labor tactics imposed under Soviet rule. Without any significant institutionalized system of prison alternatives, it seems unlikely that Central and Eastern European countries will be able to reduce their comparatively high incarceration rates any time soon.

Poland's persisting view of institutions as legitimate places for offender rehabilitation and restoration into law-abiding society is certainly not unique among countries of the world. As Empey (1982) points out, the beginning stages of a rehabilitation philosophy in America included the belief that institutions were the most effective means for preventing a child's movement into criminality and for rehabilitating those already engaged in crime. From the late nineteenth century through the mid-twentieth century Americans had great faith in institutions as places where social ills could be alleviated.

Obviously, Polish officials have not given as much thought to alternatives to imprisonment as they have to prison itself. The result is a high incarceration rate. At the other extreme on the incarceration continuum is Japan. Unlike Poland—in fact, unlike most countries—Japan does not have significant problems with overcrowded prisons. One reason, as we will discuss, is Japan's willingness to use alternatives to imprisonment.

CORRECTIONS IN JAPAN

The Penal Code of 1907 has served, with consistent modification, to orient Japanese corrections for over 90 years. The designated goals of retribution and rehabilitation are reflected in the treatment of prisoners. Although a goal of retribution might suggest imprisonment as the typical punishment, Japan actually has a very low incarceration rate. After reaching a peak in 1950 of 139 convicted prisoners per 100,000 population, the rate declined to the low 40s around 1975 and has leveled off at mid 30s since then (Correction Bureau, 1999a).

A commonsense explanation for Japan's low incarceration rate is that it uses imprisonment sentences less frequently than do other countries. But a quick look at sentences shows that Japan's low incarceration rate is not the result of its judges refusing to sentence offenders to prison. In fact, a remarkable 98 percent of persons sentenced in Japan's trial courts receive a prison sentence.

If minimal use of prison sentences does not explain Japan's low rate, we must consider other possibilities. One is that the Japanese people are simply more law-abiding than citizens of other countries, and as a result a small proportion of the population is incarcerated. Another is that Japanese officials have found alternative ways of handling offenders, so that many of those who do get in trouble are not subjected to eventual prison sentences. Actually, both these factors seem to play a role. The first, the well-behaved Japanese citizen, is a topic more appropriate to Chapter 10's elaboration on Japan. The second, alternative handling, is also discussed in Chapter 10, but deserves brief attention here as well.

Although 98 percent of persons being sanctioned will receive a prison sentence, about two thirds of them will have the execution of that sentence suspended. That may sound like a complicated way of saying most of the sentences are to probation, but the situation is even more complex than that. In U.S. jurisdictions, most suspended prison sentences require offenders to be placed on probation, in which they are supervised by a probation officer. In Japan, only about 11 percent of the suspended prison sentences are linked to probation (Research and Training Institute, 1998). Yet, unlike the situation in Central and Eastern Europe, where minimal use of community supervision is due to an inadequate infrastructure, Japan's meager use of supervised community placement is a purposeful aspect of the Japanese criminal justice system. Specifically, infrequent use of formal probation highlights a Japanese reliance on informal sanctioning.

As Chapter 10 explains, informal (from an American perspective) handling of offenders begins with Japanese police officers and continues through the Japanese courts. The result is a constant diverting of offenders away from formal processing. Nevertheless, of those offenders actually reaching the formal sentencing stage, more than one third will be sentenced to prison. Until we can explore these points more fully, it may help to think of the Japanese process in the following manner:

1. Japan's low incarceration rate means that it imprisons a low proportion of its citizens.
2. Japan is likely to divert many offenders away from any kind of correctional supervision.
3. When official supervision is deemed necessary, it will likely be in a prison setting rather than in the community.

These three points orient our discussion of corrections in Japan and allow us to look at the country's sentencing options, prison system, and community-based alternatives.

Sentencing Options in Japan

Nakayama (1987) identifies Japanese sentencing options as including execution, imprisonment (both with and without labor), major and minor fines, penal detention, and suspension of sentence. Execution is imposed only in the rare case of aggravated homicide or homicide resulting from robbery. Imprisonment is reserved for serious offenses, persons dangerous to society, and recidivists who previously failed in institutional or community treatment.

Whether sentenced to prison with or without labor, Japanese inmates typically serve a fixed term. Imprisonment with labor is the most typical type (99 percent of the imprisonment sentences), but even inmates sentenced without required labor may request a work assignment. Because most inmates request work assignment, there is little distinction between the two types of imprisonment. In the mid 1990s, most prisoners (41 percent) had a sentence term of less than two years and only about 9 percent were serving a term of more than five years. Life sentences are given, parolable after 10 years, but less than 1 percent of the inmates are serving such a sentence (Correction Bureau, 1994).

Penal detention involves a short (1 to 29 days) deprivation of liberty to be served in a house of detention. Persons convicted of minor offenses, like insult or public indecency, are the most likely candidates for this sanction (Nakayama, 1987). Fines (about $20 and up) and minor fines (under about $20) are monetary punishments that may result in imprisonment if not paid.

The enforcement of sentences to imprisonment can be suspended for a period of one to five years. As mentioned earlier, this suspended sentence of imprisonment is the most widely imposed sentence by Japan's judges. It is usually considered for offenders lacking any prior incarceration or whose period of imprisonment occurred more than five years earlier. Suspended execution of sentence can occur either with or without supervision. When accompanied by supervision, this is essentially a sentence to probation. However, in recent years only about 12 percent of the defendants actually had supervision stipulated as part of their suspended sentence. More often, supervision is not required, and the offender is simply under his or her own recognizance.

Prisons in Japan

The supervision and treatment of inmates in all Japanese correctional institutions is the responsibility of the Correction Bureau of the Ministry of Justice. A result of this highly centralized structure is a unified and coordinated corrections system. In 2000 the Correction Bureau operated seven detention houses with 110 branches, 59 adult prisons and their six branches, and 8 juvenile prisons (Correction Bureau, 1999a). In Japan, "juvenile" refers to any person under 20 years of age, but a decrease in the number of juvenile prisoners has allowed Japan to place young adult prisoners (those under age 26) in the juvenile prisons. Six of the adult prisons and branches are designated for women prisoners, while four of the facilities are medical prisons treating prisoners with mental or physical disorders. Other specialized units handle only traffic offenders, prostitutes, or foreign prisoners.

Although rehabilitation is considered more effective in a community setting, it is not ignored in the institution. Persons who are under 28 years of age, and are sentenced to adult prisons for longer than one year, will first go to one of eight regional classification centers. During the initial phase (about 15 days) at the classification center, the inmates' behavior is observed, they undergo group psychological testing, are interviewed, receive a medical checkup, and information is gathered about them from outside sources. During the 30-day middle phase, individual psychological testing is conducted, vocational skills are assessed, their behavior in groups is observed, and they receive training on group interaction. In the final stage (about 15 days), the inmates receive counseling and orientation of their transfer to a specific prison (Correction Bureau, 1999b).

Upon arrival at the assigned institution, inmates are placed in a progressive grade system that varies treatment according to the prisoner's level. This system was first carried out in 1934 in response to the Ordinance for Prisoner's Progressive Treatment. Movement begins at the lowest grades (fourth and third), where prisoners are, in principle, confined in communal cells. Through motivation and reform, the prisoners move to second and first grades, where they enjoy single cells at night, more extensive self-government, and increased privileges (Correction Bureau, 1999b; Nakayama, 1987).

Japanese prison industries are more productive and progressive than those in America. Divided into the three areas of production, vocational training, and maintenance work, prison industry lacks restrictions regarding competition with private sector. The Japanese prisoners work an eight-hour day, five days a week. They receive monetary rewards, considered a gratuity rather than a wage, of about $40 per month (in the 1990s) for their labor. Money the prisoners do not use for necessities while in prison is saved and given to them at their release.

Community-Based Services in Japan

Our discussion of Japan began by noting that its low incarceration rate is accompanied by a low percentage of persons under community supervision. This was surprising because one explanation for a low use of imprisonment might be the diversion of offenders into community-based programs rather than into prisons.

That is, in fact, what Japan does, but the release to the community is typically without any required supervision.

Because the majority of offenders are returned to the community without correctional supervision, it is not really fair to say that they are in a community-based program. Yet clearly they have been given a community-based alternative! Chapter 10 suggests reasons why Japan can rely on nonsupervision alternatives to prison, so in this chapter we focus on the more traditional programs of probation and parole.

Probation and Parole in Japan. Given the Japanese shared sense of shame and embarrassment when a group member misbehaves, it is not surprising that family and neighbors may resent offenders. Parker (1986) tells of an 1880s case where a discharged prisoner committed suicide after being rejected by family and community members. That incident moved philanthropist Meizen Kinbara to establish a private aftercare halfway house to provide shelter, employment, and guidance to released offenders with no place to return in the community. Other private individuals and organizations, following Kinbara's lead, established a number of hostels throughout Japan. Halfway houses, or Shelter Aid Services, remain an important part of Japan's corrections system, but its probation and parole service is considered the primary means for keeping the imprisonment rate low.

Japanese probation officers provide what Americans know as both probation and parole. As noted earlier, the Rehabilitation Bureau of the Ministry of Justice administers rehabilitation services for the entire country. Despite the centralized administration, Japanese probation facilities are dispersed, with 50 main offices and 25 branch offices throughout the nation.

Because probation is a complement to a suspended sentence, only offenders eligible for a suspended sentence are eligible for probation. Thus, probation has three minimum requirements: (1) the sentence must be for three years or less, or a fine for 200,000 yen (about $1700) or less; (2) the offender has not been sentenced to imprisonment in the last five years; and (3) the offense was not committed during a probation term previously ordered (Rehabilitation Bureau, 1995, p. 22).

There is no right to parole, or even to apply for it, in Japan. Instead, the head of the prison may request parole on behalf of a prisoner. The Regional Parole Board, which may also initiate its own parole examination, makes the actual decision regarding release on parole. A three-member RPB panel makes its decision upon consideration of four factors: (1) the prisoner has served no less than one third of the determinate sentence or 10 years of a life sentence; (2) the prisoner repents and has shown progress during prison confinement; (3) there is no likelihood of recidivism during the proposed parole period; and (4) society will accept the parole (Rehabilitation Bureau, 1995, p. 25).

As in the United States, persons on probation or parole in Japan must abide by certain conditions (for example, live at a specified residence, refrain from criminal behavior, avoid contact with known criminals, obtain permission before residence changes or trips). Failure to follow these restrictions on behavior can result in termination of probation or revocation of parole.

Japanese Probation/Parole Officers. Because of the large number of volunteer probation officers (see below), Japanese officers perform a different function from those in America. The professional probation officer (PPO) in Japan is a coordinator, counselor, investigator, and personnel officer. Most importantly, he or she supervises volunteer workers, who handle most of the face-to-face contact with probationers and parolees. Because the large-scale use of government-appointed volunteer probation officers (VPOs) is the most unique feature of the Japanese system, we turn our attention directly to those citizens.

PPOs have an average caseload of about 90 clients but also have the assistance of about 80 VPOs. This nearly one-to-one ratio provides a very different version of community supervision than is experienced by probationers in most other countries. The PPOs are full-time employees of the Ministry of Justice and must have competence in law, medicine, education, sociology, and other areas relevant to the treatment of offenders. In addition to their direct supervision of probationers and parolees, PPOs are also involved in crime prevention and aftercare activities.

VPOs supervise and assist probationers and parolees to rehabilitate themselves. They do this by visiting the offender's home to advise the family, assuming the supervision of a probationer or parolee who moves into the volunteer's neighborhood, and assisting the offender's family. More generally, the VPOs help educate individuals and the public about rehabilitative philosophies and promote cooperative efforts to eliminate societal conditions that encourage crime.

VPOs must be healthy, active, and financially stable citizens with the enthusiasm and time necessary for probation work. Their ranks are filled with schoolteachers, housewives, Buddhist and Shinto priests, and businessmen volunteering their service for two years. Reappointments are possible and occur so frequently that the vast majority are reappointed repeatedly. Nearly half the VPOs are over age 60 and three quarters are male (Rehabilitation Bureau, 1995).

The lengthy experience of many volunteers presents a problem with the system. Most volunteers are older than their clients, and some consider this generation gap a major problem. But despite the age difference, VPO and client often develop a trust and confidence not possible between the professional officer and the client. After all, as in America, professional probation officers have a "cop" role requiring them to investigate and report violations of probation/parole conditions. The VPO lacks such authority and can devote all his or her attention to the helping role.

When compared with the variety of community-based alternatives available in Australia, Japan seems to have a rather undeveloped program. Japan's prison system is not noticeably different from Poland's, so cannot really be offered as an example of innovation in imprisonment. Essentially, Japanese community corrections consists of halfway houses, probation, and parole. These are certainly not imaginative concepts and, except for the significant use of volunteers, they are not implemented in a unique fashion. The very commonness of Japanese corrections is notable because of the fact that the country uses them so infrequently and yet has one of the world's lowest crime rates. Do the traditional corrections systems typified by prisons, halfway houses, probation, and parole work only in Japan? The answer, of course, is more complicated than a simple yes. In Chapter 10, Japan is looked at in greater detail as we consider explanations for its seemingly effective criminal justice system.

CORRECTIONS ISSUES: PRISON ALTERNATIVES

As an aid to categorization, this chapter has concentrated on the way countries differ in their use of imprisonment as a punishment. There are, of course, other sanctions used in most countries and this chapter concludes with a few examples of those alternatives.

If correctional goals can be achieved without the use of prison, public opinion and government policy will likely be supportive of such options. In the United States various jurisdictions typically avoid imprisoning offenders through fines, sentences to community service work, placement in halfway houses, and suspended sentences with supervision provided by a probation officer. Other countries do not provide radically different options, but when and how they are used make them distinct from their American cousins. Consider, for example, the use of fines.

Fines. A financial punishment providing compensation to either the victim or society is one of the oldest forms of punishment. In the United States, fines are used extensively across the country. State penal codes usually set maximum amounts of fines for particular classes of crimes, and judges frequently impose a fine alone or in combination with another penalty (Hillsman, Mahoney, Cole & Auchter, 1987). Fines are linked to minor offenses like loitering and shoplifting, but also to such serious crimes as assault and robbery. Similar statements can be made concerning the use of fines in many countries. The primary difference is that American jurisdictions are not using fines as an alternative to prison or to probation (Hillsman et al., 1987).

The primary example of fines as an alternative to incarceration is the European *day fine.* The day fine system, which is especially popular in Germany and Sweden, is based on the idea that punishment should be proportionate to the severity of the crime but equal across individuals with differing financial resources (Hillsman et al., 1987). In other words, the seriousness of the offense and the offender's income level determine the amount of fine. The court sets the number of day fine units according to the type of offense. Then the offender's daily net income (after deducting an amount for family support and other necessary expenses) is determined. The daily net income (let's suppose it is $16.00) is multiplied by the number of day fines (for example, 85 for burglary) to determine the amount owed (which would be $1360.00). Because the number of day fine units is consistent by crime, another offender charged with the same crime (for example, 85 units) but having a lower daily net income (say, $12.00) would be punished proportionately differently (the result would be a lesser fine of $1020.00).

The day fine is the most frequently applied punishment for the majority of criminal and traffic offenses in Sweden (Amilon, 1987) and for most adult sentences in Germany (Feest, 1981; Weigend, 1983). In both countries, the fine becomes a jail sentence if the offender does not pay. When that occurs, the number of day fines imposed and unpaid equals the number of days to be spent in jail. In this manner, the jail sanction is the same for all offenders of a particular crime, because the jail time is based on the number of units, not the monetary amount.

Hillsman et al. (1987) surveyed American judges to determine the possibility of implementing a day fine system in the United States. They concluded that day fines could be used in state jurisdictions if judges had access to accurate information about the offender's economic status. Even welfare recipients, the working poor, and the temporarily or seasonally unemployed could be punished by day fine instead of incarceration. The amount might be minimal by many economic standards, but if it was substantial enough to be a punishment for that specific offender, the fine would serve its purpose.

Suspending the Sentence. The classic alternative to imprisonment has been the suspended sentence. Two types are possible: suspended sentence with supervision (typically known as probation) and suspended sentence without supervision. The latter type was exemplified by the Japanese example of suspended execution of imprisonment without supervision. Similarly, Sweden uses "conditional sentencing," wherein the court finds the defendant guilty but places no supervision requirements on that person (Amilon, 1987). Germany also provides for suspended sentences without supervision, but the actual process yields what seems to be a mid-range between the absence and presence of supervision. As a result, Germany presents a new twist on the traditional dichotomy of suspended sentence with supervision and suspended sentence without supervision.

Germany's Penal Code actually requires suspension of a sentence to imprisonment in some instances. For example, a suspended sentence must be given if the sentence is for one year or less, and if the court believes that the sentence itself sufficiently warned an offender who is not likely to commit additional offenses. According to Teske and Albrecht (1991), the court can impose two types of requirements on sentenced persons whose sentence is then suspended. The requirements, known as "conditions," oblige the offender to (1) pay money to an organization or the state, (2) perform community service duties, or (3) provide victim restitution.

The second type of requirement involves "orders." These directives are attempts to structure the sentenced person's life in hopes of preventing further criminal behavior. They sound very similar to conditions of probation in American jurisdictions, because they affect things like place of residence, use of work time, financial matters, associates, required reporting to court officials or representatives, and voluntary participation in treatment programs.

The important difference between the German and American versions is that the German conditions and orders neither imply nor require supervision (Teske & Albrecht, 1991). In other words, German offenders under a suspended sentence are held to requirements much like those for American offenders under probation, but the German is not under the formal supervision of a court official. It is possible that Germans with a suspended sentence can have attached to their conditions, or orders, the requirement for supervision by a probation worker. Yet even then German probation differs from the American version, in that probation "workers" in Germany lack the enforcement powers of American probation" officers" (Teske and Albrecht, 1991).

Variations in the use of fines and suspended sentences as prison alternatives suggest possible modifications in American procedures. Increased use of suspended sentences but without conditions or supervision, or with stipulations but without assignment to a probation officer, are strategies worthy of our consideration. Even greater potential may lie in the increased use of fines in U.S. jurisdictions. Morris (1987) expresses amazement that this capitalist country does not make better use of fines. The European use of day fines as punishment, even for a poor individual, suggests an alternative to imprisonment that would seemingly fit very nicely with some American values. Of course, other American values lean more toward retribution and incapacitation via the tradition of imprisonment. But even in that area there are good ideas to be gleaned from other countries.

SUMMARY

This chapter's classification scheme relied on the use of imprisonment in countries throughout the world. The resulting incarceration rate provides one indication of a country's preference for incapacitation as a punishment philosophy. Working only with extreme cases to lessen the problems of definition and methodology, we considered the situation in countries with a high rate (Poland), a low rate (Japan), and one with a rate at the middle range (Australia). The Australian example was especially relevant to Americans, because we share some of Australia's correctional history (for example, receiving prisoners from England) and some contemporary problems (for example, intracountry variation and racially disproportionate incarceration rates).

Poland's high incarceration rate seems partially explained by its belief that positive change can be achieved in an institutional setting, but also by the relative absence of any infrastructure for community corrections. Japan, on the other hand, uses imprisonment rather infrequently but is also unlikely to use formal community corrections agencies. Instead, Japan seems to prefer informal sanctioning in the community setting, without relying on a bureaucratic structure.

The "Impact" section highlighted the growing importance of restorative justice ideals by showing their link to traditional practices in places like Saudi Arabia. The current global sharing of information about restorative justice is a good example of how comparative studies can provide countries with new ideas and practical suggestions.

WEB SITES TO VISIT

- The International Centre for Prison Studies provides an interactive site with data on prison systems and incarceration rates in over 200 countries. Check out the information at **www.kcl.ac.uk/depsta/rel/icps/worldbrief/world_ brief.html**
- The Australian Institute of Criminology provides links to many types of correctional statistics for Australia at **www.aic.gov.au/research/corrections/stats/index.html**
- Visit Japan's Ministry of Justice at **www.moj.go.jp/english/** to keep current with information and statistics from the Correction Bureau.
- The International Corrections and Prisons Association at **www.icpa.ca/home.html** has a variety of interesting information on corrections issues worldwide.

SUGGESTED READINGS

Cook, S., & Davies, S. (1999). *Harsh punishment: International experiences of women's imprisonment.* Boston: Northeastern University Press.

Hughes, Robert. (1987). The fatal shore. New York: Alfred A. Knopf.

Johnson, Elmer. (1996). Japanese corrections: Managing convicted offenders in an orderly society. Carbondale, IL: Southern Illinois University Press.

Parker, L. Craig, Jr. (1986). Parole and the community based treatment of offenders in Japan and the United States. New Haven, CT: University of New Haven Press.

Siemaszko, A., (Ed.). (2000). *Crime and law enforcement in Poland.* Warsaw, Poland: Institute of Justice & Oficyna Naukowa.

Weiss, Robert P. and South, Nigel. (Eds.). (1998). Comparing prison systems: Toward a comparative and international penology. Amsterdam: Gordon and Breach Publishers.

Chapter 9

An International Perspective on Juvenile Justice

KEY TOPICS

- Four models of juvenile justice
- The problem of juvenile offenders throughout the world
- The welfare model in Australia and New Zealand
- The legalistic model in Yugoslavia and Italy
- The corporatist model in England and Wales
- The participatory model in China

KEY TERMS

Children's Aid Panels
Children's Hearing
corporatist model
Family Group Conferencing
help and education teams
Juvenile Justice Teams
Juvenile Suspended Action Panels
Juvenile Liaison Bureau
la dottrina
legalistic model
parens patriae
participatory model
restorative justice
welfare model

COUNTRIES REFERENCED

Australia
China
Cuba
England and Wales
Fiji
Indonesia
Italy
New Zealand
Yugoslavia

On November 12, 1934, Charles Maddox was born out of wedlock to 16-year-old Kathleen Maddox in Cincinnati, Ohio. For the first several years of Charles's life, Kathleen would disappear for days and weeks at a time. Charles would ricochet between the homes of his grandmother and aunt. In 1939 Kathleen received a five-year penitentiary sentence after she and her brother were arrested for armed robbery in West Virginia. While his mom was "away," Charles stayed with an aunt and uncle until Kathleen's release. Then, back with his mother, Charles lived in run-down hotel rooms visited by a long line of "uncles" who, like his mother, drank heavily.

After a year with foster parents, Charles was sent for by Kathleen, who had moved to Indianapolis. Again, he received minimal attention and his mother continued to receive visits from a number of "uncles." In 1947 Kathleen tried unsuccessfully to place Charles with foster parents. Instead, Charles became a ward of the county and was sent to the Gibault Home for Boys in Terre Haute, Indiana. His stay at the home was not beneficial, as his record showed poor institutional adjustment, only a fair attitude toward school, moodiness, and a persecution complex. After 10 months, Charles ran away to his mother, but she rejected him.

Burglary and theft became part of Charles's life, and eventually he was sent to the Juvenile Center. After escaping, then being recaptured, he was placed at Father Flanagan's Boys Town. After only four days there, he stole a car and made it to Johnsonville, Iowa, with stops for two armed robberies along the way. After "training" from a friend's uncle, Charles tried burglary but was arrested in his second attempt. Now age 13, Charles went to the Indiana Boys School, where he ran away 18 times during his three-year stay. His nineteenth attempt was successful, but it was not escape from his final prison (Wooden, 1976, pp. 48–49).

Charles's story highlights the classic conflict confronting society's response to juveniles. With its inception in 1899, the juvenile court in America reflected a concern for the care, protection, and treatment of children. Eventually citizens expressed concern about the informal juvenile court as a violator of due process and called for greater attention to legal procedure. More recently the philosophy of "just deserts" questions the basic concept of a juvenile justice system geared toward treatment instead of punishment. Juveniles like Charles were sent, presumably with good intentions, to institutions that responded to youths who had been neglected (Charles at the time of his first stay) and delinquent (Charles at the time of his later stays).

One question Charles's case brings up is whether a social welfare or treatment orientation is the most desirable societal response to neglected or misbehaving children. Perhaps a more compassionate societal response would have prevented Charles from falling into a pattern of delinquent and criminal behavior. Accordingly, some would argue that the justice system should have the welfare and protection of the juvenile foremost in its process. On the other hand is the argument that the welfare and protection of society must be of predominant concern in the juvenile justice system. Hence, even kids like Charles, who have endured unfortunate circumstances, should be treated the same as any other offender when their behavior threatens society.

Both positions are reasonably argued. Sometimes a spectacular case influences a preference for one position. One fact not mentioned in the foregoing account of Charles is that several years after his birth, his mother married William

Manson, who adopted Charles and gave him his last name. The idea that the juvenile justice system should have expressed more concern about the care and protection of Charles Manson, than about the welfare of society as a whole is likely to send shivers up the back of people who remember the gruesome murders committed by Manson's "family" in 1969. It is just this type of philosophical difference now discussed throughout the world. What is the best way to respond to the "problem youth" of society?

Four models of juvenile justice are readily identified: the welfare model, the legalistic model, the corporatist model, and the participatory model. These models are taken from several sources (Binder, Geis & Dickson, 1988; Pratt, 1989; United Nations, 1985) and are used here to provide a categorization format to allow description and discussion. The principles of each model are not mutually exclusive, so we must be careful not to suggest that a country following one format will disagree with the tenets of the other schemes. We will review country-specific examples falling into each model but must first appreciate the problem that juvenile offenders present throughout the world.

DELINQUENCY AS A WORLDWIDE PROBLEM

In its report on juvenile justice around the world, the International Child Development Centre (1998) noted the difficulty in determining the extent of law violations by young people. Problems are presented by differing definitions of the ages that represent a juvenile, the variation in record keeping by countries, and differences in the types of acts counted as offenses. Despite such complications, reports suggest that delinquency is considered a problem—and often a growing problem—in most regions of the world. Many Central and Eastern European countries experienced sharp increases in juvenile offenses (although the recorded levels typically remain lower than those in Western Europe) during the 1990s as they moved toward a market economy. Similarly, rapid urbanization in Africa, Asia, and Latin America has produced situations of relative deprivation, isolation, and marginalization that contribute to economically motivated, non-violent offenses in many countries in those regions (International Child Development Centre, 1998). Adding to the problem in Latin America is a high proportion of juveniles (for example, 40 percent of Guatemalans are under age 15), which are among the groups hardest hit by economic problems in the region. The turn to crime by this large and economically deprived portion of the population is not unexpected.

Reports from the Arab region have indicated a less serious problem with juvenile delinquency, though the issue is still cause for concern in several of those nations (United Nations, 1990e). Prosperous countries like Saudi Arabia and the United Arab Emirates are experiencing more difficulty than other Arab countries. Their problems have been attributed to factors like the impact of migrants seeking employment, continued urbanization, sudden affluence and a rapidly changing economy, and a heterogeneous population.

The seemingly universal nature of delinquency has been commented upon by Hartjen and Kethineni, who suggest that current data support a position that "young people everywhere seem to engage in similar kinds of behavior with strikingly similar demographic distributions" (1996, p. 161). A 12-country study

You Should Know!

SIMILARITIES IN DELINQUENCY AROUND THE WORLD

Junger-Tas (1996), reporting results from an International Self-Report Delinquency Study in 12 countries, summarized the similarities in delinquency as follows:

- Boys, in all countries, are two to four times more likely than girls to commit violent offenses.
- Boys, in all countries are 1½ to 2 times more likely than girls to commit property offenses.
- The peak ages for committing particular crimes are similar in most countries. For example, 14–15 for vandalism, 16–17 for property crimes, 18–20 for violent crimes.
- `In all countries, there was less delinquent behavior when the relationship with parents was close.
- Parental supervision is a powerful predictor of delinquency in all the countries—the less supervision, the more delinquent behavior.

of self-reported delinquency also found remarkable similarity among the countries leading to at least the suspicion that "committing delinquent acts is part of growing up for western children" (Junger-Tas, 1996, p. 13).

Although crime by young people presents similar problems for countries throughout the world, the response by justice agencies varies significantly, with each country's response reflecting the history and culture of its citizens. Nevertheless, one consistent feature is the idea that young people should be responded to differently than adults. Perhaps the earliest recognition of this point was a thirteenth-century Norwegian penal code specifying that adult thieves should lose both hands but children only one (International Child Development Centre, 1998). Country differences appear in how young offenders are identified and how they are processed in different legal systems. But we should first look at some attempts to provide standards toward which any country should strive.

The Setting of International Standards

In trying to develop rules for the administration of juvenile justice, the United Nations (UN) has provided several documents to assist and encourage countries to respond to young offenders in a humanitarian manner. Four instruments are especially relevant:

- UN Standard Minimum Rules for the Administration of Juvenile Justice—1985 (commonly referred to as the *Beijing Rules,* after the location at which the rules were developed)
- UN Convention on the Rights of the Child—1989 (commonly referred to as the *CRC*)

- UN Guidelines for the Prevention of Juvenile Delinquency—1990 (commonly called the *Riyadh Guidelines*)
- UN Rules for the Protection of Juveniles Deprived of their Liberty—1990 (commonly called the *JDLs*)

These rules and guidelines set minimum standards for juvenile justice by providing fair trial guarantees and basic procedural safeguards (e.g., presumption of innocence, right to notification of charges, right to legal representation) and by promoting the desirability for rehabilitation and reintegration of the young person.

The Beijing Rules, the JDLs, and the Riyadh Guidelines are nonbinding instruments that do not carry any formal obligations for their implementation by countries. The CRC, like all UN conventions, is a binding document that requires all signing countries to abide by its standards in its national laws, procedures, and policies. By March 2000, 191 countries had ratified or acceded to the CRC (the United States is not among them).

When agreeing to the CRC, countries are allowed to note reservations they have regarding any of the provisions. This procedure provides countries with an opportunity to avoid abiding by certain provisions as long as a majority of the other signing nations make no objection to the reservations. For example, Australia, Canada, and several other countries registered reservations regarding separation of detained children from adults. Those countries generally accept the principle involved but maintain there are situations where separation is not feasible or could even be inappropriate. Several countries following Islamic law have made reservations regarding the application of the CRC when its articles are in conflict with the provisions of *Shari'a*. Germany and the Netherlands noted that minor offenses could be tried without legal assistance (International Child Development Centre, 1998). But despite the occasional reservation, the CRC stands as an important international document that provides minimum standards for handling young offenders and has encouraged countries around the world to recognize and respect the rights of children.

Determining Who Are Juveniles

One area of historical and cultural differences that makes it difficult to compare how countries respond to juvenile offenders lies in the definitions related to the term *juvenile*. Americans can appreciate the problem of varying definitions for the minimum age of criminal responsibility, because each of the 50 states can choose its own age limits. Actually, most states use 18 as the cutoff, so there is at least consensus if not uniformity. Of course, what appears to be agreement on that point conceals the dissension on other points. For example, there is considerable variation in how the states define the circumstances under which a juvenile's case can be heard in adult court (Reichel, 2001). In some jurisdictions, transfer to adult court is possible between the ages of 14 and 17, but in a few states a child of any age can be processed by the criminal courts. And there are other jurisdictions where the determining factor is the type of crime being charged, with more serious offenses being excluded from juvenile court jurisdiction.

The variation we see in how American states handle juveniles is a microcosm of the variation found in countries of the world. Table 9.1 shows the variation in determining ages of criminal responsibility in selected countries. In at least one country (Sri Lanka) children as young as age 6 can be held criminally responsible, but in other countries the person must be at least 15 or 16 years old. The age at which people are determined to have full adult responsibility for their actions is as low as 17 in some nations and as high as 20 in others, but age 18 seems to be a common cutoff point around the world.

Given such variation, it is understandable why the UN has been frustrated in its effort to define either a minimum age of criminal responsibility or the ages to which the juvenile justice standards should apply. Because some legal systems do not even recognize the concept of the age of criminal responsibility, the UN has settled for broad statements and general guidelines. Rule 4.1 of the Beijing Rules states,

> *In those legal systems recognizing the concept of the age of criminal responsibility for juveniles, the beginning of that age shall not be fixed at too low an age level, bearing in mind the facts of emotional, mental and intellectual maturity. (United Nations, 1986)*

Table 9.1 Age of Criminal Responsibility in Selected Countries

Country	Minimum Age of Responsibility	Age of Full Adult Responsibility
Sri Lanka	6	17
Kenya	7	18
New Zealand	10	18
Turkey	11	18
Canada	12	18
Israel	12	18
France	13	19
Austria	14	20
Japan	14	20
Denmark	15	18
Spain	16	18

Note: Ages are not always easily identified since most countries have special circumstances in which the age could be lower or higher. The table is, therefore, more indicative than definitive.

Sources: Adapted from International Child Development Centre. (1998). Juvenile Justice *Innocenti Digest,* Vol. 3. Florence Italy: UNICEF—United Nations Children's Fund; and S. Mukherjee and P. Reichel (1999), Bringing to justice. In G. Newman (Ed.), *Global report on crime and justice* (pp. 65–88; Box 3.4). New York: Oxford University Press.

One intention of this rule was to encourage countries where the age reached down to the level of infancy to raise that age so that the notion of responsibility would have more meaning.

Similar generalities are used in reference to the ages comprising "juveniles" or "children." Rule 2.2(a) of the Beijing Rules states,

> *[A] juvenile is a child or young person who, under the respective legal systems, may be dealt with for an offence in a manner which is different from an adult. (United Nations, 1986)*

That is not a particularly helpful description, but it serves the UN's goal of inclusion by making sure that a broad collection of countries will determine it is possible for them to abide by the standards regardless of a country's specific definition for juvenile.

Determining the Process

The variation among countries regarding what age distinction will orient the justice system is repeated when attention turns to the procedures used to handle juveniles. The various international standards and guidelines are purposely imprecise when describing the appropriate philosophy or rationale that should direct a country's juvenile justice system. The provisions do agree that rehabilitation and reintegration of the juvenile should be given greater weight than is punishment. Consistent with that philosophy, the CRC and the Beijing Rules include specific restrictions (e.g., offenders who committed their crime while a child cannot be sentenced to death) and requirements (e.g., detention and imprisonment of a child shall occur only as a last resort and even then should be for the shortest appropriate time).

The Beijing Rules encourage the use of diversion from the formal court system for all but the most serious of young offenders. The Riyadh Guidelines consider much of youthful offending to be simply part of the maturation process and as such to require a supportive response by society that encourages behavioral change and fosters reintegration in the community. These responses suggest—even if they don't require—a particular type of juvenile justice system, and that point brings us back to the models of juvenile justice noted earlier in the chapter.

MODELS OF JUVENILE JUSTICE

It is reasonable to suspect that the four major legal traditions would each produce a subsystem for handling juvenile offenders. Things are not that simple. In fact, there is often considerable variation among countries in the same legal family regarding their response to, and even definition of, delinquents. In the common law tradition alone, we find countries emphasizing treatment (for example, Australia), justice (for example, South Africa), or administrative efficiency (for example, England and Wales). It is also important to note that juvenile justice models, like legal traditions themselves, undergo change over the years. A country's preference for a treatment approach to juveniles may be exchanged for a "get-tough" approach if citizens start demanding that change.

The four models reviewed here (see Figure 9.1) should be considered classification aids allowing for description and discussion of approaches to juvenile justice. The countries used to exemplify each model will likely have aspects of the other types as well, and at some other point in time may even have been a prime example of another model. For present purposes, though, we can use these countries as fair examples of either a welfare, legalistic, participatory, or corporatist model.

Welfare Model

The development of America's juvenile justice system was built on the doctrine of *parens patriae,* meaning that the state is obliged to serve as guardian over children who are in such adverse conditions that their health and/or basic law-abiding nature may be in jeopardy. As a result of this *welfare model* of juvenile justice, the juvenile court had jurisdiction over young people who were dependent or neglected (protection of the juvenile's health) or who had violated the penal code (protection of the juvenile's law-abiding nature). This emphasis on the child's general well-being is at the heart of the welfare model (see Table 9.2). Australia and New Zealand provide contemporary examples of the welfare model in action.

Australia. Australia has been at the forefront in juvenile justice since the nineteenth century when 1895 legislation in the state of South Australia established separate courts for trying young people. The motivation was to avoid subjecting young offenders to the stigma of being tried in an adult court (Cunneen & White, 1995). By 1918 all six Australian states had established Children's Courts with jurisdiction over both criminal matters (juvenile offenders) and welfare matters (neglected children). Despite their separate standing, Australian Children's Courts have never been as different from adult courts as have been their American counterparts. Although the Children's Courts have certainly portrayed a welfare model (tempered today with the justice model), Australia's use of diversion and community programs is the point to be emphasized in our discussion.

The primary techniques for informal handling of juvenile offenders in many Australian states have been Children's Aid Panels, Juvenile Suspended Action Panels, Community Justice Panels, and, most recently, Family Group Conferencing, police cautions, and Juvenile Justice Teams. The states of South Australia and Western Australia provide good examples of these techniques.

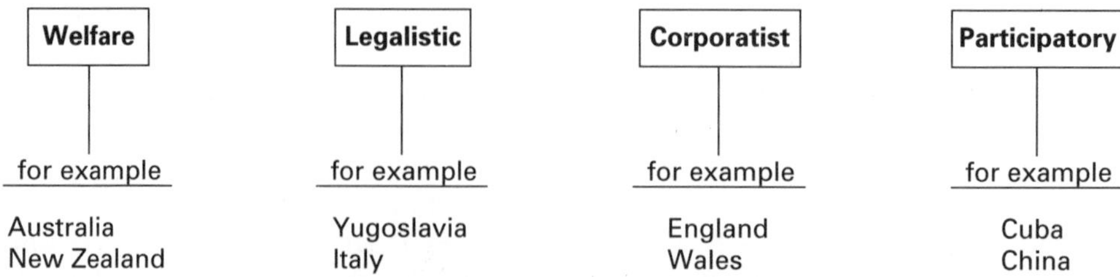

Figure 9.1 Models of Juvenile Justice

Table 9.2 Four Juvenile Justice Models Compared

	Welfare	Legalistic	Corporatist	Participatory
Key Personnel	Child-care experts	Lawyers	Administrators and bureaucrats	Community members
Use of Formal Process	Partial; prefers nonjudicial process	Full	Partial; prefers nonjudicial process	Scarce; prefers extralegal process
Prime Objective	Protection and well-being of the juvenile is emphasized, with treatment taking priority over due process.	Due process and formal action take priority over treatment, since the emphasis is on applying the law.	Emphasis is on operating an effective juvenile justice system with increased efficiency and decreased delays.	Education of all citizens and the full integration of misbehaving youth into law-abiding society are emphasized.

Prior to the early 1990s, the basic principle underlying legislation for juveniles in South Australia and Western Australia was a concern for the protection and welfare of the child. Initial legislation in the 1960s and 1970s accomplished this welfare-oriented approach by sending troubled youth through a system of successive filters consisting of the nonjudicial Children's Aid Panels, through the Children's Courts, and to community-based intervention and residential care facilities. The Children's Aid Panels were a particularly good example of the welfare approach and as such they deserve brief attention.

The Children's Aid Panels were established in South Australia in 1971 as a nonjudicial alternative to court action that would (1) support and help the child and family, (2) provide an opportunity for growth and development within the family and community, and (3) provide consistency and uniformity in handling youths in a flexible manner (Sarri & Bradley, 1980). The Western Australia version, called a Juvenile Suspended Action Panel, was first established in Perth in 1964. Both types of panels handled first offenders who were accused of fairly minor offenses. The police had an important role in determining whether a juvenile would go before a panel or the juvenile court. Arrested youths were sent directly to the juvenile court for processing, but if the police did not make an arrest they could refer the youth to a local panel. The panels consisted of a police officer and a welfare worker. The welfare worker would invite the youth and his or her parents to attend a meeting and if the parents or child refused, or if the youth denied the charges, the matter would be sent to the juvenile court. If the parties agreed, a panel meeting would be held and some sanction would be determined that everyone could accept.

In a 1992 report to the South Australian Parliament, the Children's Aid Panels were criticized as compromising individual rights in exchange for other advantages and for not having any opportunity for victim involvement in the process (McInnes & Hetzel, 1996). The report also expressed concern about the disproportionate number of Aboriginal children appearing before Children's Aid Panels and cited statistics that suggested the panels might not be effective in deterring children brought before them from further crime. As a result of the report, the panels were abolished in South Australia with the Young Offenders Act of 1993. Western Australia legislators had similar concerns and the Young Offenders Act of 1994 provided a complete revision of that state's juvenile justice process.

Legislators in both states seemed to like the idea of diversion that Children's Aid Panels provided—it was the lack of due process they had problems with. The new Young Offenders Acts in both South Australia and Western Australia provide greater opportunities for protection of the juvenile's rights, and some may even argue that these Australian jurisdictions are now more accurately an example of the legalistic model rather than the welfare model. However, keeping in mind the earlier warning about the nonexclusivity of the four models, we can still see that the procedures in Australia seem to have a welfare focus. Support for that argument is seen in the legislative recognition that misbehavior is part of growing up and by showing that sanctions handed down in Children's Courts are less harsh than they are for adults (Atkinson, 1997). Also, we find continued use of diversion programs in these as well as other Australian jurisdictions.

As Australian states searched for diversion programs that did not so obviously ignore due process rights of juveniles, they found three programs especially intriguing:

1. Police cautioning—wherein police require a young offender to complete community service work, make apologies, and abide by certain limits (e.g., curfews).
2. Family Group Conferencing (discussed later in reviewing procedures in New Zealand).
3. Juvenile Justice Teams.

Police cautioning and Family Group Conferencing are especially popular in South Australia (Atkinson, 1997; McInnes & Hetzel, 1996), but the Juvenile Justice Teams in Western Australia provide a particularly interesting modification of the earlier Aid Panels.

Juvenile Justice Teams were conceived in the early 1990s as a different way to handle young people who had committed minor offenses or were in the early stages of offending (Ministry of Justice, 1999). The teams idea was especially appealing to officials because it provided for victim participation—something the Children's Aid Panels did not do. Young offenders are sent to the teams by the police or by the Children's Court (see Figure 9.2). In 1997–1998, 15 percent of the charges filed in Children's Court were referred to a Juvenile Justice Team (Policy and Legislation Division, 2000). Upon referral offenders can choose to go through a mediation process and face the victims of their crime or can have the matter dealt with in court. If the mediation process is chosen, offenders must accept responsibility for their actions—otherwise the matter is referred to court.

The team consists of the offender and his or her family, the victim and family members, police, and a juvenile justice officer. Other people, such as a representative from the juvenile's school or an Aboriginal community, may also be

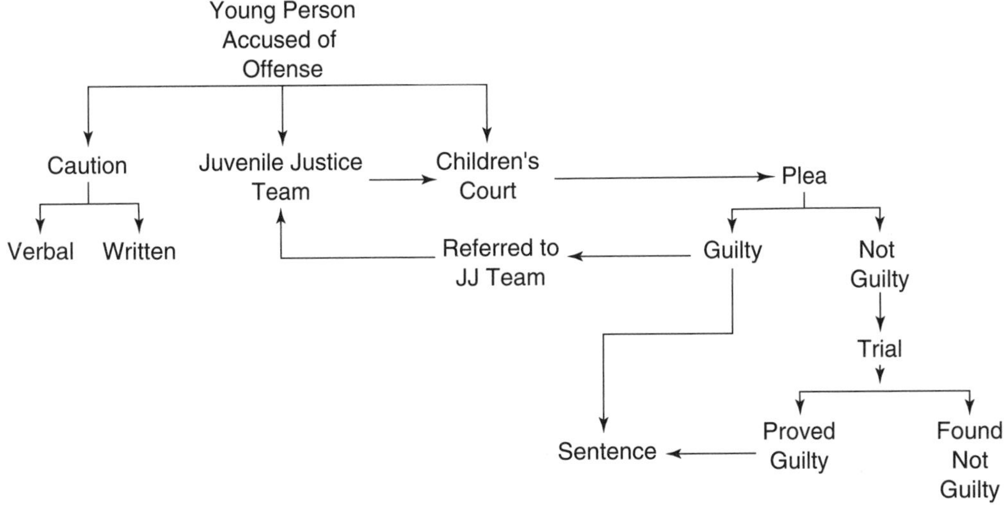

Figure 9.2 Juvenile Justice System in Western Australia. *Source:* Adapted from Children's Court (December 11, 1998). Overview of juvenile system. Available at **www.justice.wa.gov.au/division/courts/childjust.htm** (Accessed November 28, 2000).

present. At the meeting, all participants work out and agree upon an action plan for the young offender. That plan could be something as simple as a formal apology or could require community work or a monetary payment. Even family action is possible, like being grounded as part of the plan. Failure to comply with the action plan requires the matter to be referred to the formal court system. If the offender completes all conditions of the plan, the matter is disposed of and no conviction is recorded (Ministry of Justice, 1999).

The Ministry of Justice (1999) in Western Australia reports that since the teams were established, there has been a dramatic reduction in the number of young offenders involved in the justice system and a significant reduction in the number of cases processed by the courts. Victims, offenders, and parents all report high levels of satisfaction with the process.

New Zealand. The Australian use of teams provides a good example of diversion tactics that emphasize the welfare approach, but the continued presence of a formal Children's Court means the Australian system is still rather traditional. In New Zealand, the welfare model does not simply provide court alternatives but actually modifies the entire procedure for responding to youths. New Zealand's orientation toward juvenile justice stresses the well-being of children and the empowerment of families and young people. An important aspect of this approach is the use of restorative-justice principles.

Restorative justice is a penal philosophy that seeks to restore the victim, offender, and community to a position of balance that was upset by the offender's action. Restoring that balance might mean replacing or repairing property but especially refers to restoring a sense of security. The restoration and reparation is typically accomplished with conflict-resolution tactics rather than in a traditional courtroom setting. Especially popular with proponents of restorative justice are victim-offender mediation techniques.

Umbreit (1996) identified mediation programs operating in at least some jurisdictions of 11 countries. In two other countries, Austria and New Zealand, victim-offender mediation is available in all jurisdictions. The New Zealand version, especially as it applies to juvenile offenders, is our concern.

In 1989 New Zealand enacted legislation that dramatically altered the way it responded to youth crime—which, in New Zealand, refers to persons under age 17. Specifically, the family, including extended family members, was established as the locus for authority and expertise on matters of juvenile delinquency. The philosophy orienting the legislation is clearly restorative in nature because it emphasizes young offenders paying for their wrongdoing in an appropriate way. In addition, it involves families of both offenders and victims in a decision-making process resulting in solutions that help restore the lost balance. The specific format used to implement the philosophy is the Family Group Conference (FGC).

The FGC is unusual in that it plays a role in both the informal and formal systems used to process young offenders (Belgrave, 1996; Morris & Maxwell, 1993). In the informal process, police have a Youth Justice Coordinator convene an FGC without any referral to the court. If the FGC agrees about what should be done, and the youth completes the plan, the matter never proceeds to court. If agreement is not achieved, or if the FGC believes the offender should be handled formally, the police can refer the case to court.

When the police have actually arrested the young person, the formal system is initiated. If the charge is not denied, the judge directs a Youth Justice Coordinator to convene an FGC. When the charge is denied, the case proceeds to a court hearing. If the charge is proved at the hearing, the court must order an FGC and consider the outcome of that conference prior to sentencing the youth (Belgrave, 1996). In other words, at every turn in the handling of youthful offenders, the FGC has a role to play.

The FGC is composed of family members, police officials, the Youth Justice Coordinator, the offender, and the victim (or the victim's representative). The coordinator may also ask a social worker and a legal advocate for the offender to join the conference (Morris & Maxwell, 1993). Neither victims nor offenders are required to attend the conference, although conferences rarely proceed without the offender in attendance. The proceedings can result in one of only two outcomes: (1) all FGC participants must agree to the plan or recommendation, or (2) the matter must be referred to the youth court.

A specific goal of the New Zealand legislation was to increase the victim's involvement in the justice process. Morris and Maxwell (1993) and Belgrave (1996) suggest that goal has not been achieved because less than half of the FGCs had victims or victim representatives in attendance. Furthermore, many victims (40 percent) reported being dissatisfied with the outcome (Morris & Maxwell, 1993). This situation is undesirable, and New Zealand is attempting to improve victim satisfaction, but the restorative philosophy and the FGC procedure are clearly New Zealand's preferred way to respond to youthful offenders.

You Should Know!

FAMILY GROUP CONFERENCING

Maxwell and Morris (1993) describe a typical Family Group Conference as progressing through these steps:

- Introductions
- An explanation of the procedure by the coordinator
- A summary of offense facts by the police
- An opportunity for the offender to comment on the accuracy of the police statement
- An opportunity for victims (or representatives) to present their views if the offender admits the offense
- A general discussion of possible outcomes
- A discussion of options among the offender's family
- The formulation of a plan, response, or outcome by the offender's family
- General negotiation
- Agreement from the police and victim
- Recording of the agreed plan and closure of the meeting

Legalistic Model

The legalistic approach to juvenile justice emphasizes applying the law over treating the juvenile (see Table 9.2). This strategy is not necessarily less humanitarian than the welfare model; it simply stresses when and how the law is used if a juvenile is involved. Indonesia provides an extreme example of this approach, because its penal code does not yet provide for any juvenile court structure (Committee on the Rights of the Child, 1994a; United Nations, 1990d). Instead, Indonesian juveniles are granted certain privileges within the framework of the adult criminal justice system. In this manner, juveniles are accorded all the due process rights of adult offenders. However, unfortunate results of this policy include the mixed occupancy of penal facilities by juveniles and adults and the difficulty of providing discretionary justice for youthful offenders.

More typical examples of a legalistic model are offered by Yugoslavia and Italy. Both countries recognize the important role for treatment of juveniles, but each relies on a criminal justice model for dealing with young offenders.

Yugoslavia. Since the dissolution of the Socialist Federal Republic of Yugoslavia, there has been controversy and conflict regarding the geographic boundaries and official status of the former Yugoslav republics. The United States recognizes the Republic of Bosnia and Herzegovina, the Republic of Croatia, the Republic of Slovenia, and the Former Yugoslav Republic of Macedonia (the name being used until differences over the name are resolved). In 1992 the republics of Serbia and Montenegro proclaimed a new "Federal Republic of

Yugoslavia." The United States takes the position that after the Socialist Federal Republic of Yugoslavia dissolved, none of the successor republics, including Serbia and Montenegro, represents its continuation. The UN, on the other hand, has granted independent UN membership to Bosnia and Herzegovina, Croatia, Slovenia, and to the Former Yugoslav Republic of Macedonia. Yugoslavia (Serbia and Montenegro) was suspended from participation in the UN General Assembly in 1992, but it retains UN membership. For our purposes, the Federal Republic of Yugoslavia (Serbia and Montenegro) provides material for discussion of Yugoslavia's juvenile justice approach.

The first indication of the legal nature of Yugoslavia's juvenile justice system is the specification of offenses and age categories under court jurisdiction. Judicial intervention occurs only if the juvenile commits an offense defined by the Criminal Code (Committee on the Rights of the Child, 1994b). That means that petty offenses like minor traffic violations and public disorder are exempted from court control. Neither does the Criminal Code contain anything like the "status offenses" of America. In other words, the Yugoslavian court hears cases only when the young person has committed an act that would have been a crime if committed by an adult. This does not mean that Yugoslavia lacks concern about the other forms of juvenile misbehavior, but the working assumption is that "agencies other than the courts should deal with minors who have manifested their deviance, not by committing a criminal offense, but by other kinds of deviant behavior" (Selih, 1978, p. 112).

Just as the court deals with specific offenses, it also has a particular clientele. Court jurisdiction does not begin until the minor has reached age 14. In fact, no court deals with a child under 14. People 14 to 16 at the time of the offense are "younger minors" and are the first age category heard by the court. Offenders in this age category can be responded to only through corrective measures. "Older minors" are 16 to 18 years old and may receive an additional penalty of imprisonment (Committee on the Rights of the Child, 1994b).

Probably the most obvious aspect of Yugoslavia's legalistic approach is the absence of a separate juvenile court. Juveniles therefore receive the same protection given adults. There are, however, special sections for juveniles in the court systems, and a section on "Treatment of Minors" in the criminal procedure code provides special proceedings to accommodate minors (United Nations, 1990d).

Only public prosecutors can initiate proceedings against a minor between 14 and 18 years of age. They have the discretion to dismiss a case against the juvenile during pretrial proceedings. Selih (1978) says this might be done upon the prosecutor's belief that the minor's personal traits, past conduct, and circumstances of the offense warrant dismissal. In addition, minor cases also may be dropped. Making this determination requires significant data collection about the juvenile's personality, family background, school performance, and the like. As in America's version of the medical model, more importance is theoretically attached to the offender than to the offense. While officials compile the social history, juveniles may be held in a reception center, correctional institution, released to their parents' custody, or placed with another family (Committee on the Rights of the Child, 1994b).

If the prosecutor decides to proceed with the case, the judge makes plans for either a main trial or a session of the juvenile panel. The main trial, from which the public is excluded, is handled by the same judge who heard the pretrial proceedings. The goal of that requirement is to increase the judge's understanding of the history of the case and characteristics of the juvenile. The purpose of the trial is to prove that the accused juvenile was the offender, and to introduce the already gathered social information about the juvenile's rehabilitation and society's protection. Less often used is the Juvenile Panel, which has a judge (as chairperson) and two lay judges (assessors) experienced in working with youth.

The Yugoslav Criminal Code provides two special responses for dealing with juveniles: noninstitutional measures and juvenile imprisonment. The *noninstitutional approaches* are closely linked to educational measures. One is the reprimand, used for cases not needing extended care. As the first measure typically applied, critics complain about its frequent use and its lack of any special effect (Selih, 1978). Commitment to a disciplinary center for minors for several hours per day over a one-month period is another noninstitutional measure. The final one is strict supervision in the community. That supervision can be assigned to parents, to a foster family, or to social agencies, and will last between one and three years.

Four kinds of *institutional measures* are possible:

1. Commitment to an educational institution
2. Commitment to an educational reformatory home
3. Commitment to an institution for defective minors
4. Juvenile imprisonment

The educational institutions are divided between those housing neglected children under age 14, and others housing minors over age 14. Educational reformatories receive delinquent minors, whereas institutions for defective minors house the handicapped, mentally ill, and physically underdeveloped.

In principle, juvenile imprisonment is close to the philosophy of educational measures. This sanction is used only for senior minors found guilty of an offense that could gain an adult more than five years of strict imprisonment. During their imprisonment (sentences range from one to ten years), the minors undergo reeducation and receive vocational training.

Italy. The Italian penal code requires people to be at least 14 years old before they can be held criminally responsible for an act. For offenders of 14 to 18 years of age, the court must determine intent and capacity to understand—both of which must also be considered with respect to the alleged offense, the circumstances in which it took place, and the minor's personality (Committee on the Rights of the Child, 1995b).

Consistent with the civil legal tradition, the Italian legal system is not comfortable with giving a single judge wide discretionary power. As a result, Italy hesitated to follow the lead of early juvenile justice models (like that of the United States) giving one judge, operating outside the traditional due process procedures, considerable discretion in handling youthful offenders. This did not mean that Italy failed to recognize a need for differential response to juvenile offenders of the criminal code. In fact, as early as the thirteenth century, Italian cities were declaring children immune from punishment for murder and providing for their placement in houses of correction instead of prisons (Lemert, 1986).

Despite its early start, Italy was among the last of the Western European nations to set up a juvenile court. This 1934 formal achievement was preceded by developments like the 1929 creation of special sections in the Courts of Appeal that provided prosecutors with instruction and judgment on juvenile cases. Also, 1930 brought a penal code revision that raised the age of minimum responsibility from 9 to 14 while lowering the age of full responsibility from 21 to 18. The 1934 law solidified these prior actions and gave the new juvenile court jurisdiction over youths who were shown to have strayed and be in need of correction. Additional changes were made in 1977 that gave local authorities more control over the way juveniles were treated by the system, prompting increased use of community intervention and small group homes (Committee on the Rights of the Child, 1995b). The current system operates under modifications implemented in 1989.

Lemert (1986) argues that the formal establishment of an Italian juvenile court presented an intriguing conflict that continues today. Italy holds strongly to a belief in a strict interpretation of the law and a presumption that similar offenses require similar penalties. At the same time there is an understanding that some informality is desirable when responding to youths and that some individualization of penalty may be appropriate for them. The result is an awkward alliance between legality's consistency and individualization's variability. The provisions for juvenile procedures that were implemented in 1989 provide juvenile court judges with more options for handling defendants under age 18, but the context of legality remains. The resulting mixture provides Italy with a juvenile justice system offering formal rigidity tempered by informal adaptability.

Formally, Italian juvenile justice requires strict procedural legality in criminal justice for both minors and adults. The preliminary investigation is headed by a magistrate of the Juvenile Court. That magistrate is responsible for ensuring a proper and timely investigation and for safeguarding the suspect's rights. The preliminary hearing is conducted by one professional magistrate and two lay magistrates (one man and one woman). The accused is allowed to have the preliminary hearing regarded as definitive, in which case the accused is entitled to a one-third reduction in sentence (Gatti & Verde, 1997). This procedure is the closest a minor can come to having a plea bargain. In the context of the preliminary hearing the magistrate can decide to (1) hand the minor over for trial, (2) place the youth on probation, (3) apply community sanctions, or (4) rule that there are no grounds for prosecution.

When a trial occurs, the case is prosecuted by the public prosecutor attached to the juvenile court and is held, usually in private, in the juvenile court setting. The accused is questioned directly by the magistrate and, to avoid upsetting the minor, no cross examination takes place. The 1989 procedures require that specific rules be followed in juvenile court and that the court must explain to every young defendant the significance of the proceedings and the content and grounds for the court's decision.

During the criminal proceedings against minors, the prosecutor and magistrate are required to obtain information about the juvenile's personal, family, and social circumstances as well as relevant financial resources and background. This information is used to determine first if the juvenile can be charged, then the extent to which he or she is responsible, and finally to ascertain the appropriate penalty. Because these are criminal proceedings, with procedural modifications for the accused's age, the court can impose any penalty that would be applicable to an adult (with considerable discretion for reductions) as well as penalties designed specifically for minors (Gatti & Verde, 1997). Two of the specific penalties for juveniles include a judicial pardon and suspension of the trial with imposition of probation. Imprisonment is also a sentencing option, but it is typically reduced to one third of what an adult would receive and is served in special prisons for juveniles. The juvenile may be conditionally released prior to completion of the sentence.

Within this context of legality there remain some opportunities for informality (Committee on the Rights of the Child, 1995b; Gatti & Verde, 1997). For example, when an offense is not serious and is out of character, the judge can dismiss the case so as not to interfere with the young person's education or rehabilitation. Dismissal would occur only after the judge had conferred in chambers with the minor, the people exercising parental authority, and the victim. This informal option is available only at the discretion of the magistrate operating in the context of the prescribed legal procedures—and that is why Italy remains a good example of the legalistic model even with some modifications that suggest a greater concern for the offender's welfare.

The welfare and legalistic models of juvenile justice present the horns of a dilemma. If the legalistic approach seems to lack compassion and flexibility, the welfare approach may go to another extreme in lack of concern for legal protection. When speaking of the Scottish system, Martin expresses concern about "welfare totalitarianism, in which we take control of people's lives and liberties with no better justification than the belief that we know what is best for them" (1978, p. 86). Accordingly, some countries have tried to balance the desirable aspects of the legalistic and welfare models. One such attempt has resulted in what Pratt (1989) calls the corporatist approach, discussed next.

Corporatist Model

It is possible that conflict between the welfare and legalistic models could lead to a symbiotic relationship wherein the goals of each are reached through cooperation by various institutions in a country. In fact, we might argue that some countries have the cultural and bureaucratic base to achieve a success of this type. Unfortunately, just when a solution between conflicting issues seems within grasp, another variable often presents itself. This seems to be the situation giving rise to our third model of juvenile justice: corporatism.

England and Wales seemed well on the way to combining the welfare and legalistic approaches in their juvenile justice systems. In fact, Binder et al. (1988) offer these countries as examples of a combined approach. A problem with this example is suggested by Pratt (1989) when he draws attention to the importance England and Wales have given to a "justice model" of juvenile justice since the early 1970s. An important part of the justice model is increased attention to due process, right to counsel, visible and accountable decision making, and other procedures typically linked to the legalistic model. Yet the justice model goes beyond the legalistic approach, because it also requires punishment of the juvenile offender. In this manner, the public's interest in seeing juveniles get their "just deserts" is the new variable making difficult the combination of welfare and legalistic approaches.

The movement from a welfare orientation to a legalistic one, with the additional concern for punishment, provided England and Wales with a new juvenile justice approach best described as *corporatism* (see Pratt, 1989). Before explaining the meaning of this term, it will be helpful to review the developmental path that juvenile justice followed in this part of the United Kingdom.

In 1908 England and Wales established separate courts for juvenile law violators of ages 7 to 16. These courts were actually special sittings of Magistrates' Courts held at a separate place or at a different time from adult hearings (Marshall, 1978). Besides those criminal duties, the juvenile courts had civil jurisdiction in cases of neglected or destitute children. Over the years, the initial English reaction to youths has become more specific and well defined. In 1933 the minimum age for criminal responsibility increased to 8 years, and a system of" approved schools" developed to treat juveniles between ages 10 and 17. A 1963 act encouraged diversion of young offenders from the juvenile courts and again raised the age of responsibility—this time from age 8 to age 10 (Binder et al., 1988). The Children's Act of 1989 made the child's welfare the paramount consideration in any proceeding under that act, and legislation in the 1990s continued to refine the procedures for young offenders.

The Crime and Disorder Act 1998 (CDA) provides the current structure for juvenile justice in England and Wales. One of its primary changes is the abolition of a three-category division for handling minors. Prior to the CDA, minors under age 10 were considered incapable of committing a criminal act; those at ages 10 to 13 were not regarded as criminally responsible if it could be proved that they were psychologically not an adult in their criminal act; and those older than age 13 were considered fully liable but subject to different procedures and punishment. With the implementation of the CDA, a person is considered criminally responsible from age 10 onward. There is no longer any "maybe" stage where minors aged 10 to 13 could be found to lack criminal responsibility. Although people from age 10 through age 17 now have responsibility for their acts, the justice system still provides special procedures and penalties for offenders in that age category.

The steps to appearance in Youth Court begin with options available to the police. If the police decide some type of formal action is needed, the type of action depends on the stance taken by the youth. If the young person admits the offense, the police can refer him or her to the local Youth Offending Team—a program explained later. If the offense is denied by the youth, the police must either drop the case or try to prove it in court by filing criminal charges.

If the case goes to court it will be heard by a Magistrates' Court sitting as a Youth Court. That means the regular Magistrates' Court is configured to three (sometimes two) magistrates hearing the case and deciding guilt or innocence. When sitting as a Youth Court, the Magistrates' Court is closed to the public. The young person should be accompanied by a parent and may also have a lawyer present to either defend the case or to make explanations to the court. Other people present in court might include victims or members of the Youth Offending Team (YOT). The importance of those team members requires us to consider them in greater depth.

A desire to have juveniles take responsibility for their behavior was a key factor in the development of the CDA. To assist the young person in recognizing,

In the News

PUNISHING PARENTS

Have you ever wondered why parents are not punished for their misbehaving children? Actually, there have been occasions when juvenile court judges have imposed sanctions on parents, but such actions are unusual in American juvenile courts. It was also unusual in British youth courts, until the Crime and Disorder Act 1998 created the Parenting Order (see section 8-10). Implemented nationwide in June 2000, this order can be imposed by a court on a parent or guardian of

- Juveniles (10–17 years old) who are convicted of an offense
- Children of 10 and older who are made subject to an antisocial-behavior order or a sex-offender order
- Children under 10 who are made subject to a child-safety order.

Without getting into the specifics of the various "orders" (e.g., the antisocial order is applied to persons who harass other people and is intended to prevent continued harassment), the parenting order is a way to sanction parents and guardians of misbehaving young people.

The parenting order has two elements. First, the parent is required to attend counseling or guidance sessions for up to three months and not more than once per week where they receive help in dealing with their children. They might learn, for example, about setting and enforcing consistent standards for behavior for their children. Second, the court appoints a responsible officer (e.g., a social worker, probation officer, or Youth Offending Team member) to supervise the requirements of the order. Failure to comply with the terms of the parenting order is considered a criminal offense and could result in the parent being fined up to £1000 (about $1500).

The parenting orders are too new to have been properly evaluated, but pilot programs operating prior to full implementation in 2000 led the National Association for the Care and Resettlement of Offenders (2000) to rather optimistic reviews. The parenting-skills courses seemed to provide opportunities to improve parenting skills and to reduce family break-up. Parental control over children seemed to improve, and that in turn led to improved behavior and reduced offending by the children. However, there were concerns about the forced nature of the orders and the association expressed a preference for involving parents on a voluntary basis. It will be interesting to see what results are found when the parenting orders undergo a rigorous evaluation.

then taking, responsibility the CDA requires concerted effort on the part of many people and agencies. Key among those is the YOT.

Each county in both England and Wales has a YOT, which is a multi-agency grouping that has at a minimum, a social worker, a probation officer, a police officer, an education officer, and a health official. When appropriate, people from other agencies may also be included. Coordination of the YOTs at a national level is accomplished by the 10- to 12-member Youth Justice Board. Despite that national-level coordination, the YOTs are clearly decentralized, and management is at the local authority level. Local decisions are made on issues like arranging for and appointing a team manager, developing a youth justice plan appropriate for the local area, and arranging for resources available to the YOT. The YOT is responsible for providing pre-court and court services, as well as community supervision related to any type of community sanction. It is also charged with working to prevent children and young people from offending in the first place (Home Office, 1998).

In addition to providing a new mechanism for processing and supervising youthful offenders, the CDA (and the Youth Justice and Criminal Evidence Act 1999) also established some new sanctions—called *orders*—in Britain. A brief review of some of these orders provides an idea about the types of sentences available for young offenders:

- **Reparation Order.** Along with the Referral and Action Plan Orders, the Reparation Order is designed to tackle youth offending through positive intervention and in accordance with the principles of restorative justice. Under a Reparation Order the young offender must make a specified non-financial reparation, taking no longer than 24 total hours to complete, to a victim or to the community at large (*Crime and Disorder Act 1998;* §67). Activities, which are supervised by a probation officer, social worker, or YOT member, might include a written or verbal apology to the victim, cleaning graffiti, weeding the victim's garden, or doing other things that attempt to repair the damage done or are of service to the community.
- **Action Plan Order.** These orders, which last for three months, involve a short but intense program wherein the offender and his or her parents tackle the cause of offending. Each action plan is tailored to the individual's needs and may include requirements to participate in certain activities, attend specific meetings, avoid particular places, or complying with special requirements (National Association for the Care and Resettlement of Offenders, 1999).
- **Referral Order.** These orders were being piloted in 2000 and were expected to be available in all courts in England and Wales by 2002 or 2003 (Juvenile Offenders Unit, 2000). The Referral Order, which lasts from three to twelve months depending on the seriousness of the offense, is designed especially for first offenders. The youths are referred to a YOT panel that provides an opportunity for them to recognize the consequences of their acts and to become involved in a program designed to prevent further offending. The panel is comprised of YOT members, people from the local community, the youth's parents, and—if they wish—the victims. Even teachers or social workers may be asked to attend, but legal representation

is not allowed. When a program (e.g., counseling, volunteer work, school attendance) for the offender to follow is agreed upon, the YOT monitors the youth's compliance. Successful program completion results in sentence completion, but failure to comply with the program brings the youth back before the court for a new sentence.

- **Detention and Training Order.** Recognizing that some acts by young offenders will still require a custodial sentence, the CDA (§73) provides that persons at least 10 years old but not yet age 18 at the time of conviction, can be sentenced to a period of secure detention. The Detention and Training Orders (DTOs) can be for a period of 4, 6, 8, 10, 12, 18, or 24 months. Ten and 11-year-olds can receive a DTO only if they are found to be persistent offenders from whom the public needs protection. It is left to the courts to decide what constitutes "persistent." Offenders age 12 through 14 may receive a DTO if the court finds them to be persistent offenders of acts that would have justified custody under the 1989 Children's Act. A DTO for offenders age15 through 17 is possible when they commit any offense for which an adult could be imprisoned. The institution at which the DTO is served can be a training center, a young-offender institution, a youth treatment center, or any other secure facility.

Other sanctions, like probation orders or community service orders, are also available, but they do not differ in significant ways from American versions and do not need explanation here. It is apparent that the general thrust of the most recent legislation has been an emphasis on restorative justice and attempts to hold the young offenders responsible for their actions. Custody is clearly possible and, at least for youths age 12–17, can be accomplished rather easily when offenses are serious and recurring. The resulting range of sanctions provides England and Wales with an interesting combination of "just deserts" and restorative-justice principles that can be referred to as a corporatist approach toward juvenile justice.

Corporatism is a tendency found in advanced welfare societies when society itself creates social institutions that accept the duties and responsibilities formerly held by the government. As a process, corporatism can occur in particular areas, such as, according to Pratt (1989), the juvenile justice system, without affecting all of society's institutions simultaneously. From this position, Pratt posits that juvenile justice in England and Wales has moved from a welfare approach to what he calls corporatism, meaning a tendency to reduce conflict and disruption through "centralization of policy, increased government intervention, and the cooperation of various professional and interest groups into a collective whole with homogeneous aims and objectives" (1989, p. 245). As evidence, Pratt points to the increased administrative discretion encouraged by the various diversion programs in England and Wales. Movement of decision making from the courts to the administrative agencies increases efficiency and decreases delay, so the juvenile justice system can operate more effectively (see Table 9.2).

Even with the legislative changes in the late 1990s, corporatism remains an appropriate description of the system in England and Wales. The YOT, through its multi-agency cooperation, is a good example of cooperation among various professionals, and the Youth Justice Board clearly provides a centralized policy.

As administrative discretion grows, so too do the extralegal sanctions available to these agencies. Minor breaches by juveniles in community programs can be handled by the program staff without requiring appearance before the juvenile court. Social workers and other treatment personnel, who were already coopted into the welfare approach's adjudication and decision-making process, are now involved in constructing and devising the penalty itself.

Even more so than the welfare model, corporatism relies on members of the community to assist in meeting the needs of youthful offenders. In both approaches, the non-court personnel are professionals in areas like social welfare, medicine, probation, and law enforcement. But both the welfare model and the corporate model are eclipsed by the next model to be discussed here, the participatory model, in regard to the expansive role of the community in juvenile justice.

Participatory Model

The participatory model of juvenile justice involves active participation by community agencies and citizens in a concerted effort to contain the harmful behavior of young people (United Nations, 1985). The primary goal of this approach is the full integration of misbehaving youths into the mainstream of society without any

A Benign-Neglect Approach

What impact could the models covered in this chapter have on juvenile justice in the United States? None of the approaches covered here seem to allow a formal response to juvenile offenders that simultaneously meets the juvenile's needs and protects his or her due process rights. The frustration of being unable to please everyone may convince some people that no response at all ("benign neglect") is the best reaction. In fact, with tongue only partly in his cheek, Hackler (1991) suggests that juvenile justice in the United States and Canada might benefit from Fiji's more casual way of handling juvenile offenders, one that seems superior to ours in reintegrating young offenders into the community. Hackler points out that countries with more developed social control agencies can unwittingly create bureaucracies that hurt clients more than they help. In contrast, countries without such "development" may be more successful in assisting their juveniles through a period of delinquency and into a position as law-abiding adults.

Fiji is composed of more than 800 islands, but two, Viti Levu and Vanua Levu, account for over 80 percent of its land area. The capital city of Suva has about 70,000 people. As a port city Suva has its share of crime, much of which is attributable to juveniles. Yet upon inspecting the statistics for juvenile court cases, one would think that Fiji is either crime-free or its criminals

A Benign-Neglect Approach

are all adults. Hackler (1991) reports that only 12 juveniles were charged during 1989 in the Suva magistrate's court.

Hackler explains that communication links between police and community agencies have been important in Fiji since the 1970s. Police officers bring formal charges against only a few juveniles and rely instead on police connections with court alternatives. When formal charges are brought, the juvenile is taken before a chief magistrate at a regular court of law, but the preference is for informality. Consistent with the informality of police-juvenile encounters, court-juvenile confrontations in Fiji offer only casual protection of due process. A juvenile brought before a Fijian judge is just as likely to be asked about the circumstances of his life as the circumstances of his offense. The judge responds less to concerns about the proving of guilt than to the problem of how to handle juveniles in trouble.

This informality at police and court levels is repeated in the type of facilities used to house the few juveniles who are formally processed at those earlier stages. The Suva juvenile detention center houses the approximately 35 delinquents who were not successfully handled at the police or court levels. Although these are presumably the most difficult juvenile offenders, they are not kept locked up. Most attend school outside the center, while others enroll in vocational training programs or work as apprentices. The freedom of movement means that the youths occasionally abscond, but even that is responded to in a casual manner by having police contact detention center staff if they determine a runaway's location.

Admittedly, economics may be directing juvenile justice policy in Fiji. The absence of specific courts for juvenile offenders may result in greater efforts to avoid formal processing. The lack of money for a fence and reliance on a rusty jeep to chase runaways may require a nonchalant response to detention center escapes. A stronger economic base might encourage Fiji to respond more formally and legalistically to juveniles, but that will not necessarily be an efficient or effective response. As Hackler (1991) argues, Fiji's consistently informal response to misbehaving juveniles avoids the trappings of presumably advanced systems that rely on legal tradition and government bureaucracies. It may be unfair to identify Fiji's juvenile justice system as a "benign neglect" approach; but is it possible that doing less is sometimes better than doing more?

significant use of formal legal intervention. This model is especially popular in countries following a socialist political-economic philosophy. In Cuba, for example, youths under age 16 cannot be tried by ordinary courts nor be subject to penal sanctions (United Nations, 1997; United Nations, 1990d). Juveniles, Cuba believes, should be dealt with outside the scope of the criminal law and outside the court system. They participate in education and treatment programs at "schools of good conduct" operated by the Ministry of Education. Also available is placement at reeducation centers operated by the Ministry of Interior. It is possible that the setting and impact of these schools and centers are equivalent to institutional placement in other countries, but Cuba's stated policy toward juvenile offenders is one of educational evaluation and treatment.

The People's Republic of China also emphasizes a participatory approach and, more clearly than does Cuba, makes specific use of citizens and agencies outside the legal arena. China provides the primary example of the participatory model, and its system provides interesting differences from the welfare, legalistic, and corporatist approaches.

People's Republic of China. Between its founding (1949) and the 1960s, the People's Republic of China did not regard juvenile delinquency as especially troublesome. Young criminals made up only 20 percent of the criminal population in the 1950s and some 30 percent in the early to mid 1960s (Zu-Yuan, 1988). Increased economic growth and a higher standard of living since 1976 brought steadily increasing delinquency rates. By the late 1980s young offenders were reported as making up 70 to 80 percent of the criminal population in big and medium cities, and 60 to 70 percent in the countryside (Zu-Yuan, 1988).

In 1998, as juvenile crime, suicides, and other behavioral problems continued to rise, some Chinese were questioning the government's policy of limiting most urban families to one child (Kurtenbach, 1998). The one-child policy is believed to have resulted in "little emperors" who are either smothered by the attention of their well-meaning parents or are left with little supervision or emotional support since there are no siblings to rely upon when the parents are not around or are uninvolved.

China's system of responding to juvenile offenders has a legalistic aspect similar to Yugoslavia's. For example, the Chinese Criminal Code provides that persons who have reached 18 years of age (raised from 16 with the 1997 revision) shall bear criminal responsibility for their acts. Persons aged 14 to 18 who commit the crimes of murder, serious injury, rape, robbery, drug trafficking, arson, explosion, or poisoning also bear criminal responsibility, but are to receive a lesser or mitigated punishment (*Criminal Law of the People's Republic of China,* as amended in 1997).

An important document guiding the judicial response to juvenile offenders in China is the *Law of the People's Republic of China on the Protection of Minors.* This Protection of Minors Act (effective in 1992) was not modified when the Criminal Law and the Criminal Procedure Law were amended in 1997, so its provisions remain in effect as long as they to not contradict the revised laws (e.g., the age of adult responsibility).

The participatory model requires active participation by many people and agencies as everyone works toward controlling misbehavior by young people. Titles of some of the chapters composing the Protection of Minors Act (see a copy at **www.chnlaw.com**) show why China is a good example of the participatory model:

- Chapter II: Protection by the Family
- Chapter III: Protection by the School

- Chapter IV: Protection by Society
- Chapter V: Judicial Protection

The chapter on judicial protection is especially relevant as it specifies the most formal types of action that can be taken toward misbehaving minors. Rather than having a specific juvenile court, basic-level People's Courts can create special courts to handle peculiarities of various cases. With juvenile offenses presenting "peculiar cases," the People's Court in Shanghai in 1984 developed a specialized Children's Criminal Court that served as a model for the country. By the 1990s there were over 3000 special agencies (juvenile courts) hearing criminal cases involving juveniles (Committee on the Rights of the Child, 1995a). Those courts follow special trial procedures designed for minors, but each court must uphold the policy of education, reform, and rehabilitation. The emphasis on education is especially prominent for younger children committing minor offenses. The emphasis shifts somewhat to punishment for older children engaged in serious offenses.

Because China's educational response to young offenders is especially representative of the participatory model, we begin discussion with this younger group. The basic assumption is that juvenile offenders, like their adult counterparts, have failed to understand and embrace socialism. If society can simply convince the offenders that a socialist perspective and lifestyle is desirable, the craving for crime will pass. Given this conviction, it is not surprising that response to juvenile offenders is scattered among many agencies and organizations (see Table 9.2). Programs that focus on raising the moral character and sense of legality of youth as a whole, and delinquents in particular, are carried out through economic, cultural, educational, administrative, and legal means.

Chinese authorities may seem to have taken their lead from the classical school of criminology, which places great emphasis on the doctrines of rationality, free will, and deterrence, but their position is actually based on Confucian philosophy (Troyer, 1989). That philosophy is that humans are basically good and act only after thinking (that is, humans are rational). Further, humans are educable, so proper education and training will produce virtuous citizens. From that perspective, intense reliance on educating the public about laws is less a twentieth-century socialist notion than a pre-Christian, native one.

Since 1979 the Chinese have made concerted efforts toward a public legal education campaign that teaches virtually every citizen about law and the legal system. Troyer (1989) describes two phases of the campaign as being routine legal education (1979– 1985) and special legal education (1985 to the present). During the first stage, "propaganda [in the Chinese sense of that which educates and informs] workers" were assigned to teach people about the constitution, the criminal code, and other laws. The print media also played an important role in disseminating information, as did the judges and the police. In fact, some claim that legal education became the major task for patrol officers in China (Troyer, 1989). The goal in each of those efforts was to make sure young people knew what behavior was legal and illegal, and what punishment would be imposed for violating the law.

The second stage, the special legal education campaign, built on the groundwork laid from 1979 to 1985. To implement this new stage, the Ministry of Justice established legal education offices throughout the country. From these offices, 7 million "legal advocators" help citizens learn, understand, and use the laws and legal system (Troyer, 1989). The Protection of Minors Act makes clear the important role played by the media in its article 24, which encourages the press, film, television, and the arts to "create or provide works beneficial to the sound growth [of] minors." The mass media, judges, and police still play an important role in the education process, but for young people the schools have an especially prominent position.

To achieve a goal of universal citizen knowledge of law, all types of schools include law education courses. Elementary schools emphasize common legal knowledge and traffic regulations. Middle school and high school students study the constitution and criminal law. Colleges and universities emphasize legal theory and legal specialties as well as offering course work in public legal education. Although schoolteachers provide some information, officials especially like using police officers who can encourage observation of laws by telling young people of graphic criminal cases (Zu-Yuan, 1988). General deterrence is sought through the public display of crime evidence or confiscated spoils. Zu-Yuan (1988) suggests that such action can increase the citizen's attentiveness to crime while showing the power of the police in combating it.

Young people who have engaged in minor criminal activity (for example, stealing, fighting, incorrigibility) may go to special work-and-study schools administered by the educational departments in cooperation with public security agencies. Because parental permission accompanies the assignment, the schools become a special educational measure instead of a criminal or administrative punishment. At the school, students undergo a "strict disciplinary and ideological education, while studying the same subjects taught in the regular schools" (Zu-Yuan, 1988, p. 10). They spend about half the day in academic study and the other half in practical work at a school-operated factory or workshop (Myren, 1989). After two years of study, during which the students go home only on Sundays and holidays, the young people return to their original school or advance to a higher educational level.

The preferred response to juvenile offenders makes use of the "help and education team" system (Zhao, 1990; Zu-Yuan, 1988). With the close cooperation of government agencies and private citizens, young people are placed under the constant care of the help-education teams until they reform. Each help-education team has three to five members who take responsibility for helping one individual. Team members can represent teachers, parents, police officers, neighbors, government officials, or other interested citizens. They are chosen, however, because they know the person and will be able to influence by example. The constant contact with families, neighbors, and police keeps everyone informed about the "client's" progress. The team's work is not finished until the result satisfies the leaders, parents, or neighbors.

Whereas the participatory approach is especially exemplified in China's reaction to younger, less serious offenders, a similar philosophy appears even when the offender is older and the crime is more serious. Young persons who commit serious crimes go to the Surveillance and Rehabilitation Centers for Juvenile Delinquents. Whereas education is the tool for reform of younger offenders, labor is the device used by Surveillance and Rehabilitation Centers to reform the older delinquents. Still, juveniles in these correctional facilities must receive at least 24 hours per week of political, cultural, and vocational technical education. The political instruction is conducted so that juvenile offenders will come to respect the laws of the state and will work to change their poor conduct or habits (Committee on the Rights of the Child, 1995a).

The juvenile reformatories receive older offenders committing such serious offenses as stealing, fighting, rape, robbery, and damage to public property. Both boys and girls go to the same facility but stay in separate sections. Commitment is either directly by public security agencies, or through the juvenile court. The average stay is about two years, and upon release the juvenile returns home to the parents and begins either school or a job (Myren, 1989).

SUMMARY

This chapter began with a sketch of how juvenile justice agencies in America responded to Charles Manson, eventually the instigator of at least eight murders. The dilemma facing juvenile justice agencies around the world is the same regardless of the legal tradition to which the system is linked. There is, on the one hand, an interest in doing what is best for the child, and on the other hand, a need to respond in a way that protects society. These goals are not necessarily mutually exclusive, but it seems difficult to give each equal weight simultaneously. Four models of response to juvenile offenders were presented to show the variation in how countries respond to "problem youths."

Some response to misbehaving young people is necessary because delinquency is a worldwide problem. UN data were used to show how all regions of the world report problems with misbehaving youth. But nations do not agree on what constitutes delinquency, who is a "juvenile," or what is the appropriate way to respond to juvenile offenders.

The first model discussed was a juvenile justice system that concentrates on the well-being of the child. This is a basic feature of the welfare model, as exemplified in Australia and New Zealand. The states of South Australia and Western Australia passed new Youth Offender Acts in the 1990s that brought several new programs into the system. Esecially notable are the Juvenile Justice Teams in Western Australia. New Zealand's use of Family Group Conferencing presents a unique approach to juvenile justice that actually modifies the process itself rather than simply presenting an alternative. These nonjudicial responses in Australia and in New Zealand are believed to serve the best interests of the child.

The welfare approach is criticized by some for its apparent absence of concern with the rights of the juvenile. Countries following a legalistic model are also concerned about the well-being of the child, but here there is equal or more concern about protecting juveniles' rights. Yugoslavia and Italy illustrate this legalistic approach in their use of the traditional court system (Yugoslavia) or the strict adherence to formal requirements of due process (Italy). Importantly, each country has procedures (both formal and informal) that allow attention to the individual's needs despite the appearance of rigid formality or a legalistic approach.

Tension between welfare and legalistic models were said to have pushed England and Wales into a new approach toward juvenile justice—a corporatist model. An increased public interest in punishing juveniles who had committed serious crimes made it difficult for those countries to achieve their initial goal of combining welfare and legalistic models. Instead, they moved to a model wherein decision making has been moved from the courts to administrative agencies in cases where the public opinion still favors a treatment (rather than punishment) response to juveniles. The new Crime and Disorder Act 1998 is making rather dramatic changes to the youth justice system in England and Wales, and it will be important to watch how the new procedures and programs develop.

The participatory model provides the fourth approach to juvenile justice. China's system is a particularly good example of this approach, because it emphasizes an educational response to young offenders. A wide variety of agencies and organizations are responsible for the "correction" of misbehaving youth. Although a traditional judicial process also operates in China, the overall philosophy in regard to juvenile offenders is to get them to accept socialist principles through the power of community persuasion.

WEB SITES TO VISIT

- The Child Rights Information Network provides access to a variety of documents, news, and reports on children's rights. Visit their web site at **www.crin.org** for links to a variety of information arranged by topic, organization, and geographical region.
- For more information on restorative-justice programs, like New Zealand's Family Group Conferencing, see the resources listed and reviewed at **www.rji.org/rjisourc. htm**
- Read the Crime and Disorder Act 1989 for England and Wales at **www.homeoffice.gov.uk/cdact/index.htm**, and review the "Youth Justice" document at **www.homeoffice.gov.uk/cdact/youjust.htm** to understand how the system operates.

SUGGESTED READINGS

Emmins, Christopher J. (1988). *A practical approach to criminal procedure* (4th ed.). London, England: Blackstone Press.

Lemert, Edwin M. (1986). Juvenile justice Italian style. *Law and Society Review, 20,* 509–544.

Myren, Richard A. (1989). Juvenile justice: People's Republic of China. *C. J. International, 5*(3), 5–6, 22–23.

Winterdyk, J. A. (Ed.). (1997). *Juvenile justice systems: International perspectives.* Toronto: Canadian Scholars' Press.

Zhao, Peter. (1990). Violent crime and its countermeasures in China. *C. J. International, 6*(3), 11–18.

Chapter 10

Japan: Examples of Effectiveness and Borrowing

KEY TOPICS

- In what way can Japan's criminal justice system be considered effective?
- How has Japan used ideas from other countries to build its criminal justice system?
- Japanese cultural traits that help explain how and why its system operates as it does
- The use of bureaucratic informalism in Japanese criminal justice
- The structure and operation of policing in Japan
- The judiciary in Japan
- Corrections in Japan
- What may and what may not work in America

KEY TERMS

chuzaisho
collectivism
contextualism and harmony
homogeneity
honne
koban
National Public Safety Commission
National Police Agency
order
prefectural police
Summary courts
tatemae

COUNTRIES REFERENCED

Japan
United States

Japan offers an excellent opportunity to highlight the benefits of comparative study. Its example is so perfect because much of Japan's criminal justice system is borrowed; yet the adaptation was made in the context of Japan's cultural heritage. The Japanese have a long history of identifying key elements of the social institutions in other countries and modifying those ingredients so that they become workable in Japan. This is an important point to remember as we conclude this tour of comparative criminal justice. Just because something works well in one country does not mean that it is appropriate for other countries. However, the procedures and experiences a country has with the components of its justice system may suggest useful modifications in the systems of other countries. As long as the receiving country remembers to adapt rather than adopt the idea, comparative studies will benefit individual countries and the world.

This concluding chapter on the criminal justice system of Japan drives home that point. After showing why Japan is an appropriate example for such concentrated attention, we will review its history as a borrower of ideas, identify some relevant cultural traits important in what ideas were adapted and how they were adapted, and then describe Japan's criminal justice system through review of its criminal law, police, courts, and corrections.

WHY STUDY JAPAN?

Japan is an island nation perceived by many people (the Japanese included) to be quite small. Yet as Reischauer (1988) points out, size is a relative matter. Japan is admittedly dwarfed by such neighbors as China to its immediate west, Australia to the south, and by the United States and Canada to its far east on the globe. But a more accurate perspective is to compare Japan to some of the European countries: Japan's nearly 146,000 square miles of land area is considerably larger than Italy (116,000 square miles) and half again the size of the United Kingdom (94,000 square miles). Were it superimposed on a map of the United States, Japan's northern island of Hokkaido would begin just north of New York State (almost to Montreal, Canada), and the other main islands (Honshu, Shikoku, and Kyushu) would extend south into the Florida panhandle. Similar latitudes on America's West Coast would take Japan from Oregon's border with Washington to California's border with Mexico.

Since the post-World War II era, Japan has operated as a parliamentary-cabinet system. The Diet (parliament) serves as the sole lawmaking organ of the state, whereas the Cabinet (the Prime Minister and other ministers of state) operates as the government's executive branch. The majority of Cabinet ministers are Diet members, serving simultaneously as heads of government departments and directors of civil servants. The Cabinet, then, combines politics (the Diet) with administration (government departments). Japan's constitution identifies the emperor as the symbol of the state and of the unity of the people, but his position does not include powers related to government.

Japan provides an appropriate case study for our purposes because (1) its criminal justice system seems to provide an effective response to the crime problem, and (2) its effective criminal justice system owes much to the policies and procedures of criminal justice systems in other countries.

Japan's Effective Criminal Justice System

Between 1950 and 1997 Japan's crime rate dropped from about 1900 per 100,000 population to 1500 (although it steadily increased during the 1990s). During the same time period, its imprisonment rate dropped from 139 to 33 (see Figure 10.1). The decline in both sets of figures occurred while Japan was undergoing postwar industrialization, population increases (especially in the younger category), and continued urbanization. Because these factors are among those often cited as causing crime, Japan presents a contradiction that criminologists find intriguing.

Keeping in mind the cautions in Chapters 2 and 8 about cross-cultural comparison of crime and imprisonment rates, it is still instructive to see how Japanese officials view their response to crime in comparison with other countries. Comparing their own statistics with those issued by the United States, the United Kingdom, Germany, and France, Japan finds itself to be in an enviable position. Japan's crime rate in 1993 and 1994 was the lowest of the five countries, and its clearance rate was higher than all but Germany's (Research and Training Institute, 1996). Interestingly, and probably a reflection of Japan's rising crime rate,

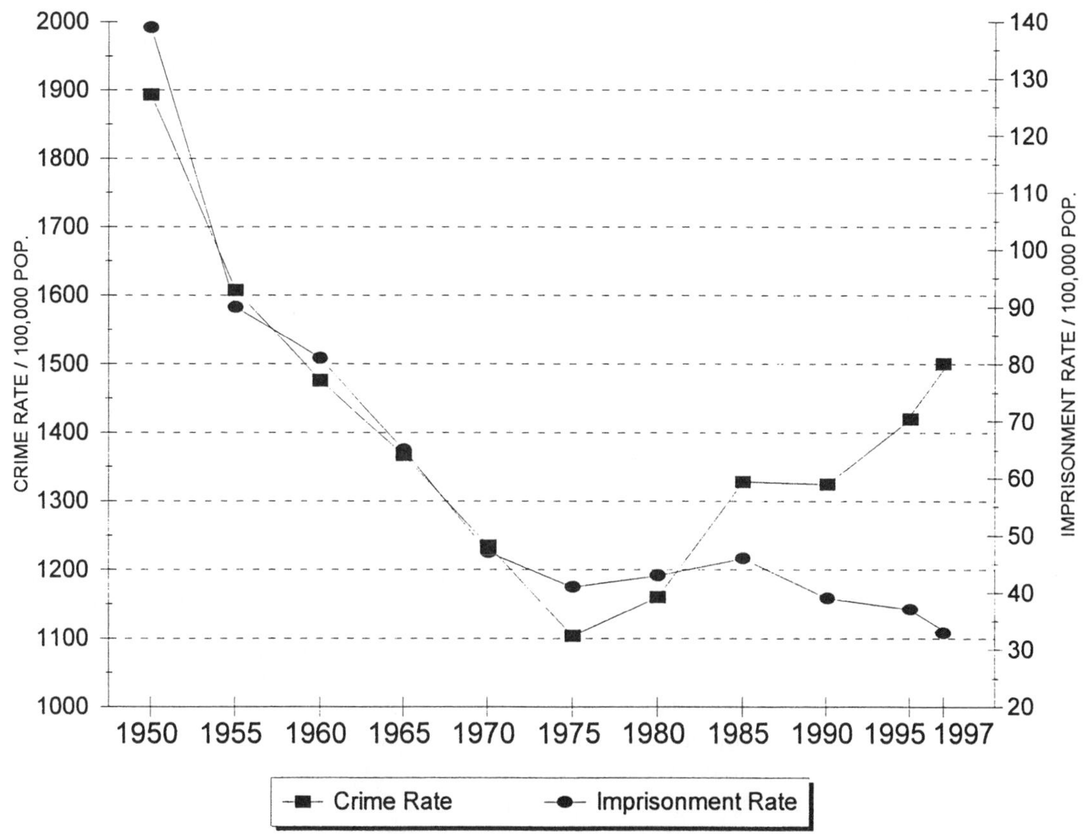

Figure 10.1 Crime and Inmate Trends in Japan. *Sources:* Correction Bureau (1995), Correctional institutions in Japan 1999. Tokyo: Ministry of Justice; Research and Training Institute (1998), *Summary of the White Paper on Crime.* Tokyo: Ministry of Justice.

more recent government reports compare homicide rates only. The 1998 report simply notes that among the five countries, for the 1994 to 1996 period, Japan had the lowest homicide rate and the highest homicide clearance rate (Research and Training Institute, 1998).

When crime does occur, and after the police catch the offender—which nearly inevitably, it appears, they do—the Japanese criminal justice system continues to stand apart from those of other nations. Over 99 percent of the offenders eventually coming before a judge are convicted. Furthermore, nearly 99 percent of those convicted are sentenced to prison. As this chapter shows, such statistics are potentially misleading, because informal control mechanisms are used at each stage regardless of the formal terminology. A 99 percent conviction rate

In the News

UNFORTUNATE CHANGES: CRIME IS UP AND CONFIDENCE IN POLICE IS DOWN

Although Japan's crime rate remains among the lowest of industrialized nations, there have been increased concerns about rising crime in the 1990s. Yoshikawa (1995) reports that police officials believe increasing crime is threatening the very foundation of public order in Japan. Especially troublesome has been an increase in violent crime, drug use, and juvenile crime (Prideaux, 2000; Stoker, 2000; Struck, 2000a).

Violent crime in Japan is at a 23-year high, and rising. The murder rate is still low by American standards—it is six times less than in the United States—but it is now higher than in England and Wales and is only slightly lower than most other European countries. Some of the increase is attributed to a poor economy (armed robbery is the fastest-rising violent crime) that has left young people with no work and few hopes for the future. But other explanations are also offered. For example, since World War II Japan has changed from a mostly rural to a mostly urban society. Family size is lower today and more mothers are working outside the home. As a result, many of the traditional informal social controls have deteriorated (Struck, 2000a).

As if the rising crime problem weren't bad enough, many Japanese are also losing confidence in their police. Stoker (2000) and Struck (2000b) report that a large number of police scandals and blunders in 2000 eroded public faith in the police. Senior officers in one prefecture were charged with covering up an interoffice drug abuse scandal while those in another chose to continue playing a game of mah-jongg rather than heading back to police headquarters after hearing a schoolgirl kidnapped nine years earlier had been found. In still other cases the police have let a suspect in a shocking schoolyard stabbing death run away from them and commit suicide, and at one police department a manual was found on how to hide misdeeds by police officers. A university expert on criminal procedure summed up the public attitude by saying, "Something is wrong, and the public is very angry about it" (quoted in Struck, 2000b). Will a continued rising crime rate and growing distrust of the police mean that Japan will someday be an inappropriate example of "effectiveness and borrowing"?

hides the fact that the vast majority of these cases are not contested by the defendant. Moreover, saying that 99 percent of those convicted receive a prison sentence seems impressive until we realize that over half those prison sentences are suspended; and in most of those cases the offender is not even placed under supervision. However, even this significant use of informal sanctioning separates the Japanese system from most others in the industrialized world.

As a comparatively safe industrialized urban society, Japan has attracted much scholarly attention. Some studies have emphasized the police role (for example, Ames, 1981; Bayley, 1991; Parker, 1984), others the law or the courts (for example, Castberg, 1990; Upham, 1987), and still others the corrections systems (for example, Johnson, 2000; Parker, 1986). A common theme, at least among those scholars who actually visited Japan for their research, is an appreciation for the apparent absence of crime and the perception of safety that is produced. Bayley (1991) presents the feeling most succinctly by titling his first chapter "Heaven for a Cop." He also wonders, as have many other researchers and authors, how Japan's justice system operates, why it is so effective and efficient, and whether some of its features are transferable to other countries. In this chapter we will examine some scholars' attempts to answer these questions.

Borrowing in a Cross-Cultural Context

Diffusion is a classic way by which innovation is shared. This is true in the broad areas of science and humanities, as well as specific areas, such as systems of justice. The way modern policing operated in early nineteenth-century America was heavily influenced by happenings and experiences in other countries. Prison construction in European countries was influenced by America's experiment with the Pennsylvania system. Roman law had specific and long-lasting impact on the legal systems of countries ranging from Europe to South America. Sometimes the influence of one country is imposed on another, but there are also occasions when ideas are freely and willingly imitated. Japan's system of criminal justice, as well as many of its other social institutions, have both imposed and imitated aspects.

In a fascinating manner, Westney (1987) provides detailed information on how Japan's Meiji Era transformation (1868-1912) relied on the deliberate emulation of Western organizations. The Japanese navy was modeled on the British; the army on the French and then on the German; the educational system on the French, the American, and the German; and the banking system on the American. And this nineteenth-century willingness to look beyond its own boundaries was simply a continuation of an earlier disposition to view foreign ideas with favor.

Japan's first sources of influence (around 300 B.C. to A.D. 500) were from the Asian continent and included important developments such as agriculture and metalworking. The fourth and fifth centuries brought specific influences from China (via Korea), and the Japanese became familiar with the philosophies of Confucianism and Buddhism, as well as Chinese written script. China continued to play the role of primary model into the eighth century, providing Japan with the basics of a centralized bureaucratic state that moved Japan into an aristocratic age.

Contacts with the West did not occur until 1543, when a Portuguese ship drifted ashore on a small southern island in the Japanese archipelago. These sailors, who brought the first firearms to Japan, were followed six years later by the arrival of the Spanish Jesuit, Francis Xavier, who introduced Christianity. By the 1630s the Tokugawa shogunate became increasingly concerned that Christian missionaries were intent on political conquest of Japan. A rigid isolationist policy was adopted, and Portuguese ships could not enter Japanese ports nor could Japanese people take trips abroad. The only countries continuing contact with Japan were China and Holland. Despite their European placement, the Dutch were acceptable to the shogunate because they made it very clear that their interest in Japan was financial rather than spiritual or political. Through the Dutch, Japan received information about the outside world, but in many respects Japan missed the scientific and industrial revolutions of the eighteenth century.

By the early nineteenth century, Japan was confronted with internal pressure for political reform and external pressure for economic contacts. Russian and British ships made occasional approaches, but the real breakthrough came in 1853, when Commodore Matthew Perry and his fleet of ships forced the Japanese government to accept a letter from the president of the United States. The Tokugawa shogunate realized the opening of Japan was inevitable, so treaties of friendship and commerce were initiated with Western countries.

Japan's period of modern history begins in 1868, when control of the government moved from the shogunate back to the emperor. This Meiji (after the reign name of the emperor) Restoration and the resulting Meiji Era (1868–1912) brought dramatic political, economic, and cultural changes to Japan. Things Western came to be defined as good, and the Japanese once again turned to other countries for ideas. Among the more important innovations was the 1890 establishment of a constitutional government modeled in the European tradition. The U.S. government structure was not deemed suitable to the Japanese, because it did not provide for an emperor. Germany and Prussia, on the other hand, operated with a kaiser, and this provided a version of parliamentary government more appealing to Japan.

Over the centuries, Japan has been remarkably skillful in its borrowing practices. Whether it was religion from China or a political structure from Germany, the Japanese took to heart Sakuma Shozan's (a Tokugawa reformer) phrase " 'Eastern morals, Western science' " (quoted in Upham, 1987). It was desirable to import and adapt Western learning, but only while protecting the Japanese spirit. That philosophy continues today and provides the heart of this chapter's argument: Countries can and should learn from each other, but things borrowed must be adapted rather than adopted. To best understand the application of this argument, we must appreciate aspects of the "Japanese spirit" that have influenced the development of Japan's justice system.

JAPANESE CULTURAL TRAITS

With Japan's increased economic prowess in the 1980s and 1990s came great interest among businesspeople around the world in everything from Japanese management techniques to the Japanese language. Concurrently, justice officials became intrigued with Japan's apparent success in responding to the crime problem. In all these areas, Japan's accomplishments were reflective of its cultural heritage. Notehelfer (personal communication, June 14, 1990) uses the analogy of the bonsai to make a similar point. Americans admire the bonsai tree for its simple elegance, its sense of harmony, and the serenity imparted by its miniaturization. In some ways the bonsai is considered a metaphor for Japanese society itself: orderly, efficient, peaceful, with citizens acting in unanimity. Yet before foreigners covet the bonsai or, by analogy, Japanese society, it is important to see how it got this way. The bonsai's beauty is the result of wiring and molding the limbs of the tree so that it does not develop beyond certain limits. The aesthetics of Japanese society may result from similar wiring and molding. We should not ignore the wires when admiring the tree.

Since every society has been shaped by its own peculiar heritage, the analogy of the bonsai can be repeated for each merely by choosing an object linked to the particular country. The danger in undertaking a discussion of any country's "wiring and molding" is to make its cultural traits stereotypes. Japan, especially, poses this danger because of its many paradoxes. For example, Japan is a conservative society with radical student groups; a contemplative self is admired by materialistic and consumerist citizens; the Japanese strive for a closeness with nature while surrounded by a serious pollution problem. Obviously it can be unwise and unfair to associate specific traits with Japan or the Japanese. Nevertheless, anthropologists and others realize that broadly stated cultural values help make sense of the complexity and variation found in all societies. If we approach the issue with an understanding of the potential problem of developing stereotypes, the search for cultural values—and even cultural traits—can be beneficial.

With that warning, we shall look at the wires before admiring the tree. That is, before appreciating the apparent efficiency and success of Japan's criminal justice system, we will inspect the cultural mold in which that system operates. We do that by considering the impact some Japanese cultural values may have on the criminal act and on society's response. A number of cultural traits have been used to understand better the success of Japan's social control mechanisms. A nonexhaustive list would include a homogeneous society, emphasis on harmony, a reliance on collectivism, and a respect for hierarchy and authority.

Homogeneity

Japan is ethnically homogeneous, with over 99 percent of its population being Japanese. The largest single minority group is the Koreans, who comprise about 0.5 percent of the island nation's population. Also noteworthy are the *burakumin* (or people of the hamlet). Although fully Japanese, these physically and culturally indistinguishable citizens are the recipients of serious prejudice and discrimination. Presumably the *burakumin* formed a social class during feudal times that was perceived as an outcast group (Hendry, 1989; Reischauer, 1988; Upham, 1987). The *burakumin* of Tokugawa times were those people engaged in defiling or dirty occupations like burying the dead or working with dead animals (for example, butchers and leather workers). Another name for this group is *eta,* meaning heavily polluted, because their work is considered contaminating in Shinto and Buddhist views.

The Emancipation Edict of 1871 granted the *burakumin* formal liberation from their feudal status of outcasts. Yet, as with minorities in other countries, in other times, legal emancipation did not have much impact on *burakumin* status. Official government policy helped perpetuate prejudice and discrimination by registering *burakumin* as "new commoners" in the family registries maintained at each citizen's place of origin (Upham, 1987). Because descent from a Tokugawa outcast is the only distinguishing feature of *burakumin*, these public registries provided easy identification of, and discrimination against, *buraku* individuals. The estimated 2 or 3 percent of today's population who fall into this group continue to have underprivileged status (Upham, 1987), which forces substantial numbers into associations with *bōryokudan* criminal gangs (Kaplan & Dubro, 1986). That process concerns Japanese justice officials, because *bōryokudan* activity has increased in recent years. Later in this chapter we will look at the *bōryokudan* more closely.

In apparent contradiction to the idea that homogeneity declines with increased division of labor, the Japanese continue to express similar values and hold tightly to common norms. When virtually all the country's inhabitants know and agree upon what it means to be Japanese, the job of social control becomes remarkably easier. However, homogeneity in itself cannot explain low crime rates. Certainly there are many examples worldwide where citizens know and agree upon particular norms yet continue to violate them. Japanese culture must provide more than simple similarity among its people.

Contextualism and Harmony

An important correlate to homogeneity is *contextualism*, or *relativism*. These terms refer to the Japanese belief that standards of morality and ethics are determined by reference to the group rather than to rigid legal codes or universal principles (Archambeault & Fenwick, 1988; Reischauer, 1988). Instead of there being absolute standards of morality, all behavioral standards are relative to the context in which people find themselves. That belief system helps explain atrocities (such as the 1937 Nanking massacre of Manchurians by Japanese forces) committed in the context of war (Becker, 1988b) by the same people who, in their own country, report more things being found than lost (Parker, 1984).

One way to view this apparent contradiction is through the concepts of *tatemae* (how things appear) and *honne* (the underlying reality). Early in the socialization process, Japanese children learn the importance of maintaining harmony *(wa)*. Yet because complete and continual harmony can be only an ideal, Japanese become rather adept at portraying harmony even where it does not exist. Often the ideal harmony that primary groups display on the surface disguises the reality of conflict underneath. The observer will usually only see the *tatemae* face, because airing of dirty laundry to outsiders brings shame on the primary group. That is, the group (whether it be the family, neighborhood, workplace, or even sport team) is faulty, because it cannot maintain harmony.

Putting the concepts of contextualism and harmony together, we can appreciate some of the control techniques popular in Japan. It is possible that in certain situations (contextualism), a person's own internal motivations *(honne)* might lead to deviant behavior. However, conventions require offender, victim, and control agent to handle the problem so that *tatemae* is achieved. Keeping this in mind will help us understand the Japanese preference for informal justice and a firm belief in social, over individual, rehabilitation. Control techniques that present harmony are more easily found outside the formal setting of justice agencies. Furthermore, because misbehavior is contextual, hence social, the treatment must also be social. Put deviants in a nurturing social environment, and they will get better, is the philosophy.

Collectivism

From the earliest life stages, Japanese learn the importance of the group to their existence and well-being. There is probably no clearer way to express the point than by noting an aspect of Japanese child-rearing practices. Misbehaving children in America are often punished by being confined to the house and made to stay with the family. In Japan, parents are more likely to put the misbehaving child outside the house. The American child clamors to be let out; the Japanese child begs to be let in. As Bayley states it, "American mothers chase their children around the block to get them to come home; Japanese mothers are chased by their children so as not to be left behind" (1991, p. 143).

The family and group orientation of Japanese society continues a sense of collective responsibility present since pre-Confucian Japan. Individualism is present, but it takes a different form than in America. A sense of personal self-worth and identity in Japan stems from the groups to which one belongs. In this sense, individualism in Japan is achieved through one's ability to create, maintain, and guard relationships. Parker (1984) exemplifies this when he notes that a Japanese is likely to introduce himself as a faculty member at Tokyo University or a worker at Toyota. Secondarily, specific occupations such as psychologist or janitor may be offered, but the group affiliation takes precedence.

The sense of collectivism attaches to family, employer, school, and other groups. The accompanying close ties to both formal and informal groups result in a sense of obligation of one toward the others. Such associations give the individual solid emotional support, but those same close ties also bring a strong sense of shame and embarrassment when a group member misbehaves. It is still not uncommon to find a boss resigning for the employee's misconduct, or parents apologizing for the behavior of even a fully grown child (Becker, 1988b). Family members experience a sense of shame and embarrassment if a member's conduct brings dishonor on the family. Importantly, such group consciousness and family identity push most Japanese to avoid actions that may bring pain, shame, and punishment on the group (Archambeault & Fenwick, 1988; Becker, 1988b).

Finally, we must note that collectivism links to contextualism because the way a reference group interprets a standard is more important than the abstract standard itself. The group is placed above the individual. For purposes of criminal justice, this means that the goal of keeping society moral and crime-free must take precedence over a goal of protecting the letter of each individual's rights in Japan (Becker, 1988b). As we see later, a criticism of the Japanese system is its apparent preference for the crime control model over the due process model. In addition, the importance of collectivism means that threatened exclusion from the group is more likely to produce conformity than is a formal punishment.

You Should Know!

THE IMPORTANCE OF CONFESSION

One reason for the effectiveness of Japan's criminal justice system is the tendency of Japanese citizens to confess their misbehavior. That tendency is also seen by some observers as one of the system's greatest problems. The predicament is outlined in Article 38 of Japan's Constitution:

> *No person shall be compelled to testify against himself. Confession made under compulsion, torture or threat, or after prolonged arrest or detention shall not be admitted in evidence. No person shall be convicted or punished in cases where the only proof against him is his own confession.*

Confession has played an important role in Japanese criminal cases since the early part of the Meiji period, when defendants could not be found guilty without a confession (Tamiya, 1983). Unfortunately, the requirement for a confession was accompanied by an acceptance of torture as a means to encourage the admission. Article 38, then, presents a dilemma wherein one horn recognizes the importance of confession and the other horn recognizes the protection against self-incrimination. To date it appears that the tradition of confession takes precedence over the constitutional protection.

Saito (1990) suggests that any efficient state system is likely to cause human rights infringements and the Japanese criminal justice system is no exception. His particular concern is with the process of pretrial detention, which Saito argues is used for interrogation and to obtain a confession. Saito's position is supported by Hataguchi, who argues that confessions are routinely admitted into evidence despite the likelihood that they are the result of police coercion (Hataguchi, 1990).

The public prosecutor's office disposes of three fourths of its cases within 15 days (Research and Training Institute, 1990), but the suspicion is that confession plays a significant role in how quickly the case is handled. Bail is guaranteed, except in a few cases, but only after the prosecutor files charges. During the detention period of potentially 23 days the suspect does not have the right to bail. Bayley (1991) suggests that because inducing confession is a key purpose of precharge detention, confession may well become a condition for bail.

Hierarchies and Order

An appreciation for hierarchical arrangements among people is the final element of Japanese culture to consider here. When discussing trends in American response to juvenile delinquents, Empey (1982) noted the importance of Americans' distrust in the 1960s of their social institutions. Japanese do not seem to have had a similar experience, and given their affinity for an ordered hierarchical society, it is not likely that they will.

The link between preferring hierarchies and faith in social institutions proceeds as follows: Japanese hierarchies, which are not just grounded in power, are of great variety and based on differing social prescriptions and social obligations. As Archambeault and Fenwick (1988) put it, group consciousness combines with a sense of order to force cooperative relationships between most segments of the Japanese community and their justice agencies. The respect for one's position leads citizens to honor and trust justice system employees. Police, courts, and corrections officials are seen as guardians of society's morals as well as enforcers of the law. As a result, the people's faith in the agents of the system, and the belief that decisions will be made according to what best serves society, allow the Japanese people to give extensive discretion to the criminal justice agents.

Because the values of contextualism, harmony, collectivism, and order are firmly grounded in Japanese culture, they help explain the Japanese response to criminal offenders and how that response differs from other countries. Importantly, however, the Japanese difference is more in the means to the end than in the end itself. For example, as with most Western systems, the Japanese corrections system is caught between the often conflicting punishment goals of rehabilitation and retribution. Western systems typically seek rehabilitation by encouraging the offender to become independent and responsible. The Japanese system encourages the offender to integrate voluntarily into the structured social order. In addition, the Japanese see the community, rather than an institution, as the more likely place for getting that voluntary integration. Because imprisonment is not considered a useful means for achieving the rehabilitative goal, a low incarceration rate is not really surprising.

Although retribution is seen as an appropriate and desirable goal, rather than following an "eye for an eye" philosophy, Japan secures the goal through "disgrace" or "reintegrative shaming" (Braithwaite, 1989). This approach would not likely work in many Western heterogenous societies, but the value of collectivism makes retribution through disgrace very effective in Japan. The Japanese desire and need for group association and acceptance make alienation from the group a harsh and meaningful punishment. Because the impact of alienation and rejection does not increase over time, there is no need to have long prison sentences.

CRIMINAL LAW

Japanese law traces its foundation to the Seventeen Maxims issued in 604 by the government of Prince Shotoku (Ryavec, 1983; Wigmore, 1936). Like the Ten Commandments, the Seventeen Maxims are more accurately a short moral code rather than rules of law. The maxims included urgings that government officials behave with decorum (Law IV) and that judges respond to cases with impartiality (Law V). The first strictly legal code was made up of short enactments between 645 and 646 in the reign of Emperor Kotoku. This Decree of Great Reform established the Chinese-like administrative organization, fixed land titles, and reformed the taxation system. Actual codification of law began with the Code of the Taiho (701), which elaborated upon the Decree of Great Reform. The Taiho Code was in turn modified by the Yoro Code of 718.

Knowledge and appreciation of Chinese society was apparent in these early days of Japan's legal growth. Not only were Chinese models used in developing those early decrees, edicts, and codes, but the Japanese also borrowed a Chinese custom for direct access to the ruler (Wigmore, 1936). In essence, this was a "suggestion box" in the form of a bell and box placed outside the palace (China) or in the court (Japan). In a 646 edict, the Japanese emperor ordered citizens to place their complaints in the box so that the ruler might call the matter to the attention of his ministers. Should there still be neglect, lack of diligence, or bias on the ministers' part, the citizen was to strike the bell to so inform the emperor. Wigmore (1936) compares this practice with the English right to petition, because it both enabled common people to seek personal justice from the ruler and kept the ruler in direct touch with public opinion.

During this early stage, Japanese law had little differentiation between civil and criminal aspects, followed an inquisitorial rather than adversarial procedure, and lacked any division between judicial and executive branches. The ruling class, being educated in the Confucian classics, was deemed morally superior to everyone else and therefore had the power to determine what constituted a crime and how serious it was. Although the codes suggest similarities with the civil legal tradition, Ryavec (1983) notes that jurists of the time referred to Japanese custom and provincial precedents more often than citing from the criminal code. This mixture of legal traditions that Europeans of the time were keeping separate continued to influence the development of Japanese law.

As this first period came to a close, rich military barons acquired semi-independence from the emperor. In the 1100s palace intellectuals lost their power, and the emperor in Kyoto was left playing second fiddle to a military feudal tenure system directed by the shogun (the commander-in-chief of the Japanese army). In theory, the emperor appointed each new shogun. Yet in fact the shogun position was as hereditary as that of emperor, and for nearly 700 years the shogun was Japan's real ruler.

The second period of Japanese law (1192–1603) began with the military shogun, Minamoto Yoritomo (Ryavec, 1983; Wigmore, 1936). Minamoto's Kamakura Shogunate (1192–1333) consolidated the new centralized feudalism and took nationwide control over all police and military agents. He also set up a court of justice (actually, a board of inquiry) and issued a legal code that, with supplementary regulations, lasted from 1232 until the end of the medieval period. Minamoto's successor, Hojo Yasutoki, established the court more firmly by ordaining the first 15 days of each month to be devoted to justice. According to the old custom, a bell was hung at the court's door and, after striking it, a complainant had his petition immediately heard.

The Kamakura shogunate's code *(Goseibai Shikimoku)* and its supplements reflected the widening range of military jurisdiction in local economic and criminal matters. Interestingly, the tendency toward common law procedures with civil law codification continued into this stage. Precedent was increasingly relied upon rather than statute, and at times civil law cases were allowed to use adversarial instead of inquisitorial procedures (Ryavec, 1983).

The third period (1603–1868) saw political equilibrium introduced by Tokugawa Ieyasu, who began the Tokugawa dynasty (1603-1868). Both feudalism and military class domination continued, but now under the control of a central federalized government. Economic and social prosperity flourished, as did the development of the Japanese legal system. While the barons (daimyo) had jurisdiction in local matters in their own provinces, they were kept well informed of the shogun's expectations in legal affairs. Ieyasu required the great barons to spend alternate years with him at the new capital in Edo (Tokyo). This policy was most helpful in keeping the barons up to date with new legislation. The barons' judges often consulted the Supreme Court in Edo in attempts to achieve uniformity of law.

One of the features of Japanese law in Tokugawa times seems unusual in comparison to our knowledge of legal systems in other countries. The four legal traditions introduced in Chapter 4 shared a belief that citizens should know the laws. Whether that knowledge comes from clearly drafted codes, immemorial custom, or divine proclamations, the people were expected to know their obligations. The laws and decisions of Tokugawa times were not circulated to the public. Wigmore (1936) suggests that this may be a result of the Confucian principle that the responsibility for justice rests with the ruler, not with the people. Because Tokugawa rulers often repeated the Confucian caution to "let the people abide by the law, but not be instructed in it" (quoted in Wigmore, 1936, p. 484), the link seems quite probable. The foregoing should in no way imply that the laws were kept secret from the public. The trial courts were open to the public, and penal laws were posted in public places. The point to remember is that the written laws were commands addressed to the officials—not the people.

The fourth period of the Japanese legal system (1868–1945) corresponds to Japan's period as an institutionalized monarchy beginning with the Meiji Restoration. The New Code of Laws was created in 1870 and then revised in 1873 to incorporate what was basically the current penal law in China (George, 1983). By the 1880s increased contacts with America and Europe brought Japan additional ideas about legal systems. Those of France and Germany were particularly appealing. With the assistance of a French criminal law scholar, the 1873 code was replaced with an 1880 version heavily emphasizing French legal principles. Yet soon after the 1882 implementation of the 1880 code, the Japanese came to appreciate German law. The Germans seemed to share Japan's view of law as a system imposed by an absolute monarch (the German kaiser and the Japanese emperor), so the 1907 Japanese code was modeled on the German code of that time. Even so, the Japanese were ever mindful of their own traditions. For example, the first three books of the new Civil Code (General Principles, Property Rights, and Obligations) resembled the German Civil Code, but the fourth and fifth books on Family and Inheritance Law were clearly based on Japanese custom (Oppler, 1977).

In its modern form (1946–present), Japanese criminal law received instruction from the United States during the Allied occupation after World War II. The 1947 constitution reflects Western influence by stipulating a separation of legislative, administrative, and judicial powers; extensive protection of civil liberties; and introducing the American system of judicial review (Hendry, 1989; Ryavec, 1983). The occupation lawyers who supervised the legal reforms had to remember that the Japanese legal system was built on a foundation using both civil and common legal traditions in the context of local custom (Oppler, 1977).

Fortunately, the occupying forces understood that the legal system could not simply be replaced with one that worked in England, the United States, or France. Using considerable input from Japanese lawyers (Oppler, 1977), a legal system was outlined that brought innovation yet maintained tradition. Hendry (1989) describes the result as another example of a Western-like exterior hiding a clearly Japanese interior. The Ministry of Justice in Tokyo serves as an analogy for itself: The brick front reflects the Western influence, but the interior of the building—like the core of the legal system itself—reflects the Japanese spirit. As we saw while discussing cultural values, part of that spirit is informality. Upham (1987) draws on the concept of informality to position the Japanese legal system in a different light than other systems. A brief review of his comments will provide a context within which we can view the specifics of Japanese police, courts, and corrections.

Law by Bureaucratic Informalism

In his excellent analysis of law's operation in Japan, Upham (1987) describes two hypothetical legal systems. The first, called *rule-dominated,* involves legal professionals using specialized techniques to find and apply unambiguous rules to certain kinds of controversy. Under this system, courts have a monopoly on dispute resolution, because only the court personnel are familiar with the specialized methods of legal reasoning. Important as these court actors are, their role is limited, because all they really need to do is find the correct rule governing the particular case before them and then apply that rule.

The second hypothetical legal system is *judge-dominated.* Here the emphasis is on judges as political actors, and the legal process becomes a forum for broad-based social controversies. Instead of simply identifying the proper rule and applying it, judges are involved in policy making. Now the court personnel, specifically the judge, have an extensive role that allows them to seek social change as they declare and form social values.

Although the rule-dominated system may remind us of the civil legal tradition, and the judge-dominated system brings the common legal tradition to mind, Upham is careful to note that his types are purely theoretical. Nevertheless, to the extent that they describe features representing existing legal systems, Upham's types provide a base from which Japan's system can be discussed. Upon searching for Japanese justice components that reflect either rule-dominated or judge-dominated aspects, Upham concludes that neither theoretical type approximates the Japanese system. Instead he suggests a model, unique to Japan, that he calls *bureaucratic informalism.*

As we saw earlier, Japanese society emphasizes, among other values, those of contextualism, harmony, collectivism, and order. Collectivism is of initial importance here because it points to a difference between the Japanese model and the rule- or judge-dominated models. Under the two latter types, individuals play a key role in either instigating the process or in having the process launched against themselves. In either event, the individual plays a central role in the judicial process. Such individuation would not set well with the Japanese. Taking individuals as the principal social unit denies that society is composed of groups, each of which is greater than the sum of its members.

The ideal characteristic of a legal system wishing to downplay the role of individuals is informality. Informal responses to misbehaving individuals confirm the view that Japanese society is harmonious and conflict-free. When sanctions are private, indirect, and ambiguous, they can be virtually invisible to society at large. In this manner, *tatemae* is securely harmonious and the group, including its disobedient members, maintains its respectable position. As we review the components of the Japanese criminal justice system, we will see several examples of

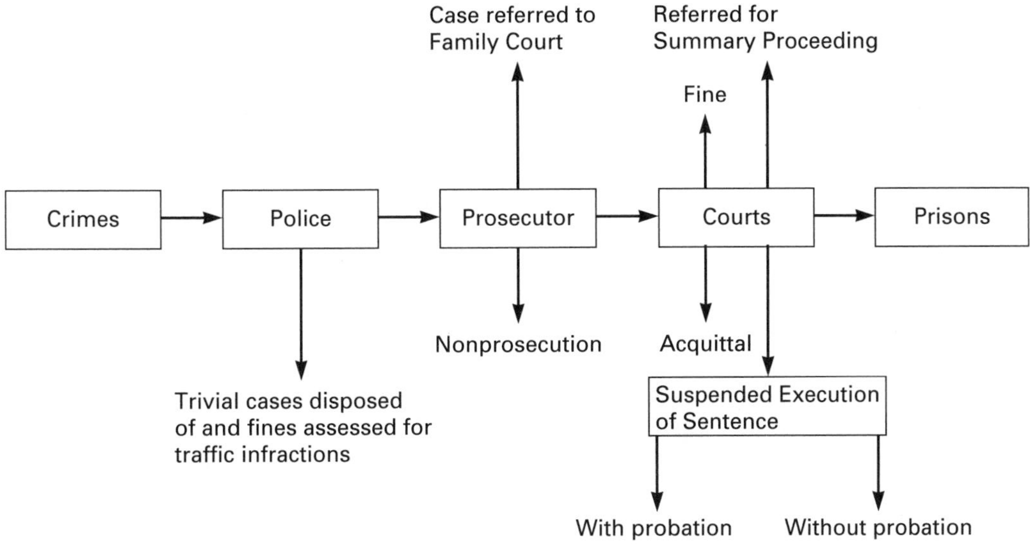

Figure 10.2 Flowchart of the Japanese Criminal Justice System for Adults

justice personnel using informal sanctions. In fact, even when the formal process is imposed, we will see prosecutors and judges preferring responses that are private and unceremonious.

The formal process of Japanese criminal justice provides the basis and structure for the observations made in this chapter. As Figure 10.2 shows, the flow of adult cases is seemingly straightforward and rather reminiscent of flowcharts for the United States. That similarity allows us to approach the Japanese system from the traditional police, court, corrections format. As we proceed through each of these stages, the informal system reinforcing the formal process is also discussed.

POLICING

The structure of Japanese policing was given close attention in Chapter 6, so discussion here can concentrate on its other aspects. Keeping with this chapter's theme of effectiveness and borrowing, we consider some reasons why law enforcement in Japan might be effective, and what, if anything, might transfer to America's police system.

Why Are the Japanese Police Effective?

The preceding heading "Why Are the Japanese Police Effective?" is somewhat misleading. It implies that the police are indeed effective, that we know why they are, and that the answer can be simply stated. It is hoped that you, the critical reader, will not be duped into such conclusions. The question is posed as a basis for discussion. If we accept Japan's comparatively low crime rate as a reflection of fact, and if we believe that the police play a role in that low rate, we can at least dismiss problems regarding the term "effective." Similarly, if we accept the idea that aspects of police organization and citizen response affect how the police anywhere complete their work, we can identify possible reasons for any police agency's effectiveness or ineffectiveness. With these cautions in mind, let us draw on studies of Japanese policing in an attempt to understand what impact the police officer may have in Japan's low crime rate. Specifically, we direct our attention to (1) the deployment of police officers, (2) the working partnership with citizens, and (3) the police emphasis on a service role. These are not mutually exclusive categories, and all obviously work in concert to provide effective policing.

Deployment of Police Officers. A long-time problem for law enforcement officials has been determining the best way to distribute their forces over a geographic area. That deployment problem determines how the job is conducted and how supervision is carried out. Once police officers are dismissed from roll call, supervisors often lose any significant ability to monitor the officers' behavior. The supervision problem was a real concern to Henry Fielding when he initiated a patrol beat in mid-eighteenth-century England. A specified patrol area allowed more exact supervision of Fielding's men, because absence from their particular area meant either a crime problem or a personnel problem.

Just as supervisors must know where their officers are, the officers need to be able to contact the supervisors. The classic scattering of officers throughout a geographic area made communication with supervisors rather difficult. The result could be officers who feel isolated and vulnerable. Boston responded to this problem in the 1870s by modifying its telegraph system in such a way that police call boxes could be positioned on city street corners so officers could notify the supervisor that they were at their post (Rubinstein, 1973). The 1880 advent of two-way communication, via the telephone call box, meant that patrolmen could make hourly contact with the station house. Still, it remained difficult for the station to contact the officer. Rubinstein (1973) describes the horns, colored lights, and bells attached to the call boxes and activated from the station house when a supervisor wanted to contact the officer. The wireless radio and patrol cars provided the next technological advance. The cars allowed officers to patrol their territory more frequently, and the radio enabled the police station to quickly notify officers of a citizen's call for help.

Today the use of patrol cars may seem not only the natural but maybe even the only way for a modern society to deploy its police. Japan has not agreed. In fact, its deployment system via the *koban* is offered by some (see Bayley, 1991; Kim, 1987; and Rake, 1987) as an explanation for police effectiveness.

Although the Japanese use patrol cars, it is the *koban* that provides the primary means of police deployment. In the city of Osaka, for example, one fifth of all patrol officers work in cars while four fifths operate from *koban* (Bayley, 1991). Tracing its origin to checkpoints the samurai established to protect the populace in feudal times (Kim, 1987), the *koban* now number about 6600 and the *chuzaisho* more than 9000 (Bayley, 1991).

Japan's reliance on static deployment through fixed posts rather than dynamic deployment via constantly moving cars occurs as much from necessity as from choice. Not only do the Japanese citizens strongly favor the *koban,* but the small proportion of Japanese land devoted to streets makes patroling by car less feasible than in other countries. For example, only 15 percent of Tokyo's land area is composed of streets, compared with 27 percent in New York City and 43 percent in Washington, DC (Bayley, 1991). Highly congested cities and streets mean that *koban* officers on bicycle or foot often beat patrol cars to scenes requiring police response.

The *koban* is a community fixture physically representing the link between police and citizen. It operates, and is perceived, as much like an assistance office as a police post. *Koban* officials spend much of their shift providing information about locations and addresses of homes and businesses tucked away in the confusing maze of often unnamed Japanese streets. They also act as the neighborhood lost and found, distribute crime prevention circulars, provide initial response to calls for assistance, and offer other services benefiting the community and citizen. The character of each *koban* is influenced by its surroundings (Bayley, 1991); in some locations it may provide a community television set, whereas in others it serves as the primary time check and alarm clock. Essentially, the needs of the neighborhood determine any unique traits found in individual *koban.*

The services provided at the *koban* and by the *koban* officers truly reflect the concept of community policing. The *koban officers,* who are not even considered to know the area until after two years at the post, spend 56 hours on duty each week. This deployment system means that every part of Japan is continually under the supervision of a *koban* (or *chuzaisho*) officer who is familiar with, and known to, the residents of that area. Not surprisingly, *koban* officers and citizens develop a strong working relationship, which serves to make the police more effective.

The Citizen as Partner. During the informal stage of police development in England and the American colonies, policing relied on the efforts of individual citizens. Whether the citizen was issuing or answering the old "hue and cry," or was more actively serving as watchman or constable, policing depended on citizen participation. The growth of professional police work in the early twentieth-century in the United States was accompanied by a philosophy that citizen involvement in policing was inappropriate. Instead, law enforcement was the duty of professional police officers who only incidentally had to interact with the law-abiding citizen. By the 1960s and 1970s, the pendulum was swinging back, and American police officials were recognizing the need for active citizen participation in crime prevention and reduction activities. In Japan, the tradition of police-citizen cooperation was never forsaken.

Building from a base that may stretch back some 600 years (see Plath, 1964, p. 142), Japan has established formal and informal associations that include crime prevention activities now linking the citizen and the police (Bayley, 1991; Kim, 1987). Crime prevention associations exist from the central government level down to the neighborhoods, but the primary organization level is tied to police station jurisdictions. Association members cooperate with the police to maintain social order through activities like distributing crime prevention literature and maintaining "contact points" where information and police assistance are available. Some crime prevention organizations may even organize civilian watches, which help monitor juvenile behavior, patrol streets, and assist police during emergencies.

Police response to these civilian efforts is one of support and encouragement. As Bayley put it, the Japanese police and their public believe each has "to work through the other in order to make the society a civil place to live" (quoted in Rake, 1987, p. 151). That cooperation requires Japanese police to place significant emphasis on nonenforcement activities and to interact with people other than those acting illegally. The result is a service orientation, which may also explain police effectiveness.

Policing as Service. Monkkonen (1981) argues that prior to the 1890s, American policing had a strong service component. Police stations served many functions now handled by social welfare agencies, and police officers provided as much service as enforcement. Between the 1890s and 1920, the public service work of police departments disappeared or was substantially diminished. Couple that with the movement toward professionalism and the disinvolvement of a citizen-partner, and the United States was left with rather isolated police officers.

Mid-twentieth-century American police officers had few occasions to interact with the helpful law-abiding citizen or even the troubled resident who had fallen on hard times. Instead, daily association was (and essentially still is) primarily with society's riffraff. Even when they interact with a supposedly upstanding citizen, it is often because that citizen has crossed the boundary into deviance. No wonder police officers are accused of having a distorted image of John and Jane Citizen. When you constantly see people's misbehavior, it is easy to assume that people are basically bad.

The deployment system for Japanese police and the citizen-police partnership provide the Japanese officer with a different view of people. Japanese police are called *Omawari-san* (the Honorable Mr. Walkabout), and their constant presence in the community gives them many opportunities to see people's good behavior. One result of this exposure to law-abiding citizens is the police officers' willingness to operate in a service capacity instead of constantly emphasizing their crime-fighter role.

The Japanese police officer's presence in the community is fittingly described by Bayley's comparison of policing styles in America and Japan: "An American policeman is like a fireman—he responds when he must. A Japanese policeman is more like a postman—he has a daily round of low-key activities that relate him to the lives of the people among whom he works" (Bayley, 1991, p. 86). The Japanese officer is consistently polite and businesslike during encounters with citizens (Kim, 1987), and the officer's presence is considered rather routine and personal. Police involvement in activities seemingly unrelated to law enforcement is accepted and expected by Japanese citizens.

One of the best examples of nonenforcement activities, and one that also emphasizes the citizen-police partnership, is the residential survey. Twice a year uniformed officers visit every residence in Japan to conduct a residential survey requesting general data about the occupants and the neighborhood (Bayley, 1991; Kim, 1987). Questions about the names, ages, occupations, and relationship of the residents are willingly answered by most people. Similarly, the respondent provides information about possible criminal activity in the area, may pass on rumors about neighborhood happenings, and might complain to the officer about municipal services. What might be considered an invasion of privacy in some

IMPACT

Wires Around the Bonsai

This chapter emphasizes the general ideas of system effectiveness and borrowing. Japan has been cited for years as an example of a country with a low crime rate and an apparently effective criminal justice system. Its success is all the more intriguing when we realize that much of Japan's system is the result of borrowing from other countries and either modifying the ideas to fit in Japanese culture or modifying the culture to accept the new ideas. The result is a justice system looked upon by other countries, including some Japan has borrowed from, as a model for improving their own criminal justice procedures. This chapter concludes with a discussion of aspects of the Japanese system that could be transported to the United States. As a contrast to that optimism, this "Impact" section provides a necessary caution. Cultural differences make the transfer of some Japanese procedures unlikely and even undesirable for many Americans. It is just as important for a country to realize what it cannot adapt as it is to understand what is adaptable.

As this chapter notes, the beauty, simplicity, and harmony of the bonsai tree are not achieved without stifling freedom of growth by using wires and cutting to train the bonsai. Similarly, the unity, order, and safety of Japanese society are accomplished by, according to American values, some inhibiting of personal freedoms. Consider, for example, the values of privacy and the right to an impartial jury.

Privacy

Reasons given for the effectiveness of Japanese police included their working relationship with citizens and their service orientation. Those concepts sound innocent enough, but some Americans might be troubled by some of the techniques used in their practice. Remember, for example, the residential survey conducted by *koban* officers twice a year. Americans might not be so willing as Japanese to share personal and neighborhood information with police officers. It is possible that surveys by American police would result in such resentment as to offset any gains made by obtaining the information.

Parker (1984) writes about *koban* officers on patrol entering a home found unlocked and empty. The officer leaves a calling card with his name on one side and a possible comment on the reverse warning the occupants about their poor crime prevention habits. Because police behavior in Japan reflects a moral norm as much as a legal one, Parker (1984) argues, such paternalism is acceptable in Japan. Many Americans might find behavior like that to be overly intrusive.

Intrusive behavior does not only take place in the citizen's home. Japanese law allows police officers to stop and question people only if they have

(continued)

IMPACT

Wires Around the Bonsai *(continued)*

reasonable grounds for suspecting they have committed or are about to commit a crime, or have information about a crime. Despite that, Bayley (1991) found it to be standard patrol procedure to stop and question anyone whenever the officer found it useful. Since most arrests are made by *koban* and *chuzaisho* officers—and most of those are the result of field interrogations—the officers become very adept at on-street questioning and are usually able to elicit information and even consents to be searched.

An Impartial Jury

Between 1928 and 1943 Japan used a jury system for criminal cases (Shibahara, 1990). In its eventual format, the jury consisted of 12 literate male jurors over 30 years of age. Their verdict did not have to be unanimous—a simple majority was sufficient. During its 15-year existence, only 484 cases were tried by jury, while defendants in over 25,000 serious cases waived their right to a jury trial (Shibahara, 1990). Obviously, the idea did not catch on.

Several conditions acted to make the jury trial a failure in Japan. On a cultural level, the jury system did not appeal to the basic national characteristic of the Japanese people. Shibahara (1990) explains that the Japanese people preferred to be tried by a professional judge rather than by their neighbors. But there were also practical problems with Japan's version of the jury. The primary one was the limited power given the jurors. Specifically, their decision was not binding on the judge. If the judge did not agree with the jury's decision, he could put the case before a new jury with newly selected jurors. Not surprisingly, most defense counsels decided that it made better sense to simply go before the professional judge. This preference for professional judges over lay jurors means the constitutional guarantee for an impartial tribunal results in a single judge, or a panel of three judges, deciding the facts and determining the sentence.

To the extent that these features of the Japanese system are important to that system's effectiveness, Americans may wonder if the tradeoff of personal rights and due process would be worth the possibly lower crime rate.

countries is typically accepted in Japan as a way for police to gain knowledge of an area and its people. The information, which is kept in large record books at the *koban*, is of great benefit in providing service and fighting crime.

The Japanese police officer's ability to play the potentially conflicting roles of authority figure and fellow citizen speaks well of both the officer and the citizen. Of course, it also reflects some of the cultural traits discussed earlier in this chapter. Police officers represent one of the hardest-working groups among hardworking people. They view their fellow officers and supervisors as an extension of their family and take enormous pride in the successful performance of their roles. For their part, the citizens' respect for authority and orderliness, coupled with an acceptance of responsibility for each other's behavior, provides an atmosphere supporting police efforts. But, of course, the police are not the extent of the criminal justice system. We must also understand the role played by the courts.

JUDICIARY

Just as Japan's policing exhibits an intriguing combination of tradition, innovation, and imitation, so too does its contemporary court system. First we will examine the historical base for the adjudication system, and then we will consider how the end result reflects aspects of Japanese cultural traits. Especially meaningful in this section is the preference for compromise and conciliation and the importance of apology.

The Japanese judicial system certainly owes some of its features to the Chinese, but there always seems to have been a glimmer of features more typically associated with European legal traditions. For example, aspects of precedent and a role for adversaries have been present since the first developmental stage of Japanese legal process, but this does not appear to be the result of borrowing. Instead, the similarity to common law is an element that seems to have developed independent of outside influence. Since the 1600s Japan's highly organized court system began developing a body of native law and practice based on judicial precedent. Though similar to the practice of *stare decisis* in English common law, Japan's development of judicial precedent cannot be attributed to borrowing from the common law tradition.

To see how judicial precedent has operated in Japan, it is necessary to describe the organization of courts. The Regency domain was divided into three jurisdictions: metropolitan, rural, and ecclesiastical. The Metropolitan Judge received all suits where the plaintiff was a townsman, the Exchequer Judge got those with a countryman plaintiff, and the Temple Judge accepted complaints from residents of church lands. When sitting as a single court, these three judges formed the Supreme Court, which had original jurisdiction in cases between parties from different jurisdictions. Actually, the men in these positions were not as busy as that description sounds. Each post was in fact held by two officials with each, in alternate months, sitting in the Supreme Court. At other times, he officiated in his own jurisdiction. Even in his home province, there were lower magistrates who heard most cases.

Within this structure, an independent system of case law developed without need to cite Chinese or any other foreign authority. To make his point, Wigmore (1936) quotes at length a case that included formal and recorded consultation between judges, a search for precedent extending back nearly 100 years, the application of precedent, and the creation of new precedent. English case law had no advantage over this aspect of the Tokugawa legal system.

The Japanese desire to appease disputes is borrowed from the Chinese principle of conciliation as emphasized by Confucian philosophy. To achieve conciliation, each Japanese town and village was divided into *kumi,* or groupings of five neighboring families, with each responsible for the other's conduct. In times of disagreement the five family heads met to settle the matter. In a dinner-party type of atmosphere, agreement was achieved in the midst of eating, drinking, and a friendly spirit. On those occasions when settlement was not reached, the complaint could be passed to a higher authority. Such appeal occurred more often in larger towns and cities. In the villages, the seeking of settlement outside the *kumi* or beyond the chief village officials was considered a dishonorable last resort.

Once a magistrate received a case from either a village or city, it could still be treated in a manner Western eyes might see as extra-legal. Wigmore (1936) provides several examples of decisions that reflect an extremely flexible view toward the law. In an 1840 case, the magistrate of Komo County was asked to order a woman (Cho) and her four male family members to stop bothering farmer Uhei and his son, Umakichi. Cho's family claimed Umakichi should marry Cho because prior relations (the exact nature of which are not specified) between the boy and girl made marriage the honorable thing to do. The magistrate investigated the case and apparently encouraged the two families to reach a settlement of their own accord. The records show that later in the same month as the first petition, Uhei asked the magistrate to dismiss the petition. Uhei explained in his second petition that the affair turned out to be unimportant and based on foolish statements. All parties were at peace, and Uhei credited the magistrate with bringing about the settlement. The petition asked the magistrate to shut his eyes to the case and not give it further consideration. Magistrate Shinomoto concurred and no legal action was ever taken.

A 1983 case (see Hendry, 1989, pp. 190–191) suggests that 140 years have not significantly modified Japanese aversion to litigation and court activities. In 1983 a family's three-year-old son drowned in an irrigation pond while he was in the care of a neighbor. The bereaved family filed a lawsuit claiming negligence by the neighbor, the contractor who had failed to fence in the pond, and against various levels of government. The District Court ordered the neighbors to pay 5 million yen, but the other parties were exonerated. The case received considerable media coverage, and the bereaved family soon received hundreds of anonymous phone calls and some 50 letters and postcards condemning them for taking legal action against their neighbors. The father lost his job, and the other children in the family were subjected to ridicule at school. The neighbors, meanwhile, appealed the court's decision. This action elicited a similarly abusive response from the public. Apparently, appealing to the courts, even in self-defense, is regarded as being as inappropriate, as are cases of disputes between neighbors.

The 1840 and the 1983 cases exemplify civil rather than criminal incidents, but the principle remains. Since the Tokugawa era, official conciliation procedures have provided alternatives to civil litigation and to criminal trials when the preferred informal conciliation efforts fail. The main difference between historical and modern procedures is the people playing the role of mediator. Where samurai and village officials served in the past, police officers and lawyers act today. As we review the formal system of handling criminal disputes, we will necessarily refer to some of the informal procedures reflecting conciliation ideals.

Pretrial Activities

There is a saying about the American criminal process that "in the Halls of Justice, justice is in the halls." The implication is that much of the everyday work by justice officials takes place away from the formal courtroom environment. Police deals with informants, prosecution favors in return for testimony, plea negotiations, sentencing arrangements, and other activities constantly take place in informal settings. At times those informal arrangements result in very formal activities (for example, a formal contract stating a plea bargain agreement), but they

You Should Know!

THE RIGHT TO LEGAL COUNSEL IN JAPAN

In the United States, a person has the right to counsel (at government expense if the person is indigent) once investigation of a crime focuses on that person (*Miranda v. Arizona,* 1966). That means, for example, suspects being interrogated by the police (*Escobedo v. Illinois,* 1964) and suspects in a police lineup (*Gilbert v. California,* 1967) have the right to the presence of counsel during that questioning and at that lineup. Once the person moves from the status of "suspect" to "defendant" (that is, once formal charges have been brought), she or he continues to have the right to counsel at the preliminary hearing (*Coleman v. Alabama,* 1970) and during any trial that could result in the defendant's imprisonment (*Gideon v. Wainwright,* 1963 and *Argersinger v. Hamlin,* 1972). In other words, in the United States both "suspects" and the "accused" (that is, defendants) enjoy the right to counsel (at government expense when necessary) from the earliest stages of the arrest process through the final stages of trial.

The constitution of Japan (see a copy at **home.ntt.com/japan/constitution/ english-Constitution.html**) distinguishes between the right to counsel for the suspect and the accused in a manner unfamiliar to Americans. Article 34 states, "No person shall be arrested or detained without being at once informed of the charges against him or without the immediate privilege of counsel." Article 37 reads, "At all times the accused shall have the assistance of competent counsel who shall, if the accused is unable to secure the same by his own efforts, be assigned to his use by the State." In this manner, anyone "arrested" or "detained" has the "privilege of counsel," but, because counsel in this case is a privilege rather than a right, the state is not obligated to pay for it. Therefore, indigents at the suspect stage, which Hataguchi (1990) says is the majority of suspects, are not provided counsel during the investigation/arrest process.

Once a Japanese suspect becomes an "accused" or defendant, Article 37 kicks in, and the state is obliged to provide competent counsel to assist the defendant during the trial phase. One result of the suspect/accused distinction is that few people held in precharge detention have access to an attorney (Hataguchi, 1990). In fact, even suspects who can afford to hire a lawyer may not see their counsel very often, because attorney access to the suspect is controlled by the investigating authorities.

may also simply remain an informal transaction. Japan's aversion to courtroom activities suggests that their "hallway justice" is even more pronounced than our own. This conclusion will be confirmed as we become familiar with the actors and actions involved at the pretrial stage.

Police Role. Japanese police arrest and refer to the prosecutor about 28 percent of the suspects with whom they have had recorded contact. Another 2 percent are arrested and released by the police, and the remaining 70 percent are not even arrested (Research and Training Institute, 1996, 1998). At the start of this chapter it was noted that Japanese police have a very high clearance rate. You might reasonably wonder how 70 percent of the suspects can avoid arrest and yet the police can claim a clearance rate of about 55 percent—compared, for example, with a U.S. clearance rate of about 20 percent for all index offenses. Much of the explanation lies in terminology.

The clearance rate for American police, as reported in the annual *Uniform Crime Reports,* reflects a suspect being arrested, charged with committing an offense, and turned over to the court for prosecution (see the FBI's *Uniform Crime Reports*). In Japan, a crime is reported as cleared when the police tell the prosecutor the crime has been solved. No arrest is necessary. Even when an arrest is made, the police need not turn the suspect over in order to "clear" the crime (Araki, 1985). By these definitions, Japanese police might well be expected to have a higher clearance rate than their American counterparts.

Japanese police have three choices in initiating cases. They can (1) "send only the evidence to the prosecutor leaving the suspect unarrested but still liable to prosecution, (2) arrest the suspect but decide not to detain him or her, or (3) arrest the suspect and recommend that the prosecutor detain him or her" (Araki, 1985, p. 609). The first situation (evidence forward, suspect not) applies to most of the cases. As mentioned, 70 percent of suspects are not even arrested. The procedure allowing police to clear a case and then discharge the suspect is established by the local prosecutor's office. Araki (1985) explains that each chief of the district public prosecutor's office develops criteria permitting police to discharge persons committing less serious offenses when the crime and criminal are determined to be nondangerous.

The institutionalization of informal sanctioning is only one indication of the significant discretion given Japanese police. Contextualism, as discussed earlier, plays an important role in understanding when and why police use their discretion to respond informally to offenses. Bayley (1991) reports that enforcement is influenced by where the offense occurred so that officers may respond according to the custom of each area (that is, contextualism). In other instances officers may believe that formal punishment would be inappropriately severe in a particular case, and respond with anything from friendly warnings to ignoring evidence.

It is apparent that those examples of police discretion can just as accurately describe American, and almost any other, police officers as well. The difference lies more in the extent to which nonenforcement tactics are used than in their form or the situation provoking them. As the 70 percent "release without arrest" statistic indicates, Japanese police officers make liberal use of policing tactics that avoid the formal justice process.

One reason Japanese officers are likely to use informal tactics stems from their collectivist culture. Because the significance of the group is accepted by most Japanese, they are also aware of the obligations accompanying group membership. One of the most basic obligations is to refrain from embarrassing the group. If that obligation is not met, the dutiful group member will do his best to avoid public display of the misconduct. The police, being fully aware of this protocol, can use it to handle the situation informally. The primary method employed is to require an apology from the offender.

Americans may consider giving an apology to one's victim to be barely a slap on the offender's wrist. Yet this is where the cultural differences come into play. When a Japanese apologizes, he or she is admitting to having failed in his or her obligation to the group, an important concept to all concerned. Were that not bad enough, an apology also forces recognition of *honne* overcoming *tatemae.* It is no easy task to admit that one is responsible for disrupting the harmony, has failed in his duty to the group, and has jeopardized his group standing. The apology, in other words, can simultaneously be a punishment for the acutely embarrassed offender and an expression of remorse to compensate the victim.

Bayley (1991) relates several stories of observed police encounters that resulted in a formal apology as the police imposed sanction. The tactic, which is always at the discretion of the officer, is used for minor violations ranging from traffic offenses and wandering drunks, to inappropriate behavior toward fellow citizens. The apology as sanction is so commonly used that *koban* officers may keep a copy of an appropriate letter of apology to be used by remorseful offenders. At the same time, it is taken so seriously by Japanese citizens and police that some offenders are simply warned instead of being required to make a formal apology.

The police preference for nonenforcement strategies in responding to offenders is not unique to this stage of the Japanese criminal justice system. Of course, there are situations that require the police to respond formally and send the case to the next stage. However, as we will see, prosecutors and judges continue both the process and the propensity for informal sanctioning.

Prosecutor Role. Prosecution in Japan falls under the authority of the Ministry of Justice and is under the direction of a Prosecutor-General, who is appointed by the Cabinet. Neither the prefectural government nor any of the other subdivisions has any control of prosecution. So, unlike the police system, which has aspects of decentralization via prefectural involvement, prosecution is fully centralized.

Following a European model, law graduates choose career paths in prosecution, defense, or judgeships after receiving their law degrees. After initial entry, each area has some levels from which to choose and others to which one can aspire. Prosecutors, for example, work at one of four court levels: supreme, high, district, and local. The workload is greatest at the district level, because that is where most criminal cases are handled.

The prosecutor's primary activity is to gather information regarding the case, and to provide information about the suspect to assist the judge in sentencing. In fact, Castberg (1990) suggests that these two activities not only define the role of prosecutors, but of police, defense, and even the trial itself. This fact appeared to be true in our discussion of the pretrial activities of police, and we will soon appreciate its pertinence to the defense and in the trial, but we must begin with the prosecutor.

Given the vigorous investigation by police, and the typical confession they are able to elicit, it may seem the prosecutor's job must require only minimum effort. Actually, there is still plenty to keep prosecutors busy because they must determine if there is sufficient evidence to prosecute, initiate specific charges, and decide if the prosecution should be suspended. Defendants in Japan cannot be found guilty solely on the basis of a confession, so prosecutors must have sufficient additional information to convince the judge of the defendant's guilt. Also, there is no plea bargaining in Japan, so determination of specific charges against the suspect is neither automatic nor always simple. Despite the time requirements for those activities, a spur-of-the-moment visit to a prosecutor's office is likely to find him pondering the appropriateness of suspending prosecution in a particular case.

The authority to suspend prosecution in a case is provided in Article 248 of the Code of Criminal Procedure:

> *If, after considering the character, age, and situation of the offender, the gravity of the offense, the circumstances under which the offense was committed, and the conditions subsequent to the commission of the offense, prosecution is deemed unnecessary, prosecution need not be instituted (quoted in Castberg, 1990, p. 60).*

Because prosecution is actually terminated in these cases, the term "suspension" is somewhat misleading. In any event, suspension of prosecution is an increasingly popular way for prosecutors to handle criminal cases. From a 1987 rate of 17 percent, suspension of prosecution increased to over 20 percent in the early 1990s and was over 30 percent by the late-1990s (Research and Training Institute, 1998).

Offenses ranging from homicide (a 1997 suspension rate of 3 percent) to gambling (a 1997 suspension rate of 34 percent) receive this prosecutorial response each year. However, as Table 10.1 shows, suspension of prosecution is especially used in cases of "traffic professional negligence" (83 percent) and embezzlement (76 percent). The "traffic professional negligence" category, which would more likely end up in a civil court in the United States, involves injuries in traffic accidents caused by a person in the conduct of an occupation (see Araki, 1985).

Article 248 is very general in setting criteria for prosecutors to use when deciding if suspension of prosecution is appropriate. Castberg (1990) suggests that "circumstances under which the offense was committed" deal primarily with aggravating circumstances, like excessive force or cruelty, which accompanied the crime. The "conditions subsequent to the commission of the offense" generally refers to apology and restitution by the suspect and forgiveness by the victim or victim's family. It is at this point that the defense attorney can begin an active role.

Defense Attorney Role. There are no public defenders in Japan, but the Japanese constitution assures anyone accused of a crime of the right to counsel, at state expense if the defendant is indigent. Indigents are represented by counsel appointed from the ranks of lawyers listed on the roll of the Japanese Bar

Table 10.1 1997 Prosecution and Suspended Prosecution Percentages by Penal Code Offense

	Prosecuted	Suspended
Total*	64	34
Homicide	62	3
Robbery	81	4
Bodily injury	73	23
Embezzlement	16	76
Larceny	56	38
Fraud	66	24
Rape	68	10
Arson	66	10
Gambling	65	34
Violent Acts	71	24
Traffic professional negligence	15	83

*Total includes more offenses than shown here. Percentages may not total 100, since options besides prosecution or suspended prosecution are also available.

Source: Research and Training Institute (1998), *Summary of the White Paper on Crime*. Tokyo: Ministry of Justice.

Federation. The low crime rate and high confession rate suggests that there is little work for defense attorneys in Japan and, in fact, few lawyers do exclusively criminal defense work (Castberg, 1990). Like the police and the prosecutors, defense attorneys assist in gathering information about the case and the defendant.

Use of the term "defendant" instead of "suspect" is important when we discuss defense attorneys, because appointment of counsel occurs after indictment. As we discovered when discussing police interrogation, a suspect's access to defense counsel at that stage is often problematic. Indigents wishing to have legal representation prior to arraignment must appeal to the Legal Aid Society or the Civil Liberties Union. Since nearly two thirds of the criminal cases involving defense counsel are for indigents, the majority of defendants cannot receive legal advice during police interrogation (Hataguchi, 1990). So there is basically no role for the defense attorney prior to indictment.

Even between indictment and the trial, defense counsel has a more informal than formal role. For example, the attorney may accompany the defendant to contact the victim, or victim's family, so that appropriate apologies can be made and reparations offered. The defense attorney can advise the defendant regarding the proper way to show remorse and the appropriate restitution to offer. If counsel can obtain written statements of forgiveness, and maybe even a victim's request for leniency toward the defendant, the prosecutor might be inclined toward suspending prosecution. Should the victim's statements and requests for leniency not impress the prosecutor, defense counsel can always use them during the trial. In fact, because so many defendants have confessed, much of the defense role during trial is to present mitigating circumstances that might convince the judge to be sympathetic toward the defendant. However, even when there is no confession and the defendant is contesting the charge, a prime defense counsel role is to provide the judge with reasons to be compassionate (Castberg, 1990).

The pretrial activities of police, prosecutor, and defense attorney seem intent on avoiding formal sanctioning of suspects and defendants. This seeking of informal responses does not stop in those cases that actually do make it to a courtroom.

Trial Options

The Public Prosecutor's Office typically handles over 2 million cases. After referring more than one-quarter million cases to the Family Courts, the prosecutors dispose of the remainder through prosecution (about 64 percent) and either suspension of prosecution (about 34 percent) or simply nonprosecution (about 2 percent). Of those cases actually prosecuted, some 90 percent are handled under summary proceedings and 10 percent go to formal trial. Of those going to formal trial, over 99 percent are convicted and, although nearly all those will receive a prison sentence, about 60 percent will have execution of that prison sentence suspended (Research and Training Institute, 1998).

To emphasize the reluctance to impose formal sanctions, consider the numbers we would obtain by using these percentages on a hypothetical cluster of 1000 offenders arriving at the prosecutor's office and not being transferred to Family Court (see Figure 10.3). Because about 360 of those would either have

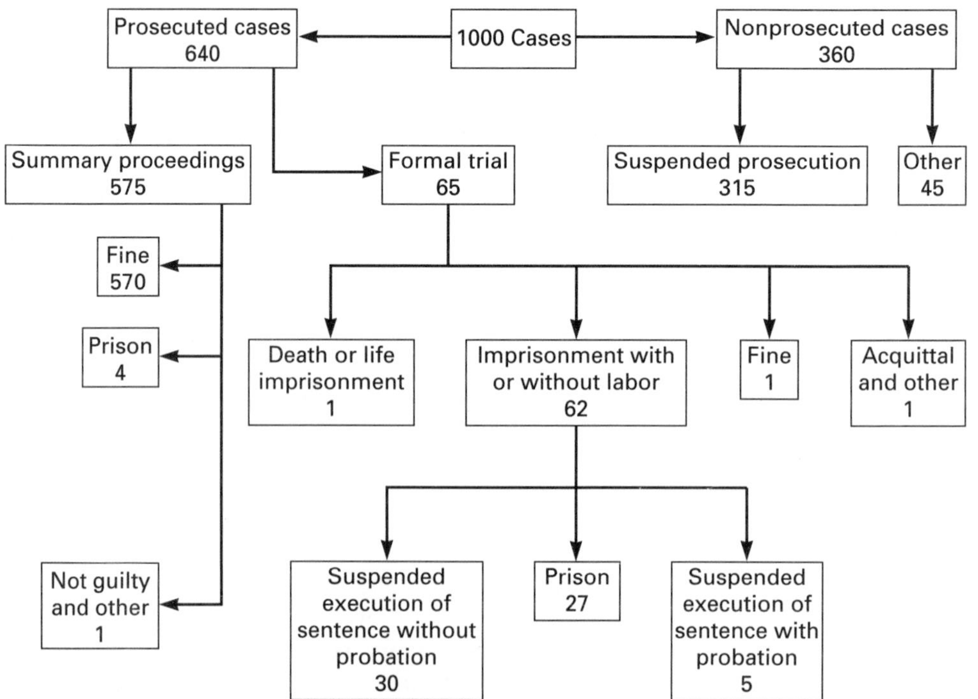

Figure 10.3 Dispositions by Prosecutor's Office of 1000 Hypothetical Cases

prosecution suspended or no action toward prosecution even attempted, only 640 would even continue in the process. Of those 640 people being prosecuted, about 575 would plead guilty and have their case quickly handled through summary procedures for which they are not even present. Of the remaining 65 people going to formal trial, almost all would be convicted and sentenced to prison—an acquittal might occur, but not often, or someone might be fined instead of imprisoned, but, again, not often. About 40 of those convicted and sentenced to prison will have the execution of their sentence suspended. And only a few of those receiving a suspended execution of sentence will be placed on probation, while the others will live in the community without any court supervision. Of the original 1000 people, then, fewer than 30 may actually be sent to prison.

It appears that the formal trial process is an infrequent occurrence in the Japanese criminal justice system. Even when adjudication is required, most of the cases are handled summarily instead of in a formal court setting. Following a brief review of Japan's court structure, we will look more closely at the summary procedures and regular trials.

Court Structure. The Japanese court system has four levels composed of two trial courts and two appellate courts (see Figure 10.4). At the apex is Japan's Supreme Court, which was the primary judicial modification in the postwar constitution. The American influence is seen in the authority given the Supreme Court, which has administrative control over all other courts and has the right to determine the constitutionality of all laws. This latter point, the concept of

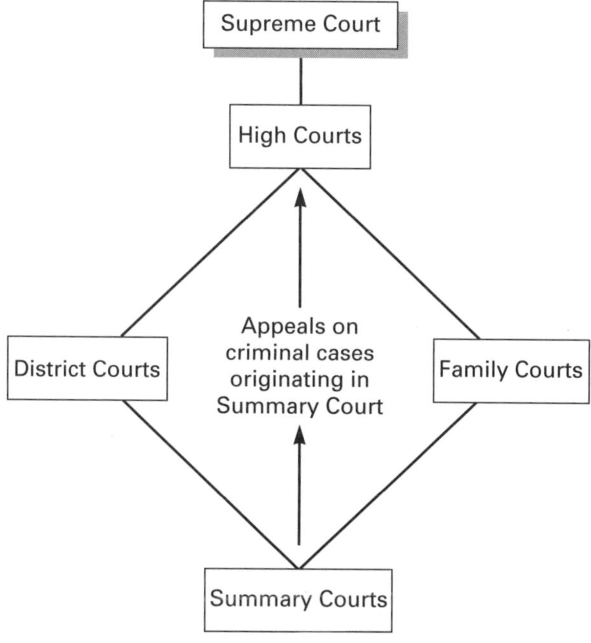

Figure 10-4 Japan's Court Organization

judicial review, presents an awkward situation, because Japan's government is essentially parliamentary in nature. In most other such systems, nothing can override the parliament, but the right of judicial review gives Japan's judicial branch the authority to do just that. Reischauer (1988) notes that the Japanese Supreme Court has been reluctant to go against the Japanese Diet's political decisions and will typically defer to what the Diet majority voted. This is in contrast to the U.S. Supreme Court's vigorous use of judicial review to shape social and political developments.

The Supreme Court consists of one chief justice and 14 justices. Cases, which are received on appeal, are initially assigned to one of three petty benches composed of five justices each. If the case concerns a constitutional issue, it is transferred to the Grand Bench, where all 15 justices sit (Castberg, 1990).

Eight High Courts, with six branches, serve as intermediate appellate courts with cases typically heard by a panel of three judges. Most of the High Court cases come on appeal from the district or family courts, but criminal cases originating in Summary Court can also go directly to the High Court (Westermann & Burfeind, 1991).

The trial level court for both criminal and civil offenses are the 50 District Courts. Each of the 47 prefectures has one District Court, but Hokkaido's size requires it to have an additional three. Equal in level and number with the district courts, yet administratively independent, are the Family Courts. These courts handle most domestic and juvenile (persons under age 20) matters. The only criminal matters heard in Family Court are those involving adults who have violated a child's well-being (typically less than 1 percent of Family Court cases).

Summary Courts, numbering nearly 600, have original jurisdiction in minor criminal and civil cases (Westerman & Burfeind, 1991). Cases heard in summary proceedings range from larceny to bodily injury, but the penalties imposed are limited to fines or short-term detention (that is, no more than three years). The popularity of summary procedures with prosecutors and offenders makes the Summary Courts a good starting place in discussing Japan's adjudication process.

Summary Courts. Japan has no grand jury system, so when the prosecutor decides to initiate formal proceedings, the defendant is indicted through the filing of an information. Since there is no preliminary hearing, the next step is for the prosecutor to choose between a summary procedure and a regular trial. If the summary procedure is used, the case is handled in one of the country's Summary Courts. These courts also conduct a few formal trials, but the vast majority of their activities are summary proceedings.

If the defendant agrees (and that agreement is required for this procedure), the prosecutor can dispose of the case by sending the Summary Court judge the defendant's consent form, the evidence related to the case, and the prosecution's sentence recommendation (Araki, 1985; Castberg, 1990). Neither party has the opportunity to appear before the Summary Court, because the judge reviews the case outside the presence of either the prosecutor or defendant. However, there is a level of protection for both sides, because defense or prosecution can apply for a formal trial if either is dissatisfied with the ruling under summary procedures. The sanctions resulting from summary procedures are fines (both regular and minor) and they are used in both violent (for example, bodily injury, assault) and nonviolent (for example, embezzlement, gambling, traffic violations) offenses.

Modified Public Trials. If the charge is not a serious one (for example, larceny), and the defendant is not contesting the facts, it is possible to have a formal, yet streamlined, trial (Araki, 1985; Castberg, 1990). These modified public trials can be held in either Summary Court or District Court, but it is much more likely to be the former. Trial procedures are simplified, and great reliance is placed on information provided by the prosecutor as being an accurate reflection of the facts in the case. The judge's written work is simplified, because this type of trial does not require written reasons for the decision, which can include fines or short-term (that is, less than three years) detention.

Regular Trials. District and Family Courts serve as the court of first instance for most contested criminal cases and for cases where the defendant or prosecutor is not pleased with the result of a summary procedure. Criminal jurisdiction of Family Courts is limited to cases of domestic relations, juvenile delinquency, and cases where adults violated laws protecting a child's welfare. The 50 District Courts have jurisdiction over all criminal cases except insurrection (which must start in the High Court), Family Court adult criminal cases, and crimes handled in Summary Court. Hearings are conducted by one judge (most cases) or by a panel of three judges (the most serious offenses and those with the most severe penalties). In either format, the court handles two general types of cases: noncontested and contested.

The noncontested cases, which are the vast majority, are typically disposed of rather quickly. A single judge examines the written and documentary evidence presented by the prosecutor and hears challenges from the defense. Because the defendant has confessed, the judge's role is basically to protect the accused's rights by examining all submitted evidence, occasionally requiring submission of more evidence, and determining an appropriate sentence (Castberg, 1990). Even though this is a formal trial setting, there is considerable flexibility regarding the admissibility of evidence. Like many of the trials under the civil legal tradition, Japanese trials are not bifurcated. That is, determination of both guilt and sentence is done simultaneously. There is no presentence investigation done for adult offenders, so the judge relies on information presented during trial to help determine an appropriate punishment for the defendant.

When the defendant contests the charges, the Japanese court system follows its most formal procedures. In this type of trial there is either a genuine dispute regarding the facts of the case or there is no confession. The judge, or judges, serve as impartial adjudicator and fact-finder (Castberg, 1990). As in countries following a civil legal tradition, Japanese judges play an active role during the trial as they decide the order of witnesses, frequently begin the questioning of those witnesses, and rule on admissibility of evidence. There are no clearly defined prosecution and defense phases in the trial, but each side may question witnesses, present closing arguments, and make sentencing recommendations.

One of the most striking differences between Japanese and American trials is the intermittent nature of hearings in Japan. Rather than having a single hearing stretch over a few hours or days, trials in Japan consist of several short, separate hearings scheduled every few weeks or months. Seventy percent of the District and Family Court trials last less than three months, but over 20 percent last for three to six months (Research and Training Institute, 1990).

Judgments

Judges in District and Family Courts have several judgment types available. The defendant can, of course, be acquitted; but this occurs in less than 0.1 percent of the cases. The extremely high conviction rate in Japanese courts must be considered in light of the system's screening process and the defendant's tendency to confess. Over 70 percent of the suspects are not arrested at all, or are arrested and then released by the police; about one third of the cases reaching the prosecutor are suspended; and some 10 percent of the cases that are prosecuted are heard in a formal trial. Even among that 10 percent, most defendants do not contest the charges. Given these circumstances, a 99.9 percent conviction rate is not quite so surprising.

Allowable sentences for convicted offenders include execution, life imprisonment, imprisonment with or without forced labor, a fine, and suspended execution of sentence. Neither the death sentence (given in 3 of the nearly 55,000 adjudications in 1996) nor life imprisonment (given 33 times in 1994) are handed down very often. Fines (including short-term penal detention) also account for only a small number of sentences (413 in 1996). By far the most frequent sentence from District and Family Courts is one of imprisonment with or without labor. The 1996 rate of nearly 99 percent is typical (Research and Training Institute, 1998).

A prison sentence in nearly 99 percent of the cases suggests that Japanese judges are quite severe. People favoring a punitive response to offenders may say it is about time somebody in the Japanese criminal justice system got tough on criminals. Actually, the preference for informal justice that we found at the police and prosecutor levels still exists in the courtroom, despite the seemingly high imprisonment rate. This is because over half those prison sentences are suspended, and less than 15 percent of the suspended executions of sentences even require probation. All types of crimes can receive suspended execution of sentences. Prison sentences for homicide, robbery, and drugs are suspended with and without probation, just as are sentences for larceny, gambling, and road-traffic violations. When the sentence is for imprisonment, or involves probation on a suspended sentence, the corrections area in Japan's system takes over.

CORRECTIONS

Corrections in Japan received specific coverage in Chapter 8, so here we will highlight those aspects of Japanese corrections that relate to this chapter's themes of effectiveness and borrowing.

History

Throughout the various shogunate periods, corrections (in its broadest sense) varied from the right of samurai to execute on the spot any misbehaving commoner (Westney, 1987) to the use of prisons *(royas)* built in the fourteenth century as both pretrial holding facilities and as places of punishments (Eskridge, 1989). Some of the later efforts, like the early nineteenth-century "Coolie Gathering Place" facility, even provided inmates with an opportunity to learn a trade (Correction Bureau, 1990). Despite that historical base, the modern era of Japanese corrections did not begin until the late nineteenth and early twentieth centuries. The push toward modernization resulted from efforts during the Meiji Restoration to increase Japan's contact with the Western world. Actually, one of the stipulations made when revising treaties with the West required Japan to improve prison administration. Japan's response, as it was in so many other areas in the late nineteenth century, was to begin a search for a model to bring home.

By 1890 Japan had joined the International Penal and Penitentiary Congress and, with the assistance of Prussian penologist Kurt von Seebach, started the country's first national training institute for prison officers (Correction Bureau, 1990). Concern about the prison employees was not matched with concern for the inmates until the 1920s and the efforts of Japanese jurist Akira Masaki. His reminiscences (Masaki, 1964) provide a review of imitation and innovation as he describes the development of modern corrections in Japan.

Masaki was sent abroad in 1928 to gather information on prison systems in other countries. Among his stops was the Hungarian farm prison, Kiss Halta, where he was impressed with the absence of iron bars and walls. The feature he would dwell upon, though, was the administrator's use of a prisoners' self-government policy controlled by a progressive stage system to modify prisoner behavior. A trip to the United States gave him an opportunity to see the classification system at Sing Sing prison (a system he found similar to the Belgian one he had earlier observed) and to visit the Elmira (New York) Reformatory, which he called "the Mecca for criminologists" (Masaki, 1964, p. 54).

American prisons at Sing Sing and Auburn (New York) and the naval prison at Portsmouth (New Hampshire) also provided Masaki an opportunity to gather more information on inmate self-government. He found the process, as used in these prisons, had several defects. Yet he believed when properly implemented, inmate self-government could be the core of a treatment system.

In 1933 Masaki was finally able to try out some of his ideas gathered while abroad. Under orders from the director of the Prison Bureau, Masaki began to set up a progressive stage system. He used the classification procedure from Belgium and the United States to set up four specific stages of inmate categorization. Following the mark system observed at Elmira Reformatory (which had come to America from Australia via Ireland), Masaki awarded prisoners marks based on their work habits, good behavior, and a showing of responsibility and firm will. The marks allowed inmates to progress through the stages; with each promotion they received more freedom and privileges.

At the second and first stages, self-government became an important aspect of the treatment plan. Inmates at these levels worked without the supervision of guards but instead under the leadership of a fellow prisoner they had selected. Unfortunately for Masaki, his program was criticized for being too lenient. Masaki admitted that some wardens forgot the need to instill a sense of responsibility in the prisoners, but he accepted the criticism and reported feelings of frustration with implementing a philosophy he believed to be correct. Today, the classification and progressive stage systems brought to Japan by Masaki remain important aspects of Japanese corrections—the use of inmate self-government is not.

Aspects of Effectiveness

Determining the effectiveness of prisons and community corrections is difficult. One type of attempt, using the concept of recidivism, judges effectiveness by whether or not a person who has been through a corrections program returns to criminal behavior. It is difficult to establish, however, just who the recidivist actually is and which program, or program part, was apparently ineffective. Is probation effective as long as the probationer is law-abiding while under probation supervision but commits a new offense after being released from probation? Is imprisonment effective if the released person does not commit a new offense within three years of being released from prison, or do we have to wait five or more years before claiming success? And if we can claim that the prison experience was effective in a particular case, isn't it important to know which prison program (for example, academic education, vocational education, drug therapy) made the difference?

In addition to the definition problems associated with the term *recidivism,* there are practical problems related to data gathering. If John is released from prison in California and moves to New Mexico, where he commits a new crime, California is not likely to hear about John's recidivism. If Mary successfully completes probation in Weld County, Colorado, and then is sentenced to a Colorado prison two years later from a different county, Weld County officials probably will not know about Mary's recidivism. The decentralized corrections system operating in the United States makes it difficult to monitor the location and recurring misbehavior of persons going through the state or federal systems. This is especially true among the various states, but can also be true within a particular state. The absence of a nationwide record-keeping process prohibits effective sharing of information among all the different corrections agencies in the country.

In countries with a centralized corrections system, the ability to keep track of current and former clients is obviously increased. As such, Japan's single system reduces some of the practical problems associated with measuring recidivism, but the definitional ones remain. The difficulty of playing with terms like *effectiveness* and *recidivism* can be seen with a brief look at Japanese suspended-sentence numbers and United States probation numbers.

Suspended Sentences. In 1993, 44 percent of the adult probationers whose probation was terminated during that year were deemed "successes" under Japanese adjustment statistics (Rehabilitation Bureau, 1995). During the same year, 53 percent of the adults left probation status in the United States under successful circumstances according to the termination statistics (Snell, 1995). Although the two percentages do not seem that dissimilar, they are figured in distinctly different ways—that is, adjustment versus termination statistics (see Figure 10.5).

Probation success in United States jurisdictions tends to be a black-and-white issue. The probationer either successfully completes the terms, conditions, and required time on probation, or has probation revoked for technical or new crime offenses. In Japan, success lies more on a continuum than being part of a dichotomy. As the Japan pie chart in Figure 10.5 shows, a person leaving probation can be said to have had a successful, moderate, or failed adjustment. "Successful adjustment" refers to persons warranting early discharge from probation and persons who have shown improved adjustment to social life. Persons having "moderate adjustment" are probationers whose standard of behavior is regarded as acceptable although it may fall short of the public's standard of behavior. For example, Yuriko Yoshioka, a young woman with substance-abuse problems and on probation for auto theft, might no longer be stealing cars but might still abuse the use of alcohol. In the United States she would likely be discharged from probation as an unqualified success, but in Japan she is counted as a "moderate" success. Of course, this means that in Figure 10.5 both the "success" and "moderate" slices of the Japanese pie chart would likely be successes in American jurisdictions—making total Japanese successes 62 percent and total United States successes 53 percent.

The Japanese "adjustment" statistics suggest an interesting way to provide more realistic feedback regarding the "success" of probation. When we identify probationers only as having succeeded or failed, the primary criteria is usually whether or not the person committed a technical violation or a new crime. However, that standard may be unrealistic. When the only successes are persons who did not violate the probation conditions (or were not caught), and the failures are only those people who committed a technical or new crime violation, we are being very restrictive.

At first glance a move away from the success or failure dichotomy might seem to mislead the public. Yet, remember that the Japanese, presumably, count

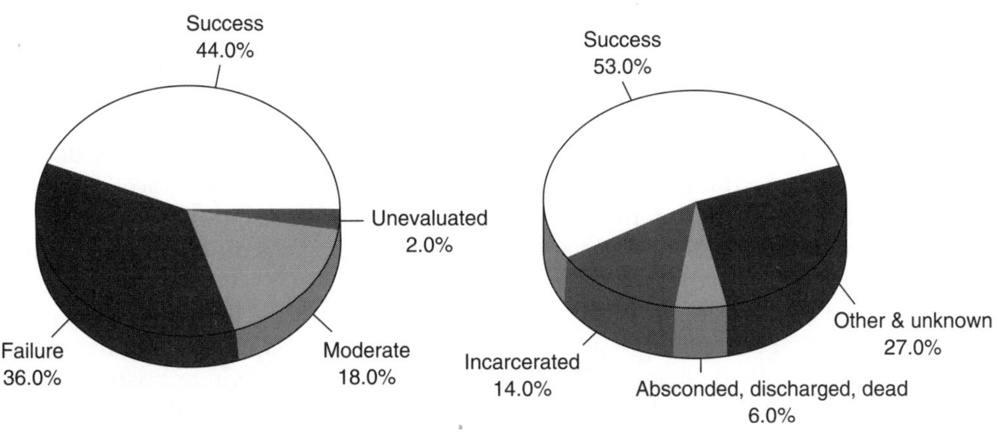

Figure 10.5 Adults Leaving Probation in Japan and the United States: 1993. *Sources:* Japan data from Rehabilitation Bureau (1995), *The community-based treatment of offenders system in Japan.* Tokyo: Ministry of Justice; United States data from T. Snell (1995), *Correctional populations in the United States, 1993* [NCJ-156241]. Washington, DC: Bureau of Justice Statistics.

as a failure those offenders "with unsatisfactory adjustments" as well as those recommitted. Used in this manner, the "failure" category would be expanded to include people who technically completed their probation "successfully" but, according to the supervisor, had not yet made an acceptable social adjustment. On the other hand, a probationer who is returned to prison because she continued to consume alcohol (though without committing a new crime) might be considered to have made a "moderate" adjustment (rather than a failure). Thus, she would be counted as success, but only a "moderate" one because her behavior "fell short of the general community's standards." All in all, the Japanese procedure seems to offer food for thought.

Prison Sentences. The effectiveness of a prison program is difficult to assess because there is not always agreement about the specific goals that imprisonment is meant to achieve. Some goals are clear enough: imprisonment in most countries is certainly designed to protect the public from presumably dangerous offenders. However, that control aspect is sometimes accompanied by an interest in treating offenders so they will be law-abiding after their release. Both the control and rehabilitative aspects require decisions to be made for the person just beginning a prison sentence.

Initial decisions about how to respond toward new prisoners are made on the basis of a classification process. The Japanese classification system, which takes about one to two months, allows effective treatment based on the prisoner's needs (the rehabilitative aspect), while the necessary level of supervision (the control aspect) is determined by the prisoner's personality.

The end result of the classification process is the prisoner's placement in one allocation category and one treatment category (Correction Bureau, 1999a, 1999b). The allocation category (see Figure 10.6) ascertains the appropriate institutional assignment as determined by the inmate's sex (class W for women), nationality (class F—there are 10 facilities for prisoners, oftentimes foreigners, needing different treatment than that of Japanese), kind of penalty (class I prisoners have a prison sentence without forced labor), age (class J indicating juveniles and class Y indicating persons under age 26), term of sentence (class L for persons with prison sentences of more than eight years), physical (class P) or mental (class M) disorders, and criminal tendency (class A offenders do not have an advanced criminal tendency and class B do have an advanced criminal tendency). That last criterion (criminal tendency) is based on the frequency of imprisonment, degree of association with organized gangs, mode of committing offense, and social attitude.

Some 80 different institutions are used to house prisoners by allocation category. In some cases the prison keeps several classes together, while other facilities receive only a single category of prisoner. For example, five prisons accept class L and class B inmates, while another two facilities receive only class L. Similarly, two institutions accept class J, Y, and A offenders, but all women prisoners will go to one of the six class W specific facilities.

Especially notable among the offenders sent to class B facilities (prisoners with advanced criminal tendency) are the *bōryokudan* (meaning "violent gang members"). These organized crime groups constitute a serious problem for prison security and treatment programs. *Bōryokudan* composed about 20 percent

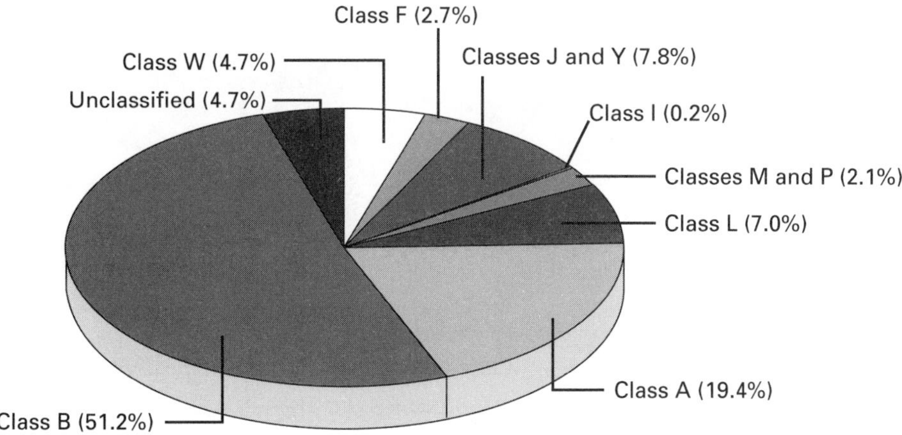

Class W = Females
Class F = Foreigners
Class I = Imprisonment without forced labor
Class J = Juveniles
Class Y = Young adults under 26
Class L = Prison sentences over 8 years
Class A = Those without advanced criminal tendency
Class B = Those with advanced criminal tendency
Class M = Those with mental disorder
Class P = Those with physical disorder

Figure 10.6 Inmates by Allocation Category: 1998. *Source:* Correction Bureau (1999), *Correctional institutions in Japan.* Tokyo: Ministry of Justice

of the prisoners placed in all penal facilities, received longer prison sentences than non-*bōryokudan* and were especially likely to be sentenced for drug, bodily injury, and extortion offenses (Johnson, 1997). Their incorrigibility and misconduct set the *bōryokudan* apart from the typical Japanese inmate, who exhibits much more compliance.

After selecting the most suitable institution, classification continues in an attempt to designate the appropriate treatment category. The seven possible categories to consider at this stage range from persons needing vocational or academic training to those needing special protective treatment (see Figure 10.7 for the related classes).

Regardless of an inmate's allocation and treatment categories, there is significant interest in providing all prisoners with a work experience. As a result, there is a 94 percent prison industry employment rate (even for those sentenced to imprisonment without forced labor) in Japan's prison system (Correction Bureau, 1999a).

The emphasis on work is seen as constructive in nature. Inmates are provided vocational knowledge and skills, and also have their will to work and spirit of cooperation through working together heightened. During a visit to some Oregon prisons, prison psychologist Takehiko Terasaki expressed surprise at the amount of free time American prisoners seemed to have (Ward, 1991). Japanese prisoners spend 40 hours per week either working or participating in counseling or academic programs. As a result, their free time is minimal.

Prison industry divides into the three categories of maintenance work, production, and vocational training (Correction Bureau, 1999b). Maintenance work

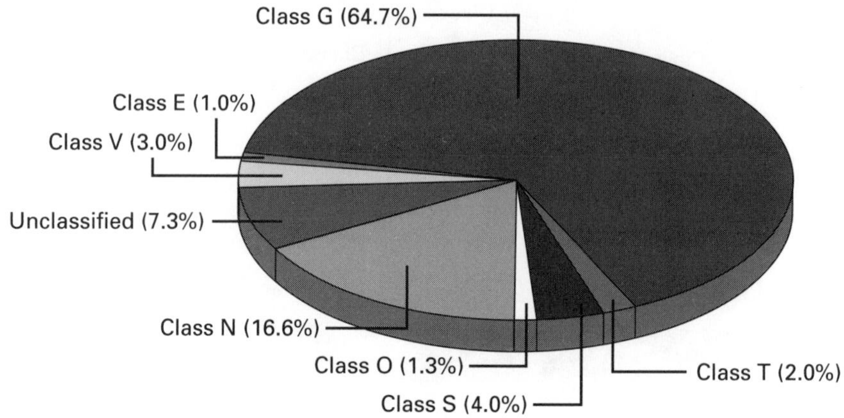

Class V = Those needing vocational training
Class E = Those needing academic training
Class G = Those needing social education (living guidance)
Class T = Those needing professional therapeutic treatment
Class S = Those needing special protective treatment
Class O = Those recommended for open treatment
Class N = Those recommended for prison maintenance work

Figure 10.7 Inmates by Treatment Category: 1998. Source: Correction Bureau 1999, *Correctional institutions in Japan.* Tokyo: Ministry of Justice.

(involving about 19 percent of the employed inmates) includes the jobs of cooking, washing, and cleaning in the facilities, as well as construction and repair work on prison buildings. The production (for example, printing, food processing, metalwork) and vocational training (for example, plastering, welding, auto repair) areas are performed in two different versions. In one, the government provides all the raw materials and facilities needed to complete a product. Those products are then sold on the open market throughout the country. In the other form, a private contractor provides the raw material and facilities and then pays the government for use of the prisoners' labor.

Profits from the prisons' work are transferred to the national treasury, but the prisoners are given a gratuity (neither called nor considered a wage) to encourage them to work. This money is set aside for the prisoners' release, but can also be accessed to buy necessities in prison or sent home for family support. Inmates wishing to do extra work are allowed to do "side jobs" for two hours a day after the normal working hours. All earnings from these jobs belong to the prisoner (Correction Bureau, 1999a).

COMING FULL CIRCLE

Japan is unique among countries of the world because of its comparatively low incarceration rate. That characteristic is all the more unusual because Japan emphasizes the same correctional objectives as most other countries: rehabilitation and retribution. But Japan seeks to accomplish these objectives by a somewhat different route than other countries take. Whereas many Western countries seek *rehabilitation* by encouraging individualism, Japan secures it through an appeal to collectivism and social responsibility. Because association provides self-identity to the Japanese, rejection and alienation from the group (that is, *retribution*) provide for society's revenge while making the offender lament.

Westerners often see the goal of retribution as conflicting with that of rehabilitation. The Japanese see it as a more harmonious relationship, because both can be accomplished in the community with the aid of other citizens. The group in Japan serves as the dispenser of guilt feelings (retribution) and the provider of social support (rehabilitation). The cultural values of contextualism, harmony, collectivism, and order make achieving correctional goals difficult and inappropriate in an institution. On the other hand, those goals are more easily and properly realized in the community. Consequently, the use of imprisonment is somewhat infrequent.

When imprisonment is required, its explicit goal is to develop in the prisoner a willingness and ability to return to society as a law-abiding and productive member. Given the general societal importance of the work group, and pride in one's work-related accomplishments, it is logical that labor would have a special role in Japanese prisons. Through work, prison officials believe, inmates can learn such values as harmony, respect for authority, and the importance of the group.

There is a sense of having come full circle with this philosophy, because these are the cultural traits identified at the start of this chapter. The homogeneity of agreed upon values means, first, that citizens are not so likely to misbehave, and second, that when norms are broken, the various agencies of social control will operate both informally and formally to emphasize and uphold those values. Even at the last stage in the process of corrections, prison officials respond to the offender in a manner designed to instill those cultural traits that seem to make a law-abiding citizen. And therein lies the essence and simplicity of Japan's seemingly low crime rate—which brings us back to the bonsai tree.

Seductively simple and harmonious, the Japanese criminal justice system seems to call for imitation. Like the gardener and her bonsai, though, criminal justice policy makers must consider the necessary role restraining wires play in making both the tree and the justice system attractive.

WHAT MIGHT WORK?

As this chapter's "Impact" section explains, the attractiveness of Japan's comparatively safe and orderly society seems partially achieved through tactics that citizens of other countries may find unacceptable. Intrusive police behavior toward law-abiding citizens, providing prosecutors with quasi-judicial duties, allowing judgments to be made without a public confrontation between defendant and judge, an apparent encouragement of self-incrimination, and severely restricted access to counsel for defense are some of the problems critics see in the Japanese justice system. Effective though they might be, proponents of due process (including those in Japan) are likely to express concern. However, this is certainly not a dilemma found only in Japan. Recall Chapter 3's discussion of the crime control model and the due process model. Japan may well exemplify the type of due process concessions that are necessary to control crime.

It is inappropriate to finish a book that hopes to encourage cross-cultural research, understanding, and appreciation with a suggestion that countries cannot effectively borrow from each other. In fact, although the "Impact" section emphasized problems such borrowing might have, this whole chapter is built on the idea that borrowing is both possible and desirable. The question is not if countries can learn from each other but rather how unfamiliar ideas can be made effective in a different setting.

A number of authors have made a variety of suggestions about adapting aspects of the Japanese criminal justice system in the United States (for example, Bayley 1991; Becker, 1988a; Castberg, 1990; Chang, 1988; Fenwick, 1982; Parker, 1986). Some of the suggestions would require as much cultural as structural change whereas others require primarily structural change. Of course the latter type is easier to implement and has the greatest chance for success because it would not pose significant challenges to cultural tradition.

For example, the centralization of policing would likely make law enforcement more efficient and effective. Yet that seemingly simple structural change directly opposes the long-held American values of decentralization and apprehension concerning a national police force. Some American communities are contracting with county or state officials to provide policing in their area, but even regional police forces in a particular state are not likely to be a popular tactic. If the United States moves away from its current decentralized multiple uncoordinated system, it seems more likely that we will model our system after that of a country like Canada and its tendency to contract with a provincial or national agency to provide police services. Alternatively, we may inventively change American police structure through increased standardization brought about by national police accreditation standards and regional training facilities.

There are, however, some aspects of Japanese policing that should be easily adapted to the American setting. Interestingly, one of the most importable tactics is the one some observers see as Japan's most effective police strategy—deployment via the *koban*. Bayley (1991) argues that Japanese-style deployment is possible in the United States because there is no compelling cultural factor inhibiting its use. Actually, several American cities have tried this approach and found it to be quite effective. Neighborhood-based foot patrols, mini- or substations (some doubling as the officer's home), and home-loan programs that encourage officers to move into troubled neighborhoods, are some of the *koban*-inspired techniques being used in many American jurisdictions. The entire push toward community or neighborhood-oriented policing so prominent in the 1990s had a distinctive Japanese quality if not a Japanese origin.

Some argue that *koban*-like deployment would be economically unfeasible throughout the United States in view of differences in population density. Even small cities, however, might make use of the basic idea. Lake Worth, Florida, is comparatively small (28,000 population), although its proximity to West Palm Beach, and an influx of tourists, present it with many big-city problems. Lake Worth police turned an old recreation department building into a ministation acting as a community center for both police officers and residents (McLanus, 1991). The ministation stays busy with neighborhood kids hanging out, residents and vendors visiting, and patrol officers using it to eat their meals and complete their paperwork. The result is a decline in drug dealing for several blocks around the ministation and a significantly more pleasant neighborhood.

With the occasional exceptions like Lake Worth, Florida, *koban*-like deployment is probably most likely to assist America's urban areas. Bayley (1991) recommends its use in places like public housing projects, major shopping malls, and around transportation and community centers. In Santa Ana, California, small storefront police posts, with Spanish-speaking officers walking downtown beats, are very similar in design and purpose to the *koban*.

Elgin, Illinois, has one of the nation's first law enforcement buildings designed specifically to support a community-oriented policing program. The building has a large public lobby providing direct public access to records, crime prevention, and meeting and interview rooms. A small museum displays the police department's history and a portion of the lobby exhibits art works from Elgin residents. The goal is to provide citizens with a police headquarters building that facilitates communication and cooperation between police and residents so that traditional barriers between police and the people they serve can be broken down. It is, in other words, a *koban* philosophy in a large public building. The city has also moved some of its officers into the community through the Resident Officer Program of Elgin (ROPE), in which the officer lives in their neighborhood in a city-provided home. The officers make themselves available 24 hours a day to help residents solve problems.

The Portland (Oregon) Police Bureau has implemented a variety of strategies that also make use of police deployment and community interaction in a manner reminiscent of Japanese procedures. In the mid 1990s the bureau aligned patrol district boundaries to closely correspond to neighborhood association boundaries and, using a five-precinct configuration, more closely aligned precinct boundaries with neighborhood coalition boundaries. Specific programs include the Neighborhood Response Team, which is a small team of officers who work on chronic call locations or other crime and livability problems referred to them by the police officer for that district. The Neighborhood Liaison Officer program connects officers to individual neighborhoods, and the Crisis Intervention Team officers receive specific training on defusing situations with mentally ill persons. To help promote order and safety, the bureau also has a Crisis Response Team formed of citizen volunteers who are trained to respond to the scene of traumatic, emotional incidents (especially, violent crimes) and assist bureau members in managing such incidents (Portland Police Bureau, 1996, 1998). The Neighborhood Response Team and Neighborhood Liaison Officer program are especially popular within the police bureau and in the community.

This discussion emphasizes ideas related to Japanese policing that may be transferable to the United States. Obviously, there are aspects of Japan's court system and corrections process that can also be helpful. Increased use of mediation, conciliation, and compromise in pretrial, and even precharge, stages could benefit from the Japanese experience. If greater use of volunteers in adult and juvenile probation, parole, and aftercare seems desirable, program directors may want to consider Japanese examples. Those in charge of providing productive work for prison inmates could benefit from examining prison labor procedures in Japan. There is no lack of possible alternatives to America's existing programs;

the challenge lies in determining which, if any, foreign approaches are possible and appropriate here.

The Japanese example is particularly relevant for Americans because the United States played such an important role in structuring the contemporary Japanese system. In fact, as Castberg (1990) points out, the criminal justice provisions in both countries are essentially the same. Differences arise because the respective courts have not interpreted the provisions similarly. For example, each country's constitution protects against double jeopardy, but Japanese courts do not interpret that provision as preventing the prosecution from appealing not guilty verdicts. Likewise, search and seizure provisions are comparably stated, but Japanese courts do not require that arrest always precede search and seizure, nor are warrantless searches and seizures necessarily invalid as long as arrest takes place closely in time (see Castberg, 1990, pp. 80–81).

The point is that imitation and innovation go hand in hand. Japan borrowed from European, Asian, and North American countries but made sure that the new ideas were compatible with Japanese culture. Ensuring compatibility may require selective borrowing, or might necessitate modifying the borrowed practice to fit a new cultural context, or could even mean using culture to gain acceptance for the new scheme. Whatever the technique, an understanding and appreciation for one's own cultural traditions is necessary for successful borrowing. Furthermore, as Japan's short-lived experiment with a jury system shows, there must be a willingness to admit when an imported idea is not working and move on to other tactics.

SUMMARY

This book followed a descriptive approach focusing on primary components of a large number of countries rather than providing a detailed description of a few countries. In this manner we showed the variability of systems but were not able to take a very close look at how any particular justice system operates—except for this chapter, which examines the Japanese system in detail. Japan warrants specific attention for two reasons. First, by all indications Japan has an effective criminal justice system, if we measure effectiveness by low crime rate. Second, Japan's criminal justice system includes a blend of foreign ideas adapted to its particular cultural history. This borrowing is one of the goals that comparative criminal justice hopes to achieve. The key to successful borrowing is to make something with a foreign origin work in the context of the adapting country. Some practices that are very effective in one setting may not work at all in another. Concentrating on Japan provides an opportunity to see how cross-cultural borrowing can work and to consider which, if any, Japanese strategies might be effective in the United States.

Because peoples' cultural traits might affect the transferability of policy and procedures, we briefly considered some of the obvious features of Japanese culture. Things like homogeneity, an emphasis on harmony, a respect for hierarchy and authority, and a reliance on collectivism help explain why and how the police, courts, and correctional agencies are effective in Japan. Upon looking at the three primary components of a criminal justice system, we saw how police deployment via the *koban* is a key feature in Japanese policing. Also important is the informal justice process that police officers and court personnel use. In fact, the reluctance to impose formal sanctions is apparent throughout the criminal justice operation and is a feature that sets the Japanese system apart from many others in the world.

This chapter's "Impact" section considers some of the problems that might be encountered if parts of Japan's system were implemented in the United States. Even after such cautions, the chapter concludes by noting some things the Japanese do that may be worthy of continued and even increased study by American policy makers. This, after all, is what comparative criminal justice is all about: what can we learn from each other and how can we work together?

WEB SITES TO VISIT

- Read a brief overview of Japan's criminal justice system at **www.jmissioneu.be/interest/crimju.htm**
- For a comprehensive and comparative review of the right to counsel in Japan and the United States, read David Suess's article at **www.law.indiana.edu/ilj/v72/no1/ suess.html#N_91_**
- See photos and read the history of the Japanese *koban* at **jin.jcic.or.jp/nipponia/ nipponia11/start.html**
- The Japan Criminal Policy Society web site at **www.jcps.ab.psiweb.com/index-e.htm** has several interesting articles on Japan's prisons.
- You'll find interesting information about the yakuza at **www.alternatives.com/Crime/YAKUZA1.HTML** and at **members.tripod.com/~orgcrime/yakuzahistory.htm**
- Visit the web sites for Japan's National Police Agency at **www.npa.go.jp/police_e.htm** and for the Ministry of Justice at **www.moj.go.jp/ ENGLISH/preface.htm**

SUGGESTED READINGS

Ames, Walter L. (1981). *Police and community in Japan.* Berkeley: University of California Press.

Bayley, David H. (1991). *Forces of order: Policing modern Japan* (2nd ed.). Berkeley: University of California Press.

Castberg, A. Didrick. (1990). *Japanese criminal justice.* New York: Praeger.

Johnson, Elmer. (2000). *Linking community and corrections in Japan.* Carbondale, IL: Southern Illinois University Press.

Parker, L. Craig, Jr. (1984). *The Japanese police system today: An American perspective.* Tokyo, Japan: Kodansha International Ltd.

Parker, L. Craig, Jr. (1986). *Parole and the community based treatment of offenders in Japan and the United States.* New Haven, CT: University of New Haven Press.

Upham, Frank K. (1987). *Law and social change in postwar Japan.* Cambridge, MA: Harvard University Press.

Westermann, Ted D., and Burfeind, James W. (1991). *Crime and justice in two societies: Japan and the United States.* Pacific Grove, CA: Brooks/Cole.

References

Abad, J. (1989). The criminal justice system of Panama. *C. J. International, 5*(3), 11–18.

Abadinsky, H. (1988). *Law and justice.* Chicago: Nelson-Hall.

Abraham, H. J. (1986). *The judicial process: An introductory analysis of the courts of the United States, England, and France* (5th ed.). New York: Oxford University Press.

Adamski, A. (1997). Criminal justice profile of Poland (ver. 1.2). Available at **www.cc.uni.torun.pl/umk/Faculties/PiA/CLCP/~raport.html.**

Adler, F. (1983). *Nations not obsessed with crime.* Littleton, CO: Fred B. Rothman.

Al-Saagheer, M. F. (1994). Diyya legislation in Islamic Shari'a and its application in the United Kingdom of Saudi Arabia. In U. Zvekic (Ed.), *Alternatives to imprisonment in contemporary perspective* (pp. 80–91). Chicago: Nelson-Hall.

Albanese, J. S. (2000). *Criminal justice: 2000 update.* Boston: Allyn and Bacon.

Ali, B. (1985). Islamic law and crime: The case of Saudi Arabia. *International Journal of Comparative and Applied Criminal Justice, 9,* 45–57.

Alobied, A. (1989). Police functions and organization in Saudi Arabia. *Police Studies, 10,* 80–84.

American Bar Association. (1988). *Criminal Justice in Crisis* (Report by the Special Committee on Criminal Justice in a Free Society). Chicago: American Bar Association.

American Bar Association. (1999). *Perceptions of the U.S. justice system, 1999.* American Bar Association. Available at **www.abanet.org/media/perception/home.html).**

American Law Institute. (1985). *Model penal code: Official draft and explanatory notes.* Philadelphia, PA: American Law Institute.

American Society of Criminology. (1995). International organized crime. *The Criminologist, 20*(6), 13–14.

Ames, W. L. (1981). *Police and community in Japan.* Berkeley: University of California Press.

Amilon, C. (1987). The Swedish model of community corrections. In *International corrections: An overview* (Tech. Rep. No. 11, pp. 11–15). College Park, MD: American Correctional Association.

Amin, S. H. (1985). *Middle East legal systems.* Glasgow, UK: Royston Limited.

Amnesty International. (1999a, April). Facts and figures on the death penalty. Available at **www.web.amnesty.org/ai.nsf/index/ACT500021999** (Accessed 26 April 2001).

Amnesty International. (1999b). The death penalty worldwide: Developments in 1998. Available at **web.amnesty.org/ai.nsf/index/ACT500041999** (Accessed 26 April 2001).

Araki, N. (1985). The flow of criminal cases in the Japanese criminal justice system. *Crime and Delinquency, 31,* 601–629.

Archambeault, W. G., & Fenwick, C. R. (1988). A comparative analysis of culture, safety, and organizational management factors in Japanese and U.S. prisons. *The Prison Journal, 68,* 3–23.

Archer, D., & Gartner, R. (1984). *Violence and crime in cross-national perspective.* New Haven: Yale University Press.

Ashworth, A. (1995). *The criminal process: An evaluative study.* Oxford: Clarendon Press.

Ashworth, A., & Fionda, J. (1994). The new code for crown prosecutors: (1) Prosecution, accountability and the public interest. *Criminal Law Review, XX,* 894–903.

Atkinson, L. (1997). Juvenile justice in Australia. In J. A. Winterdyk (Ed.), *Juvenile justice systems: International perspectives* (pp. 29–53). Toronto: Canadian Scholars' Press.

Australian Bureau of Statistics. (2000, 22 November). Prisoners in Australia. Available at **www.abs.gov.au/ausstats.**

Australian Institute of Criminology. (1996, 4 November). Lax firearm laws mean more deaths. Available at **www.aic.gov.au/media/961104.html** (Accessed 19 October 2000).

Awad, A. M. (1982). The rights of the accused under Islamic criminal procedure. In M. Bassiouni (Ed.), *The Islamic criminal justice system* (pp. 91–107). London: Oceana Publications.

Barry, D. D., & Barner-Barry, C. (1982). *Contemporary Soviet politics: An introduction.* Englewood Cliffs, NJ: Prentice Hall.

Bayley, D. H. (1985). *Patterns of policing: A comparative international analysis.* New Brunswick, NJ: Rutgers University Press.

Bayley, D. H. (1991). *Forces of order: Policing modern Japan.* Berkeley: University of California Press.

Bayley, D. H. (1992). Comparative organization of the police in English-speaking countries. In M. Tonry & N. Morris (Eds.), *Crime and justice: A review of research* (pp. 509–545) [Vol. 21: Modern policing]. Chicago: University of Chicago Press.

Beaumont, G., & Tocqueville, A. (1964). *On the penitentiary system in the United States and its application in France.* Carbondale, IL: Southern Illinois University Press.

Beck, A. J. (2000). *Prisoners in 1999* (NCJ 183476). Washington, DC: Bureau of Justice Statistics.

Beck, A. J., & Mumola, C. J. (1999). *Prisoners in 1998* (NCJ 175687). Washington, DC: Bureau of Justice Statistics.

Becker, C. B. (1988a). Old and new: Japan's mechanisms for crime control and social justice. *The Howard Journal of Criminal Justice, 27*(November), 283–296.

Becker, C. B. (1988b). Report from Japan: Causes and controls of crime in Japan. *Journal of Criminal Justice, 16,* 425–435.

Beirne, P., & Messerschmidt, J. (1991). *Criminology*. San Diego, CA: Harcourt Brace Jovanovich.

Belgrave, J. (1996). Chapter 3: The New Zealand criminal justice system and restoration. In Restorative justice: A discussion paper [Online]. Available at **www.justice.govt.nz/cepubs/reports/1996/restorative/chapter3.html#RTFToC1** (Accessed 30 November 2000).

Bennett, R. R., & Lynch, J. P. (1990). Does a difference make a difference? Comparing cross-national crime indicators. *Criminology, 28,* 153–181.

Bensinger, G. J. (1989). *Justice in Israel: A survey of criminal justice* (rev. ed.). Chicago: Office of International Criminal Justice.

Benyon, J. (1997). The developing system of police cooperation in the European Union. In W. F. McDonald (Ed.), *Crime and law enforcement in the global village* (pp. 103–121). Cincinnati, OH: Anderson.

Berman, H. J., Cohen, S., & Malcolm, R. (1982). A comparison of the Chinese and Soviet codes of criminal law and procedure. *Journal of Criminal Law and Criminology, 73,* 238–258.

Biles, D. (1986). Prisons and their problems. In D. Chappel & P. Wilson (Eds.), *The Australian criminal justice system: The mid 1980s* (pp. 238–254). Sydney: Butterworths.

Biles, D. (1993). Imprisonment in Australia. *Overcrowded Times, 4*(3), 4–6.

Biles, D. (1995). Prisoners in Asia and the Pacific. *Overcrowded Times, 6*(6), 5–6.

Binder, A., Geis, G., & Dickson, B. (1988). *Juvenile delinquency: Historical, cultural, legal perspectives.* New York: Macmillan.

Bo, J., & Yisheng, D. (1990). Mobilize all possible social forces to strengthen public security—A must for crime prevention. *Police Studies, 13,* 1–9.

Boyd, J. P. (Ed.). (1955). *The papers of Thomas Jefferson.* (Vol. 12). Princeton, NJ: Princeton University Press.

Boyd, J. P. (Ed.). (1958). *The papers of Thomas Jefferson.* (Vol. 14). Princeton, NJ: Princeton University Press.

Bracey, D. H. (1995). Police corruption. In W. G. Bailey (Ed.), *The encyclopedia of police science* (2nd ed.). New York: Garland.

Braithwaite, J. (1989). *Crime, shame, and reintegration.* Cambridge, England: Cambridge University Press.

Brewer-Carias, A. R. (1989). *Judicial review in comparative law.* Cambridge, England: Cambridge University Press.

British Council—China. (1999). A comparative overview of youth justice. Available at **www.britishcouncil.org.cn/english/governance/law3.htm** (Accessed 29 November 2000).

Broadhurst, R. (1996). Aboriginal imprisonment in Australia. *Overcrowded Times, 7*(3), 5–8.

Buck, W., & Pease, K. (1993). Cross-national incarceration comparisons inherently misleading. *Overcrowded Times, 4*(1), 5–6, 17.

Bulenda, T., Holda, Z., & Rzeplinski, A. (1990). *Human rights in Polish law and practice: Arrest and preliminary detention.* Unpublished manuscript.

Bureau of International Narcotics and Law Enforcement Affairs. (2000). *International narcotics control strategy report, 1999.* Washington, DC: Department of State. Available at **www.state.gov/www/global/narcotics_law/1999_narc_report/index.html**

Burros, B., Davidson, J., & O'Beirne, M. (Eds.). (1999). *The European Union: A guide for Americans.* Washington, DC: Delegation of the European Commission in the United States . Available at **www.eurunion.org**

Butterfield, F. (1998, 3 August). Crime data may be fudged. *The Denver Post, 2A.*

Cappelletti, M. (1989). *The judicial process in comparative perspective.* Oxford: Clarendon Press.

Cappelletti, M., & Gordley, J. (1978). Legal aid: Modern themes and variations. In J. H. Merryman & D. S. Clark (Eds.), *Comparative law: Western European and Latin American legal systems.* Indianapolis: Bobbs-Merrill.

Castberg, A. D. (1990). *Japanese criminal justice.* New York: Praeger.

Castro, J. (1991, 16 December). Eastern Europe's new bad guys. *Time, 138,* 15.

Chaldize, V. (1977). *Criminal Russia.* New York: Random House.

Chang, D. H. (1988). Crime and delinquency control strategy in Japan: A comparative note. *International Journal of Comparative and Applied Criminal Justice, 12,* 139–149.

Chappell, D. (1988). International developments in corrections: Australia in a bicentennial year. *The Prison Journal, 68*(1), 34–40.

Children's Court. (1998, 11 December). Overview of juvenile system. Available at **www.justice.wa.gov.au/division/courts/childjust.htm** (Accessed 28 November 2000).

Chwialkowski, P. (1998). Japanese policing—an American invention. *Policing: An International Journal of Policing Strategies & Management, 21*(4), 720–730.

Clark, J. P. (1989). Conflict management outside the courtrooms of China. In R. J. Troyer, J. P. Clark & D. G. Rojek (Eds.), *Social control in the People's Republic of China.* New York: Praeger.

Cole, B. A. (1990). Rough justice: Criminal proceedings in Nigerian magistrates' courts. *International Journal of the Sociology of Law, 18,* 299–316.

Cole, G. F. (1986). *The American system of criminal justice* (4th ed.). Monterey, CA: Brooks/Cole.

Cole, G. F., Frankowski, S., J., & Gertz, M. G. (Eds.). (1987). *Major criminal justice systems: A comparative study* (2nd ed.). Newbury Park, CA: Sage.

Collin, B. (1997). The future of cyberterrorism. *Crime & Justice International, 13*(2), 14–18.

Collison, C. (1991, 5 October). Expect democracy in Russia by the end of the decade. *The Denver Post,* 2E.

Committee on the Rights of the Child. (1994a, 8 March). Indonesia. In State party reports [Online]. Available at **www.unicef-icdc.org/information/portfolios/juvenile-justice/committee/indonesia.htm** (Accessed 30 November 2000).

Committee on the Rights of the Child. (1994b, 17 November). Yugoslavia, Federal Republic of. In State party reports [Online]. Available at **www.unicef-icdc.org/information/portfolios/juvenile-justice/committee/yugoslavia.htm** (Accessed 30 November 2000).

Committee on the Rights of the Child. (1995a, 21 August). China. In State party reports [Online]. Available at **www.uniceficdc.org/information/portfolios/juvenile-justice/committee/china.htm** (Accessed 29 November 2000).

Committee on the Rights of the Child. (1995b, 20 February). Italy. In State party reports [Online]. Available at **www.uniceficdc.org/information/portfolios/juvenile-justice/committee/italy.htm** (Accessed 29 November 2000).

Cook, S., & Davies, S. (Eds.). (1999). *Harsh punishment: International experiences of women's imprisonment.* Boston: Northeastern University Press.

Correction Bureau. (1990). *Correctional institutions in Japan 1990.* Tokyo: Ministry of Justice.

Correction Bureau. (1994). *Graphic introduction to Japanese corrections.* Tokyo: Ministry of Justice.

Correction Bureau. (1995). *Correctional institutions in Japan 1995.* Tokyo: Ministry of Justice.

Correction Bureau. (1996). *Prison administration in Japan.* Tokyo: Ministry of Justice.

Correction Bureau. (1999a). *Correctional institutions in Japan 1999.* Tokyo: Ministry of Justice.

Correction Bureau. (1999b). *Graphic introduction to Japanese corrections.* Tokyo: Ministry of Justice.

Corruption inquiry of Federal Police implemented by government. (1996, September-October). *C. J. International, 8.*

Coulson, N. J. (1957). The state and the individual in Islamic law. *International and Comparative Law Quarterly, 6,* 49–60.

Coulson, N. J. (1969). *Conflicts and tensions in Islamic jurisprudence.* Chicago: University of Chicago Press.

Council of Europe. (2000). *Judicial organisation in Europe.* Strasbourg, France: Author.

Cox, M. (1998, 9 December). Philly cheats on crime rate. *The Denver Post, 18A.*

Criminal Cases Review Commission. (2000). Introducing the commission. Available at **www.ccrc.gov.uk/pdf's/introduction.pdf** (Accessed 14 November 2000).

Criminal Law of the People's Republic of China (as amended 14 March 1997). (1997). Available at **l-a-law-firm.com/library/law/criminal/criminal.htm** (Accessed 2 November 2000).

Cunneen, C., & White, R. (1995). *Juvenile justice: An Australian perspective.* Melbourne: Oxford University Press.

Dahlburg, J.-T. (1995, 24 February). Pakistani court acquits Christians. *The Denver Post, 16A.*

Danilenko, G. M., & Burnham, W. (1999). *Law and legal system of the Russian Federation.* New York: Juris Publishing.

David, R. (1972). *French law: Its structure, sources, and methodology* (M. Kindred, Trans.). Baton Rouge, LA: Louisiana State University Press.

David, R., & Brierley, J. E. C. (1968). *Major legal systems of the world today.* London: Collier-Macmillan Ltd.

Davidson, R., & Wang, Z. (1996). The court system in the People's Republic of China: With a case study of a criminal trial. In O. N. I. Ebbe (Ed.), *Comparative and international criminal justice systems: Policing, judiciary and corrections* (pp.139–153). Boston: Butterworth-Heinemann.

Deflem, M. (1999, 9–11 April). *The boundaries of international cooperation: Human rights and neo-imperialism in U.S.-Mexican police relationships.* Presented at the Conference on International Institutions: Global Processes—Domestic Consequences. Available at **www.sla.purdue.edu/people/soc/mdeflem/zduke.htm**. (Duke University)

Department of State. (2000, 4 April). U.S. Justice Department official on trafficking in persons. Available at **www.usinfo.state.gov/topical/global/traffic/00040501.htm** (Accessed 19 October 2000).

Departmento de Internet Guardia Civil. (2000, 4 May). Guardia Civil organization (Translated with **bablefish.altavista.com**). Available at **www.guardiacivil.org** (Accessed 9 November 2000).

Devine, F. E. (1989). Forms of bail in common law systems. *International Journal of Comparative and Applied Criminal Justice, 13*(2), 83–95.

Dolinger, J. (1990). The influence of American constitutional law on the Brazialian legal system. *The American Journal of Comparative Law, 38,* 803–837.

Dunn, G., & Everitt, B. S. (1982). *An introduction to mathematical taxonomy.* Cambridge, England: Cambridge University Press.

Ebbe, O. N. I. (2000). The judiciary and criminal procedure in Nigeria. In O. N. I. Ebbe (Ed.), *Comparative and international criminal justice systems: Policing, judiciary, and corrections* (2nd ed., pp. 185–203). Boston: Butterworth-Heinemann.

Ehrmann, H. W. (1976). *Comparative legal cultures.* Englewood Cliffs, NJ: Prentice Hall.

Emmins, C. J. (1988). *A practical approach to criminal procedure* (4th ed.). London: Blackstone Press Limited.

Empey, L. T. (1982). *American delinquency: Its meaning and construction* (rev. ed.). Homewood, IL: Dorsey Press.

Entessar, N. (1996). Criminal law and the legal system in Iran. In R. Heiner (Ed.), *Criminology: A cross-cultural perspective* (pp. 163–171). St. Paul, MN: West.

Eskridge, C. W. (1989). Correctional practices in Japan. *Journal of Offender Counseling, Services and Rehabilitation, 14*(2), 5–23.

European Union. (2000). Incorporating the Schengen "acquis" into the European Union framework. Available at **europa/eu/int/scadplus/leg/en/lvb/133020.htm** (Accessed 12 November 2000).

Europol. (2000, January). Fact sheet No. 3. Available at **www.europol.eu.int** (Accessed 13 September 2000).

Fairchild, E. S. (1988). *German policing.* Springfield, IL: Charles C. Thomas.

Feest, J. (1981). *Cross national study of correctional policy and practice, country profile: Federal Republic of Germany.* Available from National Institute of Corrections Information Center, Longmont, CO.

Fenwick, C. R. (1989). Crime and justice in Japan: Implications for the United States. *International Journal of Comparative and Applied Criminal Justice, 6,* 61–71.

Feofanov, I. (1990-1991). A return to origins: Reflections on power and law. *Soviet Law and Government, 29*(3), 15–52.

Fooner, M. (1989). *Interpol: Issues in world crime and international criminal justice.* New York: Plenum.

Foucault, M. (1977). *Discipline and punish: The birth of the prison* (A. Sheridan, Trans.). New York: Pantheon Books.

Fox to shake up Mexico's corrupt law enforcement. (2000, 1 August). *The Denver Post.*

Frankowski, S. (1987). Poland. In G. F. Cole, S. Frankowski & M. G. Gertz (Eds.), *Major criminal justice systems* (pp. 221–261). Newbury Park, CA: Sage.

Frase, R. S. (1988). Introduction (G. L. Kock, & R. S. Frase, Trans.). *In The French code of criminal procedure* (rev. ed.). Littleton, CO: Fred B. Rothman.

French Code of Criminal Procedure. (1988) (G. L. Kock & R. S. Frase, Trans.). Littleton, CO: Fred B. Rothman.

French Ministry of Defense. (2000). Various components of the gendarmerie in France (Translated with **bablefish.altavista.com**). Available at **www.defense.gouv.fr/gendarmerie/organisation/index.html** (Accessed 9 November 2000).

French Ministry of Interior. (2000). Organization of the Police Nationale (Translated with **bablefish.altavista.com**). Available at **www.interieur.gouv.fr/police/pno1.htm** (Accessed 9 November 2000).

The French penal code of 1994: As amended as of January 1, 1999. (1999) (E. A. Tomlinson, Trans.). Littleton, CO: Fred B. Rothman & Company.

Friedman, L. M. (1973). *A history of American law.* New York: Simon & Schuster.

Friedman, L. M., & Macaulay, S. (1969). *Law and the behavioral sciences.* Indianapolis, IN: Bobbs-Merrill.

Gallup Poll. (1999, 9 December). Racial profiling is seen as widespread, particularly among young black men. Available at **www.gallup.com/poll/releases/pr991209.asp** (Accessed 29 August 2000).

Gatti, U., & Verde, A. (1997). Juvenile justice in Australia. In J. A. Winterdyk (Ed.), *Juvenile justice systems: International perspectives* (pp. 177–204). Toronto: Canadian Scholars' Press.

Geis, G., & Meier, R. F. (1985). Abolition of the insanity pleas in Idaho: A case study. *The Annals of the American Academy of Political and Social Science, 477,* 72–83.

Gelatt, T. A. (1982). The People's Republic of China and the presumption of innocence. *Journal of Criminal Law and Criminology, 73,* 259–316.

The Gendarmerie Nationale. (2000). Available at **www.info-france-usa.org/profil/glance/def97/gendarme.htm** (Accessed 9 November 2000).

George, B. J., Jr. (1983). Criminal law. In *Encyclopedia of Japan* (Vol. 2, pp. 47–51). Tokyo: Kodansha.

Gifford, D. J., & Gifford, K. H. (1983). *Our legal system* (2nd ed.). Sydney: Law Book Company.

Glendon, M. A., Gordon, M. W., & Osakwe, C. (1985). *Comparative legal traditions.* St. Paul, MN: West.

Graham, M. M. (1983). *Tightening the reins of justice in America.* Westport, CT: Greenwood Press.

Greenfield, J. (1989). *The return of cultural treasures.* New York: Cambridge.

Groves, W. B., & Newman, G. (1989). Against general theory in comparative research. *International Journal of Comparative and Applied Criminal Justice, 13,* 23–29.

Groves, W. B., Newman, G., & Corrado, C. (1987). Islam, modernization and crime: A test of the religious ecology thesis. *Journal of Criminal Justice, 15,* 495–503.

Guarnieri, C. (1997). Prosecution in two civil law countries: France and Italy. In D. Nelken (Ed.), *Comparing legal cultures* (pp. 183–193). Aldershot, England: Dartmouth.

Gun law con. (2000, 25 May [last updated]). Is the AIC deliberately misleading the media? Available at **www.ozemail.com.au/~confiles/AIC.html** (Accessed 19 October 2000).

Hackler, J. (1991). Using reintegrative shaming effectively: Why Fiji has a juvenile justice system superior to the U.S., Canada, and Australia. In *Official responses to problem juveniles: Some international reflections* (pp. 103–120). Onati, Spain: Institute for the Sociology of Law.

Hall, J. (1952). *Theft, law and society.* Indianapolis: Bobbs-Merrill.

Hall, J. (1960). *General principles of criminal law* (2nd ed.). Indianapolis: Bobbs-Merrill.

Hall, J., & Mueller, G. (1965). *Cases and readings on criminal law and procedure.* Indianapolis: Bobbs-Merrill.

Harlan, J. P. (1997). The German police: Issues in the unification process. *Policing: An International Journal of Policing Strategies & Management, 20*(3), 532–554.

Harris, M. D. (1983, 1 May). Viewing execution nets mixed feelings. *Augusta (GA) Herald,* 1B, 5B.

Hartjen, C. A., & Kethineni, S. (1996). *Comparative delinquency: India and the United States.* New York: Garland.

Harvard Law School Library. (2000, August). French legal research—courts. Available at **www.law.harvard.edu/library/index.htm** (Accessed 9 November 2000).

Hataguchi, H. (1990). A few problems of criminal trial—A defense counsel's point of view. In V. Kusuda-Smick (Ed.), *Crime prevention and control in the United States and Japan* (pp. 41–44). Dobbs Ferry, NY: Transnational Juris.

Hatalak, O., Alvazzi del Frate, A., & Zvekic, U. (Eds.). (1998). *International crime victim survey in countries in transition—National reports* (Publication No. 62). Turin, Italy: United Nations Interregional Crime & Justice Research Institute.

Hazard, J. N. (1969). *Communists and their law.* Chicago: University of Chicago Press.

Helsinki Watch. (1988). *Prison conditions in Poland.* New York: Human Rights Watch.

Hendry, J. (1989). *Understanding Japanese society.* New York: Routledge.

Hillsman, S. T., Mahoney, B., Cole, G. F., & Auchter, B. (1987). Fines as criminal sanctions. In *NIJ Research in Brief.* Washington, DC: Department of Justice.

Hitchner, D. G., & Levine, C. (1981). *Comparative government and politics* (2nd ed.). New York: Harper and Row.

Home Office. (1998, 22 December). Inter-departmental circular on establishing youth offending teams. Available at **www.homeoffice.gov.uk/cdact/yotcirc.htm** (Accessed 2 December 2000).

Hong Kong's legal system braces for Chinese rule. (1997, 7 May). *New York Times* [Online]. Available at **www.nytimes.com** (Accessed 6 September 1997).

Horton, C. (1995). *Policing policy in France.* London: Policy Studies Institute.

Hughes, G. (1984). English criminal justice: Is it better than ours? *Arizona Law Review, 26,* 507–614.

Hughes, R. (1987). *The fatal shore.* New York: Alfred A. Knopf.

Human Rights Internet. (1996). Reports (Africa; Latin America & Carribbean) on U.N. Commission on Human Rights, 52nd session. Available at **www.hri.ca/uninfo/unchr95** (Accessed November 1997).

Human Rights Watch. (1996a). *Children of Bulgaria.* New York: Author.

Human Rights Watch. (1996b). *Police abuse and killings of street children in India.* New York: Author.

Human Rights Watch. (1997a). *Juvenile injustice: Police abuse and detention of street children in Kenya.* New York: Author.

Human Rights Watch. (1997b). Legal proceedings (Saudi Arabia). Available at **www.igc.org/hrw/reports/1997/saudi/Saudi-05.htm** (Accessed 14 November 2000).

Human Rights Watch. (1997c). *Police brutality in urban Brazil.* New York: Author.

Hunter, R. D. (1990). Three models of policing. *Police Studies, 13*(3), 118–124.

Igbinovia, P. E. (1989). Nigeria. In G. T. Kurian (Ed.), *World encyclopedia of police forces and penal systems.* New York: Facts on File.

Ingraham, B. L. (1987). *The structure of criminal procedure: Laws and practice of France, the Soviet Union, China, and the United States.* New York: Greenwood, an imprint of Greenwood Publishing Group, Westport, CT.

International Child Development Centre. (1998). Juvenile Justice *Innocenti Digest.* (Vol. 3). Available at **www.unicef-icdc.org/pdf/digest3e.pdf**. (Florence, Italy: UNICEF—United Nations Children's Fund)

Interpol. (2000a). Administration and structure of Interpol. Available at **www.interpol.int** (Accessed 12 November 2000).

Interpol. (2000b, June). Stolen works of art. Available at **www.interpol.int/Public/WorkOfArt/** (Accessed 6 October 2000).

Iorio, P. (1995). Assessing a new justice system. *C. J. International 11*(1), 5–6.

Italian penal code. (1978) (E. Wise, Trans.). Littleton, CO: Fred B. Rothman.

Iwarimie-Jaja, D. (1988a). On the bench in Africa: The Nigerian court system. *C.J. International, 4*(6), 13–20.

Iwarimie-Jaja, D. (1988b). The police system in Nigeria. *C.J. International, 4*(3), 5–7.

Jamieson, A. (1995). The transnational dimension of Italian organized crime. *Transnational Organized Crime, 1*(2), 151–172. Excerpted in *Trends in Organized Crime, 1* (4), 1996, 89–94.

Jiao, A. Y. (1997). Factoring policing models. *Policing: An International Journal of Policing Strategies & Management, 20*(3), 454–472.

Jie, C. C. (2000). The legal system in China. Available at **www.enstar.co.uk/china/law/blw/legal_intro.htm**

Johnson, D. (1981). *American law enforcement: A history.* St. Louis: Forum Press.

Johnson, E. (2000). *Linking community and corrections in Japan.* Carbondale, IL: Southern Illinois University Press.

Johnson, E. H. (1997, March). *Rule violation and time in Japanese prisons: An introductory exercise in comparative criminology.* Presented at the Annual Meeting of the Academy of Criminal Justice Sciences. Louisville, KY.

Jones, T. H. (1990, May). Common law and criminal law: The Scottish example. *The Criminal Law Review,* pp. 292–301.

Jörg, N., Field, S., & Brants, C. (1995). Are inquisitorial and adversarial systems converging? In *Criminal justice in Europe: A comparative study* (pp. 41–56). New York: Oxford University Press.

Junger-Tas, J. (1996). Delinquency similar in western countries. *Overcrowded Times, 7*(1), 1, 10–13.

Juvenile Offenders Unit. (2000). Referral orders—A short guide. Available at **www.homeoffice.gov.uk/yousys/referral.htm** (Accessed 2 December 2000).

Kalish, C. B. (1988). *International crime rates.* Washington, DC: Bureau of Justice Statistics.

Kania, R. R. E. (1989). The French municipal police experiment. *Police Studies, 12,* 125–131.

Kania, R. R. E. (1990). The return of the municipal police. *C. J. International, 6*(2), 3–4.

Kaplan, D. E., & Dubro, A. (1986). *Yakuza: The explosive account of Japan's criminal underworld.* Reading, MA: Addison-Wesley.

Kayode, O. (1976). Police expectations and police role concepts: Nigeria. *Police Chief, 43*(5), 56–59.

Keenan, D. (1992). *Smith and Keenan's English law* (10th ed.). London: Pitman.

Killer revived after o.d., then executed. (1995, 11 August). *Greeley (Colo.) Tribune, A6.*

Kim, Y. (1987). Work—The key to the success of Japanese law enforcement. *Police Studies, 10,* 109–117.

Knight, C. F. (1978). Legal services projects for Latin America. In J. H. Merryman & D. S. Clark (Eds.), *Comparative law: Western European and Latin America.* Indianapolis: Bobbs-Merrill.

Koh, H. H. (1999, 14 September). The global problem of trafficking in persons: Breaking the vicious cycle on "Trafficking of women and children in the international sex trade." In Testimony before the House Committee on International Relations [Online]. Available at **www.usinfo.state.gov/topical/global/traffic/99091401.htm** (Accessed 19 October 2000).

Kolbert, C. F. (Trans.). (1979). *The digest of Roman law.* New York: Viking Penguin.

Koop, D. (1998, 24 August). Peru women's honesty gets them police jobs. *The Denver Post,* 7A.

Korn, R., & McCorkle, L. (1959). *Criminology and penology.* New York: Holt, Rinehart and Winston.

Kurian, G. T. (1989). *World encyclopedia of police forces and penal systems.* New York: Facts on File.

Kurtenbach, E. (1998, 27 December). Juvenile crime on rise in China. *The Denver Post,* 12A.

LaFree, G., & Birkbeck, C. (1991). The neglected situation: A cross-national study of the situational characteristics of crime. *Criminology, 29,* 73–98.

Langan, P. A., & Farrington, D. P. (1998). *Crime and justice in the United States and in England and Wales, 1981–1996* (Tech. Rep. No. NCJ 169284). Washington, DC: Bureau of Justice Statistics.

Lee, R. W., III. (1996). Nuclear trafficking in former communist states. *Trends in Organized Crime, 2*(1), 62–69.

Leivesley, S. (1986). Alternatives to imprisonment. In D. Chappell & P. Wilson (Eds.), *Australian criminal justice system: The mid 1980s* (pp. 255–273). Sydney: Butterworths.

Lemert, E. M. (1986). Juvenile justice Italian style. *Law and Society Review, 20,* 509–544.

Leng, S.-C. (1982). Criminal justice in post-Mao China: Some preliminary observations. *Journal of Criminal Law and Criminology, 73,* 204–237.

Lewis, C. (1999). Police records of crime. In G. Newman (Ed.), *Global report on crime and justice* (pp. 43–64). New York: Oxford University Press.

Li, V. H. (1978). *Law without lawyers: A comparative view of law in China and the United States.* Boulder, CO: Westview.

Li, V. H. (1983). Introductory note on China and the role of law in China. In J. L. Barton, J. L. Gibbs, Jr., V. H. Li & J. H. Merryman (Eds.), *Law in radically different cultures* (pp. 102–136). St. Paul, MN: West.

Lillebakken, F. (1996/1997). The Norwegian legal system: A brief introduction. Available at **www.jur.uib.no/sekr/Utland/English/ECTS/LEGAL.HTM** (Accessed 23 August 2000).

Lippman, M. R., McConville, S., & Yerushalmi, M. (1988). *Islamic criminal law and procedure: An introduction.* New York: Praeger.

Lund, D. W. (1996). Modern applications of traditional sanctions. *International Journal of Offender Therapy and Comparative Criminology, 40*(4), 347–353.

Lynch, J. P. (1988). A comparison of prison use in England, Canada, West Germany, and the United States. *Journal of Criminal Law and Criminology, 79,* 180–217.

Macdonald, I. (1987). Spain's 1986 police law: Transition from dictatorship to democracy. *Police Studies, 10,* 16–22.

Magistrates Association. (2000, 1 January). Duties and responsibilities; Current numbers; Stipendiary magistrates. Available at **www.magistrates association.org.uk** (Accessed 14 November 2000).

Maguire, E. R., Snipes, J. B., Uchida, C. D., & Townsend, M. (1998). Counting cops: Estimating the number of police departments and police officers in the USA. *Policing: An International Journal of Policing Strategies & Management, 21*(1), 97–120.

Maguire, K., & Pastore, A. L. (1999). Available at **www.albany.edu/ sourcebook/-1995/pdf/t217.pdf** (Accessed 29 August 2000).

Marcus, D. L. (1991, 23 June). Justice goes underground: Colombia's judges scared, faceless. *The Denver Post,* 17A, 19A.

Markovits, I. (1989). Law and glasnost: Some thoughts about the future of judicial review under socialism. *Law and Society Review, 23,* 399–447.

Marshall, P. (1978). As the pendulum swings in England and Wales. In V. L. Stewart (Ed.), *The changing faces of juvenile justice* (pp. 87–110). New York: New York University Press.

Martin, F. M. (1978). The future of juvenile justice—English courts and Scottish hearings. *Howard Journal of Penology and Crime Prevention, 17,* 78–90.

Martin, J., Romano, A., & Haran, J. (1988). *International Crime Patterns: Challenges to Traditional Criminological Theory and Research* (Monograph Vol. 4, no. 2). Huntsville, TX: Sam Houston State University.

Masaki, A. (1964). *Reminiscences of a Japanese penologist.* Tokyo: Japan Criminal Policy Association.

Mawby, R. I. (1990). *Comparative policing issues: The British and American experience.* London: Unwin Hyman Ltd.

Maxwell, G. M., & Morris, A. (1993). *Family, victims and culture: Youth justice in New Zealand.* Wellington, New Zealand: Social Policy Agency and Victoria University of Wellington, Institute of Criminology.

Mayhew, P., & van Dijk, J. J. M. (1997). Nationwide surveys in the industrialised countries. Available at **ruljis.leidenuniv.nl/group/jfcr/www/icvs/data/i_VIC.HTM** (Accessed 18 October 2000).

Mayr, E. (1982). *The growth of biological thought.* Cambridge, England: Cambridge University Press.

McCabe, E. J. (1989). Structural elements of contemporary criminal justice in the People's Republic of China. In R. J. Troyer, J. P. Clark & D. G. Rojek (Eds.), *Social control in the People's Republic of China* (pp. 115–129). New York: Praeger.

McCullagh, C. B. (1984). *Justifying historical descriptions.* Cambridge, England: Cambridge University Press.

McDonald, W. F. (1983). In defense of inequality: The legal profession and criminal defense. In W. F. McDonald (Ed.), *The defense counsel* (pp. 13–38). Beverly Hills, CA: Sage.

McDonald, W. F. (1997). Illegal immigration: Crime, ramifications, and control (the American experience). In W. F. McDonald (Ed.), *Crime and law enforcement in the global village* (pp. 65–86). Cincinnati, OH: Anderson.

McGuire, P. C. (1988). American law enforcement: A decentralized system with a central purpose. *C. J. the Americas, 1*(1), 13–16.

McInnes, R., & Hetzel, S. (1996, July). Family conferencing in the juvenile justice system of South Australia. *E Law—Murdoch University Electronic Journal of Law* [Online] 3(2). Available at **www.murdoch.edu.au/elaw/issues/v3n2/mcinnes.txt** (Accessed 30 November 2000).

McLanus, T. (1991). Lake Worth, Florida: A small town with a big commitment. *Footprints: The Community Policing Newsletter, III*(1 and 2), 9–11.

Merryman, J. H. (1985). *The civil law tradition* (2nd ed.). Stanford, CA: Stanford University Press.

Messner, S. F. (1980). Income inequality and murder rates. *Comparative Social Research, 3,* 185–198.

Midford, R. (1992). Imprisonment: The Aboriginal experience in Western Australia. In M. Carlie & K. Minor (Eds.), *Prisons around the world* (pp. 11–23). Des Moines, IA: Wm. C. Brown.

Ministry of Justice. (1999). Juvenile justice teams. Available at **www.justice.wa.gov.au/division/offend/3.htm** (Accessed 30 November 2000).

Mitchell, K. (1999, 11 April). Mexico offers an avenue, but fugitives still on street. *The Denver Post,* 1A, 25A, 27A.

Monkkonen, E. H. (1981). *Police in urban America 1860–1920.* Cambridge, England: Cambridge University Press.

Moore, L. (1973). *The jury: Tool of kings, palladium of liberty.* Cincinnati, OH: W. H. Anderson.

Moore, R. H., Jr. (1987). Courts, law, justice, and criminal trials in Saudi Arabia. *International Journal of Comparative and Applied Criminal Justice, 11,* 61–67.

Moore, R. H., Jr. (1988). Islamic legal systems: A comparison—Saudi Arabia, Bahrain and Pakistan. *C. J. International, 4*(3), 13–20.

Moore, R. H., Jr. (1996). Islamic legal systems: Traditional (Saudi Arabia), contemporary (Bahrain), and evolving (Pakistan). In C. B. Fields & R. H. Moore, Jr. (Eds.), *Comparative criminal justice: Traditional and nontraditional systems of law and control* (pp. 390–410). Prospect Heights, IL: Waveland.

Moran, R. (1985). The modern foundation for the insanity defense: The cases of James Hadfield (1800) and Daniel McNaughtan (1843). *The Annals of the American Academy of Political and Social Science, 477*, 31–42.

Morn, F., & Toro, M. (1989). From dictatorship to democracy: Crime and policing in contemporary Spain. *International Journal of Comparative and Applied Criminal Justice, 13*, 53–64.

Morris, A., & Maxwell, G. M. (1993). Juvenile justice in New Zealand: A new paradigm. *Australian and New Zealand Journal of Criminology, 26*, 72–90.

Morris, N. (1987). Alternatives to imprisonment: Failures and prospects. *Criminal Justice Research Bulletin.* (Vol. 3, no. 7). Huntsville, TX: Sam Houston State University.

Mozgawa, M., & Szumski, J. (2000). Promoting the rule of law & strengthening the criminal justice system. In A. Siemaszko (Ed.), *Crime and law enforcement in Poland* (pp. 87–94). Warsaw, Poland: Institute of Justice & Oficyna Naukowa.

Myren, R. A. (1989). Juvenile justice: People's Republic of China. *C. J. International, 5*(3), 5–6, 22–23.

Nakayama, K. (1987). Japan. In G. F. Cole, S. Frankowski, J. & M. G. Gertz (Eds.), *Major criminal justice systems* (pp. 168–187). Newbury Park, CA: Ssage.

National Association for the Care and Resettlement of Offenders. (1999). A brief outline of the youth justice system in England and Wales incorporating the Crime and Disorder Act 1998. Available at **www.nacro.org.uk/data/briefings/Nacro-1999090100-ycs.pdf** (Accessed 30 November 2000).

National Association for the Care and Resettlement of Offenders. (2000). The new youth justice reforms. Available at **www.penlex.org.uk/pages/nacro002.html** (Accessed 29 November 2000).

National Center for State Courts. (1999). How the public views the state courts: A 1999 national survey. Available at **www.ncsc.dni.us/ptc/results/nms4.htm** (Accessed 24 August 2000).

Neapolitan, J. L. (1999). A comparative analysis of nations with low and high levels of violent crime. *Journal of Criminal Justice, 27*(3), 259–274.

Neubauer, D. W. (1996). *America's courts and the criminal justice system* (5th ed.). Belmont, CA: Wadsworth.

Newman, D. J. (1986). *Introduction to criminal justice* (3rd ed.). New York: Random House.

Newman, G. (1978). *The punishment response.* Philadelphia: J. B. Lippincott.

Newman, G. (Ed.). (1999). *Global report on crime and justice.* New York: Oxford University Press.

Newman, G., & Howard, G. J. (1999). Introduction: Data sources and their use. In G. Newman (Ed.), *Global report on crime and justice* (pp. 1–23). New York: Oxford University Press.

NOP Research Group. (1997, 14 March). 'British justice—fair but fragile' survey suggests. Available at **www.nop.co.uk/survey/archive/public/public_10_03_97.htm** (Accessed 23 August 2000).

O'Brien, E., & Ward, J. (1970). *The foundation of Australia.* Westport, CT: Greenwood Press.

Oloruntimehin, O. (1992). Crime and control in Nigeria. In H. Heiland, L. Shelley & H. Katoh (Eds.), *Crime and control in comparative perspective* (pp. 163–188). New York: Walter de Gruyter.

Oppler, A. C. (1977). The reform of Japan's legal and judicial system under Allied occupation. *Washington Law Review, (special edition),* 1–35.

Organs from executed prisoners used for transplants in China. (2000, 9 January). *Inside China Today* [Online]. Available at **www.insidechina.com** (Accessed 14 January 2000).

Ostrihanska, Z., Balandynowicz, A., Jasinski, J., Kolakowska-Przelomiec, H., Kossowska, A., Porowski, M., Rzeplinska, I., Rzeplinski, A., & Wojcik, D. (1985). *Ordinary crime prevention and control in Warsaw.* Unpublished manuscript, Polish Academy of Sciences, Department of Criminology, Warsaw.

Packer, H. L. (1968). *The limits of the criminal sanction.* Stanford, CA: Stanford University Press.

Palmer, M. J. (1992). Policing remote areas: Difficulties and initiatives. *C. J. International, 8*(2), 9–24.

Parker, L. C., Jr. (1984). *A Japanese police system today: An American perspective.* Tokyo: Kodansha International Ltd.

Parker, L. C., Jr. (1986). *Parole and the community based treatment of offenders in Japan and the United States.* New Haven, CT: University of New Haven Press.

Pease, K., & Hukkila, K. (Eds.). (1990). *Criminal justice systems in Europe and North America.* Helsinki, Finland: Helsinki Institute for Crime Prevention and Control.

Penal Code of the Federal Republic of Germany. (1987) (J. Darby, Trans.). Littleton, CO: Fred B. Rothman.

Petrukhin, I. L. (1988-1989). Justice and legality. *Soviet Law and Government, 27*(3), 19–30.

Pew Research Center. (n.d.). Deconstructing distrust: How Americans view government. Available at **www.people-press.org/trustrpt.htm** (Accessed 24 August 2000).

Pizzi, W. T. (1999). *Trials without truth.* New York: New York University Press.

Płatek, M. (1990). Prison subculture in Poland. *International Journal of the Sociology of Law, 18,* 459–472.

Płatek, M. (1998). Penal practice and social theory in Poland before and after the events of 1989. In R. P. Weiss & N. South (Eds.), *Comparing prison systems: Toward a comparative and international penology* (pp. 263–285). Amsterdam: Gordon and Breach.

Plath, D. W. (1964). *The after hours.* Berkeley, CA: University of California Press.

Plucknett, T. F. T. (1956). *A concise history of the common law* (5th ed.). Boston: Little, Brown and Company.

Policy and Legislation Division. (2000). *Statistics 1997/98: Children's court of Western Australia.* Perth: Ministry of Justice.

Pomfret, J. (1998, 16 February). China's officers gape at America. *International Herald Tribune,* 1, 10.

Pommersheim, F. (1995). *Braid of feathers: American Indian law and contemporary tribal life.* Berkeley, CA: University of California Press.

Portland Police Bureau. (1996, September). *1996–1998 Community Policing Strategic Plan.* Available at **www.portlandpolicebureau.com** (Portland, OR)

Portland Police Bureau. (1998, June). *1998–2000 Community Policing Strategic Plan.* Available at **www.portlandpolicebureau.com** (Portland, OR)

Postema, G. J. (1986). *Bentham and the common law tradition.* Oxford: Clarendon Press.

Pratt, J. (1989). Corporatism: The third model of juvenile justice. *British Journal of Criminology, 29,* 236–254.

Prideaux, E. (2000, 27 March). Japan battles wave of drug smuggling. *Detroit Free Press* [Online]. Available at **www.freep.com/news/nw/japan27_20000327.htm** (Accessed 7 December 2000).

Prodi, R. (1999). President's welcome. In B. Burros, J. Davidson & M. O'Beirne (Eds.), *The European Union: A guide for Americans* (p. 1). Washington, DC: Delegation of the European Commission in the United States. Available at **www.eurunion.org**

Quigley, J. (1989). Socialist law and the civil law tradition. *The American Journal of Comparative Law, 37,* 781–808.

Radelet, M. L. (1999). Post-Furman botched executions. Available at **www.deathpenaltyinfo.org/botched.html** (Accessed 12 August 1999).

Rahim, M. A. (1986). *On the issues of international comparison of 'prison population' and 'use of imprisonment'* (Tech. Rep. No. 1986-41 from the Statistics Division, Programs Branch). Ottawa, Canada: Ministry of the Solicitor General.

Rake, D. E. (1987). Crime control and police-community relations: A cross-cultural comparison of Tokyo, Japan, and Santa Ana, California. *Annals of the American Academy of Political and Social Science, 494,* 148–154.

Rashid, A. (1995, 21 February). Cleric drops blasphemy case against Christians. *The Electronic Telegraph* [Online]. Available at **www.telegraph.co.uk** (Accessed 20 October 1997).

Rehabilitation Bureau. (1995). *The community-based treatment of offenders system in Japan.* Tokyo: Ministry of Justice.

Reichel, P. L. (2001). *Corrections: Philosophies, practices, and procedures* (2nd ed.). Boston: Allyn and Bacon.

Reid, S. T. (1987). *Criminal justice: Procedures and issues.* St. Paul, MN: West.

Reid, T. R. (1999, 25 February). British society tainted by racism, report says. *Washington Post* [Online]. Available at **www.washingtonpost.com** (Accessed 25 February 1999).

Reischauer, E. O. (1988). *The Japanese today: Change and continuity* (rev. ed.). Cambridge, MA: Belknap.

Reith, C. (1975). *The blind eye of history.* Montclair, NJ: Patterson Smith.

Renteln, A. D., & Dundes, A. (1994). *Folk law.* (Vol. I and II). Madison, WI: University of Wisconsin Press.

Research and Training Institute. (1990). *Summary of the white paper on crime 1990.* Tokyo: Ministry of Justice.

Research and Training Institute. (1996). *Summary of the white paper on crime 1996.* Tokyo: Ministry of Justice.

Research and Training Institute. (1998). *Summary of the white paper on crime 1998.* Tokyo: Ministry of Justice.

Reshetar, J. S., Jr. (1978). *The Soviet polity: Government and politics in the U.S.S.R.* (2nd ed.). New York: Harper and Row.

Rhoades, P. W., & Moore, E. (1992, March). *Evolution in common-law and continental police models: Do the paths converge toward a new model?*. Presented at the annual meeting of the Academy of Criminal Justice Sciences. Chicago.

Rhyne, C. S. (Ed.). (1978). *Law and judicial systems of nations* (3rd ed.). Washington, DC: World Peace Through Law Center.

Robin, G. D., & Anson, R. H. (1990). *Introduction to the criminal justice system* (4th ed.). New York: Harper and Row.

Rojek, D. G. (1985). The criminal process in the People's Republic of China. *Justice Quarterly, 2,* 117–125.

Rosen, J. (2000, 1 May). Don't end "Miranda." Mend it. *The New Republic, 18,* 20–21.

Rosen, L. (1989). *The anthropology of justice: Law as culture in Islamic society.* Cambridge, England: Cambridge University Press.

Rosenthal, E. (1998, 28 April). Increasingly, Chinese are telling it to the judge. *International Herald Tribune, 2.*

Rozalicz, J. (Trans.). (1989). *The penitentiary system in Poland.* Warsaw: Wydawnictwo Prawnicze.

Rubinstein, J. (1973). *City police.* New York: Farrar, Straus and Giroux.

Ruiz, M., Jr. (1974). *Mexican American legal heritage in the Southwest* (2nd ed.). Los Angeles, CA: Author.

Russia's system on trial, too. (1992, 25 April). *The Denver Post,* 10A.

Ryavec, C. A. (1983). Legal system. In *Encyclopedia of Japan* (Vol. 4, pp. 375–379). Tokyo: Kodansha.

SAHRDC. (1997). Torture and ill-treatment: Return of the Maoists—Midnight knocks and extra-judicial killings in Nepal. In South Asia Human Rights Documentation Centre [Online]. Available at **www.hri.ca/partners/sahrdc/nepal/fulltext.shtml** (Accessed 14 December 2000).

Saito, T. (1990). "Substitute prison": A hotbed of false criminal charges in Japan. *Northern Kentucky Law Review, 18*(3), 399–415.

Sallman, P., & Willis, J. (1984). *Criminal justice in Australia.* Melbourne, Australia: Oxford University Press.

Samaha, J. (1988). *Criminal justice.* St. Paul, MN: West.

Sanad, N. (1991). *The theory of crime and criminal responsibility in Islamic law: Shari'a.* Chicago: Office of International Criminal Justice.

Santayana, G. (1905). Patriotism (Chap 7). In *The life of reason. Vol. II: Reason in society.* New York: Charles Scribner's Sons.

Sarri, R., & Bradley, P. (1980). Juvenile aid panels: An alternative to juvenile court processing in South Australia. *Crime and Delinquency, 26,* 42–62.

Savage, J. (1997). *Cross-national variations in theft and violence: The promise of nurturant social policies.* Unpublished doctoral dissertation, University of California, Irvine.

Savitzky, V. M., & Kogan, V. M. (1987). The Union of Soviet Socialist Republics. In *Major criminal justice systems: A comparative study* (2nd ed.) (pp. 191–220). Newbury Park, CA: Sage.

Schmalleger, F. (1997). *Criminal justice today* (4th ed.). Upper Saddle River, NJ: Prentice Hall.

Schmid, A. P., & Savona, E. U. (1995). Migration and crime: A framework for discussion. *International Scientific and Professional Advisory Council of the United Nations Crime Prevention and Criminal Justice Programme, May,* 27–32. Excerpted in *Trends in Organized Crime, 1* (3), 1996, 77–81.

Schwartz, B. (1956). The code and public law. In B. Schwartz (Ed.), *The Code Napoleon and the common-law world* (pp. 247–266). Westport, CT: Greenwood Press.

Schwindt, F. (1992). Policing Germany in the nineties: Organization and function of the police in the Federal Republic of Germany. Available from Friedrich Schwindt via email at <Fritz.Schwindt@t-online.de>; no longer available online (Accessed November 1997).

Schwindt, F. (2000). Getting ready for the next century: Police in Nordrhein-Westfalen. Available at **www.polizei.nrw.de/duesseldorf/orga/englisc1.htm** (Accessed 12 November 2000).

Seay, P. A. (1998). Law, crime, and punishment in the People's Republic of China: A comparative introduction to the criminal justice and legal system of the People's Republic of China. *Indiana International and Comparative Law Review, 9*(1), 143–154.

Selih, A. (1978). Juvenile justice in Yugoslavia. In V. L. Stewart (Ed.), *The changing faces of juvenile justice* (pp. 111–134). New York: New York University Press.

Sereni, A. P. (1956). The code and the case law. In B. Schwartz (Ed.), *The Code Napoleon and the common-law world* (pp. 55–79). Westport, CT: Greenwood Press.

Shapiro, M. (1981). *Courts: A comparative and political analysis.* Chicago: University of Chicago Press.

Shargorodskii, M. D. (1964). The causes and prevention of crime. *Soviet Sociology, 3,* 24–39.

Shaw, A. G. L. (1966). *Convicts and the colonies.* London: Faber and Faber.

Shelley, L. I. (1981). *Crime and modernization.* Carbondale, IL: Southern Illinois University Press.

Shelley, L. I. (1990). The Soviet militia: Agents of political and social control. *Policing and Society, 1,* 39–56.

Sheridan, M. B. (1998, 30 May). Anti-drug cooperation in jeopardy, Mexico tells U.S. *Media Awarness Project* [Online]. Available at **www.mapinc.org/drugnews/v98.n403.a01.html** (Accessed 1 September 2000).

Shibahara, K. (1990). Participation of citizens in criminal justice in Japan. In V. Kusuda-Smick (Ed.), *Crime prevention and control in the United States and Japan* (pp. 26–31). Dobbs Ferry, NY: Transnational Juris.

Shichor, D. (1990). Crime patterns and socioeconomic development: A cross-national analysis. *Criminal Justice Review, 15,* 64–77.

Siddiqi, M. I. (1985). *The penal law of Islam* (2nd ed.). Lahore, Pakistan: Kazi Publications.

Siemaszko, A., Gruszczyńska, B., & Marczewski, M. (2000). Part Two: Facts & figures. In A. Siemaszko (Ed.), *Crime and law enforcement in Poland* (pp. 27–83). Warsaw, Poland: Institute of Justice & Oficyna Naukowa.

Single market in crime, A (1999, 16 October). *The Economist* [Online]. Available at **www.economist.com** (Accessed 14 September 2000).

Situ, Y., & Liu, W. (1996). An overview of the Chinese criminal justice system. In O. N. I. Ebbe (Ed.), *Comparative and international criminal justice systems: Policing, judiciary and corrections* (pp. 125–137). Boston: Butterworth-Heinemann.

Snell, T. L. (1995). *Correctional populations in the United States, 1993* (NCJ-156241). Washington, DC: Bureau of Justice Statistics.

Solaim, S. A. (1971). Saudi Arabia's judicial system. *The Middle East Journal, 25,* 403–407.

Something for a refresco. (2000, 28 October). *The Economist* (special insert, "After the revolution") 13.

Souryal, S. S. (1987). The religionization of a society: The continuing application of Shariah law in Saudi Arabia. *Journal for the Scientific Study of Religion, 26,* 249–265.

Souryal, S. S., Potts, D. W., & Alobied, A. I. (1994). The penalty of hand amputation for theft in Islamic justice. *Journal of Criminal Justice, 22,* 249–265.

Sprack, J. (2000). *Emmins on criminal procedure* (8th ed.). London: Blackstone Press.

Stace, C. A. (1989). *Plant taxonomy and biosystematics* (2nd ed.). London: Edward Arnold.

Stark, R., Kent, L., & Doyle, D. P. (1982). Religion and delinquency: The ecology of a "lost" relationship. *Journal of Research in Crime and Delinquency, 19,* 4–24.

Statement of Rosa. (2000, 4 April). Global issues: Trafficking. Available at **www.usinfo.state.gov/topical/global/traffic/#organizations** (Accessed 19 October 2000).

Steinberg, A. (1984). From private prosecutor to plea bargaining: Criminal prosecution, the district attorney, and American legal history. *Crime and Delinquency, 30,* 568–592.

Stephen, C. (1999). China challenges Hong Kong's rule of law. *World Capital Market Review* [Online]. Available at **pei-intl.com/Publications/HONGKONG/1999/cs0299.htm** (Accessed 2 November 2000).

Stoker, T. (2000, 13 August). 'Safe haven' Japan in grip of crime wave. *The Independent-London,* Final; PSA-2660, Foreign News Section.

Struck, D. (2000a, 10 February). Japan's violent turn. *The Washington Post,* Final, A17.

Struck, D. (2000b, 3 March). Japan's police wear tarnished badge of honor. *The Washington Post,* Final, A23.

Stuckey, G. (1986). *Procedures in the justice system* (3rd ed.). Columbus, OH: Charles E. Merrill.

Supreme Court reaffirms that police must warn criminal suspects of Miranda rights. (2000, 26 June). Available at **cnn.net/2000/LAW/06/26/scotus.miranda/** (Accessed 22 October 2000).

Sutherland, E., & Cressey, D. (1978). *Criminology*. Philadelphia, PA: J. B. Lippincott.

Sutton, J. (1990). Democratic revival from a despot's totalitarianism. *C. J. the Americas, 3*(2), 1.

Swanton, B., Hannigan, G., & Biles, D. (1989). Australia. In G. T. Kirian (Ed.), *World encyclopedia of police forces and penal systems.* New York: Facts on File.

Taiyun, H. (n.d.). The revision of the Criminal Law of the People's Republic of China. In British Law Weekly [Online]. Available at **www.enstar.co.uk/china/law/blw/art_revision.htm** (Accessed 2 November 2000).

Talbot, C. K., Jayewardene, C. H. S., & Juliani, T. J. (1985). *Canada's constables: The historical development of policing in Canada.* Ottawa: Crimcare.

Tamiya, H. (1983). Confession. In *Encyclopedia of Japan* (Vol. 1, p. 350). Tokyo: Kodansha.

Terebilov, V. (1973). *The Soviet court* (M. Saifulin, Trans.). Moscow: Progress Publishers.

Terrill, R. J. (1982). Approaches for teaching comparative criminal justice to undergraduates. *Criminal Justice Review, 7*(1), 23–27.

Terrill, R. J. (1984). *World criminal justice systems: A survey.* Cincinnati, OH: Anderson.

Terrill, R. J. (1999). *World criminal justice systems: A survey* (4th ed.). Cincinnati, OH: Anderson.

Teske, R. H. C., Jr., & Albrecht, H.-J. (1991, May). *An overview of probation procedures and statistics in the Federal Republic of Germany.* Presented at the Academy of Criminal Justice Sciences. Nashville, TN.

Thomaneck, J. (1985). Police and public order in the Federal Republic of Germany. In J. Roach & J. Thomaneck (Eds.), *Police and public order in Europe.* London: Croom Helm.

Tomkins, C., & Karim, R. (1987). The Shari'ah and its implications for Islamic financial analysis: An opportunity to study interactions among society, organization, and accounting. *The American Journal of Islamic Social Sciences, 4,* 101–115.

Tomlinson, E. A. (1999). Translator's preface. In *The French penal code of 1994* (pp. xxi–xxii). Littleton, CO: Fred B. Rothman & Company.

Tonry, M. (Ed.). (1997a). Ethnicity, crime, and immigration: Comparative and cross-national perspectives. In *Crime and justice: A review of research.* (Vol. 21). Chicago: University of Chicago Press.

Tonry, M. (1997b). Ethnicity, crime, and immigration. *Overcrowded Times, 8*(2), 1, 9–10.

Toro, M. C. (1999). The internationalization of police: The DEA in Mexico. *Journal of American History* [Online] 86(2). Available at **www.historycooperative.org/journals/jah/86.2/toro.html** (Accessed 26 September 2000).

Transparency International. (2000, 13 September). Press release: Transparency International releases the year 2000 Corruption Perceptions Index. Available at **www.transparency.de/documents/cpi/2000/cpi2000.html** (Accessed 20 October 2000).

Troyer, R. J. (1989). Publicizing the new laws: The public legal education campaign. In R. Troyer, J. Clark & D. Rojek (Eds.), *Social control in the People's Republic of China* (pp. 70–83). New York: Praeager.

Tucker, J. H., Jr. (1956). The code and the common law in Louisiana. In B. Schwartz (Ed.), *The Code Napoleon and the common-law world* (pp. 346–377). Westport, CT: Greenwood Press.

Turack, D. C. (1999). The new Chinese criminal justice system. *Cardozo Journal of International and Comparative Law, 7,* 49–72.

Turow, S. (1987). *Presumed innocent.* New York: Farrar Straus Giroux.

Ullman, W. (1975). *Law and politics in the Middle Ages.* Ithaca, NY: Cornell University Press.

Umbreit, M. S. (1996). Restorative justice through mediation. *Overcrowded Times, 7*(3), 1, 9–11.

UNIDROIT. (2000, April). International institute for the unification of private law. Available at **www.unidroit.org/english/implement/i-95.htm** (Accessed 6 October 2000).

United Nations. (1985). *Youth and crime* (Tech. Rep. No. A/CONF.121/7). Vienna, Austria: UN Crime Prevention and Criminal Justice Branch.

United Nations. (1986). *Standard minimum rules for the administration of juvenile justice.* New York: UN Department of Public Information.

United Nations. (1988). *Basic principles on the independence of the judiciary.* New York: UN Department of Public Information.

United Nations. (1990a). *Crime prevention and criminal justice in the context of development: Realities and perspectives of international co-operation* (Tech. Rep. No. A/CONF.144/5). Vienna, Austria: UN Crime Prevention and Criminal Justice Branch.

United Nations. (1990b). *Effective national and international action against: (a) organized crime; (b) terrorist criminal activity* (Tech. Rep. No. A/CONF. 144/4). Vienna, Austria: UN Crime Prevention and Criminal Justice Branch.

United Nations. (1990c). *Implementaton of the basic principles on the independence of the judiciary* (Tech. Rep. No. A/CONF.144/19). Vienna: UN Crime Prevention and Criminal Justice Branch.

United Nations. (1990d). *Implementaton of the United Nations standard minimum rules for the administration of juvenile justice* (Tech. Rep. No. A/CONF.144/4). Vienna: UN Crime Prevention and Criminal Justice Branch.

United Nations. (1990e). *Prevention of delinquency, juvenile justice and the protection of the young: Policy approaches and directions* (Tech. Rep. No. A/CONF.144/16). Vienna, Austria: UN Crime Prevention and Criminal Justice Branch.

United Nations. (1990f). *Proposals for concerted international action against forms of crime identified in the Milan Plan of Action* (Tech. Rep. No. A/CONF.144/7). Vienna, Austria: UN Crime Prevention and Criminal Justice Branch.

United Nations. (1990g). *Third United Nations survey of crime trends, operations of criminal justice systems and crime prevention strategies* (Tech. Rep. No. A/CONF.144/6). Vienna, Austria: UN Crime Prevention and Criminal Justice Branch.

United Nations. (1995). *Action against national and transnational economic and organized crime, and the role of criminal law in the protection of the environment: National experiences and international cooperation* (Tech. Rep. No. A/CONF.169/15/Add.1). Vienna, Austria: UN Crime Prevention and Criminal Justice Branch.

United Nations. (1997). *Use and application of United Nations standards and norms in crime prevention and criminal justice: Administration of juvenile justice* (Tech. Rep. No. E/CN.15/1997/13). Vienna: UN Crime Prevention and Criminal Justice Branch.

United Nations. (1999). *Global Programme Against Trafficking in Human Beings* (United Nations Interregional Crime and Justice Research Institute). Vienna, Austria: Centre for International Crime Prevention.

Upham, F. K. (1987). *Law and social change in postwar Japan.* Cambridge, MA: Harvard University Press.

van Dijk, J. J. M. (1999). The experience of crime and justice. In G. Newman (Ed.), *Global report on crime and justice* (pp. 25–42). New York: Oxford University Press.

van Dijk, J. J. M., & Mayhew, P. (1993). Criminal victimization in the industrialised world: Key findings of the 1989 and 1992 international crime surveys. In A. A. del Frate, U. Zvekic, & J. J. M. van Dijk (Eds.), *Understanding crime: Experiences of crime and crime control* (pp. 1–49). Rome: United Nations Interregional Crime & Justice Research Institute.

van Dijk, J., & Kangaspunta, K. (2000, January). Piecing together the cross-national crime puzzle. *National Institute of Justice Journal*, pp. 34–41.

Vernadsky, G. (Trans.). (1947). *Medieval Russian laws*. New York: Columbia University Press.

Waldron, R. J. (1989). *The criminal justice system: An introduction* (4th ed.). New York: Harper and Row.

Walker, J. (1999). Firearm abuse and regulation. In G. Newman (Ed.), *Global report on crime and justice* (pp. 151–170). New York: Oxford University Press.

Walker, J., & Biles, D. (1986). *Australian community-based corrections: 1985–1986.* Australian Capital Territory: Australian Institute of Criminology.

Walmsley, R. (1995). *Developments in the prison systems of Central and Eastern Europe* (Tech. Rep. No. 4 from HEUNI). Helsinki, Finland: The European Institute for Crime Prevention and Control.

Walmsley, R. (2000). *World Prison Population List (2nd Ed.)* (Research, Development and Statistics Directorate No. 116). London: Home Office.

Walsh, J. (1991, 25 November). It's a steal. *Time, 138*, 86–88.

Ward, G. L. (2000, Fall). Restorative justice: A global initiative. *Perspectives, 24*(4), 7–9.

Ward, J. (1991). Japan: Prisons in U.S. don't compare. *C. J. International, 7*(4), 7.

Watson, A. (1970). *The law of the ancient Romans.* Dallas: Southern Methodist University Press.

Weigend, T. (1983). Sentencing in West Germany. *Maryland Law Review, 42*, 37–89.

Weigend, T. (1993). In Germany, fines often imposed in lieu of prosecution. *Overcrowded Times, 4*(1), 15–16.

Westermann, T. D., & Burfeind, J. W. (1991). *Crime and justice in two societies: Japan and the United States.* Pacific Grove, CA: Brooks/Cole.

Westney, D. E. (1987). *Imitation and innovation: The transfer of western organizational patterns to Meiji Japan.* Cambridge, MA: Harvard University Press.

What if the O.J. Simpson trial were held in Russia? (1995). *C. J. International, 11*(5), 21.

Wiechman, D. J., Kendall, J. D., & Azarian, M. K. (1996). Islamic law: Myths and realities. *C.J. International, 12*(3), 13–19.

Wigmore, J. H. (1928). *A panorama of the world's legal systems.* (Vol. 1). St. Paul, MN: West.

Wigmore, J. H. (1936). *A panorama of the world's legal systems.* (Vol. library edition). Washington, DC: Washington Law Book Company.

Wilkinson, W. V., & Malagùn, E. (1995). Mexico: Structure training and education in policing. *Crime and Justice: The Americas* [Online] 8(4). Available at **www.oicj.org/public/toc.cfm?series=CJA** (Accessed 14 December 2000).

Williams, P. (1999). Emerging issues: Transnational crime and its control. In G. Newman (Ed.), *Global report on crime and justice* (pp. 221–241). New York: Oxford University Press.

Wilson, J. Q., & Kelling, G. L. (1995). Broken windows. *Atlantic Monthly, 249*(3), 29–38.

Winterdyk, J. A. (Ed.). (1997). *Juvenile justice systems: International perspectives.* Toronto: Canadian Scholars' Press.

Wiseberg, L. (1997, June). Clement Nwankwo—nightmare in Switzerland. *Human Rights Tribune* [Online] 4(2–3). Available at **www.hri.ca/cftribune/templates/article.cfm?IssueID=2&Section=1&Article=4** (Accessed 12 November 2000).

Yoshikawa, M. (1995). Crime threatens stability. *C. J. International, 11*(1), 3.

Yu, O., & Zhang, L. (1999). The under-recording of crime by police in China: A case study. *Policing: An International Journal of Police Strategies and Management, 22*(3), 252–263.

Zander, M. (1989). *A matter of justice.* Oxford: Oxford University Press.

Zatz, M. (1994). *Producing legality: Law and socialism in Cuba.* New York: Routledge.

Zawitz, M. W. (Ed.). (1988). *Report to the nation on crime and justice* (2nd ed.). Washington, DC: Department of Justice.

Zdenkowski, G. (1986). Sentencing: Problems and responsibility. In D. Chappell & P. Wilson (Eds.), *Australian criminal justice system: The mid 1980s* (pp. 212–237). Sydney: Butterworths.

Zhao, P. (1990). Violent crime and its countermeasures in China. *C. J. International, 6*(3), 11–18.

Zigel, F. F. (1974). *Lectures on Slavic law.* Gulf Breeze, FL: Academic International Press.

Zu-Yuan, H. (1988). Juvenile delinquency and its prevention. *C. J. International,* 4(5), 5–6, 8, 10.

INDEX

Numbers in italics indicate figures, tables, and boxes.

Only the first author in coauthored and multiauthored works is indexed.